# SUCCESSFUL MAINSTREAMING

# INTRODUCING THE AUTHORS

The authors draw upon a wealth of practical teaching experience, research, publication, and active involvement in professional education. All are experienced teachers of regular and special education classes at the elementary, secondary, and university levels. Their publications include journal articles, handbooks, textbooks, tests, and a variety of instructional materials for use by elementary, secondary, and special education students. In addition, they participate in a wide range of professional activities at the local and national levels. These authors share a commitment to inclusive education that facilitates success for both students and their teachers:

| | |
|---|---|
| **Fairy F. Carmack** | *Northeast Louisiana University* |
| **Joyce S. Choate** | *Northeast Louisiana University* |
| **Brian E. Enright** | *University of North Carolina at Charlotte* |
| **Susan S. Evans** | *University of West Florida* |
| **William H. Evans** | *University of West Florida* |
| **Robert A. Gable** | *Old Dominion University* |
| **Jo M. Hendrickson** | *University of Iowa* |
| **Lori Korinek** | *College of William and Mary* |
| **Virginia K. Laycock** | *College of William and Mary* |
| **Lamoine J. Miller** | *Northeast Louisiana University* |
| **James A. Poteet** | *Ball State University* |
| **Thomas A. Rakes** | *Memphis State University* |
| **Rex E. Schmid** | *Alachua County Schools, Florida* |
| **Dennie L. Smith** | *Memphis State University* |
| **Lana J. Smith** | *Memphis State University* |
| **Frank J. Sparzo** | *Ball State University* |
| **Paulette J. Thomas** | *University of New Orleans* |

# SUCCESSFUL MAINSTREAMING

## PROVEN WAYS TO DETECT AND CORRECT SPECIAL NEEDS

**Joyce S. Choate,** EDITOR

*Northeast Louisiana University*

**ALLYN AND BACON**

*Boston / London / Toronto / Sydney / Tokyo / Singapore*

Copyright © 1993 by Allyn and Bacon
A Division of Simon & Schuster, Inc.
160 Gould Street
Needham Heights, Massachusetts 02194

**Library of Congress Cataloging-in-Publication Data**

Successful mainstreaming : proven ways to detect and correct special
  needs  /  editor, Joyce S. Choate
       p.      cm.
  Includes bibliographical references and index.
  ISBN 0-205-14349-0
  1. Special education — United States.   2. Handicapped children —
  Education — United States.   3. Mainstreaming in education — United
  States.   I. Choate, Joyce S.
  LC4031.S93    1993                                    92-22770
  371.9′046′0973 — dc20                                 CIP


*Portions of this book were previously copyrighted by Allyn and Bacon in a series of
eight books called* The Allyn and Bacon Detecting and Correcting Series, *edited by
Joyce S. Choate,* © 1991, 1990, 1989.


Printed in the United States of America

10  9  8  7  6  5  4  3  2  1      97  96  95  94  93  92

# CONTENTS

**PART THREE**

**IMPLEMENTING DETECTION AND CORRECTION   367**

# CHECKLISTS AND SAMPLERS

# PREFACE

*Successful Mainstreaming: Proven Ways to Detect and Correct Special Needs and Problems* addresses the learning and behavior needs of special students *and* the teaching needs of those who teach them. It can be used in several settings — as a resource guide for inservice teachers, a practical compendium for mainstreaming courses, and a handbook for field experiences — to ultimately increase the achievement of special learners in both regular and special education classrooms. A practical complement to teaching wisdom and theory, this book is comprehensive but deliberately concise. It includes the detection of 101 special needs and more than 1,000 corrective strategies. The intent is to enable the reader to quickly translate the theories of effective teaching and special education into practical classroom strategies to improve the knowledge and skills of all students.

## ASSUMPTIONS

This book focuses specifically on the diverse learning and behavior needs of special learners in all classrooms. *Special learners* include students formally identified as having disabilities, as well as students without disabilities who demonstrate the need for special accommodations in the classroom. Underlying the structure and content of the book are these basic assumptions:

— All educators share the responsibility for accommodating the learning and behavior needs of all learners to the maximum extent possible.
— Teachers can create an environment in which students with special needs can perform successfully alongside more typical learners.
— Whether their speciality stems from learning, behavioral, experiential, or cultural differences, special learners have special needs that may require adjusted instruction.
— Targeted instruction improves the success of all learners.
— Certain instructional principles facilitate the selection of skills, concepts, topics, and instructional adjustments to meet the individual learning needs of special students.
— Effective management of both behavior and the instructional environment improves student and teacher success.
— Instruction is enhanced by professional collaboration and coordination of services.

These assumptions are incorporated into the Detection and Correction model for identifying the special needs of individual students and then meeting those needs with targeted instruction.

## ORGANIZATION

The Table of Contents is a specific, at-a-glance guide, facilitating quick location of the learning and behavior needs of special students. For ease of reference and discussion, categories of special students, specific academic skills, and instructional elements are often treated as intact units. Although they are labeled as discrete segments, in the real world neither student behaviors nor skills operate according to such tidy classifications.

The book is divided into three major parts. Each begins with a brief introduction, and each chapter ends with suggestions for reflecting on the content. The Reflections are intended for clarification, extension, and application. In each chapter, the final Reflections item refers to references and additional resources for further information.

Part One lays the foundation for understanding and implementing the corrective strategies for the subjects detailed in remaining sections. The three chapters in this part focus on mainstreaming, similarities and differences among students with and without disabilities, and some characteristics of categories of special learners. Chapter 1 briefly explains the rationale for the Regular Education Initiative (REI) and controversies surrounding it, dispels some myths, and builds a strong case for teaching for success — student *and* teacher success. Chapter 2 outlines categories of special students, both with and without disabilities, and suggests a few implications for instruction of each group. Chapter 3 reviews the teaching practices that form the foundation for what we consider to be special instruction. These teaching practices provide the framework of the corrective strategies for each of the subject areas in later chapters.

Part Two contains discussions of detecting and correcting special needs and problems in each of 10 subject areas — word recognition, reading comprehension, speech, language, written expression, spelling and handwriting, arithmetic computation, mathematical problem solving, science, and social studies. Together, these subjects comprise the content of classroom teaching and contain a vast array of concepts and skills that may pose problems but nevertheless offer opportunities for student and teacher success.

Part Three presents the means to operationalize detection and correction as three essential elements: behavior, instructional management, and collaboration. Like previous sections, it offers practical suggestions for correcting problems in structuring, managing, and enhancing instruction. The three chapters in this section offer a positive and productive view of teaching that places previous chapters in proper perspective and provides a useful overview of the detection and correction process.

## FEATURES

These detecting and correcting strategies are grounded in theory but shaped by practitioners. Their uniqueness resides in their practicality and versatility. Most can be implemented with relative ease in both regular and special education classrooms with individual students or with small or large groups. Elementary levels of functioning are emphasized, but content and strategies can be readily extended for students functioning at higher levels. Because the strategies must be adapted to fit individual students and teachers, only the most salient features are described. To keep the book clear, succinct, and practical, theories of effective instruction and special education are built into the strategies.

For the reader's convenience, a consistent format is used throughout. The concepts and principles described in the first three chapters are incorporated throughout each discussion that follows. Chapters 4 through 16 begin with a general overview, often accompanied by useful diagnostic checklists. The discussion of Detection and Correction for the components of each subject is contained on either two or four pages. Each treatment begins with a list of a few behaviors that may signal potential problems or indicate a special need for instruction. Next is a description of the subject, associated skills, and the special problems or concerns that may be related. Corrective strategies are then described for each component skill, topic, or behavior; included also are Sampler activities and useful forms, ready for duplication and immediate classroom use.

Each content chapter is written by specialists in the particular subject. Other features include:

— Comprehensive but concise and practical content
— Translations of theory into specific suggestions for practice
— A consistent and convenient format for readily accessible information
— Detailed Table of Contents permitting quick location of target topics
— Specific suggestions to identify *101* special needs and problems
— More than *1,000* practical and versatile corrective strategies
— Practical procedures for implementation with individuals or groups in regular and special classrooms
— Checklists of skills and problems for observing, recording, and monitoring performance
— Sampler activities ready to copy and use with a variety of age, interest, and ability levels
— Reflection activities for guiding readers to synthesize, extend, and apply content

The suggestions and activities have been modified and tested by several thousand teachers and their special learners. Many of the activities are also appropriate for most students, but it is the special student who must have special accommodations to maximize success in the classroom.

## ACKNOWLEDGMENTS

The inspiration, suggestions, and experiences of several thousand teachers and students are reflected in this book. We appreciate the dedication, time, effort, and expertise of those practitioners. For their guidance in articulating and refining the content, we are indebted to our field reviewers — Robert Freeland of the Kenmore Schools, Kenmore, NY, Elizabeth M. Hall of Athens State College, Athens, GA; Grant McGiffin, Assistant Superintendent of the Hampshire Regional School District, Westhampton, MA; and Patricia L. Sitlington, Iowa Department of Education, Des Moines, IA.

For his expert consultation and collaboration, a special thank-you is due Mylan Jaixen, Allyn and Bacon's Editor Extraordinaire. We are grateful to Karen Mason for sharing her production expertise as well as her special spirit. And to our families whose own special needs and problems were detected but often neglected while the book was in progress, we promise appropriate correction.

# Part ONE

## ACCOMMODATING SPECIAL NEEDS IN THE CLASSROOM

 All educators share the responsibility for accommodating the learning and behavior needs of all learners to the maximum extent possible. This holds true for both regular and special educators and both students with and without disabilities. Part One focuses on the mandate for providing quality education to *all* students, on the needs of certain groups of special learners, and on general guidelines for detecting and correcting some of the learning and behavior needs of special learners.

# CHAPTER ONE

# TEACHING ALL THE STUDENTS: A MANDATE FOR EDUCATORS

*— Robert A. Gable and Jo M. Hendrickson*

During the last quarter of the twentieth century, a number of events have contributed to dramatic changes in the course of public education. A major force in creating change in our schools was the enactment in 1975 of Public Law 94-142 (Education for All Handicapped Children Act). This landmark piece of federal legislation ushered in a new era by mandating that, to the maximum extent appropriate, students with disabilities should be taught alongside students without disabilities. Soon after, recognition grew that a substantial number of school-age children, while failing to qualify for classification as disabled, still need specialized instruction in order to perform satisfactorily. Today, these students are referred to as "at risk" and comprise a population that is receiving tremendous attention, especially among urban educators.

Another change has been in the field of educational assessment, with a shift away from norm-referenced, standardized instruments to greater use of curriculum-based measures. The bulk of available assessment tools are not sensitive enough to produce a complete and accurate picture of the instructional needs of poor-performing students (e.g., at risk and disabled). Furthermore, assessment is no longer viewed as a singular, isolated event that occurs outside the classroom under the auspices of a school psychologist. Teachers are assuming greater responsibility for making decisions about educational placement and adjusting daily instruction to align it more closely with student needs.

At the same time, teachers are discovering that quality instructional strategies are applicable to students with and without special needs. Prior assumptions of the need for two separate sets of teaching skills are being replaced by a growing consensus that much of what works with special students works with regular education students and vice versa.

Another important change is that teachers are no longer relegated exclusively to the classroom, limited in their opportunity to interact with and learn from one another. Regular and special classroom teachers are working cooperatively with their colleagues and with persons representing other professional disciplines, such as school psychologists, guidance counselors, and speech and language pathologists. Teachers are being cast in such roles as "peer coach," "cooperative teacher," "teacher assistance team member," and so on. While the responsibilities associated with these collaborative frameworks may vary, these frameworks share a common purpose — to bring two or more people together to better serve a student experiencing problems in school.

Lastly, among the most far-reaching changes in education is the manner in which students with mild disabilities are served. A major reason for this shift is what has become known as the "Regular Education Initiative" (REI). Proponents of the REI assert that the "two-box" system of regular education and special education is dysfunctional and detrimental to students. Believing that most students can be taught in the regular classroom, advocates call for a merger of regular and special education. The present system of special education in which we classify and place students would be replaced with various pupil services. These services would include technical assistance to regular classroom teachers, along with returning administrative control of special education to principals.

In calling attention to a few of the more conspicuous changes taking place in our schools, we have sought to put into perspective the subject of this textbook — quality teaching of all the students. In the discussion that follows, we examine more closely issues that relate to teaching students with and without disabilities in the regular classroom. We look at major legal and legislative actions that have influenced educational policy, discuss movement of students with disabilities into regular classrooms, and look at the reaction this movement has evoked. We dispel some of the myths that surround not only the concept of mainstreaming but also the students themselves. Finally, we explore some of the resultant changes in the roles and responsibilities of public school personnel. Discussing these topics sets the stage for succeeding chapters that focus on various aspects of instruction of students with special needs.

## THE CURRENT SCENE IN EDUCATION

Of the nearly 40 million school-age children throughout the nation, around 4.6 million now receive special education. The actual number of children and youth age 5–21 served in specific educational settings varies according to handicapping condition. According to the U.S. Department of Education, about 70 percent of all students with handicaps are in a regular and/or a resource classroom; 25 percent are in separate classes within a regular education building; and 5 percent are served in separate schools, residential facilities, or home/hospital settings. Figures on specific categories of exceptionality show that about 95 percent of children with speech impairments and 87 percent with learning disabilities are in regular and/or resource classrooms. By comparison, a little less than 50 percent of the students who have been classified as emotionally/behaviorally disordered and around 20 percent of students categorized as multihandicapped presently occupy these placements. Other students placed in regular and/or resource classrooms include those with vision, hearing, orthopedic, and health-related disabilities. These data reveal that a large number of students with various disabilities are being placed in regular classrooms and taught alongside students without disabilities.

## REGULAR CLASS INTEGRATION OF SPECIAL STUDENTS

In the past, regular and special education primarily operated as two separate and distinct enterprises. Today, the philosophical and programmatic barriers that once separated these two disciplines are being dismantled. The steady movement of students with disabilities into less restrictive settings requires regular educators to teach a significantly more diverse classroom population. This process is commonly referred to as "mainstreaming" and reflects the least restrictive environment (LRE) provision of Public Law 94-142. A "free and appropriate" education for all children is a matter of public policy. To comply with the imperative of serving students in the LRE, schools across the country are attempting to establish procedures for maintaining at-risk students and those with disabilities in the regular classroom. They are accomplishing that task with varying success.

Public Law 94-142 (PL 94-142) was never meant to ensure special services to all students who evidenced learning or behavior problems. PL 94-142 envisioned singling out only a limited number of youngsters with significant disabilities for these programming options. The problems many youngsters exhibit in school were never meant to be construed as synonymous with a handicapping condition. The original prevalence figure of 12.035 percent of the school-age population established by the federal government for allocating funds to each state to support special students still holds. The imposition of a ceiling on available funds is one reason school systems have a relatively fixed number of classrooms for special education.

A significant number of students evidence mild to moderate learning or behavior problems which interfere with their ability to make a satisfactory classroom adjustment. They do not all qualify for one of the labels required for special education services (e.g., learning disabled, emotionally/behaviorally disordered, mentally retarded). Through the years, a variety of terms have been used to characterize these students: slow learner, reluctant learner, poor achiever, under achiever, difficult-to-teach, and so on. Today, as many as 20–30 percent of the general education population may comprise the group of youngsters known as at-risk students. By most accounts, at-risk students represent a challenge equal to that of many mainstream students with handicaps.

## LEGAL ASPECTS OF EDUCATING STUDENTS WITH DISABILITIES

Litigation and legislation pertaining to the education of students with disabilities arise out of an historical context in which children with disabilities (e.g., "disorderly conduct or imbecility," *Watson* v. *City of Cambridge*, 1893) could be excluded from school or taught in segregated classes. Historically, special classes were provided for only those students for whom special training would produce skills useful to society. Even in the one-room schoolhouse, acclaimed as an early example of successful teaching of heterogeneously grouped students, the teacher or principal could choose to remove students who could not cope or were unduly disruptive. As early as 1929, recognition that some students required teaching accommodations beyond those found in the regular classroom led to the establishment of approximately 100 education programs for teachers of the handicapped. During the next 30 years, the duality in education programs for regular and special students continued to be emphasized. Monies to fund services for students with handicaps were channeled through separate administrative offices and different fiscal lines at all levels of government.

The 1960s and 1970s were marked by social unrest and societal changes that exerted powerful influence on the nature of special education and the delivery of special education services. In particular, civil rights and the fight against social, economic, and personal discrimination spearheaded the sociopolitical reform movement of the era. Litigation and legislation of the period resulted in such effects as a free, appropriate education for all children regardless of handicapping condition.

## Litigation

Much of the litigation of the early 1950s through 1975, that led to mainstreaming as we know it today, had its legal origins in the Constitution of the United States, specifically, the Fourteenth Amendment. Section 1 guarantees no citizen can be deprived of life, liberty, or property without due process of the law and that all citizens have equal protection of the laws.

The notion that what any one citizen is provided must be offered to all citizens is embodied in the Fourteenth Amendment of the U.S. Constitution. Moreover, all citizens have a right to due process and protection of the laws.

*Brown* v. *Board of Education*, 1954, was landmark litigation that had a significant impact on future court cases and legislation related to persons with disabilities. In *Brown*, the court ruled that segregating students in schools based on race, even if other educational factors appear to be equivalent, is unconstitutional. Thus, the *Brown* case rejected the notion of "separate but equal" and became a cornerstone for subsequent litigation in which parents fought for a free, appropriate education for their handicapped children. In addition to *Brown*, other litigation had momentous bearing on the definition and delivery of special education programs. Litigation of the past three decades addressed four major issues: (1) access to education; (2) accurate classification of students; (3) appropriate instructional programs, including a full range of services; and (4) procedural safeguards.

*Hansen* v. *Hobsen*, 1967, resulted in the ruling that ability grouping or tracking violated due process and the equal protection clause of the Constitution. *Diana* v. *State Board of Education*, 1970, required that children be tested in their primary language, with unfair test items eliminated and reevaluation of minority students undertaken. *Mills* v. *Board of Education*, 1972, affected educational opportunities for persons with disabilities in a pervasive way. As an outcome of *Mills*, students cannot be excluded from school because of a handicapping condition, and furthermore, they have a right to a "constructive education" which includes appropriate specialized instruction.

At about the same time, the Pennsylvania Association for Retarded Children (PARC) filed suit against the Commonwealth of Pennsylvania to gain the right for mentally retarded students to attend school. In 1971, in *PARC, Bowman, et al.,* v. *Commonwealth of Pennsylvania*, the court ruled that mentally retarded students have a right to a free, appropriate public education, regardless of the severity of their handicapping condition. Following this ruling in support of PARC, a series of cases firmly established parental rights to a fair and orderly process to determine (a) if a child has a handicap and (b) what kinds of services he or she should receive. Together, these two components often are referred to as "due process" and include the "informed consent" of parents in the evaluation and placement of their child.

Subsequent litigation has addressed the adequacy of services including the mandating of prereferral evaluations, curriculum-based assessment, and statewide inservice training of assessment personnel (*Luke S. and Hans S.* v. *Nix*, 1984); the imposition of constraints on the right of local school districts to expel and suspend students with a history of learning and behavioral problems (e.g., *Stuart* v. *Nappi*, 1978; *Doe* v. *Koger*, 1979; *S–1* v. *Turlington*, 1981; *Honig* v. *Doe*, 1988), and placing on school officials the burden of proof for changing a student's placement.

In sum, litigation has influenced educational services to students with disabilities in many ways. Court cases have clarified and supported two major themes that pertain to the education of students with handicaps — the rights to due process and equal protection under the law. Key litigation has focused on such issues as separate-but-not-equal standards, disproportionate numbers of minority children in special education, fairness in evaluation and placement practices, and in suspension and exclusion practices, and the definition and delivery of special services. Early litigation helped to set the stage for the passage of federal legislation regarded as "The Bill of Rights for Children with Handicaps" (PL 94-142).

## Landmark Legislation

Two major pieces of legislation have affected the definition and delivery of educational services to students with disabilities. These landmark legislative acts — PL 93-112, Section 504 of the Vocational Rehabilitation Act of 1973 and PL 94-142, the Education for All Handicapped Children Act of 1975 — ensure that the rights of individuals with disabilities are upheld.

Public Law 93-112 serves as a "civil rights act" for individuals with handicaps. Section 504 of the law forbids discrimination against the disabled in education, employment, housing, and access to public programs and facilities. Section 504 requires that institutions make architectural modifications to increase physical accessibility of buildings and that new structures be accessible to persons with handicaps. Regulations stipulate that employers must provide equal recruitment, employment compensation, job assignments, and fringe benefits. Discrimination is forbidden in providing health, welfare, and other social service programs. This law has had the visible effect of changing the look and accessibility of public schools; also, it has brought educators into a closer working relationship with agencies and businesses. This is especially true in regard to students with handicaps who are being prepared to work and live in the community.

In 1975 Congress enacted Public Law 94-142, the most celebrated of the legislative acts pertaining to children with handicaps, overriding President Ford's veto by a vote of 404 to 7 in the House and 87 to 7 in the Senate. This bill provided funds to state education agencies (SEAs) and local education agencies (LEAs) to meet the unique needs of children and youth with handicaps. Major provisions of PL 94-142 included the mandate for (1) all children ages 5–21, regardless of the nature and severity of their handicap(s), to receive a free, appropriate public education; (2) each child with a handicap to have a specially tailored Individualized Educational Program (IEP) based on his or her unique needs; (3) all children with disabilities to be educated in the least restrictive environment (LRE); (4) every student with a disability to have access to participate in all school activities; and (5) all children and their families to be guaranteed the rights to nondiscriminatory testing, confidentiality, and due process. The law includes a legal definition for special education and for specific categories of exceptionality and related services. Major components of PL 94-142 and its provisions are presented in Figure 1.1.

The recent reauthorization of PL 94-142 — PL 101-476, the Individuals with Disabilities Education Act (IDEA) — includes in its features the replacement of the term *handicaps* with the term *disabilities*. It emphasizes early intervention programs that address the needs of those children prenatally exposed to maternal substance abuse. Also, it places greater importance on meeting the needs of ethnically and culturally diverse students with disabilities and on incorporating transition services into the overall definition of the IEP.

In 1986, PL 99-457, Education of the Handicapped Amendments, was passed, extending many of the rights and safeguards of PL 94-142 to handicapped children from birth to 5 years of age. This law mandates services for children 3 to 5 years old, while providing states with incentives for serving children from birth through age 2. As illustrated in Figure 1.2, the law supports a child-find system to identify eligible infants, toddlers, and preschool children. Another important aspect of the law as it relates to infants and toddlers is the Individual Family Service Plan (IFSP), which is to be developed by a multidisciplinary team and the child's parents. The

**FIGURE 1.1 / Major Terms and Provisions of PL 94-142**

| Term of Provision | Definition or Description |
|---|---|
| **Special education** | Specially designed instruction, at no cost to the parent, to meet the unique needs of a handicapped child, including classroom instruction, instruction in physical education, home instruction, and instruction in hospitals and institutions. |
| **Related services** | Developmental, corrective, and other supportive services which are required to assist a handicapped child to benefit from special education. Examples: speech therapy, language development, physical and occupational therapy, recreation, social work services, counseling, psychological services, and school health services. |
| **Handicapping conditions** | Mentally retarded, learning disabled, seriously emotionally disturbed, multiple handicapped, deaf-blind, hard of hearing, deaf, speech impaired, visually handicapped, orthopedically impaired, and other health impaired. |
| **Child find** | Extensive efforts must be made to screen and identify all handicapped children 5-21 years of age. |
| **Free appropriate public education (FAPE)** | Every handicapped child, regardless of the nature and severity of the condition, must be assured a free, appropriate public education at no cost to the parents or guardians. |
| **Due process** | The child's and parents' right to information and informed consent must be assured before the child is evaluated, labeled, or placed. They have a right to an impartial due process hearing if they disagree with evaluation, labeling, or placement decisions. |
| **Parent (parent surrogate) involvement** | Parents will have continuous involvement and input into all aspects of the special education process. |
| **Least restrictive environment (LRE)** | The child must be educated in the least restrictive environment that is consistent with his or her educational needs and, insofar as possible, be placed with nonhandicapped peers. |
| **Individualized education program (IEP)** | A written individualized education program must be prepared for each handicapped child. The plan must state present levels of educational performance, long- and short-term goals, services to be provided, and plans for initiating and evaluating the services. Parents are to participate in the IEP process. |
| **Nondiscriminatory evaluation** | Students must be evaluated in all areas of the suspected disability and in a way that is not biased by their language handicaps. Evaluation must be conducted by a multidisciplinary team, and no single evaluation procedure may be used as the sole criterion for placement or planning. Students must reevaluated every three years. |
| **Confidentiality** | Results of the evaluation and placement must be kept confidential; parents (or guardians) may have access to records regarding their child and may initiate due process proceedings if they object to information on record. |

**FIGURE 1.2 / Major Terms and Provisions of PL 94-457, Education of the Handicapped Amendments**

1. Special education and related services, that is, FAPE, are mandated for all handicapped children age 3 to 5 beginning in the 1990–91 school year.

2. Individualized education programs (IEPS) are required for each child with a handicap, with instruction for parents to be included to the extent parents desire such instruction.

3. Education must occur in the least restrictive environment (LRE).

4. Due process guarantees are extended to 3- to 5-year-olds.

5. Confidentiality and nondiscriminatory testing are mandated.

6. Provision of all services must be by qualified personnel.

7. Incentives are provided for states to plan, develop, and implement early intervention services for infants and toddlers and their families

IFSP is to detail early intervention services needed for the child as well as services which may be important for family functioning. Further, PL 99-457 provides incentives for interagency cooperation in programming for handicapped infants and toddlers and their parents. Participating states are expected to provide comprehensive, coordinated, multidisciplinary interagency programs for all infants and toddlers with handicaps. One potentially far-reaching outcome of this law appears in states that are funding initiatives to provide school-based interagency programs of comprehensive care for school-age at-risk students and their families. Figure 1.2 summarizes the main components of the Amendments related to young children with disabilities. PL 93-112, PL 94-142, PL 101-476, and PL 99-457 have had monumental impact on the definition and delivery of services to students with disabilities. Together, these laws have ensured the right of children with disabilities to a free, appropriate public education and have underscored the mandate to provide that education in the least restrictive environment (LRE).

## THE LEAST RESTRICTIVE ENVIRONMENT (LRE) AND THE CONTINUUM OF EDUCATIONAL SERVICES

Educational services appropriate for students with disabilities comprise a continuum of service placement options, extending from most restrictive (e.g., hospital, residential, or total care facility) to least restrictive (e.g., full time regular education with few or no support services). As shown in Figure 1.3, the continuum of services has eight levels. Although renderings of the continuum vary by number of levels, they all have two dimensions in common. First, in any representation of the continuum-of-services model, the milder the handicapping condition(s), the less restrictive the setting. Second, the less restrictive the setting, the greater the number of students served; conversely, the more restrictive the setting, the smaller the number of students served.

In implementing the continuum of services model and in concert with the goals of PL 94-142, the aim of instruction is to advance students as quickly

**FIGURE 1.3 / Continuum of Service Placement Options**

Most Restrictive
Fewest Students

Separate Programs

1. Full-time residential, hospital, or total care setting

2. Full day special school

Very Limited or Incidental Mainstreaming

3. Part-time special school, part-time regular school

4. Full-time special class in regular school

5. Full-time special class with integration for lunch, recess, etc.

Mainstreamed Programs

6. Part-time regular class and part-time resource room

7. Full-time regular class with consultation for the teacher

8. Students with disabilities in regular education full day

Least Restrictive
Most Students

as possible through the mastery of knowledge and skills which will allow them to move into less restrictive placements. In contrast, movement of a student to a more restrictive placement is done with discretion, keeping the reintegration goals and timeline in mind. In fact, PL 94-142, as amended, now requires the educational program of a student with a disability to include a plan for making the transition to post-secondary life. Quality IEPs (versus those that simply comply with the law) include features such as transition goals and objectives, regardless of a student's age. Classroom placement must be based on the student's individual educational needs rather than on his or her disability or on the particular programs a school district may have to offer. Only when a student's handicapping condition is of such magnitude that he or she cannot be accommodated in a regular education setting are more restrictive placements, such as self-contained classrooms, special schools, or institutional settings, considered.

In examining more closely the continuum of services, the following definitions correspond to the level of service: (1) full-time residential includes 24-hour care away from home, with academic instruction and daily living managed; (2) full-day, special school placements refer to all day instruction at a school for students with disabilities; (3) part-time special and regular school includes instructional arrangements which provide for some instruction within a regular school such as a community vocational program; (4) full-time in a special class in a regular school essentially represents a placement segregated from nonhandicapped peers, but one that may afford integrated busing and incidental opportunity for interaction with peers; (5) full-time special class with limited integration provides for the regular inclusion of handicapped students with peers during nonacademic activities such as lunch, recess, music, physical education, and so on; (6) part-time placement in a special class or resource room and part-time in a regular class involves the provision of direct services by special education teachers to the student for part of the day in a nonintegrated class; (7) full-time regular classroom placement with consultation for the teacher includes adaptations made in the regular classroom and/or the procuring of resources to enable full participation in the regular classroom; and (8) full-time regular classroom placement provides very limited or no direct service support by special education personnel. Home schooling with the support of an itinerant teacher might be seen as falling between levels 1 and 2.

As shown in Figure 1.3, placement levels 1 and 2 — residential and full-day special school, respectively — are segregated educational environments. Four placement levels, 3–6, afford incidental or minimal mainstreaming possibilities or opportunities for students with disabilities to learn side-by-side with nondisabled peers. Finally, levels 7 and 8, full-time services in regular education classrooms with substantial or very limited support, are fully integrated placements.

Although school districts must be able to provide a continuum of placement options to afford a student access to the LRE appropriate to his or her unique needs, the continuum does not dictate movement sequentially through the levels. For example, a student may move from a regular classroom directly into the most restrictive setting, such as an inpatient child psychiatry unit, and be returned to a partially mainstreamed placement such as part-time in the regular classroom and part-time in a resource room. Movement of students across and between levels of placement necessitates cooperation and collaboration among regular and special educators as well as between educators and other agencies, such as juvenile justice and medical care facilities. Generally speaking, students placed in the most restrictive settings usually are not referred by the schools; instead, corrections, parents, and welfare agencies often initiate the most restrictive placements.

## Characteristics of Students with Disabilities

The traditional practice of separating regular and special teacher preparation, along with the "two-box" system of public education, has led to various misconceptions about students with disabilities. These misunderstandings often negatively influence the way people relate to the notion of a disability. In an attempt to dispel some of the more pervasive misconceptions, Figure 1.4 contains a list of myths that relate to various exceptionalities and facts meant to correct erroneous impressions. Yet differences in students sometimes do exist in connection with regular classroom placement of students with disabilities — differences that deserve our attention.

Students identified according to various disability categories are both similar to and different from regular education students. A key to teaching students with handicaps, however, is to recognize that they are a heterogeneous group. Even students diagnosed as having the same handicapping condition (e.g., learning disabilities or mental retardation) and the same level of handicapping condition (e.g., mild, moderate, or severe) represent individuals with unique learning needs. Given this caution, exceptional students often share certain behavioral and learning characteristics.

FIGURE 1.4 / The Mythology of Exceptionality

| | Myth | | Fact |
|---|---|---|---|
| 1. | A learning or behavior problem is synonymous with, and warrants such a label. | 1. | Only a fraction of the students with problems have a quantifiable exceptionality. |
| 2. | Only students with disabilities have special needs. | 2. | Many students have special needs that may be acute at times. |
| 3. | Knowledge of the cause of an exceptionality emerges from a comprehensive diagnosis. | 3. | The diagnostic process is often inconclusive with regard to causal factors. |
| 4. | Knowledge of treatment flows from understanding the cause of a problem. | 4. | The origin of many problems is unclear, yet lack of such knowledge usually does not hinder effective treatment. |
| 5. | There are few students with special needs, and students with disabilities are so different they will succeed only in separate classes. | 5. | Many students with special needs are not identified until middle school or later. |
| 6. | Exceptional students are best served in a special rather than a regular classroom. | 6. | The intrusiveness, intensity, and duration of the required treatment should dictate which learning environment is best for a given student. |
| 7. | Educating students with special needs in regular classes reduces the quality of education for other students. | 7. | Both regular and special needs students benefit from well-designed programs in the regular classroom. |
| 8. | Learning or behavior problems are immutable. | 8. | Properly treated, most problems have a positive prognosis. |
| 9. | Once a disability is diagnosed, needed accommodations are relatively easy to identify. | 9. | Educational accommodations are idiosyncratic to individual children; labels do not prescribe educational plans. |
| 10. | Performance on standardized, norm-referenced evaluation instruments is prescriptive for instructional planning. | 10. | Such tools often are of little value for day-by-day instructional decision making. |

Many teachers are uncertain about the relationship between the various categories of exceptionality and the specific learner characteristics that they must deal with in the classroom. Although we have stressed that no two students, with or without disabilities, are exactly alike, students with special needs tend to bring attention to themselves because they differ from "average" students in intensity, frequency, and sophistication of their behavioral repertoires. Figure 1.5 presents ten characteristics often exhibited by students with disabilities.

FIGURE 1.5 / **Characteristics Associated with Exceptional Learners**

1.  Reduced rate of knowledge/skill acquisition

2.  Poor retention of knowledge/skills

4.  Difficulty discriminating important aspects of instruction

5.  Attention difficulties

6.  Motivation and task-persistence problems

7.  Expressive and/or receptive language difficulties

8.  Social-skill and problem-solving weaknesses

9.  Decreased self-help skills and adaptability

10.  Atypical or inappropriate affect

Any student may demonstrate a combination of the characteristics noted in Figure 1.5; however, some categories of exceptionality are associated with certain characteristics more than others. For example, students with mental disabilities often exhibit difficulty in knowledge/skill acquisition, retention, and generalization. Students with learning disabilities may or may not manifest significant social skill difficulties and/or inappropriate affect. A student with a speech disorder may or may not have an accompanying receptive language problem. Without specific observational information on what a student can do under specific circumstances, it is extremely difficult, if not impossible, to identify educational goals and objectives and select appropriate curricular materials and teaching strategies. Regardless of a student's classification or presenting characteristics, each student must be assessed on an individual basis. Accordingly, the question of placing a student with special needs in a regular classroom is best resolved on a pupil-specific basis.

## MAINSTREAMING

Simply put, mainstreaming is the inclusion of students with special needs in the general education process. This means that students with special physical, learning, emotional, mental, and sensory needs are taught in the same classes as students without disabilities. Mainstreaming is both a concept and a process. Conceptually, mainstreaming is a commitment to educating students with special needs in the same programs as students without special needs. Procedurally, it is the placement of a student with handicaps in the least restrictive environment in which his or her unique needs can be met. From a conceptual and procedural point of view, mainstreaming is much more than the physical integration of students with and without handicaps: Mainstreaming is planning for and implementing procedures to effectively integrate students with handicaps — instructionally, socially, and temporally — in a meaningful and educationally appropriate manner.

## Research on Mainstreaming

The fact that accumulated research offers no definitive answers regarding the most appropriate placement option(s) for students with disabilities complicates any discussion of mainstreaming. Several decades of so-called efficacy studies have failed to produce a clear-cut picture of the most appropriate educational alternatives. For example, some studies suggest that students with disabilities achieve greater gains, socially as well as academically, in regular rather than in special education programs. Comparable findings have been reported on full- versus part-time regular classroom integration of exceptional learners. In contrast, some investigations reveal no significant differences in performance as a function of classroom setting and report that the instructional strategies, rather than the setting, affect pupil performance. Still others indicate that special education may be superior to regular classroom placement and the short-term improvements in achievement and self-esteem evidenced by some students upon entering the mainstream do not always last.

There are many possible explanations for the mixed results of the efficacy of mainstreaming. First, schools and school systems vary in their practice of mainstreaming. Second, uniform guidelines for making decisions about the mainstreaming process are scarce. For example, no two school systems are likely to have the same assessment information available when deliberating over a placement decision; nor will they offer the same placement options. Third, methodological differences are common in efficacy research. For example, the instruments employed to determine the effects of a particular placement may vary across studies, making it practically impossible to compare results of various investigations. Finally, the contradictory verdicts of some researchers may be attributable to the specific category of students under investigation. The disparate outcomes of research seem to indicate that regular classroom placement is beneficial for some but not all students. In any event, about 75 percent of all students with disabilities receive a portion of their daily instruction in regular classrooms, a situation that compels us to take inventory of our present practices and to be prepared to replace those which are flawed or inefficient.

## Mainstreaming and the Regular Education Initiative (REI)

The least restrictive environment (LRE) clause of PL 94-142 has been a major force behind the increase in students with handicaps being served in general education classrooms. Another catalyst is the national movement known as the "Regular Education Initiative" (REI) which has given impetus to serving at-risk students, culturally-diverse students, and students with mild disabilities in regular education settings. These and other factors point to the mainstreaming of more students with special qualities and evoke a number of questions: What is mainstreaming? How can students with disabilities be mainstreamed successfully? What exactly is the REI? How will the REI affect public education throughout the 1990s?

The mainstreaming movement is likely to be influenced significantly by the Regular Education Initiative (REI). The REI has gained significant support across the United States since the mid-1980s. It calls for restructuring regular and special education into a unified service delivery system. For the most part, students with mild disabilities will be taught in regular education classrooms with their peers. Proponents of the REI claim that students, teachers, administrators, and parents will benefit from the merging of special and regular education wherein more students will participate in the mainstream of education. For example, many at-risk students presently not served in special education would receive the services they need if existing special education support could be used to assist needy students. Advocates further assert that the REI will lead to minimizing the negative stigma of labels, increasing opportunity for modeling desired social and school survival behaviors, learning in situations that are more representative of the real world, and increasing appreciation and understanding of individual differences. While these consequences are positive, some educators question the benefits of the REI. They argue that many special students will be lost in the shuffle, that regular education teachers are ill-prepared to serve students with special needs, that there is no empirical basis for shifting to a full-integration model, and that research has yet to identify ways to effectively educate heterogeneous and diverse populations in large group settings, such as general education classrooms.

Regardless of the pros and cons of the debate, the REI is likely to continue to influence the manner in which services are provided to students with mild handicaps, those who are at risk, and those who come from culturally diverse backgrounds. In all probability, educators will need to refine existing classroom teaching skills and develop new ones in order to meet the professional and ethical challenges they will face throughout the 1990s. Among the challenges to be met are the creation and/or implementation of strategies to assess student performance on a day-by-day basis; individualize instruction in large-group situations; manage classroom behavior of diverse students; build social competence and acceptance among students; work collaboratively and effectively with team members; and cooperate with parents, businesses, and other agencies.

### Teacher Perspectives on Mainstreaming

From the beginning, many teachers have been apprehensive about the regular class integration of students with disabilities; some have vigorously resisted it. That general educators are reluctant to accept students classified as disabled into their classrooms is understandable. Because few teachers have received specialized training at the preservice level, their ability to work with special students has been seriously tested. Until recently, teachers could not count on obtaining any technical assistance in managing or instructing students with disabilities. Faced with the pressures of mainstreaming, general and special educators, administrators, and parents have engaged in widespread and sometimes contentious debate. Regardless of this disagreement, educational policy on students with disabilities is likely to shift even more toward providing instruction in the least restrictive environment. General education teachers will assume more responsibility for the education of all students, including large numbers of those formerly excluded on the basis of an identified disability, such as a language or learning disability.

Fortunately, the exchange of opinion has resulted in a better understanding of the concerns of the various participants in the mainstreaming process. Discussion among various professionals has created strong sentiment for the need for additional training, instructional resources, and technical assistance to ensure "equality of educational opportunity" for disabled students in regular classes. At both the preservice and the inservice level, regular and special education teachers should learn to assess and teach academic and social skills to all students.

### The Changing Role of Teachers

Among the most fundamental changes taking place in our schools is the redefinition of teacher roles and responsibilities. The roles of both regular and special educators have been influenced and will continue to be influenced by interpretations of the law. Recent litigation supports the propositions that more students with mild disabilities will be served in regular classrooms and that procedures for better serving students in the least restrictive environment (LRE) will become the focus of educational activity at the classroom, building, and district levels. Not only will "pull-out" programming decrease, but also suspension and expulsion will be used less as disciplinary tools. Instead, more effective ways to reduce undesirable behavior and teach appropriate replacement behavior will need to be developed.

For students with mild disabilities, the LRE translates to full- or part-time placement in the regular classroom. Until recently, the special education teacher has been primarily responsible for formulating educational programs to meet the individual needs of the student with a disability by facilitating and managing the development of the IEP. The current trend toward the full integration of students with disabilities into regular education places ever-increasing responsibility on the regular educator to design individualized education programs for these students. Much of the responsibility for successfully mainstreaming students with mild disabilities rests with the multidisciplinary team, including the regular education teacher. Fortunately, material adaptations (e.g., highlighting and outlining strategies, self-correcting materials), and instructional approaches (e.g., peer tutoring, group-individualized instruction, and curricular strategies) have been found to be beneficial not only to students with special needs, but also to general education students. These and many other proven strategies are presented in succeeding chapters.

As we have noted, many authorities believe that it is possible and desirable to bridge the gap between general and special education and to merge the knowledge and expertise of these two professional disciplines. Survey studies indicate that regular classroom teachers who express negative views toward mainstreaming often feel ill prepared and unsupported in that effort. At the same time, studies involving special educators reveal that they are relatively inexperienced in furnishing assistance to their general education colleagues. However, many of these teachers express a willingness to assume a collaborative role and to work cooperatively with their colleagues to remedy problems evidenced by their students. To ensure the success of students in the mainstream, educators must establish an alliance that combines general educators' knowledge of *what* to teach with special educators' knowledge of *how* to teach. By pooling these two bodies of information, many school districts should succeed in mainstreaming students with disabilities.

However, teacher renewal efforts that consist only of the introduction of teaching strategies to deal with diversity in the classroom are not enough. Teachers will need to augment their interpersonal and communication skills to engage successfully in a group problem-solving process. Some schools have initiated integrated inservice programs, consisting of regular classroom teachers, special education teachers, and building-level administrators, as a step toward full collaboration. All educators must recognize that students with and without special needs constitute a community of learners for whom all school personnel share responsibility. As we discuss in Chapter 16, the various collaborative approaches being initiated at the elementary, middle school, and secondary levels hold much promise for achieving that end.

## CONCLUSION

There is ample reason to be optimistic about our ability to meet the challenges we face in the schools. There is no simple solution to the many problems that confront classroom teachers and other school personnel. While we support regular classroom integration of students with disabilities, we acknowledge that not every student is best served in the regular classroom. Students with disabilities benefit from regular class placement when there is congruence between their ability to perform and the support and expectations of the classroom. In the end, it will take a change in our philosophy of education, as well as in the technology we rely on, if we are to succeed in teaching all the students. The remainder of this textbook is devoted to practical information to help teachers create a learning environment in which students with special needs, diverse backgrounds, and specific disabilities can perform satisfactorily alongside more typical learners.

## ADDITIONAL SOURCES OF INFORMATION

Kauffman, J. M., & Pullen, P. L. (1989). An historical perspective: A personal perspective on the history of serving mildly handicapped and at-risk students. *Remedial and Special Education, 10,* 12–14.

Lewis, R. B., & Doorlag, D. H. (1991). *Teaching special students in the mainstream* (3rd ed.). New York: Merrill/Macmillan.

Morsink, C. (1984). *Teaching special needs students in regular classrooms.* Boston: Little, Brown.

Prasse, D. P. (1986). Litigation and special education: An introduction. *Exceptional Children, 52,* 311–312.

Rothstein, L. F. (1990). *Special education law.* New York: Longman.

Salend, S. J. (1990). *Effective mainstreaming.* New York: Macmillan.

Schulz, J. B., Carpenter, C. D., & Turnbull, A. P. (1991). *Mainstreaming exceptional students: A guide for classroom teachers* (3rd ed.). Boston: Allyn and Bacon.

Stainback, W., & Stainback, S. (1992). *Controversial issues confronting special education: Divergent perspectives.* Boston: Allyn and Bacon.

U. S. Department of Education (1990). *Twelfth annual report to Congress on the implementation of Public Law 94-142.* Washington, DC: U. S. Government Printing Office.

Ysseldyke, J. E., Algozzine, B., & Thurlow, M. L. (1992). *Critical issues in special education* (2nd ed.). Boston: Houghton Mifflin.

# CHAPTER TWO

## SPECIAL NEEDS OF SPECIAL POPULATIONS

*— Joyce S. Choate*

All students occasionally need specific instruction to meet their individual academic needs. However, a significant number of students demonstrate learning or behavior problems that call for more specialized instruction than other students need. This chapter outlines some of the special problems that certain categories of students may experience in attempting to master academic and social skills. Whether their difficulties result from the described learning differences, experience differences, or inappropriate teaching, many of the students in each category share some common instructional needs.

Briefly described are two sets of special learners: (1) students designated as regular and remedial learners who are considered at risk for school failure and (2) students who by virtue of their learning differences are eligible for special education services. The first set of special learners contains groups of at-risk students whom teachers informally categorize according to observable clues and assumed causes of learning interference; less obvious underlying causes may include factors as disadvantaged homes (e.g., inadequate parenting, income, education, nutrition, or abuse) or early exposure to toxic elements (e.g., drugs, alcohol, lead). In the second set are special students formally classified according to diagnosed disabilities. Many students who qualify for special education services are also taught in regular or remedial classrooms, but special educators direct at least a portion of their instruction. Gifted students are treated as a separate group because their exceptionality is unique. Each group's frequently cited learning characteristics lead to implications for instruction, although they are never applicable to every student in a group.

Although entire books have been written on each of the special categories, in this discussion each category covers a single page. Each page begins with a list of problem behaviors often associated with the classification, followed by a brief description of some typical performances, the relationship of the learning or experience problem to academic difficulties, and the implications for academic progress.

All students occasionally evidence some of the Detection behaviors. Not every student with academic problems fits neatly into a category, nor does every student in a category exhibit every problem. The Detection behaviors offer clues to a possible pattern of learning needs. To identify and confirm exact problems, a teacher must consider these clues as well as a student's past and sustained performance and the results of evaluations by appropriate experts.

The Corrective Principles apply to the most typical characteristics of each category. To correct skill deficits, the teacher may have to tailor strategies to the learning needs of individual students, always consulting appropriate specialists. Confirming that any principle applies to a given student requires diagnosing and analyzing each student's skills and evaluating targeted teaching. These principles are intended as preliminary guides to help you select and modify the Correction strategies presented in later chapters.

## AT-RISK STUDENTS IN REGULAR OR REMEDIAL EDUCATION

### Cultural / Language Differences

DETECTION

Students in this group may

- Perform below capacity or exhibit *no* academic problems
- Display a restricted vocabulary
- Comprehend surface meanings only
- Use incorrect grammar and have difficulty with complex sentences
- Frequently mispronounce, rearrange, or substitute words

*Description*

Students may differ culturally in one of two ways: (1) They have a cultural background different from that of the majority of students attending their school or (2) they share the culture of the majority of their schoolmates, but their culture differs from that of the students for whom the curriculum and textbooks were developed. A language difference often accompanies a cultural difference, resulting in limited language fluency and a narrow vocabulary. Some culturally different students also are considered *disadvantaged* because they have not been exposed to the experiences that provide a foundation for academic achievement. Students who are culturally different may display academic difficulties ranging from none to mild to severe. These difficulties may resemble the problems of students with language disabilities. Their language performance is often riddled with errors in pronunciation, syntax, and vocabulary. Silent reading may be less difficult for these students than oral reading or comprehension of speech.

*Special Problems*

The major problems that cultural diversity presents in the classroom result from the students' different experiences, values, and language. These differences may interfere with students' understanding of common reference points used to illustrate concepts, their understanding and manipulation of concepts, and their ability to communicate the extent of their knowledge. Many of these students think in their primary language and then translate into English, thus slowing performance; characteristics of the first language often creep into their translations, producing errors consistent with the student's primary language.

*Implications*

The extent to which cultural and language differences impede or facilitate academic performance depends in part on the teacher's knowledge of and attitude toward multicultural issues, as well as his or her willingness to accommodate individual learning styles, to provide visual cues to explain and translate concepts, and to establish or explain common experiences prior to each lesson.

CORRECTIVE PRINCIPLES

Use these guidelines to plan and modify instruction.

1. Incorporate students' multicultural contributions into lessons.
2. Build concrete and vicarious experiences prior to each lesson.
3. Use pictures and other visual cues to explain and translate concepts.
4. Give students the written script of oral directions and lessons.
5. Involve students in structured cooperative-learning activities.
6. Provide positive corrective feedback on vocabulary and grammar.
7. Use a whole-language approach to explain syntactical differences and to bridge gaps among students' oral language, reading, and writing.

## Cumulative Deficit Skills

DETECTION        Students in this group may

- Demonstrate a pattern of steadily decreasing performance in all subjects
- Exhibit problems in all academic skills but not in speaking and listening
- Display mastery of review skills but not of new ones
- Evidence skill and/or concept gaps

*Description*   Students with this problem are often described by teachers as the ones who "got behind and can't catch up." They simply did not master the prerequisite skills before the curriculum moved ahead of them. Their problems are most obvious in the basic subjects (reading, writing, and arithmetic) but eventually spill over into most curricular areas. Because mathematics requires mastery of each step in sequence, students who miss one skill will not be able to acquire other skills. Students who struggle with basic computation will be unable to attend to problem solving.

*Special Problems*   Cumulative deficits occur when students do not master key skills at the intended point in the curriculum; skill deficits are compounded as new skills are introduced and levels of difficulty increased. Frequent or lengthy absences, a change in schools, or fragmented instruction caused by teacher error or teacher absences interrupt program and skill continuity. Narrow vocabularies, limited experiences, or lack of reinforcement at home further contribute to the problem. Some students become so overwhelmed that they simply quit trying.

*Implications*   A cumulative deficit in the basic skills eventually interferes with performance in all subject areas. Classwork is often incomplete or incorrect because students find it too difficult and/or have not mastered appropriate strategies. As these students advance in school, demands for independent classwork increase while their overall academic performance decreases. Corrective instruction must focus on targeted teaching of missing skills, regular reviews, and interactive learning with peers. Since a variety of learning and experience problems can cause cumulative skill deficits, the nature of the student's difficulty should be identified before planning a corrective program.

CORRECTIVE PRINCIPLES   Use these guidelines to plan and modify instruction.
1. Directly teach the missing skills that impede progress.
2. Temporarily slow instructional pace to permit reteaching of skills.
3. Review and reteach prerequisite skills and concepts before each lesson.
4. Teach concepts and mechanics with focused listening activities.
5. Provide a tutor for supplementary instruction in appropriate prerequisites.
6. Use cooperative-learning groups and paired problem-solving groups for new and review assignments.

## Educational Deprivation

DETECTION        Students in this group may

- Evidence gaps in academic skills and knowledge
- Apply skills inappropriately
- Either try very hard or not try at all
- Have difficulty understanding and/or expressing knowledge
- Perform slowly

*Description*    Educational deprivation results primarily from incorrect or ineffective teaching. The academic performances of these students often fall into one of two extremes: Either the student obviously exerts a tremendous amount of effort, or he or she appears to have given up in defeat. Many of these students appear to know only one strategy for each task. Many educationally deprived students also become underachievers as a defense mechanism.

*Special Problems*    The effects of inept or inappropriate teaching may be confined to a single subject or may be reflected in students' performance in most subjects. The causes of educational deprivation are varied and often suspected after the fact. The prime offenders are nonteachers, who put the textbooks and workbooks with the children and assume learning will just happen; those who teach the textbook and not the students, insisting that the entire class advance together according to the teacher's agenda; or those who emphasize the mechanics and not the process and content. Other factors include frequent teacher absences, inadequate planning, and changes in textbook series, as well as teachers' rigidity and teacher-student personality conflicts that result in aversive learning experiences. Some teachers overemphasize one skill at the expense of others, producing students who persist in using only the one strategy, while other teachers actually teach particular students that they are hopeless. Although these are initially teacher problems, they eventually result in academic problems for the student.

*Implications*    Students who conscientiously follow the instructions of their teachers without success soon lose faith in themselves and in their education. Without intervention, they are destined to experience difficulty in all subjects. The ineffective strategies these students use produce slow performance, resulting in incomplete assignments in all subjects. The teacher must compensate for inappropriate teaching of the past, impart enthusiasm for learning, improve students' attitudes, and show students that they can trust teachers and succeed.

CORRECTIVE PRINCIPLES    Use these guidelines to plan and modify instruction.
1. Identify and fill skill gaps.
2. Review and reteach prerequisite skills before each lesson.
3. Use whole-language activities to teach and reinforce concepts and build communication skills.
4. Stress process and content, rather than mechanics.
5. Carefully structure learning experiences to ensure students' success.
6. Highlight the personal relevance of each concept and skill.

## Slow Learning Rate

DETECTION

Students in this group may

- Develop skills at a slower rate than most age peers
- Require more practice and repetition than most age peers
- Have narrow vocabularies
- Take longer to perform academic tasks than age peers
- Make steady but slow progress with individualized instruction

*Description*

Students whose learning rate is slower than the rate of their peers, the pace of the teacher, and the pace of the curriculum are often termed *slow learners.* These students learn more quickly than most students with mild retardation but more slowly than average students. They often struggle to keep up and, without special provisions, fall behind. The social skills of many of these students are slightly below those expected for their chronological age.

*Special Problems*

These students need not experience difficulties if the pace of the curriculum is adjusted to their slower rate of learning. However, problems occur when the curriculum leaves them behind. Facing new and more difficult language tasks before mastering the prerequisite skills, the students accumulate skill deficits. As in the case of students with cumulative deficits, narrow vocabularies, limited experiential backgrounds, and limited reinforcement or practice at home contribute to the problem. A slow learning rate typically cuts across all areas of the curriculum, so that these students require extra guidance and accommodation in most subjects.

*Implications*

Although these students may not advance a full achievement level in all subject areas each school year, many can master the most basic skills. The skill sequence of the regular curriculum is appropriate for most of these students; however, they typically take longer to master each task. They need a slow pace of instruction that emphasizes practical knowledge and skills; they may require extra review and reinforcement for each concept. Students who learn slowly may require both supplementary instruction and special assistance as they attempt independent tasks.

CORRECTIVE PRINCIPLES

Use these guidelines to plan and modify instruction.

1. Slow the pace of instruction to match the student's learning rate.
2. Provide extended readiness and practice activities for each lesson.
3. Review and reteach prerequisite skills before each lesson.
4. Provide ample talking and listening activities to expand language skills and concepts.
5. Directly teach word meanings for all subjects.
6. Shorten assignments to manageable units.
7. Emphasize real-life skills.

## Underachievement

DETECTION

Students in this group may

- Exhibit skills below the level teachers expect
- Perform inconsistently and be distractible
- Appear to dislike and avoid the rigors of academic work
- Perform much better when topics are of high interest
- Often comprehend surface meanings only

*Description*

Underachievers usually exhibit similar performances across school subjects. They do not appear to exert much effort to perform and often seem disinterested. These students may perform voluntarily when a topic appeals to them and even show sudden skill gains, but soon lose their enthusiasm. Many of these students are easily distracted in the classroom.

*Special Problems*

The causes of underachievement are varied. The primary factor is often lack of motivation, resulting from sociocultural values in conflict with those of the school, lack of reinforcement for academic achievement, negative role models, or inability to see the relevance of the curriculum to personal goals in particular and to academic achievement in general. Teacher pressure may compound the problem. Language differences, limited exposure to positive academic experiences, limited experiential background, and inadequate educational training can also contribute to underachievement. Students who are easily distracted or too stimulated by a class full of peers have difficulty concentrating on learning and performing. Specific learning differences, such as those described in the next few pages, can also contribute.

*Implications*

Students who achieve significantly below their capacity do not develop the skills they need to progress in school. They often appear to exert little effort, and their verbal expression and understanding may be sparse. Many teachers are impatient and negative in their interactions with these students. Some teachers try to force underachievers to perform, producing a pronounced dislike for academic work. The teacher should try to identify the cause(s) of a student's underachievement. Underachieving students need improved self-concept and motivation. Involving students in planning their program, for example, allowing them to choose from an assortment of subtopics, increases their interest.

CORRECTIVE PRINCIPLES

Use these guidelines to plan and modify instruction.

1. Identify the cause of underachievement and teach accordingly.
2. Determine students' interests and plan appropriate activities.
3. Focus on activities that emphasize the usefulness of content and skills.
4. Clearly state the purposes of each learning activity.
5. Personalize the activities for relevance and meaning.
6. Involve students in planning their programs.

## EXCEPTIONAL STUDENTS ELIGIBLE FOR SPECIAL EDUCATION

### Cross-Categorical Disabilities

DETECTION

Properly identified students in this group may

- Learn and acquire skills more slowly than age peers
- Display poor retention of knowledge and skills
- Exhibit problems generalizing knowledge and skills
- Evidence problems attending to and completing tasks
- Exhibit expressive and/or receptive language difficulties
- Display little motivation and weak social, self-help, and problem-solving skills
- Evidence some of the specific problems cited by exceptionality on the pages that follow

*Description*

To be classified as having a disability, students must be evaluated as meeting their state's eligibility criteria for special education services. Instead of providing special education services according to the category of students' exceptionalities, some school systems group students generically or cross-categorically according to the severity of the disability. Students whose disability is mild to moderate and who exhibit learning characteristics of several categories of exceptionality are placed in cross-categorical settings for mildly to moderately disabled. In addition to special education, many of these students receive most or all of their instruction in a regular classroom. In the basic skills, many of these students perform below the level of their age peers. A large percentage of them experience numerous problems reading and solving word problems, and an even greater proportion find written expression particularly difficult; however, they do not necessarily exhibit problems in content subjects. These students also demonstrate some of the patterns of performance typical of one or more categorical exceptionalities.

*Special Problems*

These students qualify for special education services on the basis of their need for adjusted instruction and curricula. Among the characteristics shared by many of these students are slow rate of knowledge and skill acquisition, poor retention and generalization of knowledge and skills, difficulties discriminating important aspects of instruction, short attention span, distractibility, need for success and encouragement, expressive and/or receptive language deficits, weak social and problem solving skills, decreased self-help skills and adaptability, and atypical or inappropriate affect. These students may have limited experiences and need individual specialized instruction in one or more subjects. Some of these learning characteristics appear to complicate the tasks of the school curriculum, while others directly interfere with achievement.

*Implications*

Although these students share many needs, differences in their learning characteristics produce varied profiles of performance. Their difficulties in mastering basic skills, particularly listening, speaking, reading, and writing, often result in difficulties across curricula. The discussions of related exceptional categories give additional examples of interactions between learning characteristics and academic performance.

CORRECTIVE
PRINCIPLES

Cross-categorical or generic groupings exist because many common principles of corrective instruction apply to students with mild to moderate disabilities in several exceptional categories, as well as to nondisabled students. These principles are concerned with structuring the learning environment, building appropriate experiences and attitudes, and adjusting the content and style of instruction to the learners' needs. In addition to the general teaching practices recommended in Chapter 3, these general principles provide guidelines to plan and modify instruction for students with mild to moderate disabilities.

1. Build and recall experiences to prepare students for each learning task and to broaden language and concept knowledge.
2. Determine learning strengths and vary stimulus/response patterns according to students' needs.
3. Present short and varied instructional tasks planned to insure student success.
4. Keep distractions in the classroom to a minimum.
5. Systematically reinforce appropriate performance.
6. Consider students' interests, age, degree of disability, needs, and skills when selecting instructional methods and materials.
7. Include review material or tasks as the major portion of each activity.
8. Carefully guide students to transfer new knowledge and apply new skills to other situations; integrate instruction across subjects.
9. Incorporate instruction in receptive and expressive language into each lesson.
10. Emphasize the usefulness and relevance of each lesson and clearly state the purpose of each task.
11. Directly teach and then monitor the use of strategies to accomplish each task.
12. Involve students in structured cooperative-learning activities.
13. Teach and model appropriate social skills, and then coach their application.
14. Routinely collaborate with appropriate specialists to design and modify each student's corrective program.

## Behavior Disorders

DETECTION                 Properly identified students in this group may

- Exhibit inappropriate behaviors that interfere with academic progress
- Seem capable of achieving at a higher level
- Have difficulty attending or comprehending
- Be slow to begin or complete tasks, or perform quickly and carelessly
- Become agitated when they encounter difficult assignments
- Have problems communicating orally and/or in writing or be reluctant to do so

*Description*     Students who are classified as behavior disordered display inappropriate behaviors that interfere with their own progress and often with the progress of others. These behaviors, many of which are discussed in Chapter 14, persist despite ordinary attempts to change them. The nature of the academic difficulty depends in part upon the particular manifestation of the behavioral difficulty. When a student's performance is adversely affected, it is often reflected in unsatisfactory performance rates, inaccuracy, attention deficits, hyperactivity, off-task behavior, and inappropriate interactions with others or avoidance of interaction, and escalation of negative behavior when tasks become difficult.

*Special Problems*     The academic problems these students exhibit are often a logical outgrowth of their behaviors. Distractibility interferes with on-task behavior. Insecurity in unstructured or changed learning situations impedes performance. Overcautiousness and distrust create careful but slow workers, while impulsivity creates fast but careless workers. Low tolerance for frustration causes defeat when facing difficult tasks. Disruptive behaviors interfere with the student's own performance as well as with others' performance. Group activities overstimulate some students, while intimidating others. Depressed language functioning occurs in some behavior disorders.

*Implications*     Students in this group do not necessarily exhibit difficulties in all or even in a majority of academic areas. In fact, some become proficient readers and writers who use these skills as an escape. Many satisfactorily perform independent assignments but do not perform interactive assignments well. The major threat to academic performance is interruption in sequenced skill mastery, which may result in cumulative skill deficits.

CORRECTIVE PRINCIPLES     Use these guidelines to plan and modify instruction.

1. Contract with students for specific skills and then chart progress.
2. Plan highly structured programs, using consistent stimulus/response formats, routines, and positive reinforcement.
3. Accommodate students' attention- and frustration-tolerance levels.
4. Plan activities the student can accomplish; gradually phase in interactive activities.
5. Select bibliotherapeutic themes for lesson content.
6. Directly teach and coach students in the use of strategies for each task.

## Hearing Impairments

DETECTION
Properly identified students in this group may

- Evidence difficulty in all language skills
- Exhibit specific problems in speaking, reading, and/or spelling
- Master language skills slowly
- Display a limited vocabulary
- Demonstrate difficulty interpreting information
- Appear to tire or give up easily

*Description*
Students who are hearing impaired often evidence many of the same difficulties as those with general language disorders and some of the difficulties of those with speech disorders. Typically, their command of language is inversely proportional to the degree of hearing loss and directly related to the age at which their hearing loss occurred. Subtle phonetic differences may escape their attention, as may word meanings and complex sentences. These students have difficulty not only in learning from oral information presented in class, but also in interpreting the information because of language problems.

*Special Problems*
Most students with hearing impairments must surmount at least two barriers: difficulty learning from information presented orally and limited language facility. Their hearing problems limit their opportunity to acquire information from oral teaching and discussions. Limited language facility presents a more serious impediment because it may interfere with reading skills and with the ability to manipulate concepts and ideas. Whereas hearing students can glean incidental learning, broaden their experiences, expand their language, and reinforce concepts and skills from what they hear, students with hearing impairments are often denied such opportunities. They must strain to hear, draw from an often sparse vocabulary to express ideas, monitor their speech, struggle with subtle meanings, and reauditorize the words needed to express their ideas. Many hesitate to interact verbally, thereby limiting both improvement and demonstration of achievement. They tend to tire quickly, but they require extended time to master language tasks.

*Implications*
Language growth and development are critical for students with hearing impairments. Many of the students are closely attuned to visual stimuli as a compensatory learning strategy, so the teacher should provide them with advantageous seating and ample visual cues. The teacher should face them and clearly label each oral direction and concept in writing. In some instances, extra examples and demonstrations may be necessary.

CORRECTIVE PRINCIPLES
Use these guidelines to plan and modify instruction.

1. Integrate the academic and speech/language development programs.
2. Seat students where they can best see and hear.
3. Teach the use of sight and touch as compensatory learning techniques.
4. Present visual cues for each task; alternate auditory and visual tasks.
5. Carefully build the experiential framework before each lesson.
6. Extend the readiness and practice activities for each lesson.
7. Offer extensive training in vocabulary that carries the conceptual loads for each subject.

## Language Disabilities

DETECTION

Properly identified students in this group may

- Evidence a specific difficulty in language comprehension
- Have difficulty conversing or explaining answers
- Display problems both in understanding and in expressing language
- Pronounce words without knowing their meanings
- Have a limited or inappropriate vocabulary
- Use incorrect grammar

*Description*

Students with language disabilities share many characteristics of students with learning disabilities whose primary deficit is in language and some characteristics of students with language differences. Language disabilities are of three types: receptive, expressive, or both. Some students do not understand parts of what they receive as they listen or read. Others understand what they receive but cannot express that knowledge by verbalizing it orally or in writing. Still others experience difficulty both understanding what they receive and expressing their knowledge. Whatever the language problem, it can interfere with mastery of concepts and with oral and written demonstration of mastery of skills and concepts.

*Special Problems*

The language problems of these students are generally ones of meaning. Difficulties receiving and interpreting language interfere with understanding listening activities, oral directions, conversation, and reading passages. The language arts are particularly problematic. Because of their inability to manipulate words and ideas, these students are denied the incidental learning that occurs from various language interactions. Difficulties expressing thoughts verbally or in writing may interfere with their expressive performance and with their demonstrating what they do know and understand.

*Implications*

Because of the heavy reliance on language for instruction and for evaluating progress, students with language disabilities are unduly penalized in the classroom. To evaluate knowledge, the teacher may need to use a multiple-choice format that also requires the students to restate the selected answers. The teacher should provide numerous and concrete hands-on activities, emphasize vocabulary, and verbally label each step of each concept. Oral directions should be accompanied by visual cues, models, and several examples in which the teacher walks and talks students through the process.

CORRECTIVE PRINCIPLES

Use these guidelines to plan and modify instruction.

1. Integrate the academic and language-development programs.
2. Build a background of concrete experiences for each lesson.
3. Teach both receptive and expressive tasks with each concept.
4. Provide intensive instruction in word, sentence, and passage meanings, particularly as they apply to target concepts.
5. Supplement instruction with visual aids.
6. For evaluation, have students select answers and then restate them.
7. Provide positive corrective feedback for language skills.

## Learning Disabilities

DETECTION    Properly identified students in this group may

- Evidence inconsistent and uneven performance of tasks
- Demonstrate listening and speaking skills superior to reading, writing, and other skills
- Exhibit skill gaps
- Display attention and task-persistence problems
- Appear capable of performing at a higher achievement level

*Description*    Students with learning disabilities probably present more diverse learning characteristics than any other special group. They exhibit deficits in one or more psychological processes for understanding language. The language arts as well as mathematics and even thinking skills may be impaired. Academic weaknesses are usually counterbalanced by one or more strengths in other skill areas. In addition to academic deficits, particularly in reading (e.g., dyslexia), other frequently cited characteristics are attention deficits and impulsiveness. Social acceptance may partially explain the continued growth in the numbers of students in this category. This social acceptance may stem from the negatively-viewed causes excluded in the definition, since the learning problems must not primarily stem from physical, emotional, or retardation weakness or from environmental disadvantages.

*Special Problems*    Primarily a heterogeneous group, students with learning disabilities typically do not achieve at their capacity. Their abilities and performances seem to fluctuate both within and across skill and content areas. Many of their learning characteristics compound their academic difficulties: hyperactivity, distractibility, and attention deficits interrupt on-task behaviors; fluctuating performances frustrate both students and teachers; and apparent processing difficulties further confuse students.

*Implications*    The problems of students with learning disabilities are varied and often complex. Many instructional strategies that increase progress in one skill area also improve performance in other subject areas. Adjusting the stimulus/response requirements of classroom tasks to the students' needs increases their performance. Some students need multisensory instruction, while others need only to see the written labels for information that is presented orally. Carefully supervised and structured small-group activities can increase learning and social interactions.

CORRECTIVE PRINCIPLES    Use these guidelines to plan and modify instruction.

1. Adjust stimulus/response patterns, permitting the interchange of skills as needed.
2. Teach students strategies to compensate for specific learning weaknesses.
3. Build study strategies and independent learning skills.
4. Use visual and auditory prompts to teach each lesson.
5. Prepare brief activities and vary the types of activities.
6. Provide a nondistracting learning environment.

## Mental Retardation

DETECTION   Properly identified students in this group may

- Learn and develop skills much more slowly than age peers
- Exhibit limited vocabulary and language skills
- Need concrete objects and experiences to master concepts and skills
- Require numerous repetitions to understand and remember concepts and skills
- Have difficulty comprehending complex language and concepts

*Description*   The limited intellectual capacity of students who are mentally retarded similarly limits their language and academic skills. These students function at significantly below-average levels, both intellectually and socially. Their adaptive behavior is commensurate with their subaverage learning skills. Their learning rate is markedly slow, and many have difficulty with short-term memory. They require extended time and instruction to master tasks, although the sequence of skill mastery is that of the regular curriculum. While they may master the rudiments of such mechanical tasks as spelling, phonics, and simple computation, they learn writing, comprehension, and problem-solving skills very slowly and laboriously.

*Special Problems*   Unlike students with learning disabilities, students who are mentally retarded typically present a relatively even profile of abilities and performances. Most of the academic problems these students experience reflect their limited language and thinking skills. These students often have difficulty understanding and expressing the meanings of words and ideas. The higher levels of cognitive processing required for critical comprehension, writing, and complex problem solving are particularly difficult. These students tend to overlook subtle meanings and miss opportunities for incidental learning.

*Imlications*   Because of their slow rate of learning, these students should not be expected to attempt the pace of the regular curriculum. Slow progress permeates their academic performance. Students who are mentally retarded need direct instruction to recognize, understand, and use terms and develop skills essential to following oral and written directions, to social functioning, and to survival outside the classroom.

CORRECTIVE PRINCIPLES   Use these guidelines to plan and modify instruction.

1. Focus on the basic skills and concepts needed for real-life functioning.
2. Use concrete objects and experiences to teach concepts.
3. Teach each concept very slowly, reviewing frequently.
4. Often repeat instruction and practice for each task.
5. Extend the readiness activities for each lesson, building prerequisite skills and concepts.
6. Structure and guide opportunities for transfer and generalization.
7. Carefully segment concepts and divide sentences by thought units to facilitate understanding.

## Physical and Medical Disabilities

DETECTION

Properly identified students in this group may

- Perform at a slow rate
- Evidence a narrow vocabulary
- Demonstrate inconsistent performances across subject areas
- Exhibit skill gaps
- Display difficulty with comprehension, interpretation, or written expression

*Description*

Students with physical and/or medical problems are considered educationally handicapped only when their academic progress is adversely affected. Academic problems often reflect gaps in basic skills or concepts. Physical disabilities may interfere with students' ability to acquire and demonstrate knowledge through the usual means, while medical disabilities may reduce students' stamina and alertness.

*Special Problems*

Unlike most students with disabilities, these students confront mostly physical problems. They are often absent from school because of physical and medical complications; absences may cause skill gaps or even cumulative skill deficits. Students' performance fluctuates with their physical condition and the medications they take. The physical adjustments some students must make to accomplish academic tasks require such effort that the students perform slowly and tire quickly. Physical and health limitations may limit the range of experiences students have available to help them understand and interpret concepts. Some students exhibit difficulties in reading and written expression, while others exhibit motor incoordination that interferes with mobility or with precision in handwriting and in handling objects.

*Implications*

The nature of the physical or medical disability determines the degree, if any, of interference with performance. Debilitating conditions or disease, such as cancer or AIDS, impose obvious limits on students' performance and teacher options. However, students who are mobile, attend school regularly, and feel well most of the time do not necessarily experience academic difficulty. Changes in the physical structure of the classroom or in stimulus/response patterns, as well as the use of mechanical devices, can compensate for many physical limitations and accommodate students' learning needs. Students with slow performance, skill gaps, and limited experiences or vocabulary may require assistance from an assigned buddy.

CORRECTIVE PRINCIPLES

Use these guidelines to plan and modify instruction.

1. Adjust the physical environment to accommodate students' needs.
2. Broaden the experiential repertoire and extend preparation for each lesson.
3. Vary the stimulus/response pattern according to students' needs.
4. Rely heavily on oral activities and present short, varied reading and writing tasks to avoid fatigue.
5. Provide intensive instruction and experiences to broaden vocabularies.
6. Teach students strategies to adjust for physical and learning needs independently.

## Speech Disorders

DETECTION  Properly identified students in this group may

- Display difficulty discriminating certain sounds
- Exhibit reluctance to speak or read aloud before others
- Demonstrate the inability to speak or read aloud fluently or with appropriate voice
- Comprehend better when reading silently than when reading orally
- Express thoughts better in writing than in speech
- Exhibit no unusual academic problems

*Description*  Speech disorders are of three primary types: articulation, fluency, and voice. Each distorts the student's oral language. Articulation difficulties, or mispronunciations of certain sounds or words, are what teachers often think of when speech problems are mentioned because they are the most prevalent. Stuttering is the most common fluency problem. Voice disorders result in inappropriate pitch, intensity, or quality. Some students with speech disorders appear reluctant to read, discuss, or answer aloud. For some, particular sounds are difficult to discriminate and/or produce. Silent comprehension or listening is often easier for these students, as they are freed from the task of pronunciation and may attend to meaning.

*Special Problems*  The type of speech disorder determines the nature and degree of interference with oral reading and answering. Problems of articulation result in consistent mispronunciations of specific sounds and words. Fluency difficulties cause the repetition or prolongation of certain sounds. Voice disorders result in inappropriate pitch, intensity, or quality of voice and cause the voice to tire easily. The speech effort and distortions may interfere with oral communication. When auditory discrimination problems accompany speech disorders, students may acquire information by listening less readily than by other means.

*Implications*  Speech disorders need not interfere with academic progress. Silent or written work is seldom affected, despite possible difficulties in communicating orally. The most obvious interference with academic performance is the reluctance of students to read, discuss, or answer aloud, which limits oral interaction and the display of knowledge. Embarrassed teachers and peers erroneously tend to limit the student's opportunities to demonstrate his or her achievements. The speech pathologist should coordinate instruction in discriminating and producing troublesome sounds, while a medical specialist must designate appropriate oral activities for students with voice problems.

CORRECTIVE PRINCIPLES  Use these guidelines to plan and modify instruction.

1. Integrate and coordinate the classroom and speech/language-therapy programs.
2. Encourage oral interaction in a supportive environment.
3. Provide positive corrective feedback.
4. Provide ample opportunities to practice fluent speech.
5. Permit silent reading and written answers as needed.
6. Build language skills through listening, talking, and choral activities.

## Visual Impairments

DETECTION          Properly identified students in this group may

- Master reading and writing skills slowly
- Listen and speak much better than they read and write
- Perform slowly
- Hold books and papers at an odd distance and lose their place on the page
- Display difficulty understanding implied meanings
- Make numerous minor errors

*Description*    Students who are visually impaired learn academic skills in much the same way as their sighted peers but may learn to read and write more slowly. To the partially sighted, print may appear distorted and/or blurred. These students often must carefully study the page to make sense of it and point to each word to keep their place. Although they may write more easily than they read, they must struggle to locate and proofread their responses. These processes slow performance.

*Special Problems*    Denied the range and quantity of visual stimulation of their sighted peers, these students often bring limited experiences to the learning process. Although some exhibit advanced listening and speaking skills, many require extra concrete experiences, such as auditory and tactile examples, to expand and enrich concepts and vocabularies. The effort and time the students need to form and decipher print interfere with reading and writing performance. They may make seemingly careless errors because of their reduced vision.

*Implications*    The degree of visual impairment dictates the amount of adjustment students require for all types of classroom learning. Vision is a major channel for acquiring information both in the classroom and in the real world. Students with visual impairments must substitute or supplement with auditory information and with what they can read. Given sufficient auditory support, they can build upon their speaking and listening skills to improve academic skills. However, their slow performance and mastery of reading and writing skills interfere with their ability to maintain the pace of the typical curriculum. For the partially sighted, many classroom routines are particularly difficult to achieve; thus, these students may fall behind peers both in academic progress and in demonstrating task mastery. Shortened assignments, oral responses, and keyboarded assignments instead of written ones may facilitate progress and prevent students from tiring from strain. Compensatory techniques such as hearing, touch, or even Braille should be taught and guided as needed.

CORRECTIVE PRINCIPLES    Use these guidelines to plan and modify instruction.

1. Seat students where they can best see and hear.
2. Carefully build both real and vicarious experiences for each lesson.
3. Present auditory cues for each visual task.
4. Use auditory and oral stimulus/response patterns to limit visual strain.
5. Provide extensive training in word and concept meanings.
6. Specifically teach listening skills and emphasize them in other lessons.

## Academic Giftedness

DETECTION     Properly identified students in this group may

- Have a large and expansive vocabulary and use complex sentences and syntax
- Read and write above the level of age peers and/or below ability level
- Learn faster than age peers but display skill gaps
- Become critical readers and writers and sometimes bored with lesson content
- Perform drill grudgingly, incompletely, or not at all
- Excel in concepts but not in details or mechanics
- Frequently make careless errors

*Description*     Most students who are academically gifted read and write well beyond the level at which they have been taught. However, unless they have been directly taught advanced mathematical algorithms, their achievement in mathematics may be well below the level of their other achievements. Many have rich vocabularies and the capacity for a deep understanding of language and concepts. Unfortunately, many perform below their actual capacity level and evidence skill gaps. Special problems of some gifted students include underachievement or undetected talent. Such students may have limited vocabularies or background experiences and specific skill deficits. They may even avoid certain academic tasks. These students tend to perform drill reluctantly. Many make careless errors in computation, spelling, and writing.

*Special Problems*     Many students who are gifted prove to themselves that they can perform a task and then lose interest. Their rapid learning rate often results in disdain for meaningless drill. Skill gaps occur because many of their skills are often self-taught. They may become underachievers because of conformity with school or sociocultural expectations, inadequate experiential background, or a disability. Because some gifted students overlook details in written work, their grades, particularly in written expression and computation, may not reflect their true abilities. Educators who assume that superior ability requires no instructional accommodation pose a special threat to these students.

*Implications*     Many students who are gifted can advance rapidly when they are provided opportunities and taught specific strategies. Then they can master content independently and progress at their own rates, with fewer of the problems and behaviors typical of unchallenged students. Gifted students need to be freed from the boundaries of the regular curriculum.

CORRECTIVE PRINCIPLES     Use these guidelines to plan and modify instruction.

1. Use an individualized approach to teach each subject.
2. Fill in skill gaps as needed.
3. Offer enriched, challenging language experiences.
4. Directly teach study and research strategies.
5. Avoid repetitious drill, allowing students to advance as they are able.
6. Encourage students to evaluate, rewrite, and create text and problems.
7. Teach the debate skills and then provide opportunities for practice.

## SUMMARY

A significant number of students evidence learning or behavior problems that call for specialized instruction. This chapter briefly outlines some special problems and proposes some corrective principles to guide instruction for two sets of special learners: (1) students designated as regular or remedial learners but who are at risk for school failure and (2) students whose learning differences make them eligible for special education services. The first set contains the groups of at-risk students informally categorized by teachers according to assumed causes of learning interference. This set includes students who exhibit cultural/language differences, cumulatively deficit skills, educational deprivation, slow learning rate, and underachievement. Experience differences and/or inappropriate teaching, accompanied by some learning differences, primarily account for the academic difficulties of these groups. The corrective principles for each group focus first on compensating for the assumed cause and then on compensating for specific skill needs.

The second set of special learners includes students classified according to diagnosed disabilities. These students qualify for special education services but may be taught in the regular or remedial classroom. These groups include students properly identified as having one of these disabilities: cross-categorical disabilities, behavior disorders, hearing impairments, language disabilities, learning disabilities, mental retardation, physical/medical disabilities, speech disorders, or visual impairments. Gifted students are treated as a separate group because of their unique exceptionality. Learning and behavior differences account for the academic difficulties of these groups, although experience differences and/or inappropriate teaching compound the problems.

Each group's learning characteristics suggest Corrective Principles. Teachers should also confirm exact problems and needs, consult appropriate specialists, and adjust instructional strategies for individual learning needs. To confirm the applicability of any principle to a specific student, each student's skills should be analyzed and targeted teaching evaluated. All students occasionally evidence some of the Detection behaviors sketched for each special group. Not every student with academic problems fits neatly into a category, nor does every classified student exhibit every problem. The perfect recipe for correcting every learner's special needs does not exist! Thus, the Corrective Principles are preliminary guides to the Correction strategies presented in later chapters.

# CHAPTER THREE

## SPECIAL INSTRUCTION: SOME BASIC PRINCIPLES

— *Joyce S. Choate*

Special students require instruction in most of the same skills that other students need. Many of the same instructional procedures appropriate for other students are just as appropriate for special students. However, variations of some validated methods increase their effectiveness for teaching special students.

Several publications report on significant research associated with teaching students with learning problems. At the conclusion of this chapter is a list of selected references containing the mixture of research findings and good practice that provide the basis for appropriate teaching. The implications of this research document the efficacy or outline the development of the Correction strategies throughout this book. Refer to these resources for clarification and expanded explanations.

The twenty instructional practices that follow are applicable to most students but vital for special learners. These practices provide general guidelines for implementing the corrective strategies described in Chapters 4–16.

## 1. TEACH DIAGNOSTICALLY

Perhaps the most important practice for teaching special learners is diagnostic teaching. Diagnostic teaching begins with an initial diagnosis to identify specific skill deficits. Identification of the errors to be corrected is central to any targeted instructional plan. Three ways to identify or detect the specific skills in need of correction are (1) direct testing, using either formal or informal measures, (2) analysis of daily classroom interactions and performances, and (3) synthesis of the data from a combination of testing and analysis of classroom performance. In later chapters, specific suggestions for diagnosis in each subject and skill area are offered. Classroom observations offer the most realistic picture of a student's performance.

After the initial assessment, diagnostic teaching proceeds with targeted instruction for identified skill needs, followed by regular monitoring of skill progress. Monitoring will determine the appropriateness of methodology, measure skill gains and needs, and identify possible instructional modifications. Depending upon the skills being monitored, measuring of the effectiveness of instruction might involve calculating the rate of accuracy in answering questions, analyzing speech production trials, charting mispronunciations during reading, comparing written language samples, or analyzing mathematical errors. Regardless of the exact task and product, some type of charting or graphing of performance across several lessons is required to produce a record of growth. When performance is not consistently positive, the teacher should modify instructional procedures and continue teaching diagnostically. Implicit in diagnostic teaching is identifying individual students' learning styles and then teaching accordingly.

## 2. TEACH TO LEARNING STYLE

Diagnostic teaching includes identifying and teaching to an individual's learning style, that set of instructional conditions that facilitates a specific student's academic progress. These conditions include not only the preferred learning modality but also such features as light, sound, time, temperature, grouping, and degree of structure. Preferred stimulus/response format, of which modality is a part, is a key element of a student's learning style. The impact of format is often seen in students whose performance, regardless of knowledge level, varies according to whether the format is oral or written, multiple choice, or fill-in-the-blank.

Consider the format options in reading lessons. The instructional content might include pictures, sentences, paragraphs, stories, poems, listening experiences, or a variety of book, chalkboard, or written stimuli. The responses required of the student may range from selecting a picture or spoken word to saying or writing a letter, word, or paragraph. The types of stimulus presented and response required determine to a great extent the student's ability to understand and demonstrate knowledge. This book stresses varying the stimulus/response format as well as implementing other procedures to address individual students' learning styles. The checklist of options for accommodating students' unique learning needs and styles presented in Figure 3.1 suggests possible options and provides a format for analyzing and monitoring the accommodations and their effectiveness.

## 3. SPECIFICALLY TEACH NECESSARY SKILLS

Diagnostic and appropriate instruction requires teaching specific skills and adjusting for specific needs. Despite the current trend toward holistic teaching and integrated curricula, targeted skill instruction is essential for corrective instruction. As noted in Principle 11, skills are vital elements of the strategies for accomplishing subject-specific tasks. As soon as specific skills are mastered, they should be immediately applied in context to reading whole passages, solving word problems, writing ideas, conducting scientific experiments, and the like.

Certain skills may be especially difficult for special learners. If, despite appropriate and focused instruction, lack of a particular skill impedes students' progress, the teacher should consider several options: (1) Substitute a different skill, such as listening for reading; (2) change the stimulus/response format; or (3) guide students through the thought processes for accomplishing the task orally. When the troublesome skill is an essential one, targeted instruction must continue as students exercise one of these options at least to master concepts. Some special learners need these options to progress, particularly in the content areas. Explicit instruction in ways to circumvent and compensate for learning and behavior weaknesses is an essential element of preparing special students to learn independently.

## 4. ESTABLISH THE EXPERIENTIAL BASE FOR EACH LESSON

Needed skills facilitate task performance and continued learning, and background knowledge facilitates understanding of new concepts. Students understand and interpret concepts according to their individual experiential backgrounds. Typically, the richer and more varied the learner's ex-

## FIGURE 3.1 / Checklist of Options for Accommodating Learning Needs and Styles

**Constructive Learning Environment**

Preferential seating: (specify) _____

Group size:           ___ 1–1 w/teacher ___ 1–1 w/peer ___ small group ___ large group

Need for movement:                    ___ Little       ___ Average       ___ High

Distraction management: ___ Carrels   ___ Headsets     ___ Seating       ___ Other

Noise:                ___ None         ___ Quiet        ___ Moderate

Lighting:             ___ Dim          ___ Average      ___ Bright

Temperature:          ___ Warm         ___ Average      ___ Cool

Other: (specify) _____

**Productive Learning Schedule**

Peak learning time: ___ Early morning ___ late morning ___ Midday ___ Afternoon

Best lesson length:    ___ 5–10 min.    ___ 15–20 min.   ___ 25–30 min.   ___ 30+ min.

Need for variation:    ___ Little       ___ Some         ___ Average      ___ Much

Other: (specify) _____

**Best Stimulus/ Response Format**

| Stimulus Format | | | Response Format | | |
|---|---|---|---|---|---|
| Visual: ___ | Observe ___ | Read | Choose: ___ | Point | ___ Mark |
| Auditory: ___ | Oral ___ | Discuss | Tell: ___ | Restate | ___ Explain |
| Touch: ___ | Hold ___ | Feel | Write: ___ | Word | ___ Essay |
| | ___ Keyboard | | | ___ Short Answer | |
| | | | | ___ Word process | |
| Model: ___ | Demonstrate | | | ___ Make/construct | |
| | ___ Guide performance | | | ___ Demonstrate | |

Other: specify) _____          Other: (specify) _____

_____                          _____

**Useful Material Adjustments**

___ Vary stimulus/response format          ___ Vary instructions          ___ Vary sequence

___ Highlight essential content            ___ Use Partial content        ___ Add steps

___ Expand practice                        ___ Add self-checking          ___ Add Facilitative Learning Aids

Other: (specify) _____

**Facilitative Learning Aids**

___ Advance organizers            ___ Paraphrasing
___ Audiotapes of text            ___ Partial outlines
___ Calculator                    ___ Peer notetaker
___ Captioned films               ___ Peer prompter
___ Charted progress              ___ Peer tutor
___ Checklists of steps           ___ Question guides
___ Completed samples             ___ Self-questioning
___ Computer activities           ___ Simplified directions
___ Contracts                     ___ Strategy posters
___ Cooperative-learning group    ___ Structured notes
___ Evaluation checklist          ___ Study buddy
___ Games for practice            ___ Study guides
___ Highlighted text              ___ Summaries
___ Interactive videodisk         ___ Tape recorder
___ Manipulatives                 ___ Think alouds
___ Math number charts            ___ Timed practice
___ Mnemonic guides               ___ Verbal rehearsal
___ Organization charts           ___ Visual imagery
___ Outlined tasks                ___ Volunteer tutor

Other: ___ _____          ___ _____

perience, the more meaningful the learner's understanding and performance. For a number of reasons, many special students have had limited experience participating in a variety of activities; many also lack the types of experiences that contribute to a general fund of knowledge and language facility. Therefore, teachers must supply numerous concrete experiences to enhance understanding.

Pictures, video and audio materials, and additional oral and written examples supplement experiences. Teachers should also identify pre-existing concepts that will require modification or change. To promote understanding and use of language, the teacher should review, extend, or develop concepts and their language labels prior to each lesson. The review may also include prerequisite skills, since some special students forget how and when to apply tentatively mastered skills. Building experiences sets the stage for learning by providing a knowledge base and serving as a type of advance organizer.

## 5. EMPHASIZE AND DIRECTLY TEACH VOCABULARY

An important element of the experiential base is understanding the vocabulary that carries the conceptual load, particularly in the content areas. Semantic maps, concept maps and webs, word webs, and clustering of vocabulary assist students to understand levels and categories of meaning and to organize their thoughts. Graphic display of the semantic features of language helps students not only to connect the concepts themselves but also to relate them to a specific topic or organizational scheme. Whether the display is formatted as cartoon balloons, tree branches, or concentric circles, the basic premise is the same: Central or major concepts are surrounded by their subordinate concepts, as in traditionally diagrammed sentences.

When key words and phrases are categorized and illustrated during the introductory portions of a lesson, students receive a meaning-based structure for connecting, understanding, and focusing on concepts as they occur. As a follow-up experience, students can increase the categories of concepts for clarification or as proof of what has been learned. Using a phased approach, the teacher might begin by supplying several important concepts and then gradually reduce the number of cues until the students can fill in the map based upon what they have learned.

The visual array of concepts may provide special students with an important learning tool to help them master and remember the interrelationships of concepts. Mapping also aids language composition. When students are guided to construct maps or webs prior to developing oral or written compositions, these aids function as outlines by assisting students in organizing and clarifying their ideas and then in elaborating on those thoughts. As the compositions evolve, the maps serve as guidelines to help students self-monitor their expression.

Other options for presenting vocabulary include defining sentences, cloze-type activities in which a key term is deleted, or game formats that lead students to produce terms or match terms with definitions. Whatever the methodology, the terms that carry the major concepts should be emphasized throughout each lesson for three purposes: (1) before each lesson is discussed as an advance organizer, (2) during the lesson to clarify and elaborate, and (3) after the lesson to summarize and review major concepts.

# 6. EMPHASIZE THE RELEVANCE OF EACH SKILL AND CONCEPT

When teaching vocabulary, concepts, and skills, the teacher must establish their personal meaning and relevance in order to lend purpose to the students' learning. Students who must struggle to learn deserve to know why they must master school tasks. Both relevance to academic progress and, more importantly, personal and societal relevance should be explained, discussed, demonstrated, and documented, bearing the achievement level and interests of the students in mind. Beyond the obvious contributions of reading, writing, and arithmetic to future school learning, these basic skills promote general literacy, lifelong learning, and informed functioning in the real world. Some topics and skills are inherently more oriented toward real life than others. For example, safety, health, finance, communication, self care and self-improvement, and vocational concerns are essential skills and concepts for day-to-day functioning and survival in the real world. Carefully selecting skills and topics makes documenting relevance easier.

# 7. USE APPROPRIATE AND REALISTIC EXAMPLES AND DEMONSTRATIONS

Used regularly, demonstrations and examples that apply to the students' everyday life promote understanding and emphasize relevance. Concrete and familiar examples should be used before abstract ones. Concrete examples and objects are particularly important to mastery of some skills and concepts. For example, in mathematics, demonstrations and hands-on experiences with manipulatives are essential; in science, practical experiments build skills and illuminate concepts. Using the students' language to introduce concepts and then translating the ideas into more technical terms also enhances learning. Nonexamples are just as important as examples to emphasize the distinctiveness of examples and solidify learning.

Demonstrations that model key thought processes enhance teaching and learning. Guiding students to think about thinking and encouraging them to think aloud to reveal their mental manipulations are key procedures. Students soon become accustomed to thinking aloud and to sharing their thinking techniques with their peers when they are regularly asked, "How did you know that this answer was incorrect?" or instructed to "Prove it out loud" or "Tell us as you think your answer." Such teacher-guided efforts help students develop metacognitive behaviors and thinking strategies, making retention and transfer of skills and knowledge easier.

The actual content of examples and lessons also influences learning. For example, many skills and concepts can be learned or applied in the context of high-interest lessons, needed and real-life content, or award-winning literature. Since special students often experience difficulty catching up and then keeping up in most curricular areas, this practice uses teacher and student time and effort efficiently.

# 8. ACTIVELY INVOLVE STUDENTS

Appropriate and meaningful examples and models invite active student involvement. Students who are actively involved and engaged tend to learn more and faster. Students learn skills and understand concepts by doing. Hands-on, interactive learning appeals to the senses and provides a reason to learn. Active learning also promotes attention to task and may lessen negative behaviors. Cooperative-learning groups, as explained in the next principle, also facilitate active learning. Teachers should involve students in planning and evaluating their learning experiences; such involvement increases motivation, interest, and self-esteem as students develop a sense of personal contribution and accomplishment.

## 9. ENCOURAGE COOPERATIVE LEARNING

Cooperative-learning groups facilitate active learning; such shared learning also promotes social interaction, a much-needed experience for special learners. The idea of students functioning as teachers is not new, but it has only been validated as a teaching and learning strategy in recent years. A number of cooperative-learning studies verify that students can learn effectively from each other. Cooperative-learning groups of two, three, or five students provide a natural environment in which to learn and reinforce most skills, especially in communication, problem solving, and social studies.

The teacher must train the students to use the group format, clarify the each student's role and the sequence of instruction, and then carefully monitor the interaction of each group. Students should imitate the teacher's questions and responses to interact in the group. Research has validated variations of the cooperative learning format; for specific implementation procedures, consult publications by Slavin (1991) and Johnson and Johnson (1991). Although pairing and grouping students to apply skills and share knowledge is frequently suggested in this book, the teacher must carefully select partners and then guide and monitor their interactions to ensure that the format promotes successful experiences.

## 10. ASK APPROPRIATE QUESTIONS

Appropriate questions also encourage active student involvement and learning. The questions teachers ask determine in part the level of thinking and the degree of understanding that occur. Teachers who routinely ask literal questions encourage students to think primarily on a literal basis. To become proficient learners, students must be guided to seek answers to questions asking how and why and then to respond to such questions. Appropriate questions stimulate understanding and facilitate thinking and problem solving.

Equally important as the questions teachers ask are the teachers' responses to students' answers and questions. Teacher response partially determines the quantity and quality of students' responses and questions. Teachers who invite and discuss multiple answers and their logical defense encourage students to respond. After asking a question, teachers should wait five to ten seconds before seeking more information. Think time or wait time enhances students' responses. Prompting or cuing for answers helps students think; paraphrasing or restating answers reinforces concepts and builds positive behaviors in giving answers. Teaching students to formulate their own questions and answers not only increases their understanding of language but also builds vital self-monitoring skills.

## 11. TEACH STUDENTS THE STRATEGIES FOR ACCOMPLISHING EACH TASK

Prompting and cuing students to answer questions models the thinking strategies for deriving answers. Thinking, learning, and study strategies are critical elements of special instruction. In order to increase learning rate and volume, students need to know more than *what* to learn — they need to know *how* to learn. In many instances, skills alone will not suffice. For example, students who understand and can perform word analysis cannot systematically and effectively apply their word-analysis skills to read more fluently unless they also know which skills to apply, when, and what order. In other cases, component skills provide the best strategy for learning and performing tasks. For example, the four steps for solving mathematical problems presented in Chapter 11 form a strategy for problem solving. Thus, along with lesson content and skills, the strategies for accomplishing each task must be taught, modeled, discussed, and critiqued. In addition to subject-specific skills and strategies, effective utilization of technology offers learners strategies for learning and for demonstrating their knowledge. Strategy instruction empowers learners and special learners need that empowerment.

## 12. TEACH SELF-MONITORING

Students who learn strategies and apply them begin to take control of their own learning, becoming independent learners. They must learn to self-monitor their understanding of concepts and mastery of skills. Students use metacognitive skills to monitor their learning and self-correct, particularly during reading and writing, and during speaking and listening to a lesser degree. As an aid to developing self-monitoring skills and habits, teachers should encourage students to verify meanings in the context of what they hear, say, read, or write. For example, students should regularly ask themselves questions: Did she really say . . . ? Do I know that word? Is that what I meant to say? What will happen next? Do I need to reread? Is that sentence complete? Does that make sense?

Before, during, or after an activity, checklists, listening guides, interview guidelines, and graphic organizers assist students to monitor what they hear, say, read, or write. Graphic organizers, such as maps and webs, help students monitor their development of oral reports and written compositions. Checklists help them determine the need to reread passage parts, edit written work, follow algorithm sequences, conduct scientific experiments, adhere to classroom rules, and monitor an endless variety of behaviors specific to particular skills and content.

## 13. TEACH FOR MASTERY

Teachers should encourage students to persist until they attain mastery, particularly in the basic skills. Since language skills, for example, are required for progress in school, teaching for mastery is essential; mastery of basic number facts is prerequisite to mastery of higher-level mathematics. Many special learners do not easily retain mastery of a skill unless they frequently review and apply it. Such students require systematic instruction over time, periodic reviews, and application of a skill in many varied situations. Teaching for mastery also involves diagnostic teaching, monitoring of skill acquisition, transferring knowledge from one skill and subject to another, and reinforcing learning.

## 14. PROVIDE APPROPRIATE PRACTICE AND GENEROUS REVIEW

Review and reinforcement are important to help students master skills and concepts. All students need periodic reviews, but special learners often need more frequent and extensive review. Relate each new skill and topic to previously learned information and skills. Begin each lesson with a review of related concepts and needed skills and their relevance; build or reinforce students' experiences as needed. Repeat and review concepts often. Have students summarize everything in their own words and record their summaries or have a peer take notes; guide students to develop charts and graphs to summarize information. To promote students' understanding, memory, and use of concepts, guide students to paraphrase concepts and apply them to their lives. Use numerous visual aids, topical summaries, taped overviews, examples, and displays in the room to further reinforce important information. To reinforce skills, have students demonstrate and explain newly learned skills to peers.

Vary the format of review experiences to avoid boredom. Computer activities offer endless variations for practicing skills and applying knowledge. In addition to appropriate commercially available software, hypermedia, such as *Hypercard* or *Linkway*, can be used to create personalized review and application activities. Whether used for authoring activities directed toward specific students' needs or for integrating multimedia presentations, hypermedia allows the teacher to develop and structure reinforcement activities in a variety of appealing formats. Puzzles, games, or learning-center formats also offer changes to reduce the tedium of repetitive practice. Cooperative group projects, discussions, and structured problem-solving sessions can reinforce and apply skills and concepts as well. Reviews do not have to be teacher-directed question-and-answer sessions.

## 15. APPLY PRINCIPLES OF BEHAVIORISM

The principles of behaviorism are important ingredients of review and practice, and indeed of all classroom activities. Many of the practices cited as improving the achievement of special students incorporate the principles of behaviorism, which is based on the premise that rewarded behavior is likely to recur. When designing an instructional plan, the teacher should consider two major factors: 1) defining the behavior to be changed or improved through observation and diagnosis and 2) planning a program to systematically reinforce desired responses.

The first factor, a part of diagnostic teaching, must include setting realistic instructional goals. Lessons must be structured in small, manageable steps that will lead to the accomplishment of a designated goal. Systematic reinforcement is more complicated. The teacher must first determine what constitutes reward and punishment for a specific student, which sometimes becomes apparent by analyzing the instructional conditions that produce desired responses. This procedure is also helpful in identifying an appropriate stimulus/response format for specific students.

## 16. INTEGRATE SKILLS AND CONCEPTS THROUGHOUT THE CURRICULUM

All subjects and skills should be integrated throughout the curriculum. Integrating instruction across subjects mutually reinforces and extends skills and concepts and provides opportunities to apply learnings. Guided application also fosters transfer and generalization. Integrating the language arts is more natural and logical than separating them. With language as the common denominator of listening, speaking, reading, and writing, integrated teaching also provides a multisensory approach. When, for example, students are first taught the meaning of a new word in the context of a listening activity, they can also be guided to read the word in a similar or different context, to use the word orally or in an elaborated written context, or perhaps to use the word in a broader sense, as in a graphic organizer or verbal matrix. Such integrated experiences help students remember and understand concepts and language patterns as well as increasing their opportunities to incorporate the new language patterns into their own listening, speaking, reading, and writing. The teacher can incorporate science and social studies topics and skills into other subject lessons throughout the day to reinforce concepts and skills and to demonstrate their applicability to other areas. Mathematical problems naturally occur in many subjects; the teacher can infuse them into most other areas or can construct them from almost any subject content for specific math lessons. An integrated curriculum offers special learners needed review and repetition, shows them how to generalize skills and content, and heightens learning enjoyment.

## 17. BUILD INTEREST AND ENTHUSIASM

Unless students are interested in what they are learning and doing, the previous suggestions are of little use. Active involvement not only promotes learning but also increases interest, so give students a choice in what and how they learn. Involve students not only in the activities but also in each step of the planning process. Students often perform above their established achievement levels when a topic, skill, or method particularly fascinates them. Effective use of technology, such as interactive videos to embellish lessons or word processors to facilitate performance, may spark interest. Perhaps the most practical way to enhance interest is to establish the personal relevance of skills and topics; societal relevance can extend and reinforce personal relevance. Teacher enthusiasm is a vital element for building interest; the teacher's enthusiasm or lack of it can be contagious. Interest and enthusiasm are critical ingredients of a positive and productive learning climate.

## 18. GUIDE STUDENTS TO DEVELOP SELF-MANAGEMENT SKILLS

To benefit from the previous principles, students must learn to manage and control themselves. Self-management and control extend Principles 8 and 12 to increase students' active involvement in and ownership of their learning. Self-management skills enable self-monitoring, and, along with mastery of study and learning strategies, empower students to control themselves and their learning, both now and in the future. Students must learn to manage such elements as attention, on-task behavior, self-monitoring, peer and teacher interactions, time, goal setting, and possibly some of the other behaviors described in Chapter 14. Even with the use of the strategies described in that chapter, this principle is not easy for either the teacher or the student to follow. However, it should be a continual goal.

## 19. MANAGE THE INSTRUCTIONAL PROCESS EFFICIENTLY AND EFFECTIVELY

Teachers as well as students must develop management skills. By efficiently and effectively managing themselves and the instructional process, teachers model organization and management, structure a positive classroom environment, and increase the likelihood that both teacher and students will enjoy the teaching and learning process. Instructional management is the orchestration of all classroom activities to increase learning and also interest and enjoyment. As noted in Chapter 15, sound instructional management includes ecological assessment and instruction; preventive instructional planning; positive classroom climates; orderly settings; efficient scheduling and time management; appropriate instructional grouping; skilled use of materials, equipment, and technology; effective discipline plans and delivery of instruction; and last, but certainly not least, enjoyment.

## 20. COLLABORATE AND COORDINATE EFFORTS WITH OTHERS

The preceding principles focus on what a single teacher does or does not do with students. However, no teacher need stand alone. A variety of pro-

### FIGURE 3.2 / Review of Basic Instructional Principles

1. Teach Diagnostically
2. Teach to Learning Style
3. Specifically Teach Necessary Skills
4. Establish the Experiential Base for Each Lesson
5. Emphasize and Directly Teach Vocabulary
6. Emphasize the Relevance of Each Skill and Concept
7. Use Appropriate and Realistic Examples and Demonstrations
8. Actively Involve Students
9. Encourage Cooperative Learning
10. Ask Appropriate Questions
11. Teach Students the Strategies for Accomplishing Each Task
12. Teach Self-Monitoring
13. Teach for Mastery
14. Provide Appropriate Practice and Generous Review
15. Apply Principles of Behaviorism
16. Integrate Skills and Concepts Throughout the Curriculum
17. Build Interest and Enthusiasm
18. Guide Students to Develop Self-Management Skills
19. Manage the Instructional Process Efficiently and Effectively
20. Collaborate and Coordinate Efforts with Others

fessionals should collaborate to provide the best possible instruction for all students, particularly those with special learning needs. Collaboration and coordination save time and nurture teacher enthusiasm. As integrating the curriculum (Principle 16) enhances mastery of skills and concepts in all areas, coordinating efforts enhances expertise and progress. Such collaboration exponentially increases the chances of success for both students and teachers.

## SUMMARY

The twenty basic principles reviewed in Figure 3.2, applicable to most students but vital for meeting the needs of special learners, help educators adjust and individualize instruction in all subject areas. These instructional practices are incorporated into the corrective techniques recommended in this book. Of particular importance are Principle 1, diagnostic teaching; Principle 2, teaching to learning style (see Figure 3.1); Principle 3, targeted skill instruction; Principle 4, building experiential frameworks; Principle 6, emphasizing relevance; Principle 8, actively involving students; Principle 11, strategy instruction; Principle 18, development of self management skills; and Principle 20, coordination and collaboration. The best features of these twenty teaching practices provide the framework for the Correction strategies in Chapters 4 through 16.

## SELECTED REFERENCES

Algozzine, B., & Maheady, L. (Guest Eds.). (1986). In search of excellence: Instruction that works in special education classrooms [Special issue]. *Exceptional Children, 52* (6), 481–608.

Baruth, L. G., & Manning, M. L. (1992). *Multicultural education of children and adolescents.* Boston: Allyn and Bacon.

Bauer, A. M., & Sapona, R. H. (1991). *Managing classrooms to facilitate learning.* Englewood Cliffs, NJ: Prentice-Hall.

Borich, G. D. (1992). *Effective teaching methods* (2nd ed.). New York: Merrill/Macmillan.

Bullock, L. H. (1992). *Exceptionalities in children and youth.* Boston: Allyn and Bacon.

Clarke, J. H. (1990). *Patterns of thinking: Integrating learning skills in content teaching.* Boston: Allyn and Bacon.

Dunn, R., & Dunn, K. (1992). *Teaching elementary students through their individual learning styles: Practical approaches for grades 3–6.* Boston: Allyn and Bacon.

Flood, J., Jensen, J., Lapp, D., & Squire, J. R. (Eds.) (1991). *Handbook of research on teaching the English language arts.* New York: Macmillan.

Freiberg, H. J., & Driscoll, A. (1992). Universal teaching strategies. Boston: Allyn and Bacon.

Graden, J. L., Zins, J. E., & Curtis, M. J. (Eds.). (1988). *Alternative educational delivery systems: Enhancing instructional options for all students.* Washington, DC: National Association of School Psychologists.

Gelzheiser, L. M., & Shepherd, M. J. (Guest Eds.). (1986). Competence and instruction: Contributions from cognitive psychology [Special issue]. *Exceptional Children, 53* (2), 97–192.

Good, T. L., & Brophy, J. E. (1992). *Looking in classrooms* (5th ed.). New York: Harper/Collins.

Gutkin, T. B., & Reynolds, C. R. (Eds.). (1990). *The handbook of school psychology.* New York: John Wiley.

Houston, W. R. (Ed.). (1990). *Handbook of research on teacher education: A project of the Association of Teacher Educators.* New York: Macmillan.

Jacobs, H. H. (1989). *Interdisciplinary curriculum: Design and implementation.* Alexandria, VA: Association for Supervision and Curriculum Development.

Johnson, D. W., & Johnson, R. T. (1991). *Learning together and alone: Cooperative, competitive and individualistic learning* (3rd ed.). Englewood Cliffs, NJ: Prentice Hall.

Lewis, R. B., & Doorlag, D. H. (1991). *Teaching special students in the mainstream* (3rd ed.). New York: Merrill/Macmillan.

Lipsky, D. K., & Gartner, A. (Eds.). (1989). *Beyond separate education.* Baltimore: Brookes.

Male, M. (1993). *Creating exceptional classroom: Technology options for all.* Boston: Allyn and Bacon.

Meier, F. E. (1992). *Competency-based instruction for teachers of students with special learning needs.* Boston: Allyn and Bacon.

Pressley, M., Burkell, J., Cariglia-Bull, L., McGoldrick, J. A., Schneider, B., Snyder, B. L., Symons, S., & Woloshyn, V. E. (1990). *Cognitive strategy instruction that really improves children's academic performance.* Cambridge, MA: Brookline Books.

Reynolds, M. C., & Birch, J. W. (1988). *Adaptive mainstreaming.* White Plains, NY: Longman.

Slavin, R. E. (1991). Synthesis of research on cooperative learning. *Educational Leadership, 48* (5), 71–82.

Squires, D. A., Huitt, W. G., & Segars, J. K. (1984). *Effective schools and classrooms: A research-based perspective.* Alexandria, VA: Association for Supervision and Curriculum Development.

U.S. Department of Education. (1987). *What works: Research about teaching and learning* (2nd ed.). Washington, DC: Author.

Walberg, H. J. (1990). Productive teaching and instruction: Assessing the knowledge base. *Phi Delta Kappan, 71,* 470–478.

Wang, M. C. (1992). *Adaptive education strategies: Building on diversity.* Baltimore: Brookes.

Wang, M. C., Reynolds, M. C., & Walberg, H. J. (Eds.). (1987, 1988). *Handbook of special education: Research and practice* (Vol. 1–3). Oxford: Pergamon Press.

West, C. K., Farmer, J. S., & Wolff, P. M. (1991). *Instructional design: Implications from cognitive science.* Englewood Cliffs, NJ: Prentice-Hall.

Will, M. (1986). *Educating students with learning problems: A shared responsibility.* Washington, DC: U.S. Department of Education.

Wittrock, M. C. (Ed.). (1986). *Handbook of research on teaching* (3rd ed.). New York: Macmillan.

## REFLECTIONS

1. As outlined in Chapter 1, the Regular Education Initiative calls for general education to assume greater responsibility for the education of special students. After discussing the implications of this stance with at least three teachers of regular and special classes, summarize your position on the issue.

2. The practice of mainstreaming special students is briefly discussed in Chapter 1. Based on that discussion and on your own experiences, evaluate the advantages and disadvantages of mainstreaming from the perspective of each of the following:
   a. Students with mild disabilities
   b. Students with severe disabilities
   c. Students without disabilities
   d. Students who are academically gifted
   e. Parents of students a–d
   f. Regular classroom teachers
   g. Special education teachers
   h. School administrators
   i. Educational diagnosticians
   j. School budget officers
   k. Taxpayers
   l. Teacher trainers

3. Several myths and realities about students with disabilities are outlined in Chapter 1. Using your experiences as a framework, verify the realities and consider the implications of each for teaching special students.

4. The organization of Chapter 2 suggests differences in the learning needs of at-risk students and those who are classified as exceptional. Compare and contrast a problem in each area. Are there differences in the Detection behaviors and in the Corrective Principles? Why or why not? What conclusions can you draw?

5. Many of the Corrective Principles in Chapter 2 apply to all students. Justify the selection of the principles presented, adding principles where you deem necessary. Identify the three principles most applicable to the majority of students in an elementary classroom. Consider how each principle could be used to structure instruction for a student with a particular disability in three subject areas of your choice. Repeat this procedure for a non-disabled student.

6. A list of options for accommodating learner needs and style appears in Figure 3.1. Review this list and then, based on your learning and/or teaching experiences, add at least one option in each category. Next, use this list to analyze your own learning profile. What are the implications? Discuss your learning style with a colleague; how does your style compare with his or hers?

7. Each of the twenty teaching practices described in Chapter 3 applies to a variety of school subjects. Develop three examples of the application of one of these practices for teaching the subject of your choice.

8. The twenty teaching practices described in Chapter 3 are suggested as essential elements of effective teaching. Review these practices and rank them as more or less important for teaching special students. Reconsider the practices and rank their importance for teaching most learners. Do your rankings differ? Why or why not?

9. Cooperative-learning activities are recommended in Chapter 3. Consult one of the publications by Johnson and Johnson or by Slavin to learn more about cooperative learning. What are the advantages and disadvantages to students with disabilities? To students without disabilities? Identify

three validated formats for cooperative learning and the specific procedures for implementing each. Share your findings with a colleague.

10. Many school systems offer cross-categorical special education services, grouping together all mildly handicapped students for instruction. Reread the discussions of mainstreaming and the REI, as well as the Detection behaviors and the Corrective Principles cited for the exceptional classifications; add your own observations. Then debate the value of categorical and noncategorical training for special education teachers. Consider the advantages and disadvantages of each model to the individual students, to the other students in the class, to the teacher, and to the school system.

11. The list of learning accommodations in Figure 3.1 may be used to assess a student's learning needs. Try using the list to analyze the learning profile of the highest achiever in an elementary classroom; repeat the procedure for the lowest achiever in the same classroom. How are the two students' profiles similar? How do they differ? What are the implications for the teacher of that class?

12. Problems in learning and progressing in school tend to assume different proportions according to the student population and the perceptions of individual teachers. Interview a highly skilled regular education teacher to determine his or her perception of the important Detection behaviors and Corrective Principles for each problem categorized in Chapter 2; then discuss detection and correction of any frequent problems that are not mentioned in this book. Follow a similar procedure to interview a veteran special education teacher.

13. The Corrective Principles are suggested as guides for selecting and modifying strategies for corrective teaching. Select a hypothetical special learner; use the Corrective Principles in Chapter 2 and the teaching practices in Chapter 3 to modify a typical textbook lesson for that learner. Repeat the process for a second special learner. Compare and contrast the two lessons. For the same content, review the lesson script in the teacher's edition of the text. How do your lessons differ from the ones suggested for most students?

14. Special learners often need very focused and carefully planned lessons. Plan one or more integrated lessons for a special learner. Take the content of your lesson from the textbooks used in the student's school. Use the diagnostic information available from the school, the general teaching practices in Chapter 3, and the Corrective Principles in Chapter 2 to guide the design of your lessons.

15. Targeted lessons for special learners involve precise instruction. Implement the integrated lessons you designed for a special learner. As you teach, note the particular learning characteristics and and skill needs of the student as information for planning future lessons. Summarize the diagnostic data and the implications for subsequent instruction.

16. Several key references are listed at the end of Chapter 3. Select one of these publications to review and critique. What is the significance of the chosen reference to instruction for all learners?

17. In addition to the selected references listed in Chapters 1 and 3, the following resources address the special needs of students with learning or experience problems. Compare and contrast discussions in these sources with the information in Part I.

Clark, B. (1992). *Growing up gifted: Developing the potential of children at home and at school* (4th ed.). New York: Merrill/Macmillan.

Gearheart, B. R., Weishahn, M., & Gearheart, C. J. (1992). *The exceptional student in the regular classroom* (5th ed.). New York: Merrill/Macmillan.

Hallahan, D. P., & Kauffman, J. M. (1991). *Exceptional children: Introduction to special education* (5th ed.). Englewood Cliffs, NJ: Prentice-Hall.

Henley, M., Ramsey, R., & Algozzine, B. (1993). *Characteristics of students with mild disabilities in general and special education.* Boston: Allyn and Bacon.

Lewis, R. B., & Doorlag, D. H. (1991). *Teaching special students in the mainstream* (3rd ed.). New York: Merrill/Macmillan.

Mann, P. H., Suiter, P. A., & McClung, R. M. (1992). *A guide for educating mainstreamed students.* Boston: Allyn and Bacon.

Olson, J., & Platt, J. (1992). *Teaching children and adolescents with special needs.* New York: Merrill/Macmillan.

Salend, S. J. (1990). *Effective mainstreaming.* New York: Macmillan.

Schulz, J. B., Carpenter, C. D., & Turnbull, A. P. (1991). *Mainstreaming exceptional students: A guide for classroom teachers* (3rd ed.). Boston: Allyn and Bacon.

Wood, J. (1992). *Mainstreaming: A practical approach for teachers* (2nd ed.). New York: Merrill/Macmillan.

Ysseldyke, J. E., & Algozzine, B. (1990). *Introduction to special education* (2nd ed.). Boston: Houghton Mifflin.

# PART TWO

## DETECTING AND CORRECTING ACADEMIC PROBLEMS

 Academic curricula are filled with skills and concepts, each a potential help, delay, or hindrance to the learning progress of individual students. The chapters in Part Two address detection and correction of special problems in each of ten academic areas—word recognition, reading comprehension, speech, language, written expression, spelling and handwriting, arithmetic computation, mathematical problem solving, science, and social studies. Together, these subjects comprise the heart of academics and thus the main thrust of successful teaching and learning.

# CHAPTER FOUR

## RECOGNIZING WORDS: THE TOOLS FOR READING COMPREHENSION

— *Joyce S. Choate and Thomas A. Rakes*

Word recognition skills are enabling skills. By itself, word recognition is not reading, but rather a tool for reading. The recognition of single words leads to recognition and understanding of groups of words, which in turn facilitates comprehension, or reading. Conversely, failure to recognize a number of words interferes with comprehension. Many readiness skills, particularly visual and auditory discrimination and memory, are involved in the identification of words. The word recognition skills discussed in this chapter are often tested and taught in isolation. However, when applied to the decoding of words in the context of passages, these skills work together in a complementary manner.

## THE WORD RECOGNITION SKILLS

Certain experiences and skills prepare students to recognize words and then to read. These skills, known as reading readiness skills, can be categorized into four areas: language, visual, auditory, and motor skills. Because the first three categories are the most specific to developing reading skills, they are the ones considered in this chapter.

### Reading Readiness Skills

The language readiness skills (Skill 1) are the building blocks for reading. The vocabulary concepts are frequently the key terms in oral directions and explanations, and understanding these concepts can thus aid learning and performance in all subjects. Classifying objects and ideas helps to expand oral and reading vocabulary. Skilled oral expression is vital to the tools for classroom learning, such as the exchange of ideas, self-expression, and problem solving. The student's command of oral language is the vehicle for learning concepts, skills, strategies, and the reading process.

The visual readiness skills (Skill 2) include discrimination and visual memory of shapes, letters, and words. Together, they facilitate recognition and memory of the distinctive features of printed symbols. These skills are important to recognizing words, particularly sight vocabulary.

Auditory readiness skills (Skill 3) include auditory discrimination and auditory memory of sounds, words, and phrases. These skills permit recognition and memory of the sounds associated with printed symbols and are especially valuable in phonetic analysis. The auditory skills are also critical elements of understanding and following oral directions in class.

Mastery of reading readiness skills can facilitate the process of learning to read but cannot guarantee its success. Conversely, failure to master these skills can impede the process but does not preclude learning to read, an important point to remember when designing survival reading instruction for older students.

### Specific Word Recognition Skills

The word recognition skills discussed in this chapter — sight vocabulary (Skill 4), phonics (Skill 5), structural analysis (Skill 6), and contextual analysis

(Skill 7) — are collectively known as word-analysis skills. The first three groups of skills focus on analyzing words to decode them, relying heavily on pronunciation for identification. Contextual analysis also focuses on decoding words but emphasizes the meanings of the words. A fifth category, recognizing words across the curriculum (Skill 8), involves applying word recognition skills to decode all words encountered in the classroom.

Recognizing letters and sight words focuses on three types of sight vocabulary — letters, high-image words, and low-image words. In each case, because of the frequency of their occurrence in texts, readers are expected to recognize these stimuli instantly. Although students can learn to read without first learning letter names, this skill usually aids in the mastery of letter/sound associations. The high-image words are often the nouns and verbs peculiar to the text in use at the time, while low-image words are typically connecting words that appear with high frequency in all texts. Readers encounter these elements so regularly that if they do not immediately recognize them, reading rate and comprehension will suffer.

The phonetic-analysis skills are the sounding-out strategies used specifically for pronouncing words. Once the words are spoken, either the students must be sure that they recognize the meanings of the words, or the teacher must be sure to teach them.

Structural analysis uses the meaningful elements of words, such as prefixes, affixes, root words, and word structure, including individual syllables, compound words, and contractions. Like phonetic analysis, structural analysis is a pronunciation skill. However, if the word parts are taught as meaningful units, structural analysis can also help students analyze meanings.

Contextual analysis relies on the text surrounding unknown words for decoding clues. Use of context is both a word and a meaning analysis skill. More than the other word analysis skills, context forges the link between word recognition and comprehension.

Regardless of the subject of the text, students must integrate the various word recognition skills in an efficient and effective manner to decode words in all subjects, or, in other words, to apply word recognition skills across the curriculum. The recognition of words, whether it occurs instantly at sight or through phonetic or structural analysis, does not ensure comprehension. However, building upon the readiness skills, word recognition does facilitate comprehension.

## DETECTION OF SPECIAL WORD RECOGNITION NEEDS

Readiness skills are evaluated by formal tests of reading readiness or by informal assessment of target tasks. Word recognition skills are often evaluated formally or informally as students read passages or word lists aloud or as they select or write particular words or word parts.

### Formal Detection

The readiness test, a group test administered at the end of the kindergarten year or at the beginning of the first-grade year, usually tests receptive knowledge of vocabulary and concepts as well as visual, auditory, and motor skills. Students with special needs often fail to follow the oral directions of group tests and so do not demonstrate their achievements. Poor scores often, though not always, foretell poor reading achievement. Thus, unsatisfactory performance is cause for a more thorough diagnosis of individual instructional needs.

Group-administered standardized achievement tests usually include some measurement of sight vocabulary and phonetic analysis. Testing of structural analysis and contextual analysis skills sometimes occurs in conjunction with measures of word comprehension. Low scores on any of these word recognition tests indicate a need for analyzing a student's performance on an individual basis.

Standardized, individually administered tests of readiness or word recognition are frequently a part of the evaluation of students who are suspected of having disabilities. Performance may be reported as a global score, or, in the case of diagnostic tests, as an analysis of minute details of readiness or word recognition skills. Although these tests may yield a profile of specific needs, informal measures are sometimes more efficient for planning corrective instruction in word recognition.

## Informal Detection

Alternative formats for assessing recognition of words are of two basic types: (1) words in isolation and (2) words in context. The first format calls for the student to pronounce lists of target words; nonsense words are sometimes used as test items to screen out words known at sight and to determine if the student has applied phonetic structural analysis strategies. The second format places target words in the context of sentences or passages. Students read aloud, and their pronunciation of the words and the types of errors they make provide indices of their word recognition skills. Cloze formats for students to read orally or silently are also used to infer skill application, particularly contextual usage.

Most published informal reading inventories (IRIs) include a measure of word recognition skills, and many also measure readiness skills, thus permitting testing of oral language as well. A number of informal reading tests are designed specifically for measuring particular skills, especially phonics. Incorrect pronunciations provide clues to the skills that students are attempting to use, both correctly and incorrectly.

Checklists of possible readiness and word-recognition problems, such as the sample in Figure 4.1, serve several assessment purposes. They outline relevant skills and provide a means for recording and tracking students' progress. They can be used alone or in conjunction with other assessment procedures to structure classroom observations; analyze and record results from work-sample analyses, formal tests, and informal tests; and document student performances.

Classroom observation of students as they attempt to perform readiness tasks or to read aloud the words or passages of daily assignments often reveals invaluable diagnostic data. How students approach classroom tasks, their facial expressions during certain lessons, the number of times they ask for information to be repeated, the way they express their questions and answers, the rate at which they master new concepts — these are a few of the diagnostic indices that can be easily observed during classroom instruction. The types of errors that students make when reading aloud and their questions and answers about words offer insight into their command of the word recognition skills. Listings of behaviors that may signal a particular problem are included in Figure 4.1 and begin the discussion of each word recognition skill in the pages that follow.

**FIGURE 4.1** / **Checklist of Word Recognition Problems**

Use the checklist to analyze success and error patterns, record behaviors that signal possible problems, plan targeted instruction in the strategies for accomplishing component reading skills, and provide practice of those strategies in the context of meaningful passages. Whether the assessment technique is observing classroom behaviors, teacher tests, or standardized tests, watch for the factors that impede or facilitate total reading performance: Check skill areas in which proficiency is exhibited, circle problem areas and behaviors, and then refer to related skill areas to analyze success and error patterns.

| Target Skill | Possible Problem Behaviors | Related Skills |
|---|---|---|
| **Readiness** | | |
| ____ LANGUAGE READINESS | • Displays limited listening/speaking vocabulary<br>• Speaks in single words or phrases<br>• Has difficulty categorizing objects & ideas<br>• Does not understand direction concepts | Auditory Readiness<br>Visual Readiness<br>Word Meanings<br>All Comprehension |
| ____ VISUAL READINESS | • Does not discriminate or remember letters<br>• Does not discriminate or remember words<br>• Tends to reverse letters more often than age peers<br>• Does not recognize preliminary sight words | Sight Vocabulary<br>All Word Recognition |
| ____ AUDITORY READINESS | • Cannot discriminate or remember sounds<br>• Does not follow oral directions<br>• Frequently asks for words to be repeated<br>• Has difficulty remembering words and phrases | Phonics<br>Listening Comprehension |
| **Word Recognition** | | |
| ____ SIGHT VOCABULARY | • Confuses or does not remember certain letters<br>• Does not quickly recognize low-image words<br>• Does not quickly recognize high-image words<br>• Reads at a slow rate | All Comprehension<br>Fluency |
| ____ PHONICS | • Does not use letter sounds to decode words<br>• Does not remember the sounds of letters<br>• Cannot blend sounds to produce words<br>• Does not use context effectively | Contextual Usage<br>Auditory Readiness |
| ____ STRUCTURAL ANALYSIS | • Cannot quickly read words with common affixes<br>• Does not know the meanings of common affixes<br>• Does not recognize contractions or compounds<br>• Does not apply syllabication principles | Word Meaning<br>Fluency<br>All Comprehension |
| ____ CONTEXTUAL USAGE | • Does not use context to identify words/meanings<br>• Makes numerous errors when reading orally<br>• Displays generally weak comprehension skills<br>• Overuses or exhibits weak word analysis skills | All Word Recognition<br>All Comprehension |
| ____ SKILL APPLICATION | • Does not apply word analysis skills<br>• Overuses one or two recognition skills<br>• Displays difficulty reading words in 2+ subjects<br>• Does not use context to decode unknown words | Contextual Usage<br>All Word Recognition<br>All Comprehension |

The most common problem behaviors are listed first for each skill. Since reading is a holistic process, the significance of specific problem behaviors can be determined only in relation to the degree of overall reading proficiency. However, competence in certain reading skill areas facilitates orderly progress in reading and in other subjects as well. Specifically, language readiness, contextual usage, sight vocabulary, and application of the skills across the curriculum, when identified as problematic, are likely primary instructional targets.

Adapted from Choate, J. S. (1990). Reading assessment: A checklist of reading problems. *Diagnostique, 16* (1), 32–37, with permission.

## SPECIAL POPULATIONS

Although individuals and their unique needs are the key consideration in detecting and correcting special problems, certain features of special groups suggest possible problems that individual group members may experience in learning and applying readiness and word recognition skills. Of the reading readiness skills, language development is the most critical to reading success. Students who are most likely to display weak language skills are those whose early environments do not foster English language development and those whose disabilities interfere with orderly language development. Special learners in many groups, particularly students who have cultural or language differences, who are disadvantaged, or who have language disabilities or mental retardation, may begin the reading process with weak language skills. Thus, many special students lag behind their age peers from the start. In the absence of acuity, processing, or cognitive difficulties, visual and auditory readiness skills generally are not as problematic for special learners, although children provided with early informal visual and auditory experiences may perform better than others.

Some special learners in almost all groups exhibit difficulty applying word recognition skills effectively throughout the curriculum, in many cases because they have not been taught to do so. Educational deprivation results in specific problems in structural analysis as well. Since all the word recognition skills ultimately contribute to sight vocabulary, it is not surprising that some special learners in most categories exhibit relatively weak sight vocabularies. Students who are least likely to experience numerous problems recognizing words are those who are gifted or who display behavior disorders. Regardless of the special group needs, corrective instruction must focus on individual needs.

## CORRECTION OF WORD RECOGNITION SKILLS

Problems in mastering the reading readiness skills affect more than just day-to-day accomplishment of assignments; they sometimes negatively affect attitudes toward reading. Correcting special readiness needs of beginning students may not only facilitate reading achievement but also increase the probability of overall school success.

Difficulties in recognizing words slow and interfere with the comprehension process. The frustration caused by stumbling over words may lead to attitude problems that threaten future reading success. Many students who struggle to recognize words also spell and write poorly. Some students can recognize words in context but not in isolation, while others are distracted by the surrounding words of the context.

Some of the word recognition skills are more difficult than others for specific students to master. Students who find sight words hard to recall may need increased emphasis on phonics. Students who find phonetic analysis particularly difficult may benefit from a linguistic or word-family approach. How easily students master structural analysis may depend on whether the word parts are presented as sight units, phonetic units, or a combination of both. Whereas proficient readers use a combination of word recognition skills to decode words, students with reading weaknesses must often be taught how to combine these skills and use them flexibly.

The correction of readiness and word recognition difficulties requires focused and direct intervention. Many of the corrective strategies suggested in this chapter can be adapted to teach several skills. Words must be presented in many forms and varied contexts, with supplementary cues that are phased out as students progress. Appropriate computer practice may improve mastery of many skills. Concurrently teaching the meaning, spelling, and writing of key words as they are introduced increases the probability that the words will become usable components of students' listening, speaking, reading, and writing vocabularies.

## Key Principles

Although all of the principles presented in Chapter 3 are important guidelines for corrective instruction, the ones that probably are most critical for and specific to correcting readiness and word recognition skills are these:

— Teach diagnostically and for mastery
— Apply principles of behaviorism
— Teach to learning style
— Use multiple senses when teaching
— Teach the strategies for accomplishing tasks and self-monitoring
— Integrate reading with instruction in all the language arts
— Teach application of word recognition skills across the curriculum

Accommodating a student's learning style is an important factor, for instance, when choosing between a look-say or a phonics emphasis.

## Corrective Themes

Recurring themes in the corrective strategies include generous use of teacher modeling, active student participation, accommodations for learning styles, integrated instruction, and presenting words in isolation and in context. Placing the words in oral and written context affords opportunities for self-monitoring, as readers check their responses for congruence with surrounding words, and lessens the likelihood that students will become "word callers." Older and less able students may need to focus on fewer intricacies of readiness and word analysis. They should concentrate on contextual usage and on building a sight vocabulary of high-frequency words and content and consumer terms. The consumer terms are especially important for most students with special needs.

## SPECIFIC SKILLS AND STRATEGIES

Of the readiness and word recognition skills briefly discussed in the next several pages perhaps the most essential to both reading and academic progress are Skills 1, 7, and 8: language readiness, the foundation for reading and academic development; contextual analysis, the strategy for decoding individual words and meanings; and applying word recognition skills across the curriculum to decode, understand, and learn in all subjects.

In addition to the principles of effective instruction in Chapter 3, the Corrective Principles presented in Chapter 2 for each special category provide basic guidance for selecting and adapting strategies to teach identified special learners. However, the student's age and ability, as well as the particular reading program used, must be considered. The unique needs of the individual student must be the most important factor in planning and delivering appropriate instruction.

## 1. LANGUAGE READINESS

DETECTION

This may be a special skill need of students who

- Display a limited listening and speaking vocabulary
- Talk in single words or phrases with few descriptive words
- Do not understand directions
- Confuse left and right
- Are unable to identify words for body parts
- Have difficulty classifying objects and ideas
- Have unusual difficulty conversing with others

*Description*

Continuing acquisition and expansion of oral language is the foundation of reading development. This process is also necessary for developing language skills for clear oral and written communication. Skills associated with language development include careful listening and thinking, accurate articulation, concentration, vocabulary knowledge, self-awareness, and classification. Speaking and listening vocabulary should permit understanding and expression of complete sentences with some embellishment. Specific terms that facilitate classroom progress include direction words (top, bottom, above, below) — the heart of school assignments, instructions, and requests — and descriptive language (two big, blue books). Self-awareness is enhanced when students can state their personal data; label important body parts; and describe emotions, attitudes, actions, and body language. Classification of objects and concepts is an important learning and memory skill for storing and retrieving language information and for comparing new data with known data.

*Special Problems*

The foundation for language skills is built at home and expanded at school. The student with weak language skills often has not experienced many language-enriching opportunities — consistent positive, interactive communication with adults and children who use and expect rich, descriptive words in complete sentences, and who often read aloud to the child. Lack of specific instruction and modeling often causes unfamiliarity with color words, direction words, body-image words, and personal information. Although some gifted students are adept at classifying objects and ideas, many students must receive specific guidance to develop classification skills. Students who are learning disabled or mentally retarded may have particular difficulty interpreting body language. A general lack of background experiences and knowledge can also create problems. Certain difficulties in auditory acuity and processing can delay students' language development. Other groups of special learners who may exhibit weak language development are students who have cultural or language differences and those with language disabilities, learning disabilities, speech disorders, or mental retardation.

*Implications*

Oral language is the basis upon which other communications skills are built. Oral language also provides a background of experiences and vocabulary with which to understand reading and to develop writing skills. Instruction in oral language development must guide, model, and provide opportunities for using and expanding language.

CORRECTION

Modify these strategies to meet students' learning needs.

1. *Our Talk.* To model embellished language, as well as teach concepts, use *My Talk* to describe and explain your actions as you move about the classroom ("I am writing a big letter *b* on the board"). Use *Your Talk* to put the words to students' actions ("Good; you are drawing a nice, round circle around the letter *b*").

2. *Model Prompts.* Model appropriate language by routinely correcting, rephrasing, or expanding students' statements in a questioning voice. For example, if a student says, "Me too," you would say, "I want one too, please?" You would expect the student to say, "Yes. I want one too, please." Students soon catch your cues and begin to rephrase automatically.

3. *Direction Model.* As a whole-group activity, give each student a situation and object, such as a toy car or animal. Use the objects first to model direction concepts. Have each student copy your model; for example "Drive your car across your desk; park your car on the left of your pencil." After students catch on, give the oral directive but omit the direction word (e.g., across or left) as you demonstrate what is expected; have students label your action.

4. *Label Me.* Point to an easy body part — your thumb or foot — and ask students to name it. Present a silhouette of a body and ask students to find and name the same part. Then have them find and label that part on themselves. Eventually, have students take turns labeling you, the picture, and themselves.

5. *Personal Data.* Assign students one personal fact a week to memorize, in this order: full name, address, phone, birthday, guardians' full names, and siblings' full names. Have students practice saying and clapping each item rhythmically in small groups every day until they have mastered each fact. As each child can recite a fact, enter it on a large class poster. Also write the data in a personal data book for students to keep so they can begin to recognize the data at sight.

6. *Put Togethers.* To introduce the concept of classification, display an object that is used to contain groups of objects, such as a desk drawer. Present 3 items (ruler, pencil, coat) and discuss which ones belong in the drawer. Next, display 2 containers (e.g., lunchbox and purse) and 3 items that go in each container. Then follow a similar procedure using pictures of containers and pictures of objects they typically hold. Guide students to explain why each object belongs with its container. Follow this procedure with worksheets that require students to match objects with containers; upon completion, discuss the reasons for the students' choices.

7. *Real Classification.* Direct practical experiences in classifying. Guide students to sort the contents of a desk drawer or to group books on a shelf by color or size. Then label, discuss, and critique the groupings.

8. *Extra Practice.* • Set aside "talk time" for students to talk quietly about a choice of 2–3 topics. • Give students objects to move, or have them move themselves, to the directions of Simon Says. • Have students bring pictures that illustrate specific moods or body language; have them pantomime the pictures while peers guess which picture is being demonstrated. • Ask students to work in small groups to suggest items that could be classified with an object brought from home. • Have students use a computer program to classify pictures and objects.

## 2. VISUAL READINESS

DETECTION

This may be a special skill need of students who

- Cannot match or distinguish similar shapes and sizes
- Cannot match or differentiate similarly shaped letters
- Cannot identify a letter after seeing the letter elsewhere
- Tend to reverse letters more often than age peers
- Do not visually distinguish one word from another
- Have difficulty recognizing preliminary sight words

*Description*

The broad areas of visual readiness skills are visual discrimination and visual memory. Teachers usually notice difficulties in discriminating shapes, sizes, letters, and words through informal observation, by performance on readiness tests, or during daily lessons that require visual discrimination as a part of other tasks. Visual differentiation of letters is closely related to word identification. Students should recognize and remember letters both in and out of alphabetical sequence. Visual memory aids students in learning the letter names and words and in remembering their visual appearances. To become proficient readers, students must remember certain common words. Color and number words should be part of the preliminary sight vocabulary for beginning readers.

*Special Problems*

Although reading is a cognitive task, vision plays a vital role. Poor visual acuity or related problems requiring corrective lenses, maturational delays, and visual deficits that affect the internal processing of visual information can all cause difficulties. Many manuscript letters are easily confused. For example, *b*, *d*, *p*, and *q* have similar shapes but in different rotations. To the beginning reader, these subtle differences may be unapparent or seem unimportant. Problems involving visual discrimination of words can result from lack of attention to details or excessive attention to word length or letter height. Some students have not had sufficient exposure to letters or words. When beginning readers do not recognize at least a few words on sight, both limited experience with written language and visual perception problems or lack of visual training may be involved. Some students attend more carefully to auditory than to visual stimuli. Students who are visually impaired, learning disabled, slow learners, or mentally retarded may have particular difficulty with visual discrimination and memory.

*Implications*

Developing word recognition skills includes developing visual discrimination and memory skills. Teachers should select shapes, letters, and words on a graduated scale, beginning with easily distinguishable forms, and then moving to progressively more similar stimuli. Visual memory of letters is involved in learning the letter names, in decoding words, and in handwriting and spelling. To become efficient readers, students must develop automatic recognition responses to many letters and words. Visual skills can be enhanced by using multisensory intervention that includes seeing, saying, and writing words and letters.

CORRECTION

Modify these strategies to meet students' learning needs.

1. *Shaping Up.* Give the students 1 or 2 index cards, each showing a different component shape of letters, such as circle, slant, or curve. Display one of the shapes on a card or on the board. Ask students holding cards with that shape to come forward and match the shapes, each time verbalizing the likenesses. This format can later be extended to include more stimuli or letters or words.

2. *Tracing Shapes.* Begin by using one or more primary or letter shapes on an index card or sheet of paper. Draw the stimulus shape on the board. Have the students locate the same shape on their own papers and trace the outline of the shape using first their fingers and then their pencils. Next, ask the students to draw the shape without tracing. Later, have the students draw a smaller or larger replica of the original shape.

3. *Letter Match.* Give each student 2–5 letters cut from heavy paper. Have the students place each letter on the matching letter shown on a page in front of them. Outline the letters on the chalkboard and have students go to the board to match their letter. Focus discussion on why letters match, almost match, or do not match.

4. *Eye Catchers.* Print letters or words on index cards. Expose a card for approximately 1 second, and then have the students point to or circle the same letter or word on their papers and on the board. Students can reinforce one another by working in pairs and flashing cards to each other.

5. *Alphabet Soup.* Give students an envelope containing a mixture of 10–20 uncooked alphabet noodles. Have students work individually to match all the identical letters they can. Then guide students to trade extra letters with peers in order to create matching groups of 2 or more letters. Continue until all letters are matched. For variation, have student teams create as many words as they can.

6. *Language Labels.* Label familiar objects around the classroom or home (e.g., desk, table, chair) to make students aware of, and help them remember, the visual appearance of common words. Write the words on index cards, and tape the cards to the objects they name. For several days, have students read each card. Then remove the cards from the objects and ask students to read the cards and replace them on the objects. For practice with different formats, print the words on the board, on transparencies, or on paper, and then have students identify the objects named.

7. *Master List.* Help students keep personal lists of words as they learn them. Write words in list form and on individual index cards for students to match their words with peers' words or with moveable letters. Reward students each time they note that one of their words has been spoken or written.

8. *Extra Practice.* • Have students match cards from Shaping Up as they work independently or in pairs. • Have students make sets of 3 cards with 2 like shapes and 1 different; have them ask a peer to locate the different shape. • Give students word cards and have them match moveable letters to the words on the cards. • Have peers teach 2–3 words from their Master Lists to each other. • Give each student of a pair several letter or word cards; have the students take turns drawing cards from each other to collect as many matching pairs as they can.

## 3. AUDITORY READINESS

DETECTION

This may be a special skill need of students who

- Cannot match words with similar sounds
- Do not discriminate subtle differences in word sounds
- Frequently ask for words to be repeated
- Often mispronounce words
- Exhibit problems remembering what they hear
- Do not follow oral directions

*Description*

Skills that facilitate reading include auditory discrimination and auditory memory. Instruction in auditory discrimination usually begins with initial sounds because they typically are the easiest to recognize; ending sounds are taught after initial sounds and before medial sounds, which are the most difficult word parts to learn and to teach. Hearing the differences in sounds is an important first step in learning phonics, as is remembering sounds. Auditory memory involves encoding (hearing accurately), retention (storing the sounds), and retrieval (getting the sounds out of storage). Students must remember the sounds of letters, letter combinations, words, phrases, and oral directions. Following oral directions is particularly important as a basic classroom skill.

*Special Problems*

Students who hear the similarities or differences among sounds but do not understand the concepts of same and different may falsely appear to have an auditory discrimination problem. Dialectical differences, cultural habits, and inadequate language models can all have detrimental effects on students' discrimination of sounds, particularly final sounds. Both discrimination and memory may be affected by special speech problems or hearing losses, even slight ones. Determining which cognitive processes — encoding, retention, or retrieval — cause auditory memory problems for individual students is difficult. Factors such as a weak or different language background or general inattentiveness may contribute to auditory memory difficulties. Students experiencing auditory memory problems may appear confused, tuned out, or disinterested. They may also appear noncompliant because they do not follow oral directions. Failure to follow oral directions can be due to not listening carefully, inattention in general, distractibility, disinterest, a lack of effort, weak auditory discrimination or memory skills, or poorly explained assignments. The special groups of students who may experience auditory problems are those with language differences, hearing impairments, language disabilities, learning disabilities, and speech disorders.

*Implications*

Auditory skills are basic to reading as well as to overall academic progress. Auditory discrimination training should be confined to sounds and words that are not distorted by regional pronunciations. Efforts to increase auditory memory should focus on improving one or more of the component processes: encoding, retention, and retrieval. Most students learn best when auditory input is supplemented with visual information. Using rhythmic patterns to emphasize words and phrases helps students chunk the sounds into manageable groups. Guided practice, clearly stated assignments, visual cues, and examples will help most students follow oral instructions.

CORRECTION

Modify these strategies to meet students' learning needs.

1. *Handy Confirmation.* Select pairs of words to be pronounced. Begin with pairs that include students' names. Ask students to listen carefully to each pair of words and hold up 2 fingers if the words have different target sounds and 5 fingers if they have the same target sounds. Varying the signals teaches incidental concepts, such as continuity, left-right, up-down, and numbers. For extra practice, permit students to take turns pronouncing word pairs for peers.

2. *Watch My Lips.* As a supplementary visual cue, have students watch the first, middle, or last movements of your mouth as you pronounce each of a pair of words. Have students who experience extreme difficulty repeat word pairs and watch the movements of their own mouths in a mirror.

3. *Touch and Hear.* When working with students who continue to experience difficulty discriminating sounds, add touch to the process. Have them lightly touch your mouth and neck to feel sound likenesses and differences as you say pairs of words. Use words that are identical except for the target sounds (e.g., hit/him, mat/pat, hill/hall).

4. *Discrimigration.* Integrate auditory discrimination training with other lessons by asking, "What word in the title begins like *turkey*? What is another word in this paragraph with the vowel sound of *can*? Listen to the last sentence for the word that ends like *goat*."

5. *Hear and Say.* To introduce a reading lesson, pronounce several key words related to the topic. Have students say, but not write, the words in order and then guess the secret topic. Then have them signal each of the words in the original sequence as they read. For fun, throw in an occasional unrelated word and ask students to recall only the ones that are related.

6. *Key Rhythms.* Teach students to remember important information, especially telephone numbers and addresses, by saying and thinking it in rhythm. To demonstrate, say your phone number (or, if you prefer not to receive numerous calls, make up a number), chunking the numbers and emphasizing some as you say them: "6-8-5, 94, 94." Have the students clap the rhythm as you repeat the number. Help students develop patterns for their own phone numbers and addresses.

7. *See, Say, and Repeat.* When giving directions, include a visual representation of what is expected. Use a sample paper or printed directions that students can follow along with the oral presentation. After completing directions, call on individual students to explain the directions.

8. *The Last Word.* When giving oral directions, encourage careful listening by occasionally stopping near the end of a sentence for students to predict the last word or phrase.

9. *Extra Practice.* • Record several words on audiotape; provide 2–3 pictures for each recorded word, and ask students to circle the picture whose name contains the target sound. • Have student pairs use this procedure: After the first student says a word, the second student must say 5 additional words with the same target sound. • Record simple, humorous directions for paper-and-pencil tasks on an audio cassette and have students listen and do as they are directed.

## 4. REMEMBERING LETTERS AND SIGHT WORDS

DETECTION    This may be a special skill need of students who

- Do not remember or often confuse letters
- Do not quickly recognize low-image words
- Do not quickly recognize high-image words
- Exhibit an inadequate sight vocabulary
- Read at a slow rate
- Evidence difficulty comprehending text

*Description*    An inability to recall letters or identify basic sight words can cause students to experience serious reading problems. Half or more of the words appearing in printed material are high-frequency or sight words. Several lists have been developed based upon frequency counts of words in instructional and tradebook materials. High-frequency words are of two general types: High-image words can be pictured or described because they have concrete referents (e.g., *dog, man, run*); low-image words have vague or no automatic referents (e.g., *the, with, it*). Instant recognition of common words is essential because the burden of having to decode each word individually slows the reading rate, increases the complexity of the task, and impairs comprehension.

*Special Problems*    Problems remembering letters can stem from the similarities among letters (e.g., *b, d, p, q*), difficulty discriminating letters and shapes, or problems involving visual memory. Sight-word recall is sometimes hampered when students rely too heavily on phonetic analysis or cannot conceptualize abstract words without structural clues. In addition to being the most difficult words to recall on sight, some low-image words also are similar in appearance (e.g., *it/is, will/with, what/when*). Although high-image words are among the easiest words to recognize on sight, some students may not have been taught to pair words with their visual referents. Some learning-disabled and visually impaired students may experience particular difficulty recalling letters and sight words. Other students who may have this problem are those who are mentally retarded or who have been educationally deprived.

*Implications*    Many experts consider letter and sight-word mastery as prerequisites for learning to read. Some gifted or highly verbal students learn to read without first learning all the letters of the alphabet. However, except for a select few, students learn to read more easily and effectively when they can recognize letters. Because the high-frequency words comprise over 50 percent of all text, students must recognize these words instantly in order to read fluently without interrupting comprehension. Teaching sight words does not require the exclusive use of the look-say or whole-word approach. A variety of decoding strategies, including phonic analysis, should accompany specific instruction for developing a sight-word vocabulary. Students who experience particular difficulty mastering phonics may need to rely more heavily on their memory for letters and sight words.

**CORRECTION**

Modify these strategies to meet students' learning needs.

1. *High-Frequency Letters.* Emphasize the letters used in students names, their school's name, or other high-interest words. Have students say the letters as they trace them with a felt marker or as they underline or circle specific letters.
2. *Image Builders.* Provide visual images for association with each letter or word. Consistently pair the same picture with target letters and words during initial introduction and practice.
   - Present a picture whose name begins with each target letter (ball for *b*, zebra for *z*).
   - Provide a picture of each high-image word (girl's face for *girl*, children jumping rope for *jump*).
   - Present low-image words with high-image words and their pictures; teach articles with referents (*the* cat), linking and auxiliary verbs with action verbs or nouns (Alison *is* home), adverbs with action verbs (swim *fast*), and prepositions with nouns (*with* Mylan).

   Insert rebuses in text as imagery cues and meaning clues. Gradually phase out the use of pictures as students progress.
3. *Ghostwriting.* Have students say and "ghostwrite" target letters or words. Write each letter or word on the chalkboard, placing above it a key picture such as a dog for *d*, a cottage for *house*, or a boy for *the* boy. Have students use their index fingers to trace the letter or word repeatedly while saying its name. With each tracing, more chalk is erased, leaving the "ghost" of the original markings. When the ghost is almost invisible, have students close their eyes and try to see the letter or word, and then trace the ghost with chalk, again saying the letter or word. This activity is particularly appropriate for helping students differentiate between similar letters and words.
4. *Spell and Tell.* Teach the spelling of words as a means of reinforcing their visual appearance. Have students verbalize the configuration of each word and the letter heights, shapes, and names; students should pronounce each word over and over and then orally use it in 3 sentences. Begin with 3–5 words that are visually dissimilar. As students are able, increase the number and similarity of the words.
5. *Configured Cloze.* Present the configuration of target words in context; have students combine context with configuration to guess the missing word. If needed, list words from which students may choose.
6. *Sight Bingo.* Print 12–20 different letters or sight words in boxes on cards like numbers on a Bingo card. Call out letters or words, and have students mark their cards. Use rows of 3 or more, or the traditional across, down, and diagonal rows.
7. *Sight-Word Cloze.* Using a modified cloze format, have students either select the correct sight word from 3 choices or fill in an appropriate sight word in blanks in simple sentences. As they correctly select each word, have students trace or write the word while saying it.
8. *Extra Practice.* • Print letters or words on 3″ × 5″ index cards to use for flash recognition, flash matching, or a card game matching like letters or words. • Have students construct Configured Cloze activities for peers. • Pair students to practice rapid recognition using a tachistoscope or a computer program that flashes letters and words. • Highlight 2–5 letters or sight words a day as honor tasks; have student pairs quiz each other using several days' honor tasks on cards.

## 5.  USING PHONIC ANALYSIS

DETECTION

This may be a special skill need of students who

- Do not remember the sounds of certain letters
- Are unable to sound out unfamiliar words
- Refuse to try to pronounce unfamiliar words
- Cannot blend sounds into words
- Have difficulty discriminating sounds
- Do not remember much of what they hear

*Description*

Phonic analysis is one of several important word analysis skills necessary for decoding words. Phonics involves associating the speech sounds of letters with their written symbols. The sounds of the consonants are much more stable than the sounds of vowels. Phonetic inconsistencies are created when letters have different sounds depending upon their use in various combinations. Over 300 phonic generalizations could be used to teach students to sound out words. However, 20 or so of these are generally accepted as being useful. Of these 20, the most reliable generalizations are those associated with short and long vowel sounds and with the different sounds of *c* and *g*. For phonic analysis to facilitate the pronunciation of words, direct instruction must begin with the most useful and reliable generalizations in a whole-word context.

*Special Problems*

Difficulty applying phonic analysis to the decoding of words may result when students cannot remember the letter sounds because of visual or auditory problems or boredom with the task. Students who recall the sounds but do not apply them may not have had either sufficient opportunity to practice the skills in context or direct instruction in blending the sounds into words. Students who prefer a visual learning style or who are linguistically different often have problems using phonic analysis. Some students who have been taught to add *uh* to the single sounds in isolation (e.g., *r*uh, *t*uh) understandably have problems blending those sounds into words (rat = *ruhatuh?*). Other sources of difficulty include slow learning rates, learning disabilities, hearing impairments, mental retardation, and speech disorders.

*Implications*

For the past century, debate has raged over the degree, amount, and sequence of phonics teaching and over the approach that should be used. While most experts agree that training in phonic analysis is necessary, they disagree on the duration and approach that work best. Most specialists advise beginning with teaching consonant sounds, which are the most stable; consonants in the initial position of words seem most useful, and their use reinforces the left-to-right concept. In fact, using context together with the initial sounds of words may be enough to help students decode many words. To remember letter sounds, students must first discriminate visually among the letters and commit the distinctive appearances of the letters to visual memory. Then students must associate each letter with its corresponding sound(s), a task requiring auditory discrimination, auditory memory, and, as the final product, sound/symbol association. Although students who have difficulty mastering phonics can be taught by a linguistic or a more visual approach, they must still make the sound/symbol connection.

CORRECTION

Modify these strategies to meet students' learning needs.

1. *Mirror Sounds.* Have students watch your mouth as you exaggerate target sounds. Permit them to feel your throat as they listen to the sound. Then give them mirrors so they can practice making the sound themselves while placing one hand on their throats to check for movements like yours. Finally, make the mouth movements without the target sound, and have students guess the sound and then confirm their answers by watching their mouths in the mirror and feeling their throats as they make their sound.

2. *Sound Stories.* Use listening stories to introduce and reinforce sounds, emphasizing each word with the target sound as you display the target letter. Some publishers provide such stories with their reading programs; if these are not available, do not meet students' needs, or do not fit your sequence, modify read-aloud stories. For example, for *b*, call "The Three Bears" Buddy, Betty, and Baby, and have them bounce through the woods and up the stairs.

3. *Single Sounds.* With each of these activities, use a key picture to illustrate the target sound; stress the sound's pronunciation, highlight it with a felt marker, write it on the board, and have students write it as they say it: (a) Call out a word and have students either select or print the target sound; (b) Give students a target sound and have them say or write words using it; (c) Give students short phrases with a key word underlined, followed by a partial word in which to fill in the missing letters; and (d) Have students suggest sounds to substitute in words they know to make new words (e.g., *ran/_an, hit/h_t, mop/mo_*).

4. *Picture Match-Ups.* Pictures can be used in a variety of ways to improve phonic analysis. Have students say and write the target sound each time: (a) Show a picture and 2–3 words and have students select the word containing the sound of the picture name, (b) Show a row of pictures and have students select the pictures whose names contain the same sound, (c) Show pictures with partial words and have students fill in the letters that complete picture names, and (d) Use index cards with pictures on the back representing the word on the front of the card.

5. *Sound Blending.* To teach blending separate sounds, have students add a sound at a time to the beginning sound, as in *f___, fa__; fas_, fast.* Model the process and then have students repeat with you.

6. *Vowel Cloze.* Teach students to use the consonants with context to infer vowel sounds. Write a sentence on the board or overhead; omit 1 word, writing only the consonants. Model the strategies for concluding sounds and the selection process for letters to insert. Allow those who need extra help to choose from among 2–3 vowels. As students progress, increase the number of words with vowels omitted. Pair word analysis and spelling instruction by using sentences from spelling lessons.

7. *Sound Games.* Use target vowels to play games that follow the formats of such favorites as Concentration, Bingo, Lotto, or Go Fish. Use 2 different words with the target sound as a pair or match.

8. *Extra Practice.* • Pair students to practice substituting sounds using consonant and vowel wheels. • Have students write letters on fingerpaint bags as they listen to words on tape. • Record Sound Stories for students to listen to while they trace or write target letters. • Provide practice on a computer with a voice synthesizer. • For fun, permit students to write private "no-vowel" notes for a peer to translate.

## 6.  USING STRUCTURAL ANALYSIS

DETECTION       This may be a special skill need of students who

- Exhibit difficulty identifying word parts
- Are unfamiliar with prefixes, suffixes, and root words
- Cannot tell the meanings of affixes
- Do not recognize compound words or contractions
- Do not know where to divide words into syllables
- Also have difficulty with sight words and phonic skills

*Description*    Structural analysis involves using the meaningful parts of words to decode the words. Applying meaning-based and self-monitoring strategies is particularly helpful in structural analysis. The major types of word parts in the study of word structure include root words, inflectional endings, affixes (prefixes and suffixes), compound words, contractions, and syllables. Since structural skills are a part of both word recognition and vocabulary development, they are very important.

*Special Problems*    The most common cause of difficulty in using structural analysis as a decoding strategy is insufficient direct instruction and meaningful practice. Structural analysis, like contextual analysis, is typically taught less often than phonic and sight-word skills. Also, as new words occur in reading programs, many teachers do not present the meanings of affixes along with pronunciation. Some students who do receive instruction may have been exposed to poor teaching practices such as hunting for little words in big ones. Their teachers may have relied too much on phonic analysis or placed too little stress on vocabulary development. Some teachers force students to memorize syllabication rules rather than guiding them to conclude the most common and reliable generalizations. Since word parts should be taught as intact sight-word units, students who have problems with visual discrimination or visual memory may have difficulty mastering structural-analysis skills. Special groups of students who may exhibit this special need are those who have been educationally deprived or those who have language disabilities, learning disabilities, mental retardation, or visual impairments.

*Implications*    For many students, structural-analysis skills are more easily mastered than phonic or contextual analysis. The concrete nature of words and word parts makes structural skills easier to teach and apply. As a decoding strategy, structural analysis is much quicker than sounding out words and more easily understood than contextual analysis. Structural analysis is particularly important for students with auditory difficulties; analysis of word parts, taught as sight units, can partially compensate for less-skilled phonic analysis. With minimal appropriate instruction, students generally master the common compound words and contractions quickly. Understanding the meanings of just a few affixes can help students understand hundreds of additional words. Students reading at or above fourth-grade level should be guided to generalize the most useful syllabication rules, such as division of words by affixes, between paired consonants, or by frequent syllables. By combining instruction in structural analysis and word meanings, teachers can improve students' word recognition and word-meaning skills.

**CORRECTION**          Modify these strategies to meet students' learning needs.

1. *Compound Cover-Up.* When students cannot pronounce a compound word, cover the second part of the word, displaying only the first component. When they pronounce the first part, cover it to reveal only the second word. After that part is pronounced, have them say the parts together. Prompt students to cover the parts by saying, "cover up."

2. *Contraction Mark-Out.* Use the chalkboard to present pairs of words that form contractions. Guide students to (a) pronounce the words, (b) mark through the letters that are omitted to form the contraction, (c) substitute the apostrophe for the missing letters, (d) rewrite the pair of words as the contraction, and (e) pronounce the contraction. Have students repeat the process for word pairs copied from the board. Reverse the process by presenting contractions and guiding students to fill in the missing letters.

3. *Wordfuns.* Pair students to make up their own compounds, contractions, and new words with affixes, using words from their reading or spelling program. Have students decide what the meaning of each contrived word should be and then present them to peers. Emphasize that this activity is just for fun and that their words are not real words.

4. *Premier Prefixes* (or *Supreme Suffixes*). Twice a week, select a specific prefix or suffix from current texts for emphasis. Explain meaning along with highlighting the affix; have students locate, pronounce, and describe their own uses of the word part. Present additional words with the same affix; discuss meaning changes.

5. *Analytic Affixes.* Use known words to teach the recognition and meanings of affixes. When a word such as *unhappy* occurs in text, highlight the prefix as a unit of meaning. Guide students to conclude the meaning of *un* by attaching it to other known words. Discuss other words that include the affix and practice using them.

6. *Sight Parts.* Present common syllables as intact units to be mastered as sight words. Guide students to analyze known words and decide upon important syllables that occur frequently in their texts. Discuss meanings, if any, of the syllables as you model and guide students to highlight their distinctive features. Have students pronounce the syllables as separate units, say their meanings, write them, and spell them. Then have students pronounce and write the full words, again saying the meaning of the whole word. Lead students to conclude syllabication and accent rules for words with these syllables.

7. *Syllable Sense.* Present known multisyllable words to teach common patterns of syllabication. Select 3–5 words to illustrate a specific and consistent rule. Ask several students to pronounce the words and explain in their own words the rule for dividing that word into syllables. Then present an unknown word of similar pattern and ask students to pronounce it according to their rule. Follow this procedure for several days with new words that follow the rule before presenting and contrasting new but dissimilar rules in like manner.

8. *Extra Practice.* • Add 1–2 words with target structures to the spelling lesson each week. • Have students keep lists of common affixes and their meanings, as well as sample words. • Have students check the dictionary to label their Wordfuns as "real" or "mine." • Reward students who use words of 3 or more syllables in class discussions.

## 7. USING CONTEXTUAL ANALYSIS

DETECTION        This may be a special skill need of students who

- Do not use surrounding text to decode unknown words
- Make numerous errors when reading aloud
- Do not self-correct when reading aloud
- Overuse word analysis or display weak word-analysis skills
- Exhibit weak comprehension skills

*Description*        Contextual analysis is as much a comprehension skill as a word recognition or decoding strategy. It is probably the most efficient and effective word recognition skill, offering clues to both meaning and pronunciation. The use of context to decode words requires students to understand other words around the problem word(s). Context involves inferential thinking; readers use what they understand to determine the meaning of what is left. Both semantic and syntactic clues are available for use in decoding other words and phrases. When text is very difficult or filled with new concepts, students must apply context clues more broadly to figure out phrases and the larger ideas throughout passages. Thus, students must synthesize adjacent words, sentences, and paragraphs, or the overall context, to comprehend the passage.

*Special Problems*        Possible reasons for difficulty using context effectively include a poorly developed meaning-based vocabulary, an inability to predict and infer, and disinterest in or inexperience with the passage content. Passages that are too difficult for the student and lack of direct instruction or meaningful practice cause problems in using contextual analysis. Students who have been educationally deprived or who have a weak language background or a multilingual background often have difficulty using contextual analysis. The predictions and inferences required for contextual analysis may present problems for some students, especially those who are slow learners, learning disabled, and mentally retarded.

*Implications*        Using context is perhaps the word recognition procedure most frequently applied by proficient readers. When used properly, context can help students determine both the pronunciations and the meanings of unfamiliar words. When teamed with sight-word recognition, phonic analysis, and structural analysis, contextual analysis is a powerful decoding tool. Unfortunately, too many beginning reading programs teach sight words and phonic analysis, followed by structural analysis, and finally, almost as an afterthought, use of context. Because all of the word recognition skills should be presented and applied in meaningful context, contextual analysis should be taught as an integral part of word recognition and meaning from the first day of reading instruction. Contextual analysis is useful not only in reading but also in all other subjects. Students should be taught to use contextual clues for individual words before tackling multiple-word phrases and sentences. Effective corrective instruction must include demonstrations, discussions, and explanations of thinking strategies involved in predicting and verifying with context, as well as encouragement to use context along with other word recognition skills.

CORRECTION

Modify these strategies to meet students' learning needs.

1. *Guess and Test.* Present part of a sentence with a word missing (e.g., The little dog ___). Ask students to guess what the word will be. Finish the sentence and have them test their guesses for fit. Using the example "The little dog ____ the postman," model the thought processes for deciding which words fit, why they fit, and how to make and verify the final choice. Present similar sentences, talking students through the thought processes until they can verbalize the strategy. For practice, have students predict deleted words or words that could logically end your incomplete sentences in oral directions, discussion, or listening activities. This hypothesis/test or Guess and Test strategy is the essence of the effective use of context.

2. *Wrong Words.* As a follow-up activity to reading or listening experiences, present sentences that contain a few unnecessary words. Have students cross out the wrong words and explain their answers. For fun and extra practice, insert an occasional wrong word into oral or written directions or stories you read aloud.

3. *Skip It.* When students confront an unknown word in text, tell them to "Skip it and come back later." If the word is not decoded by the end of the sentence or passage, have students listen as you read the sentence aloud with the word deleted. Then read the sentence aloud again, but pronounce only the initial sound of the word in question. If necessary, reread the sentence, pronouncing the beginning and ending sounds of the target word. Regularly use this routine to force the use of context.

4. *Leveled Cloze.* Beginning with the easiest, these cloze formats vary in difficulty according to the deletions and number of clues provided:
   a. Our car (walked, tumbled) down the hill.
   b. Our car t_ _ _ _ed down the hill.
   c. Our car t_ _ _ _ _ _down the hill.
   e. Our car t_____ down the hill.
   f. Our car _____ down the hill

5. *Assisted Cloze.* For students who need an assisted cloze format, retype selections from passages; replace 3–8 key words with the initial letter, blend, or digraph, and a number of blanks equal to the letters in the missing word. For th_ _ format, students may also need the correct word choices provided at the t_ _ of the page or on the chalkb_ _ _ _.

6. *Extended Cloze.* Have students first read or listen to a short passage, and then use what they remember to fill in with their own words a cloze reprint of the passage with key words deleted.

7. *Sentence Fits.* Insert sentences that do not fit into a brief passage. Ask students to use context to identify the sentences to discard, explain their choices, reread with those sentences deleted to verify accuracy, and justify their answers. Later, have students mark out illogical sentences in passages and explain their answers. For variation, follow similar procedures but give students a logical sentence to insert in the best place in a passage; then have them verify, justify, and practice independently.

8. *Extra Practice.* • Have students develop extended cloze selections for peers. • Record short passages on audiotape and delete key words or an ending statement; have students listen and choose or write correct answers, then underline the passage parts that provided clues. • Generate crossword cloze puzzles for students to solve on the computer.

## 8. APPLYING WORD SKILLS ACROSS THE CURRICULUM

DETECTION

This may be a special skill need of students who

- Do not effectively apply word analysis to decode unknown words
- Overuse one or two word recognition skills
- Recognize more words in reading than in other lessons
- Exhibit problems recognizing words in two or more subjects
- Do not use context to decode unknown words

*Description*

Students should recognize words in all reading they do, not just in their specific reading lessons. Students must integrate all the strategies they learn in reading lessons and apply them to figuring out the words of texts, regardless of subject. They must develop a systematic approach to selecting the most effective strategies for decoding unknown words.

*Special Problems*

The major reason for decoding difficulties across the curriculum is the failure of some teachers to directly teach students how to read in subjects other than reading itself. Whereas teachers prompt students to apply word recognition skills during reading lessons, they often forget to do so during other lessons. Teachers in departmentalized situations may not teach reading because they do not consider it their domain. Likewise, some students do not exert the effort needed to decode other texts because they do not consider them to be their reading books. In addition to learning how to utilize each of the word recognition skills, most students must be directly guided to integrate the skills and select the ones most efficient for them and for the particular situation. Some students may have underdeveloped word recognition skills or inadequate practice applying the skills. Other students overuse one decoding skill to the exclusion of others that might be more effective. Difficult textbooks may also create problems; readability is controlled in reading textbooks but not usually in other subjects. The words in directions for independent tasks are often irregular or above the difficulty level of the task itself. Thus, educational deprivation creates problems in this area. Students who exhibit difficulties with specific word recognition skills are likely to experience similar problems across the curriculum.

*Implications*

Since word recognition skills facilitate reading of all types of texts and settings, they must be presented as such. Every lesson that requires reading should be taught as a reading lesson: Introduce each lesson by preteaching the words that occur frequently and carry the key concepts; teach the plan used by the text's author to present new words; continually teach word recognition skills; and prompt students to apply the word recognition skills they have mastered. The readability of textbooks in all subjects should be carefully checked. If the books are too difficult for certain students to read, decrease reliance on the book, provide parallel texts, tape-record difficult text, and/or present detailed study guides. Teachers may need to rewrite directions for independent tasks to make them clearer and more readable. A student should learn strategies for integrating word recognition skills systematically to decode unknown words in the most efficient manner for him or her.

CORRECTION

Modify these strategies to meet students' learning needs.

1. *WORDS Help.* Teach students this strategy for integrating and using word recognition skills effectively and systematically.

   **W**ith Context: Try the unknown word *with context.*
   **O**nly Beginning Sounds: Try *only the beginning sounds* with context.
   **R**ead Aloud: *Read aloud* beginning and ending sounds and context.
   **D**ecode by Structure: *Decode the word by structure* and context.
   **S**ound Out: *Sound out* the word if it remains unknown.
   **HELP:** Get *HELP* if nothing else worked.

   Prominently display the steps and guide students to follow them as they apply the skills. These steps represent the sequence in which the decoding skills should be applied in most cases. However, some students may need to modify the steps for specific types of words.

2. *Help System.* For times when students cannot figure out words independently, establish a system for seeking help (the final step in the WORDS Help Strategy), sequenced to build independent learning skills. For example, list or illustrate these resources in order: (1) Picture Dictionary, (2) Glossary, (3) Another book, (4) Your Reading Buddy, (5) The Teacher. Post the system and encourage students to follow it in sequence.

3. *Extra Help.* Teach students to gauge their ability to read the words in a particular text realistically. Tell them to count the number of words on a single page for which they will need help. When that number exceeds three on three consecutive pages, they should notify the teacher that they will need extra help reading the words and understanding the concepts because the readability level is too difficult for their present skill level.

4. *Preparation.* Using strategies suggested for teaching specific word recognition skills, preteach all key words prior to their use in lessons. For each word, highlight the distinctive features, place it in the context of a defining sentence, and have students write and discuss it.

5. *Subject Bank.* Have students keep a list of key words for each subject. Direct students to underline or highlight new words in the text and then add them to their banks as part of the Preparation portion of each lesson. These word banks are handy reminders of the words to review for tests.

6. *Word Direction.* Specifically teach the essential and recurring words that appear in the directions for independent tasks. If the words are too vague or difficult, rewrite the directions and/or provide illustrations. Then, routinely have several students read directions aloud, and have other students paraphrase them.

7. *Word Advocates.* Have students adopt key words to sponsor. They should give a 3-minute presentation to peers, explaining the uniqueness of their word, its meaning, how it can be remembered, and share its personal relevance.

8. *Extra Practice.* Give student pairs new words in context; have them alternate prompting each other to apply the WORDS Help strategy. • Have students teach the WORDS Help strategy to a peer or younger student. • Have student teams, using their Subject Banks, compete to locate target words in text, pronounce them, and read aloud a defining sentence. • Adapt strategies from the discussions of Word Meaning and Content Vocabulary.

# R EADINESS AND WORD RECOGNITION SAMPLERS

The samplers on the next five pages illustrate a few activities for developing and correcting readiness and word recognition skills. All are ready to copy, but you may need to adjust instructions to meet the specific needs of target students.

4.1 **Follow My Directions.** Sampler 4.1 is designed to reinforce direction words and following directions. The activity requires students to follow your oral directions explicitly to produce a surprise word or picture on the grid. Before presentation, sketch a meaningful letter, word, or picture related to a lesson on a copy of the grid. Then, formulate directions containing appropriate target terms and concepts — for instance, for *L*, Row 2, Column 5, down 10, right 3, or South 10, East 3 — for students to follow in order to replicate your word or picture. Give a blank copy of the grid to each student, review key terms, and dictate one direction at a time for students to follow and draw. When you have finished, display your word or picture for students to check their work and analyze errors. Since most students respond to this activity with enthusiasm, it can be disguised as a recreational activity, particularly for rainy days when recess must take place inside.

4.2 **No-Vowel Notes.** Sampler 4.2 is an example of Activity 6, Vowel Cloze, under Skill 5, Phonic Analysis. To provide phonics practice, emphasize the utility of consonants, and encourage use of word and sentence context, permit students to write notes in class if the notes contain only consonants. For illustration, the directions are printed at the top of the sampler with the vowels missing. Guide students to decode the directions and then write a note without vowels to a friend. Discuss strategies for writing and decoding the notes. Then, permit students either to use the form or to develop their own to write similar notes to friends at designated times in class.

4.3 **Wordfuns.** Designed for use with Skill 6, Activity 3, Sampler 4.3 illustrates structures and increases interest in structural analysis. Have students compose their own compound words, contractions, or new words with affixes. Discuss the sample(s) provided for each category on the form, and direct individual students or student teams to formulate their own words and meanings and then consult the dictionary to identify them as real or original words. This activity can be a competitive one that extends for several weeks.

4.4 **Subject Bank.** Sampler 4.4 is a form for recording key words for each subject as students identify them (Skill 8, Activity 5). Instruct students to highlight the words that carry the key concepts in each subject, discuss the words, write them in their Subject Banks, and later review them for tests. Subject Banks also can be used for independent or team sight-word practice and for a variety of word games.

4.5 **Help Poster.** The WORDS Help poster, derived from Skill 8, Activity 1, is intended for display in the classroom. Model and discuss the steps and then guide students to follow the steps in sequence (or in a sequence that meets individual student needs or is appropriate for the specific types of words) to apply word recognition skills in all subjects.

Name _____

# ↔ ↕ FOLLOW MY DIRECTIONS ↕ ↔

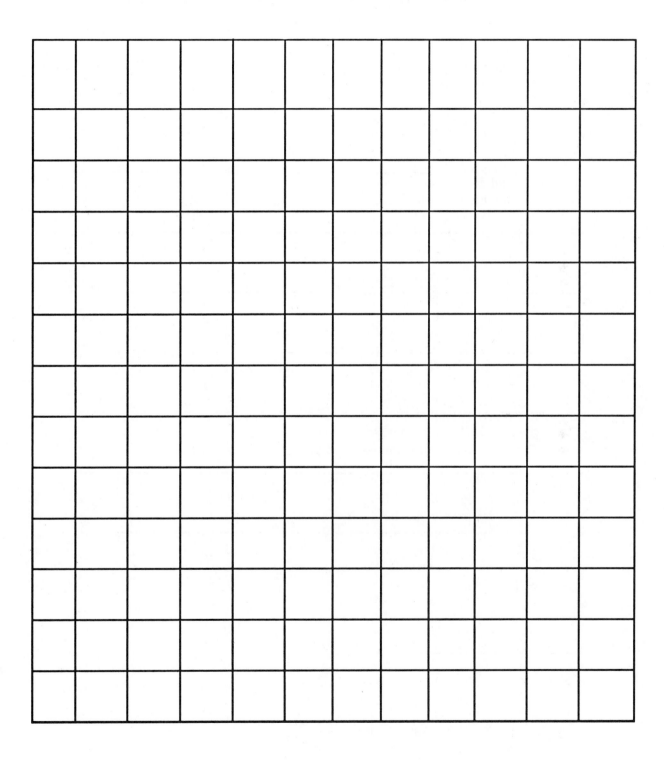

Name _____

# ✉ NO-VOWEL NOTES

D_r_ct_ _ns:  Wr_t_  y_ _r  fr_ _nd  _  n_t_,  b_t  d_n't  _s_  v_w_ls.

D_ _ r _____,

_____

_____

_____

_____

_____

_____

Y_ _ r  fr_ _ nd,

_____

Name _____

  **WORDFUNS**

| COMPOUNDS | MEANING | REAL or MINE | |
|---|---|---|---|
| 1. wordfun | have fun with words | ___ | x |
| 2. | | ___ | ___ |
| 3. | | ___ | ___ |
| 4. | | ___ | ___ |
| 5. | | ___ | ___ |

| CONTRACTIONS | MEANING | REAL or MINE | |
|---|---|---|---|
| 1. pl'ike | play like | ___ | x |
| 2. | | ___ | ___ |
| 3. | | ___ | ___ |
| 4. | | ___ | ___ |
| 5. | | ___ | ___ |

| AFFIXES | MEANING | REAL or MINE | |
|---|---|---|---|
| 1. unwork | not work or play | ___ | x |
| 2. | | ___ | ___ |
| 3. | | ___ | ___ |
| 4. | | ___ | ___ |
| 5. | | ___ | ___ |
| 6. boyish | like a boy | x | ___ |
| 7. | | ___ | ___ |
| 8. | | ___ | ___ |
| 9. | | ___ | ___ |
| 10. | | ___ | ___ |

Name _____

# 🏛 〉 SUBJECT BANK 〈 🏛

## 🏛 SUBJECT: _____

| WORD | PERSONAL MEANING | WORD | PERSONAL MEANING |
|------|------------------|------|------------------|
| ____ | _____ | ____ | _____ |
| ____ | _____ | ____ | _____ |
| ____ | _____ | ____ | _____ |
| ____ | _____ | ____ | _____ |
| ____ | _____ | ____ | _____ |
| ____ | _____ | ____ | _____ |
| ____ | _____ | ____ | _____ |

## 🏛 SUBJECT: _____

| WORD | PERSONAL MEANING | WORD | PERSONAL MEANING |
|------|------------------|------|------------------|
| ____ | _____ | ____ | _____ |
| ____ | _____ | ____ | _____ |
| ____ | _____ | ____ | _____ |
| ____ | _____ | ____ | _____ |
| ____ | _____ | ____ | _____ |
| ____ | _____ | ____ | _____ |
| ____ | _____ | ____ | _____ |

## 🏛 SUBJECT: _____

| WORD | PERSONAL MEANING | WORD | PERSONAL MEANING |
|------|------------------|------|------------------|
| ____ | _____ | ____ | _____ |
| ____ | _____ | ____ | _____ |
| ____ | _____ | ____ | _____ |
| ____ | _____ | ____ | _____ |
| ____ | _____ | ____ | _____ |

Name _____

## 🎓 WORDS Help 🎓

## A Strategy for Applying Word Recognition Skills

**W**ith Context: Try unknown word *with context*

**O**nly Beginning Sounds: Try *only beginning sounds* of word with context

**R**ead: *Read aloud* beginning and ending sounds and context

**D**ecode by Structure: *Decode the word by structure* and context

**S**ound Out: *Sound out* the word if it remains unknown

**Help**: Get *help* if nothing else worked

## REFLECTIONS

1. The reading readiness skills in this chapter are organized in three skill areas: language, visual, and auditory. Review readiness materials from your media center, reading center, school reading laboratory, or resource classroom. Compare and contrast the skills listed in these materials with the ones listed in this section. Which readiness areas receive the most attention? Why? Which ones should receive more emphasis? Why?

2. In this chapter, five specific word recognition skills are discussed: sight vocabulary, phonics, structural analysis, contextual analysis, and skill application. Compare and contrast discussions of these skills with the skills outlined in the scope and sequence charts for the word recognition sections of one or more basal reading programs. Which word recognition areas receive the most attention? Do the skill listings vary according to grade level? Why? Which ones should receive more emphasis? Justify your responses.

3. Understanding the meanings of words is considered by some to be a word recognition skill. However, in this book, word meanings are discussed under comprehension skills in Chapter 5. How do you classify word-meaning skills? Why? Is your classification the same for both able and disabled readers? Why? How will your classification affect your teaching emphasis?

4. Some of the observable behaviors that signal problems in a particular readiness or word recognition skill are listed at the beginning of each discussion. Select one of the eight skill areas; list the Detection behaviors for that skill; then observe students during instruction of that skill in regular classes to watch for these behaviors. Record any additional Detection behaviors you observe, and then ask several teachers to add to the list. Observe students in a special education class and follow similar procedures.

5. Instructional activities for teaching readiness and word recognition skills to students with special needs are often modifications of those appropriate for teaching most students the same skills. Choose a problem from one of the eight skill areas. Then locate the strategies recommended for teaching that skill in the teacher's edition of a basal reader. To identify lesson modifications, contrast the teaching activities listed in the teacher's edition with those suggested in this chapter for the same skill.

6. Only a few Correction strategies are listed for each readiness or word recognition skill. Drawing from classroom observations and/or your own experience, add to or modify the cited activities for two or more skill areas.

7. The chronological age of a student must be taken into account when planning the content of corrective instruction. Select one Correction strategy for readiness that you find appealing. Decide upon the modifications that you would plan for a very young student and for an adolescent student with the same skill needs. Justify your plans.

8. Classroom observations often yield invaluable diagnostic information. Observe a properly identified special student in his or her classroom during reading instruction. Record observed behaviors on the checklist in Figure 4.1. What tentative conclusions can you draw? What additional information do you need to confirm your hypotheses?

9. Chapter 2 presents Corrective Principles for categories of special students. Use these principles as guidelines to select and modify several corrective strategies for readiness and word recognition skills to meet the probable learning needs of a real or hypothetical special learner.

10. When enough diagnostic information is available, special readiness and word recognition lessons are easy to plan. Collect diagnostic data about

the specific needs of a special learner from school records and your own observations. Then use that information and the Corrective Principles to plan two special lessons for the student.

11. Lesson plans often must be modified during teaching. If possible, teach your lessons to the special student, adjusting your plans according to the student's responses as you teach.

12. Several reading and special education textbooks present suggestions for teaching readiness and word recognition skills to a variety of learners. For additional ideas, compare and contrast discussions in these sources with information in Chapter 4.

Burns, P. C., Roe, B. D., & Ross, E. P. (1992). *Teaching reading in today's elementary schools* (5th ed.). Boston: Houghton Mifflin.

Choate, J. S., Enright, B. E., Miller, L. J., Poteet, J. A., & Rakes, T. A. (1992). *Curriculum-based assessment and programming* (2nd ed.). Boston: Allyn and Bacon.

Choate, J. S., & Rakes, T. A. (1989). *Reading: Detecting and correcting special needs.* Boston: Allyn and Bacon.

Cunningham, P. M. (1991). *Phonics they use: Words for reading and writing.* New York: HarperCollins.

Durkin, D. (1993). *Teaching them to read* (6th ed.). Boston: Allyn and Bacon.

Fields, M. V., Spangler, K. L., & Lee, D. M. (1991). *Let's begin reading right: Developmentally appropriate beginning literacy* (2nd ed.). New York: Merrill/Macmillan.

Gunning, T. G. (1992). *Creating reading instruction for all children.* Boston: Allyn and Bacon.

Hammill, D. D., & Bartel, N. R. (1990). *Teaching students with learning and behavior problems* (5th ed.). Boston: Allyn and Bacon.

Harp, B., & Brewer, J. A. (1991). *Reading and writing: Teaching for the connections.* San Diego: Harcourt Brace Jovanovich.

Johns, J. L. (1986). *Handbook for remediation of reading difficulties.* Englewood Cliffs, NJ: Prentice-Hall.

Lapp, D., & Flood, J. (1992). *Teaching reading to every child* (3rd ed.). New York: Merrill/Macmillan.

Lewis, R. B., & Doorlag, D. H. (1991). *Teaching special students in the mainstream* (3rd ed.). New York: Merrill/Macmillan.

Rakes, T. A., & Choate, J. S. (1989). *Detecting and correcting special needs in language arts.* Boston: Allyn and Bacon.

Rinsky, L. A. (1984). *Teaching word attack skills* (3rd ed.). Dubuque, IA: Gorsuch Scarisbrick.

Rubin, D. (1991). *Diagnosis and correction in reading instruction* (2nd ed.). Englewood Cliffs, NJ: Prentice-Hall.

Schickedanz, J. A. (1986). *More than the ABCs: The early stages of reading and writing.* Washington, DC: Association for the Education of Young Children.

Vacca, J. L., Vacca, R. T., & Gove, M. K. (1991). *Reading and learning to read* (2nd ed.). New York: HarperCollins.

Walker, B. J. (1992). *Diagnostic teaching of reading: Techniques for instruction and assessment* (2nd ed.). New York: Merrill/Macmillan.

Wood, J. W. (1992). *Adapting instruction for mainstreamed and at-risk students* (2nd ed.). New York: Merrill/Macmillan.

Yopp, R. H., & Yopp, H. K. (1992). *Literature-based reading acitivities.* Boston: Allyn and Bacon.

# CHAPTER FIVE

## READING COMPREHENSION: PROCESS, SKILLS, AND STRATEGIES

— *Joyce S. Choate and Thomas A. Rakes*

Without comprehension, reading does not occur. Understanding text requires readers to use a number of the important skills treated in the following chapters. Detection and correction of reading comprehension needs can be facilitated by using a targeted approach to identify skill needs and then teaching students the strategies to accomplish manageable bits of the comprehension process. Thus, in the manner of many elementary reading curricula, this chapter discusses several facets of the comprehension process as separate but interrelated areas. However, reading is a holistic process in which many of the subskills contribute to total comprehension by interacting with each other and with the reader's background experiences. For the necessary synergistic interactions to occur, students must have regular opportunities to apply the skills in meaningful reading experiences, excluding skill-specific instruction.

## THE READING COMPREHENSION SKILLS

This chapter groups the interrelated comprehension skills into three broad categories: general comprehension, specific comprehension, and reading and study strategies. The first two categories are the traditional comprehension skills of the reading curriculum. The third category includes comprehension in other subject areas as well as the comprehension that accompanies study strategies.

The general patterns of comprehension are included in Skills 9–11, according to the mode of reading input: oral, silent, or listening. These are the primary means through which reading is evaluated and taught. Recreational reading, as a habit indicating reading attitude, is grouped with the general patterns.

The second comprehension category, addressing the more specific comprehension skills (Skills 13–16), is divided into word meanings and three levels of comprehension: literal, interpretive, and critical. Comprehension of words, both a word-recognition and a comprehension skill, facilitates understanding of phrases, sentences, and paragraphs — the parts of passages. (Another combined word-recognition and comprehension skill, contextual analysis, is discussed in Chapter 4.) Literal, or text-explicit, comprehension requires the reader to understand and recall the information specifically stated in text. Interpretive comprehension involves text-implicit understandings; the reader must use the information implied in the text to make logical inferences. The third level, critical comprehension, entails understanding and then evaluating the text. Critical reading is informed reading that carefully weighs and then judges the information.

The final category focuses on comprehending the content of subjects other than formal reading instruction, as well as on the study strategies that support comprehension and memory in all subjects. Comprehending key vocabulary means mastering the major concepts of a subject and involves applying comprehension strategies across the curriculum. Seldom taught but frequently needed, study strategies involve applying comprehension skills to permit continuous progress in all subjects.

The presence or absence of any one of the reading components discussed in this chapter can facilitate or impede understanding. The interaction of the reader with these components results in proficient comprehension.

## DETECTION OF SPECIAL COMPREHENSION NEEDS

Identifying general comprehension and study weaknesses is easy: If students do not understand what they read, they have comprehension problems; if students do not perform at a satisfactory level, they have study problems. However, determining the nature and extent of comprehension and study abilities is not so easy. Because reading is holistic, isolating precisely where the comprehension process breaks down is difficult. Study-strategy difficulties are even more difficult to pinpoint. Diagnosing reading comprehension and study habits is often educated guessing. To make the best possible guess, educators commonly use both formal and informal assessment techniques.

### Formal Detection

Formal testing of reading is typically conducted in the classroom as part of a standardized group achievement test at the end of each school year. Silent comprehension and occasionally listening comprehension are tested, but oral reading is not. Special students are often unable to demonstrate their knowledge on these tests for a variety of reasons: some read slowly and are penalized by the time constraints; many cannot visually track the correct bubble on the answer sheet; some are overwhelmed by the increasing difficulty of test items; others do not understand the questions or cannot infer the best answers from them; for many, the stimulus/response format is either unfamiliar or inappropriate. Although reported as scores for science, social studies, written expression, or mathematics, subtests for other subject areas also, unfairly, test comprehension. Study strategies are seldom explicitly tested, but their use could be inferred from the global performances. Nonetheless, valuable screening information is available from the results of such tests.

Individually administered formal reading tests are often used to identify comprehension strengths and weaknesses, particularly when a disability is suspected. These tests do not usually include measures of study strategies. Because of the standardized procedures, including directions and time limits, some special students are unable to demonstrate the extent of their reading knowledge. The test formats generally permit careful observation of the student's performance, adding important diagnostic data. However, the informal diagnostic procedures more typically yield the prescriptive data needed for teaching purposes.

### Informal Detection

A number of assessment strategies may be categorized as informal techniques; the common denominator is the absence of standardization. An informal reading inventory (IRI), a set of graded passages and questions used to determine a general reading level and sometimes a comprehension profile, is a popular assessment tool. In addition to IRIs, appropriate techniques include having students retell or paraphrase passage content, supply the missing words in passages, or verify sentences. Directly asking the student how he or she went about finding or remembering information helps in assessing study strategies. However, in most cases, it is up to the teacher to analyze a student's performance to detect comprehension and study patterns.

Checklists of possible reading study problems, such as the sample in Figure 5.1, serve several assessment purposes. They outline the component skills and offer a format for recording and monitoring students' progress. Whether used alone or with other procedures, checklists are useful for analyzing and recording work samples and test results and for documenting student performances. They are particularly valuable for structuring classroom observations and then analyzing and recording observed behaviors.

Direct classroom observations of students as they read, discuss, and perform tasks provide a wealth of diagnostic data about students' reading and study behaviors. This approach affords opportunities to compare performances across types of text, evaluate how readers interact with text and what strategies they use to obtain meaning, and confirm skill needs during actual classroom instruction. It is important to identify both facilitative factors, such as those listed in Figure 5.2, and problem behaviors. A few key behaviors that may signal a particular comprehension problem are included on the checklist in Figure 5.1 as well as at the beginning of the discussion of each specific comprehension skill. When you notice that these behaviors occur consistently and are confirmed by daily written work and test scores, you have probably found a logical beginning point for improving reading comprehension.

## SPECIAL POPULATIONS

The uniqueness of the individual student, particularly his or her distinct learning needs and preferences, must be the major consideration in detecting and correcting special reading comprehension needs. However, certain characteristics of special groups suggest possible problems that individual group members may experience in reading comprehension.

Comprehension, particularly critical comprehension, is problematic for a large proportion of special learners. In addition to students who display generally weak word recognition and comprehension skills, learners most likely to display problems reading critically are those with experiential or cognitive deficits. Weak study skills and strategies, exhibited by many types of special learners, can be partially attributed to two factors: inadequate direct instruction and meaningful practice and/or generally weak comprehension skills. Students with language differences or language or learning disabilities may exhibit a variety of comprehension problems. Cultural differences may interfere with readers' ability to extract intended meanings. Students from backgrounds that do not reinforce recreational reading are not likely to read for pleasure.

Because of its concrete nature, literal comprehension is not especially problematic for most special learners, except those who tend to overlook details in favor of more global understandings, as do some gifted or learning disabled students. Many students who are mentally retarded can comprehend literal information but experience great difficulty interpreting or evaluating text because of increased cognitive demands. Oral reading formats help some students focus attention. Students who can easily attend to task and do not have auditory deficits may not find silent or listening formats troublesome. Least likely to experience numerous comprehension problems are students who are academically gifted or have speech disorders.

**FIGURE 5.1 / Checklist of Comprehension and Study Problems**

Use the checklist to analyze success and error patterns, record behaviors that signal possible problems, plan targeted instruction in reading and study strategies, and then provide practice within meaningful passages. Whether the assessment technique is observing classroom behaviors, teacher tests, or standardized tests, watch for factors that impede or facilitate total reading performance.

| Target Skill | Possible Problem Behaviors | Related Skills |
|---|---|---|
| ____ LISTENING COMPREHENSION | • Does not comprehend listening material<br>• Does not attend to listening tasks<br>• Has difficulty following oral directions | Auditory Readiness<br>All Comprehension<br>All Subjects |
| ____ ORAL READING | • Does not comprehend what he or she reads aloud<br>• Makes numerous oral reading errors<br>• Exhibits weak word-recognition skills | All Comprehension<br>All Word Recognition |
| ____ SILENT READING | • Does not comprehend what is read silently<br>• Reads silently too fast or too slow<br>• Subvocalizes when reading silently | All Comprehension<br>Fluency<br>Study Strategies |
| ____ RECREATIONAL READING | • Seldom reads voluntarily<br>• Shows little interest in printed materials<br>• Demonstrates weak reading skills | All Comprehension<br>All Word Recognition |
| ____ WORD MEANINGS | • Displays limited listening/speaking vocabulary<br>• Does not use context effectively<br>• Frequently asks the meanings of words | Language Readiness<br>Contextual Usage<br>All Comprehension |
| ____ LITERAL | • Does not recall passage details<br>• Cannot quickly locate answers in text<br>• Does not recall facts in correct sequence | All Comprehension<br>Study Strategies<br>Conclusions |
| ____ INFERENTIAL | • Cannot identify main ideas<br>• Has problems concluding unstated events<br>• Cannot predict what is about to occur in text | Summarizing<br>Study Strategies<br>Critical Comprehension |
| ____ CRITICAL | • Cannot analyze/evaluate the content of text<br>• Does not distinguish fact from fiction<br>• Cannot detect bias or identify propaganda | All Comprehension<br>Study Strategies<br>All Subjects |
| ____ CONTENT VOCABULARY | • Performs unsatisfactorily in 2+ subjects<br>• Cannot explain technical or nontechnical terms<br>• Evidences little knowledge of word meanings | Word Meaning<br>All Word Recognition<br>All Comprehension |
| ____ STUDY HABITS | • Often submits incomplete or late assignments<br>• Cannot organize, outline, summarize, or take notes<br>• Does not apply systematic study strategies | All Comprehension<br>Strategy Application |
| ____ NOTETAKING AND SUMMARIZING | • Does not take adequate notes<br>• Cannot outline or summarize<br>• Does not organize self or materials | Study Habits<br>Strategy Application |
| ____ USING GRAPHIC AIDS AND REFERENCES | • Cannot interpret graphic information<br>• Cannot identify appropriate references to consult<br>• Does not use or locate information in references | Study Habits<br>All Comprehension<br>Content Subjects |
| ____ PREPARING FOR TESTS | • Consistently performs poorly on tests<br>• Performs better during practice than on tests<br>• Exhibits generally weak study habits | Study Habits<br>Reference Sources<br>All Subjects |
| ____ APPLICATION OF STUDY STRATEGIES | • Performs below expectancy in 2+ subjects<br>• Displays ineffective study strategies and habits<br>• Does not apply specific mastered skills | All Subjects<br>All Comprehension<br>Study Habits |

Adapted from Choate, J. S. (1990). Reading assessment: A checklist of reading problems. *Diagnostique, 16* (1), 32–37, with permission.

FIGURE 5.2 / **Checklist of Factors That Facilitate Reading Comprehension**

| ____ *MATERIAL TYPE* | | | |
|---|---|---|---|
| NARRATIVE: | ____ Factual | ____ Realistic | ____ Fantasy |
| EXPOSITORY: | ____ Science | ____ Social Studies | ____ Other (specify) |
| CONSUMER (specify): _____ | | | |

| ____ *DIRECT INSTRUCTION* | | | | |
|---|---|---|---|---|
| PRE-READING: | ____ Background | ____ Vocabulary | ____ Predictions | ____ Advance Organizers |
| DURING READING: | ____ Discussions | ____ Predictions | ____ Study Guides: | ____ Oral ____ Written |
| POST-READING: | ____ Rereading | ____ Retelling | ____ Evaluation | ____ Summarization |
| ____ *SPECIAL INTERESTS/EXPERIENCES* (specify): _____ | | | | |

Adapted from Choate, J. S. (1990). Reading assessment: A checklist of reading problems. *Diagnostique*, *16* (1), 32–37, with permission.

## CORRECTION OF READING COMPREHENSION SKILLS

Comprehension difficulties affect the reader's performance not only in reading class, but in all curricular areas. Improvements in comprehension typically occur slowly and gradually over a period of time as students begin to understand and apply comprehension strategies. Each successful comprehension experience adds to the reader's fund of general knowledge and to his or her understanding of how to learn.

## Key Corrective Principles

The factors that facilitate comprehension (e.g., Figure 5.2) provide a foundation to build upon in planning instruction that promotes reading progress. In addition, the principles in Chapter 3 offer important guidelines for corrective instruction. Probably the most critical guidelines for correcting reading comprehension are these:

— Teach diagnostically
— Teach reading as a thinking, holistic process, but teach the strategies for accomplishing the tasks
— Build experiences for reading
— Ask appropriate questions and teach self-monitoring
— Use appropriate materials and models of literature and language
— Integrate reading with instruction in all the language arts
— Teach application of comprehension skills across the curriculum

The contradictory nature of the second guideline is deliberate. Teachers must present comprehension skills in the context of interesting passages, pull out problematic skills for direct instruction, and then place the skills back in the context of whole passages for meaningful practice.

## Corrective Themes

Corrective teaching in comprehension is targeted, direct instruction that includes demonstrations, modeling, and carefully guided practice with corrective feedback. Several themes permeate the Correction Strategies suggested in these chapters. Implicit in each strategy is the assumption that the teacher will build or recall experiences related to the text. Many of the same strategies are appropriate for correcting more than one special comprehension need.

Since the language arts are used throughout the curriculum, and some form of comprehension is required in all the language arts, corrective instruction in reading comprehension should be interrelated with listening, speaking, and writing experiences. Such integration also provides more multisensory experiences. Additional themes incorporated into the corrective strategies include self-monitoring, making predictions and verifications, critical thinking skills, and structured learning strategies. Recommended in many of the strategies are student-generated questions, recitation, retelling, and expansion of ideas. Although extensive use is made of questioning — for instance, to assist readers in clarifying ideas, setting purposes, and developing metacognitive behaviors — questions should primarily be vehicles for learning rather than for evaluation. In selecting materials for skill-specific instruction, teachers should make sure that the structure of the text fits the specific type of comprehension experience desired; they should also consider the age, interests, and school and real-life needs of the students.

The SWAP strategies for oral, silent, and listening comprehension offer students a favorable reading environment (see Skills 9–11). These rights of students must be guaranteed before real reading growth can occur. Consider these SWAP activities before selecting additional comprehension strategies for special learners. Then consult the teaching practices and principles in Chapters 2 and 3 for applicable guidelines. As in previous sections, select and modify the Correction Strategies to meet the specific learning needs of individual students.

## SPECIFIC SKILLS AND STRATEGIES

Although comprehension is presented on the following pages as a series of separate skills, it is actually a global phenomenon that defies such tidy separations. For corrective purposes, however, these not-so-separate skills must be highlighted individually and the strategies for accomplishing each directly taught. Skills 12, 16, and 23 represent the ultimate goals of comprehension instruction: enjoyment of reading as a recreational activity, critical comprehension to evaluate all that is read, and application of study strategies across the curriculum for continued learning.

The unique needs of individual students are central in selecting and adapting the corrective strategies that follow. To plan and deliver appropriate instruction, teachers should also consider other elements: the suggestions in Chapters 2 and 3 for sound instruction and for teaching identified special learners; options for accommodating learner needs listed in Figure 3.1; the student's age and ability; the particular reading program in use; and the student's mastery of word-recognition skills, a direct influence on reading comprehension.

## 9. COMPREHENDING WHILE LISTENING

DETECTION        This may be a special skill need of students who

- Cannot answer comprehension questions about listening activities
- Frequently ask to have statements repeated
- Appear inattentive during listening activities
- Understand what they read orally or silently better than what they hear
- Have difficulty following oral directions
- Express dislike for listening activities

*Description*        Listening comprehension is a critical component of the total language process and of a comprehensive reading program. Students need listening comprehension skills to understand and recall literal and interpretive information and to evaluate the content of stories and other passages, assignments, examples, announcements, and the like. Recalling facts based on direct statements requires that students attend to details and sort the important from the unimportant. Inferential thinking or listening involves listeners in using the information provided to make decisions about what is not directly stated, or to listen beyond the words. Critical listening requires students to evaluate the worth, validity, and message of what they hear. Each of these tasks presupposes auditory acuity, auditory attention to stimuli, auditory memory of content, and the cognitive ability to understand language.

*Special Problems*        The learning environment, the content of the listening experiences, the delivery of the content, and the language skills of the listeners can facilitate or impede listening comprehension. Many listeners are distracted by a noisy or visually busy setting. When the content is uninteresting, thoughts tend to stray, especially when the speaker's style does not command attention. Weak language or auditory-memory skills can cause listeners to miss much of the content. Poor concentration, fatigue, neurological problems, and low mental ability can interfere with students' listening comprehension. Students who may exhibit weak listening comprehension skills include those with language differences, language disabilities, behavior disorders, learning disabilities, hearing impairments, and speech disorders.

*Implications*        Listening is a major channel for presenting direct instruction, required throughout the school day in every subject. Most activities for building background concepts prior to classroom lessons are actually listening mini-exercises. Since listening activities can be presented above the level at which students can read independently, they provide excellent opportunities to stretch students' vocabularies and comprehension skills. Unfortunately, many teachers fail to directly teach the skills of listening. Listening comprehension activities free students from the mechanics of reading, permitting them to focus on the process of comprehension and content, so these activities are particularly important for most students with special needs. Listening comprehension is an avenue through which thinking and problem solving can be improved, experiences built, vocabularies expanded, concepts taught, whole-language activities introduced, specific comprehension strategies modeled and understood, and the joys of language and reading appreciated.

CORRECTION

Modify these strategies to meet students' learning needs.

1. *Listening SWAP.* As an ongoing practice for use with every listening task, "SWAP" students these promises in exchange for their best listening behaviors:

   **S**ee: You will be given something to see while you listen.
   **W**hy: You will know why you are listening.
   **A**ttention: You will be helped to pay attention.
   **P**leasant: Listening activities will be pleasant and enjoyable.

   These promises imply elements critical to facilitating growth in listening comprehension: offering visual cues, giving students a purpose for listening, eliminating distractions, providing cues as needed, and ensuring that students find listening activities enjoyable.

2. *Instructional Adaptations.* To improve active learning during listening activities, try these ideas: Divide listening units into several short instructional periods; arrange seating to limit distractions; use many visual aids; use the names of inattentive students during lessons; increase active participation in lessons; stop to ask students to summarize content periodically; pause occasionally to ask students to predict what will happen next.

3. *Listen and Sum.* Routinely have students briefly retell in their own words what you read aloud or say. This strategy increases attention, reinforces content, builds important summarizing skills, and provides a second chance for students to hear and to check their understanding.

4. *Misfits.* Read short passages to students. In each selection, include 1–2 items or ideas that do not fit. Have students identify the misfits and explain why they are inaccurate. Insert almost logical as well as humorous elements. This activity focuses attention, builds contextual-analysis skills, and provides enjoyable listening experiences.

5. *Retellings.* As both a teaching and an evaluation activity, have students take turns retelling listening activities in sequence, one event per turn. Prompt or probe for information, showing pictures as cues if needed. Then guide students to summarize and evaluate the content.

6. *Sound Effects.* Read a story aloud, asking listeners to think of sound effects to add. Then reread the story, and have students supply special sound effects. To decide upon the appropriate sounds and make them at the proper point, students must listen carefully as well as understand. The active involvement motivates most students. Later, have students listen to taped stories and make appropriate sound effects.

7. *Rating Rules.* Guide students to develop sets of rules for evaluating listening content. Begin with very simple rules for differentiating fact from fiction. Talk through the process of analyzing obvious statements, such as "Angel's hair is green" or "Ali had snake eggs and monkey meat for breakfast," and then move to groups of statements and finally passages. As students progress, develop similar rules for rating the veracity, quality, and value of listening content.

8. *Extra Practice.* • Provide 2–5 minute adventures on audiotapes; have students listen and then write the story or retell it to a friend. • Appoint a Listening Leader each day to listen to assignments and answer peers' questions. • Have students tape Misfit passages for peers, exchange tapes, and identify misfits. • Tape articles from a weekly newspaper that specializes in sensationalism; have students listen to evaluate the content.

## 10. COMPREHENDING WHILE READING ORALLY

DETECTION

This may be a special skill need of students who

- Cannot answer comprehension questions after reading orally
- Substitute illogical words and/or mispronounce many words
- Omit, insert, or repeat words and phrases
- Exhibit weak word-analysis skills
- Ignore punctuation and do not phrase by thought units
- Read word by word and/or do not read aloud fluently
- Seldom self-correct oral errors according to context

*Description*

Reading aloud has many purposes: to assure the novice that reading is indeed occurring, to diagnose reading needs, to entertain, to inform, to share, and to use as a vehicle for teaching silent reading. That the oral reader understands the material while pronouncing it is implicit in all of these purposes. Two patterns of reading behaviors signal oral comprehension difficulties. First is "word calling," when students pronounce each word correctly but later cannot tell you what they read. The second pattern is characterized by illogical errors. When their substitutions are not reasonable, their mispronunciations barely resemble the original word and do not match context, their insertions do not add to meaning, or their errors are not self-corrected according to context, students are not likely to comprehend text. However, educators must distinguish between dialectical errors and miscues or errors that lead to loss of meaning. Unless meaning is altered, the errors are probably inconsequential.

*Special Problems*

Many students have learned to read as word callers because teachers have stressed word pronunciation more than comprehension. Students who find reading tasks particularly difficult often must exert such effort to decode each word that they lose comprehension in the process. To these students, the ever-present threat of making embarrassing errors may even compound their errors. Illogical errors often result from attempting text that is too difficult, inadequate word-attack skills, inattention to punctuation, and fear of embarrassment. Students often are so distracted by oral reading that it interferes with their comprehension. Inappropriate phrasing, an inflexible reading rate, and lack of expression can interfere with reading fluency and comprehension. Special groups who may have difficulty understanding much of what they read aloud are students who are educationally deprived and those with language differences or disabilities, hearing impairments, speech disorders, and learning disabilities.

*Implications*

Most students read best when they maintain a general equilibrium between pronunciation in context (90% accuracy) and comprehension (at least 75% accuracy). Because word recognition skills are generally easier both to teach and to learn, many beginning and remedial reading programs focus heavily upon decoding words and place too little emphasis on comprehension. Routine oral reading without comprehension can hardly be justified. Oral reading must be purposeful, not a round-robin ritual dutifully observed. However, for the majority of students, silent comprehension is a more important reading and learning skill. When students are able to read silently at a reasonable rate and comprehend what they read, fluent oral reading is less important.

CORRECTION

Modify these strategies to meet students' learning needs.

1. *Oral SWAP.* This is an ongoing activity to provide parameters for every oral reading task. "SWAP" students these rights in exchange for their best oral reading.

   **S**afe: It will be safe for you to read and make mistakes as you learn.
   **W**hy and **W**hat: You will know why you are reading and what you are looking for.
   **A**udience: You will know who your listeners are and what their task is.
   **P**reread and **P**ractice: You may preread and practice before reading orally.

2. *Pronunciation Corrections.* After oral reading is completed, try these strategies: (a) Go back and focus on the sentence in which errors occurred and have the student reread it. If the student repeats the same mistake, have the student listen while you read the sentence, mimicking the error; ask what is wrong and how to correct it. Cue the student as needed. Discuss the appearance, pronunciation, and meaning of the words. (b) If the mispronounced or substituted words are basic sight words, use strategies to improve sight vocabulary. (c) If mispronunciations are very different from the original words, teach the use of structural and context skills. (d) If substitutions appear to be the result of carelessness or random behavior, use choral reading in small groups.

3. *Pronunciation Assistants.* Have peer tutors conduct practice sessions to assist less able readers. Before a small-group reading lesson, have the tutors listen to the students read, helping them with words and discussing the stories. If necessary, designate the paragraph that a target student will be called upon to read aloud for practice.

4. *Story Shorts.* Break stories into paragraph or single-page segments. Model the procedure to be followed as a listening experience before having students read orally. Give students 1–2 guiding questions before asking them to read; have them think about the question(s) as they read, silently and then orally. Discuss the questions and how to find the answers.

5. *Chunking.* Using a discarded book, mark a passage by thought units. Place slashes between thoughts and at breathing points, and highlight punctuation. Have students read silently and then orally, pausing or emphasizing according to markings. Explain the chunking principle and have students similarly mark easy passages for peers.

6. *Read-Along-Aloud.* Ask students to read along silently while you model fluent oral reading of a passage. As you read the passage again, have students read-along-aloud with you; then have individual students orally read the passage. Later, tape passages and give small groups of students copies of the text to read-along-aloud with the tapes, synchronizing their voices with the tapes.

7. *Computer Cloze.* For a private and nonthreatening format in which students can decode words, have individual students complete cloze exercises on a computer, and then quietly read the sentences aloud. Analyze with the student how he or she found the answers, stressing the value of using context with other word-analysis skills.

8. *Extra Practice.* • Pair students to alternate giving SWAP cues and reading orally. • Tape students reading orally once a month; compare each new recording with previous ones. • Adapt silent comprehension activities as oral activities.

## 11.  COMPREHENDING WHILE READING SILENTLY

DETECTION

This may be a special skill need of students who

- Cannot answer comprehension questions after reading silently
- Are unable to retell text they have read silently
- Subvocalize while reading silently
- Understand more when reading orally than when reading silently
- Are easily distracted when reading silently
- Read silently at an inappropriate rate
- Seldom read silently for pleasure or recreation

*Description*

Reading silently, an independent task, is typically more efficient than reading orally. When students are reading silently, teachers have fewer clues than during oral reading to indicate what the readers are saying and thinking to themselves or how proficient the readers are. Subvocalizations, inappropriate rate, or inefficient eye movements may signal a problem. However, the quantity and quality of information the readers recall and interpret are the major indications of their silent reading skills. Silent reading is a means of increasing reading breadth without increasing the level of difficulty.

*Special Problems*

Among the skills prerequisite to silent comprehension are sight vocabulary, word analysis, and comprehension strategies mastered at the same level as the materials to be read. Major factors that interfere with silent comprehension include lack of interest, lack of purpose, use of materials that are inappropriate in content or level of difficulty, ineffective teaching, and distractibility. To comprehend in group situations, some students must have silence and no movement around them, while others are distracted by total silence and need constant background noise, such as music, to screen out distractions. Subvocalizations, used by some students to focus attention and mask distractions, may reflect over-emphasis on oral reading and may decrease the reading rate. A few students need the auditory input of oral reading in order to understand. In addition to students with general reading deficits, students who are visually impaired, mentally retarded, or easily distracted — such as some who are behavior disordered or learning disabled — may exhibit weak silent comprehension skills.

*Implications*

Since silent comprehension is closely related to both listening comprehension and oral reading comprehension, many of the corrective strategies for all three areas can be adapted and interchanged. As students progress through the academic curriculum, demands for independent learning, which relies heavily on silent reading, increase in all subjects. Unless students are able to understand as they read silently, both reading and academic performance in general will suffer. Students must also be interested in reading independently. Instruction designed to improve silent comprehension is of three basic types: (1) prereading experiences that build background and set purposes; (2) adjunct experiences for guided reading or application; and (3) postreading experiences for reinforcement, extension, or evaluation. Corrective instruction must improve recall of information and encourage reading for pleasure and study; it should begin with easy reading materials below the level of the students' other reading skills.

CORRECTION

Modify these strategies to meet students' learning needs.

1. *Silent SWAP.* Use this as an ongoing activity to set the parameters for every silent reading task. In return for their best silent reading efforts, "SWAP" students these promises.

   **S**ilence: Silence or distraction blockers will be provided while you read.
   **W**hy and **W**hat: You will know why you are reading and what you are looking for.
   **A**sk: You may ask for assistance any time during silent reading.
   **P**leasure: You may often choose what you want to read just for pleasure.

2. *Reading Place.* Designate a special screened-off area of the classroom as the Reading Place. Furnish the area with beanbag chairs, soft carpet, or cushions, and a generous supply of short, interesting books. At scheduled times or as a reward, have students silently read at the Reading Place for a specified period of time. Provide headsets for students to wear to screen out noise or to listen to background music.

3. *Ssshhh Technique.* To reduce subvocalizations, have students hold an index finger lightly touching their lips during silent reading (the placement for the familiar "ssshhh" sound used to call for silence). The motion provides a reminder to read quietly, while the feel of movement and breath on the finger alerts the reader to subvocalizations.

4. *Answers First.* Prior to silent reading, give students 2–5 key answers to guide their reading. After their reading is completed, have them construct questions that match the prereading answers you provided.

5. *Cognitive Interactions.* Prior to silent reading, take 3–5 minutes to involve students in cognitive interactions with the topic and content of the passage. Discuss the students' background experiences; then use techniques such as brainstorming, problem solving, and valuing. After giving them a few hints about the passage, have students predict what will happen. Then have them read silently to verify their predictions.

6. *Phrase Reading.* Provide students with passages in which you have marked meaningful phrases. Have students read the passages in a loosely timed situation. They should not only read at an increased rate but also move across the lines, taking in groups of meaning rather than each word. Model the process with sentences marked in phrases on the board before having students attempt to read in logical chunks of meaning on their own.

7. *Idea Maps.* Use idea maps to illustrate semantically how the assigned material is organized. After discussing and interrelating the vocabulary of the passage, students can more easily read and understand the material. Use a wheel to illustrate the important words and ideas. Place the story title on the hub; show key ideas as spokes and group key terms along the outer rim or under the corresponding spoke.

8. *Sustained Reading.* Have students read silently for 5–15 minutes daily. Guide them to select an interesting book; provide headsets for those who need them to block distractions. Do not require formal reporting, but permit students to share what they have read if they want to.

9. *Extra Practice.* • Have students interview peers who have finished reading a book to find out if others might also be interested in reading the book and why. • As a special favor, ask students to read a chapter or story silently and then tape 5 good comprehension questions and answers for peers.

## 12.  READING FOR PLEASURE

DETECTION        This may be a special skill need of students who

- Seldom read unassigned books and other materials
- Show little interest in printed materials
- Make excuses for not reading
- Complain about having to read
- Demonstrate weak word recognition skills
- Have difficulty comprehending as they read

*Description*        Other terms for pleasure reading are recreational reading, free reading, private reading, or personal reading. Regardless of the label, the key factor is the student's enjoyment of reading. Students who find reading pleasurable are more likely to read just because they want to, thus improving their reading skills and becoming lifelong readers. Students often need guidance in selecting books they might enjoy. Incentives, class time, teacher modeling, easy access to books, and self-selection encourage pleasure reading.

*Special Problems*        Many students are not accustomed to reading without accountability. Students may lack interest in personal reading because they have too few opportunities in school or too few good books available, or because their teacher does not value the process. Many teachers project reading as a skill-based, lesson-oriented experience that takes place only at a specific time in a certain corner of the classroom; these same teachers fail to mention that reading can be fun and also fail to make it so. Some teachers even use reading as a punitive measure, assigning additional pages, chapters, or book reports to punish inappropriate classroom behaviors. Some students favor more active recreation because they are distractible and need movement. Reluctant readers view reading as work, not play. Students who must constantly struggle to decode and then comprehend, who have primarily experienced reading as a highly structured activity using a basal reader, and who seldom see parents or teachers read for recreation, are not likely read for fun. Other special groups who may not read voluntarily are students from disadvantaged backgrounds, those who have language differences or have been educationally deprived, and students with behavior disorders and language or learning disabilities.

*Implications*        In addition to providing enjoyable school experiences, reading for pleasure can improve reading skills. Students who learn the joys of reading are likely to read often; the more they read, the more their reading skills improve. For reading to be fun, it must be easy enough for students to attend to content, rather than mechanics. Guide students to select high-interest reading materials in which they can comprehend approximately 95 percent of the content. Recommend short, action-packed passages to distractible and active students. Emphasize enjoyment, and minimize the threat of being evaluated and having to report. Since recreational reading is a vital component of a comprehensive reading program, routinely set aside time for pleasure reading. Drills and skills are of little value unless students understand the joy and value of reading. Recreational reading is a lifelong leisure activity that facilitates lifelong learning.

CORRECTION

Modify these strategies to meet students' learning needs.

1. *Reading Rec.* Set aside a few minutes every day for recreational reading in a book the student selects with your guidance to ensure ease of reading. Control distractions while all students and teachers participate; do not require evaluation or reports.

2. *Story Features.* On a daily basis, read a 5-minute feature from a good book orally to the class. Afterward, have the book available for students to finish reading individually.

3. *Listen-Along Option.* For those who continue to resist recreational reading, offer listening activities as an option. Record all but the final 5 percent of high-interest chapters or short books and place the books and tapes in a listening center. Guide the student to select a text at his or her independent reading level to read along while listening to the tape. Since the last few paragraphs or pages are not recorded on tape, students will read the final lines on their own just to discover the ending. To encourage independent recreational reading, gradually increase the amount of text not recorded. This strategy can supplement or substitute for other recreational reading activities.

4. *Reading Incentives.* Offer incentives for reading. Even older students can be motivated by the use of progress charts, stars, stickers, listing of names, prizes, and group rewards. However, incentives are fair and motivational only when all participants can attain them. Thus completed paragraphs, pages, chapters, or entire books should count as successful completion of a reading effort, according to the ability and reading history of the individual student. Groups may earn rewards, such as a special privilege for all, if they maintain 100 percent participation for a specified period.

5. *Book Clubs.* Establish a classroom book club. Take class trips to the library to locate, read, and share good books. Have students write letters to their favorite authors in care of the publisher. Many authors will respond to students' questions. Make your book club responsible for a bulletin board in a main hall of the school each month.

6. *Personal Communication.* Many students find text written by peers interesting. With permission of the authors, make stories written by students available for reading at least once a week. Permit students to substitute these stories for any recreational reading activity. Interactive journals in which each entry is at least a full page also are likely to encourage both reading and writing for pleasure.

7. *Book Bargains.* Well-stocked classroom and school libraries are necessary to make pleasure reading a realistic goal. A number of book clubs offer teachers free books in return for disseminating the publisher's order forms to class members. Ask students to request parental permission to donate any books that the children no longer read to the class library. Inside the front cover of these books, mount a book plate that displays the donor's name and the date. Enlist extra help from a school parent/teacher organization or a local business, or hold a book fair to raise money to purchase books.

8. *Extra Practice.* • Take candid pictures of students reading and post them on a bulletin board. • Designate a special comfortable spot in the room just for personal reading. • Have student teams list reasons they do and do not like to read and then compare lists. • Have students share a taped interview with a peer about a favorite book.

## 13. UNDERSTANDING WORD MEANINGS

DETECTION          This may be a special skill need of students who

- Display a limited listening, speaking, reading, and writing vocabulary
- Frequently miss vocabulary questions
- Often ask the pronunciation and/or meaning of words
- Know only one meaning for most words
- Exhibit little knowledge of word relationships
- Do not appear to use contextual analysis when reading

*Description*          An understanding of word meanings is essential to skilled word recognition and comprehension. Such understanding involves students in predicting and interpreting meanings based upon usage and their own knowledge. All three major skill areas of word recognition — phonic, structural, and contextual analysis — contribute to the development of a strong reading and writing vocabulary. Not only must students understand the words of specific passages, but they must also master strategies for figuring out meanings on their own and have the desire to do so. Knowledge and appreciation of special words, such as idioms or acronyms, generate interest in word meanings. Understanding word relationships, such as synonyms, antonyms, homophones, homograms, euphemisms, and particularly analogies, strengthens overall vocabulary usage. A constantly expanding vocabulary is an important part of progress in reading.

*Special Problems*          Underdeveloped meaning vocabularies often result from limited experiences in speaking and listening to appropriate language models. Inadequate direct instruction or stimulation, too few concrete examples and background experiences, isolated skill practice, and too few opportunities to stretch word knowledge also limit vocabulary growth. Although a typical academic strength of many gifted students, understanding word meanings may be a weakness for many groups of special learners. Among the students more likely than others to exhibit sparse vocabularies are those who have cultural and language differences, who are educationally deprived, slow learners, mentally retarded, or hearing or visually impaired, or who have speech disorders or language, learning, physical, or medical disabilities.

*Implications*          Inadequate knowledge of word meanings is readily apparent in the classroom because it interferes with students' performance across the curriculum. Some students maintain adequate reading and writing progress through the first years of school and then, as vocabulary demands increase dramatically in subject-area textbooks, achieve much less rapidly. To develop and maintain a strong vocabulary, students should receive direct instruction, involving all facets of language, on a regular basis; instruction in word meanings should be an integral part of all lessons. Sprinkling a few special words into basic language lessons can increase interest in the study of vocabulary. Categorizing relationships of words can make vocabulary development easier and more interesting, facilitate students' memory of meanings, and deepen their understanding of the words. To achieve long-term mastery, students must gain experience in seeing, hearing, discussing, and using words in different contexts as they read, write, and listen.

**CORRECTION**        Modify these strategies to meet students' learning needs.

1. *OWD.* As a simple but effective plan, introduce or have students select at least One Word a Day to master. Each word should be pronounced, discussed, used orally, written, read in context, and incorporated into other lessons during the day. Allot a few minutes each day for small groups to discuss the new word and then decide on a new one for the next day. You may want to teach OWD on Monday through Thursday but review the 4 words on Friday.

2. *Word-Mastery Guidelines.* To turn boring, ineffective vocabulary lessons into meaningful ones, follow these dos and don'ts:
   - Do introduce new words in context, use visual aids, and, when appropriate, discuss multiple meanings.
   - Do combine training in phonic, structural, and contextual analysis with emphasis on meaning to reinforce all the skills.
   - Do close each lesson by involving students in some oral or written experience that requires using each new word 2–5 times.
   - Do review new words frequently with activities that have students elaborate, combine, or reduce concepts in sentence form.
   - Do encourage the use of personal language logs, word banks, lists, and journal writing to document progress or encourage word usage.
   - Don't have students copy definitions from the dictionary and use each word in a sentence. Instead, have students use the dictionary to compare and contrast the meanings of two words.
   - Don't have students memorize meanings of words; instead, as you discuss a word, have the students decide how they can use it in their own speech and writing. Then, recognize and reward students' use of the target words in other lessons.

3. *Mapping, Webbing, And Remembering.* Whenever possible, present new words in relation to known words. Classification activities build the conceptual framework for understanding the words as well as deepening and reinforcing understanding of the interrelated terms.

4. *Concept-Analysis List.* When presenting new words or using them in a text, provide, or have students create, topical headings under which to place concepts or characteristics.

5. *Different Strokes.* Show pairs of words and ask students to explain the differences orally or in writing. Pairs might include antonyms *(find/lose)*, homophones *(miner/minor)*, or euphemisms *(plump/fat)*. Then have students tell how the word pairs are alike and how they can remember the relationships.

6. *Analogetics.* After presenting examples of simple analogies, guide students to complete a few, for example, sweet:sour::sugar:_____. Next, guide pairs of students to construct their own analogies using target words and concepts. Provide part of each analogy as a stimulus for instance, miner:_____::deer:_____ or plump:fat::_____:_____. Eventually have students develop their own analogies for single target words.

7. *Extra Practice.* • Have students use a dictionary and thesaurus to contrast word meanings. • Have student teams compete to match meanings and defining restatements. • Ask students to develop matching activities for peers. • Provide, or ask students to create, computer-generated cloze formats, analogies, or crossword puzzles of word relationships for independent practice.

## 14. UNDERSTANDING LITERAL INFORMATION

DETECTION

This may be a special skill need of students who

- Have difficulty answering who, what, when, and where questions
- Often forget details and general information
- Remember the facts but not in order
- Cannot quickly locate answers in the book
- Must reread to remember information
- Have a limited listening, speaking, and reading vocabulary

*Description*

Although comprehension is a thought process rather than discrete skills, teachers often must isolate specific skills for instruction. Instruction in literal comprehension helps students read or listen to remember directly stated or text-explicit information. Students must recognize details as they occur and recall them after reading, often in sequence. Some experts consider literal information to be the easiest of the three levels of comprehension to teach. Digestion of details facilitates higher-order comprehension. However, some students may be able to respond accurately to inferential or critical questions but not to literal questions. In most cases, teachers should include all three levels of response and intervene in specific areas when necessary.

*Special Problems*

Poor overall reading skills, including word recognition and vocabulary knowledge, or lack of concentration often cause problems in understanding literal information. Passages may be so difficult that students cannot understand them or remember the facts. If students expend too much energy decoding individual words, they will comprehend little. The memory load may be too heavy for some readers, especially when lengthy text is crammed with facts. Students must know how to sort facts in order to identify and remember the important ones. Reading too fast or too slow interferes with the recall of literal information. Weakness in sequential memory may inhibit students from sequencing events. Gifted students are sometimes so intense in their search for hidden meaning that they miss some of the obvious details as they read. As in the case of other reading skills, past teachers may not have taught the strategies for recalling facts. Students with weak language skills or hearing problems may find literal recall particularly difficult.

*Implications*

Problems in literal understanding affect overall comprehension and thus impede reading progress and progress in all academic areas, particularly fact-laden areas like social studies and science. Most learners need ready access to facts in order to store and manipulate them for further understanding. Corrective instruction must include modeling, explanation, discussion, and application. Students must master the strategies to develop a personal system of applying prior knowledge, confirming their understanding, and monitoring their reading. Special learners must focus initially on understanding the facts in sentences and short paragraphs rather than in story-length material. Once students make progress, the teacher should gradually lengthen passages and increase the level of difficulty.

CORRECTION

Modify these strategies to meet students' learning needs.

1. *Reporter Questions.* Have students read brief passages to answer just one category of the who, what, when, or where questions. Point out textual signals for facts (items in a series, middle sentences in a paragraph, key words, or the reporter words themselves). Discuss what one needs to know to understand the passage. Reinforce by highlighting the answers as they are found. Add a question category at a time as students catch on. Have students formulate similar questions for peers and grade answers.

2. *Taped Emphasis.* Tape a passage, heavily emphasizing important facts as you read. Give students a copy of the passage and ask them to mark the emphasized facts as they hear them on the tape. Check the answers with students. Listen to the tape together to correct errors. Later, have students develop similar tapes and text for peers.

3. *Cut-Ups.* Print sentences on strips or index cards; cut the sentences into phrases or 2–3 word segments. Have students arrange the pieces so the sentence makes sense, each time reading their choices aloud to confirm them. Then have students write each sentence in correct order. Use discarded texts for the same purpose, cutting sentences into phrases or separating paragraphs for students to reorder.

4. *Anticipation.* When reading a passage, have students anticipate questions about sequence by numbering in pencil the important events as they occur. Walk and talk students through the process as often as necessary. Gradually phase out actual numbering, teaching students to say numbers or signal words quietly, and finally only to think them.

5. *Given or Not?* Give students a list of 2–6 facts from a passage; ask them to listen or read to decide if each fact is or is not stated in the material. A list of sequenced facts can serve the same purpose. Have students reread or listen again, highlighting the facts as they occur.

6. *Supporting Details.* Provide 2–3 details related to a topic statement in a paragraph. Have students use the details to decide which statement is the topic sentence.

7. *Unfinished Sentences.* Use a modified cloze format after reading or listening activities. Provide 2–6 sentences that omit specific factual information. Leave a blank for students to fill in the missing details. The nearer the blank is to the end of a sentence, the easier it usually will be to fill in.

8. *Reading Trivia.* Introduce the concept and game of Reading Trivia. Have students read passages and highlight the most important facts; these are the answers to good trivia questions. Then go through a second time and highlight the less important trivia with a different color. Help students formulate questions that the marked trivia answer. Guide students through the process several times, if necessary. Later, have peers exchange questions.

9. *Extra Practice.* • Provide paragraphs cut from consumable text and have students read and underline 2–4 important facts in each paragraph. • Ask students to rewrite stories or paragraphs, leaving out unnecessary facts or unrelated information. • Have students formulate questions to practice asking peers. • Have students race to locate facts that answer oral questions. • Allow students to play Reading Trivia using their own detail questions.

## 15. UNDERSTANDING INFERENTIAL INFORMATION

DETECTION

This may be a special skill need of students who

- Have difficulty answering inference questions
- Cannot interpret text-implicit information
- Are unable to identify main ideas
- Have difficulty concluding unstated events in passages
- Cannot predict what is about to occur in text
- Have problems linking cause and effect
- Exhibit weak literal comprehension skills

*Description*

Inferential comprehension requires students to use what they already know, adding information from the text to make logical decisions or good guesses about implied information. Inferring from printed information is closely related to interpreting oral language, gestures, or nonverbal information. Types of inferences include finding the main idea, drawing conclusions, predicting events, and determining cause and effect. Finding the main idea may involve a variety of skills, including recalling details, summarizing, and drawing conclusions. Drawing conclusions requires synthesizing facts to infer relationships, judge occurrences, and predict events. Determining cause and effect becomes more complex as textual clues decrease. When cause-and-effect relationships are stated, the reader need only recall the facts; when both cause and effect are stated but their relationship is not, the reader must understand the sequence of events and draw from past experiences with the topic to infer the relationship.

*Special Problems*

Problems with inference may interfere with critical comprehension, speaking concisely and writing succinctly, finding similarities and differences, summarizing, and understanding math problems, as well as with performance in science and social studies. Inferential difficulties have several of the same causes as literal difficulties: inadequate word recognition skills, limited vocabulary knowledge, insufficient understanding of literal information, or use of text that is above students' reading achievement level. Additionally, limited mental ability or background knowledge, environmental noise and interruptions, and overdependence upon oral reading can interfere with inferential comprehension. Special groups of students who may exhibit problems in this area include those with experience and language deficits, as well as those who are slow learners, learning disabled, and mentally retarded.

*Implications*

Making inferences is difficult because students cannot always refer back to a word or phrase as *the* answer. Some experts say inferential comprehension means making educated guesses based upon the available information. Finding the main idea is particularly important because it helps readers organize, understand, and distinguish the important from the unimportant details. Corrective instruction must begin by providing additional background or prereading information to help students understand what they are about to read. Purposes for reading must be clearly stated and matched to the students' ability level.

CORRECTION

Modify these strategies to meet students' learning needs.

1. *Riddle Me.* Use riddles to illustrate inference. Have students listen to and then read a riddle. Talk through the process of sorting out possible answers and meanings and of making educated guesses based upon the information. Model and provide practice.

2. *Statement Search.* Read a passage, highlighting with a marker the first sentence, other important statements, and the last sentence; then reread the highlighted sentences to find the one that best expresses the main idea. Search in order of probability: the first, last, and middle statements, and then all others. Initially, use passages that include topic sentences; later introduce different text structures for which students must formulate a topical sentence. Model the process and then guide students, using as cues "first, last, middle, and missing."

3. *Summary Mark-Out.* Have students read or listen to consumable passages and discuss the relative importance of the words and statements. Have students reread each passage to mark through words and sentences that are unnecessary to express the ideas; ask students to repeat the mark-out process at least three times. Then have them use the remaining words and sentences to formulate a main-idea statement and/or title for the passage. Guide students to evaluate the contribution of deletions and remaining text to the main idea.

4. *Story Builders.* Set a timer; read the first few sentences of an unfamiliar story. Add the next sentence, explaining the role of facts and experience in the composition process; then alternate with students, adding and explaining sentences until time has expired. Next, have students compose a story ending and discuss their choice. Read the actual story and compare it with the students' stories.

5. *Conclusion Frames.* Present story frames before students read a passage. Ask students to predict the information that will fit in the blanks of the frame and to explain and justify their predictions. Then have students read the passage to confirm or reject predictions. As a follow-up activity, have the students use their predictions to build a different story and then compare theirs with the original. To begin this activity, present a story frame for a familiar story (omit the title and key character names for an extra exercise in drawing conclusions), and walk students through the predictions and confirmations.

6. *Predicting the Link.* Before reading a passage, state a cause, and have students predict the effect(s). Read aloud or have students read to verify predictions, and then evaluate and discuss the predictions. Go back through the passage to find and highlight relationship clues. Once students master this task, follow a similar procedure for the more difficult task of predicting the cause from stated effects.

7. *Extra Practice.* • Select passages from discarded texts to construct practice exercises for highlighting, deleting, and subtitling. • Permit students to exchange notes during class if they convey only the main idea of the message (until this becomes too distracting!). • Have students use the main ideas of previous exercises to retell passages or to develop original tales that fit the main ideas. • Using discarded texts, delete the last paragraph of passages and have students dictate 3 possible endings; then compare their endings with the original. • Mark out a few sentences in a passage; have students guess what should be there and then compare their guesses to the original passage.

## 16. READING CRITICALLY

DETECTION

This may be a special skill need of students who

- Cannot analyze or evaluate text
- Exhibit difficulty differentiating fact, fiction, and opinion
- Accept the validity of text without question
- Cannot identify authors' probable purposes
- Do not identify specific writing techniques
- Display weak skills in inferential comprehension

*Description*

To read critically, students must rely heavily on experience and prior knowledge. Critical reading can be considered an extension of inferential thinking, although no static categories can be documented. In addition to making predictions or judgments, this category includes evaluating content, answering questions creatively or by making applications, and evaluating authors' techniques. Students must interact with the text to critique its worth, validity, and true message, relying upon interpretation, personal values, affective responses, and their system of evaluation. Critical comprehension includes reading beyond the lines to evaluate the text and reading behind the lines to evaluate the author's techniques.

*Special Problems*

Perhaps the single greatest cause of weaknesses in critical comprehension is lack of direct instruction. Unfortunately, most classroom instruction focuses on literal comprehension and occasionally on inferential comprehension. At best, attempts to build critical comprehension skills often consist of tacking on a few critical questions or using the supplementary activities in basal readers labeled "extension" or "extra practice." Critical comprehension involves sophisticated thinking skills. The reading act often seems so complex to some readers that they accept the content at face value. These readers often lack the outside knowledge and reading experiences needed to evaluate text. Many students have not developed specific criteria with which to evaluate text, either on their own or with guidance. Students who have low mental abilities, poor general comprehension, or weak word recognition skills will likely experience difficulty in reading critically.

*Implications*

Critical comprehension is often considered to be the highest level of comprehension. In fact, in some reading materials, critical reading is treated as a separate skill, listed after word recognition, comprehension, and study skills. Regardless of its placement in a program's scope and sequence, most students, except for the gifted, receive little instruction in critical reading. Because it is a real-life reading skill, all students need specific instruction in critical comprehension. Those who do not read critically miss part of the enjoyment of reading because of they cannot interject themselves into the content. They are likely to become gullible readers, easily indoctrinated. To become active, thinking, questioning, and appreciative readers, students must be directly taught specific strategies for critical comprehension. Corrective instruction should begin with strategies for evaluating easy text and include guidance in developing specific criteria for evaluating text.

CORRECTION     Modify these strategies to meet students' learning needs.

1. *Classifiers.* As students read or listen to text, have them classify the content. To differentiate fact from fiction, have them classify each statement's truth value as "yes," "no," or "maybe"; use a similar classification plan to distinguish fact from opinion. Have students discuss and justify each response.

2. *Rating Rules.* Help students develop their own sets of rules for judging passage content and authors' techniques. Begin with rules for deciding if a passage is real or make-believe. Ask questions to elicit students' ideas. Write or have students write the rules; use them to judge listening activities and passages they later read themselves. Explain that even the most whimsical passage can have elements of reality and that the most fact-filled passages can include fiction. To emphasize this point, insert several fantasy statements in an expository passage. Later, develop separate criteria for evaluating characters' and authors' techniques and for judging if a passage is fact or opinion, interesting or boring, happy or sad, biased or impartial.

3. *TV Replays.* To model the process of understanding critically, videotape excerpts from popular TV programs. Present the tapes to students, instructing them to watch for specific themes such as reality versus fantasy, happy versus sad, or good versus bad. Pause and replay the tapes for discussion of key parts. Emphasize applicable criteria. Immediately after watching a tape, present a passage to critique for the same features as a listening exercise. Follow this with passages for students to read independently for the same purpose. Ask students to suggest additional programs to tape and evaluate.

4. *TV Skeptics.* Videotape excerpts of dramatic TV programs; guide students to analyze the techniques used by the actors and producers to convey messages and to create moods and special effects. Then have students listen to or read stories to identify similar techniques.

5. *Predict and Rate.* Before reading a passage, discuss what the students would like for the passage to say and why. Next, have students look at titles, pictures, and other clues to predict what the passage will say. Then have students read the passage, rate whether the author's techniques match their predictions, and decide why or why not.

6. *Provoking Propaganda.* Analyze propaganda techniques used in class events, advertisements on TV or in print, or in political texts. Have students discuss the type of propaganda used. Five popular propaganda techniques are (a) Bandwagon ("Everyone is doing it, so why not you?"); (b) Plain Folks ("This is old Humble Henry asking for your support; elect one of the real people to office."); (c) Testimonial ("These two experts recommend our product."); (d) Glittering Generalities ("Our appliances have space-age sparkle, and best of all, you'll see pride in our machines."); and (e) Transfer ("Think of the freedom and security you could have; Alarmo means better sleep").

7. *Extra Practice.* • Have students develop fact and opinion statements for an upcoming lesson to quiz peers. • Read aloud, tape, or have students read articles from a national weekly newspaper that specializes in sensationalism; have students evaluate the content. • Using Rating Rules, have students rate passages; then have peers rate their ratings. • Ask students to list their own criteria for evaluating text.

## 17. READING IN CONTENT AREAS

DETECTION    This may be a special skill need of students who

- Demonstrate unsatisfactory performance in one or more subject areas
- Show limited mastery of subject area concepts
- Do not understand many technical words
- Do not understand the special uses of nontechnical words
- Exhibit difficulty pronouncing technical words
- Display limited knowledge of word meanings

*Description*    Since the vocabulary of content subjects carries most of the conceptual load, understanding technical and nontechnical vocabulary is the most vital skill for success in any content area. Most academic subject areas have a core of technical words with special meaning and application in that context. Related science terms such as *spore, pollen,* and *asexual* are defined in the context of scientific and health-related subjects. Each subject in the major curricular areas of the language arts, mathematics, sciences, social studies, and the arts is explained in technical terms peculiar to the subject. Nontechnical terms can be used in subject-area materials in a special or technical manner. For example, *set, yard,* and *problem* are nontechnical words that take on different or expanded meanings in math textbooks. When a common word describes a technical process or function, it becomes a multipurpose word. Unlike a technical term, which has only one meaning, a nontechnical term can have multiple meanings depending on how and where it is used.

*Special Problems*    Because technical terms are used in specialized topics, students who have not been at least briefly exposed to studies in specialized areas are at a disadvantage. Even able students must master technical vocabulary in order to master content. Students with strong language skills learn technical terms more easily than students with weak vocabulary and language skills or reading problems who must struggle to master the special terms. Difficulties with nontechnical words can be caused by a limited listening, speaking, or sight vocabulary; weak contextual-analysis skills, limited background experiences in general, as well as in particular subjects; and lack of exposure to using and applying the same words in different contexts. Understanding and remembering technical and nontechnical vocabulary may be particularly difficult for students with experience or language deficits, some who are learning disabled or slow learners, and those who are hearing impaired or mentally retarded.

*Implications*    Because they carry so much of the meaning of subject areas, technical and nontechnical terms are important keys to academic progress, particularly the progress of students with learning and reading problems. Many students find it more difficult to recognize or remember different uses for a single nontechnical word than to understand the single meanings of numerous technical words. Prior to each content lesson, teachers should explain vocabulary, using content-specific examples. They must introduce the terms with examples, supported by illustrative aids and generous use of context, and with discussions, interaction, and feedback.

CORRECTION

Modify these strategies to meet students' learning needs.

1. *Term Topics.* To begin a new topic, display a chart of its major terms. As each is introduced, list the terms on the left of the chart, and on the right, list an explanatory phrase and 3 examples. As you discuss the chart, include 3 nonexamples. Later, scramble the terms and meanings for students to match.

2. *Boxing Categories.* As new words are introduced and discussed, use boxes with key terms as category headings. Categorizing words helps students see relationships and understand meanings. Always pronounce words and have students pronounce them. As a review, use box headings and present the new terms in random order for students to organize under their headings.

3. *Word Sorts.* Word Sorts can be either closed or open. Give students a list of 8–16 content words to sort. In a closed sort, provide 2–3 categories under which to classify the words. For an open sort, have students sort the words according to their own categories. Before categorizing a word, students should state or find its meaning(s). Have students support their sortings with a defining sentence from the content book.

4. *Technical Matches.* Using a bulletin board, post pictures of general areas of study, such as motion or government. Print technical terms on index cards and place them in a library pocket attached to the board. List 3–4 topical headings below the pictures. Have students pin the cards below the appropriate heading.

5. *Technical Cloze.* As a review, present several sentences in which 1–2 technical terms have been omitted. For a science lesson, you might use, "The sun's energy caused_____ to form under the glass." Have students fill in the technical words that make sense, referring to their texts as needed.

6. *Nontechnical Word Duals.* List 3 nontechnical words on the chalkboard. Beside each word, list 2 possible meanings. Have students read assigned sections of their text to determine which meaning of each term applies to the subject being studied. Have students substitute the chosen phrase for its matching word in a sentence in the text to verify their choices. After talking students through several examples, scramble the phrases for 3 additional words, and have students complete the activity independently.

7. *Nontechnical Word Call.* Print 20–30 nontechnical words on individual index cards, and number the cards. Give small groups of students 3–5 word cards each. Alternating teams, have each student take a turn. Randomly call a number to locate a word. To earn a point, the student holding the card with the winning number must pronounce the word and supply one meaning. The opposing team gets 2 points if a member can give a second meaning.

8. *Extra Practice.* • Have students form teams and quiz each other by taking turns saying terms and using them in defining sentences. • Develop Technical Matches for several subjects; place the cards in file folders for students to use individually or in teams. • Ask students to hunt for Nontechnical Word Duals in a textbook or newspaper and bring them back to share with the class. • For each subject, have students keep wordbooks of the words they learn, including page references to their texts for future reference.

## 18. BUILDING STUDY HABITS

DETECTION     This may be a special skill need of students who

- Often do not complete or are late with assignments
- Perform better during lessons than on tests
- Appear disorganized when working in class
- Cannot outline
- Do not apply systematic study strategies
- Have difficulty summarizing and taking notes

*Description*     The three major components of effective study habits are organizing for study, previewing information, and then systematically applying study techniques. Metacognition also plays an important role as students monitor their knowledge, determine the explanations they need, and attend to appropriate materials. To organize for study, students must organize themselves and methodically arrange lesson content by outlining, writing summaries, interpreting graphic aids, and using reference sources. Outlining organizes the content to be studied into logical and manageable units. Having a regular place and time to study and planning one's time are part of self-organization. Arranging in advance for ready access to study props such as pens, pencils, paper, textbooks, notes, resource aids, and the like is also an important component of self-organization. Previewing content is an integral part of organizing for study as students quickly survey the content to anticipate and gather general information as well as to decide upon the study props they need. Study techniques involve several sequential procedures that, when applied systematically, enable students to understand and recall lesson content.

*Special Problems*     The single greatest cause of poor study habits is lack of direct instruction and application in textbook materials. Many teachers present the content and then evaluate the students' knowledge, omitting the critical step of guiding and monitoring students as they work through assignments. Some students are unwilling to spend the time necessary to keep up with assignments, notes, and required reading. Organizing for study requires students to be informed, motivated, disciplined, and willing to sacrifice other activities in favor of completing assignments. Lack of encouragement at home and an improper study environment also interfere with study. Numerous special students evidence specific needs in all of the study skills.

*Implications*     Many students recognize the need for systematic study on the day before a test, too late to approach the content methodically. They must be taught organizational skills and apply them immediately in meaningful contexts if they are to transfer these skills. They must have explicit instruction in order to master specific study strategies for accomplishing critical tasks. Unless teachers routinely guide the development of study habits and pace learning experiences so students can master content and study strategies, students will not develop the study habits they need to perform in all areas. Special students in particular need early guidance to develop effective study habits.

CORRECTION

Modify these strategies to meet students' learning needs.

1. *Study Systems.* Select a study system such as PRE (see Activity 2) and teach students to use it regularly. Introduce a study system as follows: (a) discuss each student's learning style with him or her (see Sampler 15.1); (b) describe the system and explain its benefits; (c) model the mechanics and thinking procedures; (d) have students name the procedures as they mimic your model; and (e) guide meaningful practice activities, beginning with easy content before progressing to more difficult tasks.

2. *PRE as a Study System.* Previewing, Reading, and Expressing (PRE) is one of the easiest study systems to use. Display the steps on the chalkboard or a transparency and explain each step.
   a. *Previewing:* Read headings; look for questions, summaries, illustrations, and important vocabulary.
   b. *Reading:* Read to verify information gained during previewing; question yourself; self-monitor progress.
   c. *Expressing:* Talk about, rehearse, and/or write what you read. Talk-through the self-questioning process with students, and then coach students as they apply each of the 3 steps several times.

3. *Outlining Stages.* Demonstrate developing an outline several times using textbook material. Talk through the outlining process as you develop outlines on the board. Present a short, structured format. To introduce independent outlining, give students partially completed outlines; as they progress, reduce the number of completed parts.

4. *Practice Assignments.* Give students simulated assignments, and help them develop a checklist for accomplishing each task. Prompt them with questions about what materials, resources, time, and study strategies they need. Have students follow their checklist to study actual assignments.

5. *Study Drills.* Conduct 10-minute study drills in class. Give assignments and allow 3 minutes for students to organize themselves, their materials, and the work space; then, have students pretend they are at home as they begin to complete an assignment. The task becomes clearer as they get their names on paper and complete a few items. Monitor and coach as needed during the drill.

6. *Study Center.* Equip a special corner of the classroom as a study center. Have students sign up for a time for uninterrupted use of the special Study Center. Encourage students to study in a similar quiet place at home.

7. *Extra Practice.* • Have students teach a peer how to use PRE as a study plan. • Give pairs of students a syllabus and schedule for a subject to keep track of deadlines and assignments; have them make a study schedule that includes the elements of Practice Assignments. • Have students outline the story of a favorite TV show and then compare outlines. • Have student judges read outlines of stories and select the best 3 for posting in class. • Have each student develop a list of verbal cues for organizing for study and then use the list for self-monitoring. • Encourage students to use a computer program to check spelling or find words in the dictionary or thesaurus as a study resource.

## 19. NOTETAKING AND SUMMARIZING

DETECTION

This may be a special skill need of students who

- Cannot take satisfactory notes from reading or listening
- Attempt to take notes verbatim
- Have trouble stating or writing a summary
- Have difficulty organizing information
- Cannot outline text
- Do not effectively organize for study
- Do not apply a systematic study technique

*Description*

Unfortunately, notetaking and summarizing are sometimes considered to be extra skills, worthy of mention, but not essential in comparison to the many other important skills. Yet these skills support and facilitate learning throughout school and beyond. Notetaking and summarizing can also involve mapping, outlining, thinking, and distinguishing main ideas and details. Notetaking is an important study aid as well as a tool for conducting research and writing papers and speeches. Summarizing is an integral part of both notetaking and outlining. Outlining and mapping help students maintain organization within their writing and study materials. Revision and expansion occur in the notetaking process as the original notes are rewritten. Critical listening and all comprehension skills are related to notetaking and summarizing.

*Special Problems*

In order to be able to take notes, students must develop skills in listening comprehension, outlining, writing vocabulary, and general comprehension well enough to enable them to record information for later use. Weaknesses in any of these skills interfere with students' abilities to summarize and take notes. Poorly written books and disorganized teachers who do not state objectives, model, or give clear directions make notetaking difficult. Many students have simply not been taught how to outline, summarize, or take notes. The tasks are so complex and difficult that some students, unwilling to exert the effort, give up. So many variables and skills are involved that special students in many categories tend to experience difficulty mastering notetaking and summarizing.

*Implications*

Reading assigned material before it is discussed makes outlining and taking notes easier. Taking notes after reading is different from taking notes while listening. Notes taken while listening usually need to be reviewed and expanded. Students should be taught to listen for key phrases and vocabulary so that they can fill in information gaps later. Notes taken during or after reading do not always need rewriting since students have the time to reword, condense, and highlight without worrying that they will lose ideas or key points when a speaker moves on. Emphasizing process and product will help students learn the importance of study habits. Grading outlines, draft copies, and notes gives students credit for process in addition to a grade for a final product. Instruction in summarizing and notetaking should begin as early as possible, integrated with instruction in all the language arts. Many of the suggestions in the listening section may be adapted for developing skills in outlining and taking notes while listening.

CORRECTION

Modify these strategies to meet students' learning needs.

1. *Summary Writing.* Begin by showing students how to write 1–2-sentence summaries of interviews, television commercials, sports events, and everyday events. Once students understand how to write a summary, begin using reading material. After students have read a passage think out loud as you write a summary on the board. Have students contribute to a summary of another paragraph or two, again illustrating the process on the board. Have students use 3 parts in their summaries: the topic, the event or major happening, and the outcome of the story.

2. *Concept Maps.* Develop a concept map with students, using information from a textbook they are currently reading. Print a title or major topic in the center of a circle. Draw lines like wheel spokes out from the circle's hub and place key concepts or subtopics at the ends of the lines. Below these words go facts and related details about the subtopics. Like the maps and webs described earlier, the completed map shows students the general organization of the material and relationships among ideas. Use partially completed maps until students can construct their own. Have students use completed maps to write basic outlines and summaries.

3. *Summary Highlights.* Teach students to write summaries of highlighted passages. Guide students to mark the important words and phrases of consumable passages. Read a passage aloud, emphasizing key parts; next, reread the text and mark the key parts on a transparency. Read the passage a third time, and have students highlight the key points on their copies; then model how to integrate the highlighted parts into summaries. Have students verbalize what you just did. Talk students through the marking and summarizing of additional passages until they are ready for supervised independent practice.

4. *Split-Page Notes.* A split-page format is easy to use and can be applied to several types of content. Have students use only the left third of the page to write down key words and phrases while listening or reading. Soon after listening or reading, they should use the information on the left side to write more complete notes on the right side of the page.

5. *Notetaking Sheets.* Provide students with partially completed split-page notes with an appropriate number of blanks and several key ideas and phrases from material they will be asked to read. Have students read the material and take notes; then discuss the information with the students, and have them complete their notes by rewriting the notes on the right side of the page.

6. *Guided Notetaking.* As you teach content lessons, list important points on the board using Split-Page format. Give students time to copy the notes. Gradually decrease the amount of written guidance, while continuing to provide the information verbally.

7. *Extra Practice.* • Have 2 students interview peers and take notes, rewrite their notes, and summarize them. • Check notebooks weekly and give credit for keeping study notes about assigned reading. • Have pairs of students alternate highlighting passages and writing summaries from the highlights. • Tape 3-minute lectures about topics being studied; have pairs of students take notes as they listen, revise and expand their notes, and then write a summary.

## 20.  USING GRAPHIC AIDS

DETECTION    This may be a special skill need of students who

- Cannot interpret graphic information
- Appear confused when reading maps
- Have difficulty understanding charts and tables
- Exhibit problems reading graphs
- Do not interpret captions of illustrations
- Ignore most graphic aids

*Description*    Maps, charts, graphs, tables, and pictures are intended to supplement or clarify information presented in textbooks. Illustrative materials are expensive to produce and are not generally provided unless the authors and publishers believe further clarification and emphasis are necessary. However, some students either ignore or misinterpret these learning aids. For some students, illustrative material complicates the process of understanding subject-area material.

*Special Problems*    Many students experience difficulty using illustrative material because they have not received regular, direct instruction in how the information can be interpreted and used. Special attention may focus on map reading in a lesson, but map reading is then forgotten until another lesson on map reading appears in the text. Lack of experience or an inability to transfer concepts from print to graphics can cause students to be confused by the illustrations. Carelessness and lack of attention to details can also cause students to misinterpret illustrative information. Many illustrations are not accompanied by sufficient explanations for students to understand them or their relationship to the text. Some students are overwhelmed by the clutter of graphics, while others do not read or understand the titles and explanations. Many types of special students experience difficulty interpreting illustrative material.

*Implications*    The more complicated the information, the greater the need for graphic aids to clarify textual concepts, and the more likely text writers are to use them. To be useful, maps, charts, and graphs should be emphasized each time students encounter them in textbooks. Graphic aids may be used as prereading or postreading strategies. As a prereading aid, illustrative information can provide background and an information base from which to make predictions. As a postreading aid, illustrative material is helpful in expanding concepts, summarizing, or confirming predictions. Graphs and charts help explain numerical information. Maps help show geographic or territorial boundaries and relative positions of places and routes. Pictures help readers gain a more concrete understanding of topics of study. Pictures and illustrations also add interest and realism to historical and scientific information. As a general study technique, students should be taught to preview all graphics in a chapter before beginning to read the text. Studying and applying illustrative aids as they occur in text — instead of using occasional map, picture, or graph worksheets — promotes their intended use and fosters recognition of their utility and how they contribute to comprehension.

CORRECTION

Modify these strategies to meet students' learning needs.

1. *Previewing.* Before beginning a reading assignment, talk students through the unit, story, or chapter by explaining the illustrations. Discuss their relevance to the material, and have students restate or review information provided in specific aids.

2. *Graphic Summaries.* Model the process of converting summary information into a graph or chart. Construct a graph or chart of a chapter summary on the chalkboard; then discuss how to decide which format to use. Try 2 different formats and ask students to decide which format most clearly illustrates the summary information. This strategy works best using scientific or fact-filled text.

3. *Class Graphs.* Graphs increase in difficulty in this sequence: (a) bar, (b) circle, and (c) line graphs. Make a bar graph of a class activity, such as student attendance, weather data, or total books read by categories. Explain how to read the information, and call attention to the techniques for illustrating new information. Have students make a bar graph of something interesting, such as game scores or hit songs. Do the same for circle and line graphs. Take every opportunity to point out similar graphs when they appear in newspapers or textbooks.

4. *Guided Illustrations.* Using information from a textbook, give students the format and/or categories to use to construct a circle graph (show the circle and its divisions), a table (provide categories), or a map (including the sites or products). Ask students to finish the illustration using the information you provide.

5. *Graphic Switches.* Present simple information containing 4–6 items as a bar graph. Guide students to make a circle graph or a chart of the same information. Later have students convert graphic information from their textbooks into another format and explain how and why they made the change.

6. *Map Challenge.* After students are familiar with certain maps, form explorer or cross-country teams. Using a gameboard format, draw a road going across a map. Post the map on a bulletin board. Have teams take turns answering map questions for points. Each point moves the team ahead on the road. Use pins to chart explorer progress. If one team misses a question, the next team gets the question. Place each question on an index card so it can be used again with different maps. Use computer-simulation trips as a follow-up activity.

7. *Personal Charts.* Since progress charts and graphs are an integral part of corrective plans, use them not only to monitor and display individual progress but also to teach the construction and use of charts and graphs. Discuss information as it is added, take before-and-after pictures for future comparisons, have students illustrate the same information using a different format, and match the formats to similar ones in texts.

8. *Extra Practice.* • Ask students to watch newspaper and magazines for maps, charts, and graphs to bring to class and explain. • Have a weekly contest in which students vote for their favorite picture or cartoon caption; then have them practice rewriting the captions. • Have each student make a personal chart of a day's activities, and then compare charts with other students for differences in activities.

## 21.  USING REFERENCE SOURCES

DETECTION

This may be a special skill need of students who

- Have problems using a table of contents
- Cannot locate words in a dictionary
- Are unable to use textbook indexes
- Cannot use a card catalog
- Have difficulty using encyclopedias
- Are unfamiliar with a thesaurus

Description

Reference skills include two related but different areas: using textbook parts — such as tables of contents, indexes, glossaries, and appendixes — and using reference sources, including dictionaries, encyclopedias, bound indexes, and card catalogs. Neither area receives heavy emphasis, except in certain English classes or from a few teachers who have special interest in helping students use reference skills. Prerequisite skills include knowledge of alphabetical order, use of guide words, and the ability to determine key words for use in locating information.

*Special Problems*

As in the case of the other study skills, many students who do not use reference skills either have not been sufficiently taught to do so or they do not see the utility of the resources. Some teachers consider reference skills as extras to be added for more able students but ignored in favor of the basics for low achievers. Some students habitually ask teachers or peers for information rather than consulting reference sources themselves. Since some teachers assign reference activities, such as rote copying from the dictionary or encyclopedia, as busy-work or even punishment, some students avoid them because of their negative associations. Other reasons for difficulty include insufficient vocabulary knowledge, inadequate reading skills, or incomplete mastery of alphabetical order. Many special students, although capable of using reference sources, need specific instruction in this skill because the bulk of their past instruction has focused on more obvious skill needs.

*Implications*

Teachers assume that students can use book parts. Students can learn to use the locational aids in their textbooks if they are given sufficient guided instruction and regular opportunities to use the aids. Students do not have to master textbook aids before beginning to use auxiliary materials. However, the ability to locate information in textbooks by using an index and a table of contents makes using other reference sources easier. Once students have had guided instruction in using the resources, they must frequently apply the skills to build lifelong habits. A major obstacle in teaching the use of dictionaries and other sources of information is more closely associated with motivation than ability. You may have heard teachers say, "It's not that they can't, but they won't." Some students see no practical reason to use reference sources and resist doing so because of boring and negative experiences. Corrective lessons must be interesting, positive experiences that highlight the utility of reference sources.

CORRECTION

Modify these strategies to meet students' learning needs.

1. *Using Book Parts.* Emphasize the useful parts of each textbook as you teach from it. Select one part of a book that students are reading, for instance, locating page numbers or using an index, table of contents, or glossary. During 3–4 lessons using the text, incorporate use of that part with the content lesson. Model the skill and talk students through its use. Highlight headings and titles as students turn to pages to look for specific information.

2. *Contrast Search.* Focus on similarities and differences between terms and data and among reference sources. Instead of copying definitions from the dictionary, students can use the dictionary to compare and contrast target terms (e.g., *portfolio/file, capital/capitol, hypothesis/guess, fact/opinion*) or to confirm answers. Or have students compare and contrast the information available from various sources, such as glossary, dictionary, thesaurus, encyclopedia, journals, and/or books, to identify which sources to consult for different data (e.g., the difference between *county* and *parish*, the climate of Brazil, or the cause of cancer). To emphasize utility, students should share and compare all findings.

3. *Referenced Tests.* Permit students to consult a target reference source during tests in several subjects. Tell them ahead of time which source will be available to them, provide direct instruction in its use, and suggest that they practice using it. Periodically change the type of resource used. This strategy often motivates students to master reference sources by illustrating their utility.

4. *Detective Teams.* Form 2–3 member detective teams. Ask each team in turn 2-part questions about using reference sources in a textbook. Using a history text, ask, "Where should I look first for the year President Grant took office?" If a team misses, go to the next team. Then follow up by asking, "In what year did Grant become president?" The first team to find the date gets a point.

5. *Worldly Facts.* Ask students to find a specified topic in an encyclopedia. Be sure to demonstrate determining which volume to check, using the overall index, and using guide words before having students compete. After students are able to locate information successfully, add a time element. Name a topic and monitor the amount of time that student pairs need to locate it. Save your list of topics to use again another day. You can simplify the task by having students locate only the volume or by providing the volume and having students locate the topic.

6. *Reference Reports.* Have students frequently visit the library to locate information on a specific topic. Require a written record, telling where they started and each source they checked. For variation, provide a map of the library and have students plot their course. Have students explain their steps, sources, and final results to peers.

7. *Extra Practice.* • Ask students to use a textbook independently to develop questions and answers on index cards to use for Detective Teams. • Assign half the class to the traditional card catalog and the other half to the computer card catalog; have student teams compete to locate target references quietly. • Have students explain the use of a reference book to a younger student in a lower grade.

## 22. PREPARING FOR TESTS

DETECTION

This may be a special skill need of students who

- Consistently perform poorly on tests
- Appear to know more than their test scores indicate
- Perform better during practice than on tests
- Appear especially anxious before or during tests
- Do not organize for study
- Have difficulty taking notes and summarizing

*Description*

The primary method most teachers use to evaluate how well students have mastered skills and concepts is testing. Preparing to take tests involves combining study strategies to organize information for easier learning. Students must schedule reviews, anticipate and gather information, plan practice and study sessions, rehearse communicating knowledge, develop a positive attitude, and decide on appropriate test-taking skills to use during the tests.

*Special Problems*

If students are using appropriate instructional materials and tests are written at or below students' reading level, test results should reflect what students know about a topic. Certain stimulus/response formats can facilitate or impede the performance of individual students on tests. When tests are poorly constructed, teachers must share the blame for student difficulties. Many students with disabilities are not "testwise"; that is, they fail to employ test-taking strategies that permit them to demonstrate their knowledge. Because of past failures, many students who are low achievers experience tests as a source of great anxiety. Striving for near-perfect performance causes some high-achieving and gifted students to suffer text anxiety. Students who delay studying until the night before tests are often quite realistically anxious.

*Implications*

Attempting to study using scattered notes from several loose sheets, an unread textbook, and little information about the test would cause the best of students to be anxious. To be prepared for a test, students must organize well in advance, with lesson and study notes already prepared. Rereading is usually easier than initial reading and notetaking. However, a self-defeating attitude toward particular subjects or topics can be a bigger problem than learning the information. Adequate preparation can limit the worry and self-doubt many students feel before a test. Testwise students learn as much as they can about each test before it is administered: the type and number of items, most important topics, time allowed, and any sample questions. They schedule study time throughout the term so that test preparation sessions are for review, not for cramming. The best strategy for preparing students is to begin each lesson with a short review, and to teach them to plan brief daily study that includes organizing information, reviewing notes, reciting the information orally or silently, and identifying the most important information. Giving students brief trial tests as a review at the end of each lesson provides much-needed practice in taking tests, reduces anxiety, and affords opportunities for students and teachers to evaluate progress.

CORRECTION

Modify these strategies to meet students' learning needs.

1. *Personal Style.* Administer an inventory or test to determine students' learning preferences and styles (see the example in Sampler 15.1). Analyze and discuss the results with students, suggesting ways to study. Observe students to note any learning-style differences across subjects; revise study plans accordingly.

2. *Study Systems.* Select a study system or strategy, and teach students to use it regularly. One such system is PRE, or Preview, Read, Express. Using this technique, students preview by reading headings, questions, summaries, illustrations, and special terms. Then they read to confirm the preview information. Finally, they express, discuss, or repeat aloud to themselves what they have read. How you explain a study system helps determine how well students implement it. Here is one method for presentation:
   a. Discuss with each student his or her learning style (Sampler 15.1).
   b. Describe, explain, and sell the particular study system.
   c. Model both the mechanics and the thinking procedures of the system.
   d. Have students name each step as they mimic your model.
   e. Provide appropriate activities for meaningful practice; begin with easy content and progress to more difficult tasks.

3. *Response Analysis.* Guide teams of students to analyze the errors made by anonymous students on old tests and hypothesize the reasons for the errors. Have them look for error patterns, list them, and formulate a checklist of ways to avoid the errors. Then guide individual students to follow the same procedure in analyzing their own errors on previous tests. This procedure is particularly helpful for analyzing responses on trial tests in order to prepare for actual tests.

4. *Specific Tags.* Explain the implications of specific tag words that often appear on tests. For essay tests, discuss terms such as *describe*, *illustrate*, *list*, *justify*, *review*, *summarize*, and *compare*. For objective tests, explain and discuss the implications of qualifiers such as *all*, *never*, *always*, and *all* or *none of the above*.

5. *Dry-Run.* Two days before a test, give students a dry-run test. The trial test can be administered and completed individually or in small groups. After completion, discuss with students the answers, how they can be remembered, and how students should plan to study.

6. *Test the Teacher.* The day before a test, give students the opportunity to question the teacher. Have students ask questions about the topic for 10 minutes. Permit them to take notes or tape your answers if they wish.

7. *Student Quizzes.* Group students into teams and have them use their books and notes to prepare 1–15 questions and answers — an excellent study strategy. Have each team take turns quizzing the other; award points for correct responses.

8. *Think-Outs.* Write 3–5 multiple choice, true-false, or completion questions on the board. After students read each question silently, demonstrate how to determine answers by thinking out loud. Next, using different questions, ask students to think out loud as they answer. Have students repeat this procedure in small groups.

9. *Extra Practice.* • Guide students to form study groups for particular subjects. • Have students develop a checklist of study habits for peers. • Have less able students tutor younger students in 5–10 minute sessions. • Have students practice timed tests on the computer.

## 23. STUDY STRATEGIES ACROSS THE CURRICULUM

DETECTION     This may be a special skill need of students who

- Perform below expectations in one or more subject
- Display ineffective study habits
- Appear disorganized
- Cannot apply specific skills they have mastered
- Do not regulate reading rate according to task
- Exhibit little knowledge of strategies for accomplishing academic tasks

*Description*     Effective use of study strategies is critical to students' learning, independent performance, and progress in all curricular areas. Specific instruction in what various experts term learning, cognitive, thinking, or study strategies is a relatively recent development in special education, directly related to the emphasis on reading as thinking that began in the 1950s, and to renewed focus on mathematical problem solving, thinking skills in the regular curriculum, and traditional study skills. Study strategies include both generic thinking routines for accomplishing tasks in many areas — memorizing, imaging, regulating reading rate, and test taking — and specific routines for particular tasks (e.g., outlining, mathematical problem solving, and evaluating text).

*Special Problems*     The primary reason students do not use study strategies effectively is inadequate instruction. Many teachers simply do not teach study strategies, for a variety of reasons: they are not aware of their importance; they did not learn how to teach strategies in their teacher preparation programs; they do not take the time because this is not an official subject in which they grade students; and/or they consider study skills as a sophisticated topic appropriate for junior and senior high school students but not for young and/or low-achieving students. Most teachers teach students *what* to learn, but not necessarily *how* to learn. Even when teachers do provide instruction in study strategies, students may not master the strategies. The strategies may not be personalized for students' needs, students may memorize the steps without being guided to apply them appropriately and consistently, or complex strategies may be too difficult. Students who are gifted often find their own effective study strategies, but few low achievers or students with disabilities are likely to do so without guidance.

*Implications*     Learning *how* to learn is particularly important for special students, since their special needs usually include *learning* needs. Although teaching strategies throughout the curriculum may lengthen initial lessons, use of the strategies will shorten subsequent lessons. Teachers should include these elements in instruction for each study strategy: the teacher describes the strategy and its purpose and advantages; he or she models application of the strategy in the context of classroom tasks, explaining each step; the student rehearses the steps and then follows the model under teacher guidance; teacher and student discuss how the strategy works and when it should be applied; student applies the strategy to classroom tasks, revising as needed; teacher and student evaluate how the strategy affects the student's performance.

**CORRECTION**          Modify these strategies to meet students' learning needs.

1. *Self-Assessment.* Students should know their own strengths, weaknesses, and style in order to select and modify strategies that will be most effective for them. Self-assessment helps students to become actively involved in learning how to learn. Use questions such as these to guide and discuss students' self-assessment: What is my best subject and why? My best skills and why? My worst subject and why? My weakest skills and why? How do I learn best? In what type of setting? What is the best time of day for me to learn? Which study strategies do I know how to use effectively?

2. *Imagery.* To help students remember information and understand concepts, guide them to visualize. Visual images can either be realistic or contrived to facilitate comprehension and memory.

3. *Mnemonic Magic.* Constructing a word or sentence from the first letter or word of a series to be remembered aids memory, complements instruction in acronyms, and exercises students' spelling and creative skills. Discuss examples with which students are familiar, such as the acrostic, **Every Good Boy Deserves Fun** for the musical notes. When presenting important concepts and when reviewing or preparing for tests, have students compete to develop the most original mnemonic. Provide or have students develop mnemonics for each study strategy as you present it.

4. *Self-Testing.* Teach students to test themselves as they learn new information. They should pause periodically to ask themselves: Is this important enough to be on a test? What would be my answer?

5. *5 Rs.* Teach students to use the 5 Rs to monitor their own understanding when reading or during oral lessons: Do I **R**eally understand? **R**elate the information to something I already know. **R**eplay what I understand so far to see if that helps. **R**eorganize the known and identify the gaps. Consult a **R**esource or ask for help.

6. *Reading Regulation.* Regulating one's rate of reading according to purpose is an essential study strategy. Using students' classroom texts, introduce three reading rates with these tasks:

   a. Study (slow, intense reading to understand and remember): Restate everything in the first paragraph.

   b. Skimming (rapid preview to gain global knowledge): What is the main idea of this passage?

   c. Scanning (faster than skimming, to locate specific information): What is the setting of this story or chapter?

   After each task is completed, guide students to describe and list the steps they used to accomplish it. Then compare and contrast the three rates, having students describe when and why they should use each.

7. *Taking the Test.* Teach students to "Blurt Imaginary Answers to Look Certain," a strategy for taking tests:

   **Blurt**—Immediately blurt or outline the essential information you might forget; then consult your blurting as you take the test;
   **Imagine**—Imagine yourself acing the test and know that you can;
   **Answer**—Answer easy questions first and then go back to harder ones;
   **Look**—Look for key terms that signal answers or expectations;
   **Certain**—Make certain you have answered all questions.

8. *Extra Practice.* • Adapt activities from Skills 16–21. • Encourage students to develop original strategies and share them with peers.

# C OMPREHENSION AND STUDY SAMPLERS

The samplers on the next five pages illustrate a few activities for developing and correcting comprehension and study skills. The samplers can be easily adapted for a variety of situations. In some cases, you may need to adjust directions or insert information specific to the subject and student before copying.

5.1 **Oral SWAP Poster.** The Oral SWAP poster in Sampler 5.1, derived from Skill 10, Activity 1, can be displayed in the classroom to remind students of their rights during oral reading activities. Discuss each promise and remind students to request and observe the promises when they read aloud.

5.2 **Word Pairs.** This sampler is designed to expand understandings of word meanings, Skill 13, and provide meaningful practice in using references, Skill 22. Instruct students to use reference sources to compare and contrast the meanings of word pairs, each containing a familiar word and a target word. List the word pairs on the board, or write them on the sampler before copying it. Review and discuss resources to consult — dictionary, glossary, textbooks, thesaurus, encyclopedia — and then coach students as they work alone or in pairs.

5.3 **Story Guides.** This sampler presents the skeleton or frame of a traditional story to guide students through it. Students should fill in the information as they read. The sampler can also be used as a guide to retelling a story in writing or as a Conclusion Frame (Skill 15, Activity 5).

5.4 **Reading Rater.** This sampler has four purposes: (a) to promote critical comprehension; (b) to help students develop criteria for evaluating what they read; (c) to encourage students to share and compare ratings with peers; and (d) to provide a personal record of what each student reads.

  a. Explain the purpose of the activity: when students evaluate what they read, they comprehend critically.

  b. Guide students to state their criteria for evaluating whether books are enjoyable and enter them on the sampler. Discuss and write on the board some common criteria, such as illustrations. Then have individual students list their own additional criteria on their samplers.

  c. Have students review their criteria before reading, rate each book after they read, and record their rating and comments on the sampler. Allow students to share and compare ratings either in a whole-group discussion or in small groups.

  d. Have students keep samplers in a notebook as a personal record of what they have read. Periodically, guide them to evaluate their criteria for needed revisions.

Although this sampler specifies criteria for enjoyment, the first three items easily can be modified to become criteria for other elements (e.g., fact, mixed, fiction; or happy, mixed, sad).

5.5. **What Works.** This sampler provides a structure for introducing specific study strategies and for having students record the strategies that are most effective for them. To introduce a strategy, write the steps on the sampler before copying it. Have students record strategies as they learn or modify them, use the sampler for review and self-monitoring, and share and compare with peers.

# ↘ Oral SWAP ↙

## These promises swapped for your best oral reading

# **S**afe

It will be *safe* for you to read and make mistakes as you learn.

# **W**hy and **W**hat

You will know *why* you are reading and *what* you are looking for.

# **A**udience

You will know who your *audience* is and what their task is.

Name _____

# WORD PAIRS

ꙮ❯ ___dog_____ and ___horse_____ ❮

≠ _____ _____
_____barks_____ _____neighs_____
_____smaller_____ _____larger_____
_____paws_____ _____hooves_____
_____should not ride_____ _____can ride_____

= _____4 legs, tails, hair, pets, can train to do tricks_____
_____I wish I had both_____

ꙮ❯ _____ and _____ ❮

≠ _____ _____
_____ _____
_____ _____
_____ _____

= _____
_____

ꙮ❯ _____ and _____ ❮

≠ _____ _____
_____ _____
_____ _____
_____ _____

= _____
_____

ꙮ❯ _____ and _____ ❮

≠ _____ _____
_____ _____
_____ _____
_____ _____

= _____
_____

Name _____

## ☞ STORY GUIDE

TITLE:_____

AUTHOR:_____

This story takes place {*where?*} _____
_____
{*when?*}_____.

The main players are {*who?*}_____
_____
_____.

The problem is {*what?*}_____
_____because {*why?*}_____
_____
_____
_____.

The problem is solved {*how?*}_____
_____
_____
_____
_____.

In the end {*what?*}_____
_____
_____
_____
_____.

Name _____

 **READING RATER**

## Rating Rules

**+** Best books will _____
_____
_____
_____

**✓** O.K. books will _____
_____
_____
_____

**—** Bad books will _____
_____
_____
_____

| BOOK | DATE | COMMENTS | RATING |
|------|------|----------|--------|
|  |  |  |  |
|  |  |  |  |
|  |  |  |  |
|  |  |  |  |
|  |  |  |  |
|  |  |  |  |
|  |  |  |  |
|  |  |  |  |
|  |  |  |  |
|  |  |  |  |
|  |  |  |  |
|  |  |  |  |
|  |  |  |  |
|  |  |  |  |
|  |  |  |  |
|  |  |  |  |

# !!! WHAT WORKS !!!

## Study Strategies That Work For *Me*

**!Strategy!**

**Task**

_____
_____

Other Uses

_____
_____
_____
_____

**!Strategy!**

**Task**

_____
_____

Other Uses

_____
_____
_____
_____

**!Strategy!**

**Task**

_____
_____

Other Uses

_____
_____
_____
_____

**!Strategy!**

**Task**

_____
_____

Other Uses

_____
_____
_____
_____

# REFLECTIONS

1. Chapter 5 categorizes reading comprehension skills into three broad areas: general comprehension, specific comprehension, and content and study strategies. Review the discussion of each skill in these areas. Decide if any skills should be omitted and what additional skills should be included. Justify your responses.

2. Comprehension is a holistic process: understanding is more than the sum of the individual skills involved. Reconcile this perspective with this chapter's emphasis on specific skills in recommending corrective strategies.

3. Chapter 5 notes that study strategies often receive less emphasis than other reading skills. Justify this practice. Consider how and when you learned to study. How could your instruction have been improved? What are the implications for teaching special students?

4. When students read aloud, you hear what they say but do not know what they think; when they read silently, you know neither which words they can pronounce nor what they are thinking. How does this fact complicate the teacher's task? What are the implications for detecting and correcting special oral and silent reading needs?

5. This chapter presents an overview of reading diagnostic procedures. As you review those procedures, consider the group-administered reading tests you have taken. What problems did you experience in responding to the tests? How do your problems compare with those that special students might face? How might these problems affect the validity of the test results?

6. Some Detection behaviors that signal difficulties with each comprehension or study skill are listed in Figure 5.1 and at the beginning of each discussion. Observe a regular and/or a special education classroom. Record those behaviors and any others you observe. Discuss the significance of these behaviors; ask other teachers to add to the list.

7. The discussion of each comprehension skill lists only a few corrective strategies. Based on your classroom observations and/or your own experience, add to or modify the corrective strategies for one comprehension or study strategy.

8. Teaching reading to students with special needs often requires modifying strategies appropriate for teaching most students the same skills. In the teacher's edition of a basal reader, locate the instructional strategies suggested for teaching one of the skills from Chapter 5. Contrast the teaching activities listed in the teacher's edition with those recommended in this chapter for that skill. Identify and justify modifications in lessons for students with special needs.

9. Chapter 2 lists corrective principles for special populations. Select and modify several corrective strategies in Chapter 5 to meet the learning needs of a real or hypothetical special learner, using the principles from Chapter 2 as guidelines.

10. Reading lessons can occur either separately or as part of instruction in other subjects. For a special learner, plan two reading lessons: one specific reading lesson and one content reading lesson. Use the school's diagnostic information and its materials, as well as the practices and principles in Chapters 2 and 3, to select and modify your corrective reading strategies.

11. Truly individualized instruction often requires teachers to adjust lessons while teaching. With a peer or a volunteer student, practice the two reading lessons you planned for the special learner. Then teach your lessons to the student, modifying your plans according to the student's responses and needs as you teach.

12. Several reading and special education textbooks present suggestions for corrective reading instruction applicable to special learners. Compare discussions in these sources with information in Chapter 5.

Burns, P. C., Roe, B. D., & Ross, E. P. (1992). *Teaching reading in today's elementary schools* (5th ed.). Boston: Houghton Mifflin.

Choate, J. S., & Rakes, T. A. (1989). *Reading: Detecting and correcting special needs.* Boston: Allyn and Bacon.

Choate, J. S., Enright, B. E., Miller, L. J., Poteet, J. A., & Rakes, T. A. (1992). *Curriculum-based assessment and programming* (2nd ed.). Boston: Allyn and Bacon.

Collins, C. (1993). *Expanding thinking through the language arts.* Boston: Allyn and Bacon.

Ekwall, E. E. (1989). *Locating and correcting reading difficulties* (5th ed.). Columbus, OH: Merrill.

Gall, M. D., Gall, J. P., Jacobsen, D. R., & Bullock, T. L. (1990). *Tools for learning: A guide to teaching study skills.* Alexandria, VA: Association for Supervision and Curriculum Development.

Gipe, J. P. (1991). *Corrective reading techniques* (2nd ed.). Scottsdale: AZ: Gorsuch Scarisbrick.

Gunning, T. G. (1992). *Creating reading instruction for all children.* Boston: Allyn and Bacon.

Hargis, C. H. (1982). *Teaching reading to handicapped children.* Denver: Love.

Hasenstab, M. S., & Laughton, J. (1982). *Reading, writing, and the exceptional child.* Rockville, MD: Aspen.

Irwin, J. W. (1991). *Teaching reading comprehension processes* (2nd ed.). Englewood Cliffs, NJ: Prentice Hall.

Johnson, D. D., & Pearson, P. D. (1984). *Teaching reading vocabulary.* New York: Holt, Rinehart and Winston.

Lapp, D., & Flood, J. (1992). *Teaching reading to every child* (3rd ed.). New York: Merrill/Macmillan.

Lipson, M. Y., & Wixson, K. K. (1992). *Assessment and instruction of reading disability: An interactive approach.* New York: HarperCollins.

Mastropieri, M. A., & Scruggs, T. E. (1991). *Teaching students ways to remember: Strategies for learning mnemonically.* Cambridge, MA: Brookline Books.

McNeil, J. D. (1992). *Reading comprehension: New directions for classroom practice* (3rd ed.). New York: HarperCollins.

Rakes, T. A., & Choate, J. S. (1989). *Language arts: detecting and correcting special needs.* Boston: Allyn and Bacon.

Reutzel, D. R., & Cotter, R. B. Jr. (1992). *Teaching children to read: From basals to books.* New York: Merrill/Macmillan.

Schulz, J. B., Carpenter, C. D., & Turnbull, A. P. (1991). *Mainstreaming exceptional students: A guide for classroom teachers* (3rd ed.). Boston: Allyn and Bacon.

Scruggs, T. E., & Mastropieri, M. A. (1992). *Teaching test-taking skills: Helping students show what they know.* Cambridge, MA: Brookline Books.

Tierney, R. J., Readence, J. E., & Dishner, E. K. (1990). *Reading strategies and practices: A compendium.* Boston: Allyn and Bacon.

Vacca, J. L., Vacca, R. T., & Gove, M. K. (1991). *Reading and learning to read* (2nd ed.). New York: HarperCollins.

Wilson, R. M., & Gambrell, L. B. (1988). *Reading comprehension in the elementary school: A teacher's practical guide.* Boston: Allyn and Bacon.

Walker, B. J. (1992). *Diagnostic teaching of reading: Techniques for instruction and assessment* (2nd ed.). New York: Merrill/Macmillan.

Wood, J. W. (1992). *Adapting instruction for mainstreamed and at-risk students* (2nd ed.). New York: Merrill/Macmillan.

Yopp, R. H., & Yopp, H. K. (1992). *Literature-based reading activities.* Boston: Allyn and Bacon.

# CHAPTER SIX

## SPEECH: THE PROCESS OF ORAL COMMUNICATION

— *Paulette J. Thomas and Fairy F. Carmack*

The act of speaking requires precisely coordinating the organs of speech and the messages sent and received by the brain. Simply described, speech occurs through a sequence of respiration, phonation, resonation, and articulation. Air is exhaled from the lungs to the trachea. The vocal cords come together to stop the exhaled air momentarily so that air pressure increases. The trapped air overcomes the vocal folds' resistance, releasing a puff of air. The air vibrates the vocal cords and produces sound. The sound resonates in the oral cavity as the articulators shape it into speech.

Although described here in simple terms, speech is a complex process that can be disrupted by any number of factors, including neuromuscular disorders (cerebral palsy), conditions that obstruct the airway (asthma), lung tissue disorders (emphysema), structural anomalies (cleft palate), laryngeal pathologies (vocal nodules), and paralysis of any of the structures necessary for speech.

## THE SPEECH SKILLS

This chapter categorizes speech skills as articulation, voice, and fluency skills. The two articulation skills discussed represent the most common articulation errors youngsters make. Discussions of skills describe strategies for the classroom teacher to use, guided by the speech/language specialist. Because the speech/language pathologist designs the therapy program for each individual, the classroom teacher should coordinate activities with the specialist to complement the treatment.

## REFERRAL INDICATORS

Just as there are milestones in physical development, there are also milestones in the development of speech as a communication device. In order to know when to refer a child for speech problems, the teacher must be familiar with normal speech development. If a child doesn't produce sounds by the time he or she should, the teacher should seek assistance from a licensed speech/language professional.

## Articulation

Articulation is the production of speech sound resulting from coordinated, integrated movements of the lips, tongue, and jaws. The smallest unit of meaningful speech is the phoneme. Each language has specific phonemes, or speech sounds, that are combined in specific ways to form words. In the English language, phonemes are classified as either vowels or consonants and as either voiced or voiceless. Vowels, produced with a relatively unrestricted flow of air in the vocal tract, are always voiced (i.e., they result from vibration of the vocal cords). Consonants, produced with a closed or constricted air passage, may be voiced or voiceless.

Several researchers have attempted to discover the order in which speech sounds are acquired. To date, no one sequence is universally accepted. Several general conclusions, however, may be drawn about the development of phoneme production.

1. As a group, vowels are acquired before consonants and are usually mastered by age 3.
2. Consonants can be categorized as follows:
   *nasals*—sounds produced when the soft palate is lowered to allow the airstream to exit via the nasal cavity (<u>m</u>other, <u>n</u>ever, ri<u>ng</u>)
   *glides*—sounds produced while gliding from one vowel position to another (<u>r</u>ed, <u>w</u>ed, <u>y</u>et)
   *plosives*—sounds produced when the airstream is obstructed and then released quickly (<u>p</u>at, <u>b</u>ob, <u>t</u>eacher, <u>d</u>ot, <u>c</u>ot, <u>g</u>ot)
   *liquids*—consonant sounds that have the vowel-like quality of minor air turbulence in the oral cavity (<u>l</u>ed)
   *fricatives*—sounds produced by constricting the air passage so that the air must exit through a narrow channel (<u>f</u>ine, <u>v</u>ine, <u>th</u>ing, <u>th</u>em, <u>s</u>eal, <u>z</u>eal, <u>sh</u>oe, bei<u>g</u>e, <u>h</u>ello)
   *affricates*—sounds produced by the combination of a plosive and a fricative (<u>ch</u>, <u>ch</u>urch; <u>j</u>, <u>j</u>ump)
3. Sounds in the initial position in words are acquired first.
4. Consonant clusters and blends are not acquired until age 7 or 8, but some clusters are noted at age 4.
5. Individual differences account for normal variation.

For more than three decades, researchers have investigated the age at which consonant sounds are normally acquired. The age at which 90 percent of children pronounce the sound in all three word positions is presented here. About 10 percent of the population will either be delayed in acquiring consonants or will not spontaneously pronounce the target sounds without intervention.

| key word | age | key word | age | key word | age | key word | age |
|---|---|---|---|---|---|---|---|
| pat | 3 | cot | 4 | teacher | 6 | thumb | 7 |
| mother | 3 | got | 4 | red | 6 | seal | 8 |
| hello | 3 | dot | 4 | led | 6 | zeal | 8 |
| never | 3 | fine | 4 | church | 7 | vine | 8 |
| wed | 3 | yet | 4 | shoe | 7 | them | 8 |
| bob | 4 | ring | 6 | jump | 7 | beige | 8 |

These are broad guidelines to when children acquire consonants. Individual children may vary considerably within the guidelines. Teachers should always consider how well others understand the child before seeking corrective measures. Compare the misarticulated sounds with the ages presented here to determine whether the student is within the normal range. Seek professional help if the student does not correctly pronounce the phonemes at the same age as 90 percent of his or her peers, remembering that children may vary greatly in their physical, intellectual, and social development. Handicapping conditions may inhibit or delay the acquisition of speech sounds.

## Voice

One way of expressing thought or language is through oral speech, which is made possible by vocal production. The vocal folds are the main sound producers. These two bands of tissue stretch across the larynx, or voice box. When breath is exhaled, the vocal folds relax to form a V-shaped opening to let the air through. To produce sound, the vocal folds are brought together, the expelled air from the lungs vibrates the tightened folds, and sound results.

Voices vary in pitch, loudness, quality, and other less definable aspects, and listeners react to them according to their own standards. A voice that varies noticeably from the norm is regarded as disordered. Voice is considered to be defective if the vocal pitch is inappropriate for the age and sex of the speaker. Loudness is considered a disorder if the level of volume is inappropriate for the situation, inadequate for communication, or unpleasant for the listener. Deviations in voice quality are the most common and complex vocal problems. The teacher who observes any of these behaviors should refer the student to the speech/language specialist. Skill 26 gives suggestions for supplementing therapy for vocal pitch.

A child with voice problems must undergo medical examination to determine the cause of the difficulty. The child can learn to alleviate or eliminate vocal abuse and misuse through vocal rehabilitation.

## Fluency

Fluency difficulties can affect members of any society and speakers of any language. Lack of fluency is many-faceted: Some authorities describe it as an emotional or psychological problem; some believe that it results from neurological dysfunction; others see it as the result of illness or of environmental influences; some describe it in terms of the feelings of the speaker. Stuttering is characterized by uneven silences and interjections, struggle to produce sounds, repetition of sounds, or frequent, involuntary prolongation of a single sound, all of which interfere with communication. Stuttering may be accompanied by evidence of tension, such as facial grimaces or irrelevant body movements. Students with fluency problems should be referred to the speech/language specialist.

## DETECTION OF SPECIAL NEEDS

Severe articulation disorders in children are usually identified well before a child begins formal schooling. Mild articulation problems, however, may not be diagnosed until the child enters school. Screening programs usually identify children who need formal evaluation. Fluency problems probably disturb both speaker and listener more than any other speech disorder. After articulation disorders, stuttering is the most common speech disorder. Four to eight times more males stutter than females. Stuttering usually begins before adolescence. Those who stutter face limited vocational choices, since many professions require fluent speech.

Many school systems systematically screen all kindergarten and/or first-grade students for speech disorders. Teachers may find the Checklist of Common Speech Errors in Figure 6.1 useful. If the teacher notes problem areas, he or she should refer the student to a speech pathologist. The speech pathologist engages the child in conversation in order to observe the child's articulation in connected speech, noting possible articulation, voice, or fluency disorders. When a child is reluctant to speak freely with a stranger, the speech pathologist conducts a structured interview. Typically, the specialist also observes the child's rhythm and vocal quality. Students who exhibit difficulty are formally evaluated.

## FIGURE 6.1 / Checklist of Common Speech Errors

Humans are social creatures with a profound need to interact with other humans. One vehicle for communication is speech; language serves as the stimulus to communicate and structures our communication. We are judged by the way we speak — how we sound as well as what we say. Consequently, communication difficulties must be diagnosed early and remediated promptly to ensure social adjustment and future learning. A checklist of common errors assists teachers in early diagnosis of communication problems. Use this checklist to record behaviors that signal possible problems and to plan appropriate intervention. Carefully observe the student in a variety of settings, and mark problem behaviors.

| Target Skill | Possible Problem Behaviors |
| --- | --- |
| **Articulation** | ☐ Does not correctly pronounce these sounds by age 3<br>pat    mother    hello    never    wed |
| | ☐ Does not correctly pronounce these sounds by age 4<br>bob    cot    got    dot    fine    yet |
| | ☐ Does not correctly pronounce these sounds by age 6<br>teacher    ring    red    led |
| | ☐ Does not correctly pronounce these sounds by age 7<br>church    shoe    jump    thumb |
| | ☐ Does not correctly pronounce these sounds by age 8<br>seal    zeal    vine    them    beige |
| | ☐ Substitutes, distorts, or omits vowels or diphthongs at any age |
| **Voice** | ☐ Too high or too low for age, sex, and/or cultural expectations |
| | ☐ Little variation in pitch; monotone |
| | ☐ Volume softer/louder than others'; inappropriate for the situation |
| | ☐ Chronic hoarseness; frequent laryngitis; some inaudible sounds |
| | ☐ Hypernasality in conversational speech |
| | ☐ Excessive breathiness; inhales frequently |
| **Fluency** | ☐ Repeats or lengthens sounds, words, or phrases after age 5 |
| | ☐ Pauses before phrases, words, or sounds in words after age 5 |
| | ☐ Uses filler syllables between words or phrases |

Parents, daycare workers, teachers, and pediatricians can use this checklist, seeking further assistance from a licensed/certified speech therapist for an accurate diagnosis. They must obtain medical clearance to treat voice problems. Parents and/or teachers can remediate many problems under the direction of a speech therapist.

*Source:* Adapted from Thomas, P. J. (1990). *Tips for assessing speech and language: A checklist of common errors. Diagnostique, 16* (1), 29–31, with permission.

## CLASSROOM ACCOMMODATIONS

The decision to treat a child for articulation disorders depends on factors including the child's age, degree of intelligibility, and level of intellectual functioning, as well as the speech performance of the child's peers. To begin therapy, the speech pathologist designs an individualized program for the student, based on all diagnostic information. In general, therapy begins with training in acquiring sounds, followed by training in generalization. Acquisition training typically follows the sequence of auditory discrimination training and learning correct phoneme production in isolation, in words or nonsense syllables, and in phrases and sentences. Once the student has acquired the target sound, the generalization phase begins; he or she must demonstrate mastery of the sound outside the therapy room.

The classroom teacher's role is to supplement the individualized therapy provided by the speech/language specialist, coordinating the supplementary activities to fit with the individually designed therapy plan. Supplementary classroom activities should include many students, not just the student with speech disorders. The teacher should consult the therapist about when it is appropriate to require the student to speak in front of the class.

Therapy to correct voice disorders may include instruction in listening skills; in the process of speech (including anatomy and physiology); in physical hygiene, posture, and movement; in regulating respiration; and in relaxation and voice training. Therapy may require examining and changing environmental influences. Individuals who cannot use the larynx for phonation due to surgical removal or injury can be taught to articulate air resonated either by a belch or by an artificial device. Responsible, ethical professionals always obtain medical clearance before attempting to remediate voice disorders. It is imperative for the teacher to follow the specific directions of the speech/language specialist. Certain conditions require not using the voice; certain conditions require vocal practice. The safest and best course of action is to consult with the speech therapist before implementing any voice activity.

Everyone occasionally has fluency problems, but no one is dysfluent all the time. Most children between the ages of 3 and 5 exhibit normal difficulties with fluency. In addition, stutterers usually do not stutter when reciting a well-known poem or singing a song. Thus, the best course of preventive action is to focus on the message and ignore the fluency problems. According to behaviorists, calling attention to a child's fluency difficulties makes the child more likely to become a stutterer. The best response to fluency problems is to continue to listen and maintain eye contact, without finishing the speaker's thoughts or instructing him or her to "spit it out!" This chapter provides several effective strategies for increasing students' fluency. Some strategies focus on changing and creating response patterns and identifying situations that cause stress. All the strategies aim toward increasing fluency, thereby improving communication.

## SPECIFIC SKILLS AND STRATEGIES

The following pages present suggestions for detecting and correcting specific speech problems. Skills 24 and 25 provide activities in acquiring and then generalizing sounds to correct the two most common speech errors. These strategies can supplement corrective therapy. The teacher can use the samplers to follow the same sequence for other sounds; the words, phrases, and sentences for practice provide appropriate reinforcement of the target sound and should appeal to students of various ages and developmental levels. The teacher should collaborate with the speech therapist to determine whether the activities apply to particular students.

Skill 26, Voice, and Skill 27, Fluency, provide an array of activities from which the teacher may select in consultation with the speech/language therapist. The teacher should match the activities with the student's therapy program, modifying the activities to fit the student's age, specific needs, and learning style.

## 24. ARTICULATION OF S AND Z (Lisp)

**Voiceless** seal    **Voiced** zeal

DETECTION

This may be a special skill need of students who

- Substitute th (thing) for s (seal) or th (them) for z (zeal)
- Distort these sounds
- Omit these sounds in any position in a word

*Description*

The sounds s and z are continuants (i.e., sounds requiring a steady stream of air) further classified as fricatives. Voiceless sounds do not require phonation, but voiced sounds do. For the sounds s and z the tip of the tongue is elevated to the upper alveolar (gum) ridge just behind, but not touching the upper incisors. A stream of air is continuously emitted.

*Special Problems*

Inability to produce s and z sounds can have organic or functional origins. Organic causes include neuromuscular dysfunction (cerebral palsy), absence of upper incisors, paralysis of the lower lip or tongue, abnormally shortened lingual frenum (the small web of tissue under the front part of the tongue), or any condition that prevents proper placement of the articulators and/or a continuous stream of breath. Functional causes may include an inability to discriminate these sounds.

*Implications*

These sounds occur frequently in the English language. Producing them correctly contributes greatly to intelligibility; conversely, omitting fricatives or producing them incorrectly impedes intelligibility.

Ninety percent of 8-year-old students can produce s and z in the initial, final, and medial positions. Since these fricatives occur so frequently in the speech production of the English language (about 14%), correct production is essential to intelligibility of speech. Substituting th (thing) for s and th (them) for z is called an interdental lisp. When the airstream is released not from the front of the mouth but between the sides of the teeth, the resulting "slushy" sound is called a lateral lisp.

CORRECTION

Modify these strategies to meet students' learning needs.

1. *Auditory Discrimination.* Teach auditory discrimination informally, indirectly, and quickly by using minimal word pairs (i.e., words that differ in only one sound — pat/pet; hat/cat; hit/hip) in a game format. Create a bank of minimal word pairs with target sounds in the initial, final, and medial positions. Present pairs of pictures to represent each word pair. Instruct the child, "Show me (or point to) _____."
2. *Production in Isolation.* The s and z sounds are easy to teach. With the child sitting across from you, ask him or her to take a deep breath with open mouth, and then exhale as if sighing. Once the child can do this easily, work on proper placement of the articulators (see *Description* above). Make sure this activity is consistent with the speech therapist's techniques.
3. *Production in Nonsense Syllables and in Words.* Create lists of nonsense syllables with s and z in the initial, final, and medial positions. Students should read them or say them after you, mastering the sounds in the initial position before moving to the final and then the medial positions. Once students master the sound in nonsense syllables, practice using the sounds in words. See Sampler 6.5 for additional words.

|                   | *s*        |              | *z*        |           |
|-------------------|------------|--------------|------------|-----------|
| **Initial position** | sink    | sophisticated | xerox     | Zimbabwe  |
|                   | circus     | solicitous   | zombie     | Zaire     |
|                   | swim       | sanguine     | zoology    | Zulu      |
| **Final position**   | face    | glass        | nose       | confuse   |
|                   | circus     | success      | size       | graze     |
|                   | peace      | pence        | daze       | demise    |
| **Medial position**  | answer  | excellent    | visit      | altruism  |
|                   | consider   | decision     | business   | Bowser    |
|                   | decide     | precisely    | newspaper  | jacuzzi   |

4. *Production in Phrases/Sentences.* Have the student read or repeat phrases and sentences containing words with the target sound(s). See Sampler 6.5 for additional phrases and sentences.

| **Phrases** | something sinful | zoom lens |
|-------------|------------------|-----------|
|             | precinct seven   | dazzling azaleas |
|             | serene siblings  | amazing totals |
| **Sentences** | See if you can set the remote sensor. | Suzanne set a great example. |
|             | Say six seventeen times. | Azure is a dazzling color. |
|             | Summer is my favorite season. | Zorro zipped to the spot. |

5. *Generalization.* Plan experiences for three settings:
   — *In-Class Experiences.* • From coloring books, old reading books, or magazines, select five pictures of objects or actions whose names include the target sounds. • Have the child weave the pictures into an oral story, even one that doesn't make sense. • Teach the child to create acrostic poetry. • Write a number of acrostic poems, using words with the target sounds as stems. • Present a picture of an action-packed scene that includes many words with s and z sounds to stimulate conversation.
   — *At-Home Experiences.* • Play charades with the student. • All the answers should be words and/or phrases containing the target sounds. • Have your child read aloud from books by Dr. Seuss or Richard Scarry, which are intrinsically motivating. • Play a game to think of every president whose name contains the target sounds (John Adams, Thomas Jefferson, James Madison, James Monroe, John Quincy Adams, Andrew Jackson, James K. Polk, James Buchanan, Andrew Johnson, James A. Garfield, Benjamin Harrison, Lyndon Johnson). • Think of all the first names that begin with the target sounds.
   — *Fieldtrip Experiences.* • Visit the public library and look up entries in the encyclopedia that start with the target sounds. • Check out an appropriate mythology book from the library. • Read aloud or have the child read myths about Jupiter, Juno, Jason, Midas and the Golden Touch, and Charon. Discuss the stories.

## 25. ARTICULATION OF R AND L

DETECTION

This may be a special skill need of students who

- Substitute the w (wed) sound for the r (red) and/or l (led) sound
- Distort these sounds
- Omit the sounds in any position in a word

*Description*

Substituting w for r is one of the most common misarticulations. The r sound is classified as a continuant, a semivowel, and a glide. Producing a continuant requires a continuous, sustained stream of air. Semivowels seem consonant-like or vowel-like, depending on their position in the articulatory sequence (e.g., in the word *little*, the initial l is like a consonant, and the final l is like a vowel). Glides are sounds generated as the articulators move rapidly from one position to another. Additionally, their sound is not as prominent as in plosives and fricatives.

Substituting w for l is also common. The l sound is classified as a continuant and a semivowel. Children who are developing speech and language often substitute w for l, as in "ba-woon" instead of "balloon."

*Special Problems*

Difficulty in producing r and l can have organic or functional causes. Organic causes include neuromuscular dysfunction (cerebral palsy), paralysis of the tongue, shortened lingual frenum, or any condition that impedes proper placement of the articulators and/or a continuous stream of breath. Functional origins might include an inability to discriminate auditorially r and l, an inability to hear r and l, or not having learned articulatory position.

*Implications*

Ninety percent of 6-year-old students have mastered production of r and l in all positions. Young speakers often misarticulate the l sound, but the problem is easy to correct. Substituting the w for l usually results in unintelligible speech.

CORRECTION

Modify these strategies to meet students' learning needs.

1. *Auditory Discrimination.* Since substituting w for l is so common, you must determine whether the student can discriminate these two sounds. Write a list of words that contain l . Say each word once with the correct l sound and once with the w sound substituted. Ask the student to indicate whether the l sound was in the first or second word. Repeat this activity using r and w words. Create several minimal pairs (words that differ in only one sound) containing w. Write a "W" on a 3″ × 5″ card. Tape a popsicle stick to the card and hand it to the child. Ask the child to listen carefully while you say the minimal pairs. When the child hears the w sound, he or she is to raise the "W" flag. Repeat this activity for r and l words. Once the child has mastered this activity for all three sounds, mix the words to include r, l, and w words.
2. *Production in Isolation.* Check with the speech therapist who should teach the student correct placement of the articulators if you want to learn this technique.
3. *Production in Nonsense Syllables and in Words.* Create lists of nonsense syllables with the target sound in the initial, final, and medial positions for the student to read or say after you. The student should master the sounds in the initial position first, then in the final position, and then in the medial position. Later, practice using the sounds in words. Additional words for practice are on Sampler 6.3.

|                   | *r*           | *l*       |
|-------------------|---------------|-----------|
| **Initial position** | ride          | lead      |
|                   | Romeo         | listen    |
|                   | rhododendron  | lucid     |
| **Final position**   | err           | chattel   |
|                   | score         | pickle    |
|                   | door          | fatal     |
| **Medial position**  | eradicate     | elucidate |
|                   | entering      | allow     |
|                   | deterrent     | collision |

4. *Production in Phrases and Sentences.* Have the student read or repeat phrases and sentences containing the target sound. See Sampler 6.3 for additional phrases and sentences.

| **Phrases** | Rumplestiltskin | mail the letter |
|-------------|-----------------|-----------------|
|             | rolling on the river | stale lemonade |
|             | ring around the rosy | licking your lollipop |
| **Sentences** | Myrtle, was it reasonable to arrest an American hero? | The loyal follower listed the general's slifications. |
|             | The wretched photographer regretted his rash argument. | Louise listened as the long whistle blew. |
|             | Right around the block is a red house. | Low ceilings are ugly. |

5. *Generalization.* Plan experiences for three settings:

— *In-Class Experiences.* • Generate a list of animals whose names contain the r̲, l̲, and w̲ sounds. As the names are generated, write them on the board. All students should be given the opportunity to say the name of the animal that interests them most. • Write 5 words on the board that contain the target sound. Ask the children to make up a 2- or 3-sentence story incorporating all 5 words. The story need not make sense.

— *At-Home Experiences.* • Play the game Scrabble with the child. Take turns making up sentences with each word as it is created on the board. • Walk around the yard or inside the house together, giving the child a penny every time he or she correctly pronounces a word containing the target sound.

— *Fieldtrip Experiences.* • While riding in the car, read billboard advertisements, street names, and store names that contain the target sound. You can make this into a competition among all passengers.

## 26. VOICE

DETECTION

This may be a special skill need of students who display

- Pitch too high or low for age, sex, and/or cultural expectations
- Intensity louder or softer than that of other speakers
- Hoarse, nasal, or breathy voice

*Description*

Pitch is determined by the tension, width, and length of the vocal folds. Pitch rises when the vocal folds are elongated, because their tension is increased and their width at all points is reduced.

Some individuals habitually speak in loud and discordant tones that make listening unpleasant and uncomfortable. Excessive loudness may be accompanied by an unpleasant voice quality. Sometimes speakers begin at a normal volume but get louder as they continue. Students sometimes speak so softly that they cannot be understood. They often seem to produce words with little or no effort and with minimal regard for the listener.

Hoarseness is easily recognized as a low, husky, grating voice. Speakers usually appear to strain to produce even those defective sounds; their voices may break and no sound at all is produced. Because their vocal range is limited, their speech lacks vitality and variety.

Hypernasal speech, seldom regarded as normal, is usually at least mildly unpleasant. Occasionally, a speaker produces hyponasal speech that does not allow air through the nasal cavity. This may be due to temporary or chronic nasal congestion blocking the air passageway. Some students have large adenoids that partially close off the nasal passage; usually they need medical intervention.

Excessive breathiness distracts from the speaker's message. In addition, the breathy voice is usually too soft because breath is used inefficiently. Students with breathy voices must frequently interrupt their comments to inhale because their air is exhausted.

*Special Problems*

Voice problems can have organic or functional origins. Organic causes include cleft palate, hearing impairment, paralysis of the vocal folds, failure of the folds to meet adequately, lack of coordination among the components of the phonological system — breathing, phonation, and resonation — trauma or surgical modification, poor physical health, tumors, polyps, vocal nodules, edema, and laryngeal web. Functional causes may arise from vocal abuse, such as constant throat-clearing, tobacco smoking, and/or vocal misuse, such as yelling; inability or unwillingness to monitor the volume of the voice; and shyness.

*Implications*

Inappropriate pitch, intensity, or quality calls attention to the manner of speaking rather than to the content of speech, resulting in inadequate communication. A school-aged child's psychological development may be impaired because of the reaction of fellow students. Adults may not attain or advance in their chosen profession if the profession requires oral communication, as is usually the case.

Adolescent males normally experience transient periods during puberty when their pitch is too high. Loud-voiced speakers may be perceived as arrogant and overbearing, even though their social behavior may be beyond reproach. Speakers with soft voices may be viewed as ineffectual or dependent. Students with hypernasal speech often are reluctant to recite in class or carry out assignments that require speaking before a group. Students who have breathy voices may have difficulty being heard in even moderately noisy situations.

CORRECTION

Always obtain medical clearance before attempting to retrain the voice. Modify these strategies to meet students' learning needs.

1. *Optimum Pitch.* Determine optimum pitch by having students intone as low as they can, raising the level one step at a time until they reach falsetto. Use a piano or pitch pipe to match pitch levels to the musical scale to find total pitch range. The optimum pitch, considering age and physical development, is 1/4 to 1/3 above the lowest level within a student's pitch range. If 15 levels are produced during this exercise, optimum pitch is probably 4–5 levels above the lowest level. Use the piano to identify that target level for the student.

2. *Let Go.* Teach students progressive relaxation by having them contract and relax sets of muscles from the toes to the scalp while lying flat on a firm surface.

3. *Speech Breathing.* Demonstrate controlled, easy breathing for speech. Encourage students to relax the laryngeal area by yawning and by rolling their heads in a circle.

4. *Play It Softer, Sam!* Encourage students to relate personal experiences or tell about a TV program, using a soft voice in their spontaneous conversation. Listen for any increase in vocal intensity, and indicate by moving your hand downward that they should lower the volume.

5. *Louder, Please.* Direct students to say "ah" while exhaling, sustaining the tone without breaks. Encourage them to increase the volume gradually on successive trials. Tell them to stop if they feel any strain or discomfort. Repeat the exercise after vocal rest, returning to a softer volume and increasing as they can tolerate the effort.

6. *Nasal.* To help students learn about nasality, have them place their forefingers along the side of the bony parts of their noses. Have them say m (mother), n (never), ng (ring) while they feel the nasal vibrations.

7. *Less Nasal.* Retraining of the vocal mechanism may require stimulation of stronger velar (soft palate in back of mouth) action. Demonstrate for the student how to blow out the cheeks and explode the air forcefully, then easily, through puckered lips.

8. *Cool It!* When breathiness is due to chronic laryngitis, students should be taught preventative measures; be aware of sensations of tension, fatigue, and pain; and know the danger of permanent vocal damage.

9. *Breath Control.* Help students learn to control breath expulsion. Direct them to take a deep abdominal breath, clasp their hands over their diaphragms, and try to relax as they intone "ah" for as long as possible. Try this exercise at the beginning, middle, and end of every session, using a stopwatch to time each phonation; chart students' progress.

## 27. RHYTHM

DETECTION

This may be a special skill need of students who

- Repeat sounds, words, parts of words, or phrases
- Lengthen vowels and consonants, usually at the beginnings of words
- Fix the articulators in the position to produce plosives
- Pause before phrases, words, or sounds within words
- Use filler syllables between words or phrases
- Abruptly halt the flow of speech and show signs of struggle
- Cannot initiate an utterance and show signs of struggle

*Description*

Repetitions are the most common form of stuttering. They often appear at the beginnings of sentences, clauses, or verb, noun, or prepositional phrases. Normal speakers sometimes repeat themselves, but they tend to repeat phrases and whole words, not syllables or sounds.

All confirmed stutterers prolong sounds. Because normal speaking is continuous, even slight prolongations of posture or sound are conspicuous. Volume, airflow, pitch, and tension may fluctuate. Although prolongations may coexist with repetitions, they seem to develop later than repetitions and increase as the disorder progresses.

Hesitations include pauses in speaking, use of filler syllables, and stereotyped expression. Hesitation generally occurs in stutterers with full-blown stuttering block accompanied by signs of physical struggle. Filler syllables and stereotyped expressions are interjections, such as "um," "er," "ah," and "uh," used by the stutterer to fill pauses. Stereotyped expressions such as "well," "let me see," and "you know," fulfill the same purpose.

Stuttering blocks are abrupt interruptions in the flow of speech. For a time, the stutterer is literally unable to move or control the speech articulators to produce the intended word. The block occurs in conjunction with the repetitions, prolongations, or hesitations that define the speaker's disorder. The stutterer will struggle visibly to break the block.

*Special Problems*

Many stutterers describe a feeling of apprehension before they experience a stuttering block, a phenomenon known as anticipation or expectancy. Repetitions may result when stutterers cannot organize the completion of an utterance. Stutterers may use repetitions and prolongations as an anticipatory coping mechanism to stave off or postpone a perceived breakdown.

Pauses may result from stutterers' awareness of their problem. Students may be extremely sensitive to sounds or words they feel cause them to stutter. To keep from stuttering, they stop speaking before the particular word or sounds occurs. Filler syllables and stereotyped expressions may also be a postponement tactic. Stutterers may use interjections because they know that filled pauses are perceived as shorter than empty pauses. In normal speech, hesitations usually indicate that the speaker is searching for a word or expression. Hesitations may interfere the most with communication. Stuttering blocks may arise from fear associated with certain words, sounds, or situations.

*Implications*

To distinguish between normal fluency difficulties and stuttering, first define the type of repetition, prolongation, or hesitation the student exhibits. Determine frequency as a percent of occurrence per 100 or 200 words. When frequency exceeds 5 percent, the speech can be considered abnormal.

Stutterers who block often feel strained and tense. Identify and analyze students' stuttering blocks. Once students can describe and understand their blocking behavior, they will be prepared to monitor their speech and participate in therapy.

CORRECTION

Modify these strategies to meet students' learning needs.

1. *Reducing Occurrence.* Tape record the student's spontaneous speech at the beginning or end of each therapy session. Assist the student to identify repetitions, prolongations, and hesitations. Chart the data. Reward the student for reducing occurrences to target levels. Regularly repeat the activity and review progress with the student.

2. *Response Patterns.* Develop response patterns for conversations students might have during the school day and at home. Vary the interchanges so that students can initiate and respond. Encourage them to expand response patterns spontaneously. This controlled practice will build confidence for spontaneous situations.

3. *Facing Fears.* Have students describe how they feel when stuttering. If this is difficult, provide a list of possibilities from which to choose. Use this activity to initiate discussion so students identify and face their feelings as a way to overcome them.

4. *Awareness.* Provide students with a list of sounds. Have them check the ones they feel may cause them to prolong. Compare this information with data you collect from spontaneous speech samples. Analyze and discuss the findings with the students.

5. *Speech Breathing.* Demonstrate proper breathing and guide the students to practice it. Have the students lie on their backs, placing a small book on their diaphragms. The book should rise on inhalation and fall on exhalation. Gradually build up the time until students can comfortably practice for 10 minutes per session. After the technique is established, have students read aloud or speak while in the same position.

6. *In-Block Correction/Pull Out.* Instruct students to use the following steps when in the middle of a block:
   - Deliberately slow down the stuttering by repeating or prolonging.
   - Hold the stuttering long enough to regain control.
   - Discontinue the stuttering by breathing quietly and normally.

   Whenever you note that students need to use this strategy, say each step or prompt with cues such as "Slow . . . hold for control . . . easy."

# SPEECH SOUND SAMPLERS

The samplers on the next pages provide words, phrases, and sentences for practicing the sounds presented in Skills 24 and 25, as well as the other consonants. Use them in the activities described for correcting articulation of <u>s</u>, <u>z</u>, <u>r</u>, and <u>l</u>. The words range from easy to complex and should spark the students' interest. Use these samplers as spelling words and vocabulary builders in addition to oral practices of the target sound. Consult with the speech therapist, however, to select activities that complement the individual student's therapy plan.

Each sampler page contains target sounds that should have appeared by a particular age. For example, Sampler 6.1 contains words, phrases, and sentences for sounds that children should pronounce properly by age 3. The ages are identified on this page, not on the samplers, so that students will not experience additional negative reactions to their deficiencies.

6.1 **Pretty Mary Had Nine Wigs** (Age 3). Children older than 3 who do not correctly pronounce these sounds can benefit from practicing with these words, phrases, and sentences. Visit an exhibit at a local nature and science center or museum. Select two exhibits the student finds particularly interesting and read the narrative aloud. Discuss the exhibit and name concepts that contain the target sounds. Write down the concepts for later discussion, review, and practice of the target sounds.

6.2 **Brave King Gordon Felt Yucky** (Age 4). Children older than 4 who do not correctly pronounce these sounds can benefit from practicing these words, phrases, and sentences. Play "I Spy." One student says "I spy something that starts with _____." Fill in the blank with the target sound. Students must guess what the targeted object is.

6.3 **Tom Sang Really Loudly** (Age 6). Children older than 6 who do not correctly pronounce these sounds can benefit from practicing these words, phrases, and sentences. Go to a shopping mall. Have the child name all the stores that contain the target sounds. Pick an aisle in a variety store and have the child name items that contain the sound. At the bookstore, read titles of children's books that contain the target sounds. Have the child repeat the titles after you.

6.4 **Chad Shattered Jamie's Thimble** (Age 7). Children older than 7 who do not correctly pronounce these sounds can benefit from practicing these words, phrases, and sentences. As students generate a list of animals whose names contain the target sounds, write the names on the board. Give students the opportunity to say the name of the animal that interests them most.

6.5 **Some Zebras Viewed Their Treasures** (Age 8). Children older than 8 who do not correctly pronounce these sounds can benefit from practicing these words, phrases, and sentences. Play the game Scrabble with the child. Take turns making up sentences with each word containing target sounds as it is created on the board.

# <u>P</u>RETTY <u>M</u>ARY <u>H</u>AD <u>N</u>INE <u>W</u>IGS

|  | *pat* | *mother* | *hello* | *never* | *wed* |
|---|---|---|---|---|---|
| **Target sound in initial position** | pet<br>puff<br>pig<br>Pat<br>pot | met<br>monkey<br>March<br>meat<br>month | hero<br>hand<br>high<br>hurry<br>howl | nest<br>nail<br>north<br>nose<br>nothing | wisdom<br>winter<br>wasp<br>weapon<br>warranty |
| **Target sound in final position** | hip<br>stop<br>flip<br>hop<br>tap<br>up | game<br>plume<br>room<br>dome<br>assume<br>redeem | | hen<br>rain<br>done<br>tune<br>loon<br>cartoon | few<br>arrow<br>elbow<br>tow<br>crow<br>yellow |
| **Target sound in medial position** | impose<br>apart<br>deposit<br>supper<br>imperfect<br>compile | hammer<br>human<br>comfort<br>image<br>plumage<br>important | behave<br>aha<br>aloha<br>inhale<br>overhead<br>cohort | dinosaur<br>pencil<br>insect<br>dentist<br>ransack<br>intend | away<br>underwear<br>towel<br>steward<br>follower<br>underway |

**Sample phrases**

sour pickles
pay bills promptly
Pink Panther
  footprint
pick yellow pansies

comfortable home
messy bedroom
majestic mountains
murky mop water

overhauled hot rod
horrendous hurricane
howling Halloween
  ghosts
huge hippopotamus

rancid bacon
running antelopes
night manager
no money

seaworthy crew
window washer
worthless warranty
wilted wildflower

**Sample sentences**

— Mop the floor with Super Duper. Patrick has dimples. Peter Piper picked a peck of . . . Polly likes her Apple computer.

— The Saints won the game in the Superdome. Imelda imitated the manner of the Mother Superior. Mel munched on his hamburger and drank his milk. My grandmother hunted in the garden mulch for fishing worms.

— All hail the conquering hero! The overhang in the hotel was hideous. Hilary exclaimed, "Ahhh," when she beheld the wondrous sight overhead.

— Nanny noted that nothing had happened to the crane. Never say "no" to a persistent person. Johnny nailed his new poster near the torn one. Cynthia and Donna nursed the wilted plant back to a healthy green. Can anyone possibly know how a nerve regenerates?

— The wasp sting left a welt on Warren's elbow. Wanda Williams walked away from the bewitching window display. Will she win Wimbledon playing with her Wilson racket? Wouldn't it be fun to walk on water?

# BRAVE KING GORDON FELT YUCKY

|  | *bob* | *cot* | *got* | *fine* | *yet* |
|---|---|---|---|---|---|
| **Target sound in initial position** | bill | keep | gold | final | yams |
| | belt | consider | gaping | factory | yearbook |
| | big | king | gift | fever | yardstick |
| | bat | Kung fu | golly | faith | useful |
| | bold | cable | gasoline | football | yesterday |
| | balloon | killer | guest | fear | young |
| **Target sound in final position** | tube | like | tug | puff | |
| | tab | tick | dog | roof | |
| | bib | Jack | pig | loaf | |
| | slob | poke | egg | stuff | |
| | grab | look | frog | laugh | |
| | shish kebob | brake | hug | reef | |
| **Target sound in medial position** | bubble | backgammon | logjam | confirm | beautiful |
| | grubworm | record | begin | defect | canyon |
| | dabble | market | forget | before | music |
| | Flubber | doctor | dragon | muffin | union |
| | public | baker | tiger | affirmation | accordion |
| | baby | background | tugboat | after | bouillon |

**Sample phrases**

| | | |
|---|---|---|
| baseball bat | King Kong | golden grain |
| dribble on the bib | queen's castle | go for the gold |
| bingo on B–21 | combat in Africa | ugly rogue hog |
| bounce the ball briskly | nautical peacemaker | legal signature |
| blow bubbles, Becky | chocolate milk | neglected beggar |
| | | |
| ferocious forehand | tennis player | |
| famous loafer | buoyant music | |
| funny photograph | Yosemite opened | |
| comfortable sofa | onion yeast bread | |
| four-leaf clover | beautiful yacht | |

**Sample sentences**

— The baby burped after his bottle. The ebb of the tide carried the beach ball away from the boys. The linebacker blitzed the quarterback.

— The broadcast confirmed the rumors. Katie cooked too much chicken. Use your fork to break the bacon. The donkey came to a complete halt.

— Margaret has a guide dog. The ugly gang was ignorant. The guys gasped when the girl put on a batting glove.

— Don't be foolish in the forest. Steffi Graf has a great forehand. The five fell forward into the waterfall. Forgive and forget is good advice.

— The beautiful young Yolanda yodeled across the canyon. Yes, you may have some yummy Yoplait yogurt. The yearbook editor yawned at the absurd euphemism. Are there onions in Yugoslavia?

# TOM SANG REALLY LOUDLY

| | _t_eacher | ri_ng_ | _r_ed | _l_ed |
|---|---|---|---|---|
| **Target sound in initial position** | tea<br>tool<br>tummy<br>terrific<br>tall<br>tiger | | rain<br>wreck<br>Robert<br>realize<br>reward<br>ridicule | love<br>lead<br>late<br>letter<br>laugh<br>length |
| **Target sound in final position** | foot<br>ticket<br>upset<br>draft<br>gift<br>belt | ring<br>darling<br>hang<br>sung<br>joking<br>bring | dinosaur<br>solar<br>creator<br>hotographer<br>danger<br>teacher | feel<br>educational<br>olorful<br>hole<br>turtle<br>pull |
| **Target sound in medial position** | untie<br>tic-tac<br>detain<br>butter<br>quietly<br>intent | drink<br>strength<br>crank<br>Frank<br>length<br>ping pong | arrow<br>porridge<br>Gerald<br>erect<br>arrange<br>hurricane | follow<br>believe<br>hello<br>falling<br>belong<br>million |

**Sample phrases**

| | |
|---|---|
| tickle my fancy | something ringing |
| tempt the appetite | cling clang |
| lickety-split | checking the length |
| tough toenails | thinking everything |
| Tom Terrific | aching feeling |
| | |
| narrow-minded voter | lazy lizard |
| ripe strawberries | follow the leader |
| unrelenting crusader | ugly stallion |
| solar power | Larry lost |
| Red River Revel | family belief |

**Sample sentences**

— Don't step on my pet worm. Tennis is my favorite sport. Terry typed the report without mistakes. The devastating scene faded from the television.

— That cranky feeling overcame Frank. Spring Lee experienced a sinking feeling as she clung to the ledge. The doorbell clanged, "Ding dong!" A pig was making oinking noises as the boy dumped everything into the pen.

— Can you rearrange your schedule, Robin, to collect the reward money? The ornery Tyrannosaurus Rex was branded a rogue. The landlord raised the rent to a ridiculous figure. The Rex parade routed through the crowd of Mardi Gras revelers.

— The mare's foal was destined to grow into a fearless stallion. That dull individual monopolized the whole evening. The tailback looked at the goalpost. Lucille glanced at the graceful ballerina and applauded loudly.

# CHAD SHATTERED JAMIE'S THIMBLE

|  | *church* | *shoe* | *jump* | *thumb* |
|---|---|---|---|---|
| **Target sound in initial position** | check | shark | judge | thank |
|  | change | shekel | job | Thor |
|  | chum | ship | jest | thick |
|  | choose | shape | jello | think |
|  | chair | shingle | gist | thorn |
|  | chuck | sugar | gel | thunder |
| **Target sound in final position** | fetch | dish | refuge | forth |
|  | itch | mash | shortage | math |
|  | patch | fish | oblige | both |
|  | ouch | mesh | bridge | with |
|  | watch | establish | cabbage | cloth |
|  | ranch | posh | judge | mirth |
| **Target sound in medial position** | inchworm | nation | inject | birthday |
|  | picture | parachute | enjoy | cathedral |
|  | attachment | cushion | indigent | earthquake |
|  | pitcher | flashback | Bridget | monthly |
|  | untouchable | bashful | judgment | pith helmet |
|  | woodchuck | vacation | biology | Ethiopia |

**Sample phrases**

| | |
|---|---|
| scratch the itch | ship shape |
| choose to touch | flashing caution light |
| fetch the pitcher | emotional sensation |
| achieve the challeng | brash window washer |
| chicken crunch | cymbals clashing |
| challenge the judgment | thirty thousand |
| indigent gentleman | enthusiastic therapist |
| Gerald gestured | fourth birthday |
| refrigerate the fudge | thick cloth |
| garbage job | unthinkable thoughts |

**Sample sentences**

— The wreck of the Challenger touched the heart of the gentleman. Bridget became attached to the picture of the indigent underachiever. Jennifer injected the inchworm in preparation for the dissection.

— He flashed his badge and brandished his gun. The ocean waves crashed on the beach. His emotional condition was volatile. She astonished her opposition by her overwhelming margin of victory.

— Madge put the jello, the jelly, and the jam in the refrigerator. There was no shortage of cribbage players among Judy, Jim, Jill, and Jeff. Jason jumped for joy when his team scored a goal.

— Thanks for the birthday card. Both filthy boys took a bath. Nothing interested the thin girl. The thirsty man drank from the thermos. Thirty-three thugs jammed into the theater for the fifth showing of *Earthquake*.

# <u>S</u>OME <u>Z</u>EBRAS <u>V</u>IEWED <u>TH</u>EIR TREA<u>S</u>URES

| | *seal* | *zeal* | *vine* | *them* | *beige* |
|---|---|---|---|---|---|
| **Target sound in initial position** | sailor | zoo | vote | this | |
| | census | zero | value | they | |
| | soup | zebra | veer | there | |
| | circle | Xerox | volume | than | |
| | sink | xylophone | volcano | that | |
| | sanguine | Zimbabwe | vineyard | these | |
| **Target sound in final position** | house | buzz | five | smooth | garage |
| | pace | zooms | cave | tithe | mirage |
| | bus | wise | love | bathe | barrage |
| | erase | impounds | alive | clothe | triage |
| | glass | nose | cove | soothe | beige |
| | face | confuse | archive | loathe | |
| **Target sound in medial position** | pencil | magazine | convert | bother | treasure |
| | also | music | liver | weather | explosion |
| | Christmas | altruism | Volvo | mother | division |
| | sister | husband | trivial | rather | measure |
| | answer | museum | avocado | either | erosion |
| | excellent | visit | revenge | farthing | exclusion |

**Sample phrases**

| | | |
|---|---|---|
| sister sings | business newspaper | |
| solitary dinosaur | dazzling gems | |
| circus star | buzzing bees | |
| toothless smile | easy-zip zipper | |
| something simple | zippy music | |
| vindictive voter | soothing grandmother | flashing explosion |
| forgiving victim | another feather | coastal erosion |
| move everything | neither of them | unwanted intrusion |
| available van | bothering brother | treasure hunt |
| five villages | clothe that heathen | measuring tape |

**Sample sentences**

— Patrick swims the breaststroke. That's the face of a circus clown. If you want peace, work for justice. Steve decided to swim for shore. Sallie gave Sarah a surprise party.

— Did you Xerox the zoology quiz? What sizes are those blouses? The newspaper reported dismal business opportunities.

— The victim forgave her attacker. The dove dived into the lake. The wives beat the husbands in a game of Trivial Pursuit. Avarice is not a virtue.

— These feathers feel smooth. Bathe before the weather changes. The mother soothed her upset son. Is farther or further correct?

— She usually finished division problems rapidly. Protect against coastal erosion. I give my treasure with pleasure.

# REFLECTIONS

1.  Listen carefully to the articulation of a normal three-year-old child and a normal eight-year-old. Focus on sounds such as s, r, and l. Do the two children produce these sounds with equal clarity? Why or why not? Review each of the consonant sounds noting the ages at which 90 percent of the children correctly pronounce them.

2.  Using your knowledge of the sequence in which phonemes are acquired, determine whether these students should be referred for professional evaluation:

    *age*   *says*
    6       "The wabbit wan into the fowest."
    7       "My bawoon fwew up into the sky."
    4       "My baby thithter thoundth like the'th hungry."
    8       "Did you go to shursh on Easter Sunday?"
    5       "Patrick likes to play soccer."

3.  What are the four types of articulation errors? Give an example of each. Which is the most common error?

4.  List the traditional sequence of correcting an articulation error. Describe each step in your own words.

5.  What is the purpose of systemwide or campuswide screening for articulation disorders? What steps should educators take for a child who does not pass the screening?

6.  Visit points of interest in your community, such as the nature and science center, public library, art museum, university, water processing plant, recycling center, police station, post office, and so on, to familiarize yourself with local attractions and resources. You can weave this knowledge into the activities presented in this book and plan field trips for generalization activities.

7.  What three aspects of voice are discussed in this chapter? Why is it important for vocal quality to be appropriate to age, sex, and cultural membership?

8.  As you observe in elementary classrooms, you will have an opportunity to hear most of the children in the class speak. Note the percentage who speak too loudly or too softly in a specific classroom. Later, observe those same children on the playground and compare their in-class and out-of-class voices. Is this comparison important in planning correction strategies?

9.  Give a definition of fluency disorder. Why are such disorders so disconcerting for the listener?

10. A speech pathologist working with a person who stutters should attempt to understand the speaker's feelings. Some suggest that one should stutter during a verbal exchange with a stranger in order to experience the listeners' reaction to stuttered speech. Do you think this is a good idea? What benefits could there be? Could there be negative effects? Explain your viewpoint.

11. Lack of fluency can be disconcerting to the speaker. Have you ever felt that your speech was not normally fluent? What was the speaking situation, and why do you think you were not fluent at that time? How would you describe your feelings then?

12. To accommodate a severe stutterer in the regular classroom, a teacher must be aware of some basic principles. If one of the students in your fourth-grade class was a severe stutterer, how would you adjust your requirements for class participation, or what other steps would you take to alleviate the student's embarrassment? List five specific actions you would take.

13. Many resources discuss identifying and remediating articulation disorders. Compare and contrast discussions in these sources with the information in this chapter.

Andrews, M., & Summers, A. (1987). *Voice therapy for adolescents.* San Diego: College Hill Press.

Baer, T., Sasaki, C., & Harris, K. S. (1987). *Laryngeal function in phonation and respiration.* San Diego: College Hill Press.

Boone, D. R. (1987). *Human communication and its disorders.* Englewood Cliffs, NJ: Prentice Hall.

Brodnitz, F. (1983). *Keep your voice healthy* (2nd ed.). San Diego: College Hill Press.

Duran, E. (1988). *Teaching the moderately and severely handicapped student and autistic adolescent: With particular attention to bilingual special education.* Springfield, IL: Charles C. Thomas.

Hahner, J.C., Sokoloff, M.A., & Salisch, S. (1990). *Speaking clearly: Improving voice and diction* (3rd ed.). New York: McGraw-Hill.

Hegde, M.N. (1991). *Introduction to communication disorders.* Austin, TX: Pro-Ed.

Kent, R.D. (1992). *Reference manual for communicative sciences and disorders.* Austin, TX: Pro-Ed.

Leith, W. R., & Johnston, R. G. (1986). *Handbook of voice therapy for the school clinician.* San Diego: College Hill Press.

Ohde, R.N., & Sharf, D.J. (1992). *Phonetic analysis of normal and abnormal speech.* New York: Merrill/Macmillan.

Oyer, H. J. (1987). *Speech, language, and hearing disorders: A guide for the teacher.* San Diego: College Hill Press.

Rakes, T. A., & Choate, J. S. (1989). *Language arts: Detecting and correcting special needs.* Boston: Allyn and Bacon.

Sander, E. (1972). *When are speech sounds learned? Journal of Speech and Hearing Disorders, 37,* 55–63.

Shames, G. H., & Wiig, E. H. (1990). Human communication disorders (3rd ed.). Columbus, OH: Merrill.

Starkweather, C. W. (1987). *Fluency and stuttering.* Englewood Cliffs, NJ: Prentice Hall.

Sies, L. (1987). *Voice and voice disorders: A handbook for clinicians.* Springfield, IL: Charles C. Thomas.

Stemple, J. C., & Holcomb, B. J. (1988). *Effective voice and articulation.* Columbus, OH: Charles E. Merrill.

Taylor, J. S. (1992). *Speech-language pathology services in the schools* (2nd ed.). Boston: Allyn and Bacon.

Taylor, O. L. (1991). *Communication disorders in culturally and linguistically diverse populations.* San Diego: College Hill Press.

Thomas, P. J., & Carmack, F. F. (1990). *Speech and language: Detecting and correcting special needs.* Boston: Allyn and Bacon.

Van Riper, C., & Emerick, L. (1984). *Speech correction: An introduction to speech pathology and audiology* (7th ed.). Englewood Cliffs, NJ: Prentice Hall.

Wells, B. (1987). *Stuttering treatment: A comprehensive clinical guide.* Englewood Cliffs, NJ: Prentice Hall.

Wilson, D. K. (1987). *Voice problems of children* (3rd ed.). Baltimore, MD: Williams and Wilkins.

Winitz, H. (Ed.) (1989). *Human communication and its disorders: 1989 annual review* (Vol. 3). Norwood, NJ: Ablex.

# CHAPTER SEVEN

## LANGUAGE: THE FOUNDATION OF LEARNING

— *Paulette J. Thomas and Fairy F. Carmack*

All learning is based on a language system. Human interaction is facilitated by verbal and nonverbal communication. Language is the raw material that serves as the stimulus to communicate and provides the structure for our communication system. Nonverbal language serves to emphasize, confirm, or deny oral language. It is vital for social adjustment as well as future learning that communication difficulties be diagnosed early and remediated promptly.

Early correction of language disorders requires early detection. The student who does not understand language will experience extreme difficulty learning to read. Reading specialists acknowledge the association between what is printed on the page and students' speaking vocabulary. Many teachers write down the student's speech, associating speech and writing to teach beginning reading.

## LANGUAGE SKILLS

Communication is the process of transmitting and receiving information. Thus, (1) communication is active, not passive; a process, not a product and (2) communication is an interaction between a sender, or speaker, and a receiver, or listener.

## Verbal Skills

Verbal communication, whether oral or written, involves the ability to encode and decode. Encoding is the process of formulating thoughts into words in orderly sequence (or syntax) in order to transmit a message. Children with language disorders may transmit messages in which thoughts are not arranged in the expected sequence. The necessary words may be present, but the unusual sequence will cause communication to break down. Compare these two utterances: "Jason studying is for a test" versus "Jason is studying for a test."

Decoding, or comprehension, is the process of understanding the transmitted message. Children who do not understand vocabulary and/or idiomatic expressions are at a particular disadvantage in academic and social settings. Their school days may be filled with words and phrases they cannot comprehend.

For verbal communication to occur, the encoder and decoder must share a system for representing concepts. Such a system uses arbitrary but conventional symbols whose use is governed by mutually accepted rules. Both encoder and decoder must share the same system in order to communicate effectively. This chapter presents strategies to help special learners improve their encoding and decoding skills.

## Nonverbal Skills

Nonverbal communication occurs in three basic categories: prosody, kinesics, and proxemics. This chapter presents Detection and Correction strategies for these categories.

Prosody includes changes in the voice, such as pitch, duration, loudness, and rhythm. Prosodic features carry meaning and may confirm or contradict the spoken message. For example, "Oh" spoken briskly with high unchanging pitch indicates surprise. "Oh" articulated slowly, beginning with low pitch and ending with a higher pitch, indicates disbelief. And "Oh" said slowly, beginning in a high pitch and ending in a lower pitch, indicates that the speaker has experienced a revelation.

Kinesics is visual signals sent with the body: gesture, facial expression, and posture. Their meanings are determined by convention and may be culture-specific. For example, when two unrelated American males greet each other with kisses on both cheeks, they impart a very different message than two unrelated Italian men doing the same thing.

Proxemics is physical distance in interpersonal communication. Like kinesics, proxemics may be culture-specific. Communication between people less than 18 inches apart is considered in American culture to be intimate, while public distance is considered to be over 12 feet.

## LANGUAGE DIFFERENCES

Educators must be careful to distinguish between language disorders and language differences. Students with language differences do not necessarily require intervention and remediation, but students with language disorders do. A language disorder interferes with communication, calls unfavorable attention to itself, and can cause its user to be maladjusted. Language disorder is determined within the context of a speech community. Although the United States' national language is English, some speech communities use variations of the national language, or dialects. A dialect is not inferior, merely different. Politically, socially, and economically powerful people, however, tend to speak a standard dialect. In other words, if you want to be king, you must speak the king's English.

Seven major factors typically influence language behavior: race and ethnicity; social class, education, and occupation; region; gender; situation or context; peer-group association or identification; and first language culture. Racial and ethnic influences on language are related to the cultural attitudes and values of the group. Language behavior reflects social class, education, and occupation. For instance, lower-class groups use a more restricted linguistic code, and middle- and upper-class groups use a more elaborate linguistic code. Regional dialects are generally defined by geographic boundaries. Gender differences are evident in the careful and precise language use of women versus men. Language varies according to the situation or context in which it is spoken. Peer-group association or identification influences language usage, particularly among teenagers, often to the consternation of their parents. Individuals for whom English is a second language may retain vestiges of the first language in using English. The speech/language pathologist must determine whether the student has a language disorder or a language difference. Students who have mastered a nonstandard dialect do not have a language disorder, but should be given the opportunity to learn Standard American English.

## DETECTION OF LANGUAGE DISORDERS

This chapter describes language disorders in terms of observable behaviors, for example, "misunderstands idioms and figurative language," or "applies

## FIGURE 7.1  /  A Checklist of Common Language Errors

Use this checklist to record behaviors that signal possible problems and plan appropriate intervention. Carefully observe the student in a variety of settings, and circle problem areas and behaviors.

| Target Skill | Possible Problem Behaviors |
| --- | --- |
| **VERBAL COMMUNICATION** | |
| **Semantics** | ☐ Misunderstands idioms and figurative language |
| | ☐ Fails to understand multiple meanings |
| | ☐ Displays poor comprehension in reading |
| | ☐ Cannot comprehend units of distance and measurement |
| | ☐ Has difficulty answering "why" questions |
| | ☐ Exhibits below-average ability to generalize |
| | ☐ Confuses common prepositions |
| **Morphology** | ☐ Uses comparatives and superlatives incorrectly |
| | ☐ Has difficulty with subject-verb agreement in number |
| | ☐ Uses pronouns incorrectly |
| | ☐ Uses tense, aspect, or mood incorrectly |
| **Syntax** | ☐ Does not undersand passive sentences |
| | ☐ Uses run-on sentences |
| | ☐ Cannot answer simple reporter questions |
| | ☐ Uses unusual word order or phrases instead of sentences |
| **Word Finding** | ☐ Has a limited vocabulary |
| | ☐ Uses incorrect words in sentences |
| | ☐ Cannot produce the word for a known concept |
| | ☐ Uses synonyms poorly or not at all |
| **NONVERBAL COMMUNICATION** | |
| **Prosody** | ☐ Responds to variations of pitch, duration, loudness, or rhythm inappropriately |
| | ☐ Uses variations of pitch, duration, loudness, or rhythm inappropriately |
| **Kinesics** | ☐ Responds to gestures, facial expressions, or body movements inappropriately |
| | ☐ Uses gestures, facial expressions, or body movements inappropriately |
| **Proxemics** | ☐ Responds to distance messages inappropriately or not at all |
| | ☐ Uses distance messages inappropriately or not at all |

This checklist may be used by parents, daycare workers, teachers, and pediatricians. Seek further assistance from a licensed/certified speech/language therapist for an accurate diagnosis. Many problems can be remediated by teachers under the direction of a speech therapist.

Adapted from Thomas, P. J. (1990). Tips for assessing speech and language: A checklist of common errors. *Diagnostique, 16* (1), 29–31, with permission.

single interpretation to multiple-meaning words." Behavioral descriptions assist teachers, college students, and therapists in dealing with problem behaviors rather than diagnostic classifications. This should also assist teachers in working with those who have not been classified as exceptional.

## Verbal Skills

The following pages describe the development of skills in understanding (receptive) and using (expressive) language. One cannot recognize abnormal behavior without being familiar with typical behavior. The guidelines may be used with Figure 7.1, A Checklist of Common Language Errors.

We have to learn to walk before we can run. Similarly, children must understand language before they can use it, though the process of understanding does not have to be complete before a child can use language.

### Receptive Language (Understanding)

Figure 7.2 presents milestones in the development of understanding language. An adult familiar with the child should be able to answer in the affirmative at the expected age. Read over the list before doing the activities with the child, since some activities require certain props. If the child does not perform the actions at or near the expected age, the adult should seek professional assistance from a speech pathologist.

### Expressive Language (Using)

Figure 7.3 shows milestones or guidelines in children's development of language usage. When using the checklist in Figure 7.3, keep in mind that normal behavior varies widely; some children will exhibit the described behaviors earlier or later than the ages listed. If you are concerned about a child's use of language, seek help from a licensed speech/language pathologist.

**FIGURE 7.2 / Developmental Milestones for Understanding Language**

| By Age (in months) | The Child Should | Prompt |
|---|---|---|
| 10 | understand name and respond | |
| 10 | understand "no" | |
| 11 | give up an object on command | |
| 16 | obey simple commands | "Hand me the ball." |
| 17 | follow directions | "Put on your coat." (hat) |
| 18 | point to body parts on a doll | "Point to dolly's mouth . . ." (eyes, etc.) |
| 18 | point out animals in pictures | "Where is the dog?" (cow, horse) |
| 21 | respond to three commands | "Put on your hat, pick up the book, and go to the front door." |
| 24 | respond to four commands | ". . . get our lunch box . . ." |
| 27 | understand prepositions | "Put this block on the table." "Put the book behind me." |
| 36 | understand functions associated with pictured objects | "Point to the one up in the sky." "Point to the one that is good to eat." |
| 45 | respond to comparative information about objects? | "Point to the fastest swimmer." "Point to the heaviest one." |

FIGURE 7.3 / Developmental Milestones for Language Usage

| By Age (in months) | The Child Should | Example |
|---|---|---|
| 12 | imitate sounds | |
| 12 | combine two or more syllables | |
| 12 | attempt "da-da" and "ma-ma" | |
| 18 | have a 10- to 50-word vocabulary | |
| 20 | name familiar objects | block, watch, keys, cup, doll, spoon |
| 18 | use two-word combinations | "Here ball," "More milk" |
| 21 | ask for food, drink, or toilet | |
| 21 | repeat adult speech | |
| 22 | name objects in pictures | house, dog, bird, tree, flower |
| 24 | use three-word sentences often | |
| 24 | refer to himself or herself by name | |
| 24 | use pronouns (not always correctly) | |
| 24 | begin to use -ing ending | |
| 25 | use four-word sentences often | |
| 30 | give own full name | |
| 30 | refer to himself or herself by pronoun | |
| 30 | give the use of familiar objects | spoon, cup, penny, keys, comb |
| 30 | use the word "is" | |
| 31 | respond correctly to cause-effect questions | "What should you do when you are sleepy? hungry? cold?" |
| 33 | repeat a six-syllable sentence | "I can put on my coat." "John has a little dog." |
| 36 | use some plurals | |
| 37 | use indirect requests | "Can I get the doll?" |
| 37 | use an average sentence length of over four words | |

## Nonverbal Skills

Skills in sending and receiving messages nonverbally are vital. Students whose actions do not match their words or who cannot understand nonverbal messages may seem like social misfits to teachers and classmates. Students who do not understand or use prosody, kinesics, and proxemics appropriately are at a decided disadvantage, both in and out of school, since nonverbal messages confirm or deny verbal messages.

Voice inflection and length and timing of an utterance convey meaning. Students may misinterpret sarcasm and act on the literal meaning of the words. They may also be unable to understand or use humor.

Employees who insist they are open to new ideas while sitting with crossed legs, folded arms, and the body angled away from the boss contradict their verbal communication. The nonverbal message denies the verbal message.

Lecturers are usually removed from their audiences, but teachers purposefully close the distance between themselves and their students. The two interactions have different purposes: The lecturer's job is to present information, not necessarily to confirm that listeners have learned it. The teacher wants to be invited into students' intimate space to function effectively.

## CORRECTION OF LANGUAGE DISORDERS

The following pages describe techniques for detection and correction of specific verbal and nonverbal language skills. For each skill, a few strategies are suggested for corrective instruction; however, the school's speech/language pathologist should be consulted for guidance and additional recommendations for accommodating individual learners' needs.

The Correction activities for verbal language skills can be easily adapted for classrooms and for single students. The exercises reflect actual behaviors expected of students in school, so that most students, not just the target pupil, will benefit from these activities.

The Correction activities for each nonverbal skill address both understanding and using nonverbal language. Most of us learn to understand and use intonation patterns, gestures, facial expressions, postures, and appropriate distances incidentally, as we learn to communicate effectively. For those who have not learned these skills and/or for members of other cultures who wish to participate more fully in American culture, these activities should alleviate some difficulties with nonverbal communication. The activities may also help students who are studying acting to convey nonverbal messages.

## 28.  SEMANTICS

DETECTION

This may be a special skill need of students who

- Interpret multiple-meaning words in only one way
- Have sparse receptive and expressive vocabularies
- Misunderstand idioms and figurative language
- Have poor reading comprehension
- Do not appreciate verbal humor
- Cannot express future or past time accurately
- Comprehend distance and measurement poorly
- Cannot connect causes and effects

*Description*

• *Multiple Meanings:* This task requires students to interpret dual meaning words in more than one way. Students may focus on a single meaning of a word that has multiple meanings. • *Figurative Language:* This skill requires flexibility in manipulating concepts. Many culturally different students are familiar with figurative language in their own culture, but do not have the experiential foundation to understand figurative comparisons in their textbooks or in class discussions. • *Space and Time Relationships:* Some students have difficulty discussing events that do not take place here and now. Their conception of the future and past and of distance is unclear. • *Cause/Effect Relationships:* Some students have unusual difficulty with sentence constructions that require manipulating ideas. They may have difficulty recognizing the relationship and stating it correctly.

*Special Problems*

• *Multiple Meanings:* Single interpretation of multiple-meaning words may stem from difficulties in understanding abstractions. Students may prefer concrete word meanings that are frequently used or that they have experienced personally. • *Figurative Language Difficulties:* Problems with this abstract language may arise from limited vocabulary and experience. "Like a bull in a china shop" means little to a student who has seen neither a bull nor a china shop. Some students have not been exposed to the fanciful characters and plots found in children's stories. • *Space and Time Relationships:* Students may be unsure of their location in space in relation to their surroundings. This confusion is multiplied when they are asked to order space and time that they cannot see. • *Cause/Effect Relationships:* This problem involves failing to connect two events appropriately. Rigid thinking and limited vocabulary may make comprehension more difficult than expression.

*Implications*

Students with semantic problems will probably experience difficulties in most academic areas and in interpersonal relationships. • *Multiple Meanings:* Students who are unable to interpret words in more than one way will experience difficulty in the academic arena and in interpersonal relationships. • *Figurative Language Difficulties:* Problems in this area may arise after the third grade, when reading material begins to contain more figurative language. Students may be able to read all the words but not to follow the thoughts. • *Space and Time Relationships:* Students who have difficulty organizing space and time need to have abstract terms of time or space illustrated with concrete examples, such as pictures, maps, graphs, and timelines. • *Cause/Effect Relationships:* Students may have difficulty comprehending and/or expressing that one thing causes another to happen.

CORRECTION — Modify these strategies to meet students' learning needs.

1. *Dictionary Match-Up* (Multiple Meanings). Assemble pictures that represent words with more than one meaning. Print short dictionary definitions appropriate to students' reading level on 3″ × 5″ cards. Students will match the dictionary definition to the picture. Control the difficulty of this activity by varying the number of definitions and the number of pictures to be defined.

2. *Riddlemania* (Multiple Meanings). Present riddles to the students and have them explain the humor in each riddle.

3. *Word Search* (Figurative Language). Cultivate abstract thinking with lessons on choosing descriptive words. Begin with the concrete, and help the student to move on to more abstract conceptions. A hummingbird may be described as "green," "a blur of color," or "a tiny helicopter."

4. *Sense-Able Lessons* (Figurative Language). Use sensory experiences to stimulate students' use of descriptive language. Bring objects for seeing, tasting, feeling, hearing, and smelling, and compile a list of students' verbal reactions.

5. *Explain That* (Figurative Language). Discuss common idioms in class. Help students to discover the connection between the literal and figurative meanings. These examples can start the list:

   — She had two left feet. (Two left feet would cause one to be awkward.)
   — He was on pins and needles. (This would be an uncomfortable position which he would be eager to change.)
   — They were walking on eggs. (They were carefully trying to prevent a disagreeable situation.)

   Encourage the students to add other idioms to the list.

6. *Measure* (Space and Time Relationships). Measure objects in the classroom and make a bulletin board that tells that the door, for example, is 7 feet high, the desk is 3 feet wide, the dictionary is 8 inches by 10 inches, and the room is 8 yards long. State equivalents in feet and inches when applicable. Discuss how many miles it is from school to familiar places. This exercise will help students understand relative sizes and distances. Use the metric system only in areas where it is widely used.

7. *Calendar* (Space and Time Relationships). Provide sheets of paper marked in blocks for a calendar. Show students how to label the month, the days of the week, and the individual dates for that month. Then direct each student to choose personally important events for that month and write them on the spaces for the appropriate days. Events might include church, visit to friends, birthday party, spelling test, shopping, movie, piano lesson, scout meeting, or other activities. This should help students to learn to anticipate and prepare for coming events.

8. *Fables* (Cause/Effect Relationships). Read fables or stories with strong morals to the group; discuss the outcome of each. Help students to remember the events that caused the story ending.

9. *Because* (Cause/Effect Relationships). Suggest causes to the students and ask them to imagine possible effects. You might begin with these causes:

| | |
|---|---|
| The wind blew hard. | The shoes were too small. |
| He drove fast. | The wood got wet. |
| She took him a cake. | The price of oil went up. |

## 29.  MORPHOLOGY

DETECTION                    This may be a special skill need of students who

- Use comparatives and superlatives inconsistently or incorrectly
- Use -er and -est endings on irregular forms
- Omit final s on plural nouns when needed; add when not needed
- Omit final s on active verbs
- Have difficulty with subject-verb agreement in number
- Continue to use me as a subject pronoun after age 4
- Incorrectly use pronouns when two are combined by and
- Use pronouns inconsistently in other constructions
- Overuse present active or present progressive tense
- Appear confused about the stated time of action

*Description*      • *Comparatives:* Students may have difficulty in understanding and using the adjectives or adverbs which denote comparison between two objects (comparative form) and comparison among more than two objects (superlative form). They also sometimes have difficulty understanding which adjectives and adverbs do not require the -er and -est endings. • *Number:* Some students have not mastered irregular plural nouns or agreement in number between subjects and verbs. They may say, "Two bird fly away," and later, "I saw some mens in the yard." • *Case and Gender:* When children begin to talk, they often speak of themselves using me as in, "Me want to go." Children who continue to use this form after the age of 4 give warning that they will not learn correct use of pronouns easily. They appear to prefer the objective case of all pronouns using them exclusively. • *Tense, Aspect, Mood:* Some students have difficulty comprehending verb tense (past, present, future), aspect (completed, habitual, repetitive), and mood (indicative, imperative, subjunctive).

*Special Problems*      • *Comparatives:* Students who have a history of difficulties with language are likely to use incorrect morphological endings. Comparisons may be too abstract for them to learn easily. • *Number:* Some mentally handicapped and immature students display difficulty with subject-verb agreement. They may still be at the stage of concentrating on the content of the word without noticing the variation in the ending, like many normal 3- or 4- year-olds. Older students who come from homes where nonstandard English is spoken are likely to adopt what they have heard. • *Case and Gender:* Some students are slow to learn all aspects of oral language. Their social environment may model incorrect usage, except for *I*, *she*, and *he* as subjects. Informal oral conversation often contains pronoun usage that is incorrect but accepted by many groups. Incorrect use of *who* for *whom* is common, and few students feel confident they have chosen the correct pronoun even after consideration. Students must assimilate and coordinate conflicting information from home and school. • *Tense, Aspect, Mood:* Understanding or using verb phrases denoting future or past completed action requires a level of competence in sequencing words that students may not have achieved. Students need a clear understanding of relative time, but may be confused by time and space relationships.

*Implications*      • *Comparatives:* Using incorrect forms, such as *mostest*, *bestest*, or *beautifulest*, marks the speaker as immature or uneducated. This perception creates both academic and social problems and certainly interferes with success in most situations. • *Number:* Student who do not master correct usage of the final s will usually be regarded as speaking substandard English. They may have problems with reading and writing skills in school, and will definitely have difficulty entering the job market and interviewing for employment. • *Case and Gender:* Correct pronoun usage should be taught gradually, beginning with *I*, *he*, *she*, and *we* as the subjects of sentences. Diagraming sentences help students who are visually oriented. • *Tense, Aspect, Mood:* Inability to understand and use tense markers limits the efficiency of communication. Teachers should continually help students become more familiar with verb phrases.

**CORRECTION**

Modify these strategies to meet students' learning needs.

1. *Class Act* (Comparatives). Relate a simple story that tells of 3 boys (tall, taller, tallest) who go fishing and get wet (wetter, wettest) while catching fish (big, bigger, biggest); their mother puts on an apron and fixes soup and salad for them. As you tell the story, give the first adjective or adverb, and then point to the group to supply the comparative and superlative forms. Incorporate additional comparatives into the story, such as fast, tiny, red, round, sour, sweet, hot, juicy, pretty, good, and sleepy.

2. *Clap for S* (Number). Teach the students to listen for the plural *s* by playing a previously prepared audiotape. Direct the students to clap for each sentence that contains a plural noun ending in *s*. Mix sentences that do and do not contain plural nouns:

| | | |
|---|---|---|
| The cats drank milk. | I want some juice. | Put the cards away. |
| The horse ran away. | The books are there. | She saw the stars. |

3. *Two B or Not Two B* (Number). Collect two of each of the following items:

| | | | |
|---|---|---|---|
| block | basket (tiny) | box (tiny) | balloon |
| bead | bear (tiny) | bone (toy) | bell |
| button | brush (small) | ball (small) | bean |

Tell each student in turn to give you block or blocks or any of the other items. Direct the student to use both hands to get more than one.

4. *Cover It Up* (Case and Gender). Write sentences on the chalkboard with both a name and a blank in either the nominative or objective case. The student is to fill in the correct pronoun. Give choices: *I/me, they/them,* and so forth. Using the sample sentence Jane and _____ went to the store," illustrate how each nominative pronoun will fit, changing the order of Jane and pronoun for *he, she, they,* and *we.* Repeat using pronouns in the objective case.

5. *Tense Out* (Tense, Aspect, Mood) . Teach or test mastery of the three principal parts of verbs — present tense, past tense, and past participle — with a chart with three labelled columns. Write different verb forms on 3″ × 5″ cards. Mix the cards and direct the student to place the cards in the correct category. This activity can be performed by the entire class, a small group, or pairs of students.

6. *Mood Ring* (Tense, Aspect, Mood). Develop a question sequence for students to follow to determine when to use subjunctive mood:

| | |
|---|---|
| Sentence: | If I was President of the United States, I'd sleep until noon. |
| Student asks: | Am I President? |
| Answer: | No, therefore I have to use *were.* |

## 30.  SYNTAX

DETECTION

This may be a special skill need of students who

- Do not understand actor-object reversal in passive sentences
- Do not use sentence order to determine direct or indirect object
- Do not understand relationship of clauses to noun and verb
- Use run-on and incomplete sentences in conversation
- Lose the thought in long sentences with clauses
- Exhibit confusion concerning actor and object of verb
- Use statements with rising end inflection as questions
- Do not ask or answer simple reporter questions

*Description*

• *Sentence Transformation:* Some students are comfortable with subject-verb-object word order but baffled by sentence transformations. A passive-voice sentence, such as "The man was seen by the lady," may be scanned as "Man seen lady." Sentences with relative clauses and indirect objects may add more confusion. • *Complex Sentences:* Most normal children can produce well-formed sentences by around 3 or 4 years of age and comprehend higher-level linguistic constructions sometime between the ages of 5 and 10. When sentence forms deviate markedly from simple subject, verb, and object phrases, students may guess at the meaning without understanding the relationships among the words of the sentence. They may have particular trouble with oral sentences, which they must decode immediately, since the discourse is continuing and they cannot stop to study an unusual structure. • *Reporter Questions:* One of the principal functions of language is to allow us to acquire information by questioning. Normal 3-year-olds can exhaust any adult with their persistent inquiries: What's that? Why? The use of *who, when, where,* and *how* comes later in a child's language development and appears to be more difficult. The ability to respond to any of the *wh* questions appears to require more expertise in manipulating concepts and may develop even later.

*Special Problems*

• *Sentence Transformation:* Students who have difficulty in this area acquire sentence formulation rules in the same order as typical students but much later. These students have difficulty both in understanding what they hear and read and in formulating what they will say and write. • *Complex Sentences:* Students may be slow to learn to produce a complete simple sentence and may continue to use disjointed phrases to impart information that must be clarified, expanded, or qualified. Adults in their homes may use only simple sentence constructions; therefore, students may come to school having little experience with complex sentences. • *Reporter Questions:* Children whose families are unresponsive to their questioning may abandon their early attempts to gather information in that way early on. When parents respond, "Who is that?" to the child's "What that?" and then follow with "That is the doctor," they are teaching correct use of the *wh* words.

*Implications*

• *Sentence Transformation:* As students progress in school, they may learn the content but become entangled in the language of oral or written discussion. Often they follow demonstrations, pictures, and other illustrations, only to fail when asked to tell or write about the experience later. • *Complex Sentences:* Some students have difficulty recalling information if they were unsure of the meaning of the sentences they originally heard. They may not be able to mentally repeat the message to themselves (reauditorize) because they cannot reproduce the unfamiliar syntactical structures. These students will need more time to process complex sentences and frequently will not be able to communicate the information accurately. • *Reporter Questions:* Repeated questioning helps children focus on the information desired. As students become more proficient in using language, their command of questioning and answering increases.

CORRECTION

Modify these strategies to meet students' learning needs.

1. *Transform* (Sentence Transformation). Illustrate several transformations using this sentence: "Kenny drove the car. Did Kenny drive the car? Kenny did not drive the car. The car was driven by Kenny." Give simple declarative sentences for students to transform in turn: first, question form; second, negative statement; and third, passive form.

2. *Mix-Up* (Complex Sentences). Write a complex sentence on the chalkboard with the words in scrambled order; have groups of students work out the correct order.

3. *Combine* (Complex Sentences). Demonstrate combining several short sentences into one longer sentence containing all the same information:
   - Kristina went to the store. Kristina was hungry. It was raining.
   - M.J. was tall. M.J. went to school. M.J. hit his head on the door.
   - Mel is a football player. Mel plays the piano. He is big.
   - The book was Gloria's. The book fell in the mud. Gloria was sad.

4. *Expand* (Reporter Questions). Show the student how to expand a simple sentence by including *when, where, how,* and *why* an action takes place and *who* or *what* is involved. Try this simple sentence: A man gave his dog a bone. Add *when:* yesterday; *where:* downtown; *who:* owner of a store; *how:* by tossing it up in the air; *why:* the dog was hungry. (Yesterday, downtown, a man who was the owner of a store gave his dog, who was hungry, a bone by tossing it up in the air.)

5. *Who Did What?* (Reporter Questions). Diagram some complex sentences on the chalkboard to provide students who cannot identify the basic sentence with a system of organization. Then give students a list of complex sentences with directions to write beside them (a) who or what, (b) did (verb) and (c) what (direct object, phrase, or predicate nominative).

6. *Ask It All* (Reporter Questions). Display an action picture and encourage the students to ask questions about it. If they are reluctant, help by asking: Do you know where they are? Do you know what is in the box? Do you know why they are doing that? Have students frame the questions.

7. *Interview* (Reporter Questions). Let older students practice interviewing a person for a story. Another student could play a famous person, having first been prepared to answer factual questions correctly and given some freedom in responding to opinion questions. This could be an excellent social studies activity.

8. *Reverse Quiz* (Reporter Questions). Play Jeopardy, in which you will supply the answers and students will ask the appropriate question. Demonstrate with 2–3 easy examples, then try these answers for starters:

| | |
|---|---|
| She was the first female astronaut. | It boils at 212° F. |
| 911 | It's called Independence Day. |
| It means "Terrible Lizard." | She wrote *Gone with the Wind.* |
| The only state that was a Republic. | A dictionary. |

## 31.   WORD FINDING

DETECTION

This may be a special skill need of students who

- Reword and break the rhythm of speech
- Use incorrect words in sentences; have a limited vocabulary
- Cannot produce the word for a known concept
- Make false starts and reword often when giving information
- Cannot spontaneously group into obvious categories
- Use synonyms poorly or not at all in speech and written work
- Cannot sort in more than one way

*Description*

• *Circumlocution:* Most of us use circumlocution to some degree. The word itself means "talking around" and describes a speaker's efforts to complete a comment when a specific word is elusive. A child may say, "I went out to the big water where the waves are and the sand" because he or she does not know the word ocean. • *Word Association:* Some students' speech is filled with general words such as *thing, that,* and *something,* and space fillers like *you know, and then,* and *uhm.* They often resort to gestures to clarify their meaning or may abandon the effort, disguising their failure with distracting behavior, such as laughing or coughing. • *Conceptual Categorization:* This ability involves recognizing similar attributes of objects and people that are not identical. This developmental ability is related to level of intelligence.

*Special Problems*

• *Circumlocution:* Students with limited vocabularies often use circumlocutions to complete communication. The condition is more acute when a cerebral vascular accident or stroke has affected the speech and language areas of the brain. The speaker can be almost unable to produce a connected thought because of the number of circumlocutions used. • *Word Association:* Conceptual knowledge appears to be intact, since students with difficulties in this area will often describe the appearance and use of an object but be unable to produce the word. Older students or adults may be quite specific about the attributes, naming other members of its category and describing how it is different. They may even be able to name the beginning sound and the number of syllables in the word. • *Conceptual Categorization:* The child who has difficulty understanding and making abstractions will usually experience problems in categorizing. Limited vocabulary may stem from the inability to recognize commonalities in objects, words, expressions, and feelings.

*Implications*

• *Circumlocution:* The student who exhibits frequent circumlocutions needs help to build vocabulary so that communication and cognition can keep pace with experiential learning. This behavior may indicate a learning disability in the area of language, with specific problems in recalling words and organizing concepts. Teachers should concentrate on strengthening stimuli, diminishing distractions, focusing the student's attention, and providing external motivation. • *Word Association:* Students with difficulty in this area need more time to complete written assignments requiring that they structure responses with their own vocabulary. They will perform poorly when speaking spontaneously in class. They will have difficulty with activities that require verbal fluency and proficiency. • *Conceptual Categorization:* Students who are unable to create a conceptual scheme for categorization will experience great difficulty in academic subjects and problem solving in general. They may have difficulty adapting to unfamiliar social situations because they cannot find similarities with previous experiences.

CORRECTION

Modify these strategies to meet students' learning needs.

1. *In the Room* (Circumlocution). To help students retrieve words efficiently, ask individual students to name as many items in an area around school as possible during 1 minute. After time is up, discuss other items they might have included. Gradually increase the time so that the students can name more items.

2. *Thesaurus* (Circumlocution). Pair students up, taking care not to assign two students who have word finding difficulties as buddies. Each student should note the other's circumlocutions throughout the day. During a designated class period, buddies will use a thesaurus to locate synonyms that could have been used. Have the students write elusive words on a 3″ × 5″ card with 3 synonyms for each, and then learn and review the words.

3. *Pizza Pie* (Word Association). Prepare a game spinner with a category name in each wedge. Discuss the categories with students and guide them to name at least 3 items in each. The student must name a member of the category on which the spinner stops. Use these categories, or subdivide for more capable students: food (fruit, vegetables, meat); animals (mammals, fish, insects); plants (flowers, trees, field crops); or cities (in our state, out of our state, outside the country); famous people (scientists, cartoon animals, actresses, politicians).

4. *Shape, Size, Color Group* (Conceptual Categorizations). Arrange 3 blue squares of graduated sizes and 3 red circles of graduated sizes on the table. Demonstrate that the objects can be grouped by color or by size. Mix the shapes and tell students to group them in 2 different ways. Reinforce correct categorizations; reteach if the performance was incorrect. Add 3 yellow triangles of graduated sizes to the array. If students have been successful with the red and blue shapes, tell them to categorize the objects 3 ways. If they have not been successful, demonstrate and have them imitate. Add more shapes and colors.

5. *Exploring Categories* (Conceptual Categorizations). Present pictures of a giraffe and a dog. Explore similar attributes of the animals with the child and write them down. Categorize as *animals*. Add a picture of a tiger. Check each attribute listed for the other 2 animals to test whether a tiger is an animal. Follow the same procedure with pictures of other animals. When the child has mastered this task, present a picture of a tree. Go through the animal attributes so the child can determine that the tree does not have them and therefore is not an animal. Repeat this exercise with numerous categories of concrete objects, such as flowers, foods, money, balls, toys, candy, and anything else the child finds motivating.

6. *Abstract Categorization* (Conceptual Categorizations). When the child has mastered categorizing concrete objects, introduce more abstract concepts, such as feelings, democratic ideals, or entrepreneurship, which are more difficult to categorize.

## 32.  SPECIAL LANGUAGE PROBLEMS

DETECTION          This may be a special skill need of students who

- Repeat others' comments verbatim
- Repeat statements made earlier by others
- Imitate inflections as well as words
- Do not refer to themselves as *I* or *me*
- Began talking later than expected
- Do not learn new words easily
- Use only a few words or phrases for communication

*Description*          • *Echolalia:* Echolalia marks a normal stage of language development in the young child. It usually occurs after the child can produce a few functional words and has tuned in to speech as an interesting and desirable activity. The child's articulation is fairly consistent, although often imprecise, and there appears to be satisfaction in trying new sound combinations. Parents are sometimes startled by the accurate reproduction of familiar phrases — "Thank you!" "No, no, Barry," "I love you" — complete with original inflections. This is a fleeting stage for most children, who soon develop enough vocabulary and rudimentary understanding of syntactical rules to string together their own words. Some individuals, however, continue to echo what they hear and seldom produce any words spontaneously. • *Delayed Language:* This term describes language that follows the normal developmental pattern but at a slower rate. Speech is the oral expression of language and is a learned skill. Most normal children have acquired a basic understanding of the language system and intelligible, functional speech by the age of 4 or 5 without being formally taught.

*Special Problems*          • *Echolalia:* Some central nervous system disorder may have affected the echolalic child's ability to decode and encode language. These children usually do not produce their first words at the expected time but begin to repeat a few single words only after much urging from parents. They may repeat "Mama" in what appears to be a normal fashion but say it to any adult. If they develop a strong interest in an object or activity, that interest can be used to elicit vocalization. A parent can ask, "Do you want a cookie?" and the echolalic child will respond, "You want a cookie?" The child indicates that he or she wants a cookie with gestures but cannot state that desire. The child's speech reception seems to be adequate and the phonological system working well, since the words are usually clear. • *Delayed Language:* Delayed language may result from organic dysfunction, such as hearing or visual impairment, but often a specific cause cannot be identified. Problems such as central nervous system impairment, mental retardation, behavior disorder, social or economic deprivation, frail physical health, or immaturity, occurring separately or in combination, impede the normal development of language.

*Implications*          • *Echolalia:* The echolalic student needs repeated exposure to simple activities that involve the natural use of language. Sentences should be short and simple, using vocabulary related to immediate objects and activities. • *Delayed Language:* Obviously, different problems require somewhat different facilitation techniques, but the primary goal is to help the child learn to speak as effectively as possible, since the ability to communicate is a critical aspect of human behavior. Teachers can provide experiences, activities, and remedial strategies to encourage and nurture the child's developing speech and language.

CORRECTION

Modify these strategies to meet students' learning needs.

1. *Say This* (Echolalia). When students repeat a greeting verbatim, as in "Hello, Tom," say, "No, Tom, you say — 'Hello, Ms. Edwards'," dividing the words of your direction from what they are to say with a pause. In the same way, teach them to say, "I'm fine," in response to the query, "How are you?"

2. *Guess What?* (Echolalia). When students want something but do not know how to express the desire, try to determine what they want by questioning: "Do you want a pencil? Do you want paper?" Offer various items until the student indicates that you have guessed correctly. At that point, provide the appropriate sentence by saying, "You say — 'I want a pencil.' Now you try it." Do not withhold the item from the frustrated student, but repeat the sentence and praise any response.

3. *No Parroting* (Echolalia). Echolalic students often memorize commercials heard on TV or radio and deliver them with amazing accuracy. Resist the temptation to have the student perform this verbal trick for others. Provide sentences with communicative value to the student, for example, "My name is Melissa Rebecca Griffin. My parents are Ellen and Mark Griffin. We live at 415 Lakeshore Drive, San Antonio, Texas. My telephone number is 835–2126."

4. *Bingo* (Delayed Language). Prepare 8″ × 8″ cardboard cards by dividing them with a colored marker into 16 squares. In each square, mount a colored picture of an item whose name you wish to teach. Teach new vocabulary associated with holidays, study units (kitchen items, vacation trips, seasons of the year), or spelling words. Call out words from a master list, and proceed according to the rules of Bingo. The student who calls "Bingo" must name all 4 objects in the completed row.

5. *Pick a Picture* (Delayed Language). Prepare groups of pictures from magazines depicting people, chairs, cars, dogs, babies, hands, or other frequently photographed objects. Display a group of 8–10 pictures and instruct students to locate the object you describe. For example, you might instruct them to choose the picture of the greasy hand, the hand wearing a glove, or the hand with painted fingernails. Be sure that only 1 picture will satisfy the description.

6. *Colors and Shapes* (Delayed Language). Give the students cardboard triangles, circles, and squares in red, blue, green, and yellow. Spread them out on a table and instruct them to move the objects according to directions such as these: Put the red circle on the blue square, put 2 yellow squares on a green triangle, put 3 green circles over the yellow triangle, or put a blue square under a green circle.

7. *Group It* (Delayed Language). Use 3″ × 5″ cards with pictures pasted on one end. Choose 1 from each category — food, clothing, toys, plants, animals, furniture (or things in the house). Demonstrate what students are to do by placing a card on separate lines of a card chart. Then students draw cards from a stack and place them on the correct category line. It may help to talk about things we eat, things we wear, and so on.

## 33. NONVERBAL COMMUNICATION

DETECTION

This may be a special skill need of students who

- Use or respond to variations of pitch, duration, loudness, and rhythm inappropriately
- Response inappropriately or not at all to kinesics
- Do not use kinesics or use them inappropriately
- Use or respond to distance messages inappropriately or not at all

*Description*

• *Prosody:* Prosody is the voicing patterns of loudness, pitch, duration, and rhythm, which combine with verbal utterances to express such emotions as love, happiness, shame, fear, sarcasm, and the like. Prosodic features contribute to communication by confirming or contradicting the spoken message. • *Kinesics:* Kinesics may be described as nonlinguistic cues that facilitate communication, such as gestures, facial expressions, head and body movements, and posture. Gestures, arbitrary movements interpreted on the basis of convention, may be culture specific. Facial expressions and head and body movements can enhance or even replace verbal communication. Posture, or body position, also contributes to communication by confirming, contradicting, or neutralizing verbal messages. • *Proxemics:* Proxemics describes the distance between speaker and audience or between communicators. The relative level of the communicators is also important. The school principal who stands during a faculty meeting while the faculty is seated is displaying a sign of dominance; the principal who conducts the meeting from a seated position transmits an aura of collaboration. The distance may remain the same, but the tilt of the head needed to communicate changes.

*Special Problems*

Inability to understand and use prosody, kinesics, and proxemics may originate in low intellectual functioning, impaired hearing, impaired affect.

*Implications*

• *Prosody:* Students who do not understand meaning conveyed by prosodic features in oral communication invariably will have difficulty in academic pursuits and in interpersonal relationships. Much classroom learning depends on a combination of the written and spoken word. When students do not fully understand or misunderstand oral communication, they learn poorly, if at all. In interpersonal relationships, the major form of communication is the spoken word. Individuals who interpret speech without regard for the way prosody confirms or contradicts an utterance will experience social difficulties. Similarly, the student who does not use prosodic features in oral communication in the classroom or in social situations is not likely to succeed in either arena. • *Kinesics:* Lack of ability to understand and use gestures, facial expressions, and body posture is likely to impair academic achievement and interpersonal relationships. Students who cannot accurately interpret a teacher's folded arms, stiff upper body, and tapping foot may be unaware that the teacher deems their behavior unacceptable. The student who asserts, "Yes, I would like to play the game," but sits slumped over with hanging head conveys a very different message. • *Proxemics:* Like other nonverbal means of communication, proxemics serves to confirm, contradict, enhance, or diminish oral communication. The student who does not understand and use proxemics may have difficulty in academic areas and in interpersonal relationships. The adult is likely to have employment and personal problems.

CORRECTION

Modify these strategies to meet students' learning needs.

1. *Deciphering Video Puzzles* (Prosody). Videotape a short appropriate action scene from a TV situation comedy. Audiotape 2 versions of short phrases from the scene: one version using prosodic features that appear in the videotape, and one with prosody that will result in a different meaning. Play enough of the videotape for students to understand the story. When the phrase you have audiotaped is shown, press the mute button. Play the 2 versions of the audiotape and ask students to select the appropriate version. If they choose appropriately, praise them and point out why the choice was appropriate. Also discuss why the other selection would have been inappropriate. If students make an inappropriate selection, explain why the other selection is better. Replay the scene so they can see why.

2. *Fancy Faces* (Kinesics). Take individual photographs of male and female faces whose expressions convey emotions you want to teach, such as happy, puzzled, loving, forgiving, proud, fearful, surprised, relieved, and so on. Display both sets of photographs and instruct students to match the male and female faces that express the same emotion.

3. *Pigeonholing* (Kinesics). Prepare labels for the facial expressions in Activity 2. Students will attach the label to the proper facial expression.

4. *Cartoon Bubbles* (Kinesics). When students have mastered Activities 2 and 3, give them blank cartoon bubbles in which to create a phrase or sentence that the person in the photograph might say. For example, a student might write, "I'm sad because I lost my new pencil" in the bubble to be placed on the photograph with the sad expression. A variation on this activity is for the teacher to write the sentence so the student could simply match the sentence to the appropriate facial expression.

5. *Barrier Absent/Barrier Present* (Proxemics). Barriers demand distance, give an air of formality to discussion, and provide a mechanism for self-protection. Barrier-free interactions indicate openness, trust, and intimacy. Locate or create miniplays whose dialogues dictate whether the characters should erect barriers or not. Use dolls and dollhouse furnishings in the initial stages of learning if students have difficulty adopting this concept. Once they master the concept, the students should enact the miniplays themselves.

# L ANGUAGE SAMPLERS

The samplers on the next five pages provide the teacher with activities that can be easily copied and distributed. Adjust the activity for skill level or to provide additional practice using the variations described here.

**7.1** **Semantics — Multiple Meanings.** This sampler for use in Skill 28, Semantics, demonstrates that many words have more than one meaning. Direct students to use a dictionary to look up the meanings of the words and write a brief definition under the appropriate heading. Some of the sample words cannot be used as all three parts of speech. You can extend this activity by having the students write sentences to demonstrate their knowledge of the different meanings of the words.

**7.2** **Comparatives.** This activity accompanies Skill 29, Morphology, for practice in understanding and using comparatives and superlatives. The activity requires students to examine and evaluate the attributes of the objects presented. To vary this activity, instruct students to come up with their own objects to evaluate for "softness," "smelliness," and so on. For nonreaders, substitute pictures of the objects.

**7.3** **Syntax — Written Expression.** This sampler accompanies Skill 30, Syntax. Use it to help students construct complex sentences by guiding them to answer certain questions. Begin with a simple sentence and answer 1, 2, 3, 4, or 5 of the reporter questions. The student then writes (or says) the expanded sentence with the words in proper order. Students can combine answers given in the "WH bank" or generate their own answers, individually or as a cooperative learning exercise.

**7.4** **Spider Webbing.** Use this sampler to teach categorizations and associations in conjunction with Skill 31, Word Finding, or as a visual outline for students who prefer pictures to standard outlines in writing compositions. An example of this semantic map or web appears at the bottom of the page. Copy the top part of the page for repeated student use. Begin with concrete objects for ease of learning. Write a word in the center circle. In each circle radiating from the center, write one attribute that describes the central word. The student may use this single web for writing a paragraph about the central word. Create a second web using a central word in some way related to the first central word. Again enter attributes of the central word in the circles radiating from the center. Compare the two webs. If there is at least one similar attribute, then the two webs can be associated.

**7.5** **Best Friends.** This sampler, to accompany Skill 33, Nonverbal Communication, illustrates some aspects of kinesics and proxemics. Nonreaders may easily complete the activity by answering orally. A variation of the paper/pencil activity is to position students to match the pictures and conduct the activity "live and in person." Focus discussion on body positions and the distance between the people.

Name _____

# ✸ SEMANTICS—MULTIPLE MEANINGS ✸

|  | Noun | Verb | Adjective |
|---|---|---|---|
| state | 1 of 50 in the U.S. | to tell | richly equipped |
| trim | a decoration | to adorn; to cut | neat; orderly |
| diner | | | |
| short | | | |
| turn | | | |
| pink | | | |
| coin | | | |
| phone | | | |
| beat | | | |
| suit | | | |
| light | | | |
| pose | | | |
| bear | | | |
| print | | | |
| glasses | | | |
| plum | | | |
| tax | | | |

# ◀IIII **COMPARATIVES** IIII▶

| | | | |
|---|---|---|---|
| Which is the softest? | (pillow) | rock | scissors |
| Which is the smelliest? | cookie | garbage | lemon |
| Which is the slickest? | grass | ice | sidewalk |
| Which is the flattest? | dollar bill | plate | quarter |
| Which is the brownest? | cocoa | straw | wood |
| Which is the thickest? | lemonade | milk | oil |

**Arrange these in order according to the instructions.**

| | **2** | **1** | **3** | **4** |
|---|---|---|---|---|
| smallest to largest | bird | bub | dog | horse |
| largest to smallest | cow | elephant | mouse | pig |
| loudest to quietest | doorbell | fire alarm | whisper | |
| shortest to tallest | broom | match | telephone pole | |
| hottest to coldest | apple | boiling water | ice cream | |
| smoothest to roughest | corduroy | cotton | silk | wool |

# SYNTAX—WRITTEN EXPRESSION ✍

| Sentence core | When | Where | How | Why | Who/What |
|---|---|---|---|---|---|
| The men talked | last week | upstairs | quietly | to resolve | that got lost |
|  |  |  |  |  |  |
|  |  |  |  |  |  |
|  |  |  |  |  |  |
|  |  |  |  |  |  |
|  |  |  |  |  |  |
|  |  |  |  |  |  |
|  |  |  |  |  |  |
|  |  |  |  |  |  |
|  |  |  |  |  |  |

**Sentence core**
A boy threw a ball
A girl dove
The cat jumped
The men cooked

| When | Where | How | Why | Who/What |
|---|---|---|---|---|
| last week | in England | slowly | it was old | who was the teacher's child |
| at 1:00 | at school | with a grin | it could grow | who/that got lost in town |
| after lunch | out West | with difficulty | they were sad | who/that had long hair |
| Tuesday | in the yard | like a flash | it was cold | who/that was famous |
| in April | upstairs | without a word | the bell rang | who/that weighed 100 pounds |

# SPIDER WEBBING

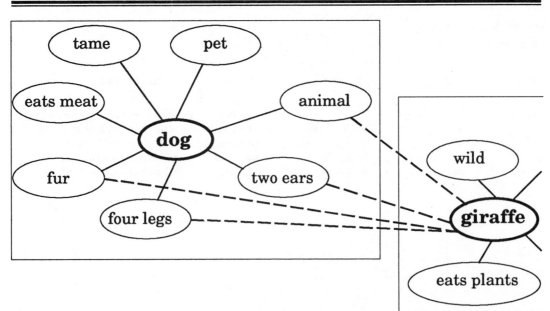

Name _____

# BEST FRIENDS

**A**                    **B**                    **C**

Which picture reminds you of best friends?        A        B        C

Why did you pick that picture?_____

_____

Cut out the pictures and arrange them so that the people look like best friends.

**PASTE HERE**

A                            A

B                            B

C                            C

# REFLECTIONS

1. Words with multiple meanings are stumbling blocks for anyone learning the English language, child or adult. List five words that have multiple meanings in common usage in your region and give three to five meanings for each. Compose sentences that illustrate each meaning and then compare sentences with a peer.

2. Figurative language is used freely in daily conversation, but the expressions may have become so familiar that they are not readily recognized as figures of speech. It is easy to recognize figurative language in poetry; however, the meaning is not always immediately apparent. Select a poem, note the figures of speech used, and explain them to the class.

3. The concepts of space and time are troublesome for all children, but especially for students with learning or language disorders. Observe a kindergarten or first-grade class early in the school day to note what activities the teacher presents to help the children develop concepts of space and time. Observe a special classroom at the same time of day and note whether the teacher uses similar activities.

4. The age and developmental level of a student must be considered when planning corrective activities. Review the strategies for Skill 28, Cause and Effect, and choose one to use with an 8-year-old student and one to use with a high school student with learning or language impairments. Explain the differences and similarities of your choices and why you selected them.

5. A great deal of teaching takes place within the normal activities of the school day. Think of five ways to incorporate the teaching of prepositions into opening exercises, lunchtime, art or music period, or playground time for each of these grade levels: first, fifth, and tenth. Consider if the activities are appropriate for the different ages and if they will be as effective as traditional drills.

6. Semantics, morphology, and syntax together are the vehicle for verbal language. After briefly reviewing the discussions in this section, explain how these three areas interact in connected discourse and how difficulties in any of the areas can impede communication.

7. Certain morphological forms are used incorrectly so often that students may hear the incorrect usage much more frequently than the correct forms. As you observe in classrooms, note the number of times morphological errors occur as students recite or talk spontaneously. If you were the teacher, how would you counteract this reinforcement of poor grammar? Refer to Skill 29.

8. Teaching the comprehension and use of complex sentence structure to students who are language-impaired may require modifying strategies used with most students. After reading the discussion in Skill 30, obtain a teacher's manual for a seventh-grade language textbook and see what activities are suggested for teaching complex sentences. Decide how you could expand or modify those activities to make them more appropriate for a student with specific language difficulties.

9. Questioning is an important way to gather information, yet the art of questioning is seldom directly taught. Choose one of the Correction activities for Skill 30 to use with a group of children as a game. Note the type of difficulties they exhibit and make up a new activity or modify one of the suggested ones to answer the need you perceive.

10. Word-finding problems affect most people at times, but some people have severe difficulty. Discuss the possible basis for this disability. Tell how you would attempt to help a second-grader and an adult.

11. A language delay and a language disorder differ; review the special language problems in this chapter and explain these differences.

12. A great deal of human communication is nonverbal. Observe a first-grade classroom, and list kinesic and proxemic messages sent by the teacher and by five students. Repeat your observation in an eighth-grade class to compile another list of messages. Be prepared to demonstrate any specific nonverbal message for your peers.

13. A number of authors offer suggestions for recognizing and remediating language disabilities. Compare and contrast the information presented in these sources with the material in Chapter 7.

Bain, A.M., Bailet, L.L., & Moats, L.C. (Eds.) (1991). *Written language disorders: Theory into practice.* Austin, TX: Pro-Ed.

Bates, E., Bretherton, I., & Snyder, L. (1988). *From first words to grammar.* Cambridge, MA: Cambridge University Press.

Bauer, A. M., & Shea, T. M. (1989). *Teaching exceptional students in your classroom. Boston:* Allyn and Bacon.

Bernstein, D. K., & Tiegerman, E. (Eds.) (1989). *Language and communication disorders in children* (2nd ed.). Columbus, OH: Merrill.

Gleason, J. B. (1989). *The development of language* (2nd ed.). Columbus, OH: Merrill.

Gudykunst, W., & Kim, Y.Y. (1992). *Communicating with strangers: An approach to intercultural communication* (2nd ed.). New York: McGraw-Hill.

Haynes, W., Moran, M., & Pindzola, R. (1990). *Communication disorders in the classroom.* Dubuque, IA: Kendall/Hunt.

Lahey, M. (1988). *Language disorders and language development.* New York: Macmillan.

Mercer, C. D., & Mercer, A. R. (1989). *Teaching students with learning problems* (3rd ed.). Columbus, OH: Merrill.

Morris, D. (1977). *Manwatching: A field guide to human behavior.* New York: Harry N. Abrams.

Nelson, C.D. (1991). *Practical procedures for children with language disorders.* Austin, TX: Pro-Ed.

Owens, R. E., Jr. (1992). *Language development: An introduction* (3rd ed.). New York: Merrill/Macmillan.

Polloway, E. A., Patton, J.R., Payne, J. S., & Payne, R. A. (1989). *Strategies for teaching learners with special needs* (4th ed.). Columbus, OH: Merrill.

Rakes, T. A., & Choate, J. A. (1989). *Language arts: Detecting and correcting special needs.* Boston: Allyn and Bacon.

Schiefelbusch, R. L. (1986). *Language competence: Assessment and intervention.* San Diego: College Hill Press.

Taylor, J. S. (1992). *Speech-language pathology services in the schools* (2nd ed.). Boston: Allyn and Bacon.

Thomas, P. J., & Carmack, F. F. (1990). *Speech and language: Detecting and correcting special needs.* Boston: Allyn and Bacon.

Wiig, E. H. (1989). *Steps to language competence: Developing metalinguistic strategies.* New York: Psychological Corporation.

Wilcox, M. J., & Campbell, P. H. (1988). *Communication programming from birth to three: A handbook for public school professionals.* San Diego: College Hill Press.

# Chapter EIGHT

## WRITTEN EXPRESSION: PROCESS AND PRODUCT

— *Thomas A. Rakes and Joyce S. Choate*

Written expression, often considered the most difficult of the language arts, is essential in nearly all subject areas. Competence in written expression depends to a great extent upon competence in listening, speaking, and reading. Writing experiences should be appropriately integrated throughout the curriculum, including in such subject areas as mathematics, social studies, science, and reading. Instruction in written expression, unlike in some other skills, should be integrated as a whole-language approach. Teachers should focus special attention on students who are non-native speakers of English or who come from a culturally diverse background.

## THE SKILLS OF WRITTEN EXPRESSION

While writing experiences should be integrated into all subject areas, three traditional subject areas are typically associated with improving written expression at the elementary level: language or English, spelling, and handwriting. Beyond the elementary level, these three areas generally fall under the single subject area of English. This chapter includes three main areas of specific skill improvement: written expression of ideas, written grammar, and writing across the curriculum. The latter section suggests ways to integrate writing with other subject areas as well as with learning experiences involving listening, speaking, and reading.

Since the 1970s writing instruction has shifted away from emphasizing grammar and correctness to a process-oriented approach focusing on content. For this reason this chapter begins with written expression of ideas. Instructional concerns involving grammar, sentence construction, punctuation, parts of speech, capitalization, and revising follow. Because written expression can be taught in conjunction with the other language arts as well as subject area content, the final segment of Chapter 8 involves writing across the curriculum. Information provided in Chapter 9 on spelling and handwriting should also be included when making decisions about writing instruction.

All aspects of writing, including grammar, are important. Without minimizing the mechanical skills, but considering developmental aspects of writing, teachers should provide students with a conceptual and experiential base in which they see generation of meaningful language. The writing process is closely connected with thinking and with the acquisition of reading, speaking, and listening skills. Written expression involves the process of generating, organizing, and expressing ideas. As a starting point, teachers encourage, guide, and support students as they use classroom experiences, good literature, subject area information, and the world around them as a basis from which they can draw ideas and inspiration. Once students feel confident about getting their ideas on paper, the process can be expanded to include more didactic instructional considerations such as grammar.

Written grammar, or mechanics, includes different types of sentences, parts of speech, word usage, capitalization, and punctuation. As presented here, these skills are emphasized during the writing process, but not as much, initially, as the generation of ideas. The writing process focuses on generating ideas through prewriting, then drafting, and then editing and rewriting, which require more mechanical skills. As a part of the refining process, aspects of written grammar are introduced, modeled, and applied to work previously generated by a class or a particular student. By beginning with generating ideas and then attending to grammar, spelling, and handwriting more directly, teachers are reflecting a philosophical stance on how students learn best. This view shifts the emphasis from the nuts and bolts of writing to generating ideas and constructing drafts before dealing specifically with grammar.

Spelling and handwriting, discussed in Chapter 9, should support and enhance writing, not inhibit its production. Unless handwriting and spelling are treated as a part of writing across the curriculum, free expression of ideas cannot become a reality for many students. This chapter presents ideas for detecting and correcting problems in the thinking, expressive process of writing.

Using writing to learn mathematics, health, or other subjects improves written expression in general and facilitates mastery of content area information. The final section in Chapter 8 includes suggestions for assisting students to use written expression in subject areas beyond specific writing lessons. Students must develop competence in writing ideas and responses in science, mathematics, health, reading, and other subjects. Teachers must provide both opportunity for and instruction in written expression, handwriting, and spelling to students as they study and learn about community helpers or the economy, giving proper assistance and expecting good writing in all subjects.

## DETECTION OF SPECIAL WRITING NEEDS

Written expression, when considered on the basis of volume or depth of ideas, is less precise and is often less valued than other curricular areas in the general performance of a specific group, grade, or category of students. Detection procedures involve both specific tests and observation of writing performance in daily assignments and other written products, regardless of the primary subject or skill involved. Assessment should focus first on the creative part of writing and then attend to the technical aspects.

### Formal Detection

Group standardized or formal tests currently offer little direction or depth in assessing written expression. Selected aspects of written expression are measured on some popular standardized tests such as the California Achievement Tests, The Iowa Test of Basic Skills, The Metropolitan Achievement Tests or The Sequential Tests of Educational Progress. The Educational Testing Service (ETS) offers competency tests that are scored using focused holistic procedures. Even these results are somewhat general, based on writing samples drawn from a limited period of time. For students in the elementary and middle grades, standardized tests generally test recognition skills or take limited samples of expressive responses. Several of these same standardized tests include recognition-level subtests of grammar or language usage. The subtest scores typically provide general information that may not be particularly helpful in planning individual intervention.

The clear message from the literature and writing experts is that written expression is best monitored and evaluated through informal assessment procedures.

## Informal Detection

Several procedures for assessing written expression are recommended and the results should be grouped into a portfolio of data on students' performance throughout the school year. By observing, analyzing, and recording students' performance as they write, teachers can identify needs in creative expression, organization, semantics and syntax, sentence formation, word choice, grammar, punctuation, and other mechanics of writing, as well as spelling and handwriting.

A teacher can evaluate a student's writing using holistic, primary-trait, or analytical scoring. Holistic scoring usually involves the use of five or six global considerations that can be adapted as students progress during the school year. In addition to teachers analyzing students' writing themselves, teachers can develop a three-to four-item response form for students to use for self-evaluation. Items such as these would be appropriate on a self-evaluation sheet:

— I proofread this paper for _____.
— I gave special attention to _____.
— I did the best job of _____.
— I need to work more on _____.

Have students complete the self-evaluation form and include it with the first draft of the paper.

A teacher could holistically evaluate a written product using items such as these:

_____ A recognizable beginning and ending can be found
_____ An overall theme or idea is reflected in the work
_____ A variety of descriptive words is used
_____ An overall order or sequence is apparent

The emphasis during holistic scoring is on the overall product, using general criteria. The criteria can be more focused depending on the type of writing being reviewed. When holistic scoring is focused, the evaluation is somewhat more specific. The results may describe the written performance in a category or level: high, low, meets expectations for this level, or some similar designation would be typical.

Unlike holistic scoring, primary-trait scoring evaluates the use of a single characteristic or trait instead of the overall writing performance. A writing sample might be evaluated for the appropriate use of summary statements, or proper punctuation, or some other specific aspect of written expression.

Analytical scoring evaluates several aspects of a writing sample, such as content, organization, sentence structure, grammar, punctuation, or use of thought units. When working with special students, conducting separate analyses of content and mechanics is particularly appropriate. Regardless of the evaluation format, both observations of students as they write and samples of their written products over a period of time should be included in the evaluation. Sample assignments, tests, and homework, specifically focused on written expression, as well as written responses from reading, science, social studies, and other lessons, should be evaluated and maintained in individual folders for review and comparison as the school year progresses.

The checklist in Figure 8.1 provides an assessment format and record form for monitoring student progress and identifying areas of written performance in which students might require intervention. In addition to the behaviors cited on the checklist, behaviors specific to a particular student can be noted in the blanks. Patterns of difficulties may suggest where corrective instruction should focus.

## SPECIAL POPULATIONS

Students do not always progress at the same rate or in the same sequence in learning to write. Special groups of students may experience difficulties more frequently or with more intensity than other groups. Detecting individual students' problems is crucial. However, knowledge of potential areas of weakness for particular groups may be helpful in the detection and correction process.

Written expression is difficult for many special learners. Students who have been exposed to limited English or little language stimulation at home, or who with identified disabilities may need highly structured, carefully paced intervention. Although students who are gifted or display behavioral disorders may experience isolated difficulties, they are less likely to exhibit multiple difficulties in written expression. However, corrective instruction should be based upon individual needs and monitored through analysis of an ongoing portfolio of written products.

## CORRECTION OF WRITTEN EXPRESSION SKILLS

For special learners, corrective instruction in written expression should begin with structured but brief exercises. Teachers should encourage students to generate ideas and put them in writing. Experiences that foster language development build skills and enhance students' appreciation of written expression as an integrated language process. Appropriate language and literature models are an integral part of language development. Perhaps the most critical principle for teaching written expression is emphasizing and nurturing the *process* of writing as the evolution of the written product through prewriting, drafting, and revising. Focusing on process emphasizes the thinking, holistic nature of writing.

Five of the instructional principles presented in Chapter 3, are especially important for guiding corrective instruction in written expression:

— Teach diagnostically
— Encourage cooperative learning (peer editing, sharing of products)
— Emphasize the relevance of each skill and concept
— Provide appropriate practice and generous review
— Integrate skills and concepts throughout the curriculum

Diagnostic teaching ensures that instruction addresses a student's developmental stage and interests. Cooperative-learning activities help students recognize written expression as a basic form of communication as they collaborate to write, edit, and share their work. Integrating instruction in writing across the curriculum permits students to generalize skills and demonstrate their content knowledge.

These instructional principles recur as themes in the strategies suggested for correcting special needs and problems in written expression. For instance,

FIGURE 8.1  /  **Checklist of Problems in Written Expression**

Use this checklist to analyze and record the written performance of individual students on informal and standardized tests or during classroom lessons. Identify specific behaviors that may reflect problems to assist in planning intervention strategies or to indicate need for more assessment in a particular area.

| Target Skill | Possible Problem Behaviors | Related Skills |
|---|---|---|
| ____ **Written Expression of Ideas** (May also include speech, language, handwriting, reading and spelling) | • Appears hesitant to begin writing <br> • Writes only a few sentences <br> • Has difficulty getting started <br> • Avoids writing <br> • Omits introductory statements <br> • Does not support major concepts with details <br> • Includes few or no original ideas <br> • Does not convey purpose <br> • Does not organize effectively <br> • Cannot use different forms of writing <br> • _____ <br> • _____ | Oral Expression <br> Vocabulary <br> Comprehension <br> Handwriting |
| ____ **Written Grammar** (May also include speech, language, handwriting, and spelling) | • Uses incomplete or run-on sentences <br> • Frequently starts over <br> • Cannot revise or edit work easily <br> • Capitalizes incorrectly <br> • Use parts of speech incorrectly <br> • Does not elaborate <br> • Cannot easily condense writing <br> • Punctuates incorrectly <br> • _____ <br> • _____ | Oral Expression <br> Vocabulary <br> Fine Motor Skills <br> Handwriting <br> Spelling |
| ____ **Integrated Writing** (May also include handwriting, spelling, reading, speech, and language) | • Appears apprehensive about writing <br> • Delays completion of assignments <br> • Is reluctant to share work with others <br> • Prefers other forms of expression <br> • Performs better using other forms of expression <br> • Has difficulty relating similar ideas <br> • Produces short, incomplete work <br> • _____ <br> • _____ | All Writing Skills <br> Reading <br> Handwriting <br> Spelling |

High-frequency problem behaviors are listed, and blanks are included in each category so that teachers can add behaviors specific to their class. Interpretation of achievement in written expression and plans for corrective instruction must be integrated with the other language arts skills — listening, speaking, and reading. Although development of discrete writing skills is essential, acquiring fluency should precede form.

Adapted from Rakes, T. A. (1990). Interactive assessment in the language arts: A checklist of related behaviors. *Diagnostique, 6* (1), 25–28, with permission.

the corrective strategies feature these elements: ample teacher modeling of how to generate and develop ideas; suggestions for integrated lessons; use of cooperative teams or work groups; experiences requiring active student participation; continual emphasis on producing and editing or rewriting material; use of literary and subject area sources for developing writing skills; and an emphasis on grammar, punctuation, and capitalization, as well as spelling and handwriting, as support skills, not prerequisites for written expression.

Written discourse is not speech written down. Writing requires a degree of precision that is not necessary in speech, where gestures, facial expression, voice tone, and inflection provide the listener with meaningful cues to understanding. Written language, lacking these cues, must use meaningful language in an organized fashion, including appropriate punctuation, capitalization, spelling, and handwriting. After teachers provide corrective instruction in a particular skill, they should have students apply that skill in a subject area lesson. When students are encouraged to use their writing skills throughout the curriculum, they master the skills more thoroughly and quickly.

## SPECIFIC SKILLS AND STRATEGIES

The following pages present suggestions for identifying and correcting specific skill needs in written expression. The section includes the most essential skills: written expression of ideas, written grammar, and writing across the curriculum. Written expression of ideas is the prerequisite; unless a student is willing to generate language there will be nothing to edit, punctuate correctly, or rewrite. The emphasis during writing should be on generating ideas, or prewriting, and getting the ideas or information on paper, or drafting. Only then does the process stress mechanics in revising or editing. This final stage in the writing process may include activities focusing on content, organization, and structure, as well as the mechanics.

In addition to the preceding principles of instruction, the Corrective Principles (Chapter 2) and the options for accommodating learner needs (Figure 3.1) offer guidance for selecting and adapting instructional strategies. Diagnostic teaching should discover additional ways to adapt corrective instruction to the unique needs of individual students.

## 34. GETTING STARTED

DETECTION

This may be a special skill need of students who

- Are hesitant to begin writing
- Would rather copy than generate language
- Have difficulty staying on the topic
- Are unable to write more than a few sentences
- Dislike writing
- Are reluctant to share written work with other students
- Prefer other forms of communication
- Exhibit little patience for or interest in writing
- Find excuses to avoid writing

*Description*

Written expression is, for most students, clearly an outgrowth of oral language. Children typically develop sentence sense and basic sentence patterns before the age of six. Although some students experience delays in language acquisition, steps taken to improve oral language typically improve written expression as well. The "getting started" step is probably the most important one for building written expression skills, expressing ideas, and maintaining interest in writing. The teacher should emphasize experiences that enable or entice students to generate language, before moving into more mechanical concerns such as punctuation or capitalization.

*Special Problems*

Students usually begin to write out of curiosity or need, or because the teacher assigns it. Some teachers' forced, tightly structured "my way" instruction simply turns students off to writing. Teachers who dwell on the mechanics of writing rather than the expression of ideas also inhibit young writers. Bad experiences in the past can cause students to shy away from beginning to write. Memories of red marks and over-emphasis upon spacing, spelling, or illegible appearance have made many students frustrated and reluctant to write. Problems with poor vision, hearing, or use of fine-motor skills can complicate the process. Language problems and communication disorders affect writing as well as other ways of generating language. Non-native speakers of English may require special assistance in dealing with language transitions.

*Implications*

In the beginning stages of writing students should all but ignore the mechanics of writing, focusing instead on the content of the ideas. Later, the students' writing can be used to teach the application of mechanics. Teaching writing means having students write frequently. However, frequent writing assignments are of little value if they are not varied, interesting, and directed to an audience. Repeated references to process writing stress that the process is more important than the product. Generation of written language involves a three-step sequence: prewriting, composing or drafting, and revising or editing. Students actually learn to write through guided practice in each of these phases. Planning and revising are just as important as composing. Each of the three steps contributes to improving written products. Teachers should take particular care to motivate students by highlighting cultural, historical, social or other differences in the classroom.

CORRECTION

Modify these strategies to meet students' learning needs.

1. *Group Stories.* Experience charts, dictated stories, or Group Stories all involve students in contributing ideas to a story as sentences that someone prints or writes on the chalkboard or transparency. Use a common experience or activity to stimulate language and solicit contributions from as many different students as possible. Reproduce the students' language as closely as possible. Have them read the story with you several times, and then copy the story with the title they agree upon. Save the story for later proofreading and rewriting, or proofwriting. Emphasize generating and using language to express ideas, not producing publishable stories.

2. *Idea Banks.* Provide a table, file box, or bulletin board for displaying or filing "Ideas for Authors." Encourage students to contribute pictures or titles of favorite topics as well as selecting topics yourself from weekly lessons. Select 1–2 students to record good ideas students have used during a particular week on cards to save as a reference. Feature "Picks of the Week" on a bulletin board.

3. *Story Openers.* Story Openers are words that stimulate students' imaginations or memories as they begin a writing project. Guide students until they feel comfortable. Instead of suggesting one opener, try to give at least 2–3 choices. When students make their own choices, they generate good writing more easily. After finishing a lesson on weather, for example, use these Story Openers: "My favorite kind of day . . . ," "After the thunder we . . . ," or "Showers of sunlight . . ." These are sentence starters; students can suggest topics as they progress.

4. *Questions.* Using a Story Opener or a topic, talk students through the process of asking questions about a topic. Guide them to compose by writing the answers to their questions.

5. *Post and Praise.* Emphasize effort more than product by displaying student work. Encourage and build pride in early written efforts. Overemphasis on detail can limit joy and creativity. After displaying work for at least a week, call an editors' conference to proofread the compositions as a group before reposting.

6. *Extra Practice.* • Ask students to bring topics from home or favorite television shows to write about. • Have students work in groups to construct Story Openers for younger students or classmates. • Have students select the best opening sentence from their texts and use them as story starters. • Capitalize on student interest in a favorite story and have them write news releases, jingles or advertisements reflecting what they like about a particular book. • Read the local paper or call bookstores to find out when an author will be visiting. Plan a trip to see the author, or have the class write a letter inviting the author to visit their class. • Begin a computerized index including the names of student authors and the titles of reports, stories, and other writing they produce. Periodically print a copy of the list to post in the room.

## 35. USING DIFFERENT FORMS

DETECTION

This may be a special skill need of students who

- Cannot write paragraphs
- Do not understand the concept of story writing
- Are unable to write descriptively
- Exhibit problems writing letters
- Hesitate to write short notes or captions
- Have difficulty generating initial ideas for writing
- Appear unfamiliar with letter writing, taking notes, and other forms
- Are hesitant to share their writing with others
- Attempt to write everything in the same manner (lack flexibility)

*Description*

The growth process in written expression includes learning to express ideas in many different forms. The ability to use different forms of written expression is called writing flexibility. Forms of writing vary and include letters, notes, compliments, acceptances, essays, stories, reports, and an assortment of descriptive or personal paragraphs and compositions. The major forms required by the classroom curriculum are utilitarian, following a structured format. The more creative forms, such as poetry, songs, and plays, can be of great interest to students, particularly if the teacher relates classroom activities to popular musicians, singers, or actors and actresses.

*Special Problems*

The greatest restriction on students' use of different writing forms is lack of proper guidance, stimulation, feedback, and modeling by teachers. Most students need specific strategies that engage them in a process they can understand and complete within a reasonable amount of time. As in nearly all writing, physical or psychological handicaps interfere with the process. However, some students master highly structured forms more readily than the more creative forms.

*Implications*

Teachers usually select the forms of writing they enjoy most to concentrate their instruction on. Share many forms of writing with students and be careful not to overemphasize your favorite types. Give students extra opportunities to use their preferred forms of writing instead of stressing yours. Once students learn to enjoy writing with confidence, you can be more directive. Older students in particular need instruction that focuses on real-life writing demands, such as completing applications. Teachers must constantly model and talk students through the various forms of written expression. Writing an answer to a question is different from writing a letter of inquiry or a book review. Model each type of expression, providing visual examples and leaving them available for continued reference. In addition to writing every day, students should have some choice in selecting topics. Vary the audience to whom the writing is addressed. Take advantage of the holidays and special cultural events that are a part of the lives of students in a multicultural class.

CORRECTION

Modify these strategies to meet students' learning needs.

1. *Letter Lessons.* Letter writing is one of the most useful and motivating writing experiences. Every letter should have a purpose. Begin by modeling a simple letter on the board, and have students take turns suggesting what they would like to say. Leave the model visible and circulate as students write a personal letter, for example:

| | | |
|---|---|---|
| Dear Mom, | | Dear Dad, |
| I love you. | *or* | Come to PTO tonight. |
| Love, | | Love, |
| Sandy | | Tommy |

As students progress, expand the contents of the letters by providing sentence and paragraph starters for students to finish. Capitalization, punctuation, and sentence-writing skills can be integrated into the proof-writing process. Provide opportunities for students to mail or deliver their letters.

2. *Special Delivery.* Have students write letters about themselves and share them with each other or with students in another class. Have the letters delivered, and arrange for the recipients to write responses. Permit note writing in class if the notes conform to your posted form for informal letters.

3. *Nice Notes.* Inform students about the occasions when thank you, acceptance, reminder, and other types of notes are important. Demonstrate what information is used in each type of note, and post several samples; then provide a situation each day that calls for writing a note. Be sure to regularly include note writing for birthdays, surprises, and special holidays.

4. *Creative Captions.* Have students write captions to fit pictures and cartoons. Create a poster or space on a bulletin board to exhibit Creative Captions.

5. *Story Segments.* Provide portions of oral or written stories, and have students write story endings or beginnings. Model the process, and then write a few sample beginnings and endings. Extend reading lessons with this technique instead of always asking questions after reading.

6. *Dear Editor.* Help students write and publish a class newspaper. Include a column for letters to the editor. For the first edition, you should be the editor as a model; thereafter, have the class select a different editor for each edition to work with you. Assign each student a different role for each edition.

7. *Extra Practice.* • Have groups of students construct special letters of inquiry, thanks, or invitation to companies or people in the community. • Provide stories or paragraphs with 2–3 sentences deleted in the middle of the text. Have students add the missing information so that the material makes sense. • Ask students to write notes to remind peers about assignments or important items to bring to class.

## 36. ORGANIZING AND REPORTING INFORMATION

DETECTION

This may be a special skill need of students who

- Have trouble selecting a specific topic for writing
- Cannot complete forms and applications
- Have difficulty staying on the topic
- Cannot gather and organize data without difficulty
- Are generally disorganized in completing assignments
- Often omit important details in written work
- Also have problems making oral presentations
- Appear disorganized in attempting other work
- Attempt to distract others or act out during writing assignments

*Description*

The formats for written reporting include formal class reports, announcements, advertisements, commercials, and stories. Special types of reporting include writing the appropriate information on a variety of forms and applications and writing an autobiography or resumé. The writing must be directed to both the intended audience and the purpose or intended use of the information. Reporting can be used to sell an idea, product, or service, or even oneself. School reports can vary in length from a few sentences to hundreds of sentences, depending on the purpose of the report, the intended audience, and the students' writing abilities.

*Special Problems*

Lack of familiarity and practice causes some students to have problems writing reports. The primary reasons for students' inability to write reports are much the same as those cited for difficulties expressing ideas in other forms (Skill 35): lack of modeling, stimulation, proper guidance, and feedback. Insufficient mastery of prerequisite writing, vocabulary, presentation, and reading skills, or of the study skills needed for writing summaries and taking notes, may also interfere with performance. Poor organization and lack of focus inhibit students' abilities to narrow a topic and then stick to it. Special students who may experience difficulty writing reports include those with cultural or language differences, behavior disorders, language or learning disabilities, or mental retardation.

*Implications*

Report writing is often less creative than story writing and includes more gathering, expanding, and combining information into an organized format. Even though mastery of study skills facilitates report writing, instruction in the two areas can take place concurrently, with an emphasis on summary writing. Correction should begin with short, interesting report formats and move toward lengthier class project. Short writing activities, such as announcements or news spots, can motivate students. Written debates about controversial issues help students focus on the topic. All students, but especially older students, need guidance in collecting and organizing data. The use of a notebook or card system and a procedure for indexing information must be taught and demonstrated, and then applied during the actual development of a report or project.

CORRECTION

Modify these strategies to meet students' learning needs

1. *ID Cards.* For real-world reporting, guide students as they collect and then write on an index card important identifying information about themselves. Include personal and emergency information and, for older students, references, school and job history, and other information they believe may be appropriate. Make a reduced copy of the card for students to keep. Guide students to transfer the data from the card to real forms, such as library cards, office record cards, or applications for jobs and driver's license or insurance forms. Later, use the cards to begin writing an autobiography or resumé.

2. *Outline Reporting.* Teach outlining as a tool for reporting. List the reporter questions: who, what, where, when, how, and why. Slowly read aloud a news article, and have students write the answers to these questions. Then guide them to add subordinate details. Finally, have students use their outlines to write the reports from a different perspective. After several guided experiences, have students choose a topic from audiotapes or books, and ask them to develop an outline report on their own.

3. *Systems.* Teach a simple system for writing a report: (a) select a topic, (b) gather references and take notes, (c) organize subtopics and notes using a map or outline, (d) write a draft of the report, and (e) proofread and revise the draft copy. This plan approaches writing as a process. Each stage requires you to guide, demonstrate, clarify, and monitor. Walk the class through several reports together before students begin independent or team efforts. You might grade progressively as specific portions are completed. By offering partial credit as they go along, you motivate students by lessening the impact of an all-or-none final grade.

4. *Minireports.* Help students write brief reports — such as announcements or short commercials for good books, past events, or trips — to place in a reading area or post on an information board. Provide students with the sources they need for the report. Initially, concentrate on outlining or charting by deciding what needs to be said. Next, actually write and then revise. Narrowing topics and gathering information can be added to the system as students progress. Provide a standard reporting format until students feel a need to expand their coverage, including what, when, where, who, and sometimes results.

5. *Packaging Reports.* Present several sources of data, such as a part of a story, related news clipping, and notes from a book. Guide students as they learn to turn the data into a short report by deciding on a topic, organizing, drafting, and revising. Have additional references available.

6. *Extra Practice.* • Have students keep daily journals to practice their reporting. • Have students identify information sources for news reports, list them, and share them with the class. • Ask students to contribute information to class reports for parents.

## 37. WRITING CREATIVELY

DETECTION

This may be a special skill need of students who

- Have difficulty responding spontaneously
- Write best using facts and information sources
- Are reluctant to write stories without ample information
- Attend to mechanics more than content
- Appear anxious when writing about personal or original ideas
- Tend to prefer factual forms of writing
- Rarely offer novel or unique responses to questions
- Prefer the familiar to trying new things

*Description*

Creative writing involves expressing personal ideas, experiences, interpretations, and embellishments of thought. Some students enjoy writing stories, poems, plays, and jingles. In fact, the more students enjoy writing, the more likely they are to write and improve their written expression. Once a pattern of consistent production, confidence, and interest has been established, targeted skills can be developed using the students' own writing. Unfortunately, some teachers believe that only targeted skill instruction is important and that imaginative, less structured writing should be limited to Fridays or a few other special times.

*Special Problems*

Teachers' attitudes and philosophies disable many would-be creative writers. When teachers place more emphasis on correctness than on expression of ideas or praise the traditional and shun the novel, students soon learn to write the teacher's thoughts, not their own. Some teachers use a single structured writing assignment to grade students on their creative expression, form, grammar, spelling, and handwriting, thereby presenting students with a stressful, uncreative, and almost impossible task. Some youngsters feel they are not creative and have little to say. Most students, however, even special students, can write creatively when encouraged to do so without fear of failure, freed of the writing mechanics, and assured that they can express what they think in their own words. Gifted students in particular often thrive on creative problem solving opportunities.

*Implications*

Students must know that they can express their ideas, free from censure. Creative writing experiences should be just that, not grammar or mechanics lessons. The students' writings, once freely expressed, are the most logical, personal, and relevant source of materials for follow-up lessons in grammar and mechanics. Therefore, the grading of the content must be separated from the grading of the grammar. To stimulate creative expression, three conditions are necessary: (1) the appropriate environment, including plenty of resources and references, a center for writing and finding ideas, and a classroom attitude conveying a supportive, nonthreatening approach to written efforts; (2) the provision of numerous experiences and strategies to stimulate creative writing of all types and in all lessons; and (3) teachers who provide an audience, guided modeling, and regular conferences. In many instances, teachers should tap students' creativity orally before having them write. Encourage students to write about their particular religious, cultural, or social customs.

CORRECTION

Modify these strategies to meet students' learning needs.

1. *Idea Generators.* As students routinely share, question, and participate in classroom experiences, watch for clues to areas of interest or excitement. Keep a list of these high-interest topics at the writing center. Many students like to write about characters in stories and books, favorite singers, sports, superheroes, animals, space, inventions, fashion, self-improvement, music, and hobbies.

2. *Special Poetry.* Directions for teaching the writing of poetry are included in most writing programs. You may be familiar with free verse, alternate-line rhyming, cinquain, haiku, and senryu formats. The two formats in which students are not required to use rhyme — acrostic and diamontic — offer opportunity to express personal ideas and are appropriate for almost any interest or ability level.

| **Acrostic Format** | Puppy and me<br>Like to run. He's<br>Always happy and<br>Yelping for more. | Cooking is my heart's delight.<br>Ovens and recipes<br>Overrun our<br>Kitchen and my tummy. |
|---|---|---|
| **Diamontic Format** | Winter<br>Cold, Wet<br>Dark, Bright, Sun<br>Swimming, Hot<br>Summer | Sad<br>Down, Lost<br>Blue, Cheerful, Singing<br>Bubbling, Playful<br>Happy |

3. *Conferencing.* Use individual writing conferences as an integral part of the writing program. Hold regular conferences for 3–5 minutes to discuss ongoing writing efforts. These guidelines may be helpful in conducting conferences: (a) Go to the students at their desks; (b) Have the students do at least half the talking; (c) Take notes about what you discuss to show your interest and provide a written record; (d) Discuss only 1–2 problems or areas of concern during one conference; (e) Ask students to retell what was discussed and summarize what action(s) they plan to take as a result of this conference. If students provide misleading or inaccurate information, allot additional time to clarify what was discussed.

4. *Simulations.* Describe simulated or hypothetical situations as writing starters. For example, have students interject themselves into a story they have read and write how their lives change and how the story changes; have them project themselves into some future or past time and write about their experiences; or describe a change in their current environment and have them react in writing. The possibilities are limitless as long as your enthusiasm is high.

5. *Extra Practice.* • Bind creative writings; have students read and/or edit the writings of peers. • Have students listen to and then rewrite taped stories. • Have students write daily in a creative writing journal. • Ask students to turn in topics to use for future creative writing assignments.

## 38.  WRITING SENTENCES

DETECTION

This may be a special skill need of students who

- Frequently write incomplete or run-on sentences
- Respond orally with incomplete or run-on sentences
- Regularly converse using incomplete sentences
- Frequently start over when writing
- Do not respond to oral and written questions in full sentences
- Have difficulty combining ideas into sentences
- Exhibit problems expanding ideas into several sentences
- Cannot differentiate among types of sentences

*Description*  Written sentence construction is largely based upon students' habitual use of complete sentences in oral language. The task requires students to think in complete idea units and to have command of a reasonable vocabulary and the handwriting skills necessary to record oral language as written language. This component also involves the more mechanical aspects of written expression discussed in Chapter 9. Teaching sentence production usually begins from an oral base and progresses somewhat sequentially from writing short, simple sentences to longer, more complex sentences. Beginning writers do not have to know the definition of a sentence in order to speak and write in complete sentences. They do, however, need a working knowledge of or feel for both semantics, the meanings of words, and syntax, the logical order of the words within sentences.

*Special Problems*  Sentence writing can be limited by any number of language or communications disorders, ranging from delayed language development to more serious, pathologically based speech and language disorders. The oral language of students who have had little exposure to rich, fluent spoken and written language often reflects their limited background. Students who speak in single words or phrases are not likely to write in complete sentences. If these same students also have done little writing, you can expect their sentence production to be unsatisfactory. Students with ample oral language who have problems writing sentences may suffer from neurological, visual, or auditory difficulties. Other students, particularly young ones, may have difficulty using fine motor skills.

*Implications*  Manuscript, cursive, keyboard, or other alternative writing formats can help students record sentences. As students begin to generate oral phrases and sentences, you may need to write the statements for them, or give them sentence starters to copy. Since written and oral language reinforce each other, teach both concurrently. Use an integrated approach combining listening, speaking, reading, and writing. Begin with writing phrases and sentences before moving students to paragraph-length assignments.

CORRECTION

Modify these strategies to meet students' learning needs.

1. *Oral Sentences.* Model speaking in complete sentences, and, whenever possible, require students to initiate and respond in complete sentences. To avoid teaching students to speak in single words or phrases as they answer your oral questions, tell them to "Pretend I didn't ask a question." Have them answer questions in complete sentences as though they are initiating a conversation by stating a fact or opinion.

2. *Sentence Builders.* Print on the board introductory phrases of sentences related to a topic or story the class is studying. Have students supply the ending of each sentence. Read the sentence openers aloud and ask students to finish each sentence orally based on what they recall from the lesson. Write each answer on the board and then have the student read the entire sentence aloud. Later, give students the sentence openers on the board, and list the words they might use to finish the sentences. Have students copy the opening and finish each sentence in writing. Vary the procedure by supplying sentence endings; have students supply the sentence openers and write each complete sentence.

3. *Too Much Sentence.* Guide students to compose sentences from groups of words. Begin by giving them sentences with 1–2 extra words inserted: "The dog sat ran the fast." Read or have students read aloud each sentence to decide which words to cross out. Model the thinking process for deciding which words do not belong. Have students practice; then present groups of scrambled words for students to rearrange into sentences. Finally, give students scrambled groups with too many words in each group; have students choose the words and arrange them into meaningful sentences.

4. *Sentence Parts.* Underline or circle the two basic parts of a sentence, explaining that one is the telling part and one is the doing part, or the subject and predicate. Guide students to mark sentences accordingly. Use these markings to highlight basic sentence patterns. Have students contribute words and topics to build simple sentences.

5. *Word Changes.* After completing a lesson, use the same text on transparencies to play Word Changes. Divide the class into 2 teams. Have the first team point to a word in a sentence. The other team must suggest a different but appropriate word to replace the target word, and then write the new sentence on the board. If a team cannot suggest a word, the other team gets the turn. Continue play until neither team can suggest further changes. Most of the text should have been rewritten with little or no meaning change. Pairs of students can also play the game.

6. *Extra Practice.* • Using a consumable text, have students underline the beginning and end of each sentence in a paragraph, and then write a sentence that fits the story using their own words. • Use a modified cloze format to encourage sentence building. • Tape sentence openers or endings, and have students tape their responses to Sentence Builders.

## 39.  COMBINING AND EXPANDING SENTENCES

DETECTION        This may be a special skill need of students who

- Frequently use short sentences
- Exhibit difficulty condensing ideas orally or in writing
- Use run-on sentences
- Tend to write excessively long sentences
- Often use incomplete sentences
- Have difficulty editing written work
- Lack flexibility in using sentences

*Description*        Sentence writing is a key ingredient in developing students' writing skills. Early writing is often filled with excessive use of the words *said, and, or,* and *but* to join sentences. Direct instruction in combining and expanding sentences will improve students' writing. Sometimes referred to as sentence reconstruction, editing, or rewriting, combining sentences involves joining two or more sentences into one meaningful sentence. Expansion refers to expanding one or more sentences or complete thoughts into two or more meaningful sentences.

*Special Problems*        Poor reading or listening comprehension, an underdeveloped writing vocabulary, and lack of writing experience can limit students' efforts in combining and expanding sentences. Students who have difficulty generating sentences (Skill 38) are likely to have similar problems combining and expanding them. Students who habitually speak in phrases or short sentences or who have cultural or language differences or general language difficulties may have special problems combining and expanding.

*Implications*        Combining and expanding sentences builds and improves skills in written expression. Knowing the parts of speech or being able to use long words is not enough to produce coherent, scholarly writing. Sentence building helps students produce paragraphs and ultimately longer works. Comprehension contributes to the ability to combine or expand ideas and words. As in the case of most writing experiences, sentence-building strategies are most effective when used in other subject-area lessons. Guided practice, which is necessary to model how to develop and rearrange sentences, can easily be provided during a history, reading, or science lesson. In addition to helping students to improve their writing skills, such practice reinforces knowledge of the subject area. Every student should be involved in an appropriate writing experience every school day. Combining and expanding can be a part of any writing experience, whether directed toward composition, reporting, notetaking, story writing, or communicating information in health, science and other subject areas. Unless students can manipulate information by combining or elaborating ideas, they will not be able to undertake writing that requires more than memorization.

**CORRECTION**

Modify these strategies to meet students' learning needs.

1. *Grown-Up Sentences.* Say 2–3 short, choppy sentences. Have students restate these sentences in order to sound more like older students or adults. Begin with very obvious examples such as "I came. I ate. I slept." The sentences may be either combined or expanded to sound more mature. Then use examples from the beginning of the preprimer book in the student's reading series or, better yet, from a simple storybook; have students restate the sentences to sound like their current reading text or a more advanced storybook. After restating the sentences, have students write the sentences.

2. *Visual Models.* Using excerpts from library or textbooks or samples from students' work, provide visual models — posters, folders, brief reprints — to reflect a specific example of writing. A model for sentence expansion or combining could also stress the accompanying punctuation:

   We were ready to go.  
   No one showed up. } We were ready, but no one showed up.

   The team was good.  
   They won the game. } The team was good, so they won the game.

   Using this format, present sentence pairs for students to combine. For students who produce excessively long sentences, a similar format can be used to shorten sentences:

   Our trip was long and we became tired and hungry before it was over and we made it home. } Our trip was long. We became tired and hungry before we made it home.

3. *Sentence Assembly.* Provide sentences written on 2–3 sentence strips or tagboard. Have students move the strips around to make good sentences; discuss and evaluate the new sentences.

4. *Jumbled Sentences.* Print the words of 3–6 sentences from a current textbook on individual cards. Include extra words that your students overuse or fail to use. Have students construct sentences and compare their sentences with those in the text.

5. *Team Interchange.* Form teams and orally give students 1 long or several short sentences. To score a point, a team has 1–2 minutes to come up with an appropriate sentence orally or in writing. Other teams may work at the same time to be ready if the first team fails.

6. *Extra Practice.* • Try the above ideas using sentence transformations. • Appoint student editors to review class work and make suggestions for combining or expanding ideas. • Have students rewrite paragraphs by expanding, combining, or reducing sentences.

## 40.  USING PARTS OF SPEECH

DETECTION

This may be a special skill need of students who

- Frequently use nouns and verbs that do not agree
- Confuse word choices when writing
- Misuse structure words
- Cannot identify major parts of speech
- Have generally weak English language skills
- Exhibit usage problems in oral language
- Reveal problems on recognition tasks involving parts of speech

*Description*

The parts of speech students must master to write fluently are nouns, pronouns, verbs, adjectives, and adverbs. Making appropriate word choices and using structure words are also important. Of the several categories of structure words, noun markers, verb markers, negatives, and question markers are the most important ones for students to master. Other categories, including qualifiers and prepositions, should be introduced, explained, and used as students progress.

*Special Problems*

Written word usage typically directly reflects oral word usage and thus students' habitual language patterns. Students from backgrounds with cultural or language differences and those with general language difficulties may have significant problems with correct word usage, even after intensive instruction. Problems result when students fail to recognize the relevance of parts of speech or when they dread writing. Inconsistent instruction is responsible for some usage difficulties. Not all teachers have made the complete transition from the grammatical teaching of their own school days to the newer linguistic orientations. Instead they retain and implement "old school" beliefs emphasizing categorization, identification, and correct usage. The result is a mixture of instruction. If students are uninterested, academically delayed, or confused by a varied background, teachers should use procedures that emphasize generating writing.

*Implications*

The teaching of grammar, and the parts of speech in particular, has changed since the 1960s. Diagraming and structured phrasing activities are no longer considered particularly useful. Although some teachers still use the traditional ordering of sentence parts, newer linguistic-based strategies approach teaching the parts of speech as a more active, usage-based experience. Teachers should base instruction on student writing or on literature instead of using impersonal exercises in recognition. Strategies that require students to manipulate language as a part of the writing process are more effective than models that use restrictive charts and sentences in isolation. Repetitive drills and practice in grammatical labeling are of little value.

CORRECTION

Modify these strategies to meet students' learning needs.

1. *Living Sentences.* Use sentence strips to print a sentence in 2–3 parts on paper. Give individual students a part of the sentence; ask them to look at their part as well as their classmates' and stand next to each other to make a sentence. After the sentence is completed, have a student write it on the board. Discuss the parts of speech in each sentence that are appropriate for the students' level. Label the parts of speech above the sample words; ask for additional examples. Emphasize capitalization and punctuation as well, if appropriate.

2. *Read-Aloud Cloze.* Using a library book or content textbook, read aloud a passage, deleting all the words of a particular part of speech, such as adverbs. Have students supply the missing words based on the context and their past experience with the passage. If the students need the visual information, have the passage available for them to see as you read. Then, identify and discuss the part of speech and the function of the missing words in each sentence. As you present new parts of speech, use the same passage and delete all the words in the new category. For practice, have students work in pairs using passages you supply.

3. *Writers' Cloze.* An entertaining and motivational way to teach parts of speech is to follow the format of Mad Libs, the consumable pads of cloze activities available from Price, Stern, and Sloan Publishers. Use a passage from a reading or content text as in the above activity. Delete every word of a certain category, but, before reading the passage aloud, have students suggest, for example, five adjectives (or describing words). Then, read the passage with the suggested words inserted. The resulting stories are usually quite humorous. For practice, construct additional similar stories for pairs of students to complete or present selections from Mad Libs.

4. *Sentence Frames.* After explaining, identifying, and using nouns and/or verbs in sentences, solicit student sentences; guide students to locate nouns and verbs. Write sentence frames on the board, omitting nouns, verbs, or both. Model the process of filling in the frames. Then have students complete sentences on their own, write them on the board, and discuss them.

5. *Personalized Intervention.* One of the best methods of dealing with parts of speech is to address specific problems in students' written work. Present special lessons to individuals or to small groups of students with similar problems. After the lesson, have students revise their own work using what they have just learned.

6. *Extra Practice.* • After a subject-area lesson, have pairs of students take turns pointing to structure words or parts of speech in their text and having classmates identify them. • Have an editor's table in class where students can read other students' papers to find examples of a particular usage. • Have students compose sentences using a posted list of words in each category and a formula you supply, such as noun + verb + adverb.

## 41. PUNCTUATING CORRECTLY

DETECTION      This may be a special skill need of students who

- Fail to use punctuation Use punctuation incorrectly
- Do not recognize the function of specific punctuation marks
- Exhibit poor phrasing during oral reading
- Tend to ignore punctuation when reading
- Often overuse certain punctuation marks
- Do not capitalize correctly
- Are careless when writing

*Description*      Punctuation provides signals to assist readers to understand written material and writers to express their thoughts as they would speak them. Some experts consider that punctuation marks function like nonverbal gestures, facial expressions, and voice intonation in oral speech. The basic punctuation marks are periods, question marks, commas, and quotation marks. After students have mastered these five, the teacher may introduce other punctuation marks.

*Special Problems*      Isolated practice without sufficient application across the curriculum causes some students to see punctuation as just another meaningless detail, like capitalization. Poor instruction helps cause skill deficiencies, but when punctuation is presented as a code to oral language, even students with general language deficits, if they speak with expression, can master it. Students who do not observe punctuation when reading orally may have particular difficulty learning to punctuate when writing. Because hearing losses may interfere with recognition of intonation, expression, and phrasing, hearing-impaired students may experience problems mastering punctuation. Gifted students who tend to overlook details may not punctuate consistently. Many students with special needs are capable of mastering punctuation because it is one of the more mechanical aspects of written expression.

*Implications*      Most students need instruction that integrates oral language with proper intonation, teacher modeling using student work on the chalkboard, and structured practice in inserting correct punctuation into text. They also need continuous guided practice in using particular types of punctuation. Teachers can provide impromptu instruction by pausing for students to suggest the correct punctuation for sentences written on the board. Students learn more effectively when teachers explain, apply, and present punctuation as a participatory experience in all subjects as a natural part of the writing process. After students have expressed their ideas in writing, have them edit for punctuation. Regular use in daily writing for both personal and academic purposes facilitates mastery.

CORRECTION

Modify these strategies to meet students' learning needs.

1. *Integrated Punctuation.* Present groups of 3–4 easy sentences that illustrate only the target punctuation marks on transparencies; highlight the punctuation marks. Have students read chorally to observe and emphasize punctuation. Next, give students copies of the sentences without punctuation; have them read each sentence aloud with you and then fill in the correct punctuation.

2. *Spotlight Punctuation.* As you present different punctuation marks, add them to a poster for class reference. To spotlight the relevance of punctuation, use sentence strips with student sentences, showing an example of each target mark. Change examples regularly to reflect samples from actual lessons. A sample poster might read

   — **A period is used for initials and titles and to end statements.**
     Mr. T. K. Jackson was Susannah's teacher.

   — **A comma is used in dates and after items in a series.**
     Jim's birthday is October 11, 1981.
     They grow corn, wheat, and beans.

3. *Punctuation Explanation.* Copy a passage that students have already read and discussed onto a transparency. Referring to posted guidelines for punctuation, help students explain the reason for punctuation marks. Have them repeat the procedure using several selections from their textbooks.

4. *Punctuation Error.* Retype passages that are familiar to the students, deleting the punctuation or punctuating incorrectly. List the number of punctuation errors at the top of the page. Have students find the errors, correct them, and decide why someone might make each error. Using transparencies, model the process; then discuss common errors.

5. *Oral Punctuation.* Read a passage to the class; pause and reread certain statements. Have students decide which punctuation marks are needed. If you use stories from a textbook, have students verify their responses in their books. Then give students consumable copies of each passage without the punctuation; have them insert punctuation in their copies with pencils as they read aloud.

6. *Punctuation Board.* Write student-dictated sentences on sentence strips to put on a flannelboard or sentence chart. Have small groups of students insert the proper punctuation in the sentences. Capitalization can also be added by providing upper-case letters on cards. Use sentences from content lessons to reinforce new content and apply punctuation in a meaningful context.

7. *Extra Practice.* • Ask students to look for punctuation in magazines, circle each mark, and orally explain its function to another student. • End each day by having pairs of students exchange dictated sentences to punctuate. • Have young students develop names for punctuation marks, such as Paula Period, Connie Comma, Donnie Dash, and Question Mark Mary.

## 42. CAPITALIZING APPROPRIATELY

DETECTION

This may be a special skill need of students who

- Often omit capitalization
- Use too many capital letters
- Capitalize at random
- Correctly capitalize only certain types of words
- Do not punctuate correctly
- Are careless about the appearance of their handwriting
- Show little attention to details when reading or listening

*Description*

Capital letters signal meaning or respect in written material, clarifying the intent and use of certain words and terms. Although they need not be memorized and recited, a few basic guidelines for capitalization are pertinent: (1) Capitalize the first letter of first and last names; (2) Capitalize the word I; (3) Capitalize the first word in a sentence; (4) Capitalize personal titles like Ms., Mr., and Mrs.; (5) Capitalize place names; and (6) Capitalize days, holidays, and months. These guidelines should be posted in the classroom, but to be valuable, they should be applied daily in writing in reading, science, social studies, and all subjects.

*Special Problems*

Many students are not familiar with capitalization. The two major reasons for problems with this skill are ineffective instruction and language problems that interfere with students' understanding of the categories of words to be capitalized. The first situation can be easily remedied with appropriate corrective instruction. The second cause is more difficult to correct because it involves conceptual weakness and often general language deficits, such as that exhibited by some students who have cultural or language differences or who are hearing impaired, language disabled, or mentally retarded. A few gifted students may capitalize incorrectly, not because they do not understand the rules or language but because they are not concerned with details. Any student who is careless or rushes through written assignments is likely to capitalize inconsistently.

*Implications*

Capitalization is generally easier for students to master than punctuation. Both skills are usually taught together because they involve similar instructional materials and related concepts. With the proper instruction, students who understand the categories of the words to be capitalized can typically master capitalization with relative ease. Use the personal experiences and writings of students, including their names and familiar places and characters, as instructional material. Target initial instruction toward one or two categories of words. Once instruction has begun, overuse of capitalization may be a greater problem than underuse. This is a good time to review the posted guidelines. Have students check the capitalization of their compositions after they have expressed their ideas. Regular editing practice will make them more likely to capitalize correctly in future compositions.

CORRECTION

Modify these strategies to meet students' learning needs.

1. *Student Directory.* Ask students to contribute to a class directory. Include information such as full name, address, title of favorite movie or book, and the names of any pets or favorite animals. Have peers check each entry to be sure that capital letters are used correctly. Reproduce the directory so each student can have a personal copy.

2. *Big or Small.* Show students names of classmates, cities, or other words that are usually capitalized written on index cards. Mix in a few words that should not be capitalized. Organize two teams and have them take turns stating "big" or "small" depending on whether the word should be capitalized or not, referring to the posted guidelines to prove their answers. Follow this isolated recognition practice with immediate application using as many of the same words as possible in context.

3. *Capital Explanation.* Copy a selection that students have already read and discussed onto a transparency. Referring to the posted guidelines for capitalization, guide students to explain why each word in the selection is capitalized. Have them locate several other selections in their textbooks and follow a similar procedure, explaining and discussing each instance of capitalization. Then, as an independent activity, give students a consumable passage to explain. Have them refer to the posted guidelines for the number of the category that explains each capital letter in the selection and write that number beside each capital letter.

4. *Capital Error.* Retype familiar passages, adding or deleting several capital letters. List at the top of the page the number, but not the type, of capitalization errors. Have students find the errors, correct them, and decide why someone might make each error. Using transparencies, model the process; then discuss common errors.

5. *Personality Caps.* Carefully explain and illustrate proper capitalization for letter writing. Next, request student input to a group letter to a favorite cartoon character, sports personality, or singer; write the letter on the chalkboard without using any capitalization. Ask students to help add proper capitalization. Leaving the letter on the board, have students work in small groups or independently either to construct their own letter or to capitalize words in a second letter you provide. Circulate as students work to provide guidance as needed.

6. *Extra Practice.* • Ask students to underline or circle all the capitalized words in a passage; then have a peer explain why each word is capitalized. • Regularly have students proofread other students' written work for proper capitalization. • Have students develop a list of words they frequently fail to capitalize or needlessly capitalize and the reason each should or should not be capitalized; then have them use their list to proofread their own work before turning it in. • Have students select a favorite library book. Give them 2–5 minutes to list on paper as many different capitalized words as they can find.

## 43. REVISING

DETECTION

This may be a special skill need of students who

- Do not correct careless errors in written assignments
- Do not revise their assignments to improve them
- Seldom use vivid and descriptive language
- Use inappropriate punctuation or capitalization
- Do not check work for spelling and organization
- Use poor grammar and sentence structure
- Turn in illegible written assignments
- Appear hurried or careless

*Description*

Revising is the third major step in the writing process, following prewriting and composing. Editing or revising written language begins with proofreading to identify elements to correct or to improve. The rewriting process includes rewording, organizing, or clarifying content, and making changes in grammar, spelling, capitalization, and punctuation. It may include improving legibility by rewriting or typing to improve the overall appearance. This final polishing step gives students a chance to pull together several language skills and apply them to a written product.

*Special Problems*

Many students are not familiar with the final stage of writing. Still others lack skills that would help them express ideas, improve wording, or spot misspellings. Even students who have mastered the skills may not take the time to edit. Those who work slowly, wait until the last minute, or hurry to finish are likely to overlook needed revisions. Rewriting requires the sometimes arduous task of recopying or rekeyboarding the product, a chore that some students avoid. To other students, editing appears to be an overwhelming task. Both lack of practice and low teacher and/or student expectations hamper many young writers. Finally, many students have never been taught how to revise their writing. They do not know how to start and then monitor the process. In addition to those whose teachers do not teach the editing process, many types of special students require focused instruction as well as encouragement to revise their writing.

*Implications*

The revision stage is a good time to present targeted lessons in grammar and mechanics. Teachers can model actual revisions on the chalkboard. With students' permission, teachers can demonstrate the revision process using students' writing on an overhead projector. Teaching students to edit and rewrite helps them become responsible for what they write and learn to improve style and quality. With each revision, they learn more about how to write. Students are also more likely to express their ideas more freely during the initial phases of writing because they do not have to worry about the mechanics at that point. With the stress of generating ideas behind them, they can attend to the finer points of form, style, and mechanics, as well as to using clearer and more vivid language. Routine revision of written products is both a skill and a habit to be developed and nurtured.

CORRECTION

Modify these strategies to meet students' learning needs.

1. *Editor's Checklist.* Give students guidelines to help them revise their writing:

   Could I easily outline my writing?
   Do I have a strong beginning and ending?
   Do my words and sentences make sense?
   Do any of my sentences sound out of place?
   Does each paragraph have a main idea?
   Do I use any words too often?
   Does my punctuation make it sound the way I say it?
   Have I capitalized the right words?
   Are the words spelled correctly?
   Is it legible and neat?

   As students become to accustomed to using a checklist, reduce the list to key terms or ideas: outline, spelling, organization, and so on. Simplify the checklist for younger or less able students.

2. *Teacher's Aide.* Ask students to be your editorial assistant for the day. Think aloud as you consider possible changes in a brief composition. Next, talk your aide through similar revisions, supplying the verbal prompts for points such as those listed in Activity 1. Then, have your assistant think the revisions aloud. Finally, have the assistant edit several papers of other students.

3. *Computer Proofwriting.* Word-processing programs can be ideal writing and editing tools. They free students to express their ideas, knowing that they can edit easily. After discussing with students the content of their writing and praising it, read their compositions aloud to them. Guide them to explain, rearrange, and organize their ideas; combine, expand or reduce sentences; or add more picturesque language. Then, have students read their product aloud, correcting punctuation, capitalization, and grammar as they read. Consider teaching students to use a companion spellchecker or editing program to assist in proofwriting.

4. *Personal Edits.* Guide students to develop their own checklists for revisions. With each student, analyze aspects that seldom need revision and those that often do; then have students construct personal editing lists citing the points they are most likely to need to revise. As students improve, revise the checklists to reflect their progress. Be sure these checklists include items involving content, organization, grammar, and language usage, as well as spelling, capitalization, and spelling.

5. *Proof Practice.* After students have become reasonably comfortable with the revising process, provide anonymous copies of poorly written passages. Specify the number and types of errors that are present but do not identify them. Have students read each passage aloud, revise it, and then read it aloud again to check the sound of their revisions.

6. *Extra Practice.* • Pair students to alternate reading compositions aloud and suggesting revisions. • Have students write passages with errors for peers to correct, as in Proof Practice. • Occasionally make deliberate errors when writing and reward students who notice.

## 44. WRITING ACROSS THE CURRICULUM

DETECTION

This may be a special skill need of students who

- Dislike writing in general
- Appear uninterested in a particular subject or area of study
- Display a variety of recognition level writing deficiencies
- Exhibit a variety of application level writing deficiencies
- Demonstrate reading problems in one or more subjects
- Have a general lack of interest in doing homework
- Indicate a limited level of language development
- Perform better on oral tasks than on written tasks
- Complete written tasks in a slow or labored manner
- Frequently request help during the completion of written assignments
- Often seek praise and reassurance during written assignments

*Description*

This section provides ideas that can be used as a part of regular lessons in content areas. Health and safety, mathematics, science, and social studies are the subjects used to show how written expression can be included as an instructional component. Though several years ago the language arts or English lesson was the only place where writing was emphasized or graded, ability to apply writing skills in all subject areas is essential to success in school.

*Special Problems*

One reason so many students cannot write effectively is that too few teachers teach writing or require students to write. Departmentalized programs are generally susceptible to single-minded teaching whereby Spanish teachers, for example, teach only Spanish; they seem to believe the language arts or English teacher is responsible for teaching writing. However, direct instruction in written expression can facilitate learning in any subject. Special learners who need more instruction and practice in writing will not get the additional exposure unless writing is an integral part of the curriculum. Students with learning disabilities are particularly prone to reading and writing difficulties. Others who experience difficulties include students with visual and auditory impairments, as well as those with motor skills deficits. Computers and touch-sensitive devices can be used to overcome some of the physical problems of these special learners.

*Implications*

The assumption that writing belongs in the language arts class and not in *my* reading or mathematics class is erroneous. Unless all teachers, regardless of discipline, are involved in improving writing skills, many students will not learn flexibility in writing. Many strategies, such as using journals or logs, can be adapted for use in many subject areas. When teaching writing, think about how this same principle or approach could be used in another subject or lesson. Research indicating the importance of having students write every day shows that writing has to be a practice across the curriculum.

CORRECTION

Modify these strategies to meet students' learning needs.

1. *Learning Logs.* The use of journals or learning logs is an excellent way to monitor learning on a daily basis. In a science, social studies, or mathematics class, have students write in their learning logs during the last ten minutes of class each day or every other day. Ask students to respond to process questions in a notebook or loose leaf binder: "What do you understand about today's lesson? What don't you understand? When did you become confused?" How can you apply today's lesson? Use different questions on different days. Read the logs without grading or marking. Give positive comments about what you read in the logs, but avoid personal references or singling students out.

2. *Documented Field Studies.* Firsthand experience is of value in studying most subjects. If the class is planning for a field trip, nature walk, color patrol, zoo day, or almost any out-of-the-room experience, have students list everything they need to do to plan, take, and describe the trip. From these planning lists, have students form committees to be responsible for locating and preparing informational briefs on things to know about a topic; writing requests for more information from companies or government agencies; developing questions to use when calling for information on the trip or event; serving as recorders, notetakers, interviewers, and drafters for final reports; and serving on follow-up teams to write thank-you notes and draft requests for more information about an area of study.

3. *Centers of Excellence.* To encourage independent writing, provide special assignments relating to the science or safety "topic for the week." Provide books, pamphlets, audiotapes, and other information for students to use and have them (1) write a poem about the topic; (2) construct a dialogue sheet reflecting a conversation between a germ and a bandage or between a helmet and a skateboard; (3) complete a "Who? What happened? How?" story glimpse; or (4) organize 4–6 mixed facts about an interesting topic and write a two-sentence summary telling what the facts mean or what happened.

4. *Who Was There?* Give students a news clipping or taped message about a recent event. Have them combine the information into one sentence containing the main idea and the people involved, plus 1–2 explanatory or supporting sentences. Post the results for others to see.

5. *Extra Practice.* • Every week, have a team or an individual write a letter requesting information or reacting to something the class is studying. Post a copy of the letter, and the responses when appropriate. • Begin a poets' corner so that students who would like to do so can go to a designated quiet area to write a poem. When students are in this area they are not to be disturbed. • Each week select 2–3 topics or areas of special interest from one subject area. Have students use a resource diary to sign and date after they fill in any information they already know about the subject. Have students share this information if they wish to do so. • Following a lesson in history or science, provide students with 5–10 answers. Form groups of 2–3 students to construct questions to match the answers. Then have groups compare how they worded their questions.

# WRITTEN EXPRESSION SAMPLERS

The samplers for Chapter 8 illustrate representative activities for developing and correcting skills involving written expression. Each page can be reproduced for use although directions may need to be altered to suit the needs of specific students.

8.1 **Print Previews.** Print Previews develop prewriting experiences. Written previews provide a structure through which expressive writing can begin. A chart is provided for students to fill in ideas as they brainstorm about something they have just heard, read, seen or recently experienced. The teacher may use a chalkboard and model placement of student ideas on the Print Previews chart. Most students will need some guidance as to the appropriate placement of key concepts or facts, incidents or overall concepts. After several guided sessions with the teacher, students should be able to complete the form and generate their own information. Post finished products written on the bottom half of the form on a volunteer basis.

8.2 **Authors' Checklist.** This checklist is to be used as a self-evaluation of written material by the author. The intent is to provide students with a nonthreatening means of reviewing what they have written and lead them into the editing or revision process. Such a checklist should not be used on every story or report. You may want to adapt items on this checklist to fit the needs of your students.

8.3 **Projected Stories.** As a prewriting or prelearning experience, Projected Stories can be used to improve thinking and combining skills as well as to facilitate revision. Before beginning a lesson in science, for example, select 8–12 important words used in the story or unit. List these target words on the board, and have students write a short story using the words without actually seeing the material. Have students construct their sentences on their Possible Sentence guide. Next, ask students to listen to or read the material. Then have students edit their stories to reflect more accurately how the words were used in the material. Encourage students to substitute words, combine ideas, or expand concepts.

8.4 **Newsbrief.** This strategy encourages students to combine ideas around a central theme. Present students with one phrase representing a primary topic and 4–5 phrases in the form of notes. Ask students to use this form to state a topic sentence. Then have them construct a brief news announcement like the ones seen and heard on television. Students who wish to may read their newsbrief to others before lunch or at some other appropriate time.

8.5 **Yours and Mine Stories.** To help students become more spontaneous and creative with language, have students bring a small picture of something they like and paste it on the form. Ask each student to look at the picture and then write 4–10 words they can associate with the picture. Have students work in pairs, selecting half of the words and sharing them with a partner. Then have students work together or individually to develop a short story using at least five of their own words and five words from their partner in one story.

# ✎ PRINT PREVIEWS

**Directions:** Gather information about something you have read, seen, or experienced. Brainstorm to create a list of ideas relating to the topic. After gathering these ideas, organize them using the chart below. Then work individually or in teams to write a preview of the topic in 25 words or less.

**KEY IDEAS:**

_____

_____

_____

**KEY IDEAS CHART:**

### Major Concepts

1. _____

2. _____

**(1) Related Ideas**                **(2) Related Ideas**

_____        _____

_____        _____

_____        _____

_____        _____

**GLOBAL CONCLUSIONS OR PREDICTIONS:**

_____

_____

**PREVIEW OF**

_____

**AUTHOR(S)_____ DATE: _____**

---

### ✎ PRINT PREVIEW:

_____

_____

---

Name _____

# ✓✓✓ AUTHORS' CHECKLIST ✓✓✓

**Directions:** After finishing your written work, use the following checklist as a guide to help you review what you have done. You may revise your work based upon these questions if you wish to do so.

**Author:** _____ **Date:**_____

**Type of work: Story** _____ **Report** _____ **Other** _____ **(Specify)**_____
_____

1.  Who is your audience? _____

2.  Is the work well organized?_____Explain:_____
    _____

3.  This work should make the reader feel_____

4.  Is the topic sentence clear and easy to find? _____ Where is it located in your work?
    _____

5.  Do all sentences make sense? _____

6.  How many descriptive words are used? _____

7.  The part you like best is _____
    _____

8.  During proofreading, how many items did you change?_____

9.  You _____ would _____ would not like to share this work with

    others because _____

    _____

    _____

**Other comments:**

_____

_____

_____

Name _____

# § PROJECTED STORIES PLANNING FORM §

**Target Words (provided by your teacher):**

_____   _____   _____

_____   _____   _____

_____   _____   _____

**Part A Directions:** After reviewing the target words, use them to create a brief story.

§_____

_____

_____

_____

_____

_____

_____

_____

_____

_____

**Part B Directions:** After reading or listening to the material, use what you have learned to revise the sentences above.

§_____

_____

_____

_____

_____

_____

_____

_____

_____

Name _____

# ❖ OFFICIAL NEWSBRIEF FORM ❖

**Directions:** Use the top half of this sheet to gather and organize the information you need to create a Newsbrief. Then write your Newsbrief on the bottom of the page.

Topic:_____

Catchy Words that grab your attention:_____

_____

Key Ideas:_____

_____

_____

Results or predictions based upon this information:_____

_____

_____

. . . . . . . . . . . . . . . . . . . . . . . . . . . . . . . . . . . . . . . . . . . . . . .

**Flash, from the news desk of:**_____ **Date:**_____

**Catchy lead sentence:** _____

_____

**❖ Story ❖**

_____

_____

_____

_____

_____

_____

_____

_____

_____

_____

_____

_____

Name _____

# ⇔YOURS AND MINE STORY FORMAT⇔

**Directions:** Paste a small picture of something you like in the space below. Then, list 8–10 words that you associate with this picture. Working with a partner, swap half of your words for half of your partner's words. Now, write a story about your picture or something in the picture using as many of your words and your partner's words as you can. You may want to share your story with someone else later.

```
┌─────────────────────────────────────────────┐
│                                             │
│                                             │
│                                             │
│             PASTE PICTURE HERE              │
│                                             │
│                                             │
│                                             │
└─────────────────────────────────────────────┘
```

**My Words**                    **Borrowed Words**

_____   _____        _____   _____
_____   _____        _____   _____
_____   _____        _____   _____
_____   _____        _____   _____
_____   _____        _____   _____

## ⇔Yours and Mine Story ⇔

_____

_____

_____

_____

_____

_____

_____

_____

_____

_____

## REFLECTIONS

1. Written expression skills in Chapter 8 are divided into two major categories: expression and grammar. Using these major headings and the subskill areas, locate a teacher's edition of a science, history, or health textbook on the level of your choice and decide how much attention is given to writing. What kinds of writing activities are included in the textbook? Explain how what you find compares to the concept of writing across the curriculum.

2. This chapter gives much attention to writing across the curriculum. Even so, most writing instruction takes place in language arts lessons. Locate a current language arts textbook and compare the instructional activities in one unit with the corrective strategies in this chapter. What differences and similarities do you find?

3. Instruction in written expression differs among schools and classrooms. Interview a teacher in a nearby elementary school. Ask what kinds of strategies he or she uses to teach writing.

4. Many teachers are uncertain about how to evaluate written products. Describe how you would suggest that the teacher should evaluate a story written by your own elementary age student.

5. Differences between formal and informal detection of writing problems are briefly discussed. What are the similarities? What additional differences do you consider to be significant, and why?

6. Three procedures for scoring written expression are described. What are their differences and similarities? Which do you prefer, and why?

7. The checklist in Figure 8.1 provides a format for analyzing written expression. Using the checklist as a guide, interview a regular elementary classroom teacher. Find out which of the behaviors he or she observes most frequently. Ask if any particular writing skills are more difficult to correct and why. Find out what is done to accommodate multicultural differences. Repeating these procedures, interview a special education teacher. Discuss your findings with at least two colleagues.

8. This chapter suggests several principles of instruction. Choose the three you consider to be most important for teaching written expression to students with disabilities; choose three for students without disabilities. Compare your selections with those of a peer.

9. This chapter presents written expression as a three-stage process. Beginning with prewriting, compare and contrast the three major stages in the writing process.

10. Observation is a powerful assessment strategy. Observe a special education student as he or she participates in a writing activity. Using your own observations and the checklist in Figure 8.1, record what you see. What assumptions or conclusions can you make about this student and his or her writing performance? What additional information would you like to have?

11. Chapter 8 discusses several major topics involving written expression. Select two or more of these — journal writing, holistic scoring, editing and revising, and so on — locate additional information in other references, and share your findings with a colleague.

12. Suggestions and/or implications for teaching special students to write are presented in several language arts and special education references. Compare and contrast information in these sources with the information in Chapter 8.

Anderson, P. S., & Flood, D. (1988). *Language skills in elementary education* (4th ed.). New York: Macmillan.

Bromley, K. D. (1988). *Language arts: Exploring connections* (2nd ed.). Boston: Allyn and Bacon.

Burns, P. C., Roe, B. D., & Ross, E. P. (1992). *Teaching reading in today's elementary school* (5th ed.). Boston: Houghton Mifflin.

Choate, J. S., Enright, B. E., Miller, L. J., Poteet, J. A., & Rakes, T. A. (1992). *Curriculum-based assessment and programming* (2nd ed.). Boston: Allyn and Bacon.

Collins, C. (1993). *Expanding thinking through the language arts.* Boston: Allyn and Bacon.

Dishner, E. K., Bean, T. W., Readence, J. E. & Moore, D. W. (1992). *Reading in the content areas: Improving classroom instruction.* Dubuque, IA: Kendell/Hunt.

Fisher, C. J., & Terry, C. A. (1990). *Children's language and the language arts: A Literature based approach.* Boston: Allyn and Bacon.

Froses, V. (1991). *Whole-language: Practice and theory.* Boston: Allyn and Bacon.

Graham, S., & Harris, K. R. (Guest Eds.). (1988). Research and instruction in written language [Special issue]. *Exceptional Children, 54* (6), 491–584.

Harris, K. R., & Graham, S. (1992). *Helping young writers master the craft: Strategy instruction and self-regulation in the writing process.* Cambridge, MA: Brookline Books.

Norton, D. E. (1989). *The effective teaching of language arts* (3rd ed.). Columbus, OH: Merrill.

Olson, C. B. (1992). *Fostering critical thinking through writing.* New York: Longman.

Petty, W. T., Petty, D. C., Salzer, R. T., & Becking, M. F. (1989). *Experiences in language: Tools and techniques for language arts methods* (5th ed.). Boston: Allyn and Bacon.

Rakes, T. A., & Choate, J. S. (1989). *Language arts: Detecting and correcting special needs.* Boston: Allyn and Bacon.

Sampson, M., Van Allen, R., & Sampson, M.B. (1991). *Pathways to literacy.* Fort Worth: Holt, Rinehart and Winston.

Stires, S. (Ed.). (1991). *With promise: Redefining reading and writing needs for special students.* Portsmouth, NH: Heinemann.

Stoodt, B. D. (1988). *Teaching language arts.* New York: Harper and Row.

Temple, C., Nathan, R., Buris, N., & Temple, F. (1993). *The beginning of writing* (3rd ed.). Boston: Allyn and Bacon.

Thompkins, G. E., & Hoskisson, K. (1991). *Language arts: Content and teaching strategies* (2nd ed.). New York: Macmillan.

Wallace, G., Cohen, S. B., & Polloway, E. A. (1987). *Language arts: Teaching exceptional students.* Austin, TX: Pro-Ed.

Wilde, S. (1992). *You kan red this: Spelling and punctuation for whole language classrooms, K–6.* Portsmouth, NH: Heinemann.

Wood, J. W. (1992). *Adapting instruction for mainstreamed and at-risk students* (2nd ed.). New York: Merrill/Macmillan.

# CHAPTER NINE

## HANDWRITING AND SPELLING: TOOLS FOR WRITTEN COMMUNICATION

— *Lamoine J. Miller, Thomas A. Rakes, and Joyce S. Choate*

Although handwriting and spelling skills are not considered a part of the core curriculum, they are support skills students must master to perform successfully in the core curriculum. Students with illegible handwriting have frequently not received adequate instruction or supervised practice or have not developed the fine-motor skills necessary to produce legible handwriting. The majority of poor spellers have not mastered word recognition skills in reading that facilitate correct spelling. The handwriting skills discussed in this chapter are usually taught during initial instruction of manuscript and cursive, then tossed aside. Handwriting skills are the most poorly and least often taught skills in the elementary curriculum. Instruction in spelling typically follows the outline in the spelling text, even though several of these procedures actually interfere with learning to spell. However, direct and focused instruction in both of these support skills with integration throughout the curriculum, can greatly improve a student's handwriting and spelling performance.

## THE HANDWRITING AND SPELLING SKILLS

Developing readiness skills in handwriting and spelling is as important as in other subject areas. Handwriting readiness includes adequate muscle coordination; a writing hand preference; gross, fine-motor, and eye-hand coordination; visual discrimination; and an understanding of left-to-right progression. Readiness skills in spelling include the ability to name and write all the letters of the alphabet, to copy words correctly, to write one's name from memory, to enunciate words clearly, to recognize common letter-sound combinations, and to write a few words from memory. Readiness skills in these two support areas overlap with readiness skills in Word Recognition (Chapter 4). This chapter will consider fine-motor skill, since it has a direct impact on handwriting and indirectly affects spelling. Visual and auditory discrimination and visual and auditory memory are also important readiness skills for both handwriting and spelling. These readiness skills are discussed in Reading Word Recognition (Chapter 4), to which the interested reader should refer for more information.

## Specific Handwriting Skills

Fine-motor coordination (Skill 45) is critical for developing legible handwriting and may affect the student's performance in all academic tasks involving writing. Legible handwriting is a key factor to communicating effectively in writing.

Writing legibly for manuscript and/or cursive lessons (Skill 46) is a major objective of direct instruction in handwriting. Direct instruction should emphasize proper grasp of the writing instrument, correct formation of letters and numerals, posture, position of the writing paper, proper spacing, and alignment. Particular attention to these skills is critical during initial instruction in both styles of writing.

Writing fluently and with flexibility (Skill 47) is a second major objective of direct instruction. Writing fluently involves writing with rhythm, smoothness, and an even flow. Writing flexibility involves students' ability to adjust their writing speed to the demands of the situation and still maintain legibility. Once students can write legibly, emphasis falls on fluency and flexibility.

Students who write left-handed (Skill 48) need instructional adjustments to learn to write legibly and fluently. The teacher must emphasize these adjustments during initial instruction in both styles of writing. Two such adjustments are correct position of the writing paper and proper grasp of the writing instrument. Proper attention to these two adjustments should prevent the typical "hooked" writing and backward slant.

Writing legibly on daily work (Skill 49) is necessary for students to perform successfully in all content areas. This long-term goal of all handwriting instruction involves the same elements of legibility as in handwriting lessons: size, slant, alignment, spacing, letter formation, posture, correct grasp of writing instrument, and position of writing paper. The teacher should frequently encourage students to apply the skills learned in handwriting lessons to all written work. Effective instruction in handwriting will require sixty to seventy-five minutes of direct instruction per week, or at least fifteen minutes per day.

## Specific Spelling Skills

The spelling skills discussed in this chapter — spelling correctly on tests (Skill 50), spelling simple and common words (Skill 51), spelling difficult words (Skill 52), and spelling correctly on daily work (Skill 53) — frequently present difficulty for poor spellers and students with special needs. Spelling correctly on tests (Skill 50) is often easier than spelling correctly on daily work. To perform successfully on the spelling test, students need only memorize the list of words. Students can accomplish this task when teachers provide regular and consistent activities.

The ability to spell simple and common words correctly (Skill 51) is necessary to successful performance in our society. Students experiencing difficulty with this skill usually have severe deficits in the prerequisite skills of reading, visual and auditory discrimination, and both long- and short-term memory. Teachers should capitalize on the students' strengths while simultaneously correcting the deficits.

Spelling difficult words (Skill 52) involves spelling "demons," or words that are frequently misspelled and difficult to remember. Students should learn these words as discrete units because of their unusual spelling. They should learn difficult words as sight words through a variety of learning strategies and through practice in isolation and in context.

Spelling correctly on daily work (Skill 53) is problematic for poor spellers, who have difficulty applying what they have learned from weekly spelling instruction to daily classroom assignments. Students fail to generalize because a week's instruction on a word list produces only minimal competence, not mastery. To master a list of words, students need ample practice and meaningful application and reinforcement. To encourage generalization of spelling skills, teachers should make spelling part of the total curriculum, emphasizing the editing stage of the writing process.

## DETECTION OF SPECIAL HANDWRITING AND SPELLING NEEDS

Teachers can easily identify students who demonstrate difficulty in handwriting. Delays in developing fine-motor skills and eye-hand coordination may contribute to students' difficulties. Teachers tend to take a wait-and-see attitude, attributing the difficulty to immaturity, when in fact lack of exposure or opportunity to develop these skills may cause the problem. Handwriting skills are typically evaluated through informal means.

Students experiencing difficulties in spelling are usually not identified until the latter part of the first grade or the beginning of the second, when formal instruction in spelling is introduced. Spelling skills are usually evaluated in the weekly spelling tests using dictated sentences.

## Formal Detection

The readiness test, administered to groups at the end of the kindergarten year or beginning of the first grade, may assess handwriting skills on a limited basis. However, few group-administered tests emphasize handwriting skills. Students with extremely poor handwriting may be evaluated individually as part of the total evaluation for students suspected of having disabilities. Commercial rating scales are available for evaluating handwriting, but they are seldom used. Teachers commonly rely on their professional judgment of students' performance as compared with their peers'.

Group-administered standardized achievement tests usually measure spelling. Usually the student must select the correct spelling of the stimulus word from four choices. Students with low scores on this test need individual diagnosis and analysis of their difficulties.

Because individually administered standardized tests in handwriting are limited, handwriting skills are seldom evaluated formally. Spelling skills, however, are frequently part of the total evaluation for students suspected of having disabilities. Individually administered diagnostic tests may provide more specific information than group-administered tests but are less specific than informal measures.

## Informal Detection

Handwriting difficulties are usually identified and evaluated through informal measures, particularly work-sample analysis and direct observation. Work-sample analysis evaluates alignment, spacing, size, and slant. Direct observation evaluates grasp of the writing instrument, posture, position of the paper, and letter formation. Both informal measures are necessary to determine specific handwriting difficulties.

Informal measures in spelling typically present words in dictation and analyze common error patterns in misspellings. The error pattern provides clues for corrective instruction. Spelling may also be assessed through two alternative formats: (1) multiple choice and (2) oral spelling. The first format presents the stimulus word with three misspellings of the word, so it indicates whether students recognize the correct spelling of the word but not whether they can recall the word and produce it in writing. The second format, oral spelling, is used less frequently because it requires total recall without visual monitoring.

Checklists of handwriting and spelling problems, such as the samples in Figures 9.1 and 9.2, provide an overview of relevant skills and a means for recording student progress. They also may be used to organize data from other formal and informal assessment procedures, work-sample analysis, and direct observation.

Direct observation of students as they perform handwriting and spelling activities in their daily assignments provides invaluable diagnostic data. During handwriting activities the teacher can observe posture, grasp of the writing instrument, formation and alignment of the letters, and position of paper for difficulties that contribute to illegible handwriting.

Students' performance on weekly spelling tests will provide clues to spelling difficulties. Teachers can observe and diagnose how the student approaches the spelling task, the number of repeats requested, the rate of response, the use of intrinsic strategies such as the generate-and-test process.

Behaviors that may contribute to handwriting and spelling difficulties are listed at the beginning of the discussion for each handwriting and spelling skill. Consistent errors that form a pattern of behavior in daily written work and are substantiated through testing will require corrective instruction.

## SPECIAL POPULATIONS

The characteristics of groups of special students, including culturally diverse students, suggest that individual members may experience difficulty learning handwriting and spelling skills. Visual discrimination and fine-motor coordination are the most critical readiness skills for handwriting success. Students with limited opportunities for tracing, cutting, and manipulating objects in their early years may lag behind their peers in fine-motor skills. Developing legible handwriting may be difficult for special learners and culturally diverse students who are economically disadvantaged, mentally retarded, or visually impaired, or who have orthopedic conditions involving the hands and arms. With proper assessment and instruction, special students and those from diverse cultures can develop legible handwriting.

The majority of mildly disabled students, particularly those who are identified as learning disabled, mentally retarded, behavior disordered, or slow learners, experience difficulties in learning to spell. In addition, student's with illegible handwriting may perform poorly in spelling, not because they cannot spell but because they form letters poorly. Students with special needs and those from diverse cultures who experience difficulty learning word recognition skills will also have difficulty learning to spell. One of the most important spelling prerequisites is the ability to discriminate accurately the sounds that one hears. If students do not associate letter sounds with the correct letters, they will not learn to spell correctly. Asian-American students have particular difficulty in this area; many sounds in the English language do not exist in their native languages, therefore, these students do not hear these sounds (Heward & Orlansky, 1992). Hearing impaired or gifted students are least likely to experience problems in handwriting.

## FIGURE 9.1 / Handwriting Checklist

Although illegible handwriting is easily detected by noting the student's performance on written assignments, an accurate diagnosis requires direct observation during the writing process. The student's posture, grasp of the writing instrument, and position of the paper must be observed directly. Use this checklist during the observation to pinpoint areas needing correction.

| Handwriting Skill | Possible Problem Behaviors | Related Factors |
|---|---|---|
| **Fine-Motor Skills** | • has difficulty cutting, coloring, and pasting | Gross-motor skills |
| | • has difficulty manipulating small items | |
| | • incorrectly grasps writing instrument | |
| | • confuses left-to-right progress | Eye-hand coordination |
| | • shows inconsistent writing hand preference | |
| **Writing Fluency and Flexibility** | | |
| ____Letter formation | • has difficulty copying letters from board to paper or text to paper | Visual defects |
| | • canot write letters from memory | Revisualizing |
| | • does not form letters from top to bottom | Poor teaching |
| ____Color of print | | |
| ____Too light | • holds pencil perpendicular to paper | Improper grasp |
| | • holds pencil too far from point | |
| | • holds pencil with point toward body | |
| ____Shaded curves | • holds pencil with point at left or right | |
| ____Heavy strokes | • presses too hard on pencil with forefinger | |
| | • uses inappropriate writing instrument | |
| **Writing Fluency and Flexibility** | | |
| ____Size of print | | |
| ____Irregular size | • grasps pencil without bending thumb | Improper grasp |
| ____Too large | • moves arm only rather than wrist and arm | |
| | • grasps pencil too far from point | |
| ____Too small | • moves fingers only | |
| | • holds pencil too near the point | |
| | • fails to slide paper up as moving downward | Position of paper |
| ____Rhythm | • writes disjointed letters | Poor teaching |
| | • mixes manuscript and cursive letters | |
| ____Speed | • exhibits slow, laborious writing | |
| **Writing Left-Handed** | | |
| ____Writing hand hooked | • positions paper incorrectly | Position of paper |
| | • grasps writing instrument improperly | Proper grasp |
| ____Backward slant | • uses push rather than pull strokes | |
| ____Letter spacing | | |
| ____Irregular | • uses incorrect paper position | Position of paper |
| ____Crowded | • uses too much slant | |
| ____Scattered | • writes with little or no slant | |
| **Writing Legibly in Daily Lessons** | | |
| ____Satisfactory performance in handwriting lessons but not in daily work | • submits illegible written work | Motivation |
| | • produces messy written work | Fluency |
| | • appears careless in written assignments | Mastery of handwriting |
| | • dislikes writing | Eye-hand coordination |
| | • exhibits slow, laborious writing | Draws rather than writes |

Adapted from Miller, L. J. (1990). Tips for Assessing Handwriting: A Checklist of Problems. *Diagnostique 16*(1), 41–44. Adapted with permission.

## FIGURE 9.2 / Spelling Checklist

Research in spelling has identified effective procedures and techniques for improving a student's spelling performance, yet many of these procedures have not been translated into classroom practice. Teachers tend to rely heavily on the format and procedures outlined in the spelling text, even though some of these procedures have been found to interfere with learning. This checklist assists teachers in identifying specific skill areas requiring correction in order to develop an effective instructional program.

| Spelling Skill | Possible Problem Behaviors | Related Areas |
|---|---|---|
| **Spelling Correctly on Tests** | | |
| **Error Pattern** | | |
| ____Vowel substitutions | • Performs poorly on spelling tests | Weak word recognition |
| ____Vowel omissions | • Performs inconsistently | skills |
| ____Consonant substitutions | • Has better weekly scores than unit scores | Poor study habits |
| ____Consonant omissions | • Generally does not spell well | Test anxiety |
| | • Has weak word recognition skills | Reading |
| **Spelling Simple and Common Words** | | |
| ____Vowel substitutions | • Spells poorly on tests and daily work | Weak memory skills |
| ____Silent letters omitted | • Has serious spelling problems | |
| ____Sounded letters omitted | • Spells word patterns inconsistently | Application of spelling rules |
| | • Reverses and transposes letters | Visual discrimination |
| | • Exhibits weak word recognition skills | Reading |
| | • Appears to be trying but not improving | |
| | • Substitutes unrelated words | |
| **Spelling Difficult Words** | | |
| ____Letter transposition | • Misspells difficult words on tests and daily work | |
| ____Phonetic substitution | • Repeatedly misspells the same words | Generalization skills |
| | • Exhibits difficulty learning homonyms | Vocabulary development |
| | • Transposes letters | Letter-sound sequencing |
| | • Generally spells poorly | Study habits |
| **Spelling Correctly in Daily Work** | | |
| ____Vowel substitutions | • Appears to be a careless speller | Motivation |
| ____Silent letters omitted | • Frequently misspells in daily work | Generalization skills |
| ____Doubled letters omitted | • Demonstrates limited proofreading skills | Dictionary skills |
| ____Single letter added | • Scores well on tests but not on daily work | Motivation |
| ____Phonetic substitution | • Writes illegibly | Handwriting |
| | • Exhibits weak word recognition skills | |
| | • Demonstrates limited vocabulary skills | |

**Teachers Comments:**

This checklist will assist in identifying and categorizing consistent spelling errors. Consistent spelling errors will overlap into several skill areas. Vowel substitutions, which are high-frequency errors, will occur in most of the skills listed. When error patterns are consistent, direct intervention is necessary to remedy the problem.

Adapted from Miller, L. J. (1990). Tips for Analyzing Spelling Errors. *Diagnostique 16*(1), 38–40. Adapted with permission.

Students with physical handicaps and gifted students are not likely to experience difficulty in learning to spell.

## CORRECTION OF SPECIAL HANDWRITING AND SPELLING NEEDS

Correcting handwriting problems will improve the students' performance not only in handwriting assignments but in other academic areas as well. Illegible handwriting by adolescents will be more difficult and challenging to correct because they may not be interested or motivated. Teachers should focus on practical situations that require legible writing, such as letters of application, application forms, and recipes for cooking.

Misspellings fall into two categories: phonetic misspellings and nonphonetic misspellings. Phonetic misspellings can be interpreted as the stimulus word whereas nonphonetic misspellings cannot be read at all. Many students study their spelling words and perform successfully on weekly spelling tests but fail to spell the words correctly in daily written assignments. These students, not having mastered the spelling words, require additional practice and reinforcement. Some students have difficulty learning to spell simple, common words. They often have significant reading problems as well. Students who have received extensive instruction in phonics may attempt to spell all words phonetically, even simple sight vocabulary.

Certain spelling words are more difficult than others for students to master. These are the spelling "demons" that contain rare, even unique, spellings of phonemes. Students need to master these words by whatever means available. Making students aware of their personal spelling demons helps them learn these words. They will have to memorize difficult words.

Direct instruction and supervised practice improve illegible handwriting. Because handwriting skills are interrelated, many of the corrective strategies presented in this chapter can improve several skills. Correcting spelling difficulties also requires direct instruction. Teaching students strategies for learning words, restructuring the weekly spelling lesson, and teaching self-corrective procedures should improve spelling performance. Encouraging students to write legibly and use their spelling words in daily assignments will provide the practice necessary to master these skills.

The following principles from the guidelines in Chapter 3 are the most critical for correcting handwriting and spelling skills:

— Teach diagnostically
— Integrate handwriting and spelling in all language arts instruction
— Teach self-monitoring
— Teach to learning style (in selecting a learning strategy for spelling)
— Apply principles of behaviorism
— Use multiple senses when teaching
— Use self-correction and evaluation procedures
— Teach for mastery
— Teach application of handwriting and spelling skills across the curriculum

In addition to the above principles, include in your teaching frequent modeling, particularly in handwriting; supervised practice; active student participation; reinforcement and corrective feedback; consideration for various learning styles; and integrated instruction in the language arts. Consider the age of the student in designing corrective programs. Older students who have years of practice in writing with an improper grasp of the writing instrument may have great difficulty changing. Focusing on correct position of the writing paper, letter formation, and slant will bring promising results. Spelling instruction, however, can be adapted to the unique needs of each student, irrespective of age. For severely disabled students, the spelling curriculum may consist of high-frequency consumer terms.

## SPECIFIC SKILLS AND STRATEGIES

The following pages present brief discussions of handwriting and spelling skills along with correction strategies. The most critical of these skills to handwriting are Skills 45, 46, and 49. Skills 50, 51, and 53 are the most essential to spelling.

The principles of effective instruction in Chapter 3 and the Corrective Principles in Chapter 2 suggest ways to select and adapt strategies to teach special learners. However, the teacher must also consider the unique needs of each student and the particular curriculum in use in order to deliver effective instruction.

## 45. FINE-MOTOR SKILLS

DETECTION          This may be a special skill need of students who

- Cut, color, and paste less proficiently than age peers
- Demonstrate weak handwriting skills
- Consistently turn in messy papers
- Have difficulty turning pages of books
- Are unable to manipulate small items easily with their fingers
- Have problems with left-to-right progression

*Description*          The fine-motor skills use the small muscles; in an academic setting, they are typically associated with eye-hand coordination. These skills facilitate students' performance of mechanical tasks and their demonstration of what they have learned. Cutting, coloring, pasting, writing, playing with small objects and puppets, and assembling models require the use of the fine-motor skills, as do writing and completing daily tasks at home and in school.

*Special Problems*          Neurological impairments, poor physical development, vision problems, physical handicaps, and lack of experiences that develop fine-motor control can cause difficulties in using fine-motor skills. Some students may never gain sufficient control of the small muscles to perform written tasks satisfactorily; they may need to use mechanical devices to compensate. If vision or muscle strength cause difficulties, the teacher should attend to these problems along with fine-motor skills. For many students who are developmentally delayed, their greatest difficulty is the correct grasp of the writing instrument. The teacher may want to investigate the variety of prosthetic aids available to assist students to grasp the pencil appropriately. Students who are disadvantaged, educationally deprived, learning disabled, physically or mentally disabled, visually impaired, slow learners, or underachievers may have problems with fine-motor skills.

*Implications*          Fine-motor difficulties can cause problems in writing and reading if students cannot master eye-hand coordination. The development of fine-motor skills should help students master the basic tasks and manipulative operations that enable them to write, draw, and otherwise respond to everyday school tasks. As they mature, most students can improve fine-motor skills with direct training. As in the case of mastering left and right, fine-motor skills should be stressed as a part of art, reading, writing, music, and physical education throughout the day. Although coloring, cutting, pasting, and similar activities help improve fine-motor skills, they take time away from direct instruction in writing. Instead, teachers should direct students to write letters and words to improve the fine-motor skills needed for writing legibly. Tracing models, tracing on onion skin paper, copying numerals and writing them from memory, and writing both manuscript and cursive letters will assist in developing the necessary fine-motor skills.

CORRECTION        Modify these strategies to meet students' learning needs.

1. *Copy Cat.* Draw a simple shape on the chalkboard. Use one of the basic shapes that make up the manuscript letters, such as a circle, open oval, or slash. Have students trace the outline several times using a different color of chalk each time. Next, have them choose the chalk color they prefer and copy the figure below the outline. Have them sit at a desk close to the board and copy the figure onto paper. For additional practice, give students an interesting picture or drawing. Have them trace a few simple but important figures in the picture. Next ask them to look back at the outline and, on a different piece of paper, draw the outline of what they have traced.

2. *Alphabet Trace.* Give each student a piece of thin paper to trace large letters on. Coordinate this activity with other readiness tasks by using letters that students are currently learning to identify or write. Have students say the letter names while tracing. To ensure correct letter formation, code the model letters with numbers and arrows indicating the sequence of strokes. Gradually fade the cues as students become proficient in writing the letters. As students progress and can stay on the lines, have them trace letters formed of dotted lines positioned close together, again saying the letter names. Gradually decrease the number of dots until students are writing the letters themselves.

3. *Trace Erase.* Give each student a thin piece of paper on which to trace large letters and the numerals 1–10. Have students trace the figures lightly, saying the letter or number. Next give them a soft pencil-shaped typewriter eraser (so as not to tear the paper) to gently erase the figure they wrote, again saying the letter or number name as they work. It usually takes several tracings with the eraser to erase most of the figure. Then have students remove the paper from the tracing stimulus and write the figure from the erasure marks.

4. *String-Its.* Use long shoelaces and large tubular pasta, about 1″ long and 1/4″ in diameter, available from most large grocery stores. With a permanent-ink marking pen, print color words, alphabet letters, or vocabulary words on each piece. Have students read the word or letter written on each noodle while they thread the lace through it to make a necklace or chain. They must read the noodles correctly to put them on the chain. Have students compete with themselves and each other to increase the length of their chains.

5. *Mechanics Instead.* If students have significant difficulty controlling the movements of the small muscles, introduce a word processor or other mechanical device for accomplishing written work. A number of software programs are available to teach touch keyboarding to those who have the control to master it. Permit students to use the machines as a reward for accomplishing fine-motor tasks that are especially difficult for them. Coordinate lesson content with other readiness tasks, by insisting that students say the names of letters or words as they work.

6. *Extra Practice.* • Provide academic activities that include painting and coloring. • Provide connect-a-dot and maze puzzles for pencil-and-paper practice. • Place at a recreational center games such as Kootie, Mr. Potato Head, and Operation; pegboards, felt boards or flannelboards; and other commercial devices that require students to fill in, rearrange, insert, and line up objects.

## 46. WRITING LEGIBLY IN HANDWRITING LESSONS

DETECTION

This may be a special skill need of students who

- Form letters incorrectly
- Write with an improper slant
- Hold their hand or pencil incorrectly when writing
- Write lines that are too heavy, too light, or inconsistent
- Write too quickly or too slowly
- Produce messy written work

*Description*

Handwriting, like spelling, is a mechanical skill that supports the other subject areas. It is the medium through which most students respond to school assignments. Both styles of handwriting are typically introduced during the first three grades. Manuscript writing, or printing, is usually taught in the first two grades; cursive, or "real" writing, is often introduced in the third grade. After third grade, manuscript writing is reviewed and practiced periodically throughout the elementary years, while cursive becomes the preferred writing style. Several combined skills contribute to legible handwriting, including size, alignment, slant, spacing, and proportion of letters and words. Although not generally considered a major subject, handwriting can facilitate or impede a student's demonstration of content knowledge.

*Special Problems*

The major cause of poor handwriting is poor teaching. In recent years, emphasis on precise handwriting has decreased to the point that formal lessons occur infrequently in most classrooms. Many teachers do not use a standard form in their own writing, and a majority have not been trained to teach children to write. They convey their disinterest to their students. Physical delays, visual-motor weaknesses, and neurological dysfunctions, in addition to lack of appropriate instruction, can interfere with the ability to write legibly. Groups of special students who may experience difficulty in writing legibly are the learning disabled, physically handicapped, and visually impaired. Impulsive and impatient students often write poorly, too.

*Implications*

Obviously illegibility earns poor grades in handwriting. Admonishing students to improve their handwriting will not suffice. Students need specific feedback on what to do to improve their handwriting. Saying "Your letters are uneven" would be too vague; instead say "all mid-line letters should be the same height" giving examples. The more specific the feedback, the more likely improvement will result. Teachers should provide demonstrations, particularly for Native American students who are predominently visual and learn by observation. Illegible handwriting implies failure to master the mechanics for recording responses in all subjects. Illegible responses are seldom acknowledged as correct; teachers who can barely decipher illegible writing award lower grades to such papers.

**CORRECTION**     Modify these strategies to meet students' learning needs.

1. *Trace and Write.* To teach letter formation, write each letter on the board. Have students trace over your letter several times and then copy it below your model. If their letters are unsatisfactory, superimpose the correct letter using colored chalk. Have students trace with the colored chalk and then copy the letter again. Repeat until corrections are no longer needed.

2. *Write and Trace.* Guide students to evaluate their own handwriting using transparent overlays. Begin by telling them the number of letters on the page that should be corrected, but not which letters. Have them locate the errors with the overlay. Then demonstrate how to remove the overlay and superimpose the correct strokes with the colored pen. Then they should write the letters again.

3. *Tell and Write.* As you teach a letter, give verbal cues for each movement. Describe each stroke as you write at the board, for instance, "start, pull, dot" for lower-case *i*. Have students repeat the cues as you write additional examples. Next, have them say the strokes as they write the same letter at the board. Finally, have students tell the strokes as they write the letter on their papers. Emphasize that all strokes begin at the top and move down and monitor students to ensure they are following this sequence.

4. *Disappearing Dots.* After introducing a letter, make a dotted outline of the letter on the board. Mark the beginning point with a tiny star or arrow. Have students trace over the dots with chalk, moving from dot to dot until they have filled in the letter outline. Have them say the strokes as they write. Then give them a page filled with dotted outlines of the letter. The outlines on the first line should contain many dots spaced closely together. On the second line, the dots should be a little farther apart. Decrease the number of dots and increase the white spaces until on the last line only the starting point is marked for students to write the letter without aid. Commercial programs that follow this format are avilable for teachers pressed for time.

5. *Alternative Communications.* Some students may never be able to write legibly. Although you should make every effort to teach them to write their signature, consider teaching alternative means of communication: keyboarding on a typewriter or computer, the use of tape recorders, or individual interviews with the teacher. Allow students who write only with extreme effort to write the first few responses of each lesson and then use the keyboard for the rest.

6. *Extra Practice.* • Have students write target letters with their index fingers in wet sand or form letters from clay. • Allow pairs of students to take turns coaching each other to write, with one student supplying the verbal cues for the partner to follow. • Have pairs of students practice reading, spelling, and writing basic sight words. • Adapt strategies from Word Recognition, Letters and Sight Words (Skill 4).

## 47. WRITING FLEXIBILITY

DETECTION    This may be a special skill need of students who

- Do not vary writing speed according to the task
- Exert the same amount of effort for every writing task
- Attempt to use one style or type of writing for all purposes
- Use inappropriate letter size for space available
- Have not mastered manuscript and cursive writing (Skill 46)

*Description*    Handwriting flexibility requires students to judge the form their writing should take and the speed and care with which they should write. In order to do this, students must have developed the basic writing skills. Completing an application, signing a library card, addressing a letter, responding to a test question, taking a phone message, taking notes in class, or printing a notice require different types, styles, and speeds of writing. As students must adjust their reading rate to the type of text and purpose for reading, they must also adjust their writing to fit the type of writing and its purpose.

*Special Problems*    Inflexible handwriting results from inflexible instruction and inadequate mastery of handwriting skills. Many students, particularly young ones or those with special needs, do not realize that different writing tasks require specific forms of handwriting. Often their teachers have insisted that they always "Write their very best," which translates to students as "Draw your letters perfectly." Some teachers fail to involve students in a program that varies handwriting for different purposes. Students who have difficulty with or are uncertain of their handwriting skills tend to stick to the form and style with which they are the most comfortable. Teachers who are unaware of the importance of rhythm in writing have permitted students to write in a disjointed fashion or use a mixture of manuscript and cursive letters, rather than emphasizing a smooth, even flow. These factors will likely interfere with fluency in writing. That students will develop their own writing style is to be expected; however, when their writing impedes their learning or is illegible, teachers must intervene. Finally, some students exhibit poor fluency due to limited perceptual-motor skills or coordination difficulties that impair their ability to adjust handwriting rate, style, and proportions.

*Implications*    Handwriting flexibility results from the integration of many skills which include fine-motor coordination, letter formation, size, and rhythm. These skills allow students to decide which written format is appropriate for each task. However, students must be taught various formats and provided meaningful practice with each. Many students are relieved to discover that, on some occasions, writing quickly and imperfectly is permissible and even advisable. Unless they master writing flexibility, students will have limited options as they encounter tasks that demand different types of writing.

CORRECTION    Modify these strategies to meet students' learning needs.

1. *3-Speed Writes.* Teach students 3 types and speeds of writing. Introduce the first speed, "slow," during a handwriting lesson. Discuss the other purposes of writing slowly and forming letters carefully, such as when writing a letter to someone students want to impress. Then, whenever you want students to demonstrate their best handwriting, tell them to use their "slow" writing. Introduce the second writing speed, "flow," as the most useful one for the majority of writing tasks, both in and out of school. Explain that this is smooth, easy writing that feels comfortable to the writer while remaining reasonably legible. Remind students to use their "flow" writing for daily assignments. Introduce the third writing speed, "go," with a game in which students race to write answers quickly. Discuss the other uses of "go" writing, such as taking phone messages and class notes. Later, when you want students to write fast, tell them to use their "go" writing. The 3 verbal cues guide students to vary their writing according to the task.

2. *Writing Rhythm.* To demonstrate the rhythm of fluent handwriting, have students listen to music and write to the rhythm. Select music to match each of the writing speeds of Activity 1. Beginning with "slow," have students write carefully to the rhythm of slow music; then discuss the purposes of this writing speed. Follow a similar procedure for "go" writing to fast music and "flow" writing to music of moderate tempo. Experiment with several moderate tempos until students find the most fluid speed that still results in reasonably legible handwriting. The teacher may count aloud to help students develop rhythm in their writing. Put the writing lesson on the chalkboard and number each letter or word by strokes. For example, the letter *a* would receive two counts. The teacher counts rhythmically while the student stays with the count to write the letter.

3. *Handwriting Samples.* Use samples of students' handwriting to illustrate types of handwriting used for different situations. Construct a poster to display in the classroom. Head the left column "Purpose" and list types of documents or situations: sign, personal note, phone message, handwriting lessons and so on. The middle column, is for "Speed," indicating which of the 3 speeds is most appropriate for the purpose. Entitle the right column "Sample" and show 1–3 examples of students' handwriting for each category in the first column. Refer to the samples as you assign writing tasks.

4. *Handwriting Checklist.* Post a handwriting checklist showing students' handwriting progress. In addition to adjusting writing speed, include size, slant, proper spacing, letter formation, neatness, and posture. Beside each name, check the features as students master them.

5. *Extra Practice.* • Highlight one form of handwriting every few weeks; "slow," "flow," or "go" to practice and maintain flexibility. • For individual feedback, write the correct letter form over the student's incorrect form with a felt tip marker to make the student aware of which specific letters or portions of letters to work on.

## 48. WRITING LEFT-HANDED

DETECTION
This may be a special skill need of students who

- Experience difficulty writing legibly and neatly
- Hook the left hand to write
- Hold the paper inappropriately for left-handed writing
- Slant letters incorrectly
- Have difficulty spacing letters and words
- Tire easily when writing
- Grip the pencil incorrectly
- Demonstrate poor posture when writing

*Description*
About 5–10 percent of students are left-handed, the average representing a few more males than females. As the number and nature of observed difficulties show, left-handed students frequently experience problems learning to write. Their problems tend to be more serious than those of right-handed students. They cannot imitate as their right-handed classmates do. They must solve problems on their own as writing is being taught, reversing the patterns of work they observe. The writing process is likely to be slow for these students since solving problems is more difficult than imitating. When they write, their body language often shows their awkwardness and intense effort.

*Special Problems*
Many of the difficulties left-handed students experience result from trying to adjust to a right-handed world. Some right-handed teachers actually create problems for these students. The writing models and directions appropriate for most students are inappropriate and even counterproductive for left-handed students. Right-handed desks make writing more difficult. Left-to-right motions are particularly awkward for left-handed students. When writing with the right hand, the left-to-right movement permits a constant view of both what is being written at the moment and what has just been written. However, when writing with the left hand, students cannot watch as letters are formed, and the writing hand partially obstructs the view of what has just been written. This difficulty interferes with self-monitoring and spacing and encourages the hooked hand, twisted neck or shoulder, and poor posture characteristic of these students. Poor posture in turn complicates the writing task. A disproportionate number of students with special needs are left-handed.

*Implications*
Before age 8, students who exhibit no clear preference should be encouraged to use their right hand, since school, work, and social conditions are generally intended for right-handed individuals. Once a preference for using the left hand for writing has been established, forcing a change to the right is not justified. Left-handed students must be taught left-handed strategies for handwriting, including paper position, slant, posture, and letter formation. The left-handed student should be seated so that the light comes over the right shoulder. The paper should be slanted to the right on the desk so that the bottom edge of the paper will be at right angles to the writing arm and down-strokes will be drawn straight toward the student. Most importantly, the writing hand should be kept below the line of writing. Instruction may need to be both specific and intense.

CORRECTION

Modify these strategies to meet students' learning needs.

1. *Chalk Talks.* The exaggerated arm movements required to write on the chalkboard illustrate and reinforce the proper motions for writing. Introduce the basic component strokes of letters — such as circles and curves and vertical, horizontal, and slanted lines — or the letters themselves at the chalkboard, verbalizing the strokes. Have students say the strokes as you demonstrate. Guide them to trace your model as they describe the strokes. Emphasize the motions as they make them. Unlike in right-handed writing, a vertical or left slant is acceptable. Providing practice using exaggerated arm movements often helps left-handed students develop proper motion and slant. Make sure the hand does not obscure the writing. When students consistently demonstrate mastery of a letter or stroke, have them write it on their papers, verbalizing the strokes. If hand, paper, or body position are incorrect or letters are poorly formed, have students return to the board and repeat the procedures.

2. *Paper Placement.* The left-handed writer must place the paper correctly at a 30 degree angle, turned clockwise and placed slightly off center to the left side of the desk. This placement, which applies to both cursive and manuscript writing is the opposite of the placement for a right-handed writer. Make sure students learn to slide the paper up on the desk as they work down so they can still control their writing as they write on the last line. If possible, the left-handed students should have a slightly lower desk or writing table so they can more easily view their work.

3. *Left-Hand Pencils.* Left-handed students should use pencils with a hard lead that will not break or smear easily. Some students grip their pencils so tightly and bear down so hard that they constantly break the lead. Because they tend to move their hand and arm over their work, they sometimes smudge their writing. Holding the pencil 1 or 1-1/2 inches from the point helps students see what they are doing. They should slant their pencils with the blunt end toward the left shoulder. Specially shaped pencils and pencil grips encourage students to grasp the pencil correctly. If these are not available, wrap a rubber band around the pencil as a grip. Insist that students keep the writing hand below the writing line at all times so the writing stays visible for easy monitoring.

4. *Model Mentors.* Seat left-handed students together, and then find a left-handed teacher or older student who has already developed satisfactory handwriting skills. Invite him or her to work with your left-handed group. The students will enjoy seeing that a left-handed person can write well and will probably gain a few hints for adjusting to a right-handed world. If no mentor is available and you are a right-handed teacher, practice writing with your left hand until you can demonstrate the movements in the air and then on the chalkboard.

5. *Extra Practice.* • Provide personal chalkboards for independent practice. • Provide activities for drawing, tracing, and clay modeling to improve eye-hand coordination. • Display charts showing hand and pencil position for left-handed writing. • Adapt ideas from Skills 46 and 47.

## 49. WRITING LEGIBLY IN DAILY WORK

DETECTION    This may be a special skill need of students who

- Submit written assignments that are difficult to read
- Produce messy written work
- Appear careless in completing written assignments
- Seem to know more than their written responses indicate
- Dislike writing
- Alternate between manuscript and cursive writing

*Description*    Writing legibly in daily work is the goal of handwriting lessons. Daily handwriting involves the same basic elements as handwriting lessons: size, shape, slant, spacing, and proportion of letters and words. Personal styles, intensity, and consistency are also involved. The position of the paper and the hand while writing not only influence legibility but may also show how much effort the student must exert to write. The handwriting that is acceptable for daily assignments is typically more fluent and less exact than that expected in handwriting lessons. However, with few exceptions, teachers should not accept unsatisfactory handwriting in any school work. If the student's writing is satisfactory in handwriting lessons, then the teacher should require similar writing in daily work. If a discrepancy does exist, note whether the student is drawing the letters rather than writing. As students progress through the traditional curriculum, the demands for handwritten responses increase.

*Special Problems*    The primary cause of illegible handwriting is ineffective teaching. Students whose performance of handwriting lessons is unsatisfactory often perform even worse in daily writing tasks. Even those who are able to form their letters perfectly for special lessons may not do so when the focus is on the content of the written response rather than on the mechanics of recording. Illegible daily assignments often result when students minds work faster than their hands, causing them to race through the writing in an effort to keep up with their thoughts. This is particularly true of gifted, impatient, and impulsive children. Physical delays, visual-motor weaknesses, and neurological dysfunctions can interfere with the ability to write legibly. Special students who may experience difficulty writing legibly include the learning disabled, physically handicapped, and visually impaired.

*Implications*    Students whose writing is not clearly legible often receive low grades in all subjects. In effect, they are being graded on their writing problems, not on their knowledge of the subjects they write about. Many students appear to be careless and in a hurry to complete their written assignments and so produce illegible writing. From such students teachers should require legible writing. However, some students with writing difficulties record responses only with great effort, write a fraction of what they know, or do not finish assignments. Teachers must view handwriting as a tool for expressing thoughts and knowledge. When that tool impedes expression, substitute alternatives such as keyboarding to improve written expression.

CORRECTION

Modify these strategies to meet students' learning needs.

1. *Writing Grader.* Consistently award 2 grades to each written assignment: one for content and one for handwriting. If work is not neat and legible, return it to students. Have them correct their handwriting using a colored felt tip pen to write over their errors. If the assignment is still illegible, have them rewrite it for their writing grade. This strategy rewards those who write correctly the first time and motivates those who do not to improve so they do not have to rewrite assignments.

2. *Twice Write.* Guide students who have writing difficulties to record their responses as a rough draft that they can read. Then have them use a word processor or typewriter to produce a final copy that anyone can read. The first version expresses ideas, while the second teaches alternatives to handwriting.

3. *Target Instruction.* Some students need specific instruction in only 1–2 elements of handwriting. In these cases, place a student's hand in yours as you write together or have students watch you model and join in as you describe strokes and form words. If a few lessons do not remedy the problem, conduct formal handwriting lessons.

4. *Contracted Writing.* When students seem to know more than their written responses indicate, implement a writing contract. First, orally quiz the students to determine the extent of the gap between what they know and what they write; discuss the problem with them. Then, agree on a certain proportion of each assignment to be handwritten legibly, with a greater portion to be keyboarded. What ratio is reasonable depends on how much handwriting problems interfere with expression. For a student with mild problems, the contract might be for the first half of each assignment to be handwritten and the last half keyboarded; a student with a more serious problem might handwrite only the first paragraph. A complex problem might even call for most responses to be given orally.

5. *Meaning and Reason.* The handwriting required for daily work should be both meaningful and reasonable. Writing a new story ending is more meaningful than copying the whole story. What constitutes a reasonable amount of writing and amount of time in which to accomplish it will vary according to students' handwriting proficiency; writing contracts can make reasonable demands on individual students. Punishing students by having them copy pages from an encyclopedia or write repeated "I shall not" lines is neither meaningful nor reasonable but instead is almost guaranteed to teach negative handwriting habits and attitudes.

6. *Letter of the Week.* • Select a letter of the week that needs improvement. All students will concentrate on that particular letter. Troublesome letters that are often written illegibly are *e, n, d, t, r, i, a, h,* and *b*. Several times during the week, select papers at random or have students exchange papers, and grade them on the letter of the week.

7. *Extra Practice.* • Encourage neatness by displaying daily spotlight papers that are written neatly and legibly. • Use individual chalkboards for students to practice their written responses. • Adapt strategies from Skill 46.

## 50. SPELLING CORRECTLY ON TESTS

DETECTION       This may be a special skill need of students who

- Perform poorly on spelling tests
- Exhibit inconsistent spelling performance
- Spell better on weekly tests than on unit tests
- Are not good spellers in general
- Have weak word recognition skills

*Description*    Correct spelling is a mechanical skill that supports written expression. Spelling words correctly on spelling tests is often easier than spelling words correctly on daily work. For weekly tests, one need only memorize a short list of words. Students must develop a study system and stay calm during the tests to succeed. Regular, teacher-directed practice sessions help most students.

*Special Problems*    Some students have heard their parents or other adults decry spelling as a difficult task and even state, "I couldn't spell either." Such statements almost give students permission to give up on spelling. Admittedly, spelling tests present a real problem for some students, especially those with language differences, auditory discrimination or processing problems, or poor visual memory. Poor performance on spelling tests can also result from test anxiety, inadequate study habits, or a linguistic dysfunction associated with phonics or decoding in general. Students with difficulties are frequently told to take their spelling words home and study them. The anxious parent drills the child on the words each evening, and the child continues to perform poorly on weekly tests. Many teachers require their students to write each spelling word some magical number of times, an ineffective practice that should be discontinued. Several common error patterns appear in misspellings: substituting vowels; omitting silent letters; omitting doubled letters; and spelling nonphonetic words phonetically. Special students who may exhibit spelling problems include the hearing impaired, language disabled, learning disabled, or speech disordered.

*Implications*    The most obvious implication of poor spelling is poor spelling grades. Many weak spellers also exhibit problems in the other language arts. Spelling skills can be taught along with related word analysis skills. Structural analysis may offer particular assistance with multisyllabic words. Intervention might involve simply reducing the number or types of words to be mastered for any one test, identifying a word study method that works for specific students and teaching it, or giving students extra practice sessions before tests. At home, parents can identify the words on the list that their child does not know, divide by four, and study only that number of words each evening, rather than the entire list. This strategy permits the student to concentrate on a few words each evening, making success on the weekly test more likely. If the student exhibits a consistent error pattern, reteaching the pertinent spelling rule or phonics generalization may be sufficient.

CORRECTION

Modify these strategies to meet students' learning needs.

1. *Sensations.* Have students with serious problems trace words in sand or on sandpaper with their fingers. Guide students to either trace the target word or spell it, without the help of prelettered patterns, pronouncing it at the same time. If necessary, pronounce the word with the student. You may need to guide students' fingers until they learn to trace and pronounce words. Move from tactile writing materials to the chalkboard and then to paper.

2. *Pretest Method.* Begin teaching a list of new words with a pretest. Immediately after the pretest, have students check and correct their own papers to determine which words they need to study. Guide them to analyze their errors to determine why they made each error. After teaching the list for 2–3 days, give a second test including only the words students missed on the first test. Again, have students check, correct, explain errors, and receive credit for correct words. Repeat until they spell all the words correctly. Retest students on the entire original list, and repeat the process as needed. When students spell 90 percent of the words correctly, begin a new list. This procedure is the most effective technique for improving students' performance in spelling.

3. *Spelling Test Guidelines.* The following suggestions help students maximize their spelling test efforts:

   a. Learn the words that seem easiest first.
   b. Develop a visual image of how each word looks.
   c. Match each word with a similar word you already know to help you remember the new word.
   d. Use any unusual letter patterns to help you remember words.
   e. Use pretend tests to prepare for spelling tests; take pretend tests in the same manner as the real ones.
   f. If words are very difficult, study only 1–2 at a time; rest 5 minutes, respell the first 1–2 words, and then add 1–2 more words. Repeat as often as necessary.

4. *Look, Say, and See.* Guide students to follow a 6-step procedure to study words:

   a. Look at the word, say it, and see it in your mind;
   b. Copy the word;
   c. Look, say, and see;
   d. Write the word without looking;
   e. Check, look, say, and see;
   f. Write without looking.

5. *Spelling Update.* Teach a few words at a time, checking retention before presenting new words. Begin by teaching and testing a core of 3–5 words. Once a word is spelled correctly on 5 consecutive daily tests, drop that word and add a new one to the cycle.

6. *Extra Practice.* • Provide audiotapes of the next spelling test for students to hear and respond to on their own. • Use progress charts to encourage continued progress on spelling tests. • Help students form study groups to study for spelling tests. • Adapt ideas from Skills 4–6.

## 51. SPELLING SIMPLE AND COMMON WORDS

DETECTION

This may be a special skill need of students who

- Are poor spellers on tests and daily work (Skills 50–53)
- Exhibit serious problems in spelling
- Reveal inconsistent spelling patterns
- Appear to be trying without improving their spelling
- Substitute unrelated words
- Demonstrate weak word recognition skills (Skills 4–7)
- Reverse or transpose letters

*Description*

Correct spelling of common words is essential to functional literacy. These words occur so often that it is not practical for students to request assistance or consult a reference for each one. When students need help spelling simple words, you must provide a personalized program. Spelling involves several language abilities, any one of which can facilitate or impede students' spelling progress.

*Special Problems*

Students who cannot spell common words despite repeated instruction and practice usually have serious deficits that complicate their ability to learn. Many of these students also have significant problems in reading and in all the language arts. Both short- and long-term memory difficulties may be involved. Some students seem unable to connect letters and sounds meaningfully due to a lack of verbal recognition or language processing. Dyslexic students experience letter and word reversals that seriously impede their spelling achievement. Students who cannot spell common words may approach the spelling task haphazardly. They do not use a systematic procedure for learning unknown words, nor are they aware that such procedures exist. Reviewing Figure 3.1, Options for Accommodating Learning Needs and Style, will provide you with suggestions for effectively meeting each student's spelling needs. In some cases, the problem is one of teaching, not learning; past instruction has simply been inappropriate to students' learning needs.

*Implications*

Teaching spelling through oral language is very difficult when working with students who are unable to spell common and simple words. Although you can dictate stories and have students copy their efforts, more direct, structured intervention will usually be necessary. In many cases, you will have to include language development along with auditory and visual intervention. You may need to offer corrective instruction for letter and sound discrimination tasks, visual discrimination, and a variety of speech tasks. Students may also need help in such areas as alphabetizing, letter formation, or handwriting. You can incorporate some of the strategies appropriate for teaching letters, sight words, and phonics into a spelling program. Use a multisensory, highly structured approach that has a set routine. Teach words as units rather than as individual letters or syllables. Use the selected method systematically and consistently. Random instruction results in more frustration than improved spelling performance. Give the selected method time to take effect. Students will need time to adjust to the new procedures. Instruction must focus on diagnosed strengths.

CORRECTION     Modify these strategies to meet students' learning needs.

1. *Recognizing Spelling Errors.* The following list of common spelling errors may help identify specific problem areas on which to focus instruction: (1) phonetically correct spellings, (2) letter reversals, (3) vowel substitutions, (4) vowel omissions, (5) consonant substitutions, and (6) consonant omissions. When you note a consistent error pattern, reteach the phonics generalization or spelling rule that applies. However, teach only the spelling rules that apply consistently or with few exceptions.

2. *Personalization.* Most students with spelling problems need individual or small-group instruction. The use of personal chalkboards (plywood painted with two coats of chalkboard paint), manipulable letters on a flannel-or pegboard, or magic markers, felt tip pens, or brush and paint maintains interest and makes spelling a different learning experience. Sampler 9.4 is an additional activity to assist students in learning these words. Although it may appear to students to be an art activity, in reality they are learning to spell these troublesome words and having fun at the same time.

3. *Multisensory Instruction.* Much like Sensations in Skill 50 these strategies involve students in seeing, saying, touching, and moving letters to reinforce spelling. Students can assemble letters cut from tagboard or plastic moveable alphabets to gain a feel for each word. A few students may even benefit from having words traced on their back as they are tracing raised outlines of words with their fingers and spelling the word aloud. In most cases, teach only 1–2 words in one 10–15 minute session. Begin the next session by reviewing the previous words; if students do not recall the words, reteach them.

4. *Image Writing II.* Emphasize each step of the procedure suggested for remembering letters and sight words (Skill 4). Write the target word on the board, placing above it a key picture, such as a red crayon for red. Students should (a) use their index and middle fingers to trace each letter of the word you wrote while saying the letter names; (b) copy the word underneath the stimulus, saying the letter names; (c) repeat steps (a) and (b) twice. After 3 tracings of the word you wrote, most of the chalk should be erased, leaving only the image of the markings. Have students close their eyes to try to see the word and then trace the image with chalk, again spelling aloud. Erase the board and have students write the word from memory. Repeat the procedure as needed.

5. *Look, Say, and See II.* Guide students to repeat a 6-step procedure several times to study words: (a) Look at the word, say it, and see it in your mind; (b) Copy the word, say each letter as you write; (c) Look, say, see, and trace and say the letters; (d) Write the word without looking; (e) Check, correct, look, say, see, and write and say; (f) Write without looking and check.

6. *Extra Practice.* • Prepare easy word-search puzzles using spelling words. • Have students play Go Fish with spelling words on index cards. • Give students groups of 3 target spelling words; have them find the one in each group that is misspelled. • Adapt activities from Skills 4–7.

## 52. SPELLING DIFFICULT WORDS

DETECTION    This may be a special skill need of students who

- Frequently misspell difficult words in daily assignments
- Repeatedly misspell the same words
- Are generally poor spellers on tests and daily work
- Transpose letters

*Description*    Correct spelling of difficult words requires concentrated effort. Although they may not be used frequently, these words show consistency in their misspellings. They are often referred to as spelling "demons" and cannot be spelled phonetically. Some examples include *recieve* for *receive, beauteful* for *beautiful,* and *stoped* for *stopped.* Adults may continue to misspell these words. Students must simply memorize these words.

*Special Problems*    Students who consistently make the same error on difficult words overgeneralize; they have probably been taught a spelling rule that does not apply consistently and has numerous exceptions. Students also may have been taught to focus their attention on the "hard spots" in words rather than to learn the word as a whole unit. They may not know that certain words are frequently misspelled and that they should be attentive to these words. Students with special needs in all areas will often experience difficulty in learning to spell these words. Disadvantaged or educationally deprived students, reluctant readers, and slow learners will also encounter difficulty. In fact, most adults must use a dictionary to verify the spelling of certain words.

*Implications*    Teaching difficult words or spelling demons to students who are unable to spell simple and common words is difficult but possible. Provide direct, structured interventions for small groups or individuals. Teach those few spelling rules that can be consistently applied. Post common spelling demons on tagboard at the front of the class for frequent reference. Make students aware that some words are especially difficult to learn to spell and encourage them to use their dictionaries to verify the correct spelling of these words. Teach students to use mnemonics. For example, "A Rat In The House May Eat The Ice Cream" will help students remember how to spell *arithmetic.* Other mnemonic strategies may be devised to aid students in learning their personal spelling demons. Posting a list of spelling demons on a poster at the front of the classroom or requiring students to keep a personal list will save the students considerable time when editing and proofreading daily assignments. Additional suggestions for assisting students in learning these difficult words may be obtained from Figure 3.1, Options for Accommodating Learning Needs and Style.

CORRECTION

Modify these strategies to meet students' learning needs.

1. *Careful Consideration.* Assist students to develop an attitude of careful thought about troublesome words. Guide students to (a) pronounce words to themselves, (b) lightly write their best guesses at the spellings of the words, (c) look up questionable words after they have finished writing, (d) correct their errors, and (e) record the words on a personal list of troublesome words for reference. To avoid classroom interruptions, assign a spelling buddy to assist in the location process. Add, or have students add, the questionable words to their spelling list for the week. Good spelling is part habit and part attitude; requiring care and cooperation can help build the proper habits and attitudes.

2. *Troublesome Patterns.* Students sometimes display spelling difficulties associated with specific patterns of words. Explain recurring letter patterns, find and discuss related words, and include pattern words in the students weekly list until the pattern is mastered.

3. *Troublesome Exceptions.* Teach students exceptions, or words spelled in a manner that is inconsistent with the language system. Underline the differences, clarify pronunciation, find words that follow a similar pattern, and have students pronounce and write the words. Have students who correctly spell the target words explain how they remember them; refer back to these spelling demons regularly.

4. *Spellademon.* Dictate ten spelling demons. Ask the students to use six of the spelling demons in a paragraph. When they finish writing, have students exchange papers and check for spelling errors. This activity also enhances proofreading skills.

5. *Catch the Teacher.* As you write instructions, directions, or sentences on the chalkboard or overhead projector, deliberately misspell some of your students' spelling demons. See how quickly students identify the misspelled word. The student who catches the error may come to the board to make the correction. The benefits of this strategy are twofold, as students are improving their proofreading skills as well. An extension of this strategy is to appoint several students as proofreaders for the week. They are responsible for making sure that anything written on the chalkboard or overhead transparency is spelled correctly.

6. *Waxed Spelling.* To add novelty and interest to learning spelling demons, try this activity. Provide each student with a strip of wax paper. Have them place the wax paper on top of their writing paper and write their spelling demons on the wax paper as you dictate. When the list is completed, have students remove the wax paper and check their spelling by coloring over their spelling words on the paper with a dark crayon. The darker the color, the more vivid the spelling words will appear.

7. *Extra Practice.* • Pick a Demon Word for the Day. Have students write a sentence using the word. • Develop sentences with demon words and their common misspelling. Ask the students to read the sentence and circle or underline the correct spelling. • Pair students to study their spelling demons. One student acts as the teacher, dictating the spelling demons to the other student and assisting in self-correction. Then have students reverse roles.

## 53.  SPELLING CORRECTLY IN DAILY WORK

**DETECTION**

This may be a special skill need of students who

- Frequently misspell words on daily assignments
- Appear to be careless in how they spell
- Spell well on spelling tests but not in daily work
- Display poor handwriting, possibly to hide spelling errors (Skill 49)
- Have weak word recognition skills (Skills 4–7)
- Seldom use a dictionary voluntarily
- Have weak vocabulary skills
- Demonstrate limited proofreading skills

*Description*

Spelling correctly in daily assignments is the goal of spelling lessons and tests; however, it is much more difficult than spelling correctly on tests. Daily attention to spelling is an unending task, like dieters' daily need to be careful about what they eat. One of the greatest dangers of allowing students to misspell words in daily work is that, in a matter of days, the misspellings may look correct to them.

*Special Problems*

For many students, misspellings reflect carelessness, lack of motivation, not being taught how to remember spellings, inadequate knowledge of proofreading and dictionary usage, a limited reading and speaking vocabulary, and difficulties associated with short- and long-term memory. Students who do not write frequently will not spell well. Practice requiring students to fill-in, circle, underline, or select the letter of the best answer gives students few opportunities to apply their spelling skills. When students view spelling as an activity only for tests, they will exert little effort to spell correctly in daily work. Auditory and visual handicaps are responsible for some spelling problems. A number of special students, including some gifted youngsters who are not concerned with details, frequently misspell words in daily work.

*Implications*

The extent to which spelling problems interfere with students' performance and progress in all areas depends in part on their teachers' grading policies. Some teachers count misspelled words as incorrect responses, even on science tests; others grade only the content of the response. The most important words for students to learn to spell correctly are high-frequency words and key terms. Remember that excessive or repeated criticism about spelling can cause some students to stop writing. Spelling is an important literacy skill, but, as adults, the students will probably have access to dictionaries or spell checkers to correct errors. Make writing an important part of the curriculum, particularly the editing stage of the writing process. Periodically have students edit each other's papers, lightly circle misspelled words, and return them to their author to correct before submission to the teacher for grading. When you provide many opportunities for students to write and rewrite their thoughts, they are continuously exercising their spelling skills beyond the weekly test. Revision activities should, however, include correction of spelling; proofreading should follow. Be sure to praise content and special efforts beyond the mechanics of spelling and grammar.

CORRECTION

Modify these strategies to meet students' learning needs.

1. *Process Emphasis.* Process writing includes, among other steps, editing or proofwriting. Editing, including a check for correct spelling on short answer as well as sentence and paragraph-length material should become second nature. Use the chalkboard to demonstrate how to go through a paper and proofread for errors, particularly spelling. If word processors are available, permit the occasional use of spellcheckers.

2. *Multi-sensations.* Spelling texts tend to favor a single sensory channel for spelling instruction. Students with other sensory strengths are forced to rely on their weaknesses in learning to spell. Teach these students a systematic multisensory strategy for learning words: (a) present the word on chalkboard or card and pronounce it; (b) students repeat while looking at the word; (c) students close eyes, revisualize word, and orally spell; (d) students check oral spelling; and (e) write the word. If students spell incorrectly at any step, start over at step (b). Repeat the cycle three times for each word.

3. *Dictionary Detection.* Demonstrate the utility of the dictionary for word spellings using the students' own words. If the dictionary seems to overwhelm students, use a picture or simplified dictionary. To begin practice, you may need to enforce somewhat unrealistic rules, such as requiring students to check the spelling of at least 3 words on a given assignment until they have established the habit. Permit students to use the spelling references during content tests, with the stipulation that spelling errors will be counted off; this often motivates students to use their dictionaries.

4. *Credited Spelling.* If necessary, award either special privileges or bonus points on students' spelling grades if students maintain or improve daily spelling through a specified time period. With students who have particular difficulty, make a contract as to timelines and rewards.

5. *Malapropisms.* Students often confuse one word for another because of faulty pronunciation or poor spelling habits. Teach commomly confused word pairs through word meaning activities, or use the wrong word in a sentence and have students cross it out and write in the correct word, for instance, "The police squab had an emergency run. The right word is s_ _ _ _ ."

6. *Buddies.* Assign a good speller as a buddy to a student who frequently misspells words in daily work. Before the poor speller may turn in work for grading, the buddy must approve it. The buddy scans the work for misspellings, marks lightly, and returns the paper to the owner for correction. Words that are consistently misspelled should be placed in a file box for additional corrective instruction.

7. *Extra Practice.* • Develop teams of students for the purpose of looking over each other's work before considering an assignment finished. • If you notice that a particular word is giving several students difficulty, periodically throughout the day say "Who can spell it?" Pronounce the word and call on the students to spell it. • Develop a Vanishing Spelling worksheet for frequently misspelled words. Initially the word appears with one letter omitted, then two, three, and so on, until there are only blank spaces for the student to write the entire word. • Adapt ideas from Skills 4–7.

# H ANDWRITING AND SPELLING SAMPLERS

The samplers on the next five pages illustrate activities for developing and correcting handwriting and spelling skills. All are ready to copy, but you may need to adjust instructions to meet students needs.

9.1 **Proper Spacing.** Sampler 9.1 can assist students who have difficulty spacing between letters and words in manuscript writing. Provide students with a copy of the sampler. Read each sentence aloud. Have students draw a mark in colored pencil wherever a space should appear. Instruct students to copy the sentences in the boxed lines provided, printing only one letter per box and skipping a box between words. Once students are proficient with the sampler, give each student a blank copy to place beneath the student's writing paper as a guide for spacing. The initial activity helps students appreciate the difficulties facing the reader who tries to read improperly spaced writing so that they become more conscious of their own errors.

9.2 **Perfect Slant.** Sampler 9.2 is designed to reinforce correct slant in cursive writing. Each student receives a copy of the sampler to place beneath his or her writing paper. The slanted lines can be seen through the writing paper, guiding the proper slant of the letters. This strategy is particularly useful when initially teaching cursive writing or when slant is a particular problem for an individual student. Adjust the width between lines to meet individual needs.

9.3 **My Spelling Story.** Sampler 9.3 has a dual purpose: to practice handwriting and to apply spelling words in context. Give students a copy of the sampler and ask them to write a story using all of their spelling words. This can be a fun activity as students develop unique stories. It provides creative writing experience and allows the teacher to evaluate students' use of words in context.

9.4 **Spelling Art.** Sampler 9.4 can help students learn their personal list of unknown words. Have students write each unknown word 1″ to 1–1/2″ high with a crayon or magic marker. Let them select a second color and outline the word with the new color. Repeat until they have used at least four or five different colors for each word. With each repetition, students pronounce the word, say each letter softly as they outline it, and say the word again. This strategy allows them to say the word, see the word, feel the word, and hear the word. The strategy actively involves students in practicing spelling words without creating unnecessary boredom. The students think they are doing art!

9.5 **My Spelling Demons.** Designed for use with Skill 52, this activity permits the student to keep a list of his/her own spelling demons. These spelling demons may be unmastered words from the weekly final test or words that are consistently misspelled in daily assignments. Add words to the list as they become problematic for the student. Set aside five minutes each day for students to study their spelling demons. Permitting students to chart their progress on words they master would be an added incentive.

Name _____

## PROPER SPACING

 1.  Mydogisacollie.

 2.  Pleasecomeandplay.

 3.  Howareyou?

Name _____

# ✎ PERFECT SLANT ✎

# ⭐ MY SPELLING STORY ⭐

_____

_____

_____

_____

_____

_____

_____

_____

Name _____

# ✿✿ SPELLING ART ✿✿

1. _____

2. _____

3. _____

4. _____

5. _____

6. _____

7. _____

8. _____

9. _____

10. _____

## 🎨MY SPELLING DEMONS

1. _____

2. _____

3. _____

4. _____

5. _____

6. _____

7. _____

8. _____

9. _____

10. _____

11. _____

12. _____

13. _____

14. _____

15. _____

16. _____

17. _____

18. _____

19. _____

20. _____

## REFLECTIONS

1. Activities for teaching readiness skills to students with special needs are often modifications of those appropriate for teaching most students the same skills. Locate the strategies recommended for teaching fine-motor skills in the teacher's edition of a readiness book. To identify modifications, contrast the activities listed in the teacher's edition with those suggested in this chapter for the same skill.

2. This chapter is organized according to two support skill areas: handwriting and spelling. Compare the skills listed in each area with the ones in the scope and sequence charts for major handwriting and spelling series. Which areas receive the most attention? Do the skill listings vary according to grade level? Which ones should receive more emphasis for special learners? Justify your responses.

3. The discussion of each handwriting skill lists some of the observable behaviors that signal problems in that skill. Review these behaviors and then observe a regular and/or special education classroom. During a writing or content lesson, compare students' writing behaviors with the Detection behaviors listed for each of the skills. Note any other deficient behaviors. Discuss the implications of these behaviors with experienced teachers.

4. When focused on a particular student with special handwriting needs, classroom observations often reveal important diagnostic and prescriptive data. Observe such a student in the classroom during writing instruction; compare observed behaviors with the Detection behaviors listed in this section for each special handwriting need. List your tentative conclusions and any additional information you need to confirm your hypotheses. If possible, observe the same student on several occasions to compare progress.

5. Spelling and handwriting are skills that support written expression. With this in mind, critique the suggestion that special students be permitted to use resources for spelling correctly on written assignments. What about all students? What is your position on permitting all students to substitute typewritten or word-processed work for handwritten assignments? Does your position differ for special-needs students? Why or why not?

6. Planning targeted writing instruction for special learners often begins with careful observation of their behaviors while they are writing and analysis of their written products. Observe a special learner to identify his or her writing needs; then use the Corrective Principles (Part I) to select and modify Correction strategies to plan two writing lessons.

7. This chapter lists a number of guidelines for corrective instruction in spelling and handwriting. Review these principles, and then observe a fourth-grade class during spelling instruction. Note which principles are being implemented. Compare your observations with the guidelines listed. Are there discrepancies? If so, do you concur with what you observed? Justify your responses.

8. For each handwriting and spelling need, only a few Correction strategies are listed. Based on your classroom observations and/or your own experience, add to or modify the corrective strategies for the special handwriting or spelling need of your choice.

9. Collect several final weekly spelling tests from poor spellers and analyze the misspelled words for error patterns. Compare the error patterns with those listed in Skill 50. Are the error patterns similar? What strategies would you recommend for correcting these spelling errors?

10. The discussion of each spelling skill lists some observable behaviors that signal problems in that skill. Review these behaviors and observe a regular and/or special education classroom. During a spelling lesson, compare

students' spelling behaviors with the Detection behaviors listed for each of the skills. Note any other deficient behaviors. Discuss the implications of these behaviors with experienced teachers.

11. Suggestions for teaching special students handwriting and spelling are presented in several language arts and special education references. Compare and contrast discussions in these sources with the information in Chapter 9.

Barbe, Walter B., Francis, Azalia S., & Braun, Lois A. (Eds.). (1982). *Spelling: Basic skills for effective communication.* Columbus, OH: Zaner-Bloser.

Barbe, Walter B., Lucus, Virginia H., & Wasylyk, Thomas M. (Eds.). (1984). *Handwriting: Basic skills for effective communication.* Columbus, OH: Zaner-Bloser.

Bender, William N. (1992). *Learning disabilities: Characteristics, identification, and teaching strategies.* Boston: Allyn and Bacon.

Bos, Candace S., & Vaughn, Sharon. (1991). *Strategies for teaching students with learning and behavior problems* (2nd ed.). Boston: Allyn and Bacon.

Choate, J. S., Enright, B. E., Miller, L. J., Poteet, J. A., & Rakes, T. A. (1992). *Curriculum-based assessment and programming* (2nd ed.). Boston: Allyn and Bacon.

Hammill, Donald D., & Bartel, Nettie R. (1990). *Teaching students with learning and behavior problems* (5th ed.). Boston: Allyn and Bacon.

Henderson, Edmund H. (1990). *Teaching spelling* (2nd ed.). Boston: Houghton Mifflin.

Heward, William L., & Orlansky, Michael D. (1992). *Exceptional children: An introductory survey of special education* (4th ed.). New York: Merrill.

Lerner, Janet W. (1989). *Learning Disabilities: Theories, diagnosis, and teaching strategies* (5th ed.). Boston: Houghton Mifflin.

Mercer, Cecil D., & Mercer, Ann R. (1989). *Teaching students with learning problems* (2nd ed.). Columbus, OH: Merrill.

Polloway, Edward A., Patton, James R., Payne, James S., & Payne, Ruth A. (1989). *Strategies for teaching learners with special needs* (4th ed.). Columbus, OH: Merrill.

Rakes, Thomas A., & Choate, Joyce S. (1989). *Language arts: Detecting and correcting special needs.* Boston: Allyn and Bacon.

Salend, Spencer J. (1990). *Effective mainstreaming.* New York: Macmillan.

Salvia, John, & Hughes, Charles. (1990). *Curriculum-based assessment: Testing what is taught.* New York: Macmillan.

Wallace, Gerald, Cohen, Sandra B., & Polloway, Edward A. (1987). *Language arts: Teaching exceptional students.* Austin, TX: Pro-Ed.

# CHAPTER TEN

## ARITHMETIC COMPUTATION: FROM CONCRETE TO ABSTRACT

— *Brian E. Enright and Joyce S. Choate*

The mathematical computation skills are the concepts and procedures for combining and manipulating numerical values to produce numerical answers. Although these are the skills that may first come to mind when basic mathematics is mentioned, computation skills take on meaning only when computation is used to solve problems. Math readiness skills build the foundation for later computation of numbers. The discussions in this chapter begin with a few important readiness skills and then move through the computation skills needed to progress through traditional math curricula and to function in society.

## THE COMPUTATION SKILLS

Mathematics readiness skills prepare students to compute and solve problems. This chapter groups these skills into two areas: understanding basic number concepts, and writing and summatizing numbers.

## Mathematics Readiness Skills

The readiness skills are the groundwork for all future learning in mathematics. In addition, students develop the concepts of basic relations at this beginning level. Understanding these concepts is essential to develop future computation and problem-solving skills. All learners — regardless of age or ability — must master basic mathematics readiness skills.

Understanding basic number concepts, Skill 54, covers a broad range of concepts and skills. Instruction begins with identifying sets of objects. Students must note the unifying features of a group of objects, as well as the objects that do not belong; that is, they must understand the relationships of objects within a set. Recognizing *more* or *less* sets the stage for introducing addition and subtraction and also prepares learners to select the correct operation in problem solving. Counting objects to 10 emphasizes one-to-one correspondence. Seeing relationships between groups, or joining sets, builds upon the ability to count to 10. Ability to demonstrate the number concepts — displaying five objects when asked to demonstrate *5* — is fundamental to understanding mathematics.

Skill 55, writing numbers and summatizing numbers, builds upon and extends the basic number concepts. To move into operational mathematics, students need to recognize and write numbers, eventually all the way to 100. Students must also be able to recognize a set of objects and instantly assign a quantity to that set, or *summatize* the set. This ability is essential to bridge the gap between counting and number-fact memory.

## Specific Computation Skills

This chapter divides computation skills into three broad groups: whole numbers, fractions, and decimals. All of the computation skills rest upon Skill 56, remembering basic number facts. Number facts are the building blocks of computation. Until the basic number facts for each operation become automatic, students can do little more than count forward or backward. Thus, number facts must be memorized.

Whole number computation, Skills 57–60, builds upon basic number facts and lays the foundation for computation of fractions and decimals. Mastery of the concept and mechanics of regrouping is essential to higher-level computation. Each of the four basic operations — addition, subtraction, multiplication, and division — has a unique algorithm sequence that students must understand and follow. These computation skills are tools for understanding and computing fractions and decimals and for later problem solving.

As a subset of the rational number system, fractional numbers describe the relationship between the number of parts an object is divided into and the number of those parts that are present or absent. Understanding fractional concepts, Skill 61, includes this basic premise, as well as converting fractions to common forms and reducing fractions to their simplest form. To compute fractions, Skill 62, students must build upon Skills 57–60 to understand and follow the algorithmic sequences for adding, subtracting, multiplying, and dividing fractions. Multiplying and dividing fractions is particularly difficult for many students because this kind of multiplication or division seems to violate students' previous understanding of those operations.

Decimal concepts, Skill 63, build upon fractional concepts but are probably easier to master than fractions because decimals stay in base 10. Decimal computation is an extension of whole-number computation, with the decimal point added. Placement of the decimal point in the answer for each operation is governed by an algorithmic sequence students must understand and follow. Computation of decimals and all other computation skills are both tools for solving problems and the means to begin the problem-solving, or decision-making, process itself.

## DETECTION OF SPECIAL COMPUTATION NEEDS

Any targeted instructional plan for computation must begin with identifying the errors to be corrected. Specific mathematics skills in need of correction may be identified in three ways: (1) by direct testing, using either formal or informal measures; (2) by analysis of daily classroom performance; and (3) by synthesis of testing and classroom performance.

### Formal Detection

Formal tests of mathematics computation are usually included in standardized achievement tests. Although such tests measure accurate computation, they do not locate the point of error. The tests may give credit for skills students do not have, such as automatic mastery of facts, while not giving credit for partial answers that demonstrate skill acquisition. Standardized tests provide useful screening information and, when they also pinpoint errors, yield important instructional information. Tests that evaluate and determine the meaning of incorrect answers offer valuable information for planning corrective instruction.

### Informal Detection

Unlike assessment in some other subject areas, informal assessment of computation skills is a relatively straightforward process. Students are given computation problems to answer from a unit test in the math textbook or from a published test, and then asked to explain their answers. Basic facts may be assessed either orally or in writing, but the rate of performance must be timed. Other formats for assessing computation skills require the student to select correct answers from choices, write the steps of the computation, think aloud while computing, or apply computation to solve word problems. Regardless of format, identifying the student's errors and successes is essential.

Analysis of students' written responses to daily classroom assignments also offers important diagnostic information. When simple computations are involved, teachers can often infer errors from incorrect answers. However, with more complex computation, the teacher may need to discuss answers with the students to confirm the source of errors.

A checklist, such as Figure 10.1, is a convenient tool for analyzing test results and daily work samples. A checklist can also be used as an outline of the important computation skills; as a form on which to record and monitor students' performance and progress; as a supplement to other measures; as a guide to analyzing and recording test results and/or to documenting performance over periods of time; and as a form to structure and record classroom observations.

Classroom observations of students performing computation activities can yield valuable assessment information. Behaviors that offer insight into students' computation abilities include the amount of time they take to compute answers; whether they need fingers or marks as crutches; questions they ask and answers they give; oral explanations of answers; how performance varies across concepts and operations; rate at which students master new concepts and mechanics; and especially the specific types of errors students make. Behaviors that may signal a particular computation difficulty are listed at the beginning of the discussions of Skills 54–64 and in Figure 10.1. When teachers observe the same behaviors on several occasions, they have confirmed a consistent error pattern needing corrective instruction. Teachers must carefully design the instruction to meet students' unique and special needs.

## SPECIAL POPULATIONS

The primary consideration in detecting and correcting special computation difficulties must be the individual student's unique learning needs and preferences. However, certain characteristics of special groups suggest possible problems that some individual group members may experience in computation.

Early mastery of the mathematics readiness skills reflects an early environment that fosters language development and awareness of numbers, as well as the absence of disabilities that interfere with participation in or absorption of such experiences. Special students in many categories, especially those who are disadvantaged or have cognitive deficits, may enter formal mathematics instruction with few readiness skills. Many special learners, including the gifted students who avoid details and drill, do not quickly learn the basic number facts. Because of their complexity and reliance upon prerequisite skills, division, fractions, and decimals will be difficult for some members of most groups.

Mathematical computation is probably the most culture-free of the basic skills, as the satisfactory performance of a wide range of culturally diverse students shows. However, computation is an exacting skill that requires

**FIGURE 10.1 / A Checklist of Common Computation Errors**

Mathematical computation is a tool that takes on meaning when applied within the context of problem solving. Computation is an exacting skill that requires both an understanding of concepts and attention to detail. Error analysis is central to planning appropriate instruction. Use this checklist to analyze and record the errors that the student frequently makes in order to identify where to begin corrective instruction.

**Mathematics Readiness**

*Understanding Basic Number Concepts*
____ Cannot identify sets of objects
____ Does not identify more or less
____ Cannot count, count objects, or demonstrate number concepts to 10

*Writing and Summatizing Numbers*
____ Does not demonstrate mastery of the basic number concepts
____ Cannot correctly count, read, and/or write numbers to 100
____ Cannot show a set number of fingers or the value of a set quickly

**Whole Number Operations**

*Basic Number Facts*
____ Counts on fingers or relies on a number line for basic computation
____ Frequently misstates simple computation answers
____ Takes more than three seconds to write the answer to a fact

*Addition*
____ Cannot instantly give the sums of the 100 basic addition facts
____ Does not correctly add multidigit numbers or more than two numbers
____ Incorrectly regroups when adding
____ Does not apply the correct algorithm sequence

*Subtraction*
____ Cannot instantly give the differences of the 100 basic subtraction facts
____ Does not correctly subtract multidigit numbers
____ Incorrectly regroups when subtracting
____ Does not apply the correct algorithm sequence

*Multiplication*
____ Cannot instantly give the products of the 100 basic multiplication facts
____ Does not correctly multiply multidigit numbers
____ Incorrectly regroups when multiplying
____ Does not apply the correct algorithm sequence

*Division*
____ Cannot instantly give the quotients of the 90 basic division facts
____ Does not correctly divide multidigit numbers
____ Incorrectly regroups in the division process
____ Does not apply the correct algorithm sequence

**Fractions**

*Understanding Fractional Concepts*
____ Does not see a relationship between the parts and the whole
____ Exhibits errors in whole number computation

*Computing Fractions*
____ Does not demonstrate understanding of fractional concepts
____ Does not find the lowest common denominator
____ Does not apply the correct algorithm sequence

**Decimals**

*Understanding Decimal Concepts*
____ Displays little understanding of the concept of place value
____ Records answers without regard to decimal values

*Computing Decimals*
____ Exhibits little understanding of decimal concepts
____ Displays difficulty reading and writing decimals
____ Omits or places the decimal point incorrectly

Adapted from B. E. Enright (1990). Mathematics Assessment Tips: A Checklist of Common Errors. *Diagnostique, 16* (1), 45–48, with permission.

attention to detail. Students with behavior disorders or learning disabilities and even some who are academically gifted, may not consistently compute correctly because of inattention to detail. When mathematics is a specific area of weakness for a student with learning disabilities, all of the computation skills are apt to be difficult. Advanced computation demands complex, higher-order cognitive processing that may exceed the capabilities of some students who are mentally retarded or slow learners. Though they may get a slow start because of weak readiness skills, students who are disadvantaged may not evidence specific computation difficulties once they have proper readiness instruction. Students with speech disorders are not particularly likely to find computation problematic. Regardless of the characteristics of the special group, individual needs must be the focus of corrective instruction.

## CORRECTION OF COMPUTATION SKILLS

Mathematics is a science of relationships of numbers and objects. Students must understand these relationships as a real part of their world in order to learn. Developing the mathematics readiness skills takes a considerable amount of time, but the time is well spent. Even use of a calculator relies upon basic number and computation concepts. The readiness skills are also important to older students as prerequisites to consumer and survival mathematics. Students must develop readiness skills before attempting computation in order to avoid misconceptions and error patterns that will follow them for years.

Measures of achievement show clear differences between students who know number facts and students who do not. Mastery of basic number facts speeds computation and permits students to focus time and attention on higher-order computation and problem-solving skills.

Certain computation skills are more difficult than others to master. Especially problematic are regrouping; the use of zero in computation; complex multiplication of whole numbers; division of whole numbers; the concept and computation of fractions, particularly multiplication and division of fractions; and placement of the decimal point. Careful, step-by-step instruction in these skills is important for all students and essential for special learners.

## Key Corrective Principles

Consistency and repetition are key ingredients of corrective instruction in the mathematical readiness and computation skills. In addition, of the principles for corrective instruction presented in Chapter 3, perhaps the most critical are these:

— Teach diagnostically
— Use manipulatives to develop basic concepts
— Apply principles of behaviorism
— Use flowcharts to develop proper algorithms
— Teach self-monitoring
— Place computation in the context of real-life problems
— Teach for mastery

Diagnostic teaching is essential to pinpoint both successes and errors to target for correction. Because mathematical computation is a detailed process, students must be taught and then coached to attend to detail.

## Corrective Themes

Controversy abounds regarding the so-called correct approach to teaching computation. Conventional wisdom proposes the exclusive use of manipulatives, or concrete objects, so that students can understand the concepts of mathematics. This approach is clearly the first choice; however, not all students learn best this way. Some students have significant trouble making the transition from understanding to doing. For these students, a second, more structurally oriented approach is needed to facilitate transfer from concrete to abstract.

Recurring themes in the corrective strategies include carefully structured and sequenced instruction so that each concept, skill, and activity build upon previous ones; consistent repetition, followed by restructuring of similar activities, for introduction and initial practice of concepts and skills prior to creative practice and application; frequent use of manipulatives; active student involvement; and the use of flowcharts. Specific instruction in algorithmic sequence is the key to successful computation. Algorithm flowcharts provide roadmaps through the skill sequences and are natural aids for self-monitoring as students work through complex computation. The student's age must be considered when planning corrective instruction. Although all students will need to master the readiness skills, once they understand the basic concepts, older and less able students may need to focus on effective use of calculators and applying computation to solve real-world problems.

## SPECIFIC SKILLS AND STRATEGIES

In the next several pages, the discussions of specific readiness and computation skills include the major concepts and skills required for computation. Perhaps the most essential of these skills to progress in mathematics are those involved in understanding basic number concepts (Skill 54), writing and summatizing (Skill 55), remembering basic number facts (Skill 56), and mastering the algorithm sequence for each of the operations. Each of the computation skills is a tool for meeting the basic purpose of mathematics — solving problems (Skills 65–69).

The principles of effective instruction in Chapter 3 and the Corrective Principles for each special category in Chapter 2 offer guidance for selecting and adapting strategies to teach special learners. However, appropriate instruction must be designed for each student's age, ability, and unique needs, with an eye toward solving real-world problems.

## 54. UNDERSTANDING BASIC NUMBER CONCEPTS

DETECTION                 This may be a special skill need of students who

- Cannot identify sets of objects
- Do not identify *more* or *less*
- Cannot count or count objects to 10
- Display difficulty joining sets to 10
- Cannot demonstrate number concepts to 10

*Description*      Basic set theory should be mastered early in the process of learning basic mathematics. An integral part of that theory involves the recognition of sets, their characteristics, their numerical value, and factors that separate them from other things. The message is that there are rules and unifying principles around which the logic of math is going to grow. Recognizing *more* and *less* involves basic comparisons and builds upon the skills of identifying sets. Youngsters first learn to count to 10 as a rote task; later, as they learn to count objects, they establish one-to-one correspondence, a concept essential to later moving up and down a numberline to set the stage for addition and subtraction. To join sets, students start off by counting one set, then the other, and lastly the sets together, physically joining sets before attempting formal addition and subtraction. To demonstrate number concepts, the expressive form of counting objects, students express a number requested of them in concrete form, for instance, by immediately holding up four fingers in response to "Show me four." This skill confirms understanding of the basic number concepts.

*Special Problems*   Lack of prior exposure is the primary cause of difficulty with all of these skills. Many children enter school with little or no experience with the basic mathematics of the world around them; they have spent little time sorting things or discussing the numeric relationships of objects. Without a solid understanding of the numeric relationships among objects, students cannot join and unjoin sets. Inability to demonstrate number concepts to 10 may reflect inadequate mastery of the other math readiness skills. Students who are physically or mentally immature may not have absorbed the mathematics experiences available to them. Students with developmental delays, especially language delays, may have particular difficulty mastering the basic concepts.

*Implications*     Students who do not understand basic number concepts will obviously have serious trouble going on in mathematics. Fortunately, the instructional implication is clear and positive. To begin, students need to sort objects by common traits and differentiate among objects by size. Instruction in counting must include touching each object while counting and later counting with the eyes. An important precursor to addition is joining sets, starting to count objects at a given number. Two critical and interwoven elements of instruction are (1) the development of the language that labels mathematical thinking and procedures, (2) ample and appropriate experience using manipulatives. Systematic practice, varying the manipulatives, is essential, as is spiraling — teaching each activity and then going back through all previous activities to permit novices time and practice for incorporating concepts.

CORRECTION

Modify these strategies to meet students' learning needs.

1. *Common Trait.* Put small sets of familiar objects with obvious common traits on a table. Working with small groups of students, have them describe the sets and the characteristics of the objects. Guide students to discover which 1–2 characteristic(s) are the same; explain that this common characteristic is the reason the objects are in the same set.

2. *Include/Exclude.* Beside the displayed set of objects, place a larger group of objects. Discuss the characteristics of each new object. Guide students to explain why it does or does not fit with the set.

3. *Set Mates.* Place 2–3 unlike objects on the table. Guide students to explain the differences. Name each item by a general feature, such as color or shape. Add items that share a general feature of the named objects. Have students discuss each new item and place it beside the object with a similar feature to form sets.

4. *Sort.* Guide students to sort the objects into 2 sets and identify the unifying characteristic of each set. Extend this to items that would sort into 3–4 sets.

5. *Size Difference.* Have 2 students who are very different in height stand next to each other. Ask students to decide who is bigger. Repeat this many times, but each time use different students so that the heights get closer and closer, forcing finer and finer comparisons.

6. *Pile High.* Have students pick the bigger of two piles of dominoes, count the number of dominoes in each set, and record the comparison on the board, using the signs < and >. Next, place 2 piles of different-sized objects next to each other. Ask which has the most objects and have students count to confirm. Display the numbers with appropriate signs; emphasize that the number of objects is the deciding factor.

7. *Straight Line.* The first step in counting objects is to place 3–4 objects in a straight line. Have students count the items, touching each item as they go. Increase the number of items as students progress.

8. *Mix and Straighten.* Rearrange the objects from the straight line. Have students touch and count the items in various arrangements: wavy line, scattered group, and so on. Next, have students touch/count items during and after putting them in a straight line.

9. *Touch and Tell.* Have students touch as they count aloud objects in the classroom (e.g., desks, books, peers). To extend Activity 8, you can even have them straighten the room as they count.

10. *Compare.* Have students count the objects in 2 sets. Record the numbers on the board; have students explain and place the > or < sign.

11. *Join 'Em Up.* Using concrete objects such as sticks, buttons, or dominoes, make 2 sets with 2–4 objects each. Have students count the objects in the first set, then in the second set, put the objects into a container, and count them all. Record values on the board; increase the number of objects and sets.

12. *Take 'Em Apart.* Separate a set of 4 objects into 2 sets — 1 object in one set and 3 in the other. Have students count to show that there are still 4 objects. Repeat with varying numbers of objects and sets.

13. *Numberless Line.* To help students move from concrete to — semiconcrete, draw a numberline without numbers. Start at the left, count 5 places, and mark that point; count and mark another 3 places. Bracket the counted spaces, then count points again. Vary the number of spaces for practice. Also use this line to teach cumulative counting. Tell students to "hold 5 in their brain" and count up from there: 5, 6, 7.

## 55. WRITING AND SUMMATIZING NUMBERS

DETECTION

This may be a special skill need of students who

- Do not demonstrate mastery of the basic number concepts
- Cannot count to 100
- Do not read numbers to 100 correctly
- Cannot write numbers to 100
- Cannot show a set number of fingers quickly
- Must count objects to tell the value of a set
- Read and write numbers in the wrong direction

*Description*

Students must recognize the numbers 1 to 100 prior to learning meaningful computation. Students must be able to look at the numbers and instantly say their names; that is, the behavior must be automatic. They also must recognize numbers both in and out of sequence. Writing the numbers from 0 to 100 requires recognition of the number/name relationship, number comprehension, and the graphics of forming numbers. Number formation is primarily a mechanical skill, but the understanding behind the writing is important as well. Summatizing is the skill of seeing a set of objects and calling their value instantly. Summatizing is a critical prerequisite to number-fact acquisition and offers support for starting to count at a preset place on a number line. Directionality is the structural way students approach mathematics. Students must orient their numbers correctly as they write. For readiness concepts and activities, moving from left to right works much as it does in reading. However, students must learn that in math they may correctly move in either direction, depending on the operation.

*Special Problems*

Inadequate understanding of the basic number concepts (Skill 54) is the primary cause of difficulty writing and summatizing numbers. As is the case with all readiness skills, lack of prior exposure is a major cause of problems. Even after formal instruction begins, some students require more teaching for longer than others to master the readiness skills. Students who are physically or mentally immature may not have absorbed the mathematics experiences available to them. Students with developmental delays, especially language or visual-motor delays, may experience particular problems mastering these skills.

*Implications*

Problems in recognizing and writing numbers will impede future progress in mathematics. As with any sight- or visually-oriented skill, instruction must focus on eliciting and practicing an immediate response to a visual stimulus. Instruction in number formation should follow the suggestions for teaching handwriting in Chapter 9, paired with the mathematics readiness program. Choral drill is probably the easiest and quickest way to practice summatizing, which is important to build mental images of numbers for later computation. The same principles for teaching the basic number concepts apply to writing and summatizing numbers: Language must be developed to label the mathematical thinking and procedures, accompanied by ample and appropriate experiences using manipulatives; spiraling permits time and practice for novices to incorporate the concepts; and systematic practice with a variety of manipulatives reinforces concepts and skills.

CORRECTION    Modify these strategies to meet students' learning needs.

1. *Flashcards to 10.* Develop a deck of flashcards with numbers 1–10 on the front and the corresponding number of items illustrated on the back. After saying the numbers, students can self-correct by counting the objects. Use similar flashcards for 11–20. Also use the cards to teach number comprehension and to reinforce recognition.

2. *Flashcards to 100.* Develop a set of flashcards to 100. Do not draw the number of objects on the reverse side, as this will distract students. Because no self-checking device is included, an adult or able peer will need to flash the cards for students.

3. *Flash War.* Have student pairs or teams compete in quick flashcard wars at the end of class. Monitor the number of each team's positive answers in the same time frame (say, 2 minutes) for continuous feedback on students' progress. Chart and display progress.

4. *Trace It.* To teach and practice number formation, give students a sheet with the number 1 repeated on it several times in large print. Review the correct movement of the pencil in writing the number. For a couple of days, have students say the name of the number as they trace it. Next, reduce the size of the number and add more practices per page. Move from a solid tracing line, to a dotted line, to separated dots, to a starting dot. Go on to number 2, but build in review for numbers 1 and 2. Repeat the procedure for all numbers to 20.

5. *Concept Sure.* To connect the written numbers with the concepts, have students match the written number to a corresponding set of objects. Use practice pages that have just a number of objects on them, and have students write and say the corresponding numeral form.

6. *20 Up.* Introduce the tens numbers to 100, one at a time (10, 20, 30, and so on). Demonstrate to students how to build a higher number: "After 19 comes 20; what comes after 20? How do you write 20 plus 1?" Demonstrate that the number "twenty-ten" is 30 and "thirty-ten" is 40. Follow procedures in Activities 4 and 5 to teach number formations.

7. *Choral Drill.* To begin each class, explain that you will display a number of fingers for only 1 second. Students are to call out the number of fingers shown. Show different numbers of fingers at random and move quickly. The entire drill should last no longer than 30–45 seconds.

8. *Expanded Choral.* The next step requires you to be nimble as you quickly show fingers for students to summatize. Show, for instance, 2 fingers; have students respond as in Activity 7. Next show 3 fingers; again have students respond. Then show the sum of the sets, 5, and have students respond. At first, you may have to add a step in which you say, "2 plus 3 equals what?" and show the total, which students call out.

9. *Extended Choral.* To transfer summatizing skills from fingers to other objects, display small objects such as cards, straws, pencils, or large pictures of objects. Follow the procedures of Activities 7 and 8 to practice instant recognition of number value.

10. *Direction.* To cue students for the direction in which they should move their eyes and/or pencils, use color-coded dots: green for *go*, yellow for *slow*, and red for *stop*. To read numbers, the green dot at the left of the page and the red dot on the right signal movement from left to right. Continue using colored dots for later computation to signal sequence and movements (e.g., to add three-digit numbers, a green dot over the ones, a yellow dot for the tens, and a red dot over the hundreds column.)

## 56.  REMEMBERING BASIC NUMBER FACTS

DETECTION

This may be a special skill need of students who

- Count on their fingers
- Frequently misstate simple computation answers
- Rely on a number line for basic computation
- Take more than three seconds to write the answer to a fact
- Make unpredictable computation errors
- Understand higher-order math but make "careless" mistakes

*Description*

Although the basic number facts are frequently played down as being unimportant in this era of calculators and computers, they are the foundation for all computation. Without knowing the number facts, students are bound to a calculator or to counting on their fingers. There are 100 essential number facts for each of three basic operations — addition, subtraction, and multiplication — and 90 number facts for division. The addition facts are combinations of any two single-digit numbers that would result in a sum (0–9 + 0–9). Subtraction facts are the combinations of any two numbers in which the subtrahend is a single digit and the difference is a single digit (0–18 − 0–9). Multiplication facts are the combinations of any two single-digit numbers that would result in a product (0–9 × 0–9). The division facts are the combinations of any two numbers in which the divisor is a single digit and the quotient is a single digit (0–18 ÷ 0–9). For each of the four operations, students must memorize the basic number facts to apply the facts to higher-order mathematics comfortably and effectively . That is, they must be able to respond automatically when asked a number fact; using a written format with the facts out of order, students must correctly answer in three seconds or less.

*Special Problems*

Limited auditory and associative memory can contribute to difficulties in mastering basic facts. Inadequate or insufficient practice of the basic facts often contributes to the difficulty. Students who originally began counting on their fingers and were never taught to leave this method may continue the practice even when it is no longer needed. In addition to the victims of poor teaching, special groups of students who may have particular difficulty mastering the basic number facts are those with language or learning disabilities or mental retardation.

*Implications*

The purpose of teaching and developing this skill is to lay the foundation for all future computation and problem-solving skills. Students who evidence difficulty in learning the basic number facts will most likely have difficulty with all future mathematics operations, as the relationship of two numbers in each fact is basic to all numerical relationships. Many beginning programs emphasize the conceptual relationship between the two numbers but then expect students to translate this understanding into memorized facts without adequate drill and repetition. Indeed, using manipulatives to introduce each set of facts is a cardinal rule; the understanding of number relationships is unquestionably essential. However, the transfer of that knowledge to mastery of facts is what renders the understanding useful. The student who instantly recalls basic number facts is freed to attend to more complex mathematics.

CORRECTION

Modify these strategies to meet students' learning needs.

1. *Manipulative Introduction.* Use manipulatives to introduce each set of facts. Pair manipulatives with the oral and written facts until you are certain that students understand the equations.

2. *Choral Drill.* Start each class with an oral practice session lasting no longer than 1½ minutes. Select a group of about 30 facts each day. At first, use common facts ($1 + 1 =$ , $5 - 4 =$, $1 \times 2 =$, $6 \div 2 =$); later, mix the facts. State the fact in the form of a question ($1 + 1 = ?$) and have the class respond in unison. Those who know the answer will respond instantly, while those who are learning will listen and repeat the answer almost instantly; this provides reinforcement for those who know the answers and extra input for those who are learning.

3. *Fact Test.* Check each student's basic fact acquisition using a written format. Write the 90 or 100 facts for a single operation in sequence in a horizontal format on both sides of a single sheet. Give students 150 seconds to do the easier facts on the first side. Instruct them to complete the page without using fingers or other counters, but to skip any fact they do not automatically recall. Check the first side. If there are 10 or more errors or omissions, do not give the second side. After students can correctly answer the facts for each of the operations in the allotted time, mix the facts for the test. Have students correct their own papers to reinforce accurate answers.

4. *Fact Ring.* Select the first 10 facts each student missed or skipped on the Fact Test. On $3'' \times 2\frac{1}{2}''$ cards record the fact as a question on the front and with the answer on the back. Punch holes in the top left corner of the cards, and attach each student's set of cards to a ring that can be opened and closed (e.g., a shower curtain ring). When time permits, have student pairs practice using their personal fact rings and checking each other's progress. Take mastered facts off the ring and replace them with the next facts from the Fact Test.

5. *Fact Race.* Have students race each other or themselves to answer target facts. The facts from each student's Fact Ring may be presented on the ring itself or on a computer exercise you design for the student, using either hypermedia or packaged software that permits selection of facts. Set a timer and have students race to answer a certain number (e.g., 10 or 20) of their needed facts. The student with the best time can then set the rules for the next race. This activity offers a game format but permits each student to compete at his or her individual level.

6. *Speed Drill.* End each class with a 2-minute Speed Drill much like the Fact Test, except that students should continue to the second side without stopping. Expect very few students to finish all the facts. However, encourage them to try to do more facts each day. Have students mark their mistakes and correct their own papers to reinforce accurate answers and to permit you to identify any error patterns.

7. *Fact Honor Roll.* Laminate a Fact Honor Roll that resembles a thermometer with blanks for students' names instead of degrees. As students improve on Speed Drills, place their names on the honor roll in ascending order to correspond with the degree of improvement.

8. *Extra Practice.* • Practice is the essence of committing the facts to memory; designate a student to design a special practice format for the week. • Have students work in pairs to practice facts using the special format. • Have pairs of students give each other practice Speed Drills.

## 57. ADDING WHOLE NUMBERS

DETECTION        This may be a special skill need of students who

- Cannot instantly give the sums of the 100 basic addition facts
- Do not correctly add multidigit or more than two numbers
- Cannot identify important place-value information
- Incorrectly regroup when adding
- Do not apply the correct algorithm.

*Description*      Besides mastering the basic addition facts at the automatic level, students must also master the concepts and procedures for more complex addition. Responding to a vertical format of the basic facts is a logical transition to more formal addition computation. The next skills, in developmental order, are adding three single-digit numbers, adding a two-digit and a one-digit number with no regrouping, and regrouping in adding a two-digit and one-digit number. Regrouping in addition refers to separating the sum of a given column into its ones and tens values. Regrouping is important for three reasons: (1) it demonstrates understanding of place value; (2) it permits mechanical performance of most addition skills; and (3) it is prerequisite to higher-level subtraction and multiplication. Common regrouping errors occur when students record the total answer for each column, record the tens below the line and carry the ones, record the ones value and leave out the tens, or record the total sum below the line and regroup as well. In order to add successfully, students must also master the sequence they should follow, or the algorithm sequence.

*Special Problems*   Students who master the basic facts but cannot count up to higher sums often have not been properly instructed to do so. Conceptual weakness is a major cause of difficulty in adding multidigit numbers, particularly when regrouping is required. Students who do not grasp the value of numbers and place value cannot advance to higher operations. Another cause of regrouping difficulties is mechanical or structural; students simply learn the procedure incorrectly and use it without regard to the concept. Students who have difficulty sequencing events and understanding cause/effect relationships often develop faulty algorithms. Students who may experience difficulty moving beyond the basic addition facts are the educationally deprived and slow learners as well as those with behavior disorders, learning disabilities, or mental retardation.

*Implications*     Students must be directly taught to continue counting or "count on" to add numbers beyond the basic facts. To correct regrouping difficulties when numeration is problematic, review numeration, emphasizing the parts of numbers and their relative values. To determine if place value is problematic, have students write numbers in expanded forms as so many hundreds, so many tens, and so many ones; inability to do this suggests that they do not understand place value. For more mechanical regrouping deficits, specifically teach the procedures for regrouping. Students who develop defective algorithms in addition and have difficulty with sequential functioning need instruction that emphasizes sequence as a dynamic aspect of addition and includes flowcharts as sequential and self-monitoring guides.

**CORRECTION**

Modify these strategies to meet students' learning needs.

1. *Manipulatives.* Use objects to demonstrate the reality of numbers: for example, 7 objects together for the number 7. Students should be able to match numbers to the corresponding sets of objects.
2. *Vertical Speed Drills.* During the final two minutes of class, continue the speed drill activities used for basic facts (Skill 56, Activity 6) but present the facts in vertical format. Encourage students to continue to practice in pairs until they have clearly mastered all facts.
3. *Count On.* To teach addition of more than two numbers or sums greater than 18, use manipulatives to reinforce the concept of "count on." Demonstrate how to add 2 numbers to get a sum and then count on from that sum to add other numbers. For example, 2 objects + 7 objects = 9; to add 8 more, continue counting from the 9. Write the equation for the action on the board and again explain how to think through the operation. Have students imitate your demonstration to add other groups of numbers and then work in pairs to practice the process.
4. *Bundle Grouping.* Once students have shown that they can match numbers and corresponding objects below 10, have them bundle objects into groups of 10 plus some other number of objects. Using boxes or cups labeled "ones" and "tens," have students place the tens bundles into that box and the remaining loose objects into the ones box. On a piece of paper, label 2 columns "ones" and "tens." Have students count the loose objects and record that value under the ones heading, then count the bundles and record that under the tens heading. The answer should equal the total number of objects.
5. *Red Box/Green Box.* Next to a sample problem, draw a green box for the ones and a red box for the tens values of column sums. When students add the ones column, they should record the sum for that column in the boxes; for example, if 7 + 8 are summed to produce 15, the 5 would go in the green ones box and the 1 would go in the red tens box. Draw a green box under the ones column and a red box above the tens column; the 5 moves from the green box next to the problem to the green box below the ones column (ones value to ones column), and the 1 in the red box next to the problem moves to the red box over the tens column (tens value to tens column). Structurally, this is an extension of Bundle Grouping in Activity 4.
6. *Draw a Circle.* When Activity 5 becomes almost automatic, eliminate the red and green boxes, instead drawing a red circle above the tens column. This will provide a bridge between high structure and no structure until students' thinking procedures change.
7. *Key Label.* To assist students in retrieving proper sequences for use in algorithms, have them make up titles or labels for steps of the algorithm. As they label, they are creating a means to call back the process through association.
8. *Problem Structure.* Diagram a sample problem for the students using lines, columns, arrows, or other tools that will clearly demonstrate a step-by-step procedure.
9. *Algorithm Flowchart.* To give students a visual picture of an algorithm and each step it contains, use a flowchart. Have the students use a place holder (e.g., a coin) to help organize their movement through the algorithm.

## 58.  SUBTRACTING WHOLE NUMBERS

DETECTION

This may be a special skill need of students who

- Cannot instantly give differences of 100 basic subtraction facts
- Do not correctly subtract multidigit numbers
- Cannot identify important place-value information
- Incorrectly regroup when subtracting
- Do not apply the correct algorithm sequence for subtraction

*Description*

Once students have mastered the basic subtraction facts in vertical format and at the automatic level, they must master the concepts and procedures of more complex subtraction. The next skills, in developmental order, are subtracting a one-digit number from a two-digit number, subtracting a two-digit number from a two-digit number with no regrouping, and then regrouping the tens when subtracting a one-digit number from a two-digit number. Regrouping demonstrates understanding of place value and in subtraction refers to borrowing, as in moving a set of tens into the ones column so the value of the ones equals or exceeds the value of the subtrahend in that same column. It is necessary to operate mechanically for most subtraction skills; the subtraction mechanics are also important to progress to division. Common regrouping errors include taking the smaller value from the greater, regardless of location; not decreasing the value of the number borrowed from; borrowing when it is not necessary; or regrouping from the incorrect column. Successful subtraction also requires students to follow the correct sequence of events, or the algorithm sequence.

*Special Problems*

Students who master the basic facts but cannot subtract more complex problems often have not been properly instructed to do so. Some beginning students appear to resist the whole notion of subtraction, preferring the seemingly more positive action of addition. A primary cause of difficulty in subtracting multidigit numbers is conceptual weakness, especially when regrouping is involved. Regrouping difficulties of a more mechanical or structural nature result when students simply learn the procedure incorrectly and use it without regard to the concept. Students who have difficulty sequencing events and understanding cause/effect relationships often develop faulty algorithms. In addition to those who have not been taught properly, students who learn slowly and those with behavior disorders, learning disabilities, or mental retardation may experience difficulty subtracting multidigit numbers.

*Implications*

Regrouping plays a bigger role in subtraction than in addition and must be introduced relatively early in the numeric sequence. The teacher must identify one of two clearly different causes of regrouping problems in subtraction. To identify both the cause of difficulty and the difficulty itself, have students write numbers in expanded forms ($238 = 200 + 30 + 8$); inability to do this suggests that students do not understand place value. Students who have not developed the required numeration skills will need to review numeration, with heavy emphasis on the parts of numbers and their relative values. Instruction for students who show mechanical deficits should develop the correct procedures for regrouping, emphasize sequence as a dynamic aspect of subtraction, and include flowcharts as sequential and self-monitoring guides.

CORRECTION

Modify these strategies to meet students' learning needs.

1. *Manipulatives.* Use objects to help demonstrate the reality of numbers: for example, 7 objects together for the number 7. Students should be able to match numbers to the corresponding sets of objects.

2. *Vertical Speed Drills.* Continue the speed drill activities used for basic facts (Skill 56, Activity 6), but present the facts in vertical format to prepare students for more formal computation. Conduct these drills during the final two minutes of class and have students continue to practice in pairs until they have clearly mastered all facts.

3. *Greater or Less Than.* Using the typical format of subtraction problems, have the students compare the ones place of the subtrahend to the ones place of the minuend. The students should mark each problem to show which number is greater. This will lead students to check the value of the numbers automatically, a behavior that must come before regrouping.

4. *Star the Problem.* Display a poster that says, "If the bottom number is bigger, then you borrow." Have the students go back over all the problems they practiced in Activity 3 and star those in which the bottom number is bigger; starred problems require regrouping. Have students star the numbers on future practice pages before attempting to subtract.

5. *Bundle Breaking.* For students who seem to have difficulty understanding that they should add 10 and not 1 when borrowing, create tens bundles. Make a tens box and a ones box. Choose any two-digit number and put the correct number of tens and ones bundles in the appropriate boxes. Next take 1 bundle out of the tens box and add it to the ones box to show the regrouping, having students break the band around the bundle to show there are 10 objects.

6. *Red Box/Green Box.* Above a sample problem, draw a red box and a green box to be used for regrouping a set of tens into the ones column (from red to green). For any problem in which the bottom number is not greater than the top number, students should draw a line through the boxes. For problems where regrouping is needed, have the students reduce the tens column by 1 and add that set of 10 to the value already in the ones column. This sum should be recorded in the red and green boxes. Subtraction should then continue.

7. *Draw a Circle.* When Activity 6 becomes almost automatic, then just draw a red circle above the tens column to continue to remind the students to reduce the value after they have borrowed. The circle is a useful reminder even for successful students, who may become overly comfortable with regrouping and forget to reduce the value of the number borrowed from.

8. *Key Label.* Have students make up titles or labels for the steps of the algorithm to assist them in retrieving the correct sequence. As they label, they create keywords that will help them recall the process through association.

9. *Problem Structure.* Use lines, columns, arrows, or other tools to diagram sample subtraction problems, demonstrating the step-by-step procedures.

10. *Algorithm Flowchart.* Use a flowchart to give students a visual picture of the algorithm and each step it contains. Have the students use a place holder (e.g., a coin or button) to help organize their movement through the algorithm.

## 59. MULTIPLYING WHOLE NUMBERS

DETECTION

This may be a special skill need of students who

- Cannot instantly give the products of 100 basic multiplication facts
- Do not correctly multiply multidigit numbers
- Cannot identify important place-value information
- Incorrectly regroup when multiplying
- Do not apply the correct algorithm sequence for multiplication

*Description*

Instant recall of the products of the basic multiplication facts precedes more complex multiplication. Responding to the basic facts in a vertical format is a transition skill. Thereafter the sequence of skills is multiplying a two-digit number and then a three-digit number by a one-digit number, without regrouping, and then a two-digit number by a one-digit number, regrouping the ones value. In multiplication, regrouping involves breaking down a product for a given column into its ones and tens values, placing the ones value under the ones column and incorporating the tens value into the next column. In addition to confirming understanding of place value, regrouping is essential to the mechanics of most multiplication. Common error patterns are exhibited by students who record the total product for each column separately below the line, record the tens value below the line and carry the ones, or record the ones value and leave out the tens. Errors occur in complex multiplication when students misplace products or make addition errors. Following the algorithm sequence is essential, particularly for multidigit multiplication.

*Special Problems*

There are two primary causes for difficulty in regrouping in multiplication. The first is conceptual weakness; students do not grasp the value of numbers and place value. The other cause is mechanical; students learn the procedure incorrectly and use it without regard to concept. Some students find the multiplication facts easier to master than the facts for other operations. Students who know but do not apply the facts to complex multiplication may not have received adequate instruction in the sequence of steps or may have developed defective algorithms. Students who have been educationally deprived, who learn slowly, or who have behavior disorders, learning disabilities, or mental retardation may experience difficulty multiplying.

*Implications*

Understanding place value is vital in multiplying multidigit numbers, perhaps even more than in addition and subtraction. Place value and regrouping must be emphasized and directly taught. The cause of regrouping errors must be identified, since there are two distinct possibilities. Review of numeration with emphasis on number parts and relative values is necessary for students who have not developed the required numeration skills. For students who show more mechanical deficits, instruction should focus on developing the correct procedures for regrouping. Having students write numbers in expanded form may reveal the cause of difficulty as well as the difficulty itself. Instruction for students who develop faulty algorithms should emphasize sequence as a dynamic aspect of multiplication. Flowcharts are particularly valuable to demonstrate algorithms and to provide sequential and self-monitoring guides.

CORRECTION

Modify these strategies to meet students' learning needs.

1. *Manipulatives.* Use objects to help demonstrate the reality of numbers. If the number is 5, put 5 objects together; if the computation is 3 x 4, present 3 sets of 4 objects and then combine the sets. Students should match these numbers to the corresponding sets of objects and to the multiplication operation.

2. *Vertical Speed Drills.* During the final two minutes of class, conduct speed drills (Skill 56, Activity 6) with basic facts presented in vertical format, to prepare students for complex computation. Have student pairs practice until they have mastered all facts.

3. *Bundle Grouping.* Once students have shown that they can match numbers and corresponding objects for numbers below 10, go beyond 10. Have the students bundle objects into groups of 10 plus some other objects. Using boxes or cups labeled "ones" and "tens," have the students place the tens bundles into the tens box and the remaining loose objects into the ones box. On a piece of paper, label 2 columns "ones" and "tens," respectively. Have students count the loose objects and record that value under the ones heading, and then count the bundles and record that number under the tens heading. The number they have created should equal the total number of objects.

4. *Red Box/Green Box.* Next to a sample problem, draw a green box for ones and a red box for the tens values of column sums. When students multiply the ones column, they should record the product for that column in the boxes: if the product of a column is 24, the 4 ones would go in the green box and the 2 tens would go in the red box. Draw a green box under the ones column and a red box above the tens column. The ones value (4) would then be moved from the green box next to the problem to the green box below the ones column (ones value to ones column). The tens value (2) in the red box next to the problem moves to the red box over the tens column (tens value into tens column). Structurally, this is an extension of Bundle Grouping in Activity 3.

5. *Draw a Circle.* When Activity 4 becomes almost automatic and students no longer misplace the parts of numbers, replace the red and green boxes with a red circle above the tens column. This will bridge the gap between high structure and no structure until students' thinking procedures change.

6. *Multidigit Review.* Because multidigit multiplication is complex, focused reviews of component skills are essential. Review the basic multiplication facts, and then emphasize the other component skills: place value, regrouping, and column addition for adding partial products.

7. *Key Label.* To assist students in retrieving proper sequences in algorithms, have them make up titles or labels for the steps of the algorithm. Labeling creates the keywords that will help students recall the process through association.

8. *Problem Structure.* Diagram a sample multiplication problem for the students, using lines, columns, arrows, or other tools to demonstrate the step-by-step procedures.

9. *Algorithm Flowchart.* Use a flowchart to give students a visual picture of the steps and the algorithm. Have students use a place holder (e.g., a button) to help organize their movement through the algorithm.

## 60. DIVIDING WHOLE NUMBERS

DETECTION

This may be a special skill need of students who

- Cannot instantly give the quotients of the 90 basic division facts
- Do not correctly divide multidigit numbers
- Make multiplication or subtraction errors in long division
- Incorrectly regroup or cannot identify place-value information
- Do not apply the correct algorithm sequence for division

*Description*

After mastering the basic division facts, students are ready for division problems with single-digit divisors. However, as a transition skill, they must first master the division facts in the traditional format $(4\sqrt{16})$. The sequence of division skills thereafter is two- and then three-digit dividends with 0 in the ones place and then in the tens place, but with no remainder, followed by one-digit divided by one digit with a remainder, building up to problems with multidigit divisors and dividends involving regrouping and remainders, until complex long division problems are reached. Regrouping is the step in division after multiplying the partial quotient times the divisor to obtain a partial product. Regrouping then uses the difference generated added to the next place of the dividend — "subtract and bring down." Students can miss this step by not subtracting or by not joining the difference to the next place of the dividend (the "bring down" part). Because the division process is complex, a variety of other error patterns appear when students have not mastered the basic division facts, subtract or multiply incorrectly, add the divisor to the dividend, subtract the divisor from the dividend, omit the remainder, or place the answer out of sequence. Many of these errors result from not following the correct algorithm sequence, particularly important in complex division.

*Special Problems*

Of the four basic operations, division is the most difficult for all types of learners. Students who master division of two-digit dividends by single-digit divisors demonstrate understanding of the basic concepts, but some may not be able to handle the complexity of multidigit division. Inadequate mastery of the basic division facts obviously increases the difficulty of the task. Regrouping difficulties may be caused by conceptual weakness or having learned the procedures incorrectly. Weak subtraction and multiplication skills interfere with accuracy. Students who do not follow the correct sequence of steps may not have received adequate instruction. In addition to students who have been educationally deprived, those who learn slowly or who have behavior disorders, learning disabilities, or mental retardation may experience difficulty dividing.

*Implications*

Teachers should build understanding with simple one- and two-digit problems, using manipulatives. However, once students understand the process, mechanics must be stressed. In fact, special students often need to overlearn the algorithms in order to recall and apply them effectively. Algorithm flowcharts are especially valuable as sequential and self-monitoring guides. The component processes of division must be reviewed, and a new skill — estimation in division — developed and practiced. To check complex problems or even to perform the computations when the demands of multidigit division obviously exceed their capabilities, students should use calculators.

CORRECTION Modify these strategies to meet students' learning needs.

1. *Manipulatives.* To demonstrate estimating, select any evenly divisible number (e.g., 25) as the dividend and a divisor that will divide equally into that number (5). Count out objects into groups equal to the divisor (5 groups). Have students find how many groups it takes to equal the dividend. This is an ideal time to show students the relationship between division and multiplication.

2. *Traditional Speed Drills.* During the final two minutes of class, conduct speed drills in basic facts (Skill 56) but with the facts in the traditional division "house," to prepare students for formal computation. Have student pairs continue to practice until they have clearly mastered all facts.

3. *Bundle Grouping.* Build on Activity 1 by having the students bundle the divisor sticks. Again find how many bundles will be contained evenly in some larger number. Next, create a problem in the traditional format. Have the students try to divide the bundle into each place of the dividend, such as a bundle of 5 into a dividend of 65. The bundle goes into the 6 one time but not evenly; there is 1 left over. Ask the students, "Should we just throw away the extra 1?" Show how to subtract the 1 and add it to the next place of the dividend. This procedure builds a bridge between the use of manipulatives and problem structure.

4. *Red Box/Green Box.* Under a sample problem, draw a green box and red box to use for the difference created when you subtract the partial product (generated by multiplying the partial quotient times the divisor and then subtracting it from the dividend). The red box should hold the difference and the green box should hold the next value of the dividend. This activity extends the Bundle Grouping of Activity 3.

5. *Draw a Circle.* When Activity 4 has become almost automatic and students no longer misplace the parts of numbers, replace the red and green boxes with a red circle to hold the value brought down from each place of the dividend. This will bridge the gap between high structure and no structure, providing a smooth transition and ensuring that students understand.

6. *Division Preview.* Because division is complex, periodic focused reviews of the component skills are essential, particularly for complex long division problems. Review the basic division facts and then emphasize the other component skills: estimation, multiplication, subtraction, rounding off to the nearest tens unit.

7. *Key Label.* To assist students in retrieving proper sequences for use in algorithms, have them make up titles or labels for the steps of the algorithm. Labeling creates the keywords that will help students recall the process through association.

8. *Problem Structure.* Diagram a sample division problem for the students, using lines, columns, arrows, or other tools to demonstrate the step-by-step procedures. Walk and talk students through the procedures using the diagram; then pair students to follow the diagram and explain it to each other.

9. *Algorithm Flowchart.* Use a flowchart to give students a visual picture of the algorithm and each step it contains. Have the students use a place holder (e.g., a coin or button) to help organize their movements through the algorithm.

## 61.  UNDERSTANDING FRACTIONAL CONCEPTS

DETECTION

This may be a special skill need of students who

- Do not see a relationship between parts and the whole
- Cannot break a set into fractional equivalents
- Attempt to add or subtract unlike fractional parts
- Leave answers in improper forms
- Do not reduce fractional answers to their simplest forms
- Exhibit errors in whole number computation

*Description*

Fractional concepts are the fundamental facts of fractions. They can be as basic as the concept that there are fractions, that objects can be broken up into parts, and that at first those parts are equivalent. A young child who has two pieces of candy can see how to share them between two people. However, that same child may have difficulty figuring out how to share those two pieces of candy among four people. Central to addition and subtraction of fractions is the concept that the fractional parts must be common in order to be manipulated easily — the denominator represents how many parts the whole is broken into, and the numerator represents how many of those parts are present. Converting fractions into a common form is the first step in both adding and subtracting fractions. As the saying goes, "You can't add apples and oranges." To convert to common form, the major step is to find the lowest common multiple into which all fractions being converted will divide evenly — the lowest common denominator, or LCD. The other aspect of converting fractions is to present the answer in simplest or lowest form; the simpler form is more acceptable because it is easier to work with.

*Special Problems*

Students frequently have difficulties with fractional concepts because they do not fully understand whole number sets. Many students are shown how to cut an apple in half, eat one half, and find what is left; however, this simple example will not help students understand the relationship between denominators and numerators unless it is greatly expanded. Students who had significant difficulty with the concept of multiple equivalent sets for multiplication will certainly have problems with multiple equivalent partial sets. Difficulty with converting fractions can result from either conceptual or operational weakness: Students do not understand that all fractions have various equivalent forms, or they do not know the mechanics of determining the LCD. Many types of special students have significant difficulty mastering fractional concepts beyond the basic notion of dividing a whole into parts.

*Implications*

Students must develop a firm grasp of the relationship of the numerator to the denominator before they can compute fractions. A variety of directed experiences using manipulatives can develop this understanding. Students who cannot convert fractions to common form cannot add or subtract fractions at all, so they will not be able to work most high-level fraction problems. Students who cannot reduce their answers produce unacceptable answers. If the difficulty is conceptual, students will benefit from experience with physically changing fractional forms. If the difficulty is operational, they should use a flowchart.

**CORRECTION**

Modify these strategies to meet students' learning needs.

1. *Split the Whole.* For each group of 4 students, cut an apple in half and then in half again to make 4 quarters. Wrap the 4 pieces back together with a rubber band. Hold up the rejoined fruit and ask what you have (1 apple). Remove the rubber band; ask if there is more fruit now. Show how the 4 equal pieces go together to make up the whole piece of fruit. Let students eat the fruit.

2. *Build the Denominator.* Building on Activity 1, explain that the number of equal pieces something is cut into is called the *denominator*. Write *denominator* on the board; have students write it on flashcards. Cut an apple in half. Ask, "How many pieces?" Say, "We broke this into 2 equal pieces, so if we write this as a fraction, the denominator is 2." Cut the apple into fourths and repeat the process; then use a banana to demonstrate thirds and sixths.

3. *Build the Numerator.* Building on Activities 1 and 2, follow this script:"We know that the number of equal parts something is cut into is called the *denominator*. Now we need to find out how many of those parts we have; that is called the *numerator*." Write the word on the board; have students write it on flashcards. Cut an apple into fourths and say, "How many equal parts have we divided this apple into? What is the denominator?" Give a piece to someone to eat. "How many of those 4 parts are left?" "The number of parts we have is the numerator, so this numerator is 3." Write the fraction 3/4 and review the relationship between the denominator and numerator. Repeat this activity with various fruits.

4. *Convert the Form.* Take 2 pieces of construction paper, 1 red and 1 green. Draw a line across the red paper, creating 2 equal parts. Draw 3 lines across the green paper, creating 4 equal parts so that 2 of the parts of the green paper cover 1 part of the red paper. Cut the green paper into fourths, leaving the red paper intact. Label each part of both colors (1/2 or 1/4). Have students cover a one-half portion of the red paper with 2 green quarters. Stress that the 2 quarters equal the half. Do this with many different fractions.

5. *Algorithm Flowchart.* Use this flowchart to walk students through procedures for finding the LCD. Later they can use it for self-monitoring.

**Finding the LCD**

## 62. COMPUTING FRACTIONS

DETECTION        This may be a special skill need of students who

- Do not see a relationship between the parts and the whole
- Cannot break a set into fractional equivalents
- Attempt to add or subtract unlike fractions
- Use the common denominator in multiplication or division
- Add or subtract denominators
- Do not follow the correct operation
- Omit steps in the algorithm sequence

*Description*        Accurate computation of fractions rests upon a deep understanding of fractional concept and the mechanics of fractional conversion. To add or subtract fractions, students must understand that the number of parts present will increase for addition and decrease for subtraction, and that unlike parts must be converted to a common form for both operations. Of the sequence of at least ten skills in adding and nine skills in subtracting fractions, the steps most often mislearned are those for finding the LCD. Unlike multiplication of whole numbers, multiplying fractions results in finding a fractional part of a number — a decrease in value; students must divide to find what will be in each part and then multiply by the number of parts they wish to find. The basic concept in dividing fractions is the division of some number by a value less than one for an increase in value; once those parts are combined, the numerator of the divisor tells how many go into each set. multiplying or dividing fractions requires a sequence of at least six skills; the steps that most often cause problems are converting mixed fractions into improper fractions before computing and converting answers to their simplest forms.

*Special Problems*        Lack of focused and appropriate instruction to meet individual learning needs is a primary cause of difficulty in computing fractions. Because fractional computation is complex and difficult to visualize, it is troublesome for most learners, and particularly for special learners. Students frequently have problems with fractional computation because they do not understand the concepts of whole number sets or of fractional sets. They must understand the relationship between denominators and numerators. Students who experience significant difficulty with the concept of multiple equivalent sets for multiplication will certainly have greater problems with multiple equivalent partial sets. Students with sequential learning difficulties frequently get the steps of the algorithm out of order or omit them, making accurate computation of fractions impossible.

*Implications*        Students who experience difficulty computing fractions will also have difficulty with algebra and geometry. However, beyond the most basic concepts, such as adding and subtracting ½, ⅓, ¼, the difficulty of computing fractions and the time and effort required for mastery must be weighed against the practicality and relevance of this skill for individual students, particularly older and less able students. Manipulatives are essential for building concepts, as are guided experiences in following the proper algorithmic steps. Having students verbalize and explain the concepts to peers reinforces understanding and helps identify errors needing correction.

**CORRECTION**     Modify these strategies to meet students' learning needs.

1. *LCD Review.* Review the algorithm flowchart for finding the lowest common denominator (Skill 61). Review reducing fractions to their simplest form as well, both before and during instruction in computation.

2. *Adding Fractions.* Use egg cartons and dried beans to demonstrate adding fractions. Cut the egg holders to form units of 2 cups, 3 cups, and so on. Give each student a 2-cup egg holder and follow this script: "How many equal parts are there? If this is divided into 2 equal parts, then the denominator for this fraction is 2." Write the denominator on the board; have each student put a bean into a part of the holder. "How many parts are filled? If there are 2 equal parts and we fill 1 part, the numerator is 1." Show the fraction ½; pair students to put their cartons next to each other. "Now you have ½ and another ½. Put the bean from 1 carton into the empty space of the other so you have 2 equal parts, both full. We write the fraction as ²⁄₂. So when we add like fractions together, we get larger fractions." Repeat using different fractions and equations; then move to algorithms.

3. *Subtracting Fractions.* Use the egg carton parts and dried beans from Activity 1 to demonstrate the concept. Give each student a 2-cup egg holder and follow this script: "How many equal parts are there? If this is divided into 2 equal parts, the denominator for this fraction is 2." Write it as a denominator on the board; have each student put a bean into each part of the holder. "How many parts are filled? If there are 2 equal parts and we fill 2 of them, the numerator is 2." Show the fraction ²⁄₂; have students take out 1 bean. "You had ²⁄₂ and you took away 1 bean, or ½. What is left? One bean is left. That means that when you have 2 equal parts and you remove 1 part, you are left with ½. So when you have fractional parts and you take parts away, you get a smaller fractional part." Repeat this process using different fractions and their equations for several days; then move to algorithms.

4. *Multiplying Fractions.* Cut and separate an apple into fourths. The example will call for ½ × ¼ or ½ *of* ¼. Verbalize each action as you work. Divide each of the fourths by the denominator 2. There are now 8 pieces separated into 4 groups; the fourths have become eighths. Take one of those groups (the ¼). The numerator of the ½ tells you how many from each group you need. Take 1 out of the group and you end up with an eighth. Thus, ½ times ¼ equals ⅛. Repeat this procedure, using different fractions, matching computations with equations, and verbalizing actions; then move to algorithms.

5. *Dividing Fractions.* Cut an apple into fourths. Verbalize each action as you work. The example will call for ½ ÷ ¼. Since the example says that you do not start with a whole unit but only half, get rid of the other half. How many pieces do you actually have? (2) How many one-fourths are there in one-half? (2) Repeat using different fractions and equations and verbalizing actions; then move on to algorithms.

6. *Key Label.* To assist students in retrieving proper sequences of algorithms, have them make up titles or labels for the steps of the algorithm. Their key words help them recall the process through association.

7. *Problem Structure.* Diagram a sample problem for students using lines, columns, and arrows to demonstrate the step-by-step procedures.

8. *Algorithm Flowcharts.* Use flowcharts to walk students through algorithms for each operation and later as self-monitoring guides.

## 63. UNDERSTANDING DECIMAL CONCEPTS

DETECTION        This may be a special skill need of students who

- Display little understanding of the concept of place value
- Leave out the decimal point
- Compute numbers without regard to column values
- Record answers without regard to decimal values
- Cannot show the relationship of the parts to the whole
- Have not mastered the concept of fractions

*Description*        Understanding fractions — the denominator as the number of parts in the whole and the numerator as the number of parts used — is prerequisite to working with decimals. The decimal system, set up in base ten, can be related to whole number values, whereas in fractions the base constantly changes as a function of the denominator. One difficult decimal concept is that the number of digits does not determine value; the value of the tenths place, not the length of the decimal, most often determines relative value. The concept of place value for computing decimals is a direct outgrowth of that for whole numbers. Students must extend their understanding of the value of each column to the right as well as to the left of the decimal point. Thus, students who have difficulty grasping the concept of place value when computing whole numbers will most likely have difficulty with place value in decimals. As with fractions, students must see the relationship of the parts to the whole.

*Special Problems*        Difficulty with place-value concepts in whole numbers causes difficulty with place-value concepts in decimals. That is, students do not conceptualize numbers as comprised of so many ones, tens, hundreds, and so on. Another common problem is that students cannot visualize tenths or hundredths of objects. Without specific demonstrations of the relevance of decimals, the concept is too abstract for some students to grasp. The idea of breaking whole objects into partial states is difficult for some students; those who have not mastered the concept of fractions will not understand decimals. In addition to those who have not been taught properly, students who learn slowly and those with behavior disorders, learning disabilities, or mental retardation may experience difficulty grasping basic decimal concepts.

*Implications*        Special learners can master decimals but may need more detailed and extensive experiences using decimal parts. However, the concept of fractions first must be taught and reviewed. Students who have not developed the necessary numeration skills will need to review numeration, with emphasis on the parts of numbers and their relative values. Since money is the most familiar and easily demonstrated decimal system, dollars and cents and their accompanying notations can serve as examples to illustrate both the concept of the decimal point and the relevance of decimals. Teachers must emphasize that the position of the digits in relation to the decimal point determines the value of the number. Students must learn and then practice reading and writing decimals before proceeding to decimal computation.

**CORRECTION**     Modify these strategies to meet students' learning needs.

1. *Fractional Review.* Review with students the relationship of parts to the whole they learned in fractions. Ask them to name items that can be divided into equal parts. Have them write sample fractions for each item on the board and then explain the fraction, stressing the meaning of the numerator and the denominator and, when feasible, sketching an example of the fractional part of the item.

2. *Paper Tenths.* Have students divide a strip of paper 10 inches long into 10 1-inch sections. Have them write the words "1 piece" on the back of the strip. Ask the students how many pieces of paper they have. Then have them turn it over, and ask how many parts the paper is divided into. Tell them in decimals, these are called tenths. Ask them to color 4 of the tenths. Write the number .4 on the board. Repeat this procedure until you have discussed all decimals .1–.9.

3. *Paper Strips.* Give each student 2 more paper strips already divided into 10 1-inch sections and labeled. Ask students to show you 3 tenths by covering 3 tenths of 1 piece of paper. Use a few more examples. Now have the students show 1 whole and 3 tenths, by holding up the 1 full strip and covering 3 sections of the other. Explain that 10 tenths is the same as 1 whole strip or the number 1. Write 1.3 on the board. Continue until 1.1–1.9 have been discussed.

4. *Decimal Chart.* Put a decimal place-value chart on the board.

   | ones | · | tenths |
   |------|---|--------|
   | 1    | · | 4      |
   | 3    | · | 5      |

   Read the following numbers to the class and, after modeling the first few, have individual students fill in the place-value chart: 1 and 4 tenths; 3 and 5 tenths; 2 and 7 tenths; 5 and 2 tenths; and so on.

5. *Chart Graph.* Using graph paper, give each student a square with 100 blocks in it, 10 × 10. On the reverse side, students should write "1 piece." Have them turn over the paper. Explain that something can be broken down into 100 pieces as easily as 10 pieces; these parts are called hundredths. Have students cover 5 hundredths, then 10 hundredths, 15 hundredths, and so on. Then write those numbers on the board: .05 = 5 hundredths, and so on. Next, have students cover the correct number of blocks as you read aloud the decimals written on the board. Write several additional hundredths values on the board and have students cover the appropriate amounts. Continue the process, but designate students to take your role.

6. *Decimal Chart II.* Display an expanded place-value chart:

   | tens | ones | · | tenths | hundredths |
   |------|------|---|--------|------------|
   | 3    | 1    | · | 4      | 7          |
   | 6    | 3    | · | 5      | 2          |
   | ____ | ____ | · | _____ |  |

   Read a series of numbers containing decimals; have students fill in the parts on the chart, and then read what they have written. Provide students with personal copies of the decimal chart and continue the process.

7. *Reading and Writing Decimals.* Provide extensive practice reading and writing decimals. Dictate numbers for students to write, and then read aloud; have them dictate numbers for you to write and them to read aloud.

## 64. COMPUTING DECIMALS

DETECTION

This may be a special skill need of students who

- Exhibit little understanding of decimal concepts
- Display difficulty reading and writing decimals
- Omit the decimal point
- Place the answer too far to the left or right of the decimal
- Use the wrong rule to place the decimal
- Demonstrate difficulty computing whole numbers

*Description*

Students must be able to compute whole numbers and understand decimal concepts to compute decimals. A firm grasp of place value allows students to place the decimal point correctly, a structural process that is a key component of the algorithm sequences. When adding or subtracting, the number with the longest decimal sets the place for the decimal point in the answer. When multiplying, the sum of the total number of places to the right of the decimal point in both numbers determines placement of the decimal point. When dividing, the decimal point is also placed with regard to the total number of decimal points in both numbers of the problem, but there are two possibilities for the mechanics of placement. When the divisor is a whole number and the dividend has a decimal, the decimal point is placed in the quotient directly above the decimal point in the dividend. However, when both divisor and dividend contain decimals, the decimal point in the divisor is moved enough spaces to make a whole number and the decimal point in the dividend is moved an equal number of spaces. The decimal point in the quotient is then placed directly over the decimal point in the revised dividend. Students must understand procedures for placing decimal points and remember to include the decimal point in their answers.

*Special Problems*

The most common errors in computing decimals are those made in computing whole numbers. Students who demonstrate errors such as those described in Skills 57–60 and do not receive appropriate corrective instruction are likely to make the same errors in computing decimals. Incorrect placement of the decimal point in addition or subtraction may result from failure to line up the decimal points when writing the problems. Errors in placing the decimal point in all four operations can result from inadequate mastery of fraction or decimal concepts or insufficient direct instruction in following the algorithmic sequences. Omission of the decimal point is a common error, particularly among students who overlook details. Because decimal computation depends upon many prerequisite computation skills with which special students experience difficulty, many special learners exhibit problems in this area.

*Implications*

Students who exhibit problems that result from place-value confusion may need intense experience with manipulatives to grasp the meaning of parts and whole (see Skill 63). To bridge the gap between the new place-value understanding and the correct structural procedure for placing decimals, give students a set of rules or summarize the rules in a flowchart, discuss the rules, model their use, and have students follow your model.

CORRECTION                  Modify these strategies to meet students' learning needs.

1. *Adding Decimals.* Teach the correct sequence for placing the decimal point when adding; provide guided practice in applying the steps:
   a. Make sure that columns are lined up; all decimal points should be in a straight vertical line.
   b. Add the numbers in each column, regrouping when necessary.
   c. Bring the decimal point straight down into the answer.
   d. Count the places to the right of the decimal point for each addend.
   e. Compare the answer to the addends; the number of spaces to the right of the decimal in the answer should equal the largest number of spaces from step d.

2. *Subtracting Decimals.* Teach the correct sequence for placing the decimal point when subtracting; guide students to apply the steps:
   a. Make sure that all columns are lined up; all decimal points should be in a straight vertical line.
   b. Subtract the numbers in each column, regrouping if needed.
   c. Bring the decimal point straight down into the answer.
   d. Count the places to the right of the decimal point for both numbers.
   e. Count to the right from the decimal point to the end of the answer. The number of spaces to the right of the decimal in the answer should equal the largest number of spaces in step d.

3. *Multiplying Decimals.* Teach the sequence for placing the decimal point when multiplying; then coach students to apply the steps:
   a. Make sure that all columns are lined up in proper order; all decimal points should be in a straight vertical line.
   b. Multiply the numbers in each column, regrouping if needed.
   c. Count the places to the right of the decimal point for both numbers.
   d. Add together the number of places to the right of the decimal in both numbers.
   e. Start at the far-right side of the product and count the same number of places as the result of step d; place the decimal point.

4. *Dividing Decimals.* Teach the sequence for placing the decimal point in division, and then guide students to apply the steps:
   *For problems whose divisor is a whole number:*
   a. Put the problem into traditional format ($X\sqrt{Y}$).
   b. Check that the divisor is a whole number.
   c. Find the decimal point in the dividend.
   d. Place the decimal point in the quotient directly above the decimal point in the dividend.
   *For problems whose divisor contains a decimal:*
   a. Put the problem into traditional format ($X\sqrt{Y}$).
   b. Check that the divisor has a decimal point.
   c. Move the decimal point to the right, making the divisor a whole number.
   d. Count the number of spaces the decimal point moved in step c.
   e. Move the decimal point in the dividend to the right the same number of places as in step c.
   f. Place the decimal point in the quotient directly above the decimal point in the revised dividend.

5. *Place the Point.* Have student pairs create and compute problems, placing the decimal point, and then challenge peers with their problems.

# COMPUTATION SAMPLERS

In the samplers on the next five pages, a few activities for developing and correcting computation are illustrated. The samplers are designed to be easily adapted for a variety of situations. In some cases, you may need to adjust instructions or insert information specific to the skill level and student before copying.

10.1 **Personal Number Line.** The number line makes numeration more concrete. Use it in the conventional ways as well as to illustrate each number concept and pair the numbers with the number words. Use with the activities for Skills 54 and 55 and to introduce addition and subtraction. Display an enlarged copy, and give each student his or her own copy.

10.2 **Just the Facts.** This sampler provides the form to structure several activities for Skill 56:
a. fill in the target facts and operation before copying for speed drills or tests;
b. fill in the target facts and operation before copying and then give to students to practice or review before speed tests;
c. after students have mastered the facts for more than one operation, fill in mixed facts, copy, and give as a review speed drill;
d. give students a blank form; have them fill in the facts they have mastered and add to the form as they master more facts; and/or
e. have students fill in the facts they do not know and practice them.

10.3 **The Steps.** Sampler 10.3 provides the form to structure Key Label activities outlining and labeling the algorithm sequence for Skills 57–60, 62, and 64. For each skill, begin by modeling the process; then have student pairs use the form to label the steps, describe the action, and give an example of each step. Students should keep their completed forms to use for self-monitoring. Copy and display several examples for each skill.

10.4 **Reverse Computation.** This activity reverses the computation process, giving students the answer and asking them to provide at least 10 equations that result in that answer. Vary the operations and level of difficulty according to students' ability and the operations currently being studied; give specific instructions to customize the form orally or write them on the form before copying. For example, given the answer *16* and instructions to construct addition equations, the equations would be $1 + 15$, $2 + 14$, $3 + 13$, and so on. However, more advanced students could use fractions and all four operations to write such equations as $7\frac{1}{2} + 8\frac{1}{2}$, $22\frac{1}{2} - 6\frac{1}{2}$, $\frac{1}{4} \times 64$, $2\frac{5}{8}$, and the like. The activity exercises and reinforces computation skills and concepts in an interesting and challenging format, especially when students compete to develop unique equations.

10.5 **Math Log.** Sampler 10.5 is designed to increase awareness, encourage meaningful practice, and highlight the utility of computation. Give a copy of the form to students and instruct them to keep a log of the computations they use outside math class, enter the equations, and describe the circumstances that prompted the computation. Periodically, have students share their logs.

# PERSONAL NUMBER LINE

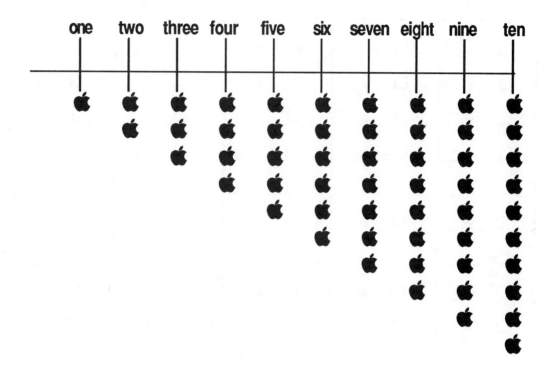

| | | | | |
|---|---|---|---|---|
| 1 = | one | = | | |
| 2 = | two | = | | |
| 3 = | three | = | | |
| 4 = | four | = | | |
| 5 = | five | = | | |
| 6 = | six | = | | |
| 7 = | seven | = | | |
| 8 = | eight | = | | |
| 9 = | nine | = | | |
| 10= | ten | = | | |

Name _____

# ☞ JUST THE FACTS

| ☐ = | ☐ = | ☐ = | ☐ = | ☐ = |
|---|---|---|---|---|
| ☐ = | ☐ = | ☐ = | ☐ = | ☐ = |
| ☐ = | ☐ = | ☐ = | ☐ = | ☐ = |
| ☐ = | ☐ = | ☐ = | ☐ = | ☐ = |
| ☐ = | ☐ = | ☐ = | ☐ = | ☐ = |
| ☐ = | ☐ = | ☐ = | ☐ = | ☐ = |
| ☐ = | ☐ = | ☐ = | ☐ = | ☐ = |
| ☐ = | ☐ = | ☐ = | ☐ = | ☐ = |
| ☐ = | ☐ = | ☐ = | ☐ = | ☐ = |
| ☐ = | ☐ = | ☐ = | ☐ = | ☐ = |

| ☐ = | ☐ = | ☐ = | ☐ = | ☐ = |
|---|---|---|---|---|
| ☐ = | ☐ = | ☐ = | ☐ = | ☐ = |
| ☐ = | ☐ = | ☐ = | ☐ = | ☐ = |
| ☐ = | ☐ = | ☐ = | ☐ = | ☐ = |
| ☐ = | ☐ = | ☐ = | ☐ = | ☐ = |
| ☐ = | ☐ = | ☐ = | ☐ = | ☐ = |
| ☐ = | ☐ = | ☐ = | ☐ = | ☐ = |
| ☐ = | ☐ = | ☐ = | ☐ = | ☐ = |
| ☐ = | ☐ = | ☐ = | ☐ = | ☐ = |
| ☐ = | ☐ = | ☐ = | ☐ = | ☐ = |

Time___Date__    Time___Date__    Time____Date__    Time___Date__

**THE STEPS**
**for**

_____

| KEY LABEL | ACTION | EXAMPLE |
|-----------|--------|---------|
| _____ | _____ | _____ |
| _____ | _____ | _____ |
| _____ | _____ | _____ |
| _____ | _____ | _____ |
| _____ | _____ | _____ |
| _____ | _____ | _____ |
| _____ | _____ | _____ |

## Sample Problems

|  |
|--|
|  |
|  |
|  |
|  |
|  |
|  |

Name _____

# ↔ REVERSE COMPUTATION ↔

## Answer ↔ Equation

• _____   = ➡ _____   ☐ _____
= ➡ _____   ☐ _____
= ➡ _____   ☐ _____
= ➡ _____   ☐ _____
= ➡ _____   ☐ _____

• _____   = ➡ _____   ☐ _____
= ➡ _____   ☐ _____
= ➡ _____   ☐ _____
= ➡ _____   ☐ _____
= ➡ _____   ☐ _____

• _____   = ➡ _____   ☐ _____
= ➡ _____   ☐ _____
= ➡ _____   ☐ _____
= ➡ _____   ☐ _____
= ➡ _____   ☐ _____

• _____   = ➡ _____   ☐ _____
= ➡ _____   ☐ _____
= ➡ _____   ☐ _____
= ➡ _____   ☐ _____
= ➡ _____   ☐ _____

• _____   = ➡ _____   ☐ _____
= ➡ _____   ☐ _____
= ➡ _____   ☐ _____
= ➡ _____   ☐ _____
= ➡ _____   ☐ _____

## $+ - \times \div$ **MATH LOG** $\div \times - +$

| Date | ➤ Use | Equation |
|------|-------|----------|
| _____ | ➤ _____ | _____ |
|  | _____ |  |
|  | _____ |  |
| _____ | ➤ _____ | _____ |
|  | _____ |  |
|  | _____ |  |
| _____ | ➤ _____ | _____ |
|  | _____ |  |
|  | _____ |  |
| _____ | ➤ _____ | _____ |
|  | _____ |  |
|  | _____ |  |
| _____ | ➤ _____ | _____ |
|  | _____ |  |
|  | _____ |  |
| _____ | ➤ _____ | _____ |
|  | _____ |  |
|  | _____ |  |
| _____ | ➤ _____ | _____ |
|  | _____ |  |
|  | _____ |  |
| _____ | ➤ _____ | _____ |
|  | _____ |  |
|  | _____ |  |
| _____ | ➤ _____ | _____ |
|  | _____ |  |
|  | _____ |  |
| _____ | ➤ _____ | _____ |
|  | _____ |  |
|  | _____ |  |

# REFLECTIONS

1. Much of the difficulty youngsters have with readiness is rooted in their initial development. Discuss this idea with others. Try to identify students in kindergarten or first grade to whom this applies. Also discuss an alternative to current practices of student placement.

2. In some areas, a large proportion of the students entering school lack basic experiences that produce number awareness. Consider what might be done in these cases and explain, using the readiness skills outlined in this chapter.

3. Similar difficulties occur in whole number computation across the four basic operations. Which skills in this chapter cite the most similar behavior? Why do you think this is so? Compare and contrast the Correction strategies across all the whole number operation skills.

4. Problems in computation tend to assume different proportions according to the student population and the perceptions of individual teachers. Interview a highly skilled regular education teacher to determine his or her perception of the important Detection behaviors and Correction strategies for each computation skill; then discuss detection and correction of any frequent problems that are not mentioned in this chapter. Follow a similar procedure to interview a veteran special education teacher.

5. Teaching and learning computation are structured processes. Based on your experience and the discussions in this chapter, for which computation skills do you think instruction is the most difficult to provide for students with disabilities? For students without disabilities? For which skills is instruction easiest? Why?

6. The Corrective Principles in Chapter 2 are suggested as guides for selecting and modifying the mathematics strategies in this chapter. Select a hypothetical special learner; using the appropriate Corrective Principles as guidelines, plan a modified computation lesson for that learner. Repeat the process for a second special learner. Compare and contrast the two lessons. For the same content, review the lesson script in the teacher's edition of a basal math textbook. How do your lessons differ from the ones suggested for most students?

7. Identifying computation errors is basic to planning corrective instruction. Using the checklist in Figure 10.1, analyze the work samples of a special student. Then observe that student at work in the classroom and record your observations on the checklist. Summarize your diagnostic findings.

8. Skilled help in providing corrective instruction for special learners is always welcome. Volunteer your services to plan one or more special computation lessons for the special learner you observed. Take the content of your lesson from the basal or other materials currently used in that school. Use the diagnostic information you collected in the previous activity, data available from the school, and the Corrective Principles to guide the design of your lesson.

9. Computation of fractions is a complex process. Select one operation of fractions and design a lesson to introduce it. Be sure to include the use of manipulatives and the transfer to a visual model. Determine all prerequisite knowledge students will need, and create a quick pretest to assess these skills.

10. Teaching fractional computation can be frustrating to teachers and students alike if students have not mastered prerequisite skills. Find an appropriate class to try your pretest from the previous activity. Make sure to give the test enough in advance that you can either change your lesson

or prepare students who have not mastered prerequisite skills. Then teach your lesson to the class and evaluate mastery. What types of errors are the most common? How would you correct those errors?

11. At least cursory mastery of decimals is essential to understanding and computing our monetary system. Repeat Activities 9 and 10, but select a decimal operation around which to design a pretest and lesson. Teach the lesson, evaluate mastery, identify errors, and suggest corrective strategies for those errors.

12. A number of mathematics and special education textbooks address the computation needs of special learners. Compare and contrast discussions in these sources with the information in Chapter 10.

Ashlock, R. B. (1990). *Error patterns in computation: A semi-programmed approach* (5th ed.). Columbus, OH: Merrill.

Cawley, J. F., Hayes, A. M. F., & Shaw, R. A. (1988). *Mathematics for the mildly handicapped: A guide to curriculum and instruction.* Boston: Allyn and Bacon.

Choate, J. S., Enright, B. E., Miller, L. M., Poteet, J. A., & Rakes, T. A. (1992). *Curriculum-based assessment and programming* (2nd ed.). Boston: Allyn and Bacon.

Cruikshank, D. E., & Sheffield, L. J. (1992). *Teaching and learning elementary and middle school mathematics* (2nd ed.). New York: Merrill/Macmillan.

D'Augustine, C. H., & Smith, C. W. Jr. (1992). *Teaching elementary school mathematics.* New York: HarperCollins.

Enright, B. E. (1989). *Basic mathematics: Detecting and correcting special needs.* Boston: Allyn and Bacon.

Enright, B. E. (1985). *ENRIGHT computation series* (Books A–M). N. Billerica, MA: Curriculum Associates.

Griffiths, R., & Clyne, M. (1991). *Books you can count on: Linking mathematics and literature.* Portsmouth, NH: Heineman.

Heddens, J. W., & Speer, W. R. (1992). *Today's mathematics* (7th ed.). New York: Merrill/Macmillan.

Kutz, R. E. (1991). *Teaching elementary mathematics: An active approach.* Boston: Allyn and Bacon.

Mann, P. H., Suiter, P. A., & McClung, R. M. (1992). *A guide for educating mainstreamed students.* Boston: Allyn and Bacon.

Post, T. R. (Ed.). (1988). *Teaching mathematics in grades K–8: Research-based methods.* Boston: Allyn and Bacon.

Reys, R. E., Suydam, M. N., & Lindquist, M. M. (1992). *Helping children learn mathematics* (3rd ed.). Boston: Allyn and Bacon.

Schultz, J. B., Carpenter, C. D., & Turnbull, A. P. (1991). *Mainstreaming exceptional students: A guide for classroom teachers* (3rd ed.). Boston: Allyn and Bacon.

Silbert, J., Carnine, D., & Stein, M. (1990). *Direct instruction mathematics* (2nd ed.). Columbus, OH: Merrill.

Spikell, M. (1993). *Teaching mathematics with manipulatives.* Boston: Allyn and Bacon.

Thomas, D. A. (1991). *Children, teachers, and mathematics.* Boston: Allyn and Bacon.

Willoughby, S. S. (1990). *Mathematics education for a changing world.* Alexandria, VA: Association for Supervision and Curriculum Development.

# Chapter ELEVEN

## MATHEMATICAL PROBLEM SOLVING: THE GOAL OF MATHEMATICS

— *Brian E. Enright and Joyce S. Choate*

Problem solving is the primary function of mathematics education. Students must learn how and when to use the computation and fact skills they develop, or those skills will be of no use at all. Solving problems involves the application of reading, computation, and a host of other skills specific to the process. As a process, problem solving takes a long time to develop. It is a process that begins when students first encounter their world and have to make choices between competing alternatives, and continues to develop throughout their lives. Problem solving is the culmination of mathematics because it applies all skills in a meaningful way. Students learn each new operation in order to solve problems. As the central focus of mathematics, problem solving lends meaning to all that students do with numbers. Solving problems is a real-life skill, essential to adequate functioning in school and throughout life as well.

## THE PROBLEM-SOLVING SKILLS

A successful problem-solving program should focus on systematically teaching students strategies for solving problems. Rather than learning fragmented skills, as many basal programs seem to suggest, students must learn a coherent model or procedure. Together and in sequence, four skills basic to problem solving comprise such a model: (1) reading, (2) organizing data, (3) selecting operation(s) and solving, and (4) evaluating answers. The steps begin with reading with understanding mathematics problems independently, Skill 65. Although this step may seem fairly obvious, many students do not read well enough to comprehend mathematics problems; they may have difficulties with fluency and/or vocabulary. Students must also locate the main question of the problem and rewrite it in their own words, an indication of how well they understand the question being asked. Students can learn the component parts of a problem and what to look for in future problems by creating their own word problems. The skills involved in recognizing words, understanding word meanings — particularly technical and nontechnical terms specific to mathematics — and comprehension in general, discussed in Chapters 4 and 5 as Skills 4–23, are vital for students as they attempt this first step for solving problems.

The second step of problem solving, organizing data (Skill 66), builds upon the first. Students with special needs often have difficulty sorting data, particularly separating relevant from extraneous data. Finding facts within problems and then organizing those facts in a coherent manner is problematic for students with sequential learning problems. Likewise, determining the importance of any fact requires the student to make a judgment about that fact in its context. This skill also involves, to a lesser extent, finding and using data from tables and graphs.

The third step for solving problems focuses on the single greatest mathematics need of all students but especially of special learners: selecting the appropriate operation to use to solve the problem. The best instructional approach provides sequential activities that lead to the selection process. After students have learned how to pick the correct operation, they must learn how to apply that decision to a working equation. This basic equation then sets the stage for the computation phase of problem solving: completing the equation to compute the answer.

The fourth step in solving problems is evaluating the correctness of the answer, Skill 68. The emphasis is on determining how reasonable the answer is in relation to the question asked. Students with special needs often lose sight of where they were trying to go during the process of problem solving; consequently, they often end up some place altogether different. To be sure they have followed the correct path, students must compare their answer with the data the problem was seeking. Though the procedure is not difficult, many special learners seem to avoid it.

The ultimate proof of problem-solving skills is students' application of the four steps to solving problems across the curriculum and in real life. This is the final problem-solving skill discussed.

## DETECTION OF SPECIAL PROBLEM-SOLVING NEEDS

Throughout the country, elementary- and intermediate-level students are having significant difficulties with problem solving. Even in situations in which students perform near or at grade level in computation, they consistently fall far below the mark in problem solving. Estimates based primarily on results of formal tests indicate that nearly half of all students are failing to learn to solve simple problems. More important than *whether* students experience difficulty is *where* in the problem-solving process their errors occur.

### Formal Detection

Formal tests of mathematics achievement are a major component of most standardized achievement tests traditionally administered to entire classes at the beginning or end of a school year. Most of these formal tests include a substantial section on solving problems. Whereas these tests are fairly accurate measures of *whether* students can successfully complete all the steps to solve problems, they do not tell *where* any errors occur.

Students with specific reading disabilities are often unduly penalized by group-administered standardized achievement tests. Although such tests are appropriate as a global measure of students' abilities to perform the first step of problem solving, they yield no clues to what the students know about the later steps for solving problems. The time limits of such formal tests also restrict the performance of some special learners, as does the format in which students must transfer their answers to bubble sheets.

Individually administered formal tests of problem solving are often included in the evaluation of students who are suspected of having disabilities. Results may be reported as a global score, indicating *whether* there are difficulties, but seldom as a detailed analysis of *where* difficulties occur. Both group and individually administered formal tests point out the students who need special help, which is useful screening information. However, measures that pinpoint errors provide more useful information for planning corrective instruction.

### Informal Detection

The options for informally assessing students' mastery of problem solving are varied, but each centers around the four steps for solving problems and, for corrective purposes, must include error analysis. The most straightforward format is to present problems at the appropriate readability level and have students produce the answers, showing their work for each of the four steps. Teachers can then analyze where any errors occur by examining the responses to each of the four steps. To discover how an error occurred, just ask the student to explain how he or she came up with the response. For variation, have students select the correct responses to each of the four steps from several choices. Giving students the correct responses for three of the steps and having them complete the missing step is another way to isolate problematic skills, particularly when the missing step varies from problem to problem. Students can be given problems orally and asked to respond orally, justifying their responses for each of the four steps. A related procedure involves having students think aloud as they solve problems. Whichever format is chosen, the key to a thorough diagnosis is identifying errors.

Analyses of students' written responses to classroom problem-solving activities also provide useful diagnostic information. Although errors sometimes can be inferred through careful study of incorrect solutions, the analysis is easier and more exact if classroom assignments require responses to each of the problem-solving steps.

Checklists, such as the sample in Figure 11.1, are a convenient tool to facilitate analysis of test results and daily work samples. Checklists can serve several assessment purposes. They outline the specific problem-solving skills and provide a useful format to record and monitor students' performance and progress. Checklists can be used alone or with other measures to analyze and record results from formal and informal tests, document performance on an ongoing basis, and structure and record classroom observations.

Observing students in the classroom as they solve problems provides particularly valuable diagnostic information. Their oral reading performance, their successes and errors in various computation activities, the questions they ask and the answers they give during class discussions, their oral explanations as they justify answers, their verbal instructions as they tutor a peer in problem solving, the rate at which they master new concepts, and especially the specific types of errors they make — these behaviors offer insight into students' problem-solving abilities. Behaviors that may signal a particular problem-solving difficulty are listed in Figure 11.1 and at the beginning of the discussion of Skills 65–69. When teachers observe significant behaviors on several occasions, they can isolate and confirm error patterns in order to plan corrective instruction.

## SPECIAL POPULATIONS

When detecting and correcting special needs in any area the unique needs of the student must be the primary consideration; problem solving is no exception. In addition to their individual learning needs and preferences, students considered to be members of special populations may, by definition, exhibit characteristics that make them likely to experience particular difficulties in solving problems.

Problem solving is difficult for all students, and particularly for special populations. Many special learners do not learn easily from incidental experiences. To facilitate their learning, experiences need to be somewhat controlled, explained, and repeated over and over until understanding occurs.

## FIGURE 11.1 / A Checklist of Common Problem-Solving Errors

Problem solving, a multistep process, gives computation meaning. Assessment must therefore also be a multistep process that considers each of the skills and steps. This checklist identifies common errors students exhibit when attempting to solve problems. Once an area of need is located, the common mistakes will assist in establishing the student's error pattern, which pinpoints where instruction is needed. Use this checklist to analyze and record the errors that a student frequently makes in order to plan appropriate corrective instruction.

**Reading**

_____ Stumbles over words while reading problems

_____ Does not independently comprehend written math problems

_____ Cannot identify the main question of the problem

_____ Asks numerous questions about the meanings of words

_____ Knows the facts but cannot put them together

_____ Exhibits generalized reading problems

**Organizing Data**

_____ Cannot identify important details

_____ Does not delete extraneous data

_____ Does not compare each fact to the question

_____ Pulls numbers out of context to compute

_____ Displays inadequate organizational skills for most classroom tasks

**Selecting Operations and Solving**

_____ Appears to choose an operation at random

_____ Did not properly identify the main question

_____ Fails to set up equation correctly

_____ Computes incorrectly

_____ Writes incomplete or grammatically incorrect sentences

_____ Frequently acts without a plan

**Evaluating Answers**

_____ Produces answers that do not match the question

_____ Does not self-correct errors

_____ Frequently gives answers in class that do not relate to questions

_____ Often loses the place in a lesson

_____ Does not attend to details

_____ Displays a short attention span

Adapted from B. E. Enright (1990). Mathematics assessment tips: A checklist of common errors. _Diagnostique, 16_ (1), 45–48, with permission.

As might be expected, the same groups of students most likely to experience difficulties recognizing words, understanding word meanings, and comprehending are also likely to experience those same problems when attempting to read math problems, Skill 65. Special groups whose characteristics may include an impulsive or disorganized approach to learning tasks are apt to approach problem solving in the same way. Thus, students with behavior disorders or learning disabilities may display problems with the second step of problem solving, organizing data. Other special groups for whom the second step may be difficult are those who overlook details, find literal comprehension difficult, or have not been taught how to organize data. The most difficult of the problem-solving steps, selecting the correct operation (Skill 67), is the step in which most special groups exhibit weaknesses.

Because it can be directly taught until it becomes habit, the fourth problem-solving step, evaluating answers, is problematic for fewer groups of special students than the other steps. Applying the four steps to solving problems in other subjects and in everyday life depends on the extent to which students are encouraged to do so, as well as on their mastery of the skills. Since mathematics is a relatively culture-free discipline, cultural differences are likely to affect only the reading required in the first step. Other special groups that are not particularly noted for difficulties in solving problems are the physically disabled, medically disabled, and speech disordered. However, without adequate direct instruction, they too are likely to experience difficulties.

## CORRECTION OF PROBLEM-SOLVING SKILLS

Since a significant number of students of all types experience difficulty solving problems, how should we go about correcting this situation? Systematic teaching is especially necessary when dealing with special students, who typically have difficulty organizing the learning process. Special-needs students are not good at integrating random pieces of information into their learning system. Although the isolated lessons found in most basals are well developed, they do not meet the needs of many special learners, who cannot fit the lesson into what has come before or what will come after.

A fragmented approach tends to confuse rather than enlighten the learner. A systematic approach helps students apply their skills. No one strategy is useful in solving all kinds of problems, and different students may apply different strategies to solve the same problem. The specific strategy a student chooses is not as important as whether the student uses it within a sound procedural model. Students must become familiar with various strategies and learn to apply them systematically.

### Key Corrective Principles

Teaching problem solving step by step is the key principle for corrective instruction, while providing guidance and opportunities to apply those steps to everyday problems renders them meaningful. Although all the guidelines for corrective instruction presented in Chapter 3 apply to teaching problem solving, probably the most critical for correcting difficulties in solving problems are these:

— Teach the strategies for accomplishing each step
— Teach diagnostically and for mastery
— Teach students to attend to detail
— Teach self-monitoring
— Develop paired problem-solving skills
— Use interesting materials at appropriate readability levels

Teaching each step of the problem-solving process and then activating each of those steps to solve whole problems will give students a general learning and study strategy for solving all problems. Teaching diagnostically permits teachers to identify errors during instruction and plan focused correction.

## Corrective Themes

Solving problems is a systematic and sequential process. Consequently, the steps and activities in this chapter are cumulative. They should be used in the order in which they are presented, although the amount of time spent on each activity may vary from setting to setting. These activities only begin an important process; field testing has shown that they improve students' understanding of the problem-solving process.

Many of the corrective principles are incorporated into the corrective strategies in this chapter. They appear in such recurring themes as modeling, paired learning, teaching problem solving as a systematic sequence of steps, teaching the strategies to accomplish component skills, analyzing and then correcting errors as they occur, focusing on topics of interest to students, solving real-life problems, and encouraging students to generate their own problems. Relevant and real-life problems are important for all special learners, but especially for older and less able students whose most pressing need is to develop consumer skills.

## SPECIFIC SKILLS AND STRATEGIES

The next several pages outline and discuss the four steps of problem solving. The first step, reading and understanding the problem (Skill 65), is the precursor to all others, but teachers can circumvent reading mechanics in extreme situations by reading the problems to the student, emphasizing the question. Skill 67, selecting the operation, is probably the most difficult to teach and learn because it involves complex thinking skills. However, students must master all four steps to solve problems both in and out of school.

Teachers who work with special students must be prepared to invest a significant amount of time before they see any progress in students' ability to solve problems. When selecting and adapting strategies to teach special learners, teachers should consult the Corrective Principles in Chapter 2 and the principles of instruction in Chapter 3. However, the student's age, ability, and unique needs must be central in planning appropriate problem-solving instruction.

## 65.  READING MATHEMATICAL PROBLEMS

DETECTION

This may be a special skill need of students who

- Stumble over words while reading problems
- Do not independently comprehend written math problems
- Ask numerous questions about the meanings of words
- Cannot identify the main question of the problem
- Know the facts but cannot put them together
- Exhibit generalized reading problems

*Description*

Problems to be solved must be written at a student's independent reading level. If the material either is at a higher readability level or contains significant vocabulary at a higher level, students will be unable to comprehend and solve the problems. Controlled readability and vocabulary are even more important for students with special needs. After reading the problem, students must locate and understand the main question, often found at the end of the problem and usually followed by a question mark. Students who cannot locate the main question can go no further because it determines everything they must do throughout the rest of the problem-solving process.

*Special Problems*

The causes of reading difficulty are as varied as the number of reading difficulties themselves. A large proportion of students with special needs experience serious problems in reading, as noted in Chapters 4 and 5. For students who can decode the words, two issues are central: locating the main question and then understanding it. Locating the main question is usually a mechanical process that students can think out if they have received and understood the necessary instruction. Some students may be fairly competent readers in other areas but not in mathematics. Because the cognitive demands for solving problems are much greater than for computation, students who are slow learners or mentally retarded may experience difficulty. In addition to students with specific reading disabilities, other special groups for whom the first problem-solving step may be problematic are the educationally deprived and the learning disabled.

*Implications*

Students who have significant difficulties with reading and vocabulary cannot use the appropriate grade-level materials to learn problem-solving skills. As in all areas, vocabulary should be directly taught and reviewed before each lesson. However, when the material is entirely too difficult, possible accommodations include presenting the problems orally, pairing special students with peers who can easily read the materials, or rewriting the problems at a lower level. Students who cannot locate the question will need specific instruction. Begin with simple directions for locating the sentence with the question mark, move to finding sentences that pose questions in "if/then" form, and finally guide students to apply a systematic strategy. Students who experience more conceptual difficulties will need extensive training in both reading comprehension strategies and basic mathematics principles.

CORRECTION      Modify these strategies to meet students' learning needs.

1. *Vocabulary Drill.* Some students have difficulty with technical or subtechnical vocabulary used in math problems. Develop a set of flashcards of the difficult words for students to learn as sight words. Have student pairs practice the words, find their meanings, write the meanings on the reverse sides of the cards, and use each word in a sentence. The meanings of technical terms are usually included in the glossary of the basal mathematics book.

2. *Taped Problems.* Recruit volunteers to tape problem-solving lessons from textbooks. As students listen to the tapes, they can follow along in the written materials, marking where necessary. Students can replay the tapes to get full meaning and to begin to master the essential sight vocabulary.

3. *Clue Scan.* Present three simple problems on a transparency and have students read aloud in chorus. Then discuss the clues that point to the question: a question mark, the last sentence, and words such as *how much, how many, find,* or *solve.* Highlight clues in each problem as students find them; list them on the board as well. Then introduce the skill of scanning (rapid vertical, or zigzag reading) to locate specific information. Coach students to scan problems for clues; list and discuss clues and how students found them.

4. *Question Search.* Have students practice finding questions that are clearly stated and followed by a question mark. Explain that the question is frequently but not always followed by that punctuation. If the materials are consumable, have students highlight with a felt marker first the clues, next the question mark, and then the question itself.

5. *Rewrite the Question.* One way of knowing whether the students have a firm grasp of a problem's main idea is to have them rewrite the question in their own words. Do not have students select an operation at this point; this will come later. Have students work in teams of two or three, rewrite questions, and compare with other teams the different combinations of words they used to say or ask the same thing.

6. *Draw a Picture.* When students have a partial idea of what is being asked in a problem, having them draw a picture of the action within the problem often helps. The quality of the artwork is of no concern, but the drawing may help clarify what the problem is all about. Then have students find the question the picture illustrates.

7. *Build a Model.* To clarify and expand partial understandings, have students build a model of the problem with manipulatives. The objects used are not important; what is important is for the students to build a total model, beginning with the pieces that they know and filling in as the problem becomes clearer. Have students work in pairs, since each will probably view the problem from a slightly different perspective and can add something to the model. Encourage students to think aloud (quietly) as they build their models.

8. *Student Problems.* Having students create their own problems helps them identify all the main elements. They can base problems on information from almanacs and encyclopedias or on events of interest from newspapers or magazines.

9. *Extra Practice.* • Have students compete to locate problem clues and questions. • Have students generate problems (e.g., about sports) for peers to locate the question. • Use student problems for Activities 3–7.

## 66. ORGANIZING DATA

DETECTION          This may be a special skill need of students who

- Cannot identify important details
- Do not delete extraneous data
- Do not compare each fact to the question
- Make incomplete lists
- Pull numbers out of context to compute
- Display inadequate organizational skills for most tasks

*Description*    Facts are the details in a problem that make the overall plan specific. Facts are always exact and complete, leaving nothing to speculation. Students who cannot sort out facts cannot use the given information to solve the problem. Organizing the data in a problem involves literal comprehension (see Skill 14): understanding the details in sequence. It may also involve sorting relevant from irrelevant details. The ability to screen out extraneous data is essential to organizing information into useful sets. Thus, problem solving is a process of choosing between and among competing data.

*Special Problems*    Some students, including many types of special learners, have never learned to be organized. They approach all tasks the same way: rush in, make conjecture, and rush out. These same students typically have difficulty developing and applying the computational algorithm sequences. They often get steps and facts out of order, leave facts out, or fail to notice missing or extraneous facts. These are the students who forget assignments and often demonstrate their disorganization in their study habits and, most obviously, in their notebooks. Although lack of organization may stem from insufficient early training in the home, it most certainly reflects classroom training. Besides inattention to details, difficulties organizing the data in a problem can result from three other factors: (1) the student has weak literal comprehension skills; (2) the student does not fully understand the main question of the problem; or (3) the problem is overloaded with factual information. In addition to students with specific reading disabilities and those overwhelmed by the cognitive demands of problem solving, special groups who may not effectively organize the data are students with behavior disorders, hearing impairments, language differences or disabilities, and learning disabilities, as well as some academically gifted students.

*Implications*    Students who have difficulty identifying salient details will have difficulty with all upper-level mathematics as well as with other subjects requiring them to manage facts and details. They will fail at problem solving because they are working with the wrong information. Many students require specific instruction in the mechanics of extracting information from tables and graphs, a related subskill. A corrective program in organizing data must include a system for overall organization, with specific strategies for organizing facts. Guiding students to organize notebooks and keep records of assignments is helpful. Practice in analyzing tasks that students perform every day helps them attend to details. Teaching students to use organized lists of steps helps them organize the data of story problems.

**CORRECTION**

Modify these strategies to meet students' learning needs.

1. *List the Facts.* Have students go through sets of word problems to list every fact they find, number each fact, and write each on a separate line. This will emphasize that the facts are separate: each one adds information to a problem, but some are more useful than others. By listing the facts, students will extract data from a large mass of information, organize the data, and evaluate it.

2. *Create Your Own.* To emphasize the utility of facts, guide students to the endless sources of facts that are available: almanacs, encyclopedias, record books, newspapers, and magazines. Have student teams select a few facts on a given topic, list the facts, and write a problem using them. Have teams exchange problems, find the same facts, and then use those facts to create a different problem to exchange. Do this activity each day at the end of class for 5 minutes. After a few days, increase the number of facts.

3. *Insufficient Data.* Introduce the notion of insufficient data in problems by presenting problems in which a key variable is left out. Have the students identify the missing variable, explain how it affects their ability to solve the problem, and supply the information. Have student teams create their own problems, deleting a key variable, and then exchange problems to identify what is missing. If they succeed, have the original team provide the missing variable to help solve the problem.

4. *Concentration.* Select several problems at the students' independent reading level. Write each on an index card. On the reverse side of the card, write two facts from the problem and one fact that is not found in the problem. Ask students to select the fact not found in the problem.

5. *Reverse Problem Solving.* Using the problems from the preceding activity, have students select 2–3 facts from each problem and write a totally different problem. This will show students that facts are meaningful only in the context of a given problem. If a student creates a problem that makes a previously useful fact extraneous, amplify the importance of context. Have students exchange problems and confirm that the facts are appropriate.

6. *Compare and Contrast.* Select a number of problems at each student's independent reading level. Have students underline each fact in the problems, circle the main question, and then compare each underlined fact to the main question to decide if that fact is related to the question. Guide students to think aloud about the relationships.

7. *Omission.* Write problems on index cards, leaving a blank where a key fact should go as a context clue. Write each missing fact on a separate card. Have students match the cards and explain their choices.

8. *Table List.* Display and discuss this list of steps for reading tables, and then provide guided practice: (a) Move your finger down the first column till you find the object you seek; (b) Move your finger across that row; (c) Read across columns till you find the right one, and stop; (d) Use a ruler if you need it. Develop a similar list for reading graphs.

9. *Extra Practice.* • Give student pairs consumable copies of word problems in which to highlight facts; save the highlighted problems for practice of later problem-solving steps. • Adapt the above activities for team competition. • Have student teams create tables and graphs of their own using information from school: attendance, average grades, age, height, and so on.

## 67. SELECTING OPERATIONS AND SOLVING EQUATIONS

DETECTION    This may be a special skill need of students who

- Write down one of the facts as the answer
- Appear to choose an operation at random
- Do not pay attention to the sign in an equation
- Have not properly identified the main question
- Demonstrate computation difficulties
- Frequently act without a plan

*Description*    When students translate terms into action in selecting an operation, they are using the language of the problem to determine which operation they need. They must sort the problem into one of several categories and sometimes sort even further as they subdivide categories. Selecting an operation is the most difficult step in problem solving because it requires the use of critical thinking skills. Once students select the correct operation, they must put that operation and the corresponding facts into a complete statement called an equation. Like a sentence with its subject and predicate, an equation must have two sides. On one side of the equal sign, the action is demonstrated, showing the relationship between facts. On the other side, a statement of the consequence is formed, worded in the same way the answer would be but without the number. The statement of consequence should be compared carefully to the main question at this point since it should answer the main question of the problem. Thus, the relationship set up on one side of the equal sign results in the consequence on the other side, and the consequence answers the question asked. Computation skills must then be applied to solving the equation.

*Special Problems*    Students who cannot translate terms into action may have one of a number of problems: difficulty reading the necessary vocabulary, difficulty locating the main question, little understanding of each operation, and/or inadequate skills in computing whole numbers, fractions, and decimals. Frequently, students who have the greatest difficulty constructing equations do not fully grasp the concept of cause and effect; they cannot follow the logic of an if/then relationship. Because the task is complex, many special students have great difficulty with the cognitive demands involved in selecting the correct operation and performing the required computations.

*Implications*    Students who cannot select the correct operation simply cannot solve the problem. They must be directly taught the strategies for sorting problems into categories and then subsorting them into additional categories as needed. Students who cannot generate an equation will have significant problems with putting facts into proper order and performing the indicated computations. These students will have even greater difficulty as they progress to higher-level courses, in math and other subjects, that require the organizational skills represented in the generation of equations. Mastery of this process is in part a function of how the concept is presented. Teachers must approach equation-writing skills in a step-by-step manner, providing practice in isolation and building systematically on what has already been learned. Presenting skills one at a time is essential for the development of learners who have special needs. However, equally important is the need to help students synthesize these skills.

CORRECTION

Modify these strategies to meet students' learning needs.

1. *Preparation.* Begin each problem-solving lesson with a review of the necessary operations, providing corrective instruction for observed computation errors (see Skills 54–64). Use activities from Skill 65 to direct practice in finding the main question in problems.

2. *Vocabulary Clues.* Present and explain the words *total*, *compare*, *distribute*, and *difference*. Make poster cards with these words, and place them on four different tables or desks; read a problem, and have a student decide which table to place it on. Ask peers to confirm placement and describe the thinking process for making the decision. Select several examples of each problem type, randomly mixing types, and repeat this sorting process.

3. *Team Sort.* Present problems written on index cards for student teams to sort into the proper categories, verbalizing the decision process; have them exchange cards and repeat the procedures. The practice is critical to developing the thinking skills needed to select the correct operation.

4. *Subsort.* Since this activity is difficult, it must be covered slowly, with systematic review. Use the cards from the preceding activity. Discuss an addition problem and a multiplication problem and how they both find totals. Next, list the facts for each problem, crossing out any extraneous facts. Label each fact as an *addend* or a *factor*. If all needed facts are addends, put that card in the *add* pile; if one of the facts is a factor, put the card in the *multiply* pile. Begin with single-step problems, and progress to comparative problems and distributive problems. Think aloud as you model each step; then have students follow your model, thinking aloud as they work.

5. *Equation Cards.* Select sample equations from the math text, focusing on a single operation. Explain each equation, its parts, and their functions. Read the problem as the relationship of fact A to fact B, resulting in the answer. Next, prepare problems on individual index cards (or use the ones from the preceding activity) and write an equation for each card. Read each equation as a similar relationship, and relate the process to equations students have been using. Repeat the process.

6. *Structured Teamwork.* Use the problem cards to guide pairs of students through the process of writing equations for each of four categories.
   a. For *total* equations, have student pairs draw a card from the *total* pile, review the problem, find the question, justify its placement in that pile, and list the relevant facts. Provide a blank equation (__ + __ = __) for students to fill in the parts and practice.
   b. For *difference* equations, have students select cards from the *difference* pile. Follow the same procedures used for the *total* pile, supplying an appropriate blank equation (__ − __ = __).
   c. To mix the two formats, provide blank equations for both addition and subtraction and mix problems from the two piles. Have students examine the problem, sort it into the appropriate operation, and go through the steps to write the equations.
   d. For *multiplication*, follow similar procedures using blank multiplication equations. Mix the formats for the three operations, and have students sort for operation and then write the equations.

7. *Extra Practice.* • Adapt the above activities for team competition. • Have student teams construct word problems for specific equations. • Use computation practice activities from Skills 54–64.

## 68. EVALUATING ANSWERS

DETECTION    This may be a special skill need of students who

- Produce answers that do not match the questions
- Frequently give answers that do not relate to the questions
- Often lose their place in the lesson
- Do not pay attention to detail
- Exhibit a short attention span

*Description*    Frequently, low scores on achievement and other tests are related to the students' lack of attention to detail and poor proofreading skills. Confirming that the question answered is the question that was asked in the first place is important in problem solving. Sometimes students go off on tangents and return at the wrong point, moving on through the process solving a different problem. One way to check this is to stop at some midpoint and compare the answer to the original question to see if it makes sense. Again, all the steps in problem solving build on one another; thus, the very first step of understanding the problem is essential to the final step, comparing the answer to the question for logical fit.

*Special Problems*    Students often feel they need to rush through a large number of problems when teachers stress quantity rather than quality. Many teachers talk about the importance of checking answers but do not teach the process as a problem-solving strategy. Some students, particularly special learners, compute very slowly and spend a disproportionate amount of time with this mechanical step of comparing answer to question. Some students have simply learned over time to be careless. Irrelevant and uninteresting problems diminish students' concern for accuracy. Students who are more likely than others to omit this final step are those who display weak computation skills or overlook details; who are educationally deprived, behavior disordered, or learning disabled; and even some who are academically gifted.

*Implications*    Checking the answer is a time-honored routine in mathematics, but one that must be directly taught, modeled, monitored, and developed as an automatic habit. Students must be taught to reread the problem, rephrasing the question as a statement that includes their answer. They can then judge the logic of the statement, repeating the problem-solving steps when the resulting statement is illogical. When the statement is logical, they should check their computation to ensure that their answer is precisely correct. One way to relieve the burden of computation for those students who compute slowly or incorrectly is to provide them with calculators. Teachers should stress that it is not the sheer number of problems completed that counts but the number completed correctly; after students learn the correct process, they will have plenty of time to increase their pace. The use of interesting and personally relevant problems is likely to improve students' performance of each step in solving problems, particularly in this last step as they seek to ensure that they have found the solution to meaningful problems. Comparing the answer to the question as the final step in systematically solving problems should be specifically taught and implemented in all practice.

CORRECTION

Modify these strategies to meet students' learning needs.

1. *Check Computation.* This is an appropriate time to thoroughly check each student's ability to perform all necessary operations. Have students explain their computation, thinking each step aloud. As you note errors, institute corrective procedures for the particular error from Chapter 10.

2. *Calculator Time.* Carefully demonstrate how to use a calculator for each operation. Provide plenty of practice, as this powerful tool can be helpful if used correctly and dangerous if used incorrectly. Permit students who compute slowly to use calculators to check their computation; then have them compare their answers to the question to evaluate their logic.

3. *Match Time.* Use the problem cards developed for selecting the correct operation (Skill 67). Create 2–3 answers for each problem, only one of them correct. Have student teams brainstorm to pick the correct answer, without calculating, by studying the relationship of each possible answer to the question. Next, have them check themselves by solving the problem.

4. *Estimation.* Read problems aloud and have students race to estimate the answer. Have them explain why they think their answer is fairly accurate and how they arrived at their conclusion. Next, give them 2–3 choices, none of which is precisely correct, to compare to the estimations. Then have students actually solve the problems to confirm estimations. Guide a discussion comparing the strategies students used to estimate answers.

5. *Custom Problems.* Problems that students create are often more interesting to them than the ones in a book. Guide a discussion of the types of story problems that appeal to students. List the appealing features on the board. Next, specify an operation and have students use that operation to create story problems for peers to solve. Have peers present the solutions to the problem's author and explain and justify their answers. This activity can also be used to highlight other steps of the problem-solving process. Keep a file of problems the students have developed for review and extra practice.

6. *Change-a-Line.* Give student teams five problems. Instruct them to change one fact or event to develop a new problem, rewrite the problem, write the solution, and give the problem but not the answer to another team. Have teams compete to correctly solve the problems. Then have them evaluate both the answers and the problems themselves. This activity emphasizes all four steps of problem solving as students reread, organize, select and implement the operation according to the new information, and evaluate answers. Again, keep a file of the students' revised problems for review and extra practice.

7. *Extra Practice.* • As this is the last step in problem solving, guide students to apply all four steps to solve many problems; they should carefully study the problem, find the question, select useful facts, determine an operation, generate the equation, calculate the answer, and check that answer. • Since a significant amount of practice is required, base problems on topics of interest to students; ask what they enjoy reading about and then you or the students can develop or select problems accordingly. • Have student pairs race to solve problems from the files in Activities 5–6.

## 69. APPLYING PROBLEM-SOLVING SKILLS

DETECTION

This may be a special skill need of students who

- Do not solve problems except during math class
- Display little interest in solving problems
- Frequently ask for answers to math problems in other subjects
- Display weak problem-solving skills
- Demonstrate weak computation skills

*Description*

Solving problems should not be confined to specific mathematics lessons. For the problem-solving process to become meaningful and useful, students must routinely apply the skills to solve problems as they arise in other classes and in everyday life. First they must learn to identify problems that can be solved mathematically. After discovering a problem, other skills include describing the problem in story form, identifying the question, organizing the data, developing the equation, solving the equation, and evaluating the answer. When students apply the problem-solving process to real situations, the process assumes personal relevance. Establishing relevance in turn increases interest. The true teacher of mathematics teaches and encourages problem-solving all day, seizing every opportunity to guide students to identify, solve, evaluate, and share problems.

*Special Problems*

Problem-solving, with its heavy cognitive demands, is not a process many students approach eagerly, not even the the highly skilled. Some students who do not apply problem-solving skills outside mathematics lessons simply have not been encouraged to do so. Students who have not completely mastered the steps of problem solving or who demonstrate generally weak computation skills are not likely to attempt to solve problems without strong inducement. Without specific guidance, students who do not readily recognize problems that can be solved mathematically may overlook or ignore opportunities. Some students do not automatically transfer the learning from mathematics lessons to other situations and problems. Other students who may exhibit reluctance and/or experience special difficulty applying problem-solving skills are the educationally deprived and those who are mentally retarded or learning disabled.

*Implications*

In order to help students develop the habit of applying problem-solving skills to real problems as they occur, teachers must remain constantly alert to appropriate opportunities. Many special learners need direct instruction, modeling, talk-throughs, and prompting to master the initial step, the identification of problems. Special students may also require substantial and consistent encouragement to seek and then solve problems. Corrective instruction must include sharing and discussing each step of the application process. After each problem is solved, students should be guided to evaluate collaboratively the value and relevance of both the problem and its solution, as well as what they learned during the process.

CORRECTION

Modify these strategies to meet students' learning needs.

1. *Academic Problems.* Highlight the utility of problem-solving skills by identifying classroom and academic problems to solve. Throw out leading statements and questions: I wonder how much time we have before recess. What fraction of your spelling assignment have you completed? What score must you make to raise your grade a full letter? How much colder is it today than it was yesterday? Challenge students to apply their problem-solving skills to respond.

2. *Problem Seek.* As a group activity, guide students to identify problems to solve mathematically throughout the school day. Initially present leading statements and questions as in the previous activity, prompting students to identify problem elements. Ask one student to write the problem story on the board, another to explain the question, and others to explain the remaining three problem-solving steps. Next, reward students for generating leading statements and questions, again walking through the four steps. Keep a card for each problem, noting the name of the student who identified it, to use for review and practice.

3. *Real-Life Problems.* Instruct the students to write about real-life mathematical problems they solve outside math class: on the playground, at home, or at school but in other subjects. Have students present their real problems for the class to solve and justify their solutions. These real problems can emphasize the usefulness of problem-solving skills because they will be more relevant and interesting to the students than textbook problems. Maintain a file of students' real problems for review, extra practice, and use with future classes.

4. *Language Arts Problems.* Routinely infuse problem-solving into the language arts curriculum. Guide students to apply their skills to accomplish tasks like these: Explain how story characters could use mathematics to solve their problems; estimate how many lines or pages will be needed to write a given composition; determine the speed at which one must speak to describe a particular object in a given time period; measure one's personal writing rate; compose story problems for a peer to solve.

5. *Science Problems.* Problem-solving is an integral part of the study of science. As problems are identified in science lessons, develop a problem-solving journal in which students take turns writing the problems and solutions for peers to evaluate.

6. *Social Studies Problems.* Guide students to identify, solve, and share problems involving data comparisons; financial computations; measurement of size, distance, and time; and behavioral analyses.

7. *Problem Journals.* Guide students to develop a journal of the problems they encounter and solve mathematically. The form in Sampler 11.4 may be used or adapted to structure the journal initially. Journals may be exchanged with peers and then discussed and evaluated, or they can be interactive journals in which peers or the teacher routinely exchange written comments. The journal entries provide a permanent record of the students' use of and growth in problem-solving skills. Thus, the journals also provide a problem-solving portfolio that teachers and students can use collaboratively for assessment and for planning additional instruction.

# P ROBLEM-SOLVING SAMPLERS

The samplers on the next five pages include activities for developing, correcting, and increasing interest in problem-solving skills. They can be adapted to the interests, age, abilities, and skill needs of a wide range of students. Thus, you may need to adjust directions or modify or insert information to individualize the activities before copying them for classroom use.

11.1 **Problem-Solving ROSE.** The poster in Sampler 11.1 reflects the four steps of problem solving in this chapter. Although the acrostic is not flashy, it helps students remember the steps in sequence. Discuss the Sampler as a poster and display in the classroom to remind students of the master strategy for solving problems. Give students personal copies for reference.

11.2 **Problem-Solving Frames.** Sampler 11.2 has a dual purpose: It guides students both through problems as they read and solve them and through the process of composing problems. Patterned after the four-step master strategy for solving problems, this framework also reinforces the master strategy.

11.3 **Custom Problems.** This sampler helps students create custom problems, Skill 68, Activity 5. Prior to copying and distributing the sampler to students, enter the operation around which the problems should be built. Then, discuss the criteria for interesting problems. After students have created the specified number of problems, they should exchange problems with peers to solve and evaluate. Keep a file of the problems generated by this activity to use for review and with future classes.

11.4 **Real-Life Problems.** Designed for use with Skill 69, Activity 3, this sampler provides the format for developing and recording the real problems students solve outside math class. Although students may require some coaching to identify and then write the problems, opportunities abound for problem solving at home, on the playground, and in other school subjects. This should be an ongoing activity in which students add to their real problem file as the problems occur and then share their problems and solutions with peers.

11.5 **Math Plays.** Math Plays place problem solving in a familiar format that is a favorite of many youngsters. The format consists of cloze activities in which the types of words to insert in the blanks are specified. The blanks are strategically placed to draw ambiguous and humorous answers. Without showing his or her partner the story, the student requests the type of word required for each blank. After all blanks are filled, the student reads the story with the partner's answers inserted, sometimes producing hilarious results. After reading the story, students should solve the problem by following the questions given. Once students become familiar with this problem-solving format, they can generate their own Math Plays. Student enthusiasm for this activity is contagious. Students eagerly solve each problem so that they can solve more, practicing and improving problem-solving skills, use of context, and reading and writing skills, and enjoying the process. Both teachers and students should maintain a file of Math Plays to use over and over with different words and numbers.

**PROBLEM-SOLVING ROSE**

*A Master Strategy for Solving Problems*

# **R**ead for the Question

# **O**rganize the Facts

# **S**elect the Operation & **S**olve

# **E**valuate the Answer

Name _____

# PROBLEM-SOLVING FRAME

## SCENE

_____
_____
_____

- **First Fact**_____
  _____

- **Second Fact**_____

  Other Facts_____
  _____

- **Main Question**_____
  _____

- **Operation**_____

- **Equation**_____

- **Evaluation**_____

## SCENE

_____
_____
_____

- **First Fact**_____
  _____

- **Second Fact**_____

  Other Facts_____
  _____

- **Main Question**_____
  _____

- **Operation**_____

- **Equation**_____

- **Evaluation**_____

**CUSTOM PROBLEMS**

### Rules for Good Problems

════════════════                    ════════════════
════════════════                    ════════════════
════════════════                    ════════════════

**1. OPERATION:**_____

    Facts:


    Question:

    Equation:

    Solution:

    Evaluation:

**2. OPERATION:**_____

    Facts:


    Question:

    Equation:

    Solution:

    Evaluation:

**3. OPERATION:**_____

    Facts:


    Question:

    Equation:

    Solution:

    Evaluation:

Name _____

# ✳ **REAL-LIFE PROBLEMS** ✳

1. **SETTING**_____

   Facts:


   Question:

   Operation:
   Equation:
   Solution:

   Evaluation:

   ✳ HOW PROBLEM SOLVING HELPED_____

   _____

2. **SETTING**_____

   Facts:


   Question:

   Operation:
   Equation:
   Solution:

   Evaluation:

   ✳ HOW PROBLEM SOLVING HELPED_____

   _____

3. **SETTING**_____

   Facts:


   Question:

   Operation:
   Equation:
   Solution:

   Evaluation:

   ✳ HOW PROBLEM SOLVING HELPED_____

   _____

## ▌▌▌▌▌ MATH PLAYS ▌▌▌▌▌

**1.  YOUR NEW HAIRDO**

(Your name) _____ has a new hairdo. (Your name)_____ is wearing (#)____ (nouns[1])_____ on top and (#)____ (nouns[2])_____ in back. The hair is cut (#)_____inches in front, (#)_____inches on the sides, and (#)_____ inches in back. How much longer is the longest part than the shortest part? How strange does (your name)_____ look?

- Main question?
- Key details?
- Equation?
- Answer?
- Evaluate your answer: Draw a picture of (your name)_____ in the new hairdo.

**2.  THE VACATION**

(Your name)_____ and (friend's name)_____ took a trip to (place)_____ to (verb)_____. They took (#)____ (noun[1])_____, (#)___ (noun[2])_____, and (#)___ (noun[3])_____ with them. They left on (day)_____ at (time)____ and arrived on (day)_____ at (time)_____. How long did the trip take? Were they still friends when they arrived?

- Main question?
- Key details?
- Equation?
- Answer?
- Evaluate your answer: Would you really take this trip? Why or why not?

**3.  THE PICNIC**

(Your name)_____ and (#1–49)____ friends went to (place)_____ for a picnic. They saw (#)____ (nouns[1])_____ and (#)____ (nouns[2])_____. For lunch they shared a bag of (color)_____ (nouns[3])_____. There were (#50–100)_____ (nouns[3])_____ in the bag. How many (nouns[3])_____ did each person eat for lunch? How many people asked for seconds?

- Main question?
- Key details?
- Equation?
- Answer?
- Evaluate your answer: Was the meal healthy? How do you know? What should you order for dessert?

**4.  YOUR STORY:**_____

- Main question?
- Key details?
- Equation?
- Answer?
- Evaluate your answer.

## REFLECTIONS

1. The chapter divides problem-solving skills into four steps that constitute a systematic strategy for solving problems. Compare and contrast this approach with that of at least two basal textbooks.

2. Observable behaviors and skills are cited for each of the steps of problem solving. Scan each discussion to locate these relationships. Which steps cite the most similar behaviors and skills? Why do you think this is so? Follow a similar procedure to compare corrective strategies across the problem-solving steps.

3. Both teaching and learning mathematics are complicated processes. Based on the discussion of special mathematics needs in this chapter and on your own experience, for which difficulties in problem solving is mathematics instruction the most complicated to provide for students without disabilities? Why? For which is it easiest? Why? What about instruction for students with disabilities?

4. Many of the corrective strategies in this chapter apply to all students. Justify the selection of the ones presented, adding, deleting, or modifying strategies where you deem necessary.

5. Problems in mathematics tend to assume different proportions depending on the student population and the perceptions of individual teachers. Interview a highly skilled regular education teacher to determine which Detection behaviors and Correction strategies in this chapter he or she considers most important; then discuss detection and correction of any frequent problems not mentioned in this chapter. Follow a similar procedure to interview a veteran special education teacher. How do their perceptions compare with yours?

6. Problem-solving banks can be invaluable for teaching and practicing the steps of problem solving. Try some of the strategies suggested in this chapter to create problems for such a bank. If you have your own class, have your students help by contributing problems developed around areas that interest them. If they are hesitant, suggest sports or hobbies to get them started; then try to get them to move on to other areas, such as current events. Use the bank for class activities and as the foundation of a cumulative problem-solving bank for future classes.

7. Sampler 11.5 presents an entertaining activity that spurs interest and builds skills in problem solving. Review the sampler, and then create a Math Play of your own; present your Math Play to at least two peers and two children for their stories and solutions.

8. Newspapers and magazines are replete with articles of interest to students. Routinely clip out such articles and group them around common themes or areas of interest. File the clippings in folders labeled "Problem Starters for Football" (or Fashion, Rocks, Trivia, and so). These folders will be the beginning of your bank of ideas that will encourage students to generate problems. Students can use the clippings to find facts and create problems using those facts.

9. The Corrective Principles in Chapter 2 are suggested as guides for selecting and modifying the mathematics strategies in this chapter. Select a hypothetical special learner; using the appropriate Corrective Principles as guidelines, plan a modified problem-solving lesson for that learner. Repeat the process for a second special learner. Compare and contrast the two lessons. For the same content, review the lesson script in the teacher's edition of a basal math textbook. How do your lessons differ from the ones suggested for most students?

10. Teachers often know how but do not have time to plan special mathematics lessons for special learners. Volunteer your services to plan one or more

problem-solving lessons for a special learner in a nearby classroom. Take the content of your lesson from the materials currently in use in that school. Use the diagnostic information available from the school and the Corrective Principles to guide the design of your lesson.

11. A number of mathematics and special education textbooks address the problem-solving needs of special learners. Compare and contrast discussions in these sources with the information in Chapter 11.

Bitter, G. G., Hatfield, M. M., & Edwards, N. T. (1993). *Mathematics methods for elementary and middle school: A comprehensive approach* (2nd ed.). Boston: Allyn and Bacon.

Cawley, J. F., Hayes, A. M. F., & Shaw, R. A. (1988). *Mathematics for the mildly handicapped: A guide to curriculum and instruction.* Boston: Allyn and Bacon.

Charles, R., & Lester, F. (1982). *Teaching problem solving: What, why and how.* Palo Alto, CA: Dale Seymour.

Cruikshank, D. E., & Sheffield, L. J. (1992). *Teaching and learning elementary and middle school mathematics* (2nd ed.). Columbus, OH: Merrill/Macmillan.

D'Augustine, C. H., & Smith, C. W., Jr. (1992). *Teaching elementary school mathematics.* New York: HarperCollins.

Enright, B. E. (1989). *Basic mathematics: Detecting and correcting special needs.* Boston: Allyn and Bacon.

Enright, B. E. (1987). *SOLVE: Action problem solving* (Books I–III). N. Billerica, MA: Curriculum Associates.

Heddens, J. W., & Speer, W. R. (1992). *Today's mathematics* (7th ed.). New York: Merrill/Macmillan.

Howell, K. W., & Morehead, M. K. (1987). *Curriculum based evaluation for special and remedial education.* Columbus, OH: Charles E. Merrill.

Hyde, A. A., & Hyde, P. R. (1991). *Mathwise: Teaching mathematical thinking and problem solving.* Portsmouth, NH: Heineman.

Kane, R. B., Byrne, M. A., & Hater, M. A. (1974). *Helping children read mathematics.* New York: American Book.

Krulick, S., & Rudnick, J. A. (1988). *Problem solving: A handbook for elementary school teachers.* Boston: Allyn and Bacon.

Kutz, R. E. (1991). *Teaching elementary mathematics: An active approach.* Boston: Allyn and Bacon.

Lacy, L., Marrapodi, M., Wantuck, L., Wickenden, B., Witten, T., & Zimmermann, M. (Consultants). (1983). *Problem solving in math* (Books A–D). Cleveland, OH: Modern Curriculum Press.

Panchyshyn, R., & Monroe, E. E. (1986). *Developing key concepts for solving word problems.* Baldwin, NY: Barnell Loft.

Post, T. R. (Ed.). (1988). *Teaching mathematics in grades K–8: Research-based methods.* Boston: Allyn and Bacon.

Reys, R. E., Suydam, M. N., & Lindquist, M. M. (1992). *Helping children learn mathematics* (3rd ed.). Boston: Allyn and Bacon.

Schultz, J. B., Carpenter, C. D., & Turnbull, A. P. (1991). *Mainstreaming exceptional students: A guide for classroom teachers* (3rd ed.). Boston: Allyn and Bacon.

Silbert, J., Carnine, D., & Stein, M. (1990). *Direct instruction mathematics* (2nd ed.). Columbus, OH: Merrill.

Thomas, D. A. (1991). *Children, teachers, and mathematics.* Boston: Allyn and Bacon.

Willoughby, S. S. (1990). *Mathematics education for a changing world.* Alexandria, VA: Association for Supervision and Curriculum Development.

Vacca, J. L., Vacca, R. T., & Gove, M. K. (1991). *Reading and learning to read* (2nd ed.). New York: HarperCollins.

# CHAPTER TWELVE

### RELEVANT SCIENCE:
### TOPICS, PROCESS, AND STRATEGIES

— *Thomas A. Rakes and Joyce S. Choate*

Science, unlike the basic skills of reading, writing, and mathematics, is generally considered a content subject, meaning that mastering content is the goal of study. However, the study of science also includes learning process skills and applying them both to master the content of a planned program and to learn concepts outside school. Teachers should use the information and strategies from previous chapters on the language arts, mathematics, and other areas in planning scientific study. Although they are not always directly addressed in science materials, these skills are often required in scientific study and can be taught concurrently. In the coming century, science will be treated not as a body of knowledge but as an evolving process of ideas and information that directly affects how people live. Teachers must take care to capitalize on multicultural strengths students bring to class. A student's familiarity with a particular geographical or cultural environment affects both interest and learning rate.

## THE SKILLS OF SCIENCE

In addition to the science skills discussed in this section, this chapter addresses three major categories of science content: (1) life science, (2) earth science, and (3) physical science. A final section on integrating the three areas is called "Understanding Science Across the Curriculum." Science content and skills are interrelated. The science skills are (1) information acquisition skills — observing, listening, reading, studying, and directed experimenting; (2) information processing skills — organizing, analyzing, measuring, classifying, predicting, and communicating; and (3) integration skills — synthesizing, hypothesizing, experimenting independently, generalizing, and evaluating. Corrective strategies are organized around the three major content categories, and the science skills are included in the activities suggested for each category and in the final section on science across the curriculum.

Teaching both science content and science skills is appropriate. The skills of science provide the means to master the content. A variety of schemes classify the skills and strategies used in understanding science, but all of them include higher-order thinking skills. No matter how these thinking skills are labeled, the process begins with acquiring information and ends with integrating the information. Figure 12.1 shows the classification of science skills used throughout this chapter. In theory, the three groups are sequential; in practice, the order of skills within or between the groups may vary. The needs of the learner, the nature of the concepts involved, and the demands of the teacher determine which skill is used, regardless of sequence.

## Information Acquisition Skills

Information acquisition includes both obtaining and expanding information. Of the five subskill areas under information acquisition, three involve basic listening, reading, and study skills previously discussed. The remaining skills, observation and direct experimentation, appear in Chapter 12 for the first time. Students who have not mastered these basic skills will have

**FIGURE 12.1 / Science Skills**

| Information Acquisition | Information Processing | Integration |
| --- | --- | --- |
| • Observation | • Organization | • Synthesis |
| • Listening | • Analysis | • Hypothesis |
| • Reading | • Measurement | • Independent Experimentation |
| • Study | • Classifiction | • Generalization |
| • Directed Experimentation | • Prediction | • Evaluation |
| | • Communication | |

difficulty working independently, so study or observation teams may be necessary. Observation and directed experimentation are essential in science, since they are the beginning stages for many projects and scientific studies. When some special learners observe the number of details or the complexity of the task being viewed they may be hindered. Both observation and direct experimentation also include recording information. Recording could be used to combine science and writing lessons. Directed experimentation involves research conducted with clear parameters. Teachers can use directed experimentation to introduce topics, present discrepant events, confirm theories, and formulate questions for additional study.

## Information Processing Skills

Information processing skills include six related functions: organizing ideas; analyzing information; measuring properties and data; classifying information; predicting outcomes; and communicating objective information by speaking, writing, demonstrating, or performing. Organizing ideas involves arranging data, whether sequentially or in some other format, to make it comprehensible and useful. Analysis occurs throughout the process of understanding scientific concepts and principles, as learners assess what they know and what they need to know and then decide how to go about obtaining data. Analysis may include comparing and contrasting, breaking elements into their smallest units, identifying changes during a period of time or space, and taking stock of what is presently known about an object or event. Measuring information can be dealt with directly by teaching students to use measurement instruments and techniques. Measurement involves identifying the best unit and method of measurement to accomplish the goal, using that unit and method to measure, selecting and following the proper procedures for organizing and recording the data, and interpreting the measurements. Quantification of data relies heavily on competence in basic mathematics as well. Classifying information is a key component of understanding concepts and of organization. Grouping ideas by common properties is important not only in science, but also in other subjects such as mathematics, English, and health. Like making inferences and drawing conclusions after reading or listening, predicting outcomes includes anticipating events and relationships. Students should be able to draw on previous experiences and hands on practice with concrete examples to predict outcomes. Effective communication includes effective speaking and writing. Demonstration or presentation skills are also a part of communication.

## Integration Skills

Students must integrate and apply scientific information in order to use their knowledge. The subskill areas are synthesis, hypothesis development, independent experimentation, generalization, and evaluation. Synthesizing ideas based on observations and experiences requires students to classify, organize, and think critically. Critical reflection, another vital element of synthesis, permits students to weigh and interweave data to form new relationships. Effective synthesis enables students to connect and combine information into an integrated whole. Developing hypotheses is similar to formal prediction. Relying heavily upon previously mentioned acquisition and processing skills, a formal hypothesis makes an informed guess about future events. Hypotheses serve as advance organizers for directed experimentation and represent the initiation of the planning stage for designing original experiments. Unlike directed experiments, which are devised by a teacher or suggested in a textbook, independent experiments are designed by students themselves. Generalization and evaluation are the two most meaningful integration skills. When students transfer concepts from one event to another they can apply their scientific knowledge. Evaluating the worth and logic of information and principles supports conceptual change. Evaluation establishes personal and societal relevance and thus renders scientific knowledge useful.

## DETECTION OF SPECIAL SCIENCE NEEDS

Assessment of achievement in science is often less precise than in reading or mathematics. However, the general methods for detecting special needs in science are essentially the same: (1) synthesizing data already available, (2) conducting direct formal and informal testing, (3) interviewing students, and (4) observing students in the classroom.

## Synthesizing Available Data

A review of students' report cards, cumulative records, old science tests, standardized test results that include science content, and teacher comments can yield an indication of past achievements in science. In particular, comparing students' progress across subjects and among teachers can be revealing. When performance fluctuates depending on the teacher, the teacher who elicited the best performance should be interviewed to identify how he or she increased the student's progress. When several past teachers have cited specific skill strengths or weaknesses, the present teacher knows where to begin corrective instruction.

## Formal and Informal Detection

Direct testing can be carried out by using formal or informal procedures. Standardized tests have been criticized for testing information, not such process-related abilities as the science skills presented in this chapter. These tests measure few of the skills for acquiring information. Most formal tests present written information and ask questions designed to test readers' knowledge of what they just read. Standardized science test scores can be useful but are not appropriate as a single source of information on which to base corrective instruction. Informal or teacher-made tests are often more appropriate tools, but they also have their advantages and disadvantages.

Informal tests in science include nonstandardized tests supplied with science textbooks, content or group reading inventories, and traditional teacher-made tests. In classes where textbooks provide the core of the science program, the tests that accompany the science textbooks can be used to assess students' understanding of content and, to some extent, their use of science skills. The way they are used determines the effectiveness of textbook tests. When used for grading purposes alone, they are not very valuable, but when they are used for prescriptive purposes, these tests can help identify both content and skills in need of direct instruction. Some teachers draw many of the questions from the tests that accompany a textbook, adding and deleting according to the material covered in class. When assessing process skills, a checklist such as the one in Figure 12.2 is a useful diagnostic aid.

Another way to assess students' science achievement and interests is to interview former teachers and the students themselves: How much time is spent studying science? Which of the science skills are the strongest? What particular skill problems did you note? Which topics were of greatest interest? The interviews can help teachers determine how well students have performed and in what tasks. An orally administered inventory of science interests, either published or teacher-constructed, can also add information to the interview process. See Sampler 12.1 for such an inventory.

Direct observation of students as they participate in classroom science lessons can often yield the most valid and reliable assessment data. Observations are particularly valuable for identifying the specific needs of special students. One convenient method for structuring classroom observations is to use a checklist, such as the one provided in Figure 12.2. A popular way to handle the accumulated information is to maintain a portfolio of each student's work samples and test results, as well as notes from conferences or daily observations.

## SPECIAL POPULATIONS

Without instructional accommodation, mastery of science content and skills can be a problem for special learners. Of the information acquisition skills, reading about science is particularly difficult for many students, while directed experimentation is not. Of the information processing skills, communicating orally or in writing present the most difficulty and measurement the least. Because of their complexity, integration skills are difficult for many special learners.

## CORRECTION OF SCIENCE SKILLS

Special learners may require fewer and less dramatic accommodations in science than in any other academic subject. In fact, carefully structured and supervised activity-based science classes seem tailor-made for mainstreamed special students. Corrective strategies recommended in this chapter can often be adapted for use on various levels and in many instances, across different topical or subject areas. Fourteen principles for teaching science, listed in Figure 12.3, are used throughout the activities that follow. Most of these principles are appropriate for all learners, but they are particularly important for teaching science to special learners.

Adjusting instruction for specific needs, the final principle in Figure 12.3, is essential for both students' and teachers' success in science. In planning to ways to accommodate special learners, the *information acquisition* skills are relatively easy to adjust by substituting one for another. When involving

FIGURE 12.2 / **Checklist for Detecting Special Needs in Science**

| Skills | Student Behaviors | Observed | Reported | Comments |
|---|---|---|---|---|
| **Information Acquisition** | | | | |
| **Observation** | • Attends to stimuli<br>• Distinguishes relevant features<br>• Describes observations<br>• Other: | | | |
| **Listening** | • Attends to stimuli<br>• Understands details<br>• Listens critically<br>• Other: | | | |
| **Reading** | • Recognizes and understands word meanings<br>• Comprehends details<br>• Makes inferences<br>• Reads critically<br>• Other: | | | |
| **Study** | • Works independently<br>• Organizes for study<br>• Follows a routine<br>• Locates additional information<br>• Other: | | | |
| **Directed Experimentation** | • Follows directions<br>• Observes and describes<br>• Draws conclusions<br>• Other: | | | |
| **Information Processing** | | | | |
| **Organization** | • Organizes self and materials<br>• Sorts and groups data<br>• Follows a plan<br>• Other: | | | |
| **Analysis** | • Identifies unique features<br>• Compares and contrasts<br>• Describes relationships and patterns<br>• Other: | | | |
| **Measurement** | • Chooses correct instruments<br>• Selects appropriate methods<br>• Understands basic mathematics involved<br>• Other: | | | |

| Skills | Student Behaviors | Observed | Reported | Comments |
|---|---|---|---|---|
| **Information Processing (Cont.)** | | | | |
| **Classification** | • Identifies salient features<br>• Groups by commonalities<br>• Other: | | | |
| **Prediction** | • Anticipates relationships<br>• Identifies cause and effect<br>• Predicts outcomes<br>• Other: | | | |
| **Communication** | • Orally explains under-<br>standings<br>• Writes understandings<br>• Demonstrates or performs<br>• Other: | | | |
| **Integration** | | | | |
| **Synthesis** | • Classifies information<br>• Combines information<br>into a new whole<br>• Other: | | | |
| **Hypothesis** | • Predicts outcomes<br>• States predictions<br>• Other: | | | |
| **Independent Experimentation** | • Plans experiments to<br>test hypotheses<br>• Conducts experiments<br>to test hypotheses<br>• Other: | | | |
| **Generalization** | • Uses deductive logic<br>• States scientific principles<br>• Applies principles to other<br>phenomena<br>• Other: | | | |
| **Evaluation** | • Critiques the logic of<br>information and principles<br>• Critiques the worth of infor-<br>mation and principles<br>• Modifies conclusions when<br>appropriate<br>• Describes personal<br>relevance<br>• Describes societal relevance<br>• Other: | | | |

**FIGURE 12.3 / Fourteen Principles for Teaching Science to Special Learners**

1. Use an activity-based format to teach concepts and skills

2. Choose important survival topics and apply them to everyday life

3. Use realistic and relevant experiments and examples

4. Establish the experiential base for each topic

5. Emphasize and directly teach vocabulary

6. Limit each lesson to the most relevant information

7. Provide generous review activities with each lesson

8. Integrate science with other subjects

9. Carefully structure the content and format of the program

10. Provide response prompts and teach self-monitoring

11. Encourage parents to reinforce the science program

12. Keep up with scientific advances

13. Build interest and enthusiasm

14. Teach specific skills and adjust for specific needs

students in science, always be alert for opportunities to adjust the approach and reteach. Use advance organizers to prepare students for tasks, state no more than three specific purposes for the observations to focus students' attention, and lead students to verbalize their observations. Use concrete examples, place key vocabulary in context, and eliminate distractions. Zero in on the particular meaning appropriate for the lesson, and do not spend time developing multiple meanings. Limit the length of informational units, and use varied and appropriate formats. Be sure the reading level of science materials is appropriate. Provide extra assistance or alternate methods of acquiring information if the reading level of materials is beyond students' abilities.

In science, *information processing* skills are critical to experimentation and evaluation. Because scientific study is based upon observing, recording, and analyzing information, students must have guided activities in which they can predict and verify by measuring or classifying. To be successful, students need many demonstrations, interactive experiences, and hands-on activities. Students can make predictions, which are so vital in science, only when they are able to acquire information and make judgments. As a part of processing information, students must receive frequent opportunities to communicate their findings and guided practice in doing so. Let students choose whether to report findings orally or in writing.

Science is the *integration* of skills and ideas. Synthesizing information is a critical thinking skill that leads to developing hypotheses, evaluating, generalizing, and evaluating. Because science content is so broad, even common terms such as *ecology* or *energy* can involve multiple areas of scientific information. Structured experiments with plenty of concrete examples promote mastery of science concepts and skills.

## SPECIFIC SKILLS AND STRATEGIES

The sections that follow begin with suggestions for improving science skills in the area of *life science*. This section includes topics learners will find relevant: ecological concerns, health and nutrition, and living things. The next section, *earth science*, deals with astronomy, weather, and the earth. The third section on *physical science* contains topics related to energy alternatives, technology, and using machines. The final section on *science across the curriculum* includes activities based in science but appropriate for use in conjunction with other subjects and skills. Although the fourteen key principles listed in Figure 12.3 are not mentioned in every activity, be sure to incorporate these principles into your lessons.

Many classrooms have become multicultural settings as students from the Caribbean, Central America, the Far East, and other regions enter the schools. Teachers must give special attention to language and cultural differences. In science, teachers should ensure that cultural diversity is reflected in posters, audiovisual materials, books, bulletin boards and displays, grouping and seating arrangements, topical and project activities, and the selection of resource persons. Science is a natural area for studying diversity.

## 70. UNDERSTANDING LIFE SCIENCE

DETECTION

Mastery of key concepts may be difficult for students who

- Do not observe carefully
- Reveal poor listening and reading habits
- Cannot classify or predict
- Experience difficulty analyzing and hypothesizing
- Cannot explain the interdependence of living things
- Have limited experiences outdoors
- Are unaware of different pollutants
- Know little about natural resources
- Demonstrate little concern for the preservation of nature
- Exhibit inappropriate personal habits

*Description*

Life science is the area of science of the most immediate value to special learners. Its content helps students understand and care for themselves and others. Developmentally, life science is a particularly appropriate introduction to science. Teaching and learning about living things involves a mixture of classroom and outdoor experiences. Life science deals with plants, animals, and the human body, including ecology and health and nutrition. Although all science skills are necessary, listening, communicating, and particularly observing, predicting, and generalizing facilitate learning. These basic skills also prepare students for using other science skills later in the study of more complex topics. Studying living things also provides an excellent context for demonstrating, studying, and sharing the diversity of life in a positive, multicultural setting.

*Special Problems*

A primary cause of difficulties in the life sciences is lack of meaningful experiences with living things and the outdoors. Cultural differences may mean that students need to spend a great deal of time gaining background through field trips, tapes, pictures, supplementary books, and demonstrations. Students who have difficulty understanding about animals or plants need experience. Learners respond to topics involving their personal and cultural interests. Purposely devote time and attention to topics such as the human body, ecology, or nutrition. Highly personalized lessons also enable students to improve skills while studying something they like. Predicting and visualizing the future effects of our actions may be particularly difficult for special students, but life sciences topics are easily related to daily life.

*Implications*

Teaching principles 1–5 from Figure 12.3 can help students become excited about science. Provide background information using local examples and points of reference before moving to distant resources and/or unusual animal and plant life. When students are indifferent to the use of resources partially because their teachers do not provide personalized, hands-on activities, they cannot master concepts or apply skills. The basic topics and activities in this section can be easily adapted for special learners.

**CORRECTION**      Modify these strategies to meet topical and learning needs.

1. *Plant Eaters* (Observing, studying, classifying, predicting, hypothesizing, generalizing, evaluating). Begin by displaying samples of fresh fruits and vegetables. Encourage discussion about how they are grown and which foods are grown in the region where the students live. Have students predict how each food is grown — above ground, below, on stalks, on trees, and so on — and then verify their predictions. using the information acquisition skills. After they identify a few foods that are grown locally, have student gather information about the plants by observing, listening, reading, viewing tapes, or study and research. Form teams or pairs of students to search for answers to target questions about regional conditions that permit the plants to flourish and then chart their answers. Help students contact someone at a local produce market and practice using questions to find out information. To integrate concepts with social studies, guide students to discover the regions of the country where local products are shipped. Repeat the activity for students' favorite produce that is not locally grown.

2. *Parks and Nurseries* (Observing, organizing, analyzing, classifying, predicting, generalizing, evaluating). Before planning a trip to a park, nursery, or garden, invite a resource person to explain what is done there and the types of plants involved. Guide students to prepare questions ahead of time. To prepare for the field trip, help students develop an outline of what to look for and what questions to ask to guide them while they tour. Plan who will be in charge of taking notes and pictures and of writing the thank-you note. Assign students the task of identifying 1–3 plants they consider the most desirable based on beauty, utility, hardiness, cost, and care. Arrange for a guide to accompany the students during the tour to help them fill in their outlines as they go. Later, have students discuss and defend their choice of desirable plants.

3. *Animal Inquiry Center* (Observing, studying, measuring, communicating, synthesizing, hypothesizing, generalizing, evaluating). Place at a supervised center an ant farm; an aquarium with fish, a snake or insects; or a cage with a rabbit or gerbils. Provide one or more times each day for 1–3 students to observe the animals for 5–10 minutes during feedings or wakeful periods. Designate a specific purpose for each observation, and give students a checklist of elements to analyze. Activities at this center allow animal study in the classroom; the possibilities for teaching and reinforcing skills and concepts are limited only by the age, interest, and ability levels of the students and by the teacher's guidance and purposes.

4. *Using Your Senses* (Observing, directed experimenting, analyzing, predicting, classifying, generalizing, evaluating). Establishing the relevance of sensory organs is usually no problem because their functions can be readily observed and personally experienced. There are a variety of ways to provide practical experience using the five senses. In each case, stress the role of the senses in acquiring information. As a matter of practice, identify and avoid students' allergies and dietary restrictions. Accompany each experience with diagrams of parts and functions, working models, or videotapes to illuminate concepts, and labels and verbalization of the process, first by the teacher and then by students. Conclude each experience by discussing how each sense contributes to acquiring information and self-knowledge and to enriching life.

— *Taste.* To illustrate the four different tastes (sweet, salty, sour, and bitter), add sugar, salt, lemon, and vinegar to four containers of water. Dip a cotton swab into each liquid, apply to students' tongues, and ask students to identify each taste. Provide diagrams showing the four regions of the tongue that detect different tastes (tip of the tongue for sweet, front sides for salty, back sides for sour, and back center for bitter). Have students repeat the tasting to verify the diagram.

— *Touch.* Create a Touch Box or Feeling Bag filled with several textured objects; have students take turns describing and then guessing what they feel inside the box or bag; conclude with discussions of how touch helps them understand.

— *Sight.* Show a black-and-white picture and a color picture of a similar scene or object and have students compare what they see. Shine a flashlight across the room first with the lights off, and then with the lights on. Next, have students observe in a mirror the change in their eyes as you move a light toward them; lead a discussion of the purpose of changes in size of the eye's pupil with a question such as, "Why do you wear sunglasses?" Follow with lessons on eye safety and care.

— *Sound.* Begin by discussing which sounds students consider the most pleasant and unpleasant. Use a variety of supervised experiments to demonstrate that vibrations cause sound and to introduce the concepts of quality, pitch, and intensity and why they vary. Let students manipulate stringed musical instruments, rubber bands, tuning forks, small objects on a drum, and simple flutes for illustration. Guide students to verbalize what is occurring in each case. Then present a diagram of the ear and explain each step of the process of hearing as students repeat their experiments. Conclude with lessons on the long-term effects of loud music or industrial noises and proper care of the ears.

— *Smell.* Demonstrate the function of smell in tasting by having students compare taste when they hold their noses and when they do not; discuss the implications for eating something pleasant or unpleasant or for tasting when students have a cold. Call attention to the odors from the school cafeteria, and have students identify the ones that make them hungry and those that do not. Discuss associations and effects on appetite. Have students smell several different perfumes and then discuss why these fragrances are not as distinct as food odors. With some students, this also may be a good time to discuss unpleasant body odors and personal hygiene.

5. *The Recycling Revolution* (Observing, studying, analyzing, integrating). Class or independent projects, in recycling can improve local conditions, increase awareness and commitment, raise money, and actively involve students in the learning process. Since recycling projects are also important lessons in citizenship, they should be included in discussions of social awareness and responsibility. Beginning with the trash can in the classroom, and moving to garbage from the school cafeteria and from students' homes, and then to litter along the roads to and from school, have students identify the types of trash that can be recycled instead of left to litter or contaminate the land. Videotape a variety of local scenes, including a local garbage dump or landfill. As students identify each type of trash, guide them to investigate its recycling potential through study, analysis, and interviews. Use news items to present the array of possible recycling projects (e.g., certain types of plastic). Then have students decide on a manageable large-group project or a few small-group

projects to recycle items such as aluminum cans, paper trash, or glass bottles, and determine how any revenues will be used. Emphasize environmental improvement, rather than earnings.

6. *Water Purity* (Observing, analyzing, communicating, generalizing, evaluating). Have teams of three students collect water samples from at least three different sources, such as taps at home and school and a mudpuddle or ditch. Have all team members view samples under a microscope. Designate one team member as Describer, a second as Artist, and a third as Recorder. The Describer should view each sample and describe what he or she sees while the Artist sketches the sample from the description; the Recorder should retell on tape or write a summary of the description. After they have analyzed all samples, have students compare the sketches and recordings. Although the school samples are from the same source, they will probably notice differences because the time, exact locations of samples, and perceivers' tastes, vary. Through demonstrations and directed study, guide students to identify and evaluate impurities. To extend concepts, invite a resource speaker, or use this activity to introduce chemicals or single-cell life.

7. *Ecological Survey* (Listening, reading, directed experimenting, organizing, classifying, communicating, integrating). Organize students into pairs or teams and have each team select ecological issues to investigate. Guide teams to prepare 3–8 item questionnaires to survey the knowledge of students and teachers about their ecological topics. Put responses into categories to organize results and make them easy to interpret. Help the teams decide on numbers and categories of students and teachers they will interview and hypothesize which ones will know the most about the topic. After the data are collected, guide students to organize, synthesize, and interpret their results by categories. Ask students to dictate or write summaries and make simple charts of their findings. Use the summaries as news releases for the school paper or to post on a school bulletin board. Some results may indicate the need to investigate factors that influence certain groups' knowledge. Screen information to make sure it will not embarrass anyone before it is posted.

8. *Principles of Safety* (Listening, reading, analyzing, communicating, synthesizing, generalizing, evaluating). Have students develop or modify safety rules, guidelines, and procedures in their room or school. First, have students identify all rules that involve safety, from not running in the hall or classroom to cafeteria rules to emergency evacuation procedures. Have students list, discuss, and evaluate how these rules contribute to student safety. Next, have students suggest modifications to the rules, and even new rules, that might improve school safety. List the improved rules and periodically review and refine them.

## 71.  UNDERSTANDING EARTH SCIENCE

DETECTION          Mastery of key concepts may be difficult for students who

- Do not observe carefully
- Have difficulty classifying and/or analyzing
- Exhibit problems predicting and synthesizing
- Experience problems generalizing or evaluating
- Have had few experiences in the outdoors
- Demonstrate little knowledge of land, rock, and water resources
- Cannot read a thermometer
- Appear uninformed about astronomy
- Show a lack of knowledge about weather

*Description*          Earth science can be unusually interesting to special students. They can conduct experiments, projects, and small-group and independent studies on such topics as rocks, sources of water, forests, of weather, and the planets and stars. Most of these topics, while not being of immediate value to students, are still highly motivating. Weather studies are often a favorite. Of the science skills that must be applied in learning earth science, the most important are observing, analyzing, classifying, experimenting, and generalizing.

*Special Problems*          While students find topics dealing with space and technology interesting and full of unusual information, studying about the earth is not generally as well received. Cultural, religious, ethnic, and geographic differences can affect learner interest. A number of reports have focused on students' limited knowledge of geography. Establishing the personal relevance of studies of rocks, land masses, and sources of water is difficult. Some parents can share little knowledge with their children; teachers often shy away from earth science because it seems dull or uninteresting. Some students live in areas where they are not exposed to different types of rocks, forests, and bodies of water. Limited travel opportunities and some disabilities restrict how much information some students have about land and water. Students who have not visited parks or seen different parts of the country will have difficulty generalizing about an oil spill or the size of a lake or river. Difficulties in analyzing and classifying interfere with studying earth science.

*Implications*          To personalize content, begin with an analysis of land and outdoor resources in your immediate region. Always consider multicultural differences and take advantage of any background students bring to class. It does students who live inland little good to study about an ocean if they do not know the difference between a river and a lake or a spring. Students can learn about rocks directly through hands-on analysis that allows them to experience the textures, weight, and appearance of something real. Teachers can address relevance by pointing out the products of rock, wood, and water. Integrate conservation with earth studies so that students develop a sense of responsibility for the environment and for others. Lessons involving temperature and weather offer opportunities for students to practice measuring, analyzing, predicting, and evaluating information of immediate interest. Take advantage of the fact that many students have some knowledge about weather, temperature, and seasons. Land and water are more difficult to conceptualize.

CORRECTION               Modify these strategies to meet topical and learning needs.

1. *Clay Concepts* (Observing, studying, analyzing, synthesizing, evaluating). Ask students to study pictures of local or prominent land areas and draw what they see. Have them explain which features are most noticeable. Guide teams of students to make clay models of the land features, using their pictures and a raised relief map as references. Pair this activity with a social studies lesson to investigate the sociological effects of land formations.

2. *Which Is Which?* (Listening, reading, studying, analyzing, communicating). Help students write 1–2-sentence descriptions of at least four different land areas, such as islands or mountains. Place the descriptions on index cards. The same formations can be used several times but with descriptions written or dictated by different students. Form teams to take turns reading descriptions for others to identify.

3. *Rock Displays* (Observing, reading, studying, classifying). Locate samples of different types of rocks, beginning with ones found nearby. Provide books about rocks for references. As students study a particular type of rock, display a sample in a shoebox top with its name and key features written beside it. When students become familiar with the samples, remove a few, and ask students to match the rocks with the correct names.

4. *Water Uses* (Observing, studying, classifying, generalizing, evaluating). Begin a chart with three headings: Oceans, Lakes, and Rivers. As students learn about them, add the names of examples under the correct category. Students can also add information about size, uses, and location on cards or directly on the chart with the name of the body of water.

5. *Types of Wood* (Observing, listening, reading, analyzing, classifying). Guide students to classify trees as coniferous (softwood) or deciduous (hardwood). As they study different types of trees and their uses (there are many more types of deciduous trees than coniferous), have students complete a class listing by type, for example:

| *Coniferous* | | | *Deciduous* | | |
|---|---|---|---|---|---|
| cedar | fur | larch | ash | birch | oak |
| hemlock | pine | spruce | cypress | maple | poplar |

If possible, add a picture or drawing and a leaf of each tree to the listing. Discuss the major differences between the two types of trees. This activity can also involve writing to students in other regions and exchanging leaves or collecting leaves when visiting other areas.

6. *Hunting for the Forest in School* (Observing, analyzing, classifying, communicating). Encourage students to compete to find forest products. Provide categories, such as foods, chemicals, and lumber. Extend the search outside the school, and recognize students who make many or unique contributions.

7. *Reading a Thermometer* (Observing, listening, reading, measuring, communicating). To review reading thermometers, bring a large thermometer to class and place it out of direct sunlight but where students can read it. Explain how thermometers work. After students locate the present temperature, call out various temperature readings for students to find on the thermometer. Individual simulated thermometers are useful learning aids.

8. *Understanding Temperature* (All information acquisition, processing and integration skills). To demonstrate the effects of temperature, have students predict and record results as they perform activities such as these.

   — Put containers with thermometers in various places.
   — Make a thermometer and explain how the liquid behaves.
   — Make frost, icicles, ice, and/or popsicles; then place them in the sun.

9. *Predicting Precipitation* (Observing, analyzing, predicting, generalizing, evaluating). Have students describe situations when they needed to predict precipitation. Show videotapes of local weather reports, and discuss what the forecasters look for. Then begin a daily program of study: Have students watch the morning weather forecast on television, periodically observe clouds and temperature outside, record their observations, analyze them, and conclude the signs that foretell precipitation. Later, designate a different student to predict precipitation each day; have peers evaluate the value of the signs used and the accuracy and value of the predictions.

10. *Storm Watch* (Observing, listening, reading, organizing, communicating). Set aside an area on a bulletin board for students to post short news reports or their own retellings of television and radio descriptions of local storms.

11. *Documentary Evidence* (Observing, organizing, communicating, generalizing, integrating). Have students take pictures of activities occurring during various weather conditions: peers at work on experiments or projects, animals, field sites, playground activities, and scenes at a shopping center or on a highway. Guide students to analyze the pictures to identify the effects of weather on themselves and others.

12. *Local Storm Analysis* (Observing, listening, reading, communicating, generalizing). Provide information about the types of storms that occur locally, how they are formed, and the damage that can result. Discuss the effects of such storms on property and people and their activities. Guide students to analyze the resulting problems and then classify those problems using headings such as Transportation, Power, Property, Life, School, and Home. Compare and contrast local storms with those that occur in other regions. Have a student delegation contact the local police and fire departments or civil defense director to find out what plans have been made for storm disasters in your area.

13. *Accuracy of Weather Sources* (Observing, listening, analyzing, predicting, evaluating). Each morning, have a student tell what one source, such as one report on a television or radio station, predicts as the weather for the day. Guide students to plan three things they should and should not do according to the forecast. Have them evaluate the accuracy of forecasts the next day by comparing them with the weather that actually occurred. If appropriate, students can compare forecasts on television with forecasts in a newspaper or almanac to evaluate accuracy.

14. *Weather Comparisons* (Observing, listening, reading, analyzing, measuring, communicating, evaluating). Media obtain their weather information from different sources. Conduct telephone or letter surveys of local media to identify whether their source is the National Weather Service or a private weather service. Ask students to compare weather forecasts from media that use the same source. Have student teams use information from two or three different newspapers, television

stations, or radio stations. Over a 10–30 day period, chart each forecast and compare the results the next day. Guide students to develop a system for evaluating and recording accurately.

15. *Seasonal Relationships* (Observing, analyzing, classifying, communicating). List the four seasons on the board. Have students name words related to each season as it occurs in their area. Use these words to begin the study of the seasons. For some regions, a partial listing might look like this:

| Summer | Autumn | Winter | Spring |
|--------|--------|--------|--------|
| hot | leaves | cold | green |
| humid | windy | snow | flowers |
| swimming | Halloween | ice | baseball |

16. *Seasonal Differences* (Observing, listening, reading, analyzing, classifying, communicating, evaluating). Ask students to locate photographs taken during a particular season — summer, for example. If possible, they should bring pictures of themselves and their families during a summer activity, or they can use pictures from magazines. Have students interpret events in each picture by describing how the picture would differ according to each season, emphasizing weather and and health. Have students decide which season is best for the activity or event in each picture.

17. *Planetary Information Center* (Observing, listening, reading, studying, communicating, synthesizing). Develop a planetary information center containing (1) pictures or drawings of each planet in our solar system, (2) student-authored descriptions of each planet, (3) trade books about the planets, and (4) activities on the planets for students to complete. Have students develop part of the contents of the center themselves. Encourage students to work in pairs at the center both to expand their own knowledge and to add to the information at the center.

18. *Star Search* (Observing, listening, studying, analyzing, synthesizing, hypothesizing). Identify several stars that can easily be viewed in your area. Have students locate the stars on a star map and describe how to locate them. Then make arrangements with a local astronomy club to sponsor a Star Search night for the students. Ask club members to bring telescopes and help students use them. Have students describe the stars they want to view, tell where they are located, and then try to locate them. Have extra adults available to guide students, prevent accidents, and keep students on task.

## 72. UNDERSTANDING PHYSICAL SCIENCE

DETECTION    Mastery of key concepts may be difficult for students who

- Demonstrate poor observation skills
- Do not predict or analyze easily
- Have difficulty generalizing or evaluating
- Are not technology literate
- Exhibit wasteful habits
- Appear to know little about how machines work
- Are unfamiliar with water, wind, and solar power
- Take sources of energy for granted
- Cannot explain the value of different energy sources

*Description*    The physical sciences may be the most difficult for special learners because they encompass many complex concepts and because ideas and technology change almost daily. Except for the basic laws of physics, innovations and research are reported at such a pace that the knowledge base of science textbooks is outdated before printing. In the physical sciences the skills of predicting, measuring, analyzing, generalizing, and evaluating are most important.

*Special Problems*    The sheer complexity of nuclear energy or robotics, or for that matter of simplifying such topics, makes portions of physical science difficult. Many students are unaware of their dependency on nonrenewable fuels such as coal and gas. Few students see sunlight, water, or wind as a source of energy. The principles involved and their interrelationships are complex, too complex for some special learners to see their relevance. Understanding force and work, for example, requires measurement skills. Without a conceptual base and minimal mathematics skills, students will have difficulty analogizing, hypothesizing, and generalizing about, for example, nuclear power and its relationship to the ecology and to the growing need for energy. Unless they live near a nuclear facility, many students will have little experience with which to discuss radiation or declining forest lands, even after reading and talking about them.

*Implications*    Since textbooks cannot keep pace with the changes occurring in some areas of physical science, and since the concepts are complex, teachers should select topics for study carefully. Use supplemental materials such as articles, materials from government agencies, tapes, and demonstrations. Areas involving machines, magnetism and electricity, sources of energy, and energy conservation can be taught as interesting, understandable topics related to daily life. Study of nonrenewable fuels can be integrated with social studies, exploring locations, shortages, and alternatives in a meaningful way. Students with physical disabilities will be particularly interested in biotechnology. More than any other area of the sciences, teaching physical science requires teachers to build background concepts and move ahead in small conceptual units. Principles 6, 7, 12, and 13 in Figure 12.3 are especially important when teaching physical science.

CORRECTION  Modify these strategies to meet topical and learning needs.

1. *Why Fossil Fuels?* (Observing, listening, reading, studying, organizing, communicating, synthesizing, generalizing). Explain that fossil fuels contain energy from plants and animals that, through the process of heat and compacted earth over millions of years, changed into coal, natural gas, and petroleum. Show samples or pictures of fossils and then drawings depicting their layers in the earth. Have students handle several pieces of coal and notice the black deposits on their hands. Discuss why coal is not a clean source of energy. Then have students critique videotapes showing fossil fuels being extracted and refined. Guide student to answer these questions: Why is burning petroleum not a clean source of energy? What are fossil fuels called *nonrenewable fuels?* Why would you not want to live next to a rig, mine, or refinery? What couldn't you have or do without fossil fuels?

2. *River Power* (Observing, directed experimenting, analyzing, communicating). Have students work in pairs to find out what happens when water is dammed. First, pack a 1″ layer of dirt in a 9″ cake pan. To represent a river, make a trench down the middle with your finger. Tilting the pan about 25 degrees, slowly pour a stream of water into the trench, beginning at the top of the pan and using a second 9″ pan to catch the water. Next, use half a popsicle stick to create a dam about 2″ from the top of the pan. Again slowly pour water, beginning from the top of the pan. Then ask students to describe what happened. Discuss how to prevent overflow and what effects the dam would have on people and animals above and below it.

3. *Old Faithful* (Observing, listening, experimenting, communicating, generalizing). Heat a whistling teapot of water and have students watch the steam as it rushes out. Hold a ruler near the steam, test it for heat, and then have students touch the ruler to feel its warmth. Discuss the similarity with geothermal energy and then read about Iceland's use of geothermal energy. Guide students to compare their school's source of heat with geothermal energy.

4. *Collecting Solar Energy* (Observing, listening, experimenting, predicting, analyzing, communicating). After discussing solar collectors and reflectors, demonstrate how to capture energy. Fold two 4″ × 4″ pieces of construction paper, one white and one black, and a 4″ × 4″ piece of aluminum foil to form miniature puptents. Place equal pieces of chocolate candy under each tent, put them all in direct sunlight. Ask students to predict which piece of candy will melt first, justifying their predictions. After a few minutes, have students observe the results. Point out that some paper caught more energy from the sun and melted the candy rapidly. Ask: Which of these colors would work best as the surface of a solar collector? Why? Have students view pictures or examples of solar collectors to verify answers.

5. *Collecting and Using Wind Power* (Observing, listening, reading, organizing, analyzing, communicating, synthesizing, evaluating). Use a blow dryer on sand and familiar examples such as sailboats and hats on windy days, to illustrate the strength of wind. Guide student teams to predict the problems of using wind as the main energy source. Have them evaluate the feasibility of using a windmill for the school's energy. Then have them identify five other locations in your area that would be good locations for windmills, justifying their selections.

6. *Magnetic Attractions* (Observing, directed experimenting, analyzing, classifying, predicting, communicating, evaluating). Place an assortment of small metal and nonmetal objects on a table. Have student teams predict which items a magnet will attract. Divide these items into two groups. Ask students to use a small magnet on each object to test predictions. Discuss common properties of the objects, uses of magnets, magnetizing other objects, and how to identify other objects in the room that a magnet will or will not attract.

7. *Using Electrical Energy* (Observing, analyzing, communicating, predicting, synthesizing, generalizing, evaluating). Have student committees acquire various information about electricity while using electricity: read a page, watch or listen to a tape, or complete a computer activity. The next day, assign the same tasks to different committees. This time, simulate a power failure in the classroom; turn the electricity off or do not permit its use. Have committees describe alternative ways to achieve their tasks, and how electricity would have helped. Then have them rank the ten most important uses of electricity. Have the groups compare and critique lists and develop rules for using electricity safely. Have students repeat the process at home and then compare and discuss listings.

8. *Target Behaviors* (Observing, listening, analyzing, predicting, communicating, evaluating). Help students develop two lists, one titled "User" and the other "Actions." Ask students to think of all the ways they use energy. Then discuss how they can use less energy. A list might begin like this:

| *User* | *Actions* |
|---|---|
| light switch | Turn off lights when not in use |
| refrigerator | Don't leave the door open |
| doors | Close doors (quietly) behind you |
| television | Turn off when not being watched |

9. *Making Good Judgments About Energy* (Observing, analyzing, classifying, communicating, evaluating). Give students a list of 4–8 different energy sources: sun, wind, garbage, petroleum products, and so on. Have students work in pairs to divide the list according to these categories: renewable/nonrenewable; clean/dirty; efficient/inefficient; safe/potentially unsafe. Ask students explain and defend their choices and describe three ways to conserve each resource.

10. *Using Force* (Observing, listening, experimenting, analyzing, predicting). Explain that moving something requires force. Demonstrate force by showing several simple actions in the classroom. To demonstrate how force feels, fill two empty milk cartons, the first with rocks and the second with paper or cloth. Have students use a pencil to push each container 10–12 inches. Ask: Which was harder to move? Why? Which required the most force to move? Why? Have students think of their own examples to contrast varied amounts of force. End by pointing to objects in the classroom and having students predict which ones will require the most force to move and defend their predictions.

11. *Understanding Gravity and Friction* (Observing, listening, predicting, communicating). Explain and discuss gravity as a force that causes things to move together. Demonstrate the pull of gravity by throwing a ball or bean bag into the air or letting water run down a surface. Show a videotape of a space flight to demonstrate the results of decreased

gravitational pull. Have each student find a certain number of illustrations of gravity to share with peers. To demonstrate friction and lubrication, have students rub two fingers together, first without and then with a coating of cooking oil, and describe the differences. Discuss the need to reduce friction, as on squeaky doors, and have each student try to open an empty jar with their hands covered with soap. Mention examples such as special shoes and snow tires. Emphasize safety factors, and have students suggest two more examples each.

12. *Machines and You* (Observing, listening, organizing, analyzing, measuring, communicating, evaluating). Encourage students to keep a record of the machines they use during a one-or two-hour period of time. Then guide them as they work in pairs to determine the amount of time and effort saved, their dependence on the machines, and the value of the machines. Ask for volunteers to report to peers.

13. *Machines: Then and Now* (Observing, listening, studying, analyzing, measuring, communicating, generalizing, evaluating). Comparing old and new toys or tools of the same type can be an interesting activity. Display pictures or use actual items, such as a nonelectric eggbeater, can opener, lantern, or curling iron. Have students decide how the old items were used, how much time and effort were required, how good the items are, and how they have been improved. Have students list the characteristics that make each newer item better than the old: weight, speed, size and so on. Conclude by having students summarize their evaluations.

14. *Information Exchange* (Reading, communicating, generalizing, evaluating). Connect pairs of computers by modem and have student partners make an interactive journal entry each day or take turns writing lines to tell a story. If classroom computers can access information services by modem, give student pairs missions to accomplish. In either case, conclude the activity by having students evaluate the information exchange and suggest ideas for additional information exchanges.

15. *Water Farming* (Observing, listening, reading, analyzing, predicting, communicating, integrating). Display a tomato and ask how students can tell where it was grown. Explain that aquaculture involves growing plants in water instead of soil. Guide students to compare growing methods by growing two or three plants in water and two or three similar plants in soil. Prompt them to develop their hypotheses and then observe and record growth and daily care. At the end of three weeks, have student teams identify situations and locations in which aquaculture or traditional agriculture would be most appropriate.

16. *Technology Display* (Observing, reading, organizing, communicating, analyzing, generalizing, evaluating). Display such items as an old calculator, telephone, camera, radio or 8-track tape player. Ask students to get their parents to help them find items to bring that represent improvements in function and design. Work with students to label each device with student name, the name of the device, a list of improvements over earlier models, and 1–3 problems that the new model still has. Have students from other classes view the display.

## 73. UNDERSTANDING SCIENCE ACROSS THE CURRICULUM

DETECTION    Mastery of key concepts may be difficult for students who

- Cannot use information acquisition skills
- Demonstrate problems with information processing skills
- Are unable to apply integration skills
- Appear unable to provide examples for concepts
- Need extra opportunities for applying and discussing
- Do not apply basic skills in content areas
- Demonstrate difficulties relating information
- Lack background experiences in several areas
- Need integrated studies involving thinking skills

*Description*    Science skills and content are used in nearly all subjects, and in social studies, health, and the language arts in particular. Scientific information can provide the basis for high-interest reading and study on topics ranging from animals to asteroids. Most students enjoy the topics and mysteries of science, which can be used as a catalyst in other subjects. Students can practice and apply the three categories of science skills during a discussion on the different types of native dwellings or on historical events beginning with the first moon walk. From studying sounds using different musical instruments to learning mathematics while measuring temperature and weight, integrating science across the curriculum can benefit all students.

*Special Problems*    The lack of a prop or material can make science teaching inconvenient. In most instances, however, integrating science instruction involves basic tools and objects found at school or at home. The greatest problem may rest with teachers rather than students. Consideration for cultural differences means that teachers must be willing to pace and organize instruction so that all students can master the concepts. Certainly, students can benefit from cross-curricular lessons. Teachers, on the other hand, are sometimes reluctant to "get off the subject." Some teachers have such low expectations for some students that they do not try to integrate studies. While introducing too many concepts can confuse students, science across the curriculum means simplifying ideas, not complicating learning. Published textbooks are a part of the problem because they do not often integrate knowledge across subject areas.

*Implications*    If students like science, carry this interest over to other subjects. If they do not, use a subject they prefer to form links with science. The activities that follow are primarily science-related but make connections with social studies, language arts, health, mathematics, and other subject areas or topics. Capitalizing on student strengths and adjusting for weaknesses is easier when concepts and skills can be reinforced or expanded in more than one subject area. The process goes in both directions; be alert to opportunities to develop science-related concepts and skills during lessons in other subjects. Emphasize cultural diversity by integrating science with areas such as social studies, music, and art.

CORRECTION    Modify these strategies to meet topical and learning needs.

1. *Investigative Inquiry* (Language arts: Reading, organizing, communicating, generalizing, evaluating). After several activities that identify local sources of air pollution and identify the ones most likely to affect students negatively, select 1–3 methods of controlling or preventing a particular type of air pollution. Help students construct group letters asking for details about what a company or agency is doing about air pollution. Include 3–4 specific questions in each letter. For example, students could send letters to car manufacturers, local and national government agencies, and companies located in or near the area. When responses arrive, guide students to evaluate the effectiveness of each remedy. Also, have students share replies orally, and display copies of the letters and their responses.

2. *Food Journals* (Language arts: Listening, reading, analyzing, classifying, communicating, integrating). To reduce the tendency to eat too much of certain foods and not enough of others, guide students to keep an individual and interactive food journal. Demonstrate the process as a group activity after a favorite lunch at school. In addition to the amount, frequency, and types of food consumed, encourage students to write about the texture, flavor, and nutritional value. Provide a few sample entries of your own as examples. Permit students who have difficulty with written expression to dictate their entries using a tape recorder. Have students make entries for everything they eat each day, including snacks, and classify what they eat by categories you provide, depending on age and ability levels. Read journal entries 1–2 times each week but do not mark them. Instead, offer discreet oral comments to students on what they write. This activity will increase students' awareness of their eating habits and encourage writing. After the first week, have students analyze their eating patterns, and guide them to suggest changes they should make.

3. *Scientific Stories* (Language arts, health: Listening, communicating, synthesizing, evaluating). Locate books in the school or public library that tell historical stories about presumed causes of illness. Read the stories to students for five minutes each day. Tell students to listen to identify and explain what people thought the cause was and why. Have students compare the cause in the story with what is known today about the cause of the illness and then evaluate the logic and accuracy of information in the story. Encourage students to read and study about the people and diseases in the story, sharing information with their peers.

4. *The National Weather Service* (Language arts: Observing, reading, studying, organizing, communicating, generalizing). Ask teams of two or three students to write letters to the National Weather Service requesting information about instruments they use to forecast the weather. When the information arrives, have the teams summarize in writing the purpose of a particular instrument, describe how it works, and judge its value. Then have the teams exchange reports and orally report on another team's instrument. If possible, include pictures, or have a weather specialist display sample instruments.

5. *A Concept of Scale* (Mathematics, geography, art: Observing, analyzing, measuring, communicating). To help students develop a sense of the relative sizes of different land formations and areas, have them observe, feel, and describe the features of a designated area on a raised

relief map. Next, provide information about the dimensions of the features. Round off the numbers, and make or have students make scaled cut-outs of specific sites. Then have students compare the sizes of different mountains, deserts, and other features, as well as the sizes of similar land types from different parts of the country. When possible, use local landmarks and buildings as reference points to help develop a realistic concept of size and distance.

6. *Classroom Temperature Record* (Mathematics: Observing, analyzing, measuring, communicating, evaluating). Ask students to chart classroom temperatures at the beginning, middle, and end of the day. Have them take turns reading and recording temperatures for a two week period. Explain how to combine the three readings for a daily average. Repeat this experience during a different season, and have students compare the differences in average temperature and in daily fluctuations to identify and then explain patterns. These temperatures can also be compared with outside temperatures locally and in other locations listed in the newspaper.

7. *How Long is a Kilometer?* (Mathematics: Observing, listening, directed experimenting, organizing, measuring, communicating, synthesizing, generalizing). Use the distance from the school to a familiar place several miles away to teach the conversion of miles to kilometers (divide by .6). Next, have students measure (in millimeters) the length of the school's baseball or football field, walk from one end of it to the other, and convert measurements to kilometers. (The exact size or distance is not important.) Use these two distances as reference points to help students determine and visualize the sizes of and distances between planets, orbits, and other heavenly bodies. Assign such tasks as finding the distance from here to Mars in football fields or in "school-to-post-office" units. Guide student teams to make models of the relative distances on calculator tape, and post the models around the wall or on the floor for ready reference.

8. *Chart Reading* (Mathematics: Observing, reading, studying, analyzing, measuring, communicating). Display a chart showing the amount of electricity common appliances use in kilowatt hours. Ask pairs of students to read the chart and answer 4–8 questions such as these: (1) Which appliance uses the most energy? The least energy? (2) Which uses more energy — a clothes dryer or an electric stove? A washing machine or a microwave oven? (3) At 22 cents per kilowatt hour, how much could you save by cutting annual use by 50%? (4) What can you personally do to conserve energy where you live?

9. *Ocean Spotlights* (Social studies, geography: Observing, listening, analyzing, measuring, communicating). List the five major oceans on the board, and show students where each is located on a map or globe. To help students remember what is near each ocean, say, repeat, and have students repeat the name of each ocean and the key adjacent countries, states, or cities. Some students should concentrate on only the Atlantic or Pacific Ocean, discussing the coast and two or three states that border it. To enhance concepts, compare approximate sizes of land masses or bodies of water.

10. *Surveying Local Fuel Supplies* (Social Studies: Observing, listening, reading, directed experimenting, organizing, analyzing, communicating). Guide students to develop a 4–8 item fuel survey. Have students use the survey to interview officials from local manufacturing com-

panies, factories, and power companies. Then have students analyze the results and report back to the class. Include in the survey such questions as these:

— What are the sources of energy you use?
— How is your fuel transported here?
— Which type of fuel do you use the most? Second?
— What problems do you associate with the fuels you use?

11. *Picture Concepts* (Social studies: Observing, listening, reading, studying, organizing, classifying, predicting, generalizing, evaluating). Create a scrapbook of problems and solutions, with left pages for problems and right pages for their solutions. Begin with a list of events that might create environmental problems: floods, volcanoes, fires, droughts, logging, hunting, building, and so on. Have students find or draw pictures of people, animals, plants, and places that would be affected most by each type of problem; paste these pictures on the problem page; and take turns describing the range of effects. Guide students to suggest solutions to these problems and paste appropriate pictures on facing right pages. Each two-page entry can be extended to include additional examples, personal photos of problems or solutions, written descriptions and explanations, and news clippings of events. Share the scrapbook with other classes or with families during an open house or parents night.

12. *Community and State Resources* (Social studies: Observing, listening, reading, synthesizing, generalizing). In many communities, local health departments, hospitals, private physicians, school nurses, dentists, rescue squads, fire companies, and others offer free demonstrations, school kits, and printed material on the proper care of teeth, skin, or eyes, or on proper emergency actions. Determine which materials or procedures are appropriate for particular students and take advantage of them. Welcome personal visits, loaned tapes, and free literature. In advance of each visit, outline the students' needs for the speaker and give students information about what they are going to see. Prepare students to ask questions and take notes. Help students develop a class list of vital services with addresses, telephone numbers, and a brief statement about the services provided. Guide students in discussing the importance of particular agencies or services.

# S CIENCE SAMPLERS

Copy these samplers for classroom use, adding or deleting information and adapting the process for use in other content areas.

**12.1**    **Polling Science Interests** (Reading, communicating, measuring, organizing, and synthesizing). Sampler 12.1 involves students in developing their own poll of science interests. Have students respond in writing or orally, reading the survey aloud to students who need this help. Form a student committee to tally and rank the results. Use the topics students find interesting for experiments and focus projects.

**12.2**    **Collective Bargains** (Observing, organizing, classifying, communicating, synthesis, generalization, and evaluating). This activity can involve students in collecting safe and available substances for study, including samples of rock, earth, plants, seeds, and other plentiful materials. Facilitate communication by using display boards, reports, poster contests, manipulative experiments, or individualized learning folders.

**12.3**    **Sight and Sound** (Observing, listening, and communicating). Used as a stimulus for targeted observation, Sight and Sound can focus on sights or sounds of any appropriate type, for instance, musical sounds, happy sounds, sad sounds or others. Have students use Sampler 12.3 for recording and describing what they see or hear. After a few minutes or so, ask students to work in teams of 2–4 to compare their records of frequency of occurrence or duration, similarities, differences, or other aspects.

**12.4**    **Measures of** _____ (Observing, directed experimenting, prediction, communicating, measuring, independent experimenting, and evaluating). Measures of temperature, distance, or time can help structure directed or independent experiments. Sampler 12.4 can be used to record (1) temperature in 3–4 different sections of a room; (2) temperature of water in 3–4 different water fountains during different times of day; (3) time required for water to freeze at specified temperatures below freezing; (4) time required for seeds to sprout; (5) time required for ice to melt on glass, wood, or paper; (6) length of the longest foot or pencil in class. When appropriate, have students track their measurements over a 1–2 week period. Repeat some experiments during a different season or in a different location, or make comparisons based on the week, location, or time of day or year.

**12.5**    **Uses of Science** (Observing, independent experimenting, organizing, measuring, predicting, synthesizing, and evaluating). Help students learn about the importance of science in everyday life. Select a topic of interest to students that has concrete applications in their lives. Topics can be as generic as skin or as specific as a brand of candy bar. Have students follow this procedure: (1) brainstorming sources and then uses; (2) predicting needed improvements; and (3) drafting a letter or interview questions and using them when contacting a manufacturer about a process or product.

**SAMPLER 12.1**

Name _____

# ▋⫼⫼ A POLL OF SCIENCE INTERESTS ▋⫼⫼

By:_____ Date:_____ Grade:_____

**Directions:** Answer each of the following items.

1. Things I like about science are _____

   _____

   _____

2. Things I do not like about science are _____

   _____

   _____

3. Television shows I like best are _____

   _____

4. I would like to visit _____

   _____

5. I would like to collect _____

   _____

6. The last thing I studied in science was _____

   _____

**Directions:** Put **1** next to your favorite topic, **2** next to your second favorite, and **3** next to your third favorite topic.

7. I would like to know more about

   ___ animals     ___ planets   ___ energy    ___ plants and flowers

   ___ the earth    ___ weather ___ machines

   ___ Other _____

# ◆ COLLECTIVE BARGAINS ◆

**Directions**: Use this form to record information about your collection. Then list your items using the categories you think are best.

Field Examiner:_____ Today's Date_____

Item(s):_____

| Item Description | Date Located and Details | Other_____ |
|---|---|---|
| _____ | _____ | _____ |
| _____ | _____ | _____ |
| _____ | _____ | _____ |
| _____ | _____ | _____ |
| _____ | _____ | _____ |

Classification System Used:_____

Number of Categories:_____

| List of Categories | Number of Samples |
|---|---|
| 1. _____ | _____ |
| 2. _____ | _____ |
| 3. _____ | _____ |
| 4. _____ | _____ |
| 5. _____ | _____ |
| 6. _____ | _____ |
| 7. _____ | _____ |
| 8. _____ | _____ |
| 9. _____ | _____ |
| 10. _____ | _____ |

# ✹ SIGHT AND SOUND ✹

**Directions**: Decide what information (time, measurements, description, etc.) you will need and use this form to record your notes.

Researcher:_____ Date:_____

Observation Target:_____

| Event/Source | Description of Sight/Sound | Duration | Time |
|---|---|---|---|
| _____ | _____ | _____ | _____ |
| _____ | _____ | _____ | _____ |
| _____ | _____ | _____ | _____ |
| _____ | _____ | _____ | _____ |
| _____ | _____ | _____ | _____ |
| _____ | _____ | _____ | _____ |
| _____ | _____ | _____ | _____ |
| _____ | _____ | _____ | _____ |

| List of Similarities | List of Differences |
|---|---|
| _____ | _____ |
| _____ | _____ |
| _____ | _____ |
| _____ | _____ |
| _____ | _____ |
| _____ | _____ |
| _____ | _____ |

**S** **AMPLER 12.4**

## ≋ **MEASURES OF**_____ ≋

**Directions:** Use the following categories to record information for your project. Add more categories in the blanks if necessary. You may not need all categories for all projects.

**Researcher**_____ **Date**_____

**Description of the Study:**_____

_____

_____

_____

**Predicted Outcomes:** _____

_____

_____

**Observational Data:**

Dates      Location      Time      Event       Results      Other_____

_____

_____

_____

_____

_____

_____

_____

_____

_____

# ⚹ USES OF SCIENCE ⚹

**Directions:**  Use this form to record information about interesting uses of science.

Researcher:_____ Date:_____

Object or Product Studied:_____

Current Uses:_____

_____

_____

Possible Future Uses:

_____

_____

Possible Letter or Interview Questions:_____

_____

_____

_____

Inquiry Method:　　__ Letter　　__ Phone Call　　__ Other_____

Date of Inquiry:_____　　　　　　Date of Response:_____

Summary of Response Content:_____

_____

_____

_____

_____

_____

_____

## REFLECTIONS

1. Prior misinformation often interferes with acquiring new information. Along with one or more peers, consider the science topics in the first section of this chapter. What are some misconceptions associated with the topics in the area you choose? List these, and decide on several strategies to replace these inaccurate concepts.

2. Similar Detection behaviors are listed for several of the topics in this chapter. Analyze the topics for similarities and differences in behaviors, and explain your analysis. Suggest additional behaviors that might indicate possible problems in understanding the content of each topic.

3. Students' age partially determines what instructional activities are appropriate. Identify five corrective strategies in this section that you believe would be best for teaching a 7-year-old student about ecology. Which ones would be most appropriate for teaching the same topic to students representing an ethnic group that is different from your own?

4. Some teachers use textbooks to determine the science curriculum. Review the second-and fourth-grade science texts in use in a school in your area. Modify a lesson from one of the textbooks for a real or hypothetical special student. Be sure to include teaching principles from Chapter 12 in your lesson.

5. Carefully structured questions help special learners focus on science concepts and guide their thinking. Construct such a set of questions about one of the science topics in this chapter. Develop questions that would be appropriate as advance organizers to introduce the topic.

6. Special students often require extra review activities and demonstrations in order to master a topic. Game activities can be used to interest students in a topic and then to review concepts and apply skills. Choose one life science topic and develop a game that highlights the most important concepts. Try out the game with a peer or a special student and make modifications as needed.

7. Observing, analyzing, classifying, and generalizing are particularly important skills for mastering many concepts in earth science. Review the recommendations in this chapter for teaching these skills, and plan how to integrate them as you teach the concepts for an earth science topic.

8. Some of the concepts in science are difficult to teach unless explanations are accompanied by some type of demonstration. Videotape an important example of earth science in action in your neighborhood or city. If possible, tape activities that might relate to two or three different topics. As you tape, explain each scene. Formulate questions to present students as advance organizers before they view the tape. If possible, use the tape with a group of students.

9. When focused on a particular student with special needs, classroom observations often reveal important diagnostic and prescriptive data. Observe such a student in a classroom during a science lesson; compare observed behaviors with the Detection behaviors listed in the checklist in Figure 12.2. List your tentative conclusions and any additional information you need to confirm your hypotheses.

10. Experienced teachers usually develop a collection of activities that they have found to be effective. Interview one or more experienced teachers to identify experiments for one earth science and one life science concept. Modify the experiments for a real or hypothetical special learner. Be sure to ask how the teacher addresses multicultural differences.

11. A learning center can provide excellent opportunities for independent, hands-on science experiences. Develop one or two center activities for two science topics or concepts of your choice.

12. Advances in technology are occurring too quickly to be recorded in most elementary science textbooks. Suggest at least three readily available sources teachers can use to update their knowledge of technology.

13. Some teachers adhere closely to the topics and activities suggested in their science textbook. Review an elementary-level science textbook being used in your area. Locate the physical science topics. Then, practice teaching one or two lessons to a peer or to a special learner. What modifications are needed for your lessons to be more effective?

14. The skills checklist in Figure 12.2 can be used to assess students' skills in any area of science. While observing in a local classroom, use this checklist to identify whether students can apply each of the skills during a life science or earth science lesson. Are some skills emphasized more than others?

15. For more information about using correction strategies to improve science learning, consult several of the following books.

Abruscato, J. (1992). *Teaching children science* (3nd ed.). Boston: Allyn and Bacon.

Doris, E. (1991). *Doing what scientists do: Children learn to investigate their world.* Portsmouth, NH: Heinemann.

Esler, W. K., & Esler, M. K. (1989). *Teaching elementary science* (5th ed.). Belmont, CA: Wadsworth.

Gega, P. C. (1990). *Science in elementary education* (6th ed.). New York: Macmillan.

Jacobson, W. J., & Bergman, A. B. (1991). *Science for children: A book for teachers* (3rd ed.). Englewood Cliffs, NJ: Prentice-Hall.

Kameenai, E. S., & Simmons, D. C. (1990). *Designing instructional strategies: The prevention of academic learning problems.* Columbus, OH: Merrill.

Mercer, C. D., & Mercer, A. R. (1989). *Teaching students with learning problems* (3rd ed.). Columbus, OH: Merrill.

Polloway, E. A., Patton, J. R., Payne, J. S., & Payne, R. A. (1989). *Strategies for teaching learners with special needs* (4th ed.). Columbus OH: Merrill.

Rakes, T. A., & Choate, J. S. (1990). *Science and health: Detecting and correcting special needs.* Boston: Allyn and Bacon.

Schulz, J. B., Carpenter, C. D., & Turnbull, A. P. (1990). *Mainstreaming handicapped students: A guide for classroom teachers* (3rd ed.). Boston: Allyn and Bacon.

Wassermann, S., & Ivany, J. W. G. (1988). *Teaching elementary science: Who's afraid of spiders?* New York: Harper & Row.

Wood, J. W. (1992). *Mainstreaming: A practical approach for teachers* (2nd ed.). New York: Merrill/Macmillan.

Smith, L. J., & Smith, D. L. (1990). *Social studies: Detecting and correcting special needs.* Boston: Allyn and Bacon.

Watts, M. (1991). *The science of problem-solving: A practical guide for science teachers.* Portsmouth, NH: Heimemann.

Zeitler, W. R., & Barufaldi, J. P. (1988). *Elementary school science: A perspective for teachers.* White Plains, NY: Longman.

# CHAPTER THIRTEEN

## SOCIAL STUDIES:
## TOPICS, PROCESS, AND STRATEGIES

— *Lana J. Smith and Dennie L. Smith*

Special instruction in the social studies should not only develop a knowledge base but also accommodate the many developmental, academic, and social levels of students with special learning needs. These students are likely to have difficulty meeting the demands of society if they are unable to use social science knowledge in a technological and changing economic world community. At the very least, these students must be able to function effectively in all social milieus, including home, school, work, and the larger society.

## SOCIAL STUDIES GOALS

The social studies have four main goals:

1. Development of citizens who participate intelligently in a democratic society by making thoughtful decisions and by contributing to efforts to improve the human experience;
2. Transmission of cultural heritage, developed through analysis of the historical problems and events that formed the democratic values that shape and sustain our way of life, and building appreciation for a pluralistic and interdependent world;
3. Enhancement of critical and creative thinking abilities as students make decisions and engage in problem-solving activities related to the people, environment, and world around them;
4. Expansion of self-realization, a better understanding of human relationships, and the development of interpersonal skills that will aid individuals in reaching their potential as human beings.

## SOCIAL STUDIES SKILLS

Skills are an integral aspect of the social studies, not isolated entities. The basic skill framework for this chapter comes from the scope and sequence of social studies skills developed by a task force of the National Council for the Social Studies. The skills are divided into three major categories, as outlined in Figure 13.1. These three major categories are identified with each activity in this chapter and are referred to as Strands 1, 2, and 3. Teachers should note that these skills can be adapted and used for all learners at elementary, middle, and high school levels.

Students who have not mastered the basic academic skills of Strand 1 will have difficulty acquiring information and will not be able to learn new information independently unless teachers can design special situations to circumvent the basic skills.

Strand 2 skills, which involve organizing and using information, are often referred to as thinking skills. Classifying, interpreting, analyzing, summarizing, synthesizing, and evaluating information are the primary activities in the development of these skills. Lack of experience in these activities con-

**FIGURE 13.1 / Social Studies Skills**

| Strand 1:<br>Acquiring<br>Information | *Reading* | *Study* | *Information<br>Search* | *Technical* |
|---|---|---|---|---|
| | • Comprehension<br>• Vocabulary<br>• Rate of reading | • Find information<br>• Arrange informa-<br>tion in usable<br>form | • Library<br>• Special references<br>• Maps, globes,<br>graphics<br>• Community<br>resources | • Computer<br>• Telephone and<br>television<br>information<br>networks |

| Strand 2:<br>Organizing and<br>Using Information | *Intellectual Skills* | *Decision-Making Skills* |
|---|---|---|
| | • Classifying information<br>• Interpreting information<br>• Analyzing information<br>• Summarizing information<br>• Synthesizing information<br>• Evaluating information | • Identifying decision situations<br>• Securing factual information<br>• Recognizing implicit values<br>• Identifying alternatives<br>• Taking action |

| Strand 3:<br>Participating<br>Socially | *Personal Skills* | *Social and Political<br>Group Interaction Skills* | *Participation Skills* |
|---|---|---|---|
| | • Expresses convictions<br>• Communicates feelings<br>• Adjusts behavior to<br>group<br>• Recognizes mutual<br>relationships | • Contributes to group<br>climate<br>• Participates in making<br>rules<br>• Serves as leader or<br>follower<br>• Participates in group<br>actions<br>• Resolves group conflicts | • Informed on social issues<br>• Identifies social action<br>situations<br>• Works with others to<br>decide actions<br>• Works to influence<br>social powers<br>• Accepts responsibilities |

tributes to special students' difficulties in this area. Many students are able to participate and develop skills through these activities even when they are unable to read or write well. In fact, these become the coping and survival skills for special students who are severely limited in the academic areas.

Strand 3 skills emphasize interpersonal skills, social development, and individuals' participation in group life. Although social skills are developed throughout the school curricula, the responsibility for teaching these skills directly falls to the social studies curriculum. Because the special student often has difficulty in being accepted as a participant in society, these skills are equally important as the more academic areas. These skills also contribute directly to an individual's happiness and sense of worth, giving him or her a sense of accomplishment and the determination to meet the next challenge.

## DETECTION OF SPECIAL NEEDS

The social studies skills and concepts to be taught in each grade are generally available in curriculum guides, adopted textbooks, and guidelines developed by professional organizations, such as the National Council for the Social Studies. Determining which students have deficiencies in these skills, the levels at which these skills should be taught, and the specific disabling conditions can be accomplished by (1) synthesizing available data, (2) acquiring data through direct testing by both formal and informal means, (3) observing students' behavior in and out of the classroom, and (4) interviewing students and resource people who have pertinent knowledge regarding students' performance levels.

## Synthesizing Available Data

Previous achievements in social studies should be reviewed by examining cumulative records, past report cards, and standardized test results and, if possible, asking former teachers of special students. Identifying performance patterns and compiling a synthesis of available information will reveal a composite picture of target students, providing implications for instructional interventions in social studies.

## Direct Testing

Performance in social studies can be measured to some degree by both formal and informal tests. The level of achievement revealed by testing is not as important as students' strengths and weaknesses in specific tasks and content objectives.

### Formal Testing

Formal tests of achievement in social studies, provided on some standardized achievement batteries, are useful for making comparisons of students' performance on a national or regional basis and for identifying students in need of more thorough analysis. Generally, gauging performance over time and in comparison with peers, a more informal approach to assessment, is more useful for the classroom teacher.

### Informal Testing

Some social studies textbooks supply informal tests that can assess students' mastery of both content and important skills. Informal testing techniques, such as the Group Reading Inventory (GRI) and cloze procedure, help assess students' strengths and weaknesses in their ability to read and use their assigned textbooks. Most reading methods textbooks include instructions for developing these tests.

Teachers can construct other informal tests using criterion-referenced formats based on the present curriculum. Data from these assessments can be compiled into student profiles that yield information on individuals' strengths and weaknesses, mastery of specific skills, progress, and appropriate instructional grouping placement. The more systematic and ongoing the assessment, the more useful it is for teachers in making instructional decisions.

## Observing Behavior

The most convenient and reliable means of conducting observations is to use a checklist of behaviors and skills. Figure 13.2 is an example of such a checklist. Teacher observation of behavior and performance under specified conditions show what elements contribute to students' progress. Anecdotal records, profiles, or checklists that permit a holistic look at how students are developing in the social studies are typically useful for designing instruction.

## Interviewing

New approaches to assessment emphasize finding out how students perceive learning tasks. Students' own analysis of how difficult they find the social studies material can reveal specific problems they may be having. Another format is to have students recite what they have learned, or retell what they have just read. Teachers can compile interest inventories, using topics from the textbook's table of contents, and ask students to rank them in order of their interest in learning about them. Discussions with other teachers who have worked with students often provide insight. In addition, parents, siblings, friends, and other people who know students well can provide information about social dynamics within and outside the classroom. Knowledge of students' prior experiences and familiarity with their immediate environments can provide helpful information about what has shaped the social development of the learner.

## Portfolio Development

Portfolio development is the most comprehensive approach to student assessment. Although there are numerous types of assessment formats, the most complete picture of the special student's performance emerges when all diagnostic information is synthesized. With that profile in hand, teachers may select strategies likely to correct individual students' special needs in social studies. Information on students' performance in the classroom over time should then become part of a portfolio, reflecting a closer and more valid assessment of individual students' progress than any one method can yield.

## SPECIAL POPULATIONS

Many of the concepts of social studies are particularly relevant to the needs of special learners but, without instructional adaptation, their skill deficits may keep them from mastering concepts. The information acquisition skills, especially reading and study strategies, are difficult for many students with language and learning disabilities, hearing impairments, and mental retardation. The organizing skills may pose special difficulty for students who are mentally retarded or learning disabled. Interpersonal and social participation skills, a notable area of concern for students with behavior disorders, challenge many types of special students. However, the social studies present an appropriate forum for developing social concepts and skills.

## Figure 13.2 / Checklist for Detecting Special Needs in Social Studies

Student's Name _____ Observer _____ Date _____

| Skills | Student Behaviors | Observed | Reported | Comments |
|--------|-------------------|----------|----------|----------|
| **Information Acquisition** | | | | |
| **Reading** | • Recognizes and understands word meanings<br>• Comprehends details<br>• Makes inferences<br>• Reads critically<br>• Other: | | | |
| **Study** | • Locates information in text and other resources<br>• Outlines and/or summarizes<br>• Takes notes<br>• Organizes for study<br>• Works independently<br>• Other: | | | |
| **Information Search** | • Uses card catalog<br>• Uses special reference sources<br>• Interprets maps, graphics, and charts<br>• Uses community resources<br>• Other: | | | |
| **Technical Skills** | • Operates a computer to enter and retrieve information<br>• Accesses information through telephone and television<br>• Other: | | | |
| **Information Processing** | | | | |
| **Classifying** | • Identifies most salient features<br>• Groups by criteria<br>• Places data in tabular form<br>• Other: | | | |
| **Interpreting** | • States Relationships<br>• Notes causes and effects<br>• Draws inferences<br>• Predicts outcomes<br>• Recognizes value dimensions<br>• Other: | | | |
| **Analyzing** | • Identifies unique features<br>• Identifies relationships and patterns<br>• Detects bias<br>• Questions credibility of sources<br>• Other: | | | |

| Skills | Student Behaviors | Observed | Reported | Comments |
|--------|-------------------|----------|----------|----------|
| **Information Processing (Cont.)** | | | | |
| **Summarizing** | • Extracts significant ideas<br>• Combines concepts to form conclusions<br>• Restates ideas in concise form<br>• Other: | | | |
| **Evaluating** | • Selects pertinent ideas<br>• Estimates adequacy of information<br>• Tests validity<br>• Describes personal relevance<br>• Describes societal relevance<br>• Other: | | | |
| **Decision Making** | • Identifies decision-making situations<br>• Recognizes relevant facts<br>• Recognizes implicit values<br>• Identifies alternative courses<br>• Takes action<br>• Other: | | | |
| **Relating Interpersonally and Participating Socially** | | | | |
| **Personalizing** | • Expresses convictions<br>• Communicates feelings<br>• Adjusts behavior to fit groups<br>• Recognizes mutual relationships<br>• Other: | | | |
| **Interacting in Groups** | • Contributes to group situations<br>• Participates in making rules<br>• Participates in group activities<br>• Other: | | | |
| **Participates in Political Events** | • Keeps informed on issues<br>• Identifies social action situations<br>• Works to influence social decisions<br>• Accepts citizenship responsibilities<br>• Other: | | | |
| **Additional Comments:** | | | | |
| **Summary of Observations:** | | | | |

## CORRECTION

Corrective instruction is most effective when targeted to individual students' needs and previous learning. Adaptations, variations, and individualized instruction can help special students learn effectively. The outline in figure 13.3 summarizes 12 basic principles for developing mastery of social studies content and skills. These principles are appropriate for all learners, but they are particularly important for special learners.

The final principle in Figure 13.3, teaching to and adjusting for specific needs, is essential for students' and teachers' success in a social studies program. Key strategies to adjust instruction for Strand 1 skills include (1) preparing students for reading by building interest, connecting with past experiences, and setting purposes; (2) teaching key vocabulary prior to reading; (3) teaching the comprehension skills and practicing them in functional contexts; and (4) applying reading skills to other materials and contexts. Other strategies include providing focused study guides, dictating oral summaries, reading material to students, rewriting text at lower reading levels, and using alternative forms of acquiring information, such as listening, video, roleplays, field trips, demonstrations, and modeling by students and teacher, to circumvent reading as the primary means of acquiring information.

Strand 2 skills require extensive experiences in perceiving similarities and differences, comparing and contrasting, moving from the concrete to the abstract, and developing questioning skills, as well as frequent rehearsal of what is learned. Evaluating the veracity of information is important in decision making; thus students must learn to identify alternatives and choose among them, based upon the students' values and the best evidence available. Simple charts of pros and cons or "the best that could happen" and "the worst that could happen" are good beginnings for helping students learn to make decisions. The process of carefully analyzing options can be demonstrated even to large groups until students internalize the process, transfer it to their personal lives, and apply it as a useful personal skill. The interpersonal and social participation skills of Strand 3 can be especially difficult

**FIGURE 13.3 / Twelve Principles for Teaching Social Studies to Special Learners**

1. Choose topics that have personal relevance
2. Build on what students already know
3. Directly teach the skills needed for the task
4. Establish safe learning environments
5. Develop activity-centered lessons
6. Promote inquiry learning
7. Teach to learning styles
8. Provide positive and informative feedback
9. Encourage parental involvement
10. Stay knowledgeable about current events
11. Promote effective social interaction
12. Both teach to and adjust for specific skill needs

for special learners. Opportunities to express personal convictions in socially acceptable forms can be a natural part of every classroom activity. In planned activities, roleplaying can be particularly useful for teaching appropriate social behaviors. Other techniques for teaching positive social behavior include contingency contracting, self-monitoring and evaluating with charts and journals, and behavior modification using both social and material reinforcement.

## 74.  PERSONAL GROWTH

DETECTION     Mastery of key concepts may be difficult for students who

- Do not understand that personal growth and change occur constantly
- Are not aware of their own strengths and weaknesses
- Do not have positive views of themselves
- Have difficulty controlling emotions and feelings
- Cannot empathize with others
- Have difficulty interacting socially with others
- Lack appropriate social behaviors

*Description*     Growth and change are inevitable and constant. Not only do all people change physically over time, they also change emotionally, intellectually, and socially. In order for students to assume productive roles in society, they must understand, adapt to, and accept the changes occurring in their lives and appreciate the differences of people around them. These tasks are not easy even for those who are developmentally on target. Among the social concepts relevant to adapting to change are healthy self-concepts; awareness, acceptance, and relative control of feelings and emotions; knowledge of personal history in relation to human history; self-respect and respect for others; and social interaction and participation in work and play with others who are different from oneself.

*Special Problems*     When a variety of changes occur in a short time, they can be overwhelming. Students do not always understand what is happening to them and often do not have the language base to discuss abstract feelings and emotions. Limited language proficiency can affect the ability to engage in introspection and create difficulty in describing and expressing conflicting emotions. Limited experiential backgrounds, conflicts in family and cultural value systems, and different language backgrounds can also interfere with students' understanding of common reference points and examples used to illustrate social concepts. Often students with special needs have been caught in failure syndromes focusing on their weaknesses while suppressing perception of their strengths. If problems have been particularly severe, students may have been socially isolated to relieve tension or overly protected by well-meaning parents.

*Implications*     Positive and successful experiences with peers and skilled teachers can lead to the self-confidence needed for taking increasingly more challenging social risks and can help in moving students to higher levels of self-actualization. Opportunities to analyze, reflect on, and discuss difficulties with others in safe classroom environments are important for students to begin to share the more personal elements of their lives.

CORRECTION

Modify these strategies to meet topical and learning needs.

1. *Growth Ruler.* (Strand 2, Skill: Analyzing Information)
   Using a strip of adding machine paper with the student's name printed on one end, note the student's height with a mark and date. Each month, measure the student again and note the date. Students can make comparisons with other students, determine the average student height, compare their height to the average, and determine differences between boys and girls.

2. *All About Me.* (Strand 2, Skill: Summarizing Information)
   Using Sampler 13.1, have students fill out the information and then organize and summarize it in small groups.

3. *Baby Challenge.* (Strand 2, Skill: Classifying Information)
   Ask students to bring a baby picture and keep it a secret from the rest of the class. Separate 3 pictures from the 3 students' names and challenge the rest of the class to match them. Ask students to share the characteristics they used to match the pictures with the names, such as eyes, ears, hair, and the like.

4. *My Time Line.* (Strand 1, Skill: Classifying Information)
   Ask students to draw a time line with a year designated for each year of their lives (or use Sampler 13.5). They should then label significant events that have occurred at given points in their lives. If students have photographs of significant events, they could bring those to share also. CAUTION: Be sensitive to adopted students and those who cannot fill in details of their backgrounds.

5. *Headlines.* (Strand 1, Skill: Arranging Information)
   At the end of the school day, ask students to explain important events or activities that occurred during the day in the classroom, school, community, or world. Develop an appropriate headline. At the end of the month, challenge students to develop a headline for the month. At the end of the year, review the headlines.

6. *Strangers Beware.* (Strand 3, Skill: Personal Skills)
   Organize a roleplaying activity, asking a student to play a parent explaining to a child the importance of not talking to strangers or taking anything from strangers at any time, especially walking to and from school. You may want to coach students with the dialogue. The roleplaying could be extended by having a stranger try to give one of the students a ride home in his new car.

7. *My Special Day.* (Strand 3, Skill: Personal Skills)
   Establish a time when each student is spotlighted. Each student should bring in 3–5 objects about him- or herself to show and explain to the class. Encourage the class to ask questions about the objects; this gives the student an opportunity to express him- or herself further. Compliment the child by telling something he or she has done well.

8. *Cartoon Emotions.* (Strand 2, Skill: Interpreting Information)
   Cut out comic strips from the newspaper, post them on a bulletin board, and ask students to note the emotions of the various characters. Point out that the artist uses various techniques to show emotions, especially using the mouth and eyes. List emotion words such as *happy, sad, angry, sleepy, tired, joyful, kind,* and *loving.* Ask the students to match the words to emotions portrayed and explain their choices to the rest of the class.

9. *Feeling Drama.* (Strand 2, Skill: Interpreting Information)
Write feeling words on index cards, distribute them to students, and ask them to act out the feeling while other students try to guess the emotion. Students could do this in teams and think of other emotions.

10. *Color Me Yellow.* (Strand 2, Skill: Interpreting Information)
Provide a number of different colors of paper disks and discuss their implied emotions: blue = sad, depressed, lonely; green = calm, neutral, smooth, rested, nature's color; yellow = happy, gay, bright, sunny, excited; red = angry, upset. Ask students to select a color that reflects their feelings at the moment and tell why. This can be done each morning for a week or more by having students place colored disks on pictures of themselves on the bulletin board. Set aside time each day to discuss their selections. Students can also change colors appropriately throughout the day and explain why. You might also participate in this activity to warn students on bad days or to reflect pleasure with their performance.

11. *Welcome to Class.* (Strand 2, Skill: Classifying Information)
Ask students to pretend that a student their own age from another country or even another planet will soon visit their classroom. Make a list of questions that the student would like to ask and some of the information that could be passed on to the visitor. To extend the activity, have students write a group letter asking some of their questions and explaining their country.

12. *More Alike.* (Strand 2, Skill: Interpreting Information)
Explain to students that you are going to make a list of things that are similar and different about class members. Write the 2 headings on the chalkboard and invite students to contribute ideas. Ask: How are we alike? How are we different? Students' comments concerning their differences and similarities may include observations about their clothes, height, weight, hair, voice, sex, or fingerprints. Have students summarize what they have observed, and ask whether they believe people are more similar than different or vice versa.

13. *Being Different.* (Strand 2, Skill: Summarizing Information)
Select a student volunteer and leave the room with him or her. Make large red dots on the student's forehead and cheeks with watercolors. Return to the room, asking your volunteer to return shortly after. Students will probably laugh or stare at the volunteer. After a brief discussion, explain to students that many prejudices are formed because of outward appearances, physical handicaps, or practices from other cultures.

14. *History or Tradition?* (Strand 1, Skill: Vocabulary)
Write the word *history* on the chalkboard. Discuss and define the word, explaining that history consists of important past events that have been recorded. Write examples and nonexamples of historical events on slips of paper. Have each student draw one, decide if it is an example of history, and, if the class agrees that it is, come to the board and place it under the word *history*.

15. *Changing Times.* (Strand 2, Skill: Interpreting Information)
Ask students to identify some changes that have occurred in their lives and why they think those changes occurred. Have students bring photographs of themselves at different ages or other old photographs and compare them to the present.

16. *I'm Sorry.* (Strand 3, Skill: Social Participation)
Organize a roleplay by explaining that sometimes one hurts someone's feelings and an apology is in order (e.g., you accidentally spilled water on a person's schoolwork). Ask students to list on the chalkboard situations requiring an apology. Have students act out the situations and say, "I'm really sorry" or "I did not mean to hurt your feelings." This activity can be extended for students to learn to say "thank you" in other situations.

17. *Spotlighting Strengths.* (Strand 3, Skill: Personal Skills)
Have each student make a large personal shield, containing his or her picture and other personal information, such as favorite food, music, pets, and places. Provide an opportunity for each student to be spotlighted for compliments. The featured student will stand while the rest of the class gives a few compliments for the teacher to write on the personal shield.

18. *Picture Us.* (Strand 3, Skill: Group Interaction)
Ask students to bring pictures from magazines that illustrate social situations. Attach each picture to a large chart and give students an opportunity to explain the social situation. Emphasize the proper behavior and rules that people must follow in order to live together.

19. *Dealing with Anger.* (Strand 3, Skill: Personal Skills)
Explain that people do not have to use violence when confronted with situations that make them angry. Discuss with students situations that have made them angry. Reactions may have been to throw something, hit someone, or use insulting language. Using short roleplay activities, have students practice talking with the individual to clear up the misunderstanding. Students could also practice apologizing to each other.

20. *Social Greetings.* (Strand 3, Skill: Personal Skills)
Introduce students to the fundamentals of greeting people through a short roleplaying activity. Explain the importance of shaking hands for both boys and girls and of looking at the other person's face and eyes. Have students practice asking and responding to the question, "How are you?"

## 75. EXPANDING COMMUNITIES

DETECTION

Mastery of key concepts may be difficult for students who

- Have had limited travel experiences
- Exhibit prejudices toward different cultural groups
- Have difficulties understanding the medium for exchanging goods in society
- Cannot relate money to the process of consumption and production
- Are not aware of how laws are made or enforced
- Cannot differentiate levels of government
- Have not experienced a variety of forms of communication and transportation

*Description*

The approach in teaching social studies that focuses on the expanding community is based on the way elementary students progress through developmental stages of social awareness, beginning with life at home and expanding to their neighborhood, community, state, country, and world. As students learn concepts in and about these expanding social environments, they can begin to apply them to other social studies learning in broader contexts.

*Special Problems*

Lack of knowledge of expanded environments often comes from students' lack of experience and travel opportunities. Teachers often fail to tap the richest classroom resource for offering real and vicarious experiences — the multicultural experiences of a diverse student population. In addition, social studies is not often given priority in the early elementary grades, especially for special learners who may be struggling with basic reading and language tasks. Thus, students may not have had opportunities to develop these skills.

*Implications*

Learning activities should provide concrete experiences with historical and geographic concepts corresponding to students' observed skill needs and backgrounds. As much as possible, teachers should give students opportunities to select their level of involvement from several alternatives. Students usually select activities that interest them and are within their capabilities. Special learners must first become comfortable with their immediate social situation and peer group before progressing into more abstract learning. Thus, if special students have not developed the skills and knowledge presented in the Personal Growth area, they may find the material in this section difficult and frustrating. The learner must understand certain concepts before being able to compare and contrast ideas and to attach new learning of the more difficult concepts to previous learning.

**CORRECTION**        Modify these strategies to meet topical and learning needs.

1. *Home Address.* (Strand 1, Skill: Arranging Information)
   Write the school address on the chalkboard and explain the meaning of each line. Have each student address an envelope to another classmate at his or her home. Help the students write short letters describing the neighborhoods in which they live. Take the students on a field trip to a neighborhood mailbox or post office to mail the letters. Ask students to bring their letters to school when they receive them at home.

2. *School Neighborhood Map.* (Strand 1, Skill: Map Making)
   Take students on a field trip to observe the neighborhood around the school. Point out major landmarks, businesses, houses, streets, and open land for the students to observe and label. Upon returning to class, introduce students to map-making symbols (boxes for buildings, lines for streets, dotted spaces for open land, and other symbols for specific landmarks). Have each student make a map of the school neighborhood.

3. *Neighborhood Services.* (Strand 2, Skill: Analyzing Information)
   Provide a list of activities that may or may not be available in certain neighborhoods: mail a letter, buy clothes, get a haircut, buy gas, catch a bus, get help for a fire, play football, observe wild animals, fish, hunt, climb trees, and so on. Ask students to label each activity "yes" or "no" as it pertains to their neighborhoods.

4. *Other Neighborhoods.* (Strand 2, Skill: Analyzing Information)
   Ask students to collect or find in reference books pictures of neighborhoods in other cultures. Ask, "How are the neighborhoods alike and different?" Emphasize housing, business, geography, activities, landmarks, and multicultural aspects.

5. *Urban/Rural Living.* (Strand 2, Skill: Analyzing Information)
   Make 2 headings on the chalkboard: *Urban* and *Rural.* Ask students to list things that are alike and different for these neighborhoods. Emphasize buildings, activities, industry, and land forms. Go through the list again and label whether these things are found in their neighborhoods with "yes" or "no."

6. *Name Your Neighbor.* (Strand 2, Skill: Classifying Information)
   Explain to students that neighbors are people who live close to you. Ask students to name some of their neighbors on a chart on the chalkboard. Have students complete the chart by indicating if the neighbors have children, are elderly, or come from other cultures, and what type of work they do. Explain to students that neighbors usually share things and do good deeds for each other. For example, a neighbor may pick up your mail or feed a pet when you are out of town. Give students an opportunity to discuss some of the good deeds that neighbors can do for each other.

7. *Country Neighbors.* (Strand 2, Skill: Synthesizing Information)
   Explain to students that countries such as the United States have neighbors, Mexico and Canada. Show the countries on a map. Country neighbors have conflict just as people have conflict. What are some conflicts that develop between home neighbors and countries? (Home: noisy pets or garbage piling up; countries: boundaries, travel, immigration, pollution, and products) How do countries and people settle their conflicts?

8. *Fences for Neighbors.* (Strand 3, Skill: Group Interaction)
   Make a fence using classroom chairs and set up a roleplay to explain

why neighbors build fences. Fences are more often found in cities, where people have small lots. Before initiating the roleplay, ask students to develop reasons why people build fences, such as privacy and security. Invite students to act out the situations.

9. *Student Neighbors.* (Strand 2, Skill: Evaluating Information)
Explain that students sitting next to each other are neighbors. Ask the class to describe good and bad student neighbors.

10. *Disaster Aid.* (Strand 2, Skill: Interpreting Information)
Explain to students that, during the pioneer days, neighbors used to help each other build barns in barn raisings. In modern times, we usually don't help people build, but we do help in times of critical need. Ask students to identify times of critical need, such as a blizzard, tornado, flood, fire, or crime. Students can finish the activity by drawing neighborly activities that might occur during a disaster. If a local or world disaster occurs, organize students to help.

11. *Mapping It Out.* (Strand 1, Skill: Maps)
Explain that marketplaces to exchange goods have existed in all parts of the world since ancient times. Make a list of all the shopping areas in town. Locate each on a map and place a marker to label it. Have students determine which shopping area is most convenient to where they live. Discuss how often they or their families go there and what differences would result in their lives if it were not there.

12. *Go Shopping.* (Strand 2, Skill: Decision Making)
Take a field trip to a local shopping area. Give each student a hypothetical amount of money to spend on an outfit of clothing, including shoes, pants, blouse or shirt, and accessories. Have students keep notes on where they found each item they would have bought, how much they would have spent on it, and where the item was made. Compare students' experiences. As a variation, give each student an assigned item to find: shirt or blouse, shoes, or belt. Ask students to list each store that offers this item and compare the highest price and the lowest price they found.

13. *Whose Law Is This?* (Strand 2, Skill: Evaluating Information)
Our laws can be local, state, or federal laws. Explain this to students, using examples to illustrate the point. For instance, federal and state laws are enforced at the local level, but local laws are not enforced at the federal level. List laws students know about, such as the speed limit, and have students decide what levels govern their enforcement. You could also use Sampler 13.4 to have students list all the laws they know, the questions they have about laws, and what level of government is responsible for each law and its enforcement.

14. *My Way/Our Way.* (Strand 2, Skill: Summarizing Information)
Organize a roleplay for students to experience the differences between democratic and dictatorial forms of government. Play the leader roles yourself. First, play the dictator in common classroom activities such as lining up to leave the room, seating arrangements, playground activities, and so on. Make some blatantly arbitrary decisions to emphasize the power of dictators. Then switch roles and use democratic processes for making decisions in the above situations. Let students vote on some decisions, with the majority ruling. Discuss the differences between the two forms of government.

15. *Who Leads Us?* (Strand 2, Skill: Classifying Information)
    Collect pictures and list the names of leaders the students know. Classify pictures and names by the levels of government each represents.

16. *Mapping It Out.* (Strand 1, Skill: Maps)
    Find or draw a grid map of the community and guide students to locate its centers of transportation. Have them label these locations with symbols: an airplane for the airport, a bus for the bus depot, and so on.

17. *Plan a Trip.* (Strand 2, Skill: Synthesizing Information)
    Ask each student to plan a trip. Specify the kinds of information students should research, make decisions about, and share with the class: location, number of miles to be traveled one way and round trip, means of transportation, time trip will take, clothes they will need to pack, and so on.

18. *What Was That?* (Strand 2, Skill: Summarizing Information)
    Tape-record a sentence or series of sentences that tell a short story. Whisper the information to 1 student and have that student whisper it to another student until all have heard it. Ask the last student to say what he or she heard. Compare this to the tape recording. Discuss the implications for communication.

19. *Braille.* (Strand 1, Skill: Arranging Information)
    Bring examples of Braille to class and have students experiment with reading it. Discuss how this form of communication is used. To extend the activity, teach students to write in Braille and have them write a paragraph.

20. *Sign Language.* (Strand 2, Skill: Interpreting Information)
    Learn the American Sign Language alphabet, teach students the basic signs, and use them with the class for an entire day. Discuss with the class their feelings about not being able to communicate orally.

21. *Timely Events.* (Strand 2, Skill: Synthesizing Information)
    Using one of the time line formats in Sampler 13.5, have students make a time line of the history and development of communications.

22. *Computers All Around.* (Strand 1, Skill: Technical Skills)
    Ask students to observe for a full day to determine how many times and in what ways their lives are touched by computer technology. Examples will include clocks, radios, television, mail, banking, grocery checkouts, cash registers, and the like. Discuss the implications for their lives now and in the future.

## 76. TOWARD A SMALLER WORLD

DETECTION

Mastery of key concepts may be difficult for students who

- Do not understand the relevance of world events to their personal lives
- Have had limited contact with persons and places outside the United States
- Do not know why countries must have strong allies
- Are not aware that people have different appearances, values, and cultures from their own
- Do not know how the environment influences life
- Are not aware of significant world problems
- Do not recognize the importance of establishing harmony within oneself as well as with others

*Description*

Today's students must contend with such vital concerns as protecting the environment, controlling population growth, monitoring technological advances, and solving world conflict. Harmony in our smaller world hinges upon people working cooperatively to meet challenges. Special learners cannot be exempted from these problems because of their difficulties; ways must be found to help them understand the issues, participate in the decision-making process, and cope with inevitable changes. Current situations are always rooted in the past, making historical perspective important for building concepts related to a shrinking world. The study of ancient Egypt, the U.S.'s nearest neighbors, and other currently significant countries are appropriate for this unit.

*Special Problems*

While past events are often perceived as irrelevant and even boring to today's students, teachers must nonetheless help students find the relationship of the past to the present, lest they ignore history and be doomed to repeat it. Limited contact with other people and places contributes to students' inability to accept and live cooperatively with those different than themselves. In addition, students are often unaware of events and places outside their immediate environment or feel they are remote from their own lives.

*Implications*

To be effective, instruction must include ample learning opportunities involving interactions of all types. Structure listening, viewing, speaking, reading, and writing activities, and include such skills in all activities. Television and newspaper and magazine articles will provide the most current information, as textbooks will often be dated. Select events and places for study that illustrate changes through time in order to develop students' knowledge of and appreciation for the contributions of many cultures to the collective wisdom of the human race.

CORRECTION

Modify these strategies to meet topical and learning needs.

1. *Around the World in a Week.* (Strand 2, Skill: Summarizing)
Ask students to collect newspaper articles of events that occur in other countries for 1 week. Make a list of the major events on the chalkboard and discuss which are most likely to have impact on other countries and particularly on students' lives.

2. *Relevance Research.* (Strand 1, Skill: Information Search)
Assign individual students or cooperative groups a major historical event, and have them read about it. Ask students to make a list of all the ways this event affected the future and their lives. Have students report orally, and encourage the rest of the class to add to the lists.

3. *What If . . . ?* (Strand 2, Skill: Synthesizing Information)
Choose several historical events for students to reinterpret in terms of what might have happened if things had been changed in some way: What if Columbus had disappeared at sea instead of finding the Americas? What if nuclear weapons were not controlled?

4. *Play It Again.* (Strand 2, Skill: Interpreting Information)
Form students into groups, and ask them to choose a historical event to roleplay as it might have occurred in ancient days and then as it might occur today. Encourage simple costumes and props, and videotape the presentations.

5. *Cultural Inquiry.* (Strand 2, Skill: Summarizing Information)
In order to understand any culture, students must obtain information about its government, religion, education, arts, economics, history, technology, and social organization. To summarize information about a specific culture, ask students to draw large circles for each of these concepts, and fill in the data for each. The concepts could be modeled by the teacher to provide clarity. Display the summary circles for the class to review.

6. *Cultural Exchange.* (Strand 3, Skill: Group Interaction)
Divide the class into 3 groups, each representing a different culture. Give each group a specific nonverbal behavior that makes them different, such as wanting to be close while talking to you, always looking away while talking to you, covering your mouth while talking, and using 1-word sentences. Ask students to play the role of their culture and attempt to get others to join it. After the experience, discuss the unusual behaviors of the different groups or cultures.

7. *Lost in a Strange Land.* (Strand 2, Skill: Decision Making)
Have students imagine that they are visiting another country and cannot speak the native language. They are staying in a hotel and want to wander around the city. Point out that they may get lost and need to return to the hotel. Have groups of students discuss what they could do to communicate where they are staying. (Clue: They could take a matchbook from their hotel with them or learn the name of the hotel.)

8. *New Handshake.* (Strand 3, Skill: Social Participation)
Challenge students to invent a new handshake for their class. Ask students to teach the handshake to others in the school during recess. Discuss the idea that cultures share particular habits and practices.

9. *Cultural Costumes.* (Strand 2, Skill: Classifying Information)
The way people dress establishes cultural identity. Have students collect pictures of different costumes in various cultures and post on a bulletin board. Ask students, "What would happen to a person's dress if he or she moved to another culture?"

10. *Egyptian Vocabulary.* (Strand 1, Skill: Vocabulary)
The study of ancient Egypt and its contributions to the modern world can give students historical perspective. Place the following vocabulary on the chalkboard and have students pronounce the words and draw pictures or give examples: *Nile River, Rosetta stone, papyrus, pyramid, pharaoh,* and *mummy.* Use Sampler 13.3 to explore students' knowledge of Egypt before and after study.

11. *Egyptian Life.* (Strand 2, Skill: Evaluating Information)
Give students a map of Egypt and the surrounding countries, blank except for the Nile River. Explain that Egypt has practically no rainfall. Form groups of 3 to locate cities on the map and determine how people made a living in Egypt.

12. *Pyramid Building.* (Strand 3, Skill: Group Interaction)
Divide the class in groups of 3, and ask them to construct pyramids from clay blocks. Have them make lists of things the Egyptians would probably place inside, and then of things from their culture they would place inside today. Compare Egyptian burial practices with those of other cultures.

13. *Pharaoh's Power.* (Strand 3, Skill: Group Interaction)
Explain that the pharaoh's power was absolute in most kingdoms in ancient Egypt. Have a student play pharaoh, and let the others pose problems for the pharaoh to decide on. You may need to coach the pharaoh to make unpopular decisions. Compare and contrast the powers of pharaoh and president. Discuss and compare making decisions and solving problems the way the pharaohs did with other, more democratic or scientific ways of making decisions. Use Sampler 13.2 to demonstrate contrasting approaches.

14. *Pen Pals.* (Strand 2, Skill: Personal Skills)
Have students exchange letters with students in another culture (if possible, a currently important country about which students may have limited knowledge), sending pictures and describing school life. Vary the form of communication by sending audio- or videotapes.

15. *Typical Kid's Day.* (Strand 2, Skill: Analyzing Information)
Ask someone who is familiar with life in Russia to compare a typical day for a Russian student to that of a U.S. student. Discussion should include differences in how we live, customs, education, religion, and attitudes.

16. *Stereotype Demolition.* (Strand 2, Skill: Analyzing Information)
Students have accumulated many stereotypical ideas about Russians. Ask them to call out their first impressions when Russia is mentioned, and write them on the chalkboard. Discuss each one and determine the extent of the bias. Have students research some of the ideas to determine how accurate they are. Ask students to trace where and how they developed these ideas. You can use Activity 13.3 and/or 13.4 to structure this activity.

17. *Invent a Way.* (Strand 2, Skill: Synthesizing Information)
Using Sampler 13.2, have students choose a particular environmental problem and design an invention for solving it to benefit the environment. Have them draw or make their inventions and display and explain them to the class.

18. *Population Growth.* (Strand 3, Skill: Social Participation)
The world's population will double in the next 50 years. Ask students to imagine that the classroom represents the world. Move students to

various parts of the room to take up the space. Invite another teacher's class into the room and make the comparison of doubling the world population. Discuss the consequences of having twice as many students in the classroom-world.

19. *Feast and Famine.* (Strand 3, Skill: Social Participation)
Explain to students that many people in Africa and India do not have adequate food supplies. Around lunchtime, take the students to the lunchroom to watch others eat while they do not eat themselves. Discuss with students how they felt.

20. *Food Shortage.* (Strand 3, Skill: Social Participation)
Food and health care cost money and are thus not available in many countries. Assign monetary value to tokens and distribute them randomly—2 blue to one student and 1 red to the next—for students to exchange for food and health care. Two blue tokens will purchase a cookie and a bandage; about half the class will have enough while the other students will not have the necessary tokens to make the purchase. Discuss with students their feelings about this activity.

21. *Lifeboat.* (Strand 3, Skill: Group Interaction)
Explain to students that the world is like a giant life raft with room for a certain number of people. Give students occupations, such as lawyer, doctor, scientist, construction worker, farmer, teacher, banker, and student. Use a large string to draw a life raft with limited food and water. Suggest that 2 people must be sent off on a smaller raft due to shortage of supplies. Students must decide as a group who is to be sent off and explain why.

22. *Family Tree.* (Strand 3, Skill: Social Participation)
Illustrate the effects of population growth by using the students to represent 2 families, the Smiths and the Joneses. The Smith family has 2 children per generation and the Jones family has 1 child per generation. Ask students to play the roles of the families in front of the class to illustrate these patterns of population growth. The Smith family's 2 children will have 2 children; the Jones family's 1 child will have 1 child. Students will see how quickly the families grow and the effect this has on population growth.

## 77. SOCIAL STUDIES ACROSS THE CURRICULUM

DETECTION

Mastery of key concepts may be difficult for students who

- Have difficulty understanding their social world
- Do not readily perceive relationships
- Cannot give examples to express concepts
- Have mistaken interpretations about the world around them
- Cannot collect data to support their thinking
- Lack historical or time perspective
- Have poorly developed notions of cause and effect

*Description*

Social studies concepts and skills are by no means confined to the specific curriculum areas history, geography, economics, and the other disciplines at the core of this teaching area. Social studies content is evident to some degree in all subject areas, and current educational trends reflect this integration across the curriculum. Social studies content can have rich and meaningful connections to the language arts program of reading, writing, listening, and speaking. Music, literature, and the arts reflect a culture's values and customs and provide both a means for understanding the way people have adapted to their environments and a sense of a civilization's human spirit. Mathematics and science provide contexts in which students can learn and apply economic and problem-solving concepts. Thus, integrating subject matters can stimulate thought processes and encourage creative solutions to human problems.

*Special Problems*

Special students often have difficulty transferring what they have learned to other contexts. Thus they may need additional time and attention to develop the complex and sometimes ambiguous concepts of the social studies in other areas. Often, too, students have developed strong erroneous interpretations that they must unlearn with careful guidance.

*Implications*

Often students excel in one subject area, which can become the catalyst to develop an important social studies idea and increase students' motivation to learn. Therefore, teachers must know students' strengths and weaknesses and be alert for opportunities to connect their experiences and previous learning to new material and ideas across subject areas. These connections provide students with contexts for learning social studies in depth because they are the glue necessary for application in the real world. Teachers can share the challenge of finding across-the-curriculum opportunities with students. The tasks selected and the problems to be solved must be familiar, concrete, and related to students' needs and interests.

CORRECTION

Modify these strategies to meet topical and learning needs.

1. *Humidity All Around.* (Strands 1, 2, & 3; Science)
Have students watch television weather reports and note the daily humidity index. Arrange to work with a class in a different area of the country to compare the humidity indexes. Discuss the differences and what causes them. Point out the effects of the different humidity levels on housing, clothing, health, vegetation, and so on, in the two areas. Data can be exchanged by computer modem, conference calling, or facsimile transmission. Encourage and find opportunities to exchange information using modern technology.

2. *Spring's in the Air.* (Strands 1, 2, & 3; Science, Art, Language Arts)
Discuss geographic differences in the arrival of spring. Examine changes in nature as well as photographs and pictures of spring-like conditions. Have students notice that, like people, no two flowers are exactly the same. Ask students to develop an art project around the concept of a magic flower garden. Begin by talking about seeds, soil, water, air, and the sun's influence on the growth of flowers. Have students paint a garden with tempera paints on one side of the classroom or actually grow flowers in a classroom garden. Then guide them to study animals and insects that might visit their garden and discuss the impact of pollution on people, plants, and animals. Finally, they can write a story about one of the insects or animals who lives in the garden.

3. *Build a House.* (Strands 1 & 2; Math)
Have students design two types of houses suitable for different climates. Have student groups calculate the approximate cost of materials for the two houses. Develop a list of supplies and costs for students to use. Discuss how the costs differ and why.

4. *What's the Biggest?* (Strand 2; Math, Science)
Use geography data for math problems and application of science concepts. Have students solve the problems in pairs. Use questions like these: Tiger City's population is 8,902, Zebra Township's, 9,066. Which is larger and by how much? Colorado's average rainfall is 15 inches, New Jersey's, 46. Which state gets more rain and how much more? West Texas gets 12 inches of rain each year, while East Texas gets 46. How much more does East Texas get, and what differences would this make in the climate, vegetation, crops, and terrain?

5. *Mail Messages.* (Strand 3; Language Arts)
Review with students the names of relatives who live in other cities and states, and place colored tacks on a large map to show the locations. Ask students to write a friendly letter to one of these relatives. Have them write, proofread, and correct the letters and then mail them. Encourage them to ask questions in their letters about differences in their cities and states. Mail the letters, and have students share responses in class.

6. *Cultures Rainbow.* (Strands 1 & 2; Reading, Language Arts)
Make a rainbow across a wall or bulletin board, and place under it a table for books about different cultures and by authors of different races. After several students have read the same book, ask them to report what they found out about the culture. Encourage them to find out information about the authors. Make a pot of gold filled with stickers at the end of the rainbow. When students finish a book, they may have a sticker.

7. *Community Ads.* (Strands 1 & 2; Language Arts, Art)
   Collect pictures and brochures of places in your city where people might like to visit. Form students into small groups, and assign each group a place to locate on a city map. Then have them write an advertisement about the place to convince people to visit it. Students can also design and create a brochure of their ad.

8. *Country Challenge.* (Strands 1 & 2; Art)
   Have each student select a country and make an artistic representation of it using any medium they choose: clay, crayons, string, salt maps, and son on. Have students exchange projects and challenge each other to find the country on maps and globes.

9. *Aurora Who?* (Strands 1 & 2; Science)
   Have students investigate the phenomenon of Canada's aurora borealis. Use Sampler 13.4 to begin the study and to form cooperative learning groups.

10. *Endangered Species.* (Strands 1 & 2; Science)
    Investigate the endangered species of a neighboring country (e.g., Canada or Mexico). What has caused the endangerment? Are people there concerned? What steps are being taken to prevent extinction?

11. *How Long Will it Take?* (Strands 1 & 2; Math)
    Estimate how long it would take to go from New York City to Los Angeles at an average speed of 80 miles per hour.

12. *Mosaics.* (Strands 1 & 2; Art)
    Sometimes Canada is referred to as a mosaic. Have students investigate why it is described this way. Have them make a mosaic and display their creations.

13. *Piggy Bank Pets.* (Strand 3; Art, Math)
    Using recycled materials, have students work in pairs to design piggy banks. Challenge students to find items at home that could be made into eyes, ears, and legs of the piggy. Ask students to solve mathematical problems related to saving their money. For example, if students saved a quarter a week for a year, how much would they have at the end of the year? If students saved $200, invested 1/2 of it and received an 8 percent return, how much money would they have?

14. *Wildlife Report.* (Strand 2; Science)
    Ask students to investigate the effects of various forms of pollution on wildlife. Discuss examples of oil spills, large forests dying from air pollution, and contaminated waterways prior to their research.

15. *Animals' Families.* (Strand 1; Science)
    Research what other animals live in families, for how long, and what their relationships and responsibilities are. Compare and contrast the various animal families. For variation, assign a specific animal to each class member.

16. *Piñata.* (Strand 3, Art)
    Countries have traditions and customs that differ and are important to their cultures. For example, children in Mexico often break a piñata before Easter and Christmas. Using a large paper sack and papier-mâché, challenge students to make a piñata in the shape of an animal, fill it with candy, fruit, and toys, and take turns trying to break it with a broom handle.

17. *Water Sample.* (Strand 2; Science)
    Collect samples of water from local areas, such as lakes, wells, ponds, and rivers, for students to compare with the water they drink. Ask

students to compare the samples through sight, smell, and analysis with a microscope; discuss possible ways that water can be contaminated or polluted in their state. Students could research state and federal laws related to water pollution. Students can also use plastic tubs filled with water, adding a variety of different pollutants, such as cooking oil, food coloring, soap powder, or coffee grounds. They should determine how to remove the pollutants and clean up the water. Provide coffee filters, net scoops, and other possible tools for cleaning the water. Ask students to draw conclusions from their experiments in cleaning up the water.

18. *Gauge It.* (Strand 2; Science, Math)
Have students make a weather chart for the bulletin board and post each day's weather. Devise a rain gauge to place within easy access of the classroom, and have students note the precipitation they measure daily on the chart. At the end of the month, have them summarize the information and determine averages for the numbers of rainy, sunny, and cloudy days and for the amount of precipitation per month.

19. *Climate Map.* (Strand 1; Science, Math)
Collect weather maps from local or national newspapers over a period of time. Ask students to make bar graphs of the high and low temperatures for their state over a 7-day period. Have students explain the weather patterns they observe for a week. Students could compare their home state with another state of their choice and make bar graphs showing comparisons.

20. *Travel Game.* (Strand 1; Math)
Provide students with a state map and problems on the distances between cities. Students will compute the distance between 2 cities with the scale on the map, using strips of paper or rulers. Have students challenge each other by asking how far a certain city is away from another city.

# SOCIAL STUDIES SAMPLERS

The five samplers that follow can be quickly and easily used to supplement the suggested activities in this chapter. Some activities suggest use of a particular sampler. In other activities, a sampler may not be specifically mentioned but can nonetheless add or modify the activity. The samplers are relatively open in format to allow for a wide range of modifications.

13.1 **All About Me.** Use this activity early in the year to get to know students. Compile and analyze the information to discover common interests to help you group students and select books likely to be hits. If students can read and answer the questions on their own, you will be able to ascertain limited diagnostic information about their ability to read, comprehend, respond appropriately, spell, and write. You may want to place the completed sheet in students' folders for easy reference throughout the year. Use of this sampler is most appropriate during units on personal development.

13.2 **Problem Solving.** This sampler presents a simple model for identifying, analyzing and solving problems. Its use is specifically suggested in activities 76.13 and 76.17. However, this model is useful in any context, whenever students are confronted with making decisions. Once students have become familiar with this model, help them transfer this thinking process to any situation presenting a problem to be solved.

13.3 **Idea Tree.** This sampler encourages a free-flowing, creative approach to thinking. It may also be useful in stimulating and revealing background knowledge and experience as well as how well they have understood concepts in a particular subject. Its use is suggested in activities 76.10 and 76.16. In addition, teachers will find this format useful for developing limited, synectic-type associations which will release students from structured answers and linear thinking.

13.4 **Developing a Learning Plan.** You can introduce almost any topic using Sampler 13.4. It reveals students' depth of background information and teaches them to approach new topics independently with an organized plan for learning. Use of this sampler is particularly appropriate with activities 75.13, 76.16, and 77.9.

13.5 **Time Line and Sequence.** Sampler 13.5 uses three variations of time and sequence concepts. One or more of the formats can be used with activities 74.4, 75.21, and others focused around time concepts.

## 🦬 ALL ABOUT ME 🦬

**All About** _____
                          Name

Age _____        Color Hair _____    Color Eyes _____

Brother(s) _____        Sister(s) _____

_____                        _____

Good Friend _____        Pet's Name _____,

.............................................................................

**Favorites:**

    Game        _____

    Animal      _____

    Food        _____

    Color       _____

    Ice Cream   _____

    Hobby   •   _____

    TV Show     _____

.............................................................................

**Subjects I like to read:**

Animal      Science Fiction   History        Science      Space

War         Love              People         Monsters     Sports

.............................................................................

**The most exciting thing that has ever happened to me was** _____

_____

_____

_____

**361—**

Name _____

# ⊕ PROBLEM SOLVING ⊕

**Directions:** Use the following outline to solve any individual or group problem. Try getting creative ideas from other students.

1. Identify the Problem: Explain the problem in detail by answering who, what, when, where, and why questions.

   _____

   _____

2. Complete an "I wish. . . ." statement about the problem.

   I wish that_____

   _____

   _____

3. How many different ways can this problem be solved? Make a list of possible solutions.

   A. _____

   _____

   B. _____

   _____

   C. _____

   _____

4. Which solution will solve the problem? Explain the reasons for each possible solution. Select the best solution.

   Best Solution: _____

   _____

5. What is the action plan to try the solution: When, where, etc.?

   Action Plan: _____

   _____

   _____

6. Did it work? _____

Name _____

# 🌳 IDEA TREE 🌳

**Directions:** Complete the blanks for the Concept Tree to stimulate creative thought by linking words and ideas. Start at the bottom of the tree on the single line with any word such as music, family, money, happiness, neighbor, conflict, work, play, sharing, etc.

**Concept Tree 1**

_____ _____ _____ _____

_____ _____

_____

_____
^ Start Here

**Concept Tree 2**

_____ _____ _____ _____

_____ _____

_____

_____
^ Start Here

Name _____

# ☙ DEVELOPING A LEARNING PLAN ☙

**Directions:** Use the following outline to develop a plan for learning about any topic.

### Step 1

Name of Topic_____

### Step 2

What I know about this topic:          What I don't know about this topic:
                                                  (Use questions)

_____          _____

_____          _____

_____          _____

_____          _____

_____          _____

_____          _____

### Step 3

Select an area(s) from the Don't Know section to learn more about this topic. Circle the areas you choose.

### Step 4

What are you going to do to learn more about these areas?

_____

_____

_____

### Step 5

Explain what you found out: _____

_____

_____

_____

# ⌐|⌐|⌐|⌐| TIME LINE AND SEQUENCE |⌐|⌐|⌐|

**Directions:** As you read a section in a book, note the dates and important events on the lines below.

## Time Line 1

Time
Beginning_____          Ending_____

Events


_____          _____

## Time Line 2

Time
Start_____          Finish_____

Events


_____

## Time Line 3

Time
First_____ Last

Events


_____

# REFLECTIONS

This chapter presents Detection and Correction strategies for special students who are learning about themselves in their immediate surroundings, expanding their relationships into larger communities and contexts, encountering a smaller world, and exploring social studies concepts across several curriculum areas. Many suggestions for teaching about these key concepts are contained in social studies texts. Compare and contrast discussions in these sources with the information and activities in this chapter.

Banks, J. A. (1990). *Teaching strategies for the social studies: Inquiry, valuing, and decision-making* (4th ed.). New York: Longman.

Barell, J. (1991). *Teaching for thoughtfulness.* New York: Longman.

Benninga, J. S. (1991). *Moral, character, and civic education in the elementary school.* New York: Teachers College Press.

Chapin, J. R., & Messick, R. G. (1992). *Elementary social studies: A practical guide* (2nd ed.). New York: Longman.

Clark, J. H. (1990). *Patterns of thinking: Integrating learning skills in content teaching.* Boston: Allyn and Bacon.

Ellis, A. K. (1991). *Teaching and learning elementary social studies* (4th ed.). Boston: Allyn and Bacon.

Evans, J. M. & Brueckner, M. M. (1990). *Elementary social studies: Teaching for today and tomorrow.* Boston: Allyn and Bacon.

Kaltsounis, T. (1987). *Teaching social studies in the elementary school: The basics for citizenship.* Englewood Cliffs, NJ: Prentice-Hall.

Kameenui, E. J., & Simmons, D. C. (1990). *Designing instructional strategies: The prevention of academic learning problems.* Columbus, OH: Merrill.

Maxim, G. W. (1991). *Social studies and the elementary school child* (4th ed.). New York: Merrill/Macmillan.

Michaelis, J. U. (1992). *Social studies for children: A guide to basic instruction* (10th ed.). Boston: Allyn and Bacon.

Polloway, E. A., Patton, J. R., Payne, J. S., & Payne, R. A. (1989). *Strategies for teaching learners with special needs* (4th ed.). Columbus, OH: Merrill.

Savage, T. V., & Armstrong, D. G. (1992). *Effective teaching in elementary social studies* (2nd ed.). New York: Macmillan.

Schulz, J. B., Carpenter, C. D., & Turnbull, A. P. (1990). *Mainstreaming handicapped students: A guide for classroom teachers* (3rd ed.). Boston: Allyn and Bacon.

Smith, L. J. & Smith, D. L. (1990). *Social studies: Detecting and correcting special needs.* Boston: Allyn and Bacon.

Van Cleaf, D. W. (1991). *Action in elementary social studies.* Englewood Cliffs, NJ: Prentice-Hall.

Wood, J. W. (1992). *Adapting instruction for mainstreamed and at-risk students* (2nd ed.). New York: Merrill/Macmillan.

# Part THREE

## IMPLEMENTING DETECTION AND CORRECTION

 Essential to successful implementation of the detection and correction process are the three elements that lend it substance: proficient behavior management, effective instructional management, and productive collaboration. Behavior management strives to direct students' behaviors so that learning can take place; instructional management orchestrates detection and correction efficiently and effectively; and collaboration mobilizes expertise to develop and deliver successful instruction and maintain its integrity. These three elements, the focus of Part Three, combine to energize and control the quality of the detection and correction of special problems.

# Chapter FOURTEEN

## MANAGING CLASSROOM BEHAVIOR TO ENHANCE TEACHING AND LEARNING

— *Frank J. Sparzo and James A. Poteet*

This chapter focuses on some general principles and procedures for changing behavior. Its major message is that teachers can place themselves in a favorable position to change social and academic behaviors if they pay close attention to what students do and the situation or context in which they do it.

Although this is a very practical message, it is neglected in education. Teachers are bombarded with terms from psychology, sociology, and elsewhere that many find more confusing than helpful. The basic problem appears to lie in where one looks for an explanation of behavior. Although the language varies considerably, many professional and lay people search for explanations of behavior by focusing on factors thought to reside in some way within the person. When attempting to explain behavior, proponents are inclined to use words such as *attitude, aggression, mood, elation, interest, alienation, motive, self-concept, intention, belief, information, psyche, habit, intelligence,* and so on. There are hundreds of such terms. For example, to say that a student who is truant, criticizes school, and turns in assignments late has a negative attitude toward school may be appropriate if *negative attitude* is used as a summary description of the behaviors — truancy, criticism, and late assignments. But attributing the behaviors to a negative attitude that resides somehow within the student is a fictitious explanation, because negative attitude and the behaviors, although expressed differently, actually mean the same thing.

"Explanations" of this sort are commonplace. Rather than invoking psychological labels to explain behavior, the approach in this chapter, derived from behavior analysis, focuses on student performance and the situation or context in which it occurs. By its very nature, this approach spawns practical teaching strategies because it points to environmental arrangements that can be made to promote learning. Although this chapter emphasizes basic principles and procedures and their application to social behaviors (e.g., hitting and fighting), the principles and procedures can also be applied to academic instruction and achievement. The first step is to describe a basic way to analyze behavior.

## AN ABC ANALYSIS OF BEHAVIOR

Whenever we want to change student behavior in a deliberate and systematic way, we must focus on the behavior to be changed (the target behavior) and the events that come before and after it. Events that come before behavior are called *antecedent, cuing,* or *A events,* while those that follow are termed *consequent* or *C events.* The *B* part of the analysis refers to the *behavior,* whether social, academic, motivational, or motor, that concerns us.

If, for example, you present a problem to a student, the problem is an A event, the student's response to the problem is a B event, and feedback that follows the behavior is a C event. An ABC analysis can be applied productively to a wide range of human and nonhuman behavior. Consider the following examples. The first one focuses on academic performance, the second on social behavior.

— *Example 1:* Mr Jones asked his students to determine the cost of the bottle when a bottle of liquid costs $10.00, and the liquid alone costs $9.00 more than the bottle. Some students said that the bottle cost $1.00. Mr. Jones said, "Remember that the liquid costs $9.00 more than the bottle. Nine dollars is not nine dollars more than one dollar." After several additional attempts, Mr. Jones provided another clue: "Try thinking algebraically." A student immediately said, "The bottle costs $.50." "Right!" said Mr. Jones.

— *Example 2:* Jean hit her classmates from time to time. After specifying the ways in which Jean hit others, Ms. Elliott, Jean's teacher, explained the following plan to her: Jean would owe five minutes each time she hit someone. Owed time would be paid back after school. Jean's rate of hitting declined.

In the first example, Mr. Jones's presentation of the problem and his clues were antecedent (A) events, the students' attempts to solve the problem were behavioral (B) events, and the corrective feedback from Mr. Jones served as consequent (C) events. With respect to Jean's hitting, the teacher's specifying and explaining were A events, instances of hitting were B events, while lost time for each occurrence of hitting was a C event.

## More About Antecedents

Why does a student answer a question when asked? Or why does a student cause a disruption in one classroom but not in another? The answers lie in the student's past learning experiences as well as in the current situation. People learn to respond to environmental cues because they have been rewarded, or reinforced, for doing so.

The process by which an individual learns to respond to the "right" antecedent stimuli or events and not the "wrong" ones is termed *discrimination*. To teach discrimination, one rewards an action when a particular stimulus or event is present but not when other stimuli or events are present. Thus, only a certain stimulus or event comes to cue the action. Most of the time, however, several antecedent events cue an individual's actions, as they do, for example, when a person enters an elevator after the up light comes on, the doors open, a tone sounds, and the individual observes others moving in the direction of the elevator.

What has been described is similar to what occurs when a person does one thing in one situation but the opposite in another. Such inconsistent behavior is sometimes viewed as hypocrisy. But what has actually happened? The person has learned to discriminate between the situations: In the first setting, the person has probably been rewarded for acting in a certain way; in the other setting, acting in a contrary way has brought rewards. Note that the explanation for the difference is sought mainly in environmental or contextual circumstances, not within the person in the form of a characteristic or trait called hypocrisy.

The relationship between an ABC analysis and such complex situations as instruction, modeling, and rule-following behavior is shown in the following table:

|              | Antecedent Event | Behavior Event | Consequent Event |
|--------------|------------------|----------------|------------------|
| **Instruction** | Teacher's question | Student answers | Teacher says, "Good" |
| **Modeling** | Coach shows good form | Student imitates | Student praised |
| **Rules** | Directions for experiment | Student follows them | Successful experiment |

## More About Consequences

Most of the time, what comes after an act is more important than what comes before it. We are often unaware of how much we are affected by the events that follow or accompany our actions. We normally engage in thousands of social, academic, motivational, and motor acts each day, many of which are followed by consequences that maintain our actions or make them more or less likely to recur. These consequences include reinforcement, extinction, and punishment.

### Reinforcement

There are two types of rewards, *positive* and *negative*. Both maintain or increase behavior, but they do so in different ways. If something is presented after a behavior and the behavior increases — in frequency, duration, force, or likelihood — the event is a positive reward. If something is removed or prevented from occurring after a response and the response increases, the event is a negative reward. For example, a student does a good deed because in the past good deeds have been followed by various forms of appreciation. These forms of appreciation are positive rewards — they were presented after behavior and behavior was maintained or increased.

Now consider this example: A student repeatedly hands over her lunch money to a bully. This is an instance of negative reward because the behavior, surrendering money, was maintained by the removal of something, presumably the bully's threats.

Does the following episode illustrate positive or negative reward? A student scampers to his seat each time he hears his teacher approaching the classroom. You should say negative reward, because the episode fits the definition: Something is prevented from occurring (a possible reprimand from the teacher) by a behavior (scampering), and the student's behavior is likely to continue under similar circumstances in the future.

### Discontinuation of Reward (Extinction)

When a reward that has maintained a particular behavior is consistently withheld or discontinued, the behavior is likely to decline in frequency. For example, if a teacher who has given attention to a student's tattling now ignores all instances of it, tattling will probably be eliminated, at least in the presence of the teacher. Note that extinction is not synonymous with simply ignoring a behavior, because extinction is withholding attention *previously given*.

Social events are not, of course, the only events that can be involved in an extinction procedure. If an apparatus fails to work despite several efforts to repair it, one quickly learns to stop using it.

### Punishment

Like extinction, punishment also reduces or eliminates behavior. But because it can cause detrimental side effects, it should be used sparingly and with caution. For example, although punishment might effectively eliminate a response, its use might well elicit negative emotional reactions that linger far beyond the punishing incident itself. Fortunately, as we shall see, there are a number of ways to reduce behavior by using positive reinforcement.

There are two types of punishment, *positive* and *negative*. As in the case of reinforcement, *positive* means to *present*, while *negative* means *to remove*. But in the case of punishment, behavior is reduced or eliminated, not increased. Consider these definitions: If an event is presented after a behavior and the behavior is reduced or eliminated, the event is a positive punisher. If, on the other hand, an event is removed after a behavior and the behavior is reduced or eliminated, the event is a negative punisher. Thus, reprimanding a student for an action is an example of positive punishment, if the action is reduced: reprimanding is presented after a behavior and the behavior is reduced. Taking away recess time (1–5 minutes) after each instance of misbehavior is an example of negative punishment, if undesirable behavior is reduced or eliminated: recess time is removed after undesirable behavior and the behavior is reduced.

Figure 14.1 summarizes these procedures. The left column shows two procedures for increasing behavior; the right, three procedures for reducing behavior.

**FIGURE 14.1 / Reinforcement, Extinction, Punishment**

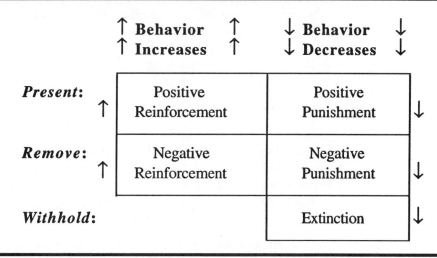

|  | ↑ Behavior ↑ Increases ↑ | ↓ Behavior ↓ Decreases ↓ |
|---|---|---|
| *Present:* ↑ | Positive Reinforcement | Positive Punishment ↓ |
| *Remove:* ↑ | Negative Reinforcement | Negative Punishment ↓ |
| *Withhold:* |  | Extinction ↓ |

## Checking Your Knowledge

See if you can determine whether the following situations illustrate positive reward, negative reward, extinction, positive punishment, negative punishment, or none of these.

1. Jim ignored his friend's attempts at gossip. Consequently, his friend no longer gossips in front of him.
2. Lori used to greet her colleague with friendly comments. Lori's greetings were met with sarcasm. Consequently, Lori no longer speaks to her colleague.
3. Ms. Peters increased creative writing by acknowledging her students' innovative compositions but not routine ones.
4. Jessica got a big hug immediately after completing her spelling worksheet.
5. Frank liked to do the grocery shopping when he was first married. Almost invariably, though, his wife criticized his shopping — he forgot items, paid too much, got the wrong brand, and so on. Consequently, Frank no longer does the shopping.
6. Because a student found classwork quite aversive (punishing), she began to daydream.
7. Whenever little Weston jumped up and down on the sofa while watching TV, it was turned off for one minute. He stopped after it was turned off several times.
8. A comedian has dropped several jokes from his repertory because audiences make little or no response to them.
9. A politician has learned to choose her words carefully to avoid angering her constituents.

Now compare your answers with ours: (1) Jim extinguished his friend's attempts at gossip by withholding attention. (2) Lori stopped greeting her colleague because her comments were positively punished; sarcasm was presented and Lori's greeting responses were eliminated. (3) Ms. Peters positively rewarded innovative responses. (4) Without more information we do not know how the hug affected Jessica's subsequent spelling assignments, so we cannot say any principle is illustrated. Remember that a reward, as well as a punisher, is identified by its effect on behavior, not by whether something looks like a reward or punisher. (5) Positive punishment (nagging criticism) appears to have been the key factor in eliminating Frank's trips to the grocery store. (6) The student's daydreaming, at least initially, was negatively rewarded: something aversive was taken away as daydreaming began. (7) Negative punishment accounts for the cessation of Weston's jumping: something was removed and behavior stopped. (8) The comedian's audiences have extinguished the telling of certain jokes. (9) Because the politician prevents anger by speaking cautiously, her constituents have negatively rewarded cautious speech.

## Hidden Influences

We sometimes see students do things for which they get no reward. This is a time when some are prone to search for causes inside the student: "Jimmy doesn't do his schoolwork because he's unmotivated (or has low self-esteem)." The use of such labels tends to stop inquiry into the real reasons for behavior. The next time you think you are observing someone behaving without rewards, consider three important possibilities:

1. The student may be engaging in escape or avoidance behavior — that is, negatively reinforced behavior. What the student is escaping from or avoiding may not be readily apparent.

2. The behavior you are observing may be rewarded only occasionally, and you are unaware of the occasions. In fact, studies of reinforcement schedules, that is, specifications of the way rewards occur in time, indicate that persistent or habitual behaviors are maintained by occasional reward.
3. You may not be aware of the events in the student's life that are functioning as rewards.

Rewards (and punishers) can be conveniently classified in four broad categories, although the categories overlap somewhat. A few reinforcers in each category are listed:

| Social | Activity | Tangible | Primary |
|--------|----------|----------|---------|
| Attention | Playing | Toys | Sleep |
| Touching | Free time | Money | Food |
| Smiles | Thinking | Books | Water |
| Praise | Reading | Coupons | Sex |

These categories have considerable practical value. They call attention to the enormous range and variety of things that serve as consequences for our actions, although the lists under each category provide only a slight hint of that range and variety. What students find rewarding can be quite individual. Some students respond very positively to a kind word or praise (social reward), some relish free time (activity reward), others will do almost anything for access to the family car (tangible reward), while some especially like sleeping (primary reward). Moreover, rewards can be almost anything, not just things controlled by the teacher. For example, the laughter of other students, seeing the teacher upset, the sound of a dropped book, and being sent to the principal's office can all function as rewards for various behaviors.

## NINE STEPS TO SYSTEMATIC BEHAVIOR CHANGE

The next stage is a general plan for increasing and reducing behavior. Although the plan is presented in nine steps, the number of steps is not sacred. Sometimes, for example, the plan can be easily implemented by simply specifying a behavior (step 1), applying a strategy (step 7), and noting the result (step 8). On other occasions, most or all the steps in the plan are necessary. Sometimes, too, the entire plan can be put into effect quite easily in a few minutes, as in the case of the elementary school teacher described in the next section. At other times, the plan may extend over several weeks. In any event, you should apply the plan and the principles more like an artist than a mechanic. There are no hard-and-fast rules to be applied without careful analysis and an appreciation for the complexity of human behavior.

The nine steps to behavior change are

1. Define the behavior of concern
2. Observe and record behavior
3. Set attainable goals
4. Identify potential rewards
5. Select teaching procedures
6. Rehearse key elements
7. Implement plan
8. Monitor plan
9. Maintain and generalize gains

The plan is appropriate not only for changing someone else's behavior but also for changing one's own. It can be applied when there is too much, too little, or inappropriate behavior. Overeating and monopolizing conversations are instances of too much behavior; low academic performance and social withdrawal are examples of too little behavior. Breaches in etiquette are considered inappropriate behaviors. What is too much, too little, and inappropriate behavior requires a judgment call on your part. Falling behind in one's studies, for example, is not necessarily a problem in and of itself. It is a rare student who is always current on assignments.

## THE NINE-STEP PLAN IN PRACTICE

Teachers and parents in every culture bring about change in their own and others' behavior easily and naturally with little or no awareness of the principles and practices presented in this chapter. But sometimes they get stuck. That is when the plan can be quite helpful.

Consider the case of an elementary school teacher who was having problems with noncompliant students. The children were having difficulty moving from one activity to another. The problem was especially evident during transition from free play to story time — the children simply ignored requests to put their toys away and settle down for story time. They sometimes took 10 minutes or more to comply. Their teacher was unknowingly *rewarding problem behavior* because she read stories to the children immediately after long delays.

Since story time was a strongly rewarding activity, the teacher decided on the following plan. When free time came to an end, the room lights would be turned off for two minutes. When they were turned on again, all toys were to have been put away and everyone was to be sitting quietly, awaiting story time. Should any child fail to comply with the requirements, story time would be postponed to a time later in the day. (Note that this is a negative punishment procedure and the opportunity for stories was not eliminated for the entire day.) The teacher was to rehearse the new procedure, roleplaying positive and negative instances of behavior, several times before implementation. She was also to occasionally praise the children for their efforts.

Implementation went smoothly and the plan was quite effective. Although the teacher was unaware of the general plan described here, all of its elements were used:

| *The Nine Steps* | *Description* |
| --- | --- |
| 1. Define behavior | Toys put away; sitting quietly |
| 2. Observe/record behavior | Problem occurred daily |
| 3. Set attainable goals | Children ready for story when lights turned on |
| 4. Identify potential rewards | Story time was an established reward; praise effective |
| 5. Select procedures | Lights back on; positive reward (story) for compliance; praise by teacher |
| 6. Rehearse procedures | Several roleplays |
| 7. Implement plan | Done after roleplay |
| 8. Monitor results | Plan successful from start |
| 9. Maintain gains | Cuing with light gradually eliminated (fading); additional stories occasionally read for compliance; praise continued |

Remember that an ABC analysis is appropriate when we want to change behavior in a deliberate and systematic way, as is the case in the described episode. Before the plan was implemented, the teacher's directives (A events) were not very effective in getting students to put toys away and settle down (B events). The teacher was rewarding problem behaviors by reading stories after delays occurred (C events). Subsequently, the teacher's requests (A events) became associated with a new event, lights off (A event), while compliance (B event) was rewarded with story time and teacher praise (C events). In effect, the teacher began rewarding appropriate rather than inappropriate behavior!

Unfortunately, not all situations are as simple as this one. Complex situations require more attention to each step in the plan.

## A CLOSER LOOK AT THE GENERAL PLAN

Although space limitations allow only a brief look at each step of the plan, the literature listed at the end of the chapter can provide details.

### Step One: Define Behavior

Before behavior can be observed in a deliberate and systematic way, it must be clearly defined. Many behaviors are relatively easy to define and observe, such as when a student calls out your name, repeats an error in long division, or asks a question. On the other hand, behaviors such as tattling, shyness, aggression, noncompliance, and arguing are not so easy to define.

Good definitions have three essential features:

1. The definition should be clear and specific. Any number of people should be able to understand and apply your definition — they should be able to agree when the behavior occurs and does not occur. You should be able to count the behavior (how often it occurred in, say, 1 minute, 5 minutes, 30 minutes) or to determine the amount of time involved (the behavior lasted 17 minutes). Good definitions describe behaviors that can be seen, heard, or touched. Terms that only infer or imply behaviors should be exchanged for terms that refer to directly observable action. For instance, "poor attitude" might refer to making negative comments about the teacher, noncompliance, and failure to complete assignments. In the interest of clarity and specificity, address these behaviors, not "poor attitude."
2. The definition should include all major components of the behavior to be changed. Suppose you are concerned about a socially withdrawn (shy) student. Realizing that the characteristics of social withdrawal vary from person to person, you observe the student in various situations over a period of several days. You judge the following behaviors to indicate social withdrawal: student goes to and from school alone, spends free time by him- or herself, sits apart from others during lunch, does not initiate conversations, and does not volunteer answers in class. If these five behaviors are actually the major components of the student's withdrawal, a definition based on these behaviors would fulfill the second criterion of good definitions.
3. The definition should be socially valid. Socially valid definitions incorporate behaviors that are socially or educationally important. As an example, consider a student who occasionally slouches in his or her seat. If slouching is not harmful to the student or others, the validity of a definition requiring the student to sit up straight at all times is open to question.

## Step Two: Observe and Record Behavior

After you clearly specify the behavior or performance, you are ready to estimate its current level or amount, allowing you to see what happens to it after you change procedure.

There are three basic ways to observe behavior: automatic recording (e.g., videotaping it), product or outcome recording (e.g., evaluating achievement test results and student compositions), and direct observation (observing behavior as it is occurring). Direct observation is appropriate when behavior does not leave a product, as in class discussions, or when the use of equipment, such as a video camera, is not feasible. Here are five procedures for direct observation. All require good definitions of behavior.

1. *Narrative Recording.* This involves writing down, using abbreviations or shorthand, most of what a student or group is doing as it is occurring in a block of time (e.g., 15–30 minutes). Narrative recording is sometimes called ABC Recording because one can subject the narrative to an ABC analysis, possibly revealing problem behaviors as well as their antecedents and sustaining consequences.

2. *Frequency Recording.* Like product recording, frequency (event) recording is widely used by teachers. It involves counting discrete behaviors, or behaviors that are similar in duration and have a clear beginning and end. Frequency recording might include counting the number of times a student swears, interrupts, tattles, volunteers, makes self-references, or compliments others. (When teachers record the number of correct answers on tests, they are using product recording because students' responses occurred earlier.)

   Sometimes you must consider not only the number of times a behavior occurs but also the amount of time spent observing it. Suppose you observed a student hit others 10 times during a 30 minute period on the first day of your observations. On the second day you noted only 5 hitting incidents, but spent 50 minutes observing. Because you observed for different lengths of time for the two days, response rate would convey a more accurate picture of hitting than frequency. Response rate is determined by dividing the number of responses (hitting) by the amount of time spent observing. In this example, the response rate was 0.33 per minute on the first day; 0.10 per minute on the second.

3. *Duration Recording.* Duration recording means determining how long behavior lasts. Minutes talking on a long-distance telephone call and time logged on a computer are duration measures. Teachers can use duration recording to determine time spent reading, being off-task, talking, or staring out the window.

4. *Latency Recording.* Latency, like duration, is a temporal measure. In this technique, the elapsed time between the onset of a signal or cue and the student's response to it is recorded. Latency recording is an appropriate measure when teachers are concerned with compliance, or the time it takes a student to begin a task after a request is made.

5. *Momentary Time Sampling Recording.* In this technique, a period of time is divided into manageable units (e.g., 2, 10, or 20 minutes). At the end of the interval, the teacher observes whether a given behavior has occurred or not. For example, a teacher might take a few seconds at the end of every 15-minute interval to count the number of students who are off-task or in their seats. Note that one observes only some incidents of behavior, those that occur at the end of a specified period of time. Time sampling is easy to use—a watch can be set to sound a low tone at specified intervals—and can be applied with little interference in your daily activities. The procedure is appropriate when behavior occurs at a moderate rather than a low rate, since you would not observe much of the behavior if it seldom occurred.

With practice, you should find direct observation techniques increasingly easy to use. Displaying the information you collect on a simple chart or graph will be profitable. Charts and graphs that show performance over several days can diminish a tendency to interpret slight variations in performance as more important than they are. The information displayed can have beneficial effects on students and their parents. Simply recording a behavior can be an important factor in changing it. Consider the example of a couple and their son who was known to be aggressive in school. Until their son's aggressiveness was observed systematically, the parents denied the seriousness of the problem. In fact, communication between home and school had completely broken down. When the parents and their son were shown a simple graph of the number of aggressive acts across 10 school days, they changed their view of things rather drastically. It is hard to deny good, systematic data. Subsequent intervention was successful, due in no small way to this change in perspective.

The term *baseline* refers to the target behavior before intervention. In the case of aggression cited above, the number of aggressive acts for 10 days is *baseline data*. Baseline data allow you to determine what effect, if any, your strategies are having on the target behavior, since you will be comparing the student's behavior during intervention (step 7) with behavior prior to intervention (step 2). Observing and recording current baseline behavior may take a few seconds or several days, depending on its variability. You would not need to take baseline data for the completion of homework assignments, for example, if a student has not turned in assignments for several weeks. On the other hand, many behaviors — such as verbal abuse, level of academic performance, or athletic skill — may fluctuate from day to day. In these cases you will need to observe behavior over several days to establish baselines.

A hypothetical example will provide a summary. Suppose a teacher is concerned about a student who verbally abuses his peers. The student, Tim, calls his classmates names and keeps up a steady stream of derogatory remarks: "Here comes big nose!" "How'd you get so stupid?" After carefully defining *verbal abuse*, the teacher collects baseline data by simply counting the number of incidents.

Frequency over five days is as follows: 15, 6, 6, 16, and 17. Because this is a busy teacher, he can not observe for an equal amount of time each day,

**FIGURE 14.2 / Response Card for Tim**

| Student's Name | Tim |
|---|---|
| Behavior | Verbal abuse; name calling; making derogatory comments |
| Where/When | English class; third period |
| Probable Reinforcers | Social: attention from others; students respond defensively |

| Day | Frequency | Time | Rate per Minute |
|---|---|---|---|
| 2/8 | 15 | 10:00–10:50 | .30 |
| 2/9 | 6 | 10:10–10:30 | .30 |
| 2/10 | 6 | 10:05–10:35 | .20 |
| 2/11 | 16 | 10:18–10:50 | .50 |
| 2/12 | 17 | 10:05–10:47 | .40 |

FIGURE 14.3 / Graphs of Frequency and Rate of Verbal Abuse

FREQUENCY BASELINE

RATE BASELINE

so response rate is a better measure than response frequency. The teacher records his observations on a card, such as the one shown in Figure 14.2.

We can get an overall impression of these data by placing them on a graph. In Figure 14.3, frequency of verbal abuse is shown on the left graph; rate of abuse is on the right one. The two graphs of the same behavior differ considerably. In fact, the frequency graph is misleading: It shows a decrease in verbal abuse from the first to the second day, when the rate actually remained the same. Clearly, then, one should report response rate rather than frequency when opportunity to behave or time to observe are not constant from one observation period to the next.

## Step Three: Set Attainable Goals

The key question at this point in the plan is this: What can I realistically expect performance to look like after intervention? Any answer to this question must be educationally and ethically sound. Thus, the plan should be in the best interest of the student — goals that are too high or too low do not qualify — and must make use of the most humane procedures possible. Involve students in goal-setting whenever you can, and provide enough intermediate rewards to sustain activity until goals are reached.

## Step Four: Identify Potential Rewards

Motivation is a concept that covers a broad spectrum of interests, ranging from genetic and physiological factors to so-called psychogenic and cognitive motives. Teachers who want to change behavior should view motivation practically, in terms of reinforcement.

When identifying possible rewards, keep in mind the categories of reinforcers mentioned earlier: A *social reward* is any act by a person — such as a smile, a spoken word, a gesture, a hug — that follows a behavior and makes it likely to occur again. Teachers can influence the likelihood of many kinds of student performance by following the performance with a smile, words of praise, or other forms of attention and recognition. An *activity reward* is a behavior that maintains or increases another behavior. For example, a teacher might grant free time or access to a computer to reward a student for doing something the student is less likely to do, such as completing a map assignment. Consider an example of how this important principle, sometimes called the *Premack* principle, worked in a resource room where the students were said to be unmotivated. Although the students were not completing many assignments, they were given access to other activities they enjoyed. Motivation to complete assignments increased markedly when the teacher provided access to the preferred activities only after assigned tasks were completed. The only change in the classroom was when the activities were provided. A *tangible reward* is a physical, nonedible object. Tangible rewards include marks of progress (grades, smiling-face stickers, gain scores on a chart), awards, books, points or tokens, and so on. A *primary reward* is one that is necessary for survival, such as food and water. Teachers should refrain from using primary rewards except under special circumstances. Good programming focuses on social and activity rewards.

The following suggestions can help you locate rewards that will motivate students, but remember that we can determine whether something is a reward only by seeing its effect on behavior.

1. Watch what the student *does* in a variety of settings. Students who spend a lot of time reading, lifting weights, or collecting things tell you by their actions what they like. These activities might be helpful in applying the Premack principle.
2. Interview the students as well as others, such as parents, friends, or former teachers who know them well. Keeping in mind the four reward categories, ask a series of gently probing questions in each category. You should end up with a list of potential rewards in each category.
3. Provide plenty of simple records that let students see their progress. Success and signs of progress are powerful motivators for most students.
4. Take note of the student's friends. They may be able to provide some social support for behavior change.
5. You might get some leads by noting what the student's friends and associates enjoy.
6. If appropriate, watch for payoffs that follow persistent misbehavior.
7. Try reward sampling. Perhaps you have sampled food in a supermarket and found yourself buying it, or watched an entire television program because you were attracted by one of the segments introduced at the beginning of the program. In like manner, let your students sample parts of activities. If the samples are attractive, later access to the activities might well be reinforcing.

## Step Five: Select Teaching Procedures

If you have followed the general plan to this point, you have a record of student behavior along with a list of possible rewards. The interventions that will follow provide a means to deliver rewards. But before applying strategies, consider several principles for selecting and using rewards:

1. Be clear about the behavior to be changed to improve your chances of rewarding it in a consistent manner.
2. Avoid the use of rewards to which the student has ready access apart from your program. Students are not likely to be motivated by extra computer time, for instance, if they have ready access to computers at home.
3. Avoid controversial rewards. For example, some parents will object to the use of food or money as incentives.
4. Tell the student how the plan will work and how to earn rewards.
5. Whenever the appropriate or target behavior occurs, reward it

immediately. Reward small gains at first, even though the behavior might only approximate the desired outcome.

6. After the behavior is well established, make reinforcement less and less frequent by rewarding only occasionally.

7. Prevent satiation. When a person repeatedly receives a reinforcer, it may lose its effectiveness, at least temporarily. Satiation can be dealt with by (a) allowing students to select from a variety of rewards, (b) using rewards in small amounts, and by (c) using points or tokens to be exchanged for other rewards.

### Strategies for Increasing Behavior

The first four of the strategies that follow, focusing on events antecedent to behavior, are usually easier to apply than the others. If appropriate, try them first. Be consistent in your application of the strategies, and don't be surprised if things don't run smoothly at first. Stay with your plan until you have a reasonably clear idea why it is not working. You are strongly urged to consult the references at the end of the chapter, especially Sloane (1988) and, for those interested in a more advanced treatment, Bellack and Hersen (1985), which elaborate on strategies only touched on here.

1. *Instruction.* One form of instruction involves spoken or written directions that state what a person is to do. "Turn in your worksheets" and "Please face front" are examples of instruction. Most students respond appropriately to this kind of instruction, but some do not. In this case, teachers must turn to more effective methods or combine instruction with other strategies.

2. *Situational Changes.* The setting in which behavior occurs has a profound influence on the behavior. Consider the difference in people's actions in church and at a party, or before and after the advent of television in the home. Teachers can alter the classroom setting to increase a wide range of behaviors, as these examples illustrate:

   - Because Mr. Bennett's students had to request toys and materials when he deliberately placed them out of reach, they have increased their use of language.
   - Liz is studying much more successfully since her teacher and parents set up distraction-free study areas in school and at home.
   - Ms. Taylor posted a new requirement for essay questions: "No writing, only outlining, for the first 15 minutes of the exam." She has noted distinct improvement in the organization and clarity of student essays.

3. *Prompting and Fading.* A *prompt* is an added cue or supplemental stimulus to help a student respond to a new stimulus. *Fading* is the gradual elimination of the prompt. Consider these examples:

   - When drama students forget their lines, a teacher cues them from off stage (verbal prompting).
   - A basketball coach positions his players by pointing to where they should be during practice (gestural prompting).
   - A gymnast is guided by a beep sound each time part of her body strays too far off the perpendicular during practice on the balance beam (mechanical prompting).

   Teachers should fade prompts as soon as possible. The gymnast's goal is to perform well without the aid of the beeper.

4. *Modeling.* People are influenced in subtle and not-so-subtle ways by what they observe others say and do. The person who provides a sample of behavior, whether directly, or symbolically in books or on television, is *modeling* the behavior; those who behave similarly are engaging in *imitative action.* We learn much of our appropriate and

inappropriate behavior by imitating the behavior of models. Students imitate their teacher's pronunciation or solutions to geometry problems, their coach's golf swing, the clothing styles they see on television, and their friends' aggressive actions. Modeling is especially effective when combined with other strategies for change.

5. *Differentially Reward Appropriate Behavior* (DRA). DRA is selectively rewarding one behavior while ignoring other behaviors. It is the premier strategy for changing performance. Teachers use DRA when they mark one answer right and ignore other answers to a multiple-choice question, or acknowledge constructive criticism while ignoring whining and complaining.

6. *Successive Approximation* (Shaping). Successive approximation is a procedure by which teachers encourage a new behavior (one the students cannot perform) by rewarding responses as students get closer and closer to a final performance. It involves changing behavior a bit at a time, or small step by small step. Shaping is not recommended when instruction, situational changes, prompting and fading, or modeling will bring about the desired performance. Good teaching materials and methods, such as computer-assisted and mastery systems of instruction, incorporate the essential features of shaping.

7. *Contracting.* A contract is an agreement between two or more people that specifies in writing a relationship between behavior and consequences. The relationship is usually in terms of if/then. For example, a contract might say, "If you complete at least 80% of your daily assignment in math, then you may work on your television project for 15 minutes at the end of the day." Contracts can be very effective vehicles for changing behavior. They have been applied to a wide range of problems, including truancy, fighting, arguing, drug abuse, and failure to complete assignments. They bring people together to discuss problems and their solutions, provide a record of who promised what to whom, and support student commitment to change (committing oneself in front of others can strengthen the commitment). A contract should be honest, in the sense that all parties must honor it when it is in effect. Opportunities for negotiation and renegotiation should be provided, and all parties should perceive the contract as fair.

8. *Point Systems.* Points, often in the form of tokens or plastic coins, are generalized rewards that can be exchanged for other rewards called *backup rewards.* A point system of rewards has much in common with the use of money in our daily economy. In fact, a point system is a sort of token economy. Point or token systems include points to be exchanged, backup rewards, and rules that specify the relationship between the behaviors that earn points and the backup rewards for which points can be exchanged. Point or token systems can be quite effective in improving both social and academic performance. Because they take considerable time and effort to plan and implement, you should avoid a point system unless one or more of the above procedures fail to work.

## Strategies for Reducing Behavior

Strategies for reducing behavior are listed in order of preference. When selecting procedures, start with the first two, and, if necessary, work your way down the list.

1. *Instruction.* Simply telling them to stop doing something will work for most students. But, as teachers know, stronger action is sometimes necessary.

2. *Situational Changes.* Teachers can reduce (or increase) behaviors by making situational changes, as these examples illustrate:

    • Ms. McKinnon has learned that students make fewer errors when she stands in the middle of a circle of students than when she stands in front of them.

- A teacher changed the seat assignments of two students who talked constantly before the change.
- School officials have discovered that cleaning up immediately after an act of vandalism suppresses additional incidents.

3. *Differential Reward of Other Behavior* (DRO). DRO means delivering a reward at the end of an interval of time during which inappropriate behavior is absent. Any other behavior is rewarded, so long as the student refrains from the inappropriate action. For example, time watching television might be reduced by providing a reward after each 30-minute segment away from television — one rewards any acceptable behavior so long as television-watching is absent.

4. *Differential Reward of Incompatible Behavior* (DRI). Rewards can be provided for an act that is incompatible with a misbehavior, in the sense that the two behaviors cannot occur at the same time. Suppose a student walks about the room, taps peers on the head, and interrupts others. Using DRI, a teacher might reward one or two behaviors that are incompatible with the undesirable behaviors. Rewarding the student for staying in his or her seat and on-task should do the trick. Though finding socially valid incompatible behaviors to reward is often difficult, DRI can be a valuable strategy, especially when several behaviors need to be reduced or eliminated.

5. *Extinction.* Extinction is a procedure by which we withhold rewards that have maintained a behavior in the past. For example, we maintain temper tantrums and gossiping by giving them various forms of attention. Consistently withholding all forms of attention — saying nothing and not looking in the direction of the tantrum or acknowledging the gossip — should eliminate the inappropriate behaviors. When you use extinction or punishment, also reward a related, appropriate behavior (e.g., extinction for tantrums *and* reinforcement for handling frustration in an appropriate manner, or extinction for gossiping *and* reinforcement for positive talk). Extinction has its problems: In the social sphere, it is difficult to withhold all attention; target behavior may get worse before it gets better; the student may become aggressive; and effects are usually delayed.

6. *Response Cost.* This procedure, the removal of a reward or privilege when an undesirable act occurs, is a negative punishment procedure. Because a reward is removed when an undesirable act occurs, teachers have an important opportunity to give the reward back for acceptable behavior. For example, two minutes might be deducted from recess each time misbehavior occurs. If behavior is reduced, response cost has been at work. Teachers and parents know response cost as "taking away privileges."

7. *Time Out (TO).* TO is a negative punishment procedure. Unlike response cost, whereby a particular reward is taken, TO removes access to a variety of rewards contingent on misbehavior. Consider this example: Each time Billy takes something belonging to another student, he must return it and go to another part of the room, or to a place outside the room, for 5 minutes. Billy finds the time out place safe but boring, devoid of all rewards. Some guidelines for implementing TO are these: In private, show the student how TO will work; give one warning ("If you do that again, you will go to TO"); if your warning is ignored, lead the student to TO calmly, ignoring complaints; if possible, ignore disruptions, such as talking or yelling, by the student in TO; permit the student to leave when time is up, provided he or she is acting appropriately — not talking or yelling — for at least 15–30 seconds prior to release. If the student is not acting appropriately, he or she remains in TO for another minute. As before, behavior should be acceptable for the last 15–30 seconds; upon return to classroom, catch the student being good and reward appropriate behavior.

8. *Reprimanding.* Reprimands are statements, such as warnings, rebukes, expressions of disapproval, saying "no" or "stop," that reduce the behavior

they follow. Reprimands, unlike instructions or directions, come after rather than before an act. Because reprimands are a form of positive punishment and can lead to negative side effects, use them sparingly and, if possible, in private.

9. *Overcorrection.* Overcorrection is a positive punishment procedure. It consists of two components, although the second component is found more often in classrooms. *Restitution overcorrection* consists of requiring a student to correct, actually overcorrect, the effects of misconduct. If a student is rude to others despite attempts to eliminate the problem by the techniques described, he or she might be required to apologize to the person he or she was rude to as well as to others who may have witnessed the rudeness. *Positive practice overcorrection* requires a student to practice, actually overpractice, correct forms of a behavior in the setting in which misconduct occurs. In the case of rudeness, the student might repeatedly practice talking politely to the person he or she has offended. No reinforcement of any kind should accompany overcorrection. Restitution and positive practice overcorrection are sometimes used together. Overcorrection can take a lot of time to administer, and some students will not comply with its requirements.

10. *Negative Practice.* This punishment technique requires the person to engage in incorrect behavior to the point of fatigue or aversion. One mother stopped her daughters from jumping on their beds by requiring them to continue doing so beyond the point of enjoyment. In a school setting, throwing paper wads, swearing, and other behaviors might be eliminated similarly, away from the view of peers.

### A Final Note About Strategies

Good plans for changing behavior typically provide a variety of reward options for students and incorporate two or more strategies (e.g., instruction, modeling, and praise; or DRO, approval, and response cost). Further, good plans gradually eliminate artificial or contrived procedures, such as points or tokens, in favor of more natural ones, such as the enjoyment of tasks for their own sake or recognition by others. When positive punishment is used, approval from the proper authorities may be necessary.

## Step Six: Rehearse Key Elements

People often learn more quickly when they are shown as well as told what to do. This step calls for practicing or roleplaying key elements of your plan, for example, practicing a time-out procedure in private before implementing it, or showing parents how to record mock data in a home-based contract plan. Try to involve all key players — the student, teachers, and parents. Rehearsal enables participants to experience conditions much like those they will experience when the plan is put into effect. Immediate feedback can then be provided. Such feedback is unlikely when people are merely told what to do.

Some teachers may feel uneasy making such comments as "That's a good job," "Exactly," "Nice going," and so on. For these teachers, private rehearsal or practice may keep them from sounding phony when they use such expressions in the classroom.

## Step Seven: Implement Plan

Put the plan into effect when you are fairly certain you have the cooperation of all key players.

## Step Eight: Monitor Plan

Monitor calls for observing the target behavior using the same methods from step 2 of the plan. Comparing observations from steps 8 and 2 will help you judge what effect, if any, intervention is having on the behavior. Use the results of this comparison to make needed changes in the plan, but do not change the plan until you are fairly certain why it isn't working. Here are some important questions to ask: Is the behavior clearly specified? Are initial standards for reinforcement too high or so low that the student has become sated with the rewards? Have rewards been selected and used appropriately? Is the plan being applied in a consistent manner?

## Step Nine: Maintain and Generalize Gains

Once behavior has changed in the desired direction, take steps to assure that the changes are retained and, if appropriate, generalized, or transferred to new settings. Applying effective strategies in different settings is one way to promote retention and generalization. If, for example, DRO is effective in reducing a student's swearing in one classroom over a period of time, you might recommend it to another teacher who is troubled by the student's swearing. If DRO also reduces the student's swearing in the second classroom, generalization has occurred. That generalization is successful is even clearer if the student stops swearing in a third setting without being exposed to DRO. Incorporating elements that your classroom has in common with other settings is another way to promote retention and generalization. For example, students will experience many delays in receiving reinforcement in everyday life. Rather than permitting students to claim backup rewards twice each day in a point system, introduce delays in reinforcement by scheduling exchanges at the end of the day, then after two days, three days, and so on.

## SPECIFIC BEHAVIOR PROBLEMS

The next section of this chapter consists of nine specific problem behaviors that general and special education teachers face from time to time. Each behavior can be subsumed under a more general category. For example, "Unmotivated to Learn," "Unsatisfactory Homework," and "Inattention," which are discussed first, can be subsumed under the more general category, "Performing Academic Tasks," because low academic motivation, failure to turn in homework, and inattention interfere with academic performance.

The specific behaviors, along with the suggested general categories to which they are related, follow, with the general categories in parentheses.

1. Unmotivated to Learn (Performing Academic Tasks)
2. Unsatisfactory Homework (Performing Academic Tasks)
3. Inattention (Performing Academic Tasks)
4. Swearing and Name Calling (Verbal or Communicative Behavior)
5. Hitting and Fighting (Aggression)
6. Cheating (Dishonesty)
7. Inadequate Social Skills (Social Interaction)
8. Attention Seeking (Immaturity)
9. Low Self-Esteem (Sense of Self)

Many problem behaviors can be placed under each general category. For instance, noncompliance, being out of seat, and talking without permission fall under *Performing Academic Tasks* — they all have a bearing on academic performance. Lying and stealing can be categorized under *Dishonesty*, while tattling, temper tantrums, and overdependence are indicative of *Immaturity*. Something similar can be said for each of the remaining general categories. Categorizing problems is arbitrary for the most part. For instance, although lying and cheating may be seen as forms of dishonesty, one might argue that they are really forms of immaturity. However, a discussion of illustrative problems under each category might well be helpful when you encounter similar problem behaviors in the general category.

The discussion of each behavior problem begins with a list of Detection behaviors—acts closely associated with the problem behavior. The discussion moves on to a brief *Description* of the behavior. Next, some *Implications* or problems associated with each behavior are mentioned. These implications are largely based on interpretation and logical prediction. The next section, *Controlling Factors*, identifies some factors that often account for the problem behaviors.

The order in which *Correction* procedures are presented reflects a strong preference for reinforcement over aversive (punishment) procedures. Although it is not cited here, a substantial amount of research supports this preference.

When applied with care, these procedures have a reasonably good chance of working. You will need to use common sense, however, at each step in the process. Consider, for example, negative practice. Many behaviors, such as fighting, are not good candidates for negative practice. As another example, a teacher, in order to encourage reading, assigned the book *Helter Skelter* (about torture and murder) to a student with serious emotional disabilities. This was hardly a display of common sense.

When selecting procedures, start with those listed first whenever you can. Combine strategies when it makes sense to do so. Regardless of the procedures you apply, always acknowledge gains in student performance with positive attention and approval: praise, recognition, honors, announcements, displays of achievement, and so on.

At this point you might review the example of the nine-step plan in practice presented earlier. View the discussions of problem behaviors as background information for applying the plan. For example, information about the academically unmotivated learner (Problem 78) may help you define *unmotivated* (step 1) as well as select procedures for helping students (step 5). The information about homework (Problem 79) can also be incorporated into a nine-step plan. It can, for instance, help you clarify the problem and identify situational factors that may work against your efforts to improve the quality of homework. It may also help you select strategies to improve homework, including some that promote home-school cooperation and cooperative learning in the classroom.

Add strategies you have found useful to those listed for each problem area. Whatever you decide to do with the discussion of specific problem behaviors, keep in mind that the principles in this chapter are applicable to a wide range of human action.

## 78. UNMOTIVATED TO LEARN

DETECTION

Watch for these behaviors:

- Students' achievement level is low relative to their capabilities
- Students do not begin assignments or turn in incomplete or sloppy work
- Students make negative statements about school

*Description*

Lack of academic motivation is not directly observable; rather, it is a characteristic inferred from behaviors that can be seen. Thus, teachers detect lack of motivation in what students do such as making negative comments, and do not do, such as not performing assignments they are capable of doing. When students' academic progress is adversely affected by these factors, we can say that they are unmotivated to learn academic tasks.

*Implications*

The strongest implications of low motivation are deficient knowledge and skills and lethargy toward school work. Unmotivated students may not see the relationship between the curriculum and making their way in the world at large.

*Controlling Factors*

Low academic motivation is related to several factors. First, the student may have a history of academic failure; academic work may have brought more punishment than success. Second, teachers, parents, and others may not know the motivators or rewards that work best with the student, or may use them ineptly. Third, students may be turned off by a serious mismatch between the demands of the curriculum and their interests or level of skills. Fourth, significant others in the student's life may be negatively rewarding low motivation. For instance, students may neglect their studies to avoid being called "teacher's pet," "a sell-out," and so on.

CORRECTION

Try one or more of these procedures.

1. *Match Academic Tasks and Student Skills.* Determine whether the curriculum should be adjusted to match the student's knowledge and skills. When tasks are too difficult, check to see that the student has the prerequisite skills to complete assignments. You may have to do a task analysis in which all skills prerequisite to a task are listed. After you determine which prerequisite skills the student can and cannot perform, you must teach the needed skills before you can make a fair assignment.

2. *Identify Rewards.* Locate rewards in the manner suggested earlier in the chapter (step 4 of the plan) and build them into your plan of action. Focus on activity, tangible (points and other signs of progress), and social rewards. Given the nature of this problem, your success in identifying and using rewards will be a critical feature of your plan. For advanced students, low motivation may be due to assignments that are too easy.

3. *Reward On-Task Behavior (DRA).* On-task behaviors are those that relate directly to an assigned task, such as adding numbers or writing an essay when those tasks are what the assignment calls for. Once you and the student are clear about what being on task means, provide rewards for time the student spends on task. A timer set at various intervals is easy to use. If the student is on task when the timer sounds, he or she earns a reward. Start with intervals that will enable the student to earn rewards. If, for example, the student stays on task for an average of 10 minutes before the implementation of your plan, start with 7-or 8-minute

intervals. You can gradually lengthen the intervals later. When the student is able to stay on task for a reasonable period of time, provide additional rewards for correct answers.

4. *Token System.* Provide a point or token for completing each task or component of a task. Students then exchange the tokens they earn for backup rewards. Whatever you offer as backup rewards must be attractive to the student.

5. *Successive Approximations (Shaping).* Sometimes you will have to divide an assignment into unusually small steps. Students should then be rewarded — simple corrective feedback may work — as they progress from one step to the next. If you can find good programmed materials, consider using them. Favor programs that have been tested on students and have been shown to work.

6. *Emphasize Practical Learning.* Devise activities that require the practical use of learning. For example, let the student determine the area of the gym floor for a mathematics activity. Some students will be motivated to learn elementary physics if it is related to music and sound systems. Consider asking students to list out-of-school activities that they might like to do to earn money, possibly during summer months. Help them list, from least to most difficult, the academic skills needed to do the jobs well. Then set up a program for learning the skills. Offer assistance in helping them find the jobs they want.

7. *Contracts.* A series of contracts specifying work to be completed and rewards to be earned could be quite effective. You are advised to consult an appropriate reference for assistance (see the references listed at the end of the chapter). Writing good contracts can be tricky business. For example, if you delay in providing promised rewards or demand too much from the student, you may discourage rather than promote learning.

8. *Cooperative Learning.* Try various forms of cooperative learning. Research on cooperative learning indicates that it can be quite effective in increasing achievement in a variety of subject areas. The idea behind cooperative teaching is that groups of students with mixed levels of ability are rewarded on the basis of the success of the entire group. Thus, consider placing the student in a small group to work on an academic task that requires cooperative effort from all participants. Provide individual rewards, such as free time, following successful completion of the task.

9. *Introduce Novelty.* The *novelty effect* refers to the motivating effects of novel stimuli. You can capitalize on this effect by playing a surprise game from time to time. As an example, call for volunteers to participate in an academic game, but do not at first reveal the nature of the task. Then ask volunteers to complete an assignment that is academic but unusual in its requirements. Let all who succeed select a reward from an array of attractive rewards, such as free time, visiting another room, going with you to another building, and so on. If you apply the suggestions we have made for identifying rewards, you should have plenty to offer students.

## 79.  UNSATISFACTORY HOMEWORK

DETECTION        Watch for these behaviors:

- Students do not turn in or complete homework assignments
- They may not understand or attend to assignments
- Students may offer excuses for not doing homework

*Description*        Homework refers to assigned tasks that students are to complete after school hours. The tasks are an extension of classroom learning and can be distinguished from extracurricular and voluntary intellectual activities.

*Implications*        There is considerable disagreement about the role homework plays in academic and social development. Although research concerning the link between homework and achievement is inconclusive, most administrators, teachers, and parents think that homework is a necessary part of schooling. A reasonable position is that homework has positive effects on learners when it is assigned and evaluated properly.

*Controlling Factors*        Students have difficulty with homework assignments for a variety of reasons. Some see little relationship between homework and classroom learning. These students, and those who have already mastered the content of the assignment, see homework as busywork and a waste of time. Some students lack the prerequisite knowledge and skills to complete the assignment on their own. Too much homework discourages some students, while after-school interests, such as TV, keep others from their assignments. Using homework as punishment certainly contributes to the problem, as does failure to evaluate and return assignments.

CORRECTION        Try one or more of these strategies. Several of the strategies simply call for making situational changes.

1. *Schoolwide Policy.* A schoolwide policy should help prevent too much homework in a single subject and discourage the use of homework as a form of punishment. The policy should stress the need to evaluate and return all assignments.
2. *Letter to Parents.* Send a letter to parents early in the year explaining the homework policy and informing them how homework will work in your class. You might make suggestions for study arrangements at home and ask parents to control access to play, TV, and other distractions until their children have completed their homework. Remember the Premack principle discussed earlier.
3. *Prerequisite Skills.* You must make sure students have the prerequisite skills necessary to complete an assignment before making the skills part of the assignment. One way to check for prerequisite skills is to have students complete tasks that are similar to those in the assignment before they go home to work independently.
4. *Clear Assignments.* Make assignments clear to all students. If necessary, have students copy the assignment from the chalkboard. Show how homework is linked to learning in the classroom so students will not think it is busywork. You may also have to individualize assignments for both advanced and less advanced students. Assignments that are not challenging will bore advanced students, while less advanced students will become discouraged by assignments that make demands above their level of competence. Consider outlining daily assignments a week or more in advance.

5. *Evaluation.* Although you need not grade all homework, you must evaluate all homework. If you cannot, consider making fewer assignments. Written comments on student papers, both positive comments and constructive criticism, are instructive and are highly motivating to most students. Provide this kind of feedback as often as possible.

6. *Reassignment.* Reassign homework when it is not turned in or when students need additional practice. When reassigning homework, you might indicate only the number of correct and incorrect answers on the front page of the returned assignment, and then ask students to find and correct all errors.

7. *Home-Based Contracts.* Because homework is ordinarily completed at home, teachers should seek the assistance of the students' parents when homework problems persist. Home-based contracts have important advantages, if they can be arranged. Contracts and their negotiation can

   — Incorporate a wide range of incentives, many of which are not available in the school setting;
   — Increase communication between school and home;
   — Promote parental involvement in the formal education of their son or daughter.

8. *Charts/Graphs.* Charting or graphing homework completion can be quite useful. Seeing the ups and downs of performance over time will motivate many students.

9. *Provide Novelty.* Because novelty can spark student interest, use it when you can. For example, make a homework assignment in which students supply the question for each answer you give them. As another example, let your students stipulate the homework assignment. You may have to provide a set of guidelines to help them do this.

10. *Credit for Tutoring Others.* Some students will profit from helping others master concepts and skills. On occasion, consider giving students homework credit for tutoring others, that is, let the student substitute tutoring for a homework assignment.

11. *The Good Homework Game.* Assign students to teams whose members are fairly well matched in motivation and skills. Each team member receives a grade for each homework assignment, with A grades earning more points than B grades, and so on. The team with the highest number of points gets to select from an array of attractive rewards. As a variation, each team selects a variable number of rewards from the array, depending on the number of team points earned. The team with the second highest number of points, for example, selects fewer rewards than the team that came in first. You may have to invent a way to keep students from giving too much help to other team members, or the achievement of some members of a team will suffer. One possibility is to require a minimum average team score on a homework quiz as a prerequisite to selecting rewards.

## 80. INATTENTION

DETECTION

Watch for these behaviors:

- Students are easily distracted, unfocused, impulsive, and generally inattentive
- Students may daydream, fidget, forget, or lose things
- Sometimes students may also appear hyperactive — in constant motion, very talkative

*Description*

Many young children have difficulty focusing attention and sustaining action. Later, most of these children respond well to controls that are administered in a consistent manner. If, however, some or all of the foregoing behaviors remain for more than six months despite well-executed and consistent efforts to reduce inattention, the student's behavior may be characterized as an attention deficit disorder (ADD). If the student is also hyperactive, then the behavior may be characterized as an attention deficit with hyperactivity disorder (ADHD).

*Implications*

Roughly five percent of the population exhibits attention deficit disorder. The incidence is higher among those with learning disabilities. Recent evidence indicates that ADD lingers into adulthood, although it was once associated with childhood. Both ADD and ADHD can seriously interfere with learning and social adjustment.

*Controlling Factors*

As in the case of many problems in human adjustment, there is disagreement about the causes and treatment of ADD and ADHD. At present no medical tests can confirm the existence of the disorder. Thus the existence of ADD and ADHD is inferred from the behaviors exhibited by the person. Medications, such as ritalin, dexedrine, and others, are often used to control the symptoms of the disorder. The position taken in this chapter is that medication, a last-resort measure in most cases, should be properly prescribed and monitored, and used in conjunction with well-executed behavioral interventions.

The following discussion focuses on mild inattention, the kind of inattention all teachers see in students from time to time — talking to others, behaving inappropriately, orienting one's body and eyes away from the lesson, and a variety of off-task behaviors. The interventions listed may also be appropriate for students with ADD and ADHD.

CORRECTION

Try one or more of these procedures.

1. *Private Talk.* Discuss the matter with the student privately. Try to solicit information that will help you understand the problem.
2. *Use Prompts.* There are a variety of physical, visual, and auditory ways to control a student's attention. Proximity and touching the student's hand are powerful attention-getters. Tapping on the chalkboard and saying, "Everyone look at this," can also work. When giving instructions, insert such phrases as, "And the next step is really important," or "Listen carefully to what I'm going to say next." Change the tone and volume of your voice to emphasize key concepts. Try inserting long pauses before particularly important points. Include a little humor in the lesson, and praise students for noticing your subtle plays on words. In written directions, make important letters, words, or instructions stand out by using highlighters, colored chalk, large or bold print, and so on.

3. *Use the Student's Name.* Directly focus students' attention to tasks by using their names: Paco, do you understand? Bill, what do you make of what was just said? Lajuana, can you explain the instructions to Dane? Miho, listen carefully because you will be asked to explain this to Mikey who is absent. Use students' names in examples you present in class: That word begins with the same sound as Pam. Ali is taller than Angel; let's measure to see how much taller. Suppose Mylan is taking a trip to Alaska; how will he know which clothes to pack? The use of students' names helps focus attention and may also make lessons more meaningful.

4. *Situational Changes.* Have the student sit near you or work with a peer who is popular, calm, and pays close attention to tasks. Remove or minimize as many distractions as possible. For example, if the student is distracted by scissors during a writing lesson, keep the scissors on your desk and make them available only if the student has paid attention to the proper tasks. Place the desk of a student who is easily distracted away from the windows, or provide a study carrel. Listening to quiet music on a headset may block out distractions for some students.

5. *Increase Rate of Task Completion.* Concentrate on increasing the student's rate of completing tasks. Completing tasks increases attention automatically. Shortened assignments, individual tutoring, and extra time to do assignments are often necessary.

6. *Active Lessons.* Whenever possible, actively involve students in lessons by presenting participatory activities. Active learning not only helps students attend but also may make the concepts more memorable. In addition, such purposeful movement may benefit students who require more movement than others. Cooperative learning experiences that involve interactive learning also help students attend to task.

7. *Other Situational Changes: Provide a Calm and Structured Environment.* For students who have serious problems with inattention and hyperactivity, keep the classroom as calm, quiet, and structured as possible. If necessary, establish strict routines at school and encourage parents to use similar routines at home. Try to inform the student of schedule changes ahead of time. Parents may also need to change the kind of TV programs they allow the student to watch—from violent, stressful programs to calmer, more informative or humorous ones.

8. *Insist on Order.* Help students remember where they should be, what they are to do, and where they are to place things by insisting that they become more organized and orderly. For example, show them how to keep a notebook of activities, and insist that they return things to their proper locations.

9. *Social Skills Training.* Some students will profit from training designed to help them follow directions, correct errors without complaint, and interact with others in a thoughtful and polite manner. Try some of the suggestions for improving social skills that are presented for Problem 84.

10. *Regular Exercise.* Some inattentive and overactive students might well profit from some form of regular exercise that requires persistent attention, such as tennis or soccer.

## 81. SWEARING/NAMECALLING

DETECTION

Watch for these behaviors:

- Students use words and phrases that are offensive to others
- Students use derogatory names

*Description*

Swearing and namecalling involve the use of offensive language directed at others. Classifying a word as obscene or derogatory depends upon circumstances. Words acceptable to one person may be unacceptable to another. For instance, an exclamation like "Good Lord" is simply the vernacular to most people, while others might take offense at the expression. One's tone of voice may also be a factor. For example, "You dummy," could be an expression of endearment or a derogatory remark, depending on how it is said.

*Implications*

Students who resort to swearing and derogating others risk social rejection. Teachers who permit such behavior in their classes risk loss of respect from students and parents.

*Controlling Factors*

Swearing and namecalling can result from imitation, frustration or anger, and attention from others.

— Abusive language may be largely the result of imitation. Students' friends, and family members, as well as people in the media, may serve as models.
— Abusive language may be what students resort to when angry, frightened, or excited.
— Abusive language may be positively rewarded by various forms of attention that follow its use. Responding to abusive language with surprise, shock, or laughter can reward the abuse.
— Verbal abuse is sometimes used as punishment. For example, if calling someone "stupid" puts a stop to that person's actions, the namecaller is likely to resort to similar language in the future. Namecalling is negatively rewarded in such cases.

CORRECTION

Try one or more of these procedures.

1. *Private Talk.* Discuss the problem with students in private. They may not be aware of the extent to which their language offends others. Focus on the offensive language as a problem to be solved, not as personal or moral failings. Identify the specific words that are objectionable, even it it makes you a bit uneasy, and suggest substitute words and actions. For example, students could say "Stop it!" when they are frustrated or angry. They can learn to ignore someone, walk away, or count to 10 rather than resorting to abusive language. To help students become more aware of the language they use, suggest ways in which they can monitor their speech. For example, they might simply count the number of times they use certain words in a particular setting. Follow students' cooperative action with various forms of approval.
2. *Situational Changes.* If others in class swear or use abusive language, make such language off-limits. Post a specific rule. We cannot expect a student to refrain from offensive language if others are allowed to engage in it.
3. *Reward Appropriate Behavior (DRA).* Ask students to devise a list of positive things to say about others. Then praise them when they speak more positively.
4. *Reward the Absence of Swearing (DRO).* Consider letting students earn a point for each specified period of time they go without swearing, or

provide a reward whenever they swear less than a certain number of times in the specified period. When enough points have been earned (require a small number at first), the student or the entire class receives a reward.

5. *Ignore Abusive Language (Extinction).* Abusive language is likely to decrease in frequency if it is ignored consistently. Because everyone must ignore the abusive language, if you try this procedure in a class setting, you will have to ask class members to ignore each instance of abuse. Tell them to say nothing and look away. If the class cannot comply, select another procedure.

6. *Owing Time (Response Cost).* Students can owe time (2, 5, or 10 minutes) each time they swear or derogate others. Time can be deducted from recess or free time, or can be paid back after school hours. Consider providing the student a number of points and taking back a point each time verbal abuse occurs. At the end of the hour (day, two-day period, week), the student gets to exchange the remaining points for attractive backup rewards.

7. *Time Out (TO).* Consider using TO if the above procedures are ineffective. Send students to the time-out area immediately after each instance of swearing or namecalling. Permit them to leave when time is up, usually 2 to 15 minutes, provided that they are acting appropriately: not shouting, swearing, and so on. If students are behaving inappropriately, they must remain in TO for another minute. Behavior should be acceptable for 15 to 30 seconds prior to release. If it is not, have the students remain for another minute. As before, they must engage in acceptable behavior for the last 15 to 30 seconds. Rehearse the procedure with students in private before applying it. When students return from time out, catch them being good and reward them in some way.

8. *Reprimanding.* If you use reprimands, do not get personal; refer only to the verbal behavior. Hostile statements like "What's wrong with you?" and "Can't you do anything right?" do not get at specific action and should be avoided. You might say, "Deb, those words are not permitted in here!" or "Clean up your language, Deb!" Be firm, but stay calm. If you begin to lose control, walk away until you calm down.

9. *Overcorrection.* Require an apology. Require students to apologize repeatedly to the person they verbally abused and to others who witnessed the abuse (restitution overcorrection). The students might be required to practice appropriate words and phrases over and over again (positive practice overcorrection). Practice should occur in private and under supervision. Sometimes using both forms of overcorrection is effective to reduce a behavior. In this case, students would apologize and practice appropriate language.

10. *Make a Recording.* If all else fails, consider audiotaping students' abusive language, with their knowledge, and ask the student and the school principal or the student's parents to listen. Once you have applied this technique, simply making a move toward the recorder might well encourage the student to refrain from offensive language.

## 82. HITTING AND FIGHTING

DETECTION

Watch for these behaviors:

- Students engage in physical contact causing pain or discomfort to others or themselves

*Description*

Hitting includes such physical acts as punching, slapping, pushing, kicking, tripping, and pinching that inflict pain or make someone feel uncomfortable. When hitting involves reciprocal action, it is called fighting.

*Implications*

Teachers are concerned about hitting and fighting because such acts induce other aggression, cause serious injury, and disrupt the educational process.

*Controlling Factors*

Some professionals believe that frustration is the major cause of aggression. When some people become frustrated, they attack the perceived source. Treatment consists of reducing frustration by eliminating its source. Others believe that failure to learn appropriate social skills accounts for many, if not most, cases of aggression. This is the position taken in this chapter.

Negative reinforcement is probably behind many instances of hitting and fighting. The process is similar to the process that rewards scolding or nagging. Teachers and parents soon learn that if they scold or nag, the student will stop doing something, at least for a short time. Thus, they are likely to scold in the future because the scolding removes something annoying. Similarly, fighting and hitting work to reduce unpleasant events in a student's life. Allowing a student to be rewarded when he or she hits and fights is likely to encourage hitting and fighting as a means of dealing with annoying events.

Hitting and fighting often provide positive consequences as well. For example, pushing another student out of the cafeteria line to get one's food quickly results in positive reinforcement for aggression. Attention for being a class bully is also positively rewarding.

When you are confronted with of aggression, then, the trick in most cases is to keep it from paying off.

CORRECTION

Try one or more of these procedures. However, you should seek professional assistance if you think the hitting and fighting might result in serious harm to others.

1. *Private Talk.* In private, state clearly what hitting and fighting mean. Does hitting mean slapping, punching, finger-poking and shoving only? Is chasing someone in a situation that is not playful acceptable? Make certain students know what is off limits. Do not assume that they are aware of all the ways in which they act aggressively. Remember the characteristics of good definitions discussed earlier: They must clearly and specifically state all the major components of behavior and be socially valid as well.
2. *Situational Changes.* If possible, separate the student from those he or she hits. If students spend time with others who model aggression or watch aggressive models in movies or on television, find ways to reduce their contact with these models. Consider involving students in athletic activities, such as track and field or gymnastics. An athletic coach could be a key figure in redirecting aggression.

3. *Reward the Absence of Hitting (DRO).* Work individually with students to determine how long they can go without touching or hitting. Then give them a point and praise each time they go without hitting during the specified period of time. Points can be exchanged at the end of the morning or day for other rewards.

4. *Roleplay Appropriate Behavior (DRA).* Determine the particulars of the student's last aggressive act. Taking the role of the student, point out how he or she might have responded without hitting: walking away, ignoring provocation, counting to 10, resolving the conflict, reporting to an adult, and so on. Then reverse roles and provide feedback for appropriate action. Try to meet with the student regularly to evaluate progress.

5. *Paying Fines (Response Cost).* Each morning, give young students 10 or more tokens in a container. Reclaim a token for each hitting episode. Students can exchange the remaining tokens for attractive rewards at the end of the day. Consider combining this procedure with response cost at home. If parents will cooperate, tokens can be exchanged for privileges at home. Thus, parents would provide privileges for tokens from school and remove privileges for each reported incident of hitting, for instance, by allowing 15 minutes less time at play or watching TV. A similar strategy could be tried with older students. Parents, for example, might fine their son or daughter each time an act of aggression is reported. If the student does not receive an allowance or earn money, the removal of other privileges might work just as well.

6. *Owing Time (Response Cost).* Inform students and their parents that students will owe 5–15 minutes for each incident of hitting. The most effective procedure is to have the student pay back time after school. Otherwise owed time could be paid back as time not spent at an enjoyable activity during school hours.

7. *DRO and Response Cost.* Students could earn rewards for each period of time they go without hitting (DRO) and lose rewards, such as minutes from free time or a portion of their allowance, each time they hit (response cost).

8. *Time Out (Negative Punishment).* Each time students hit or fight, send them to the time-out area for 5–10 minutes.

9. *Contingent Exercise (Positive Punishment).* If possible, require students to sit on the floor and stand up 10–15 times in rapid succession each time they hit. This procedure should be done in private and should be considered a last-resort measure. Get appropriate consent before using this technique.

10. *Physical Restraint (Positive Punishment).* Aggression may call for immediate action. Use the following procedure only under extreme and unexpected circumstances to prevent serious self-abuse or physical harm to others: Gently place the student who is hitting on the floor, holding the limbs and torso so the student cannot move them, for two minutes. Try to release the student only when he or she has relaxed. If you release a student who is struggling and acting aggressively, you will reward the aggression. You may require help to carry out this procedure. Be alert to the possibility that attention and physical contact from you or others could function as a reward rather than punishment for hitting. Establish a policy for dealing with extreme situations *before* they arise.

## 83.  CHEATING

DETECTION

Watch for these behaviors:

- Students copy from others, use crib notes (cheat notes), take credit for someone else's work, or deliberately break the rules.

*Description*

Cheating is a form of dishonesty. Cheating, lying, and wandering — that is, not being where one is supposed to be — often occur together. Like lying and stealing, cheating may be hard to change because it is often difficult to confirm.

*Implications*

Although cheating may be rewarded with immediate gains, it also may lead to negative consequences. The chronic cheater may fall behind in learning and be shunned by other students. Those who make a practice of cheating may be striving to attain unrealistic goals, hold an unrealistic view of their potential, or experience feelings of dejection and low self-esteem.

*Controlling Factors*

Students cheat to gain a variety of positive and negative rewards — to do well enough to get approval from peers and adults, to escape prolonged study, or to avoid a painful sense of failure following a low grade. Some students find it easy to cheat because cheating is an acceptable practice in their peer group; they may feel that everybody does it.

CORRECTION

Try one or more of these procedures.

1. *Analyze Why Cheating Occurs.* Try to determine why students cheat. For example, if cheating involves several students, part of the problem may lie in class requirements. If assigned tasks are too difficult, you may need to change your expectations, provide tutoring and supplemental study questions, introduce programmed materials, and so on. In other words, analyzing why cheating occurs can provide leads for making important situational changes in your classroom.
2. *Establish Rules about Cheating.* Make it clear to all that cheating is not permitted. State rules positively when you can: desks clear of notes, eyes on your own paper, talking permitted after the exam, and so on. Also make the consequences for cheating clear. Punishment can range from redoing an assignment, to redoing a larger assignment, to receiving no credit, to loss of privileges and failing the exam.
3. *Private Talk.* Talk with the student about your suspicions. State only what you saw, and remain calm. Try to convey the notion that you think the student is an honest person who has made a mistake. Try to discourage others from labelling the student "cheater." Some students will need professional help in dealing with unrealistic goals set by themselves or by significant others, such as their parents and family members. If students are distressed, and their behavior suggests a serious and prolonged reaction to pressure, consider seeking assistance from a school psychologist or counselor.
4. *Situational Changes.* If you suspect that several students are cheating, remove as many temptations as possible. For example, separate desks during a test, and move around the room monitoring performance. Some teachers find such monitoring repugnant, preferring to assume that students are trustworthy. But failure to take appropriate steps to eliminate cheating can put unfair pressure on those who want to be honest but see others benefitting from cheating. Reduce your monitoring as soon as you can. In fact, although it might take considerable

effort, consider an honor system of some kind. In the process, students could learn many valuable lessons about character and social responsibility.

5. *Redo Assignment.* Do not give students credit for assignments or tests on which they have cheated. Instead, require them to redo the entire assignment, even if you must construct a new, comparable assignment or test.

6. *Reward Appropriate Performance (DRA).* Find ways to reward students for completing assignments on their own. Sometimes merely providing additional instruction or special tutoring will do the trick: Since knowledgeable students see no need to cheat, this procedure is highly recommended.

7. *Redo Larger Assignment.* If the preceding strategies do not work, require students to redo a larger, comparable assignment — being reasonable — even if the new assignment makes more work for you. Several applications of this procedure can have a sobering effect on a student.

8. *Response Cost (Negative Punishment).* If Procedures 6 and 7 do not work, consider adding to them the removal of rewards when students cheat. For example, the grade a student earns on a redone assignment might be lowered by a few points. Be cautious: Lowering grades for disciplinary rather than academic reasons can destroy their meaning.

9. *Reading Assignment.* Ask a librarian to suggest a book about cheating or other forms of dishonesty. Make sure that the book is appropriate for the student's independent reading level. If reading the book in class would be embarrassing, the student can read it at home or in the library. Make a point to discuss the book with the student. Perhaps you can incorporate its contents into a writing assignment. If you think it might be helpful and will not make the student uncomfortable, ask him or her to review the book in front of a supportive audience, possibly another class. Public statements extolling the virtues of good character can have lasting effects on the student.

10. *Referral.* Sometimes cheating persists even after a variety of well-planned interventions have been tried. If you find this to be the case, refer the student to an appropriate professional.

## 84. INADEQUATE SOCIAL SKILLS

DETECTION

Watch for these behaviors:

- Students have unusual difficulty establishing and maintaining interpersonal relationships
- Students persistently exhibit one or more of these characteristics: may be shy or withdrawn; have difficulty initiating social interactions; seldom compliment others; avoid asking and answering questions; falter in conversation; fail to comply with appropriate requests; have difficulty sharing, cooperating, and participating; are over- or under-assertive; may be considered rude or ill-mannered; show flat or inappropriate emotional reactions in social settings.

*Description*

Social competence is a broad and complex topic. The discussion here focuses on some of the characteristics associated with inadequate social development. Students who are having difficulties getting along with others exhibit a variety of deficiencies, some of which are listed above.

*Implications*

Socially competent people are effective in their interactions with others and are generally well-liked. They meet people easily and convey the impression that they respect the views and opinions of others. Good social skills enable people to pursue their goals successfully in a variety of settings. Because other people are so closely tied to one's accomplishments, self-esteem, and happiness, the student who lacks social skills is likely to experience lifelong difficulties. In fact, interpersonal deficiencies are closely linked to a variety of behavioral and emotional disorders.

*Controlling Factors*

People learn appropriate and inappropriate social behavior in a variety of ways, especially by direct reinforcement of their actions and by observing and imitating the behavior of others. As an example of direct reinforcement, consider a child who is complimented by his or her parents for giving others a chance to talk during conversations around the dinner table. If such direct reinforcement is given consistently, the child will learn one of the characteristics of effective communication. Many of our social skills are learned through imitation. Children who behave in an altruistic manner have probably observed important people in their lives behaving similarly. Both the children and those they imitate must be rewarded in some way for their actions, or their altruism is not likely to last. Now consider a child who frequently observes his or her parents trying to resolve their differences by hostile confrontations, criticizing and accusing one another. If using similar tactics to resolve conflicts with others pays off, the child may well end up with deficient communicative skills.

CORRECTION

Try one or more of these procedures.

1. *ABC Analysis.* Observe the student in a variety of settings. Pay attention to all three components of the model: antecedents or context, behavior, and consequences. Is the student having difficulty making friends? If so, what specific skills are lacking? Difficulty starting conversations? Difficulty in asserting him- or herself? Being too blunt in expressing his or her opinions? Under what circumstances are the problem behaviors occurring, and what are the consequences? Consult a school psychologist or counselor or other appropriate professional if you need help in assessing social skill deficits. A variety of commercially available

checklists can help you identify problems. Many programs for teaching social skills are also available.

2. *Situational Changes.* Do what you can to promote the development of social skills by suggesting environmental changes. For example, if the students have difficulty making friends, consider helping them become involved in school or after-school activities that will put them in contact with others. Activities to consider include the art club, a social club in the community, organized games, school plays, and the like.

3. *Teach Necessary Social Skills (DRA).* DRA is the single most important strategy we can recommend for helping students overcome social problems. Your observations of students should provide information about specific deficit social skills. Teaching social skills involves some or all of the following components:

   a. Private Talk. Talk with students in private about your observations. Let them do most of the talking as you offer to help them develop specific social skills. Perhaps they need to learn to assert themselves, they may need assistance in making friends, or possibly they do not know how to invite someone home after school.

   b. Instruction. You will need to provide information about the social skill in question, why it is important, and how it should performed.

   c. Roleplay. Ask students to roleplay a situation. Suppose, for example, a student lets others interrupt, allows classmates to take his or her place in line, and avoids meeting new people. After you describe a situation, interrupt the student as he or she is talking and note how the student handles the interruption. Provide feedback, keeping it as positive as possible.

   d. Modeling. Continue roleplaying, but this time let the student interrupt so that you can demonstrate an appropriate response. When the student interrupts you, for example, you might say, "I'm not finished yet!" or "Hey, I was talking first!" Repeat the sequence — instruction and reverse roleplaying — until the student feels comfortable and masters the response. Vary the situations, and encourage the student to improvise rather than imitate your actions too closely. After the student has learned to respond appropriately to interruptions, move on to the next specific problem — losing his or her place in line — and repeat the whole process. Do the same for additional skills to be learned.

   e. Application and Followup. Ask the student to practice what he or she has learned in actual social settings. Help the student pick a specific situation in which to try the new skill. Provide followup support as the student lets you know how each new skill is working.

4. *Discourage Negative Private Dialogues.* Students may carry on internal verbal dialogues, or private conversations with themselves, that disrupt social relationships. When approaching classmates, for example, a student might think, "They think I'm ugly." If students let you in on their private world, suggest replacing such negative thoughts with positive ones.

## 85. ATTENTION SEEKING

DETECTION

Watch for these behaviors:

- Students draw attention to themselves by clowning, talking silly, interrupting others, and so on.

*Description*

Many students show off from time to time. Teachers become concerned with those who show off at unacceptably high rates. In addition to the characteristics listed above, show-offs may tap their feet, snap or strum their fingers, make howling noises, or generally behave in inappropriate ways.

*Implications*

Students who habitually seek attention in inappropriate ways disrupt the learning process for themselves and others. The instructional implication is that the teacher must devise a plan to bring attention to appropriate rather than inappropriate behaviors.

*Controlling Factors*

Students clown because their behavior draws various forms of attention. For example, other students laugh at the attention-seeking student, talk about that student, and imitate his or her actions. Because attention can increase behavior even when the attention appears to be negative in nature, the teacher's reprimands might also encourage showing off. The fact that even occasional attention is likely to maintain clowning makes matters worse.

CORRECTION

Try one or more of these procedures.

1. *Private Talk.* Let students know how they can be recognized in the classroom: by distributing and collecting materials, monitoring activities, tutoring, and so on. If appropriate, encourage them to participate in extracurricular activities that provide an audience, such as dramatics, sports, or musical performance. Be specific about what is inappropriate behavior — giggling, tapping on objects, mocking, and so on. In the interest of clarity, you may have to demonstrate some of these behaviors. Your talk might be even more convincing if you have counted the number of clowning incidents over several days and now show the student these data on a chart or graph. Do not be extreme. Let students know that occasional clowning is acceptable; frequent clowning is not. Consider this plan: Tell the student that he or she is to stop the disruptive action immediately when you signal that the behavior is getting out of hand with a private, unobtrusive gesture. Rehearse the procedure if you think it will help. End the session when you are convinced the student understands what is acceptable behavior and what is not.

2. *Situational Changes.* If possible, separate students who clown from those who encourage the clowning, assign them a seat in the back of the room where fewer students can see them, or seat them near you. Ask others to ignore such students' antics by turning away and saying nothing. You may have to provide some incentives for the other students, such as free time or additional access to a favorite activity. You might ask students who clown to observe classmates who are popular among their peers but do not show off. You will have to choose students whom the attention-seekers like and respect, as well as conduct followup meetings should the students take your suggestion. If simple situational changes are not feasible, try one or more of the following procedures.

3. *Reward Appropriate Behaviors (DRA).* DRA is the single most important strategy for diminishing attention-seeking behaviors. When students who tend to clown engage in appropriate behaviors, which you identified in your private talk, reward them in some way. Rewards should be frequent during initial stages of the plan. Consider asking these students to give a series of reports in front of the class. Provide clear guidelines so that they will stay on the topic and provide a good learning experience for themselves and fellow students. If DRA does not work, consider adding DRO. You will now provide rewards for appropriate behavior and for the absence of inappropriate behavior, when it is absent over a specified period of time.

4. *Negotiate Contracts.* Involve students in the construction of a series of contracts. The contracts should clearly specify appropriate behavior, privileges, and responsibilities. Test the initial contract by putting it into effect for a few days only. Make needed changes in the second contract, and try again. Sample contracts can be found at the end of this chapter.

5. *Response Cost (Negative Punishment).* If the foregoing procedures fail, consider using response cost, whereby students owe 5–10 minutes each time they show off. The students pay back accumulated time after or during school hours. DRO can be combined with response cost, if need be. You will now remove a reward or part of a reward (e.g., in the form of points or minutes) for each instance of clowning and provide a reward in the absence of unacceptable behavior over a specified time period.

6. *Time Out (TO).* For younger students, consider TO if all else has failed to this point. If TO alone is ineffective, try adding a response cost procedure. You will now send the student to TO for a brief period of time at the beginning of each disruptive act and remove a reward of some kind, possibly 5–10 minutes from recess or a favorite activity. TO and response cost are negative punishment procedures.

7. *Reprimanding.* Try firm but calm reprimands if the student fails to respond to the foregoing procedures. Because reprimanding students in front of others may be counterproductive, reprimand in private whenever you can. Try to end your encounter on a positive note.

8. *Negative Practice (Positive Punishment).* The following suggestion may be of help should you decide that negative practice is appropriate. When the student engages in any of the unacceptable behaviors, quietly tell the student to stay in at recess or after school. Away from the view of others, require the student to practice showing off repeatedly in an empty classroom. Specify the sequence of behaviors the student is to practice. Practice should continue to the point of boredom or aversion. Avoid unnecessary talk and any use of reinforcement. When the student rejoins the class, find ways to reward him or her for good performance. Because negative practice is positive punishment, it should be considered a last resort. Before trying it, ask yourself: Have I carefully tried the alternative procedures? If not, choose another strategy.

## 86. LOW SELF-ESTEEM

DETECTION          Watch for these behaviors:

- Students may make self-depreciating remarks, set unrealistically high goals, lack confidence, verbalize in low tones, or avoid eye contact.
- Students may appear unaware of their talents, have deficient skills, or compensate by showing off, boasting, or criticizing others.

*Description*     Low self-esteem refers to evaluating oneself as inadequate or inferior. Self-esteem can be interpreted as an aspect of self-concept. In addition to self as knower (the intellectual self), self-concept consists of a person's perception of who he or she is as a physical organism, as a family member, as a student, and as a peer (one's self-identity); of what he or she wants to be (self-ideal); and of his or her worth and dignity as a person (self-esteem).

*Implications*     Everyone experiences feelings of diminished worth from time to time. Such feelings are quite normal as we undergo the ups and downs of life. These feelings are of concern only when they extend over time and are associated with general feelings of unhappiness and depression. Thus, when teachers observe prolonged and serious unhappiness and depression in students, they should seek professional assistance. Self-concept studies show a clear association between positive self-acceptance and healthy adjustment, while negative self-acceptance is associated with maladjustment.

*Controlling Factors*     In a general sense, self-esteem is a result of interacting with one's physical and social environments in ways that lead to positive reinforcement. More specifically, self-esteem is largely learned from our successes in mastering early developmental tasks, such as walking and talking, and, especially, from our interactions with important people in our lives: parents, friends, and teachers. As children get older, peers and the development of knowledge and skills become increasingly important in determining their sense of worth.

Some writers assert that low self-esteem leads to poor academic performance. But the essential sequence may be quite the opposite: Failure in school, and in other places, is responsible for low self-esteem. Finally, be alert to the possibility that students' self-depreciating statements may be maintained by the attention and reassurances that follow them, that is, by positive reinforcement. In addition, if the statements enable students to avoid tasks, they may resort to them again in the future because they have received negative reinforcement.

CORRECTION          Strategies for altering self-esteem focus on enabling students to experience much more success than failure and on encouraging them to make more positive than negative self-statements.

1. *Private Talk.* Try to determine specific areas in which students feel inadequate, and suggest ways in which they can gain success in these areas. If students make self-depreciating statements, let them know that you are concerned because they may come to believe the statements. If you think a self-report questionnaire might identify problem areas, ask a school counselor to recommend one.
2. *Academic Success.* Students are not likely to feel good about themselves if they are doing poorly in school. If students are not performing as they should, your basic task is to arrange things so that such students will have many academic successes.

3. *Identify Talents.* Many students have hidden talents just waiting to be discovered — in art, music, writing, drama, broadcasting, politics, sports, math, carpentry, horsemanship, community service, and so on. Students may need help in identifying their special talents. Becoming competent in one or more areas is very likely to improve one's self-image.

4. *Success Conferences.* Meet with students whose self-esteem is low on a regular basis to acknowledge recent successes. Consider asking such students to write positive self-descriptions from time to time. Read each paper and add supportive comments: "I agree, you surely are good in math" or "I thought the second paragraph of your essay was hilarious."

5. *Ask for Advice.* Ask students to advise you in areas in which they feel comfortable. For example, a student might help you plan a field trip, organize activities, and so on.

6. *Reward Positive Self-Statements.* Students who feel inadequate may engage in thoughts about themselves that elicit negative emotional reactions. For example, when confronted with a new task, such a student might think, "I could never do that." If the student tells you about these thoughts and if you think this procedure might help, suggest thoughts that are incompatible with the negative ones. People can actually think themselves into a more pleasant (or unpleasant) mood. Rather than "I could never do that," you might suggest that the student think, "I'll give it a shot and see what happens. If I fail, so what? Lots of people fail when they try this for the first time." Be sure, however, that students have the prerequisite skills to tackle the task. Teaching them effective problem-solving strategies will reduce the risk that they will fail and boost their self-esteem as well. You might also suggest that students make a point of complimenting themselves when they deserve it: "I think I handled that situation very well!"

7. *Enlist Parental Support.* Students' sense of worth is not likely to improve if important people in their lives are counteracting your efforts in school. Contact your school counselor or local mental health agency, who can suggest teaching materials and procedures to assist parents who want to respond to their children in more positive ways.

8. *Establishing Friendships.* If appropriate, help students make new friends. Supportive friends can do wonders for a shaky self-image.

9. *Cooperative Learning.* Ask a student who has low self-esteem to join another student in carrying out an assignment that extends over several days. You will have to select the other student with care. Such cooperative efforts can have good effects on a student's self-image.

10. *Peer Tutoring.* Ask the student to tutor others. Tutoring younger children may be especially beneficial.

# ◼C LASSROOM BEHAVIOR SAMPLERS

The following samplers illustrate the kinds of forms teachers and parents find useful when implementing behavior change programs. You may wish to alter them, or construct others, as your plan develops.

For help in designing additional forms, including some that focus on academic performance, see books by Alberto and Troutman, particularly Chapter 4, and Kaplan, particularly Chapter 14, listed at the end of this chapter. These authors also discuss charting and graphing.

14.1 **Frequency/Rate Record Card.** This form is useful when you need to count instances of a behavior. One column is for frequency, and one is for rate per minute, hour, day, and so on. Also see Figure 14.2 and the accompanying discussion for an example of a comparable form.

14.2 **Parent Report Card.** Parents may find this form useful. The behaviors and check marks on the sampler are for illustrative purposes only. Teachers can easily convert the form for classroom use.

14.3 **Simple Contract.** This form shows a relatively simple contract, one that may be appropriate when several teachers are concerned about the same student. Note the time period designation at the top of the form. Initial contracts should usually extend over short time periods (1–4 days) until implementation problems are worked out. The few entries that appear on this example indicate how the form can be used with a particular problem behavior. The form can be easily changed to fit a variety of classroom situations.

14.4 **Responsibility Contract.** This contract is more elaborate than the one shown in Sampler 14.3. Note the emphasis on assigning responsibilities and keeping careful records. As an example, with respect to student responsibilities, *Who* refers to the student's name, *What* might refer to math homework, *When* might mean whenever homework is assigned by the teacher, and *How Much* might refer to the acceptable level of performance for each assignment. As you can see, contracts can assign responsibilities to several people.

14.5 **Reward Interview.** This form suggests a format for interviewing a student and others who know him or her well. The main purpose is to identify potential rewards, motivators, or incentives. Primary rewards are not included because most teachers should avoid using primary rewards such as food. Interviews should be conducted individually to preserve the independence of the responses. Ask each person a series of gently probing questions in each of the categories. You should end up with several lists of rewards. Then decide which rewards are feasible for your plan. But remember, rewards can be identified only by observing their effects on performance.

Name _____

# |||||||||| FREQUENCY/RATE RECORD CARD ||||||||||

Student's Name_____

Target Behavior_____

Where _____

When _____

Rewards Maintaining Behavior_____

_____

| DAY | FREQUENCY | TIME | RATE/DAY |
|---|---|---|---|
| | | | |
| | | | |
| | | | |
| | | | |
| | | | |
| | | | |
| | | | |
| | | | |
| | | | |
| | | | |
| | | | |
| | | | |
| | | | |
| | | | |
| | | | |
| | | | |
| | | | |
| | | | |
| | | | |
| | | | |

Name _____

# ♥♥ PARENT REPORT CARD ♥♥

Student's Name_____

| BEHAVIOR | M | T | W | Th | F |
|---|---|---|---|---|---|
| (Out of bed on time) | | ✔ | ✔ | | ✔ |
| (Makes bed) | ✔ | ✔ | ✔ | | |
| | | | | | |
| | | | | | |
| | | | | | |
| | | | | | |
| | | | | | |
| | | | | | |
| | | | | | |
| | | | | | |
| | | | | | |
| | | | | | |
| | | | | | |
| | | | | | |
| | | | | | |
| | | | | | |
| | | | | | |
| | | | | | |
| TOTAL POINTS | | | | | |

# ✳✳ **SIMPLE CONTRACT** ✳✳
for Period _____ to _____

## Behavior to be rewarded:

✳_____

## Ratings

| Class/Period | Teacher | Rating | Signature |
|---|---|---|---|
| Language | | | |
| Math | | | |
| Science | | | |
| Social Studies | | | |
| Art | | | |
| Physical Ed. | | | |
| Lunch | | | |
| Other (specify) | | | |
| | | | |

Total = _____        Average = _____

### Rating Scale
1 = Flagrant violation
2 = Many incidents
3 = More than 1 incident
4 = Only 1 incident
5 = HURRAH!!!

✳ Privileges:   4 or better average per day = _____

3 or better average per day = _____

# ☞ RESPONSIBILITY CONTRACT ✍

for Period _____ to _____

Student's Name _____

Teacher's Name _____

‖‖‖‖‖‖‖‖‖‖‖‖‖‖‖‖‖‖‖‖‖‖‖‖‖‖‖‖‖‖‖‖‖‖‖‖‖‖‖‖‖‖‖‖‖‖‖‖‖‖‖‖‖‖‖‖‖‖‖‖‖‖‖

## RESPONSIBILITIES – Who/What/When/How Much

‖‖‖‖‖‖‖‖‖‖‖‖‖‖‖‖‖‖‖‖‖‖‖‖‖‖‖‖‖‖‖‖‖‖‖‖‖‖‖‖‖‖‖‖‖‖‖‖‖‖‖‖‖‖‖‖‖‖‖‖‖‖‖

STUDENT:                              TEACHER:




\*\*\*\*\*\*\*\*\*\*\*\*\*\*\*\*\*\*\*\*\*\*\*\*\*\*\*\*\*\*\*\*\*\*\*\*\*\*\*\*\*\*\*\*\*\*\*\*\*\*\*\*\*\*\*\*\*\*\*\*\*\*\*

## PRIVILEGES — Who/What/When/How Much

\*\*\*\*\*\*\*\*\*\*\*\*\*\*\*\*\*\*\*\*\*\*\*\*\*\*\*\*\*\*\*\*\*\*\*\*\*\*\*\*\*\*\*\*\*\*\*\*\*\*\*\*\*\*\*\*\*\*\*\*\*\*\*

STUDENT:                              TEACHER:




_____

Bonus arrangements: _____

How behavior will be observed: _____

By whom: _____

Who will keep records: _____

Who will provide privileges; when: _____


_____        _____
Signed                          Date

_____        _____
Signed                          Date

**S**AMPLER 14.5

Name _____

## ✳ ✳ ✳ REWARD INTERVIEW ✳ ✳ ✳

|  | STUDENT | PARENT | OTHER | OTHER |
|---|---|---|---|---|
| **SOCIAL** |  |  |  |  |
| **ACTIVITY** |  |  |  |  |
| **TANGIBLE** |  |  |  |  |

## REFLECTIONS

1. Consulting appropriate references is an excellent way to learn more about the analysis of behavior. The references that follow will get you started. For example, several of them provide additional strategies for changing behavior. Try to determine which of these strategies might be appropriate for problem behaviors discussed in the chapter.

2. An ABC analysis can be a powerful classroom ally. As a test of this statement, select a particular student to observe — one who is off-task, for example. You will first have to define *off-task*. Pick a particular time of day at which to observe the student over several days. Pay particular attention to the behavior and to what typically happens before and after it. Can you determine what cues the behavior? What rewards maintain it? Chances are the student is being negatively rewarded by the avoidance of work and positively rewarded by the activities he or she engages in while off-task. Your task is to identify the specific positive and negative rewards at work for this student. Once you have done an ABC analysis, you will be in a position to design a plan (possibly a nine-step plan) to help the student.

3. This chapter makes a case for clear, objective behavioral definitions. Suppose a teacher claims that a student doesn't complete assignments because the student is "just plain lazy." Given the point of view expressed in the chapter, what is wrong with the teacher's explanation? Suggest a more plausible one.

4. The situation or context in which behavior occurs has an important bearing on that behavior. Thus, teachers can increase or reduce behaviors simply by altering situations or contexts. One teacher, for example, switched a highly motivating activity from the morning to the afternoon schedule and thereby eliminated the afternoon doldrums that plagued the sixth-period class. A principal discovered that students eat less junk food during school hours since the vending machines have been removed from the school building. Try your hand at listing situational changes that might improve student performance.

5. Some people say that changing behavior by the deliberate use of reinforcement is a form of bribery. Given the broad range of consequences that affect our lives, do you agree? What is bribery? Can a society function without various systems of reward?

6. Punishment can elicit negative emotional reactions that linger well beyond the punishing incident itself. List some other disadvantages of punishment.

7. This chapter recommends that desirable alternative behavior be taught whenever extinction or punishment is used. Suggest some alternative behaviors for each of these: arguing, stealing, and tattling.

8. Prompting is a short-cut method to bring about behavior change. Identify several prompts you have used in teaching. How do you usually fade them?

9. Charting provides an overall picture of student performance. Select an academic or social behavior to chart or graph. After you have a clear definition of the behavior, observe it in some systematic way. With respect to inappropriate talking, for example, you might try frequency recording or momentary time-sampling. After several days, chart or graph your data.

10. Students can apply the nine-step plan for self-management. Discuss some of the ways they might use the plan to improve study skills or performance in other areas. For example, how might self-monitoring promote the good performance of a dancer? Of a musician? Of a math student?

11. The principles presented in Chapter 14 can be widely applied in daily life. In a home setting, give an everyday example of negative reinforcement involving a social consequence. Here is one of many possible answers: Dan practices the piano 15 minutes each day to avoid his parents' reprimands. Because the behavior (piano playing) is being maintained by the prevention of something (the reprimands), the answer fits the definition of negative reinforcement given earlier. Note that reprimands are essentially social consequences. Now give an example of positive reinforcement involving a social consequence in a school setting.

12. Research Press (Box 31779, Champaign, IL 61821) has produced an outstanding film, *Harry*, showing how the principles of changing behavior described in this chapter are used to transform a young man from an uncontrolled, institutionalized person to one capable of some adjustment outside the institution. *Harry* would be an excellent film to show and discuss in a faculty meeting. Various techniques such as positive reinforcement, time-out, and extinction are nicely demonstrated. Note especially that behavior change sometimes requires a massive effort and that, in the hands of skilled people, the systematic use of behavior principles really works.

13. Experienced teachers can be rich sources of knowledge about education. Ask a teacher to suggest some promising procedures to use in response to specific behavior problems. Compare his or her suggestions with those in this chapter.

14. A number of resources address special classroom behavior problems. Compare and contrast discussions in these references with the information in this chapter.

Alberto, P. A., & Troutman, A. C. (1990). *Applied behavior analysis for teachers* (3rd ed.). Columbus, OH: Merrill.

Baldwin, J. D., & Baldwin, J. I. (1986). *Behavior principles in everyday life* (2nd ed.). Englewood Cliffs, NJ: Prentice-Hall.

Bellack, A. S., & Hersen, M. (Eds.). (1985). *Dictionary of behavior therapy techniques.* New York: Pergamon Press.

Charles, C. M. (1992). *Building classroom discipline* (4th ed.). White Plains, NY: Longman.

Coleman, M. C. (1992). *Behavior disorders: Theory and practice* (2nd ed.). Boston: Allyn and Bacon.

Kaplan, J. S. (1991). *Beyond behavior modification: A cognitive-behavioral approach to behavior management in the school* (2nd ed.). Austin, TX: Pro-Ed.

Kazdin, A. E. (1989). *Behavior modification in applied settings* (4th ed.). Pacific Grove, CA: Brooks/Cole.

Rosenberg, M. S., Wilson, R., Maheady, L., & Sindelar, P. (1992). *Educating students with behavior disorders.* Boston: Allyn and Bacon.

Sloane, H. N. (1988). *The good kid book: How to solve the 16 most common behavior problems.* Champaign, IL: Research Press.

Sparzo, F.J. (1985). *Changing behavior: A practical guide for teachers and parents.* Bloomington, IN: Phi Delta Kappa Educational Foundation.

Sparzo, F. J., & Poteet, J. A. (1989). *Classroom behavior: Detecting and correcting special problems.* Boston: Allyn and Bacon.

Sulzer-Azaroff, B., & Mayer, G. R. (1991). *Behavior analysis for lasting change.* New York: Holt, Rinehart and Winston.

# CHAPTER FIFTEEN

## INSTRUCTIONAL MANAGEMENT FOR STUDENT AND TEACHER SUCCESS

— *William H. Evans, Susan S. Evans, Robert A. Gable, Lamoine J. Miller, and Rex E. Schmid*

This chapter provides the framework for establishing educational settings that are efficient, effective, and rewarding. It provides an ecological approach to detecting and correcting instructional programs, addressing the ways home, community, and school affect performance in the classroom. Most importantly, it illustrates that instructional management is a multifaceted process that must constantly change to meet the needs of students, parents, and teachers.

## ASSUMPTIONS

The concepts and principles in this chapter have been drawn from a vast body of professional literature. The focus is on providing practical and effective techniques for detecting and correcting instructional problems. The basic assumptions underlying this chapter are these:

— Each student has unique needs that must be met in the instructional program.
— Instructional settings are affected by teacher and student behaviors, as well as by elements from other environments.
— Not every instructional problem warrants an elaborate intervention.
— Variables in the home, community, and school have a direct bearing on the classroom and must be addressed in developing and implementing an instructional management program.
— Many instructional problems can be prevented by careful planning.
— Learning is best accomplished in orderly settings that use instructional procedures and materials appropriate to the students' interests and stages of learning.
— Teaching can be an intensely rewarding experience.

## ORGANIZATION

In this chapter the discussion of ecological instructional planning covers procedures that may be used to identify, or target, instructional problems. Practical assessment strategies for examining these targets are also suggested. The effects that home, community, and school have upon classroom performance are emphasized. This chapter presents a variety of strategies for increasing cooperative relations among parents, members of the community, school administrators, and teachers, as well as a comprehensive analysis of methods teachers can use to correct instructional problems. Preventive planning, discipline, classroom organization, time management and scheduling, instructional grouping, materials, and individualized instructional plans are all addressed. This chapter, offers practical suggestions for detecting and correcting instructional problems. Because each problem and setting demand a unique solution, these suggestions will not answer every instructional difficulty encountered in the classroom. However, in an effective instructional environment, where the parts are harmoniously arranged to support the whole, education becomes a richly rewarding experience for all.

## ECOLOGICAL INSTRUCTIONAL MANAGEMENT

*Instructional management* is the process of blending instructional and environmental variables to produce rewarding educational conditions that result in a maximum amount of learning accomplished in an efficient manner. While this is the goal, the reality is that even for the best teachers, there will be times when very little seems to be accomplished or when any amount of effort on the part of students or teacher seems inadequate. In classrooms with effective instructional management, these days are the exception rather than the rule.

One of the most formidable challenges in instructional management is deciding upon a starting point for intervention. All too often it seems that students and teachers alike are surrounded by insurmountable problems. A host of difficulties — such as home and peer problems, learning and behavior problems, inadequate facilities and materials, and time constraints — interact to produce a tangled, chaotic web of instructional and personal problems. A cyclical process in which home problems combine with seemingly random and uncontrollable forces in the school produces classroom problems of considerable magnitude. What results is a lack of learning and student dissatisfaction, which, in turn, produce other serious problems that affect motivation and behavior across environments.

Instruction is complex. Rarely is an instructional problem completely isolated from all other elements of the environment. Rather, students' behaviors are shaped by their environment, including physical setting, values, and past experiences. This interaction between student behavior and environment means that instructional management be must viewed ecologically. Then instructional management becomes a task of carefully orchestrating diverse behavior and environmental variables to produce a setting that enhances and promotes learning.

By assuming an ecological perspective, we recognize that altering one element in an environment can produce corresponding changes in other elements. While these changes may produce the desired result and eliminate the problem at hand, they may also cause unanticipated consequences. Teachers should be aware of these consequences. In classrooms, the physical conditions of the classroom and school are not easily separated and compartmentalized from the past experiences, behavior, and values of teachers and students. The classroom is a focal point where these variables converge: Home problems; learning difficulties; the attitudes of teachers, students, administrators, and parents; seating arrangements; lighting; room temperature; and instructional materials all influence the educational environment. Therefore, one of the first steps in effective instructional management is the comprehensive examination of the exact nature and interaction of all elements in the instructional environment.

## ENVIRONMENTS THAT AFFECT THE INSTRUCTIONAL SETTING

The physiological, psychosocial, and physical environments exert a great influence upon the classroom environment. These environments combine in novel ways to affect the behavior of students and teachers, thus making each classroom unique. This uniqueness necessitates the analysis of the exact nature of each instructional setting.

## Physiological Environment

The physiological environment encompasses nutritional, health, and biophysical conditions. Children who are ill, who suffer from an inadequate diet, fatigue, allergies or physical impairments, or who are taking medication or consuming illicit drugs will not learn well. While some of these elements may be beyond the immediate control of the teacher, they nevertheless must be successfully managed if optimum learning is to occur. The best attempts at implementing an instructional program will be thwarted unless the physiological environment is successfully managed. The most clever material and the best lesson will all be for naught if a child has significant, unmanaged physiological deficits.

## Psychosocial Environment

The psychosocial environment includes individual values, expectations, emotions, past learning history, and interpersonal interactions. While many of these conditions are inferred from behavior, they nevertheless significantly affect how people approach tasks and evaluate events. School performance may be affected if the values of children and parents are dramatically different from those of teachers and school officials. Likewise, teachers, parents, and students can have unrealistic expectations of what should take place in the classroom or of each other's role in supporting the instructional program. Major problems result if these expectations differ significantly or if they contribute to the development of a grossly inappropriate instructional program. The instructional program is also affected by past student performance and interpersonal problems. Instructional plans for a high-achieving student in math, for example, would differ significantly from those constructed for a student with a long history of failure or an extremely serious parental or peer problem. As a result, while instructional planning has a lot to do with the presentation of material, it also is significantly affected by values, expectations, and motivation.

## Physical Environment

The physical environment includes things used in daily living. In the home, the physical environment includes things such as books, television, radios, and household appliances; in the classroom, desks, instructional materials, lights, and heat. Clearly, the physical environment affects behavior in the classroom. Colorful, nicely arranged classrooms that have ample and appropriate instructional materials help establish an environment that is conducive to learning and promotes teacher and student satisfaction. The physical environment of the classroom is what is typically thought of when discussing instructional management. Materials, instructional groupings, the physical layout and condition of the room, and seating arrangements influence behavior and must be carefully considered in instructional planning. These factors constantly interact with elements of the psychosocial and physiological environments to produce unique instructional settings.

## INSTRUCTIONAL PLANNING

Instructional planning is a dynamic process. Behaviors and environments interact to produce unique, ever-changing settings. A reading program that was appropriate in September may not be appropriate in February. The goal of instructional planning is to produce a stable classroom ecosystem, one in which there is a balance between all of the elements of diverse environments. This balance is very difficult to achieve and maintain due to constantly changing conditions. When balance is lost, learning suffers and education becomes burdensome. If instructional planning is to be effective, teachers must realize that students are not all stamped out of the same mold. Each one is unique and constantly changing. Educational interventions, therefore, must be carefully formulated so as to consider their effects upon all elements of the ecosystem.

## Targeting Problems

The first step in the intervention process is to determine whether a problem is serious enough to warrant an intervention. The goal is to intervene only in problems that have a serious and adverse effect on instruction. Anything else wastes valuable time and energy that could be spent on more critical elements of the instructional program.

The effect that the current program has upon the teacher and student is perhaps the most critical factor in determining the existence of an instructional problem. When a student is not learning or is obviously dissatisfied with the instructional program, there is undoubtedly a serious problem. Likewise, a serious problem may exist when a teacher is unhappy with the effectiveness or implementation of the educational program. The crucial question is how dissatisfied must a teacher be, or how much or how long must a student not learn, for there to be a problem? The seriousness of an instructional problem depends on what is expected or required for skill mastery. Research has shown, however, that a number of critical teacher and student behaviors, as well as classroom conditions, facilitate effective implementation of the instructional program. Critical student behaviors include effort, motivation, time, behavior, expectations, and organization:

— Does the student spend too much or too little effort completing tasks?
— Is the student sufficiently and appropriately motivated to engage in and complete assigned tasks and to behave in an expected manner?
— Does the student have and use an appropriate amount of learning time?
— Does classroom behavior match school and teacher expectations?
— Does the student organize assigned tasks to maximize learning?

Critical teacher behaviors include effort, motivation, plan, expectations, and organization:

— Does the teacher spend too much or too little effort implementing the instructional program?
— Is the teacher sufficiently and appropriately motivated to conduct the instructional program?
— Does the teacher have an organized, efficient plan for use of classroom time?
— Are the teacher's expectations of students appropriate and positive?
— Is the instructional program organized in an appropriate manner?

The answers to these questions help determine the vitality and appropriateness of an instructional program. Each of these variables results in some teacher or student behavior. Instructional problems, manifested in behavior, reflect deficits in one or more of these areas. Each of these variables must be systematically examined in order to determine the origin and nature of the problem. This analysis involves examining the amount as well as the severity of behavior.

## Amount of Behavior

The amount of behavior a student exhibits may have a direct impact on the student's academic performance. Behavior may be judged by *frequency* (the number of times the behavior occurs within a specified time period), *latency* (the length of time it takes for a behavior to occur once it has been promoted), or *duration* (the length of time the behavior lasts). While judging the amount of behavior is not difficult, determining what amount should be expected is. Violent behavior, such as physical assault, cannot be tolerated in any amount because such behaviors make instruction impossible. Standards for less severe acts, such as talking out of turn, can be established by comparing with peer behavior to determine an acceptable range. The amount of teacher behaviors can also be assessed. The teacher controls such behaviors as positive or negative comments, the amount of time devoted to tasks, the number and timing of warnings, and the number and types of questions asked and assignments given, which contribute significantly to the classroom environment. Unfortunately, teachers often assume that the problem in an instructional setting resides wholly within the student. As a result, the teacher may initiate a quest to determine the exact nature of the student's problem. In truth, some of the problem may be due to student behavior; however, a certain amount also may be caused by teacher behavior, parental expectations, or environmental conditions in the school or home. Therefore, examining teacher as well as student behavior is always a good idea. Teachers who encounter students with persistent behavior problems should use the strategies in Chapter 14 to manage these behaviors successfully.

## Severity of Behavior

The severity of a behavior problem is best judged according to the specific situation. What may be a problem in one setting may not be viewed as a problem in another. One key factor is how much the teacher can tolerate specific behaviors. Tolerance may be affected by environmental conditions such as fatigue and the difficulty of the activity. Everyone is less tolerant when tired or ill. Often times frustration and inappropriate behavior result when students attempt new and difficult tasks. An analysis of the severity of behavior must also examine whether the behavior is appropriate to the setting, as well as its intent and magnitude. However, determining the exact degree of severity of a problem is not always easy. What appears to be an extremely severe problem often appears less serious several days later. Also, our tolerance for many noxious behaviors is constantly changing, so that we permit behaviors we once considered inappropriate. Added to this is the problem of determining intent and magnitude of the behavior.

The difficulty of evaluating how severe instructional and behavior problems are means that teachers must carefully and thoroughly assess the student's whole environment. The student's skill level, teacher tolerance, perceptions of the severity of the problem by other professionals, parents, and students, and demands and expectations present in the setting, all serve as standards against which the specific problem is judged. While this judgment process is far from exact, it does allow teachers to examine the difference between what is expected and what is actually happening. This examination helps determine which problems are serious enough to warrant intervention.

Critical teacher behaviors must also be examined. Analysis of a problem may reveal that some teacher behaviors, as well as student behaviors, contribute to classroom difficulties. For example, a derogatory comment made to a student about a failing grade or personal attribute is a serious act that could have a dramatic effect upon the student's educational environment. Clearly, teachers must avoid pointing fingers or affixing blame. Rather, they should carefully analyze the interaction between behavior and environment, reviewing how interventions may affect both student and teacher.

## Interventions

The intervention process requires precisely defining the apparent problem and the conditions associated with it. We must define the changeable, observable, and measurable conditions in the environment, such as lack of relevant rewards or work that is too difficult, that may contribute to the problem. Effective instructional planning includes gathering information from many sources and settings. Indeed, effective ecological planning requires analysis of the behavior and of the perceptions of everyone associated with the problem. For this reason, a collaborative team should identify targets for the instructional program. Collaboration focuses a wide array of expertise on a problem to obtain a more complete view of the environment. The team should examine the setting of the problem to determine specific environmental conditions and behaviors that may contribute. The purpose of the intervention is not simply to stop the targeted behavior but rather to change it into an appropriate behavior. Targeting becomes the process of identifying not only what must be decreased but also what must be increased. Once the targeted behavior has been identified, determine how to assess it. You can streamline assessment by collecting only relevant data; assessing the environment, not just the student; keeping data collection simple; and assessing learning as well as performance. If observation is required, methods for recording may include event, duration, and latency; permanent products; or anecdotal notes. Initially, collect data to detect problems and select targets for intervention. Then you can determine long-term goals and short-term objectives and continue to collect data so you can refine and adjust programs to meet the changing needs of the student and environment.

## MANAGEMENT PRINCIPLES AND THEMES

Good teachers know their subject areas thoroughly, for without this knowledge, they cannot impart accurate and timely information to students. It is possible, however, to have a complete grasp of a subject area and yet thoroughly fail to communicate the content to students. *Knowing how* to teach is as important as *knowing what* to teach.

In order to know how to teach, one must know how to assess the conditions under which learning occurs. Teachers must analyze not only the student but also the environments surrounding the student and others' behavior. The challenge is to assess the student's entire environment, understanding that it will be constantly changing.

Selecting appropriate targets and realizing both that not all problems are caused by students and that not all problems require intervention are central. Once detected, significant problems can be corrected through interventions that address the entire educational environment. Teachers who consistently practice the instructional principles summarized in Figure 3.2 provide a good educational environment. Other essential principles for establishing, implementing, and maintaining a positive instructional management program are these:

— *Establish a positive learning climate.* The teacher should establish a climate that encourages learning and focuses on meeting students' individual needs.
— *Structure an orderly setting.* Teachers must establish an effective room plan and environment that accommodate the needs of both teacher and students. If the room is not organized, the classroom appears cluttered, materials are difficult to locate, and instructional time is wasted.
— *Implement Preventive Planning.* Critical to the success of any classroom is preventive instructional planning. Careful planning can eliminate a great deal of misbehavior and increase learning.
— *Efficiently schedule and manage time.* If the teacher does not use time carefully, students and teachers waste valuable time and energy in a disorganized instructional program.
— *Appropriately group students for instruction.* Consistently instructing each student individually is impossible, so instructional groupings are necessary and desirable.
— *Use materials and equipment effectively.* Materials and equipment for students to use must be selected carefully and adapted to meet their individual needs.
— *Deliver appropriate instruction.* Match the instructional methods to the students' stage of learning and consider their cultural backgrounds as well. Appropriate use of methods, materials, and positive grading tactics will create an environment that fosters student success.
— *Develop an effective discipline plan.* Students cannot learn in settings where the teacher's time is spent resolving behavior problems rather than teaching. A discipline plan that clearly defines teacher expectations and consistently applies consequences supports task-oriented behavior and discourages disruptive behavior.
— *Intervene in the total school setting.* Correcting a student's learning problems may require the efforts of more than one teacher. The correction of instructional problems must encompass a host of variables from inside and outside the classroom. When home, community, and school efforts are well organized and in harmony with the classroom instructional program, the potential for student learning is enhanced.
— *Capitalize on home and community resources.* Establish a relationship among home, school, and community. A wealth of resources and services present in a community often go unused. Harnessing even a small number of these resources and services could have great impact on an instructional program. When home and community are involved in the school program, everyone gains.

## SPECIFIC MANAGEMENT THEMES AND STRATEGIES

The key management principles just enumerated are discussed individually on the next several pages. As in previous chapters, each discussion begins with a list of behaviors that may signify a problem and then offers suggestions for correction. Suggestions for modifying these correction strategies may be obtained by reviewing Figure 3.1. The themes and strategies apply to multicultural as well as special populations. These principles are closely related to the behavior management strategies presented in Chapter 14. For assistance in managing specific behavior, refer to the correction strategies in that chapter.

Even the best of teachers will become frustrated when they have difficulties dealing with students, parents, and professional peers. The final section of this chapter examines ways of preventing teacher burnout and methods for resolving the inevitable conflicts that occur in teaching. This material should help the teacher establish an efficient and effective classroom. Implementing these strategies should make teaching and learning fun and rewarding.

## 87. ESTABLISHING A LEARNING CLIMATE

DETECTION

Watch for these problems:

- Behavior management has replaced academic learning as the classroom goal
- Disorder and disruption are common in the classroom
- Achievable goals have not been established
- Students simply give up when frustrated
- The classroom is cluttered and messy
- Instruction is frequently interrupted
- Students complain that work is too difficult

*Description*

A classroom learning climate consists of the collective attitudes, beliefs, and behaviors contained within its walls. The first and most important function of any classroom activity is to impart the academic knowledge and skills students need to become functioning citizens. The values, expectations, and beliefs of students and teachers must be carefully considered in any education program. Successful classrooms are characterized by a climate that recognizes and honors academic achievement.

*Special Problems*

In some classrooms, learning becomes a lower priority than discipline, as the teacher sends the message that academic achievement is less important than behaving in a specified manner. Children who are noisy, disruptive, and inattentive prevent effective teaching. Unfortunately, many teachers tolerate these behaviors in the mistaken belief that they cannot change some children or that their hands are tied by potential legal liabilities. In such instances, the teacher examines how the instructional methods are presented. Several additional factors appear to have major impact on classroom climate. First, the climate of the school as a whole shapes the climate in individual classrooms. Traditional expectations of students, values held by the faculty and administration, and parent opinion place pressure on individual teachers to maintain certain classroom climates. Second, the norms of the school tend to be maintained over time, with new faculty members being socialized into prevailing patterns of behavior. Third, the physical condition of the school and maintenance policies make statements about the commitment to learning. If the administration is ineffective, unorganized, unstructured, and inconsistent in applying discipline policies, then the entire school climate is affected, as evidenced in individual classrooms.

*Implications*

The teacher must establish and maintain a positive learning environment that has structure, expectations, and consistent reinforcement of those expectations. The environment must be warm and supportive, demonstrating care and concern for children. These conditions support learning, establishing secure working conditions, and build confidence in students. Maintaining a relatively low level of student anxiety is also part of the teacher's role. Students should be concerned only about living up to their potential, not letting others down, and acting in their own best interest.

CORRECTION        Try these strategies.

1.  *Focus on Achievement.* Determine lesson objectives, materials, and methods, and limit students to options you provide. Present objectives in writing, post them on classroom walls, and send them to parents. Describe performance standards for assigned materials. State expected standards and provide opportunities to achieve them. Keep the classroom organized and businesslike. Model a commitment to academic achievement by being on time and prepared to teach. Have materials ready, organized, and maintain a focused lesson. Aim for a balance of high and medium success levels in student responses by varying difficulty levels. Chart and post increases in student skill levels to boost motivation. Devise a variety of ways to recognize academic progress, and use them frequently.

2.  *Deal Effectively with Disorder and Disruption.* Set and enforce classroom behavior limits. Select reasonable, enforceable consequences for disruptive behavior and communicate them to students. Point out choices students have. Make disruptive students realize their choice to misbehave will result in a self-imposed consequence. Design and implement incentive plans. Develop contingency plans for unexpected emergencies.

3.  *Create a Climate in Which Every Student Can Attain Academic Success.* Permit students to choose among several ways to accomplish a task. Give the students responsibility for planning and producing an academic product. Periodically require students to complete projects—long-range activities that must be organized, conducted, and reported over a period of time ranging from a few days to several weeks.

4.  *Provide Timely and Appropriate Assistance.* Give clear, brief directions for learning tasks. Have students paraphrase exactly what they are supposed to do, when it is to be done, and what they are to do with the completed work. Display models and reminders when students must follow several steps in sequence.

5.  *Manage Movement and Materials.* In the elementary grades, teach children to enter and exit the room in orderly lines. Give signals to indicate the kind of movement expected in the classroom. Enforce a policy for pencil sharpening. Establish a system of passes for out-of-room movement. Develop a system for distributing materials. Insist that children replace materials and clean up after an activity is completed.

6.  *Minimize Distractions.* Reduce procrastination. Keep instructional tasks short while still attaining the learning objective. Break long tasks into a series of shorter elements and set a deadline. Provide an incentive for completing a task. Reward neatness. Teach responsibility by assigning specific roles to each student.

7.  *Foster Accurate Self-evaluation by Students.* Break the teaching unit into smaller units that have starting and ending points. Post progress charts to provide tangible feedback to students. Reward satisfactory work habits often. Prepare a display, and select a "Student of the Week" based on work performance. Call parents to inform them of how well their child is achieving in the classroom. Ask parents to praise the child.

## 88. STRUCTURING AN ORDERLY SETTING

DETECTION

Watch for these problems:

- The classroom is crowded, distracting, and messy
- The classroom environment lacks structure
- The students do not know where to find materials
- The students exhibit noisy, disruptive behavior
- Classroom activities are not carried out efficiently

*Description*

Creating an orderly setting is the first step in establishing an environment that is conducive to learning and to preventing behavior problems. An orderly and attractive environment can have a positive effect on behavior by improving the level and quality of student interactions, so that the teacher and students can carry out daily activities efficiently without excessive noise or disruption.

*Special Problems*

To maximize efficient use of classroom space, teachers should carefully plan the physical layout of the classroom, using furniture, equipment for special activities, and walls, ceiling, and floor space appropriately. Without some guidelines for daily activities within the classroom, student movement, seating positions, personal space, individual duties, and daily routines can interfere with classroom instruction. The size of the classroom and type of class, whether regular or special will determine if areas may be designated for specific activities. The teacher's desk should face the classroom so the teacher can see the whole classroom and all students. Student desks or tables may be arranged in a variety of ways. Effectively managing movement and planning individual student duties and daily routines are also important elements of an efficiently run classroom. Students who are constantly moving around the room are not on task and may distract others. Undesirable behaviors, such as hitting and loud talking, may result when students are constantly roaming the classroom. Teachers must not, however, impose a rigid system that requires all students to sit constantly in their seats. Rather, they should foster individual initiative and curiosity while encouraging personal responsibility. Structured routines can do a great deal to establish a pattern of appropriate and productive behavior. Too much routine, however, can produce a deadly monotony in which the excitement and exuberance of learning is slowly but surely pulverized. A routine becomes a rut, and dissatisfaction and lethargy set in.

*Implications*

Plan the physical layout of the classroom carefully, designating areas for specific activities, determining what furniture to include and arranging it, decorating areas for different purposes, and organizing teaching and student materials for easy access. The teacher must remember that students can learn both in and out of their seats. The goal of instructional management is not to force students to sit, but to ensure that they learn when they are in their seats. Management techniques that reduce student movement and foster routines are tools to be used in implementing the educational program. Their purpose is to help, not handcuff, the teacher and students. The teacher must recognize when change is needed and implement the change in a timely manner.

**CORRECTION**

Try these strategies.

1. *Structure the Large-Group Area.* Before arranging desks and other classroom areas, structure the large-group instruction area.
2. *Create Small-Group Areas.* Small groups you form based on common needs are appropriate for teaching new skills and conducting reading and math instruction. Small-group instruction should take place in an area free from noise and distraction.
3. *Provide Individual Student Areas.* Each student needs a place to call his or her own, to store personal materials, and to sit during individual or group activities. Students who are highly distractible may need to have a very private area, such as a study carrel, or to be placed close to the teacher. If you use a carrel, present it positively as a place to learn.
4. *Organize a Teacher Area.* The teacher's desk should be well-kept, organized, and decorated attractively. Place it so you can see everyone.
5. *Establish a Paraprofessional/Volunteer Work Area.* If the classroom is large enough, paraprofessionals should have their own working space, situated across from the teacher area to allow additional monitoring of students.
6. *Develop a Recreation Area.* A recreation area may be used as a reward for students who have completed their work.
7. *Equip an Audiovisual Area.* Set up a separate center for audiovisual equipment, including a computer, tape recorder, language master, VCR, or overhead projector for use by individuals or small groups.
8. *Use Resources.* Use bulletin boards and other wall space to display work, post class rules, provide schedules and feedback charts, list daily assignments, highlight new skills, or instruct. Displays should be appealing, catch the students' interests, and be changed frequently.
9. *Encourage On-Task Behavior.* More distance between students generally leads to increased levels of on-task behavior. Seat students with academic or social problems near peers who model appropriate academic and social behavior.
10. *Facilitate Cooperative Learning Activities.* Build in flexibility to allow students to work together on projects, assist one another, and share experiences and knowledge. Some students from diverse cultures particularly benefit from such activities.
11. *Plan for Traffic Control.* High-traffic areas should be free of congestion. Consider traffic patterns when deciding on locations of the pencil sharpener, self-correcting stations, teacher's desk, and frequently used materials.
12. *Establish Routines.* Use effective techniques such as correcting work while circulating, allowing the quiet row to line up first, and establishing routines for the beginning, transition periods, and end of the day. End the day on a positive note to promote enthusiasm for returning the next day.
13. *Discover the Problem.* Observe carefully to discover the time, place, and individuals involved with an instructional problem. What appears to be a generalized problem may be related to a specific time, area of the room, instructional activity, or student.
14. *Consider Possible Solutions.* A sketch of the problem area may suggest a variety of changes in traffic patterns, location of a learning center, student seating, or scheduling. Before instituting a change, consider whether it will create new problems.

## 89. IMPLEMENTING PREVENTIVE PLANNING

DETECTION        Watch for these problems:

- Teacher has low expectations of students' academic performance
- The instructional program is confusing or poorly organized
- Inadequate time is allotted for classroom instruction
- Teacher offers little or no feedback to students
- The classroom situation is one in which praise is ineffective

*Description*    Preventive planning can eliminate a significant number of instructional and behavior management problems. Classrooms in which preventive planning is not practiced are chaotic, forcing the teacher into a reactive role. Learning becomes a matter of chance and the teacher is almost certain to be dissatisfied. Preventive planning involves coordinating all elements of the instructional program.

*Special Problems*    Teachers sometimes take credit for students' success but blame inadequate achievement on the student's lack of ability, weak motivation, or poor home environment. They then ignore structures and procedures that have been demonstrated to improve academic success. While there is no one best instructional system, the teacher must organize learning activities around some system. Otherwise, disorganization, disruptive behavior, teacher stress, and low achievement will result. Teachers have control only of the time students are physically in their classroom, and not all that time can be devoted to instruction. A teacher can use every possible moment of instructional time and still find little actual learning by students. Learning requires presentation of academic instruction and active participation. No matter how much time teachers spend on instruction, students will not learn unless they are actively participating.

*Implications*    Effective teachers, believing that all students can learn, take responsibility for their student's academic performance. An administration that insists teachers take responsibility for students' achievement and supports them in this responsibility, influences how low achievers are perceived. Time is the most important commodity the teacher has. All teachers should spend the maximum available time on academic instruction. Engaged time is the part of learning time during which the student is paying attention and on task. Motivating students during engaged time depends on several factors, which may not be controlled by the teacher. A student who is fatigued, hungry, or anxious will be difficult to motivate. However, teachers control many important factors related to motivation: selecting tasks, offering rewards and feedback, pacing, grouping, and providing advance organizers. To be effective, praise must be desirable to the student, follow performance of a specific behavior, identify the target behavior, and be convincing. Effective teachers give the class skill objectives and expect all students to attain the standard, giving some students extra time, practice, feedback, and instruction. The teacher must direct, structure, and pace the learning, ensuring continuity, and maintaining maximum engaged time.

CORRECTION

Try these strategies.

1. *Give Low Achievers the Same Number of Chances to Perform as High Achievers.* During class discussion, alternate between calling on a high and a low achiever. Give ample time to respond; count to 10, if necessary. Give as much corrective feedback to low achievers as to high achievers. Do not praise low achievers for marginal performance, but avoid being more critical of failure in low achievers. Prompt low achievers toward correct responses. Guiding students to appropriate answers is a technique all effective teachers use. Do not substitute seatwork and drill for interactive teaching which should establish understanding before students attempt independent work. Tolerate few interruptions when working with low achievers. Be enthusiastic.

2. *Implement Effective Instructional Strategies.* Carefully review the teacher's edition of the text to identify objectives for the teaching unit, revising them to fit specific student needs. Establish a minimum standard for each objective. Communicate to students what the standards are and how students can achieve them. Develop a method for sampling student progress. Provide enrichment opportunities for brighter students. Provide regular remediation that is teacher directed and peer assisted.

3. *Manage Learning Time.* Structure space to accommodate group activities and minimize disruptive movement in the classroom. Plan instruction for every moment allocated to teaching, stating the objective of each activity. Establish routines to maximize time in academic activities. Start and stop each element of the routine on time. Reduce transition time between activities. Discourage interruptions during instructional time.

4. *Effectively Motivate Engaged Time.* Select learning tasks appropriate to the group. Use advance organizers. Pace student work rate. Move as briskly as the group can manage successfully. Monitor student reaction for signs of confusion, and provide feedback to engage students again. Circulate among students to check on progress, prompt, and reinforce engagement. Vary grouping for instruction. Use small-group and individual instruction for enrichment, extension, or remediation. Praise students, but only when they are actively engaged. Make assignments challenging. Hold students accountable by stating exactly what you expect, specifying consequences for incomplete assignments, and following through.

5. *Use Praise Effectively.* Teacher praise must reinforce a student's performance of a specific behavior, identify the behavior being reinforced, and be convincing. Provide clear stimuli; students must understand what is being asked in order to respond. Praise should immediately follow performance of a desired behavior and should be specific, stating the particulars of the student's performance. Adjust the frequency of praise.

6. *Implement Interactive Teaching Practices.* Establish performance standards for each learning unit. Initially teach the content and then provide interactive practice, expecting all students to respond. Give immediate feedback. Assign independent practice that students can understand.

## 90. SCHEDULING AND MANAGING TIME

DETECTION    Watch for these problems:

- The classroom environment lacks structure
- The teacher has not developed an appropriate schedule
- The teacher does not adhere to a regular schedule
- Students do not know what they are supposed to do
- Students never seem to get everything done
- The teacher does not deal effectively with paperwork

*Description*    How teachers and students manage time has much to do with their success in the classroom. Efficient and appropriate use of time enables student learning and achievement. In fact, student achievement is closely related to the amount of time they spend actively engaged in appropriate academic activities. Teachers who obtain poor achievement from students frequently use too much class time for noninstructional activities and/or for noninteractive tasks.

*Special Problems*    Teachers vary widely in how they allocate time. Organizational and transition times account for much of the noninstructional time during the day, including opening activities, lunch money collection, announcements, passing out materials, restroom breaks, clean-up time, and the like. Teachers often do not realize how much time they spend on noninstructional activities until they analyze it in detail. For example, a 9:30 reading period may actually start at 9:40 after chairs are arranged in the reading circle and materials are passed out. A recurring 10 minute deviation becomes 50 minutes over the course of a week. When all noninstructional time is totaled, it may amount to as much as 10% to 30% of the day. A predetermined schedule prevents loss of instructional time and allows students to predict what will happen next, avoiding confusion and incomplete assignments. Time allocated to subject areas is important, but time that students are actively engaged in a relevant task is what enables academic success. Pulling students out of a regular class for additional help in another class, while it may have a number of benefits, can become problematic if instruction is fragmented or if the schedule is not carefully arranged. As a result, some students may receive less instruction than they need in an important academic area. Moreover, students may receive conflicting instruction if methods, materials, or approaches of the special teacher are incompatible with those of the regular teacher. Teachers often find it difficult to keep track of who was out of class during which lesson. The irony is that schools are really attempting to help these students.

*Implications*    Teachers must develop a schedule that allots time for various classes and activities during the school day and adhere to it as much as possible. Teachers must manage noninstructional time and teach students to do the same. With practice, students can learn to perform organizational tasks and handle transitions efficiently and quickly.

CORRECTION                 Try these strategies.

1.  *Establish a Daily Schedule.* The daily schedule should allow the maximum time for instruction in every content area; activities should offer the greatest possible learning potential.
2.  *Designate Key Time Slots.* Schedule the most important activities of the day when students are at their peak, usually in the morning. Compensate for lower levels of alertness in the afternoon by requiring more student participation, more hands-on tasks, and so on.
3.  *Provide Flexibility.* Build flexibility into the schedule to allow for individual variations in learning, revising the schedule for each student as needed. Set aside times to work with each student individually during the week.
4.  *Alternate Tasks.* Design the schedule to alternate highly preferred tasks with less preferred tasks. In secondary schools, use this principle to plan activities within the class period.
5.  *Establish Opening Routine.* Establish a routine to open each day, or period in secondary classes, so that students know exactly what to expect. Have an activity on each student's desk so students don't wander about the room. The activity should be one that will begin the day or period on a positive note, such as a riddle, or puzzle. Meanwhile, you can check homework or complete noninstructional tasks. Begin the daily activities according to the schedule.
6.  *Post Schedules.* Post a weekly schedule for the class and give each student a daily individualized schedule with time cues. Although routine is important, build variety into the schedule.
7.  *Organize and Prepare.* Make sure to prepare lesson plans and materials and grade papers before the school day begins. Model organized behavior for students.
8.  *Seek Assistance.* Enlist the help of others in planning and adhering to daily schedules. To avoid interruptions, try posting a sign with a note pad outside the classroom door: "Our time is valuable. Please leave a note or see me after school."
9.  *Actively Involve Students.* Make sure students are motivated, attending, and engaged in learning by using tasks that require active response. Ask questions, encourage students to explain answers, and provide frequent opportunities to respond. Materials and assignments should match student abilities in all subject areas.
10. *Correct While Circulating.* While moving through the class, check student papers, thus providing immediate feedback and reducing the need for later grading. Note correct responses and write suggestions for improvement on the student's paper.
11. *Use Self-Correcting Materials.* Self-correcting materials assist in reducing the time teachers must spend grading. Use answer keys at a checking station, peer checking, and instructional materials with attached answers. Posting and reiterating rules, as well as spot checking, will eliminate much of the desire to cheat.
12. *Establish Priorities.* Not all paperwork is of equal importance. Some may be completed by teacher aides or volunteers. Other paperwork, however, is critical for legal or program reasons.

## 91. GROUPING FOR INSTRUCTION

DETECTION

Watch for these problems:

- All of the low-ability students are placed in one group for instruction
- Students are not engaged in the assigned task
- Instruction wanders and has little focus
- Instructional groups function in turmoil
- Students do not know what to do

*Description*

Grouping refers to how a class of students is organized to participate in instruction. As educators learn more about individual differences, interests, and abilities, they diversify how they teach. Teachers may divide students into three or more ability groups, working with each in turn while the others do seatwork. In planning instruction, the teacher may use some, all, or a combination of the following methods: lecture, demonstration, discussion, learning activity, instructional game, and drill.

*Special Problems*

How to group students is a critical instructional decision. While some tasks and skills can be taught individually, much daily instruction is best conducted in a group. However, inappropriate grouping of students leads to frustration for both teacher and students. Lecturing is a strategy in which the teacher tells the students what is to be learned. If poorly planned, it lacks stimulation and fosters disruptive behavior. In demonstration, the teacher shows what is to be learned. Demonstrations are most effective with medium to small groups. The most commonly used and misused group in secondary and elementary education is the discussion group. Teachers must focus and direct the discussion to prevent it from turning to irrelevant topics. Teachers who use learning activity groups, must give explicit instructions; otherwise students will be confused about the assigned task. A criticism of the instructional game is that it mimics reality poorly; real-life situations are not as simple as those practiced in the game. Drill groups, formed on the basis of past performance, are moderate to small in size. An important consideration in forming a drill group is the students' readiness. If the students lack the background to do the drills, then they will likely practice and learn errors.

*Implications*

Teachers have experimented with many kinds of groups. Most teachers can plan and deliver good lectures. However, they must have a firm grasp of the content and organize it to interest all students. Clarity is vital. The strength of an effective demonstration is that it provides a concrete example to illustrate facts and make abstract concepts more meaningful. Discussion is most successful when students are organized by interest into small groups. Discussion groups work best if the students feel free to contribute and believe their comments are valued. In learning activity groups, students manipulate objects or equipment under teacher supervision. Several small groups usually work to accomplish a specific task. The instructional game group provides extensive opportunity to practice and improve communication and decision-making skills, encouraging active involvement. Drill aids retention and builds mastery. If students understand a concept and are able to apply it, they will remember the material longer and more completely than if they do not drill.

CORRECTION          Try these strategies.

1. *Establish Ability Groups.* Many schools have high, medium, and low ability classrooms for students of the same age. When low achievers work in a group without the assistance of more able students, their achievement suffers. Effective use of ability groups follows these guidelines:
   a.  Use whole-class, heterogeneous groups for initial instruction.
   b.  Use whole-class, heterogeneous groups for regular practice and skill reinforcement.
   c.  Use homogeneous ability groups for corrective instruction.
   d.  Use homogeneous ability groups for enrichment activities following lecture, demonstration, or direct instruction.
   e.  Use a balance of homogeneous and heterogeneous groups.
2. *Use Lecture Groups.* Relate new information to what students have already learned. Use advance organizers. Begin the lecture with an attention grabber. Project confidence and mastery of the material. Present content in a logical and ordered sequence. Use questions during the lecture to get student feedback. Monitor nonverbal behavior to determine whether students are receptive. Use voice inflection, body movement, and gestures to emphasize key points.
3. *Arrange Demonstration Groups.* Plan demonstrations carefully. Prepare a study guide for students. Students should answer questions about what they experienced during and after the demonstration. Make sure every student can clearly see and hear the demonstrations. Ensure that the demonstration is relevant to other instruction. Begin demonstration with a brief overview. Elicit participation by students. Conclude with a short question-and-answer session, and provide opportunities for immediate practice.
4. *Facilitate Discussion Groups.* Structure discussion groups: Prepare objectives and organize content to provide a framework for discussion. Provide background information and resources, augmenting student discussions with additional information. Use preplanned questions to guide discussion. Encourage interaction among students. Accept student contributions as worthwhile. Stimulate unwilling students to participate. Keep digression to a minimum.
5. *Implement Learning Activity Groups.* Prepare students for activity group. Assign students to groups of two or three. Provide time for groups to complete assigned activities, requiring them to maintain a record of activity and findings. Conduct followup discussion after the activities. Allot time for presenting reports and findings.
6. *Plan Instructional Game Groups.* Relate instructional games to ongoing classroom instruction. Firmly establish the rules of the game. Provide direction during the game as needed. Evaluate each group's performance.
7. *Use Drill Groups.* Make certain students have an adequate understanding of the concept or skill before using drill groups. Match complexity of drills with individual attention spans and performance levels. Circulate among drill groups to answer questions, troubleshoot, and give feedback. Make certain students do not perceive drill activities as punishment for academic performance. Evaluate the work of the drill group and give feedback within one or two days.

## 92. USING MATERIALS AND EQUIPMENT

DETECTION     Watch for these problems:

- Teachers are unaware of materials available in the classroom
- Guidance is needed to establish budgetary priorities
- Some students appear to be victims of a flawed curriculum
- Commercial materials are poorly suited to most special-needs students
- Classroom learning does not always endure or find its way into daily usage
- Few technological innovations are implemented

*Description*     Some 70% of all students with disabilities receive a portion of their instruction in regular class settings. Figures suggest that only about one-third of these students are making satisfactory progress. Another 20% to 30% of the student population evidence learning problems but are ineligible for special education services.

*Special Problems*     The huge number of students who fail to learn through traditional methods and materials shows that teachers must know how to analyze and adapt curricula. When funds are available, selecting appropriate materials may be difficult because the marketplace is flooded with attractive, seemingly appealing materials from which to choose. Too little emphasis is given to the curricular modifications needed to accommodate special-needs students. Although equipment may be available for teachers to use to enhance student learning, many teachers are hesitant to use it. Since students spend from 75% to 90% of their instructional time using commercial products, being able to detect and correct shortcomings of instructional materials and equipment is critical for special and regular classroom teachers alike. While many materials look promising, their educational effectiveness may be questionable. Students' ability to apply newly acquired skills in real life situations is the basis for judging instruction. Few instructional materials encourage generalization, so teachers must correct this shortcoming. Educators are recognizing the relationship among learners needs and abilities, teaching strategies, and curricular content more than ever before.

*Implications*     To learn about curricular needs, first determine exactly what material — traditional and nontraditional — and equipment is available by conducting an inventory. Doing so will provide a basis for making later decisions about buying and/or adapting instructional materials. Teachers must select instructional materials wisely. Classroom materials can be grouped into several categories: core instructional materials, drill and practice materials, and free-time activities or enrichment materials. Generally, little money should be spent on diagnostic tests, drill and practice, or free-time materials. Well sequenced validated core curricula in reading, spelling, arithmetic and so on usually should be the priority. Teaching materials, "tools of the trade," must measure up to the rigorous demands of daily instruction. Teachers must possess the skills of detecting and correcting faulty instructional materials. Without curricular adaptation, individualized instruction is likely to remain more a promise than a reality for an increasingly diverse population of school-age students.

CORRECTION

Try these strategies.

1. *Assess What Is Available.* Categorize available materials: Record name and publisher, skills taught, quantity and teaching arrangements, classification of the material (drill and practice, core), strategies for presenting the material, analysis of its apparent usefulness, and location in the classroom.

2. *Establish Budgetary Priorities.* Concentrate on core materials. Once core materials have been acquired, select supplemental materials. Add to your materials by collaborating in the purchase of core materials with colleagues, seeking sample materials from publishers, or other companies, and borrowing materials from libraries.

3. *Analyze Instructional Materials.* Ask questions before purchasing: Do the materials allow for evaluation and placement of students? Are procedures for monitoring student progress provided? Good materials include behaviorally stated objectives; content that corresponds with those objectives; organization from simple to complex; some redundancy; and provision for teaching across the stages of learning: acquisition, proficiency, maintenance, and generalization. The materials should provide ample practice of skills distributed across lessons; give clear directions; prompt appropriate and varied responses; provide clues that can be faded across time; offer immediate reinforcement for correct responses and remedial feedback for mistakes; adapt to various instructional arrangements; and emphasize maintaining knowledge and skills and adapting them to new learning situations.

4. *Take Corrective Steps To Improve Instructional Materials.* Changes in materials usually encompass both the content and the measurement system. If content is not appropriate, correct to accommodate individual objectives. Few materials are well-suited to specialized instruction; most require adaptation: Modify written and verbal directions, shorten sentence length, replace difficult vocabulary, highlight key words, use contingencies, and allow for overlearning. Fade corrective procedures as soon as possible.

5. *Promote Durable Instruction.* Program to help students generalize across settings, conditions, stimuli, reinforcers, and persons. Teach problem solving and increase difficulty level. Teach to apply previously learned skills to new situations. Initiate training so that the student practices problem-solving strategies under conditions that compare to real life.

6. *Make Use Of Technological Innovations.* Use audiotutorial programming for individualizing instruction, providing a bridge between regular group and remedial one-to-one instruction, and for independent teaching. Use computer applications to promote quality student performance. Promote learning centers to individualize instruction more than conventional paper and pencil materials permit.

7. *Carefully Adapt the Curriculum to Individual Student Needs.* Instruct students systematically; give every student opportunity to respond; correct frequency and complexity of responses individually; reinforce correct responses enthusiastically and provide immediate feedback on errors; limit the number of concepts introduced; emphasize depth over breadth; and incorporate redundancy into the curriculum.

## 93. DELIVERING APPROPRIATE INSTRUCTION

DETECTION

Watch for these problems:

- All students are expected to progress through the curriculum at the same rate
- Students are moved from one skill to the next regardless of skill proficiency
- Skills that students learn are not maintained, generalized, or applied over time

*Description*

The traditional model of classroom teaching usually includes grade-level sequencing and dividing subject-area instruction into units characterized by group pacing, whole-class instruction, and independent seatwork. Students are expected to progress through the curriculum at the same rate as age peers with the same amount of instruction and practice, regardless of their proficiency.

*Special Problems*

This model has persisted in public school teaching over the years and may be appropriate for average students. However, this lockstep approach may not meet the needs of students with learning or behavior problems. Students do not learn at the same rate or come to school with the same set of readiness skills. Moreover, learning and behavior problems may be partially due to the lockstep curriculum imposed on these students. As the curriculum becomes more difficult, some students are unable to master new skills and maintain the learning pace. The rapid pace does not permit these students to maintain, generalize, or practice the skill over time, and therefore they do not achieve mastery. They are advanced to the next task or next grade with a fragmented set of skills. The same pace advances other students too slowly; these students become bored and uninterested. Both kinds of students, whether they are undertaught or overtaught, complete tasks less frequently and may misbehave. These students become curriculum casualties, eventually experiencing learning and behavior problems. In addition, if students are evaluated haphazardly or infrequently, the problems will go undetected and grow in magnitude and severity.

*Implications*

All students can master the prescribed curriculum if they are given enough time and appropriate instruction. Teachers must vary learning times to allow individual students to master skills and become proficient. The six stages in the process of developing skills are sequential: acquisition, fluency, proficiency, maintenance, generalization, and application and adaptation. Once the student has been appropriately placed in a curriculum and/or skill group, direct instruction offers an effective, organized approach to individualizing instruction. It leads students through a process that helps them learn and master simple skills, complex skills, and independent study skills. If students are appropriately placed in the curriculum, with their individual learning rates and styles considered and direct instruction provided, they have a good chance of academic success. Continuous evaluation of student progress is critical, so teachers should grade student work and provide constructive feedback as immediately as possible.

CORRECTION Try these strategies.

1. *Accommodate Stages of Learning to Meet Individual Needs.* Stage 1 is acquisition, when the skill or behavior is first introduced. Students may give many incorrect responses and few correct responses. Instruction is designed to improve skill accuracy. Stage 2 is fluency, when rate becomes an important issue. Students need to practice skills. At stage 3, proficiency, students use the skill accurately and comfortably and continue to practice. Stage 4, maintenance, ensures that improvements will persist naturally after formal programming and reinforcement are eliminated. The teacher must review or require the use of a skill or behavior periodically to ensure it is being maintained. Stage 5, generalization, refers to changes that continue in conditions other than the original training conditions. Stage 6, application or adaptation, involves modifying skills to use in new situations without needing directions. Application or adaptation is achieved by providing opportunities to meet many new situations, discriminate key elements, and formulate an appropriate response.

2. *Individualize Programming Using the Direct Instruction Model.* Direct instruction includes teaching the exact behavior of concern; sequenced and systematic instruction and well-organized assignments; setting clear and precise performance goals; frequent and direct feedback to students about performance; arranging consequences for appropriate or inappropriate performance; active and frequent responding; and practice until mastery. Direct instruction does not mean repetitious, rote, meaningless, isolated learning. To use direct instruction in the classroom, follow these steps:
   a. Determine skills to be taught, and establish performance goals.
   b. Prepare students for instruction by using advance organizers.
   c. Model or demonstrate the skill. Most students learn better if they can see a skill performed and then imitate the steps.
   d. Provide controlled practice and feedback. Students should have many opportunities to practice the skill while receiving individual, frequent, specific, and corrective feedback on their performance.
   e. Encourage generalization. Skills must be generalized to real, meaningful situations and maintained over time. Require skill application in a variety of situations.

3. *Ensure Educational Success.* Vary the types of activities used. Differentiate instruction. Provide students who are having trouble keeping up with the group with individualized instruction, using peer tutoring or cooperative learning. Set and communicate high expectations. Students tend to learn as much or as little as their teachers expect. The level of achievement and unique needs of each student should guide instruction. Teachers should change course whenever necessary to meet the changing needs of each student.

4. *Continuously Evaluate Students in a Timely and Positive Manner.* A constant stream of failing grades should sound a warning bell. To continue giving failing grades without discerning the fundamental cause for failure is clearly inappropriate. Accentuate the positive. Note correct responses and strengths in students' answers to foster participation. Suggestions for improvement can be given kindly, sandwiched between positive comments.

## 94. DEVELOPING EFFECTIVE DISCIPLINE PLANS

DETECTION          Watch for these problems:

- Students do not follow directions and are unable to demonstrate the expected classroom routines
- Students fail to respond to teacher requests
- Students lack self-control in academics and classroom conduct
- Students lack a clear understanding of teacher expectations
- Strategies for decreasing or eliminating inappropriate student behavior are sometimes misunderstood

*Description*        It sometimes appears that nothing less than sorcery is needed to establish and maintain a well-organized, smoothly operating classroom. Teachers are challenged daily to instruct students with diverse abilities, suppress attempts by some to disrupt that instruction, and maintain a climate conducive to learning and positive social interaction.

*Special Problems*   Teachers who fail to develop and implement an effective discipline plan often spend an inordinate amount of time attempting to gain control of their class. In fact, the school year may be well advanced before the class appears to have some form of discipline and order. In such classrooms, students ignore teacher directions, fail to respond to teacher requests, and frequently behave in ways that are not conducive to learning. If rules have been established, they probably are stated negatively rather than positively: "Do not speak without permission," rather than "Raise your hand for permission to speak." Teacher expectations are unclear so students are confused. Students appear to have little control over their classroom behavior. The teacher has not established clearly defined routines or does not follow established routines consistently. Learning cannot occur in settings where an unacceptable level of misbehavior requires the teacher to spend most of the time resolving behavior problems rather than teaching. Consistently unmanageable students who exhibit inappropriate behavior and lack of self-control may require interventions beyond the teacher's expertise. In such instances, the teacher should seek help for the student through counseling or other professional services.

*Implications*       Teachers who have little difficulty managing their classrooms have developed efficient, effective discipline plans. They have established procedures for managing routine activities, such as transition time, passing and collecting materials, and establishing classroom rules. They state classroom rules positively, post them for everyone to see, and review them frequently. They clearly define consequences for breaking rules and consistently apply them. They punish students sparingly and only immediately after the misbehavior. When behaviors are particularly disruptive and difficult to control, these teachers use strategies such as the nine-step plan detailed in Chapter 14 to correct these behaviors.

CORRECTION    Try these strategies.

1. *Script out Classroom Routines.* Many teachers use classroom scripts, step-by-step written directions for student behavior. Scripting helps in dealing with routine events: submitting class assignments, responding to teacher requests, using time out, requesting teacher assistance, and so on. The script is a permanent product that can be easily reintroduced to the same or new students.

2. *Use Peers to Prompt Appropriate Behavior.* Most students can positively influence peers' behavior. A strategy that combines teacher direction with peer participation is peer challenge. Each time a target student misbehaves, ask the student's peers to help: "James seems to be having a problem. Who can tell him what the problem is?" Verbally reinforce students who respond positively to this question, and have classmates join you in reinforcing the student for accepting and following the recommendations.

3. *Use Goal Setting for Self-Control.* Self-control procedures can produce changes in academic performance and classroom behavior. State goals positively and in detail so that both you and the students can easily tell when they have been reached. Gradually shift responsibility to the student. At first you will determine objectives and select and administer reinforcers while students simply comply. In succeeding phases, shift determination of the reinforcer and then of the academic task to students.

4. *Establish Classroom Rules.* State behavior positively, for instance, "Raise your hand for permission to speak." Establish 4 to 5 general classroom rules and 1 to 2 for special activities. List several examples of behavior that does not comply with the rules. Implement training exercises to give each student the opportunity to state and perform the desired behavior and obtain feedback. Establish consequences for rule violations and follow through.

5. *Use Punishment Sparingly.* In most cases, positive strategies work well, but they will not always suffice. Judicious punishment can be an effective component of a sound discipline plan. Use time out judiciously, whether you deny the student access to classroom reinforcers or physically removed the student from the setting. Reprimands are common punishment. Statements that specify a single target behavior and say why it is unacceptable can be highly effective. Consider using response cost, either alone or with token reinforcement, to punish an inappropriate act. However, avoid overdependence on punishment. Exercise care in using reduction strategies, and always promote desirable behavior when eliminating an unwanted behavior. Another concern is the use of corporal punishment. While there is a precedent for the use of corporal punishment in schools, serious ethical and legal considerations argue against its application. Corporal punishment is at best a last resort that may harm the teacher as well as the student.

## 95. INTERVENING IN THE TOTAL SCHOOL SETTING

DETECTION

Watch for these problems:

- Excessive punishment is used in the school
- The school lacks an organized curriculum across subject areas and grade levels
- School curricula lack relevance
- There is little meaningful teacher and parent input in the development of the instructional program
- Poor communication exists between parents, students, teachers, and administrators
- Student failure and retention rates are high
- School leadership is ineffective
- School staff members have developed negative expectations

*Description*

The manner in which the classroom instructional program is implemented is affected by the organization of the total school program. Schools that are effective foster classrooms that are effective. The individual teacher cannot implement an effective instructional program when the total school program is disorganized and incoherent. Curricula, discipline, grading, materials, and even the skill levels of students are elements of the educational program controlled not solely by the teacher but at the school or district level.

*Special Problems*

In too many cases, discipline is punitive and designed solely as a means of responding to inappropriate behavior. Discipline becomes a reaction to student behavior and fails to promote appropriate responses. Chaos reigns when this type of discipline program is enforced in an entire school. The diverse needs of students require a school curriculum to be relevant, allow numerous choices, and match students' unique needs. A curriculum that lacks teacher-parent input and organization across subject areas and grade levels becomes irrelevant. The effect on student performance is high failure and retention rates. Services and settings should be just as varied as the school curriculum. Movement to a more restrictive setting must be based upon the real needs of the student and not upon the convenience of school staff. Teacher behavior is affected by negative expectations. Teachers provide more negative feedback if they believe that students are incapable or unwilling to learn. As a result, students fail to achieve and develop negative attitudes about learning and school. This cyclical pattern produces frustration for both students and teachers.

*Implications*

Successful schools expect and encourage student growth; seek participation by the community, parents, and students; and provide teachers an active role in the development and implementation of the instructional program. Teachers and administrators have a commitment to increased student learning and growth. The curriculum is constantly developing through the input of students, teachers, and parents. These schools are well-managed places where the instructional program is organized to meet the unique needs of each learner. Successful schools provide a broad array of relevant educational and extracurricular experiences and have a carefully coordinated discipline program. The leaders establish a climate in which all resources are directed at providing a relevant, safe, effective, and satisfying instructional environment.

CORRECTION

Try these strategies.

1. *Develop a Comprehensive Discipline System.* The system's discipline program should be fair and effective; provide a range of interventions and rules for application; have as its central goal preventing inappropriate student behavior; be a means to assist in implementing the instructional program, rather than an end in itself; and reflect beliefs of teachers, students, and parents.

2. *Develop a Relevant, Multifaceted Curriculum.* Focus on agreed-upon goals and objectives. Parents, teachers, and even students should assist in identifying goals during the curriculum development process. Develop a hierarchy of skills for each academic area and grade level, thus providing continuity across grade levels.

3. *Offer an Array of Services and Settings.* Some students are best served in a setting with little formal structure, while other students may need a broad array of supportive educational and social services and may be best served in a highly structured classroom with a low student-teacher ratio.

4. *Frequently Evaluate Student Progress.* Students who experience success in school are more likely to enjoy and profit from the instructional program. Frequent assessment allows opportunities for students to experience success and alerts teachers to instructional problems so they can intervene in a timely manner. The school's challenge is to institute evaluation procedures that allow students frequent opportunities to meet achievable goals on relevant tasks.

5. *Plan for Effective and Coordinated Leadership.* In most cases, successful leaders encourage prudent experimentation; provide resources and organization to the entire instructional program so that the school's goals can be met; build morale among teachers, staff, and students; and share responsibility for development and implementation of the educational program. They value the opinions of staff, students, and teachers; provide ample opportunities for relevant professional development; and quickly and freely recognize effort and achievements. Teachers may effect change by demonstrating innovative practices in their classrooms and then collaborating with administrators and colleagues to improve the innovations and implement them in other appropriate settings. Collaboration is a critical factor for intervening in the total school setting. Effective consultation and collaboration strategies are described in Chapter 16.

6. *Communicate Positive Expectations.* Successful schools encourage individuality and coordinate services and efforts. Teachers and administrators share a professional attitude that encourages active participation. Instructional problems do not simply validate negative expectations, but rather serve as opportunities for learning. Encouragement, effort, and shared responsibility are the hallmarks of these schools. In short, effective schools foster positive expectations and a climate in which learning will occur and satisfaction will result.

## 96.  INTERVENING IN THE HOME AND COMMUNITY

DETECTION        Watch for these problems:

- Students are often tardy or absent
- Students fail to complete homework
- Students show signs of tiredness, excessive illness and hunger, and wear inadequate or inappropriate clothing
- Parents or students justify breaking rules
- Teachers receive reports of abuse or illegal activity

*Description*      Students' experiences at home and in the community have a dramatic effect on the behavior and values they bring to the classroom. Problems occur if these behaviors and values differ significantly from those expected in the school setting. Moreover, the best instructional intervention has little chance of success if there is a significant problem or lack of resources in the home or community.

*Special Problems*     When a significant home or community problem affects school performance, the question is not whether to intervene but who should intervene, initially and later on. Classroom problems may be due to lack of basic necessities, such as food, clothing, or housing, or result from an unstable family environment. Students from dysfunctional families are often tardy or absent, fail to complete homework assignments, and frequently show signs of fatigue, hunger, and excessive illness. The relationship between home and school is frequently poor. In some cases, parents will attempt to justify and support the student's inappropriate behavior. Parent-school communication is also incomplete and irrelevant when schools adopt impersonal form letters as their primary means of communication with parents. An opportunity to establish a close relationship between home and school has been missed.

*Implications*      The classroom teacher can easily address such interventions as providing instruction or tutoring concerning homework. Other, more serious problems, however, require involving professionals with the time and expertise to address them comprehensively. The teacher does not have the expertise to single-handedly solve all of the student's problems. Attempting to do so almost ensures making a difficult situation much worse. Teachers who suspect that a lack of resources is creating problems should discreetly inform appropriate school authorities. Even more discretion must be exercised when approaching parents about the need for social services. Embarrassment, guilt, blame, rejection of services, and ugly confrontations may ensue if parents are approached in an inappropriate manner. Assist parents in establishing a home environment that supports and enhances the educational program. Home tutoring can greatly assist in the learning and use of academic tasks when school officials provide guidelines for parents in setting up such a program. Develop a comprehensive range of personal, direct methods of communication. While form letters notifying parents of school events and activities do have a place, direct communication with the home is critical.

**CORRECTION**

Try these strategies.

1. *Refer Students to Social Service or Community Agencies.* Form a team including the parents whose task is to provide the best learning environment for the child. Team meetings should identify needs of the student and family, agencies that can meet these needs, and responsibilities of team members in obtaining these services. Identify available resources. Be aware of social and health care services available in a community. Often, community mental health centers provide booklets that detail private and public services and their eligibility requirements. Armed with this information, a teacher can be a knowledgeable member of the team.

2. *Obtain Needed Educational Resources and Services from the Community.* Seek volunteers. Classroom volunteers can come from service agencies, colleges and universities, guilds, retirement centers, government, and private industry. Collect information from businesses and agencies about occupational training. These sources may be used for field trips and to provide summer and after-school employment. Request donations of material, labor, money, and scholarships from businesses, civic groups, and public and private agencies. Before soliciting these resources, examine school district policies and assess the school's needs.

3. *Facilitate Home-School Cooperation.* Encourage parents by informing them of daily opportunities in the home to teach and foster student skills. Initiate a parent education program that shows parents how to use daily activities to teach and enhance the skills and concepts taught in school. Parents and teachers should exchange information on successful strategies, and tactics to avoid. The program should establish a climate that rewards personal responsibility, initiative, and hard work. Inform parents and students of your policies and expectations concerning completion, accuracy, and grading of homework. Suggest ways that parents can facilitate the completion of homework: designating a time and place for doing homework and encouraging the student to bring home necessary materials. A daily checklist may help parents to check homework for accuracy and neatness and to offer encouragement and recognition for effort.

4. *Establish a Home Tutoring Program.* Provide guidelines for parents in establishing a home tutoring program. These may include coordinating carefully with the classroom teacher; using the same instructional procedures as used in the classroom; dealing with only one clearly defined skill; holding short lessons of perhaps 15 minutes; and rewarding rather than punishing the child's efforts.

5. *Facilitate Frequent, Positive, and Personal Home-School Communication.* Conduct parent conferences that encourage free exchange of ideas and expectations. Establish clear goals, avoid placing blame and using jargon, develop rapport, and identify agreed-upon strategies. Issue frequent oral and written progress notes that detail the student's successes and the skills addressed, not failures and problems. Effective communication leads both to effective strategies and to an educational climate in which parents and teachers work together on mutually established goals. In such a setting, education becomes an effective partnership.

## 97.  EARNING JOY AND SATISFACTION FROM TEACHING

DETECTION

Watch for these problems:

- Teacher has no sense of humor
- Teacher displays inappropriate sense of perspective
- Teacher complains but does not solve problems
- Teacher resists personal involvement
- Teacher's sense of self-worth appears to be decreasing

*Description*

Teaching is not an easy profession. At best, a teacher training program gives an individual entry-level skills. Following this training, teachers must work diligently to acquire the tools to be successful. The first year in the classroom is marked by long hours of preparing lessons, constructing materials, and experimenting with techniques. Each succeeding year planning and management become easier, as experience and practice sharpen skills and judgment. In general, an individual must "pay dues" for three to five years before earning the title of *teacher*.

*Special Problems*

For some teachers, basic job rewards gradually dwindle and then cease. They lost their enthusiasm for leading an eager group of children through a new experience and watching as understanding replaces wonder. Teaching becomes tedious. Each day is endured, every Monday dreaded. This condition is most often referred to as burnout. *Burnout* is attitudinal, emotional, and physical exhaustion. It does not occur suddenly, but develops gradually and usually goes unnoticed until a serious problem exists. A number of indicators point to impending problems: feelings of fatigue, depression, boredom, or apathy; changes in regular sleeping, eating, or exercise habits; irritability, forgetfulness, and inability to make decisions; chronic and unresolved problems with intimate relationships; development of physical symptoms, such as chest and back pains, headaches, ulcers, increases in blood pressure or heart and respiration rates; calling in sick, daydreaming or not caring about the quality of one's performance; a general lack of concern for others; student relationships marked by overindulgence or harsh punishments; feeling controlled by the clock; and noticeably lower self-esteem and self-confidence.

*Implications*

Develop a sense of humor. Next to intelligence, a sense of humor may be the most useful attribute a teacher can possess. It can be armor against daily stress, a tool for resolving interpersonal conflict, or medication for curing emotional hurt. • *Refocus your perspective.* Having perspective means knowing the appropriate relations of the parts to the whole. Too often teachers are so involved in the details of managing a classroom and the individual needs of children that they lose sight of how everything is related. • *Rekindle your problem-solving skills.* Successful, satisfied teachers have strong problem-solving skills. They never discuss difficulties without proposing at least one solution. They invest their energy in finding solutions to problems. • *Become personally involved.* Complete teachers have a strong sense of personal involvement. They exult when students strive and succeed and are downhearted when they fail. Such teachers are advocates and advisors, expecting the best from the children in their care. • *Rebuild your self-worth.* To work effectively with children, teachers must have a strong sense of personal value. If students are to have a strong self-concept and sense of their value as unique human beings, their adult models must exhibit genuine feelings of worth and confidence.

CORRECTION

Try these strategies.

1. *Practice Good Health.* Some risk factors are unavoidable; preparedness is the only defense. Factors such as age and heredity are beyond control, but you can influence their effect through better overall health and by reducing behavior that aggravates uncontrolled risks. Reducing blood pressure, smoking, cholesterol, and weight will reduce risk.

2. *Know Your Limits.* Frequently, teachers add unnecessary stress to their lives by taking on more than they can handle. Before agreeing to do a task for which you have limited time or skills, evaluate how much time is available, what energy will be required, and what skills are needed. The results should assist in making a realistic decision and reducing your stress.

3. *Manage Your Time.* Analyze your time to identify inefficient use and waste. Set priorities and rank tasks from most important to least. Each evening, list tasks to be completed the next day. Delegate less important items to someone else so that you can devote your time to important tasks. Make good decisions quickly. Manage paperwork in a smooth, orderly progression, handling each item only once. Set deadlines and mark them on your calendar at frequent intervals as a reminder. Don't overcommit yourself; learn to say "No!" Putting items back where they belong takes only a moment, but saves much valuable time later. Group similar tasks in school, home and business activities. Doing it right the first time in relationships, paperwork, and production can save you a vast amount of time.

4. *Develop a Hobby.* You can focus all your effort and attention on teaching for only a finite period of time before quality begins to erode. Become involved in other activities. Hobbies can divert your attention from teaching and be most refreshing.

5. *Appreciate Your Accomplishments.* Some people seem to feel guilty about enjoying recognition for doing a good job, while others feel shortchanged if their efforts are not noticed. Always enjoy praise when it is given. The pleasure serves as encouragement and helps to neutralize the effects of stress.

6. *Share with a Buddy.* Develop a close relationship with at least one colleague with whom you can share confidences. For example, a first-year teacher may feel isolated in a school and somewhat insecure about how to handle a difficult problem. Discussing such feelings with a buddy is vitally important to managing stress.

7. *Pamper Yourself.* Take time for yourself. A few minutes to perform a relaxation exercise during your preparation period, lunch break, or recess will provide respite from the continuous routine and stress of teaching. Have lunch with a friend, shop the mall, read a book, ride a bicycle, or what ever you desire, but make sure you schedule individual time each day.

8. *Tip the Scales.* When possible, take on assignments you can do well. This enhances your reputation as a "doer," brings recognition and praise, and improves your self-concept and ability to cope with stressful events.

9. *Recognize Your Value.* **Teachers make a difference** in the present and future quality of their students' lives and, in turn, affect entire families. Making a positive difference is not quick or easy. Changing human behavior takes persistent hard work, with no assurance that the change will endure. Teaching requires an orientation toward people rather than things, continuous effort to improve, and confidence, self-assurance, and a positive attitude. The rewards, however, are worth the effort.

# INSTRUCTIONAL MANAGEMENT SAMPLERS

The samplers on the next five pages illustrate activities for correcting instructional management difficulties. All are ready to copy, but you may need to adjust instructions to meet your unique needs.

15.1 **Checklist of Learning Patterns.** Appropriate instruction is a central element of instructional management. Teaching to a student's learning style facilitates learning and may minimize discipline problems. Although comprehensive learning style inventories are available, Sampler 15.1 presents a brief checklist you can use to determine a student's learning patterns.

15.2 **My Progress Chart.** This chart is designed for primary and intermediate students to chart their daily progress in a particular area of difficulty, whether an academic behavior, such as basic sight words, math facts, or correct spelling words, or a social behavior that needs improvement. For primary students, a bar graph is appropriate, while intermediate students may use a line graph. This chart provides feedback and permits students to see their progress.

15.3 **Good Behavior Chart.** This chart can help you manage students who consistently exhibit behaviors that interfere with the instructional program, such as talking out of turn, roaming the class, and so on. Use group contingencies to manage these behaviors. Divide the class into two teams, making sure there are an equal number of students on each team who exhibit the target behaviors. Make and post charts for both teams. Identify inappropriate behaviors and label across the top of the chart. List student names down the left-hand side of the chart. Set up contingencies. For instance, the team with the least number of checks at the end of the day earns 15 minutes of activity time, while the losing team must continue to work on school tasks.

15.4 **Analysis of Teacher Class Time.** Class time is the number of minutes students are actually present in your classroom. If you feel pressed for time to cover all subjects and/or content and to complete routine classroom tasks, analyze your class time. Keep a record for one week on the amount of time you spend on each activity. Include time spent on noninstructional activities such as attendance report, lunch count, changing from one activity to another, and recess. Such an analysis will help you identify areas you can streamline to gain more instructional time. Once you have completed the analysis, select a correction strategy from Scheduling and Managing Time (Skill 90) to assist you in managing your time more efficiently.

15.5 **Checklist for Managing Teacher Time.** Respond to the statements on the checklist as honestly and accurately as possible. Once the checklist is completed, note items checked in the *never* and *sometimes* columns. These are the target areas you need to change to manage your time more efficiently. Rank the importance of these items, and select one to work on immediately. Make a concerted effort each day to improve your performance on that item. When you have achieved to your satisfaction, move to the next item.

Name _____

# ✓ CHECKLIST OF LEARNING PATTERNS

Student's Name _____

**ADDITIONAL COMMENTS**

**1. Time on Task** Estimate the amount of time this student to an academic task.
____Same as most in class    ____5 to 10 minutes
____10 to 20 minutes    ____Less than 5 minutes
____Time varies by task (explain)_____
____Time varies by other factors (explain)_____

Describe student's behavior when not attending to task:

**2. Learning Rate** Estimate how quickly the student masters new concepts in the subjects where his or her performance is strongest and weakest.

| Strongest: | | Weakest: |
|---|---|---|
| _____ | Faster than most of the class | _____ |
| _____ | Same as most of the class | _____ |
| _____ | Same as most in lowest group | _____ |
| _____ | Slower than lowest group | |

Describe behavior when student does not comprehend:

**3. Stimulus** The student learns and remembers best what he or she:
____Sees    ____Reads    ____Hears    ____Does    ____Writes
____Combination_____

Example lessons:

**4. Stimulus** The student learns fastest by these methods of instruction:
____Demonstration    ____Discussion    ____Guided Reading
____Discovery    ____Other_____

Example lessons:

**5. Response** This student answers most items correctly when responding by:
____Saying    ____Choosing    ____Filling in blank    ____Writing
____Showing    ____Other_____

Example lessons:

**6. Stimulus/Response** The student performs best when the lessons include these materials:
____Worksheets    ____Computer Games    ____Tape Recordings
____Workbooks    ____Computer Drill    ____Active Games
____Flash Cards    ____Board Work    ____Passive Games
____Other_____

Examples:

**7. Study Strategies** The student effectively applies study strategies to accomplish tasks in these areas:
Specify_____

Describe:

**8. Settings** The student learns and performs best when the setting is:
____One-to-one with teacher    ____One-to-one with peer
____Large Group    ____Small Group    ____Other_____

**9. Structure** The structure that seems to promote the student's learning performance is:
____Rigorous    ____Formal    ____Informal    ____Permissive

Describe:

**10. Effective Lesson** Describe a recent lesson in which the student mastered a new concept at a rate that equaled or exceeded your expectations according to learning factors.
Subject: _____    Concept: _____
Stimulus: _____    Response: _____
Setting: _____    Structure: _____

*Source:* From *Curriculum-based assessment and programming* (2nd ed.). J. S. Choate, B. E. Enright, L. J. Miller, J. A. Poteet, and T. A. Rakes. (Boston: Allyn and Bacon, 1992). Copyright 1992 by Allyn and Bacon. Reprinted by permission.

Name _____

✻ MY PROGRESS CHART ✻

**Behavior**

20
19
19
17
16
15
14
13
12
11
10
9
8
7
6
5
4
3
2
1

1  2  3  4  5  6  7  8  9  10  11  12  13  14  15

**Days**

# ★ GOOD BEHAVIOR CHART

### Team_____

**Behaviors**

**Students**

**445 —**

Name _____

# ✎ ANALYSIS OF TEACHING CLASS TIME ✎

Date _____

| Class Activities (Min.) | | | | |
|---|---|---|---|---|
| From | To | How I Spend My Time | Minutes I Wasted | Why |
| | | | | |
| | | | | |
| | | | | |
| | | | | |
| | | | | |
| | | | | |
| | | | | |
| | | | | |
| | | | | |
| | | | | |
| | | | | |
| | | | | |
| | | | | |
| | | | | |
| | | | | |
| | | | | |
| | | | | |
| | | | | |
| | | | | |
| | | | | |
| | | | | |
| | | | | |
| | | | | |
| | | | | |
| | | | | |
| | | | | |
| | | | | |
| | | | | |
| | | | | |
| | | | | |
| | | | | |

Total Time Wasted _____

# CHECKLIST FOR MANAGING TEACHER TIME

**Directions:** Read each statement and respond accurately and completely. Honest answers will help you identify areas in which you can manage your time more efficiently.

| | Never | Sometimes | Frequently | Always |
|---|---|---|---|---|
| 1. I keep my desk and teaching area clear and neatly arranged. | | | | |
| 2. I put materials where they belong as soon as I have used them. | | | | |
| 3. Each evening I list and prioritize tasks to be completed the next day. | | | | |
| 4. I set deadlines on major tasks and mark them on my calendar. | | | | |
| 5. I do tasks correctly the first time to avoid doing them over. | | | | |
| 6. I group similar tasks to save time. | | | | |
| 7. I have learned to say "No" and don't overcommit myself. | | | | |
| 8. I devote my time to important tasks and delegate less important items to others. | | | | |
| 9. I make decisions quickly and with a minimum of hesitation. | | | | |
| 10. I set time aside daily for myself. | | | | |
| 11. I set priorities and rank tasks from most to least important. I complete most important tasks first. | | | | |
| 12. I handle paperwork efficiently in an orderly progression that allows me to handle each item only once or twice. | | | | |

# REFLECTIONS

1. Ecological assessment is not a single isolated event; rather, it examines a complete picture of students and their environment to select targets for intervention. What steps would you take to conduct an ecological assessment of a behavior problem?

2. Observe experienced teachers in each of the following settings: elementary, middle, and high school. Record the instructional management techniques each teacher uses. Compare your observations with techniques described in this chapter. Are there discrepancies? If so, how would you correct them?

3. Observe a student in elementary school, another in middle school, and one in high school who are experiencing problems; identify at least five possible behavior and environmental targets for each. After selecting these targets, interview each student's teacher and, if possible, parents or guardians to determine their opinions of possible targets. Compare and contrast the information.

4. Conduct an ecological assessment of the environments of each student in question 3. List the factors in each environment that influence the problem. Describe how the assessment process changes in relation to the age of the student.

5. Many students difficulties are the product of either an ineffective discipline system or a curriculum that is ill-suited to their abilities and interests. Describe the steps you could take to remedy a flawed discipline system and an inadequate curriculum.

6. List at least 10 critical factors that elementary, middle, and high schools must address in developing and implementing an effective educational program. Compare and contrast the factors among the three levels of schooling.

7. Interview students to determine how particular school-based extracurricular activities affect their performance in the educational program. Ask how they would improve extracurricular activities in their school.

8. Interview school and social service personnel, and compile a list of services available in your community. Describe how individuals qualify for these programs and the difficulties they might encounter.

9. Interview teachers and parents of elementary, middle, and high school students, and compile a list of at least five impediments to home-school interaction and five ways that this relationship could be enhanced. Compare and contrast the differing perceptions of parents and teachers.

10. Observe and interview a teacher and an administrator from a local elementary, middle, or high school, and develop a list of 10 school practices that hinder or enhance development and implementation of an effective educational program.

11. Teachers can enhance student achievement by incorporating recently developed strategies into classroom practices. Describe five of the strategies discussed in this chapter that address low-achieving students in particular.

12. Establishing and adhering to classroom routines and schedules that maximize opportunities for quality instruction is important. Develop a schedule and list of classroom routines that would be appropriate for students at each level: elementary, middle, and high school.

13. Students acquire an expectation of success or failure in the classroom. Describe how you might use three motivational strategies to remedy the negative perception some students hold.

14. As students grow older, they often become increasingly more responsive to classmates than to adults. In what ways might you take advantage of the influence that students exert on one another's behavior?

15. The physical arrangement of the classroom has a significant influence on daily instruction. Draw a floorplan that reflects the current layout of your classroom. What changes might improve teaching and learning? Modify your plan to reflect appropriate changes.

16. Observe elementary, middle, and high school classrooms, and develop a comprehensive list of ways in which preventive planning tactics, expectations, discipline plans, time management, and instructional materials and methods hinder and enhance the educational program. Compare and contrast procedures across levels of schooling.

17. Several professional textbooks present suggestions for implementing effective instructional management strategies. For additional ideas, compare and contrast discussions in these sources with information in Chapter 15.

Borich, G. D. (1992). *Effective teaching methods* (2nd ed.). New York: Merrill/Macmillan.

Charles, C. M. (1992). *Building classroom discipline* (4th ed.). White Plains, NY: Longman.

Choate, J. S., Enright, B. E., Miller, L. J., Poteet, J. A., & Rakes, T. A. (1992). *Curriculum-based assessment and programming* (2nd ed.). Boston: Allyn and Bacon.

Christopher, C. J. (1992). *Nuts and bolts: Survival guide for teachers.* Lancaster, PA: Technomic Publishing.

Collins, C. (1987). *Time management for teachers: Techniques and skills that give you more time to teach.* West Nyack, NY: Parker.

Dunn, R., & Dunn, K. (1992). *Teaching elementary students through their individual learning styles: Practical approaches for grades 3–6.* Boston: Allyn & Bacon.

Evans, S. S., Evans, W. H., & Mercer, C. D. (1986). *Assessment for instruction.* Boston: Allyn and Bacon.

Evans, W. H., Evans, S. S., & Schmid, R. E. (1989). *Behavior and instructional management: An ecological approach.* Boston: Allyn and Bacon.

Good, T. L., & Brophy, J. E. (1992). *Looking in classrooms* (5th ed.). New York: Harper Collins.

Jones, V. F., & Jones, L. S. (1990). *Comprehensive classroom management* (3rd ed.). Boston: Allyn and Bacon.

Kerr, M. M., & Nelson, C. M. (1989). *Strategies for managing behavior problems in the classroom* (2nd ed.). Columbus, OH: Merrill.

Male, M. (1993). *Creating exceptional classrooms: Technology options for all.* Boston: Allyn and Bacon.

McLoughlin, J. A., & Lewis, R. B. (1990). *Assessing special students* (3rd ed.). Columbus, OH: Merrill.

McQueen, T. (1992). *Essentials of classroom management and discipline K–12.* New York: Harper Collins.

Paine, S. C., Radicchi, J., Rosellini, L. C., Deutschman, L., & Darsch, C. B. (1983). *Structuring your classroom for academic success.* Champaign, IL: Research Press.

Parkay, F. W., & Hardcastle, B. (1990). *Becoming a teacher: Accepting the challenge of a profession.* Boston: Allyn and Bacon.

Sparzo, F. J., & Poteet, J. A. (1989). *Classroom behavior: Detecting and correcting special needs.* Boston: Allyn and Bacon.

Wang, C. M. (1992). *Adaptive education strategies: Building on diversity.* Baltimore: Brookes.

Wood, J. W. (1992). *Adapting instruction for mainstreamed and at-risk students* (2nd ed.). New York: Merrill/Macmillan.

# CHAPTER SIXTEEN

## COLLABORATION IN THE SCHOOLS: ENSURING SUCCESS

— *Robert A. Gable, Lori Korinek, and Virginia K. Laycock*

This chapter examines various aspects of school-based collaboration and discusses ways to detect and correct problems that might stand in the way of successful mainstreaming. Before beginning that discussion, however, it is well to remember that what happens on the playground, in the home, and in the community has a significant bearing on classroom performance. Accordingly, teachers should keep in mind that strategies for carrying out school collaboration easily can be adapted to working with parents and agency personnel outside the school. With little modification, the same strategies have proven successful in strengthening the partnership between home, school, and community.

The 1970s and 1980s witnessed events that have significantly influenced educational policy and classroom practices. Historically, schools operated according to a dual system, with separate general and special education classes. Students judged to be disabled generally were excluded from instruction provided to students without disabilities. In some cases, these students were denied access to public schooling altogether. As a result of legal and legislative actions, along with changes in thinking about students with disabilities, much of that has changed. Today, the majority of students with disabilities are being moved into regular classrooms and taught alongside students without disabilities. No longer a novel idea, mainstreaming still poses an immense challenge to teachers, administrators, and students alike.

The decision to mainstream a student with disabilities should depend on the "goodness-of-fit" among the situational demands of the classroom, the demonstrated capabilities of the student, and the nature of the intervention(s) required to establish and maintain satisfactory pupil progress. That congruence can be an elusive goal. While ensuring a quality education for all students sometimes is more a promise than a reality, we have made significant progress toward achieving that end.

Longstanding barriers that separated general and special education gradually are being removed. Survey studies show that more regular education teachers are receiving preservice preparation for dealing with special students in the mainstream. Universities are introducing more unified training programs so that prospective regular and special educators now participate in some overlapping courses: Mainstreaming the Special Student, Introduction to the Exceptional Student, Diagnostic and Remedial Reading, Multicultural Education, and so on. In the schools, the traditional roles and responsibilities of public school personnel are being examined and, in many instances, redefined. Mistrust that too long served to maintain the separation of programs in regular and special education is lessening. School divisions are exploring innovative funding and service delivery options to accommodate a larger segment of the special needs-student population, so that fewer will "fall through the categories." A sense of shared responsibility for all students is beginning to emerge in many schools.

This chapter explores peer collaboration as a means of successfully integrating students with disabilities and retaining those with special needs.

First, we compare and contrast alternative collaborative approaches to help teachers and administrators choose an approach to begin collaboration. Second, we discuss ways teachers can ensure that a student's problem is fully examined and correctly identified. Third, the skills of peer problem-solving that lead to zeroing in on appropriate interventions are detailed. Lastly, we offer some strategies that teachers may find useful in sustaining the momentum of school collaboration.

## EMERGENCE OF COLLABORATION

The success of mainstreaming rests on the proposition that, given reasonable support, general educators can teach most exceptional and at-risk students in the regular classroom. As schools grapple with the myriad issues associated with mainstreaming, one approach that is gaining momentum is to provide technical assistance to teachers working with special-needs students through various collaborative frameworks. Although it originated in the 1960s, collaboration gained prominence as a legitimate service delivery option in the mid-1980s. Today, various programs of collaboration and consultation provide *prereferral intervention* or *teacher assistance* to teachers at all grade levels. Peer collaboration between regular and special educators is in keeping with administrative and instructional options envisioned in Public Law 94-142; it is also a proven way to deal effectively with the challenges of mainstreaming.

There is mounting recognition that operating schools according to a "two-box" system that separates students with and without disabilities is of little benefit. But many are reluctant to accept peer collaboration as a way to provide specialized instruction in the regular classroom. In an era of diminishing resources and escalating demands, redefining the roles and responsibilities of school personnel poses a real challenge. The demands associated with peer collaboration provide both administrators and classroom teachers with legitimate grounds to resist. With the growing pressure to resolve the ills that many believe have befallen public education, the tremendous benefits of collaboration to general and special educators and administrators are not always easy to see.

Some of the issues in peer collaboration include finding an approach that fits the climate of a particular school, gaining teacher support, arranging for release time, scheduling various meetings, delegating decision-making responsibilities, and providing teachers the recognition they deserve for team participation. Further, most authorities agree that the hierarchical nature of our schools underscores the importance of gaining administrative support for collaboration. Even after personnel receive the necessary training and a collaborative program is introduced, sustaining the momentum can be difficult. Finally, the students in whom teachers invest so much time and effort are usually left out of the process; ways must be found to involve them more fully in the mainstreaming process.

Notwithstanding the very real obstacles, persons from every professional discipline can contribute to and profit from a collaborative relationship. The number of classroom teachers and other personnel involved in collaborative relationships is increasing rapidly. Their dedication and enthusiasm is strong testimony to the wisdom of introducing collaboration in the schools. That collaborative efforts on behalf of one student spill over onto other students in the class attests to the quality and practicality of the knowledge being exchanged. In sum, collaboration presents an opportunity to further both student and teacher success by increasing the organizational and educational options available to students with disabilities. The steps to achieving integrated regular classroom instruction for students with special needs and problems follow.

## DETECTION AND CORRECTION IN THE COLLABORATIVE PROCESS

The four key steps for implementing school-based collaboration are (1) Selecting a collaborative approach, (2) identifying problems and planning interventions, (3) involving students, and (4) maintaining momentum. In the next few pages, the most common obstacle to achieving each step is considered along with suggestions for possible solutions.

Collaboration can occur in a variety of configurations. The array of collaborative models outlined in Figure 16.1 emphasizes the options in the first step as well as the first potential obstacle — deciding which collaborative approach to implement.

FIGURE 16.1 / **Alternative Collaborative Approaches**

| Approach | Teacher Assistance Team | Child Study/Resource Team | Intervention Assistance | Behavioral Consultation | Collaborative Consultation | Peer Collaboration | Cooperative Teaching |
|---|---|---|---|---|---|---|---|
| **Configuration** | • Small group | • Small group | • Dyad initially, small group if necessary | • Dyad | • Typically dyad | • Dyad | • Dyad |
| **Participants** | • Teachers | • Administrator, teacher(s), special educator, specialists | • Classsroom teachers and specialists | • Teacher and specialist | • Teacher and specialist(s) | • Teachers | • Teacher and specialist |
| **Unique Features** | • Focus on problem identification and brainstorming interventions<br>• Teacher selection of intervention(s) | • Prereferral support<br>• Referral for special education evaluation if interventions fail | • Multistage system with individual consultation and interdisciplinary teaming | • Problem-solving interview defining antecedents and consequences of behaviors<br>• Focus on behavioral techniques for data collection and intervention | • Parity, reciprocity, shared decision making and resources<br>• Teacher Implementation | • Structured, problem-solving dialog<br>• Self-questioning and metacognitive strategies | • Joint planning and instruction by both teachers in the mainstream classroom<br>• Teaching roles change according to needs and expertise |
| **Selected References** | Chalfant, Pysh, & Moultrie, 1979; Chalfant & Pysh, 1989 | Hayek, 1987 | Graden, Casey, & Christenson, 1985; Graden, 1989 | Fuchs & Fuchs, 1990; Gable, Friend, Laycock, & Hendrickson, 1990 | Friend & Cook, 1990; Idol, Paclucci-Whitcomb, & Nevin, 1986; West, 1990 | Pugach & Johnson, 1988 | Bauwens, Hourcade, & Friend, 1989 |

## 98.  SELECTING A COLLABORATIVE APPROACH

DETECTION

Watch for this obstacle:

- Teachers are sometimes unaware of alternative options and unable to choose an approach to begin the process of collaboration

\*\*\*\*\*\*\*\*\*\*\*\*\*\*\*\*\*\*\*\*\*\*\*\*\*\*\*\*\*\*\*\*\*\*\*\*\*\*\*\*\*\*\*\*\*\*\*\*\*\*\*\*\*\*\*\*\*\*\*\*\*\*\*\*\*

### COMMENTS OF A SECONDARY SCHOOL TEACHER

"I have really tried everything I can think of to help this student, but nothing seems to work. I'm sure I'm not the only teacher who's faced this type of problem, and I wish I could talk to others who have come up with some successful ideas. I just don't know where to go for assistance."

\*\*\*\*\*\*\*\*\*\*\*\*\*\*\*\*\*\*\*\*\*\*\*\*\*\*\*\*\*\*\*\*\*\*\*\*\*\*\*\*\*\*\*\*\*\*\*\*\*\*\*\*\*\*\*\*\*\*\*\*\*\*\*\*\*

CORRECTION

Consider these possible solutions.

1. *Become familiar with major collaborative models or structures that could be adapted for implementation.* A number of different arrangements or structures have been developed to bring school personnel together for collaborative problem solving. Each structure offers a way to provide direct and immediate support to classroom teachers whose students pose instructional or management problems. Each collaborative structure also makes educational programs more responsive to students who are experiencing difficulties in mainstream classrooms. Teachers and at-risk students can receive prereferral support, or quick assistance prior to the pursuit of formal special education evaluation, which may prevent the need for later, more intensive intervention. Even when students have identified disabilities and are receiving direct special education services, collaborative approaches enable more effective integration into general education classes. For students who can function successfully, collaboration can ease the transition out of special and into regular education.

    The major collaborative approaches that have been described in the literature and replicated in the field are presented in Figure 16.1. Each approach is depicted in terms of its primary configuration (dyad or small group), key participants (classroom teachers with or without other specialists and administrators), unique features (distinctive purposes or procedures), and selected references (developers and proponents).

    In behavioral consultation, collaborative consultation, and peer collaboration, two individuals engage in dyadic problem solving. Peer collaboration pairs teachers as partners, while behavioral consultation and collaborative consultation typically involve a classroom teacher with a specialist: a school psychologist, special educator, or related service professional. Intervention assistance begins with similar dyadic interaction between a teacher and specialist but progresses to small-group problem solving if the situation warrants. Teacher-assistance teams and child study/resource teams use a small group arrangement to support teachers and facilitate problem solving. Child study/resource teams and intervention assistance teams include teachers, administrators, and specialists, whereas teacher assistance teams involve only classroom teachers.

With all of these options, colleagues support the referring teacher in clarifying the problem, pinpointing intervention goals, generating alternative solutions, planning the intervention, and monitoring its effectiveness. The classroom teacher retains responsibility for implementation. A cooperative teaching arrangement differs from the others in that a classroom teacher and specialist engage collaboratively in actual service delivery as well as instructional problem solving. Both professionals are present in the mainstream classroom and actively participate in teaching, behavior management, and evaluation.

Approaches such as collaborative consultation and cooperative teaching are highly flexible, allowing the specific participants to structure their problem-solving interactions. Other approaches, such as peer collaboration, require specialized training in a predefined, problem-solving sequence.

2. *Recognize the resources available for use or creation of collaborative support systems.* Teachers may find several different collaborative options available within their schools and be able to choose among them according to their personal preferences and/or the nature of the problems they experience. Other teachers may find few collaborative structures in place in their schools. All schools must have a child study team as a required component of the special education process, and teachers should be able to request assistance with difficult-to-teach students without seeking special education per se. Some collaborative arrangements require more extensive administrative support than others. Even when leadership is not forthcoming, many teachers can create their own collaborative consultation or cooperative teaching groups by pursuing supportive relationships with interested colleagues. Some existing mechanisms, such as departmental or grade-level teams and mentor teacher arrangements, can be easily reshaped to provide opportunities for collaborative problem solving.

3. *Assess colleague readiness and get started with those who are willing.* Not all teachers will choose to participate in collaborative activities. Some may object to the time required for interactive problem solving, claiming it takes away from more critical teaching responsibilities. Others may be reluctant to share difficulties or ask for assistance, because they fear that admitting their needs will reflect negatively on their perceived teaching competence. Still others may resent having to make instructional modifications for students with special needs in their classrooms. Finding colleagues who are genuinely interested in pursuing some collaborative approaches is a critical first step. Even one or two committed teachers can begin to make a difference.

## 99.  IDENTIFYING PROBLEMS AND PLANNING INTERVENTIONS

DETECTION

Watch for this obstacle:

- Few guidelines exist that would enable teachers to identify precisely a student's problem or select an appropriate intervention

\*\*\*\*\*\*\*\*\*\*\*\*\*\*\*\*\*\*\*\*\*\*\*\*\*\*\*\*\*\*\*\*\*\*\*\*\*\*\*\*\*\*\*\*\*\*\*\*\*\*\*\*\*\*\*\*\*\*\*\*\*\*\*\*
COMMENTS OF AN ELEMENTARY SCHOOL TEACHER

"I feel so frustrated; Bill is not a bad kid, but he can be so disruptive in class sometimes, I really don't know what to do any more. It's driving me crazy. I wish I could put my finger on exactly what is going on."

\*\*\*\*\*\*\*\*\*\*\*\*\*\*\*\*\*\*\*\*\*\*\*\*\*\*\*\*\*\*\*\*\*\*\*\*\*\*\*\*\*\*\*\*\*\*\*\*\*\*\*\*\*\*\*\*\*\*\*\*\*\*\*\*

These comments are symptomatic of the feelings of many classroom teachers as they struggle with the demands of daily instruction. While we all can identify with the frustration being expressed, we know too little about what is happening in the classroom to venture a possible solution.

CORRECTION

Consider these possible solutions.

1. *Seek support and assistance from one or more colleagues.* Remember that you do not need to go it alone. Many times teachers struggle in silence to resolve a classroom problem for which a colleague has an immediate solution. Ironically, we seek the opinion of others on countless subjects of a personal nature but are reluctant to ask advice about our students. Generally you should talk with colleagues with whom you already have a positive relationship. Practically every personal relationship is built upon mutual trust and respect, two basic ingredients of successful collaboration. In seeking assistance, look for teachers who have characteristics in keeping with effective collaboration, including regard for the unique qualities of each student, the conviction that every student can benefit from teaching, and a sense of accomplishment when a student achieves a specified goal.

2. *Together, focus discussion on specific aspects of the problem.* Among the most critical aspects of peer collaboration is the process by which two or more persons work together to identify the problem. Problem solving is usually accomplished through discussion that leads to a detailed understanding of the exact nature of the problem. Often inexperience will cause teachers to formulate a plan before they obtain a full and complete picture of the problem. A dialogue that is too superficial usually leads to misidentification of the problem. That misidentification makes the proposed solution much less likely to fit the problem, so that the outcome will not be satisfactory. Accordingly, the process of identifying a problem is divided into two discrete operations: (a) focusing and (b) pinpointing the problem.

   a. Focus on the problem can be achieved through a series of verbal exchanges between the teacher initiating the contact and the teacher(s) facilitating or providing assistance. The initial goal, however, is to establish mutual acceptance and trust that encourages a sense of positive interdependence among participants. In securing that relationship, participants must display empathy for the difficulties a teacher is experiencing and avoid making statements that might discourage frankness in talking about the situation. Teachers who are liked and respected by their colleagues are especially successful in achieving such a relationship. Finally, if a satisfactory resolution to a problem is to be achieved, participants must share the commitment and responsibility for achieving that goal. The person serving as facilitator usually assumes responsibility for indicating the purpose of the meeting and for specifying the format for the discussion: describing the agenda of the meeting, reviewing the problem situation, and presenting other salient information. The major goal is to identify the problem and to choose an appropriate strategy for dealing with it.

b. The problem-solving process itself usually consists of a series of questions posed by the teacher who has assumed the role of facilitator. The purpose is to encourage an exchange of useful information that leads to pinpointing a possible pattern in the problem behavior as well as the probable relationship of the behavior to specific environmental events. The questions that are at the core of the problem-solving process are worded like this: Can you give me an example? What exactly do you mean by disruptive behavior? How else might she react? Open-ended questions usually are preferable to those that elicit only a "yes" or "no" reaction. Communication skills such as asking general-to-specific questions, clarifying and paraphrasing information, and redirecting discussion to salient points regarding the problem maintain focus. The facilitator usually "mirrors" the language of the referring teacher, using the same terms to avoid value clashes or miscommunication. Also, all participants must recognize that both objective and subjective aspects of a problem warrant attention. Our perceptions of a situation are influenced by various factors, not all of which are consonant with the available evidence. In the earlier example, Bill may be so congenial that the teacher cannot see that he instigates other students in the classroom to misbehave. By following these procedures, the facilitator can secure enough specific facts regarding the problem to produce a precise definition.

3. *Conduct a thorough analysis of the problem.* Once you have established a clear definition of the problem, one that is expressed in observable and measurable terms, you can begin to analyze the problem. Problem analysis includes giving some thought to the temporality of events, according to the following format:

a. Discuss events that precede the problem: the way the class entered the room, the instructions a teacher gives to begin a lesson, the subject matter itself, and so on.

b. Discuss events that occur at the same time as the problem: teacher and peer responses to Bill's disruptive acts, for example.

c. Discuss events that follow the occurrence of the problem: what the teacher ordinarily does to deal with the problem, and Bill's reaction.

d. Discuss possible extraneous events occurring outside of the classroom — a fight on the playground, conflict between parents, or a special holiday — that may influence the behavior of the student.

The causes of some student problems may be beyond the reach of public school personnel; still, you can devise a plan to address those aspects of the problem that are manifest in the classroom and that the school can control.

4. *Select an appropriate intervention.* After you have analyzed the problem, shift discussions to brainstorming to create a list of possible interventions. Under the direction of the facilitator, generate as many ideas as possible without commenting on or prejudging the worth of any of the suggestions until the brainstorming portion of the meeting ends. Instead, participants seek to generate as many solutions as possible, with everyone encouraged to contribute. Ordinarily, the facilitator is the designated recorder and is responsible for listing the ideas that surface from the discussion.

   In order to capture the events that may be connected with the problem, some system of recordkeeping is essential. Teachers have created various written forms for conducting the problem-solving process to:

   a. facilitate the collection of information in a consistent manner;
   b. decrease the prospect of lost data (a forgotten detail that may later prove to be significant);
   c. introduce a degree of objectivity to the review or further discussion of the case; and finally
   d. to allow faithful replication of the problem-solving process in the future.

   Although by no means a foolproof instrument, Figure 16.2 illustrates one way for teachers to organize the problem-solving process.

   After participants are satisfied that they have created a sufficient number of possible interventions, subject that list to more careful scrutiny. At this time, raise several questions:

   — Which strategies best fit the problem and the student?
   — Which strategies are most compatible with existing classroom routine (e.g., instructional schedule, class groupings)?
   — Which strategies are in keeping with the philosophy of the referring teacher?
   — Which strategies are most feasible with available resources?
   — Which strategies appear least intrusive into the overall operation of the classroom?

5. *In establishing priorities, strengthening desirable behavior should be uppermost on the list.* Any plan of action should be designed to reinforce positive qualities displayed by the student. Even when the aim is to eliminate a noxious behavior, such as Bill's disruptions, it is essential to work on promoting a replacement — something for which the student can obtain acceptance, such as hand-raising.

6. *Decide on a method of evaluation and choose criteria.* In formulating an action plan, it is important to incorporate a means for evaluating the effectiveness of the intervention, along with preselected criteria against which you can judge if and when the goal has been met. Although the problem-solving session generally will take about 30 minutes, participants should remain flexible regarding the time set aside for meeting.

7. *Be patient.* Patience is a critical attribute in collaboration. The collaborative process often falters after an intervention has been chosen. A teacher who is frustrated by repeated episodes of disruptive behavior is likely

to be impatient for change. For that reason, it is imperative that the facilitator preach the virtues of patience and underscore the fact that the action plan may take some time to work. Recognize from the beginning that it may take more than one plan to arrive at an effective solution. A written format such as the one presented in Figure 16.2 is useful for structuring the process of identifying problems, planning interventions, and monitoring and evaluating them.

**Figure 16.2  /  Problem-Solving Worksheet**

Facilitator _____     Initiator _____
Participants _____     Date(s) _____
_____
_____     Time(s) _____
_____
_____     _____

*General Information/Source(s)*

_____
_____
_____
_____
_____
_____
_____
_____
_____
_____

**I. Problem Identification**          Excess(es) _____ Deficit(s) _____
                                       Other _____

   a.  Definition(s)

_____
_____
_____
_____

   b.  Multiple examples

_____
_____
_____
_____
_____
_____

**II. Problem Analysis**

   a.  General setting events

_____
_____
_____
_____
_____

   b.  Before events

_____
_____
_____
_____
_____

   c.  During events

_____
_____
_____
_____
_____

   d.  After events

_____
_____

**FIGURE 16.2 / Problem-Solving Worksheet** *(continued)*

Current strategies

_____

_____

_____

_____

_____

### III. Intervention

a. Possible solutions

_____

_____

_____

_____

b. Probable outcomes

_____

_____

_____

c. Appraisal

_____ Suitable?　　_____ Resources available?　　_____ Intrusive?

_____ Acceptable?　　_____ Practical?　　_____ Compatible?

_____ Other factors: _____

d. Prioritized Plan

_____

_____

_____

_____

_____

e. Change criteria/source

_____

_____

_____

### IV. Implementation

a. Participant responsibilities

_____

_____

_____

_____

b. Evaluation procedures

_____

_____

_____

_____

c. Timeline

_____

_____

_____

_____

### V. Followup Schedule

_____

_____

_____

_____

## 100.  INVOLVING STUDENTS IN COLLABORATION

DETECTION

Watch for this obstacle:

- Teachers sometimes fail to take advantage of the contributions that students themselves can make to assuring the success of mainstreaming

\*\*\*\*\*\*\*\*\*\*\*\*\*\*\*\*\*\*\*\*\*\*\*\*\*\*\*\*\*\*\*\*\*\*\*\*\*\*\*\*\*\*\*\*\*\*\*\*\*\*\*\*\*\*\*\*\*\*\*\*\*\*\*\*\*

### COMMENTS OF A SPECIAL EDUCATION TEACHER

"Rita seems to be at the periphery of academic and extracurricular activities; she rarely asks questions or volunteers answers and seldom interacts with classmates."

\*\*\*\*\*\*\*\*\*\*\*\*\*\*\*\*\*\*\*\*\*\*\*\*\*\*\*\*\*\*\*\*\*\*\*\*\*\*\*\*\*\*\*\*\*\*\*\*\*\*\*\*\*\*\*\*\*\*\*\*\*\*\*\*\*

CORRECTION

Consider these possible solutions.

1. *Become familiar with ways that classmates can be involved in mainstreaming students with special needs.* Students without special learning and behavior problems are a readily available and abundant resource for facilitating the transition of students with special needs into regular classrooms. There are several reasons for increased student involvement in various aspects of mainstreaming. First, most students are willing to accept assistance from classmates that they might resist accepting from adults. Second, in the course of the school day, students spend more time, in more places—cafeteria, playground, lavatory, corridors, library—with each other than with adults. Third, the opportunity to work directly with peers can foster respect and acceptance while building social skills, essential ingredients for effective mainstreaming.

   Students from the regular classroom can serve in various roles, ranging from simple to complex. Regardless of the particular assignment, however, the students selected to collaborate in mainstream programs should possess several important attributes, including strong interpersonal skills and a positive disposition. Select students who are reliable and not easily discouraged and who have a good attendance record. Remember that students participate in collaborative programs strictly on a voluntary basis. It is generally advisable to obtain administrative support and parental approval before implementing special programs that rely on the students themselves.

2. *Take advantage of the fact that regular class students can contribute substantially to formulating a sound reintegration plan.* Students can provide a unique perspective on classroom demands that includes aspects adults might overlook. Also, students can share ideas that may be useful regarding various accommodations a special student may need, such as clarification of assigned work, preview of key vocabulary or concepts in science, or use of a ground-floor lavatory.

3. *Teach classmates to extend various kinds of assistance.* Once a special student enters the classroom, classmates can offer support and encouragement during the first several weeks, a time that is especially difficult for any new student. Give one or two students the responsibility of serving as buddies to provide gentle reminders regarding the daily schedule or classroom rules, check the student's understanding of homework assignments, or even offer special tips on test preparation. Teach

classmates to serve as peer tutors and to provide supplementary instruction in the form of drill and practice activities, such as reviewing spelling words or drilling addition facts.

In every instance, general and special classroom teachers should collaborate in properly preparing students for their new roles. Give students ample opportunity not only to gain a complete understanding of their responsibilities, but also to practice them under conditions that resemble those they will encounter in the classroom as closely as possible. Role playing is especially helpful in assuring that students can correctly perform a particular task.

4. *Provide ample cooperative-learning experiences.* Cooperative learning is a popular form of instruction in which students with and without special needs can perform equally well on different tasks. Generally, the teacher introduces the objectives of the lesson to the entire class, and then places students in heterogeneous groups and gives each group an assignment. As students work singly and together to complete their assignment, the teacher moves from group to group, monitoring, troubleshooting, and offering assistance when necessary. Finally, the individual accomplishments of each student are evaluated, along with the performance of the group. The positive interdependence that emerges from the cooperative-learning experience can provide special students a group identity and a real sense of belonging, as well helping to expand their social skills.

5. *Involve special students in the collaboration process.* Perhaps most importantly, special students who are being mainstreamed should participate in the reintegration process. Mainstreaming students with disabilities and special needs takes time and effort. Success requires that teachers take part in a series of planning meetings and IEP meetings, during which time important decisions about instruction are made. Decisions to make special accommodations should include the students themselves; they too should become part of the solution! Participating in the process can motivate students and improve their ability to solve problems. Of course, on occasion it will not be suitable for a student to be a stakeholder in the decision-making process; however, teachers should take full advantage of the myriad contributions that students with and without special needs can make to ensuring the success of the mainstreaming process.

## 101. MAINTAINING MOMENTUM

DETECTION          Watch for this obstacle:

- Teachers are often frustrated in their efforts to maintain the momentum necessary to sustain collaborative relationships with others

\*\*\*\*\*\*\*\*\*\*\*\*\*\*\*\*\*\*\*\*\*\*\*\*\*\*\*\*\*\*\*\*\*\*\*\*\*\*\*\*\*\*\*\*\*\*\*\*\*\*\*\*\*\*\*\*\*\*\*\*\*\*\*\*\*\*\*\*\*\*
### COMMENTS OF A MIDDLE SCHOOL TEACHER

"Our early attempts to work together seemed to be going so well; but now it is hard for us to meet, and when we do, we seem to be pulling in opposite directions."

\*\*\*\*\*\*\*\*\*\*\*\*\*\*\*\*\*\*\*\*\*\*\*\*\*\*\*\*\*\*\*\*\*\*\*\*\*\*\*\*\*\*\*\*\*\*\*\*\*\*\*\*\*\*\*\*\*\*\*\*\*\*\*\*\*\*\*\*\*\*

The initial rewards of collaboration can fade when teachers confront many competing demands or experience the inevitable conflicts that occur when individuals try to solve complex problems cooperatively. Ensuring the vitality of collaborative support systems once they have been established requires continued attention to minimizing resistance, solidifying relationships, scheduling time, monitoring and refining interactive processes, and gathering administrative and parental support. The following considerations and suggested strategies can help maintain collaborative momentum in each of these areas.

CORRECTION          Consider these possible solutions.

1. *Overcome resistance by encouraging colleagues to participate according to their own levels of readiness and commitment.* Collaboration cannot be mandated. Because collaborative relationships are strictly voluntary, the challenge is to encourage collaboration at whatever level of readiness teachers exhibit. Responding to teacher inquiries about the process and urging them to talk with others who have participated or to observe problem-solving meetings are examples of ways to build positive experiences. Assuring others that the collaborative process is teacher-centered may help to alleviate apprehension over loss of autonomy. Although consultants or team members facilitate and contribute to problem solving, the referring teacher retains ultimate responsibility for defining the problem and selecting interventions. Allowing teachers to define the parameters of their involvement and appreciating incremental progress toward greater collaboration will help teams to move beyond inevitable resistance.

2. *Solidify relationships, while staying open to new ways of working together.* Collaboration and team building are developmental processes. It takes time to overcome initial obstacles, clarify expectations and procedures, and establish a sense of team identity. By staying focused on student needs, teams can avoid some of the conflicts — attempts to overpower, territorialism, and personal style — that frequently contaminate collaborative efforts. Colleagues learn to value the diverse perspectives and complementary strengths that enable them to generate creative solutions to problems.

Dyads or small groups should remain flexible and open to new ways of working together. Whatever the collaborative structures and problem-solving processes established initially, they are likely to evolve and change over time to accommodate different instructional challenges and more advanced collaborative skills.

3. *Search for creative ways to schedule time for collaborative problem solving.* One of the most frequently cited barriers to successful collaboration is time. Schools that value and promote collaboration have to provide the time for teachers to work together; meaningful collaboration cannot happen on the run. Some schools schedule common meeting times for all faculty. Others attempt to have common planning periods for teachers on the same team. Floating substitutes, paraprofessionals, or volunteers can be assigned to cover classes while teachers meet with one another. Teachers may agree to combine their classes for appropriate activities so that one of them can participate in an important meeting. Some teachers are relieved of bus, hall, or lunchroom duties to free them for conferences. If teachers have to schedule collaborative meetings before or after school, compensatory time or other incentives can be provided. Recognizing that collaboration is not only legitimate but also essential as a teaching function allows school-based professionals to explore creative ways of scheduling collaborative sessions.

4. *Regularly monitor and refine collaborative processes.* Because collaborative support is highly personalized and constantly evolving, participants should reflect frequently on the quality and effectiveness of their interactions. Whether collaborative problem solving occurs in a dyad or in a small group, participants can evaluate themselves, their colleague(s), and the team as a whole. The emphasis is on formative evaluation that yields insight into ways to refine collaborative processes.

Figure 16.3 provides examples of questions that each member of a dyad or collaborative team might address after a problem-solving meeting. Respondents have the opportunity to identify both perceived successes and challenges to effective team functioning. They also specify the interactive behaviors of teammates that they personally find most and least helpful for collaborative problem solving.

Figure 16.4 is an example of a rating scale for evaluating overall team functioning. Participants might complete this scale several times each year to monitor the perceived effectiveness of their collaborative efforts. This scale is especially appropriate for small-group approaches, such as teacher-assistance, child study/resource, or intervention assistance teams.

Regular and systematic monitoring of collaborative initiatives contributes to a sense of shared ownership and accountability. When participants can openly discuss their perceptions of team strengths and weaknesses, the climate of mutual acceptance and trust is enhanced. Teachers and specialists then use their collaborative skills to shape their support structures to be as helpful as possible, according to their current needs and specific settings.

5. *Keep parents and administrators informed and cultivate their support.* In many ways, collaborative approaches in the schools represent a change from conventional practice. Anticipate the reservations that some parents, administrators, and others might have about consultation and

**FIGURE 16.3** / **Collaboration Self-Check**

Name of Respondent _____ Role on Team _____

Student's Name _____ Date _____

### Questions for the Collaborative Team to Address after a Problem-Solving Meeting

1. Overall, do you feel the team problem-solving process functioned smoothly?

   ____ yes          ____ no

2. With what aspects of the teaming were you most satisfied?

   _____

   _____

   _____

   _____

   _____

3. What aspects of the teaming do you feel need improvement?

   _____

   _____

   _____

   _____

   _____

4. How satisfied were you with your own participation in the teaming?

   _____ Very Satisfied          _____ Satisfied          _____ Dissatisfied

5. In order to help you participate more effectively in team problem solving, list what you would like team members to do:

   More of _____

   _____

   _____

   _____

   Same as _____

   _____

   _____

   Less of _____

   _____

   _____

   _____

**FIGURE 16.4 / Collaborative Team Dimensions Scale**

Date _____ Team Members _____

Circle the number that most nearly describes how you view the current functioning of your collaborative team on the listed dimensions. The letter(s) are abbreviations for the following responses:

SA = Strongly Agree     A = Agree     U = Undecided     D = Disagree     SD = Strongly Disagree

1. All members participate actively.                                          SA   A   U   D   SD

2. Communication is clear and jargon-free.                                    SA   A   U   D   SD

3. Members actively attend (i.e., ask relevant questions, paraphrase, and elaborate).                                    SA   A   U   D   SD

4. Comments are focused and relevant.                                        SA   A   U   D   SD

5. Student problems are clearly identified.                                   SA   A   U   D   SD

6. A specific, measurable intervention goal is defined.                       SA   A   U   D   SD

7. Brainstorming results in a wide range of intervention alternatives.                                                   SA   A   U   D   SD

8. Evaluation of alternatives is suspended until the list is completed.                                                  SA   A   U   D   SD

9. Everyone's ideas/opinions are sought as input to decisions.                                                          SA   A   U   D   SD

10. Specific strategies are selected for intervention.                        SA   A   U   D   SD

11. Conflicts/disagreements are dealt with and worked through.                                                           SA   A   U   D   SD

12. A plan for measuring the success of the intervention is developed.                                                   SA   A   U   D   SD

13. Members are accepting and open-minded.                                    SA   A   U   D   SD

14  Team interaction helps task achievement.                                  SA   A   U   D   SD

15. The facilitator helps task achievement.                                   SA   A   U   D   SD

16. Adequate time was allotted for the meeting.                               SA   A   U   D   SD

Comments:

_____

_____

_____

_____

_____

_____

_____

_____

teaming as emerging support systems for teachers and students. Share concise information on the origins, purposes, and potential benefits of collaborative problem solving with the major stakeholders early in the process. To the maximum extent feasible, involve them in selecting and adapting collaborative approaches for implementation in their schools. Parents can be encouraged to participate in problem-solving meetings dealing with their children's needs. Principals can observe or actually become members of school-based collaborative teams.

Gathering and sharing basic information on the effectiveness of collaborative efforts is essential for advocacy. The satisfaction of teachers who have received assistance and parents whose children have been served can be captured through simple structured interviews or surveys. Documenting the number of teachers and students served is also helpful. Student performance data, such as attendance, assignment completion rates, grades, frequency counts of target behaviors, and so on, that show improvement resulting from collaboratively planned interventions, is especially convincing.

## CONCLUSION

Previous chapters have covered an assortment of procedures for dealing effectively with students' learning and adjustment problems. In contrast, this chapter has discussed collaboration in the schools and focused on the process by which two or more professionals can work together to better serve a student with problems. Successful collaboration requires that public school personnel have positive individual attributes and strong problem-solving skills, along with precise knowledge of classroom interventions. By combining these skills, regular educators, special educators, and others can equip themselves for the new roles that they must assume in our changing schools.

## REFERENCES AND SOURCES OF ADDITIONAL INFORMATION

Bauwens, J., Hourcade, J.J., & Friend, M. (1989). Cooperative teaching: A model for general and special education integration. *Remedial and Special Education, 10* (2), 17–22.

Chalfant, J. C., Pysh, M., & Moultrie, R. (1979). Teacher assistance teams: A model for within-building problem solving. *Learning Disability Quarterly, 2,* 85–96.

Chalfant, J. C., & Pysh, M. (1989). Teacher assistance teams: Five descriptive studies on 96 teams. *Remedial and Special Education, 10* (6), 49–58.

Cook, L., & Friend, M. (1990). Pragmatic issues in the development of special education consultation programs. *Preventing School Failure, 35* (1), 43–46.

Dettmer, P., Thurston, L., Dyck, N. (1993). *School consultation and collaboration for students with special needs.* Boston: Allyn and Bacon.

Friend, M., & Cook, L. (1992). Interactions: Collaboration skills for school professionals. New York: Longman.

Friend, M., & Cook, L. (1990). Collaboration as a predictor for success in school reform. *Journal of Educational and Psychological Consultation, 1* (1), 33–40.

Fuchs, D., Fuchs, L., Bahr, M., Reeder, P., Gilman, S., Fernstrom, P., & Roberts, H. (1990). Prereferral intervention to increase attention and work productivity among difficult-to-teach pupils. *Focus on Exceptional Children, 22* (6), 18.

Gable, R. A., Friend, M., Laycock, V.K., & Hendrickson, J.M. (1990). Interview skills for problem identification in school consultation. *Preventing School Failure, 35* (1), 5–10.

Graden, J. L. (1989). Redefining "prereferral intervention" assistance: Collaboration between general and special education. *Exceptional Children, 56,* 227–231.

Graden, J. L., Casey, A., & Christenson, S. L. (1985). Implementing a prereferral intervention system, Part I: The model. *Exceptional Children, 51,* 377–384.

Hayek, R. A. (1987). The teacher assistance team: A prereferral support system. *Focus on Exceptional Children, 20* (1), 1–7.

Idol, L., Paolucci-Whitcomb, P., & Nevin, A. (1986). *Collaborative consultation.* Austin, TX: Pro-Ed.

Johnson, D. W., & Johnson, R. T. (1986). Mainstreaming and cooperative learning strategies. *Exceptional Children, 52,* 553–561.

Morsink, C. V., Thomas, C. C., & Correa, V. E. (1991). *Interactive teaming: Consultation and collaboration in special programs.* New York: Merrill/Macmillan.

Pugach, M. C., & Johnson, L. J. (1988). Rethinking the relationship between consultative and collaborative problem solving. *Focus on Exceptional Children, 21* (4), 1–8.

Villa, R. A., & Thousand, J. S. (1990, April). The power of student collaboration or practicing for life in the 21st century. Paper presented at the 68th Annual Council for Exceptional Children Conference, Toronto, Canada.

West, J. F. (1990). Educational collaboration in the restructuring of schools. *Journal of Educational and Psychological Consultation, 1* (1), 23–40.

# FINAL THOUGHTS

In bringing to a close discussion on detecting and correcting special needs of students with and without disabilities, several thoughts come to mind. Some authorities argue that more changes have occurred in our schools in the past decade than during the previous one hundred years. As never before, the classroom skills of teachers are being severely tested, and some are struggling to discover new ways of managing and instructing an increasingly diverse population of students. Regular classroom teachers, special classroom teachers, along with administrators, supervisors, and support personnel, are being cast in new and unfamiliar roles. Without exception, everyone associated with public education faces challenges that are likely to remain well into the next century. Yet this is an exciting time to be a part of the educational process, recognizing the promise that tomorrow holds for all students.

In the preceding chapters, the authors have sought to put into perspective what is occurring in schools across the country. People with knowledge of various content areas who are experienced in teaching students with special needs have shared a wealth of useful information. Others have addressed the changing role of public school personnel and provided guidance to teachers assuming new responsibilities for directly instructing and collaborating with their colleagues to better serve students with special needs. Throughout, we have attempted to draw upon our backgrounds in classroom teaching, administration, and research to ensure that the content is both consistent with accumulated literature and of practical use. Together, the chapters in this volume have been written to better equip teachers to face the challenge of the 1990s—teaching for both student *and* teacher success. We hope that we have come close to achieving that high goal.